Contributing Authors

Henry E. Adams — University of Georgia
Arthur J. Bachrach — Arizona State University
John R. Peace — University of Florida
Irwin A. Berg — Louisiana State University
Sidney W. Bijou — University of Illinois
Jeanne E. Brown — University of Southern California
Jack R. Butler — Purdue State University
Raymond B. Cattell — University of Illinois
Hubert S. Coffey — University of California and Berkeley
Ralph Mason Dreger — Louisiana State University
Albert Ellis — Institute for Rational Living, Inc.
Ann Magaret Garner — University of Nebraska
Jules D. Holzberg — Wesleyan University
Leonard S. Kogan — The City University of New York
Stanley G. Marcoff — Illinois State University
Joseph D. Matarazzo — University of Oregon
Boyd R. McCandless — Indiana University
Gerald R. Pascal — University of Mississippi
L. A. Pennington — Dun the Illinois
Leticia A. Dyer — Louisiana State University
Herbert C. Quay — University of Illinois
William A. Quigley — Arizona State University
George Saslow — University of Oregon
Donald N. Sloane — University of Illinois
William U. Snyder — Ohio University
Charles Van riper — Western Michigan University
John G. Watkins — University of Montana
Walter L. Wilkins — Naval Medical Neuropsychiatric Research Unit, San Diego
Richard A. Young — Indiana University

Contributing Authors

Henry E. Adams   University of Georgia
Arthur J. Bachrach   Arizona State University
John R. Barry   University of Florida
Irwin A. Berg   Louisiana State University
Sidney W. Bijou   University of Illinois
James E. Birren   University of Southern California
Joel R. Butler   Louisiana State University
Raymond B. Cattell   University of Illinois
Hubert S. Coffey   University of California at Berkeley
Ralph Mason Dreger   Louisiana State University
Albert Ellis   Institute for Rational Living, Inc.
Ann Magaret Garner   University of Nebraska
Jules D. Holzberg   Wesleyan University
Leonard S. Kogan   The City University of New York
Stanley S. Marzolf   Illinois State University
Joseph D. Matarazzo   University of Oregon
Boyd R. McCandless   Indiana University
Gerald R. Pascal   University of Mississippi
L. A. Pennington   Danville, Illinois
Felicia A. Pryor   Louisiana State University
Herbert C. Quay   University of Illinois
William A. Quigley   Arizona State University
George Saslow   University of Oregon
Howard N. Sloane   University of Illinois
William U. Snyder   Ohio University
Charles Van Riper   Western Michigan University
John G. Watkins   University of Montana
Walter L. Wilkins   U.S. Navy Medical Neuropsychiatric Research Unit, San Diego

Richard David Young   Indiana University

AN INTRODUCTION TO

CLINICAL
PSYCHOLOGY

EDITED BY

Irwin A. Berg, Ph.D.
Professor of Psychology and
Dean, College of Arts and Sciences
Louisiana State University

L. A. Pennington, Ph.D.
Clinical Psychologist
Danville, Illinois

Third Edition

THE RONALD PRESS COMPANY • **NEW YORK**

Copyright © 1966 by
THE RONALD PRESS COMPANY

Copyright 1954, 1948, by
THE RONALD PRESS COMPANY

All Rights Reserved

1
G-B

Library of Congress Catalog Card Number: 66–20081
PRINTED IN THE UNITED STATES OF AMERICA

Preface

This Third Edition of *An Introduction to Clinical Psychology* provides a survey of the clinical psychologist at work and some understanding of the problems he deals with along with the opportunities and responsibilities he faces. As was true of the two previous editions, the editors have sought to have the Third Edition serve broadly to orient the clinician-in-training and to provide definite information for medical specialists and social workers. The book will give those in cognate disciplines information concerning the backgrounds, duties, and activities of the clinical psychologist.

While new chapters have been added and all retained chapters have been revised and updated, the original framework of the book has been continued. The first chapter sets forth the historical development, current problems, and professional responsibilities of the field. This forthright historical orientation allows the teacher and the advanced student to develop and apply selected conceptual frameworks that illustrate the trend in the synthesis of clinical and experimental findings.

Part I describes the tools with which the clinician works. No effort has been made to depict every instrument known to the psychodiagnostician. On the contrary, the emphasis is placed upon the rationale, the problems of reliability, validity, objectivity, and restricted areas of usefulness of these instruments. After these delimiting attributes have been weighed, the reader meets at the descriptive level the most frequently used tools. Here the editors take full responsibility for the exclusion of projective test protocols, among others, from the discussions.

Part II approaches clinical activities with hypotheses, or "best guesses," to be checked and rechecked by recourse to the scientific method operative in the clinical laboratory. Although first mentioned at this point, the emphasis throughout the book is centered upon the problem approach, in contradistinction to testing for testing's sake. We do recognize that new techniques uncover new problems and permit the devising of more meaningfully phrased hypotheses. But to give a battery of tests for the battery's sake is unlikely to result in the invention of new methods. The clinician is on safer ground if he early learns to formulate "guesses," some of which can today be tested by available instruments. The others then serve as distress signals for research study. This interaction between hypothesis-test and hypothesis-experiment is viewed as a two-way approach that in the long run will yield far greater dividends than the routine operations of the technician.

Part III presents views and background information and describes illustratively the techniques of clinical psychologists in the field of psychological treatment. Some overlap in certain portions of these chapters will be noted; in this way, the differences in emphasis will become more evident and so serve an instructional purpose.

Part IV stresses the psychologist's ever present role as a research worker in the clinical laboratory. For most psychologists, the scope of this role has yet to be fully ascertained or exploited. By exploring experimentally and statistically the vast resources available to him, the psychologist will discover the broad areas in which he is able to function effectively.

In a book by several authors, there arises the problem of consistency in approach. Because clinical psychology, as we view it, still leans heavily upon different frames of reference and because many clinicians differ in their uses and interpretations of so-called procedures, the editors have purposely fostered the development of a text that portrays these nuances. No pretense at over-all eclecticism is made. The book reflects the diverse views and methods of practicing clinicians as turning about a hard core of established fact. That these views may change, perhaps converge in due time with the continued push into the realm of science, is highly probable. But this is not yet an actuality.

Clinical psychology has matured in self-awareness and in asserting its position of equality with psychiatry and other disciplines. It now clearly fosters rigorous training in science as opposed to the softer road of psychological artistry. And maturity, too, is reflected in the concern with matters of ethical behavior. These trends, among others, are evident in the pages of this Third Edition.

Throughout the volume, the equality of all members of the professional team and the functions of the psychologist in interviewing, psychodiagnostic examining, report writing, psychotherapy, counseling, and research have been portrayed as aspects of an ongoing, unitary process that is the lifeblood of clinical psychology.

Gratitude is expressed to all contributors, publishers, and others whose cooperation and suggestions, in and out of official channels of consultation, have facilitated the development of this new edition.

IRWIN A. BERG
L. A. PENNINGTON

Baton Rouge, Louisiana
Danville, Illinois
April, 1966

Contents

Part III. TREATMENT APPROACHES

Part IV. THE CLINICIAN AND RESEARCH

AN INTRODUCTION TO

CLINICAL PSYCHOLOGY

1

The Meaning of Clinical Psychology

RAYMOND B. CATTELL *

THE AREAS OF THE CLINICIAN'S ACTIVITIES

The student who contemplates the calling of a clinical psychologist needs to take stock both of its present functions and status and of its past and probable future development. Its present activities cover a quite extraordinary breadth of skills and specialties. The role of a clinical psychologist covers the diagnosis and treatment of neurotics and psychotics, advising on delinquency, analyzing school retardation and educational adjustment, and treating such problems as alcoholism and sex deviation. Clinical principles enter into good vocational guidance, the more sophisticated aspects of vocational selection, industrial management, and marriage counseling. The clinician must concern himself with matters as diverse as the sociology of suicide; the neurology of brain defects and damage; the etiology of stuttering, epilepsy, and cerebral palsy; truancy from school; sensory defects; psychosomatic disorders; geriatrics and problems of aging—and so on through a kaleidoscope of behavioral difficulties.

Correspondingly, his resources, in terms of therapy, must include a command of the principles of classical psychoanalysis; group therapy; non-directive, client-centered approaches; chemotherapy by tranquilizers and hallucinogenic drugs; physiological and surgical possibilities using EST and leucotomy; hypnosis; psychodrama; existential analysis; Jungian, Alderian, and Rankian methods and Horney's "character analysis"; socio-

* Raymond B. Cattell, Ph.D. D.Sc. (University of London), Research Professor of Psychology, and Director, Laboratory of Personality and Group Analysis, University of Illinois.

logical and anthropological ecological treatments; and, last but not least, the recent developments in behavior therapy.

It is not my purpose here to enlarge on these, since the remaining chapters of this book will clarify their apparently bewildering variety, and there are recent ample surveys in such books as Ford and Urban's *Systems of Psychotherapy* (1963),[1] Masserman's *Current Psychiatric Therapies* (1962–64), Kogan on social work (1960), Allensmith and Goethals (1962) on the schools and mental health, and others. However, my purpose in this opening chapter requires that I begin by indicating what the clinical psychologist actually does, as a basis for rapid, but hopefully not superficial, review of how he needs to be trained, what his professional status has been and is likely to be, in what ways he can organize his working conditions and teamwork for best service, why he must have good contact with research trends, what the special satisfactions of such a career can be, and how the subject has developed and is likely to develop in the next decade or so.

THE HISTORICAL EMERGENCE OF THE CLINICAL PSYCHOLOGIST

Those who take it for granted that the clinical psychologist is the natural specialist to handle the activities described above may need to be reminded that such functions have not always been his. Even today, these services are quite differently arranged and divided in countries in which psychology has developed, as a science, less vigorously than in America. It was equally possible for these functions, viewed in a broad perspective of culture and history, to have been developed as an extension of the activity of the priest, minister, or religious organization (see McCann, 1962; Tweedie, 1963); of the teacher (at least with children); or of the medical doctor. As it happens, the only area where relations are still in a state of flux and complication, especially in certain countries, concerns the sharing of the task with medicine. Consequently, the relation of psychiatrist and clinical psychologist deserves special and sympathetic analysis later.

Some writers on historical trends in psychology (e.g., Kelly, 1947) place the birth of clinical psychology as late as 1917, but this might better be described as its adolescent "confirmation," by the formation of the first professional organization concerned with the study of clinical problems. The literal starting point, in the modern sense of psychology, that is, omitting the usual references to philosophic beginnings in Paracelsus, Galen, or Aristotle, was surely when Witmer established the first psychological clinic, in 1896, at the University of Pennsylvania (Brotemarkle, 1947). (We are told that what sparked action was the challenge of a

[1] See references at end of chapter.

public-school teacher seeking help for a chronically bad speller!) Sir Francis Galton's activities with individual measurements and family histories a generation earlier, however, had the spirit if not the service function of psychology applied clinically to the individual case. Soon after this, in the first decade of our century, we witnessed an almost explosive growth of psychology applied to the adjustment and guidance problems of the individual. This period is remembered by such landmarks as the Binet test and Whipple's *Manual of Mental and Physical Tests* (1910), and its passing into the vast experiment in 1916–18 in the application of tests to military selection under Yerkes (1921).

In contrast with the present activities of clinical psychologists, as illustrated in America in the fifties and sixties, the thirty years following World War I saw the practicing psychologist, however, relatively restricted to (1) diagnostic work only and (2) the realm of cognitive phenomena—mental defects as causes of school backwardness, sensory defects, and special school disabilities. Freud, it is true, in *The Future of Lay Analysis* (1927), had even at this early stage gone so far as to say that medical training was not necessary for, and in practice might even be a distraction from, the acquisition of the highest skills in therapy by psychoanalysis. Although, consistent with this position, many outstanding lay analysts entered therapeutic practice in this period, theirs was nevertheless not the usual pattern for the psychologist in the clinical field. Psychologists held back from therapy partly because they were not satisfied with the experimental scientific standing of the methods—notably psychoanalysis—by which they were invited to conduct therapy. At the same time, the organizational compromise adopted as practicable in the early American Child Guidance Clinic tended to channel the efforts of the psychologist into ability and achievement diagnosis and those of the physician—commonly a psychiatrist and the clinic director—into the handling of emotional problems.

The objections to freezing this into a standard pattern were stated by the present writer, when taking up the direction of the first child-guidance clinic in Britain to be directed by a psychologist (Cattell, 1932). The first objection was to the excessive training period required of the psychiatrist, in virtually piling a Ph.D. in psychology on an M.D., a level of educational investment that only a handful of individuals can hope to attain. This points to the need for some division of the totality, and it was suggested that a more natural division can be drawn between the physical and mental examination and treatment of the individual. This plan had in fact been successfully followed in the writer's clinic, where the school medical officer and the psychologist met to integrate, in case conferences, across this less arbitrary frontier. Another objection was that the natural growth of psychology as a science, even though it was then weak in the areas of emotional adjustment, personality, learning principles and laws, and the understanding of pathology, would necessarily end by bringing the cognitive and emotional fields into such conceptual and methodological integration that it would be absurd not to have the psychologist—or some other one practitioner—handle both together. The thirty years since this forecast was made have undoubtedly brought it visibly much nearer to realization.

It was inevitable that the growth of psychological practice should bring some searching mutual appraisals by psychiatrist and psychologist. Questions regarding the status of psychiatry as a branch of science were raised, for example, by Terman (Cattell, 1932), who concluded "psychiatry will not be pulled out of the mire until it lays down the requirement of two or three years of solid training in psychology . . . including personality testing and statistical methods." This remains as apposite today as when written twenty years ago. Conversely, the psychiatrist doubted the "bedside manner" of the psychologist and the adequacy of his general training in pathology.

The issues as to what types of practitioner are likely to emerge and best fit the public need have been discussed from the standpoint of different specialties very adequately by Gregg (1948), Heiser (1945), E. L. Kelly (1947), Kern (1951), Lerner (1963), McGuire (1962), Menninger (1947), Moreno (1963), Pennington (1953), Roe (1949), and others. Most of these apparently agree with the present writer's assertion in the 1948 edition of this book that the old practice of first sending the client at the child-guidance clinic to a psychometrist to have his abilities examined and then to a psychiatrist for a "mental and emotional" examination and, finally, consuming the expensive time of both of these practitioners in a conference to join the severed halves of the client's personality is not a very intelligent procedure. The more we know about personality, the more we realize the absurdity of sundering it into artificial independent segments. For example, scholastic performances and abilities are sensitive indicators of dynamic adjustment, and, conversely, the treatment of scholastic disabilities is, more often than not, a problem of therapy of the total personality.

Admittedly, specialization must exist, because our minds are small, but at least we can draw the divisions wisely. A boundary drawn through the center of the personality is as unsatisfactory and productive of costly misunderstanding as a national boundary running through a densely populated industrial region.

Those cognizant of this struggle over the birth of a new practitioner and who attempt to dramatize it into a conflict of individuals, however, are guilty of a misstatement of actual conditions as well as disservice to the growing cooperation of all specialists in the clinical field. For, in view of the professional tensions and difficulties that might have arisen from the strain of growth, it is evident that the great majority of those concerned have met the needs of adjustment and of enlightened progress admirably. Academic psychologists, it is true, have muddled the opportunity for training clinical artists, and psychiatrists have been slow to recognize that psychology is the basic science in these fields of practice, but, as Menninger (1947) well says, "Psychiatrists should not be surprised that psychologists are not yet fully accustomed to their new clinical role. Psychologists similarly should not be surprised if the medical profession, jealous of its historical and traditional responsibilities, is somewhat slow in welcoming the psychologists." But socially the situation improves, and one meets increasingly from the field such reports as that by Vernon (1946) that "resistance to consulting psychology is declining and cooperation . . . with informed members of the medical profession . . . no longer offers any difficulty."

THE LEGAL STATUS AND PROFESSIONAL STANDARDS OF THE CLINICAL PSYCHOLOGIST

The clinical psychologist has in effect won the functional position logically indicated above as his—at least in America, Australia, Britain, Japan, Holland, and Scandinavia. And, though he is far from this in more conservative countries (in some Latin countries, still occupying the role of a minor handmaiden or technician to the physician), they are clearly moving in the new direction, in step with the expansion of psychology as a science.

The three aspects of clinical psychology that we may call the service role, the training need, and the problem of legal professional status are necessarily very closely interrelated. They form a healthy or a vicious circle according to circumstances. The existing training determines what services can be given; the service determines the status and emoluments; and these attractions, in turn, determine how many years of training recruits to the profession will put in for such positions. It can easily be recognized that the areas of professional work and service designated above demand highly intelligent persons, trained to a doctorate level, but the actual training and salaries still have to adjust to this in many parts of the world. Let us, however, defer studying the training problem until the next section, while we consider the professional standards and community relations of those who have already attained to representing reasonably adequate prototypes of the clinical psychologist.

In the last twenty years, the clinical psychologist has made his way into a widening circle of community services, which are briefly summarized in Table 1–1.

Table 1–1. Professional Resources Available in Numerous Psychological Service Centers as Surveyed by Trow (1950) * and Indicative of the Numerous Specialists Met by the Clinical Psychologist

Medical	(hospital, clinic, private physician)
Psychiatric	(mental hospitals and child guidance clinic)
Rehabilitation	(vocational counselors, occupational therapists, physical therapists)
Special	(specialists in speech, reading, and hearing disabilities)
Social	(family service agencies, child care, foster home representatives, social service workers)
Recreational	(corrective therapists, recreational specialists, camp counselors)
Education	(subject-matter specialists in colleges, high schools, trade schools)

* Based upon material presented by W. C. Trow (1950), in *The American Psychologist.* Reprinted with permission granted by the American Psychological Association, publishers of *The American Psychologist.*

These community services call for the interaction of the psychologist with many types of patient, with psychiatrists and physicians, teachers, speech pathologists, social workers, psychiatric nurses, ministers, magistrates and lawyers, pediatricians, prison officials, employment officers, industrial personnel and management, military officers, and, not least important, the man in the street, as a parent. It is vital that all of these have a reliable image of the psychologist and his functions and that he, in turn, have a definite and appropriate set of attitudes, in etiquette and ethics, for all practical situations.

In this connection, many psychologists in the early days of the profession met at some time or another the expressed or implied criticism from psychiatrists that a psychologist does not have that "regular indoctrination" concerning the relation to colleagues and patients that ensures that he will "automatically" assume the cloak of ethical behavior, or, at least, of professional etiquette, which is assumed to be second nature to the medical man. This is doubtless largely a matter of time, and the requisite standards are now becoming crystallized as the profession becomes of age. What is overlooked by some who appreciate the importance of the matter, however, is that it could be undesirable to enforce too early a mere imitation of the pattern set by the medical practitioner. For it is entirely possible that there are certain important differences in manners and modes of relationship that must come with this new profession of ours. The matter is receiving considerable thought from leaders in the field, and a number of practical suggestions have been made, which need to be critically examined. For example, Dr. James G. Miller (1948) suggested a system whereby clinical psychologists and psychiatrists would be trained together from the first year of graduate school. This might do much to assist in the spread of what one might call the "fraternity outlook." On the other hand, it might harm more than it helps, for the clinical psychologist might also absorb what must be described as the psychiatrist's rather indifferent attitude toward involvement in research.

For the time being, the main questions have been solved, at least on paper, in terms of the code of ethics drawn up by a committee of the American Psychological Association (1953, 1963), setting forth ethical standards pertaining to six areas of professional behavior: public responsibility, client relationships, teaching, research, writing and publishing, and relationships with colleagues and other professional persons. These recommendations recognize that the clinical psychologist, to focus our attention on him once again, by the very richness and complexity of the lives of the people with whom he works, encounters unusually subtle moral and ethical questions. Among these are the following items: the maintenance of proper technical standards, the recognition of limitations in knowledge of psychological techniques, the correct bounds of the therapeutic relationship to the client, the protection of the confidential relationships to the client, the communication of information to professional co-workers and agencies, the use of clinical materials in teaching and writing, the relationship to advertising, and the problem of fees. These and many others from day to day can raise problems in ethical behavior and professional conduct.

Naturally, the biggest problem, as in every new profession, has been the elimination of charlatans, which has to be done firmly as regards those who prey upon the public with definitely unscientific or dangerous methods, yet considerately in regard to somewhat unconventional approaches that may nevertheless have virtue. Fortunately, both the American Psychiatric Association (See Committee on Clinical Psychology . . . etc., 1949) and the American Psychological Association have reached a position (Ad Hoc Committee, 1952), in which psychotherapy by clinical psychologists under adequate medical safeguards is approved.

The magnitude of the problem, and its importance to American psychologists, is brought out by the fact that the number of psychologists in the clinical division of the APA—about 6,000—is now greater than in any other division, and far above the average of all other divisions. It is not surprising that the American Psychological Association has taken active steps to support and guide in every state the official certification of practicing psychologists, which has made such strides in the last ten years. As of 1966, more than half of the 50 states have licensing or certification laws for psychological practitioners by statutory act.[2]

[2] *Certification* restricts the use of a professional title such as "certified psychologist" to those who have been legally accepted as meeting the educational and training standards specified by state law or other certifying agency. It prevents noncertified persons from using the legally defined title but does not prevent them from practicing psychology. While *licensure* has the same provision concerning the use of a professional title, it also limits the practice of psychology as defined in the legal statutes of a state to those who have been granted a license. Connecticut issued certificates

The beneficial effects of certification and of the further definition of the professional code of ethics (American Psychological Association, 1963) are already apparent in wider recognition of the psychologist and his functions, and more confident use of his services. Pediatricians and physicians in general, for example, have recognized that the psychologist can handle their type of problem sometimes more aptly than the fully pathologically oriented psychiatrist, while, on other frontiers such as in industrial psychology, there has been an increasing elimination of practitioners not really qualified to handle the scientific complexities personnel work presents.

Another direction in which the beneficial effects of certification have become quickly apparent is the increased assurance with which students obtaining the Ph.D. clinical degree have entered private practice. Several aspects of this professional field are well discussed by Blau (1960). Readers interested in the related topic of psychologists in psychotherapy should read the bulletins of "Psychologists Interested in the Advancement of Psychotherapy" (Section 2, Division 12, 1964). This group, now over 1,000 in membership, began its activities in 1960 and has passed a number of important and specific resolutions including a request to health insurance companies not to discriminate against patients of psychologists, and another to the APA to take positive steps on public relations "to promulgate models for [psychological services] and disseminate information" and "to inform NIMH [National Institute of Mental Health] that those parts of the regulations governing new mental health centers which state that a psychiatrist will be responsible for the clinical programs and the medical responsibility for every patient must be rested in a physician are unsatisfactory to psychology" (1964).

The birth pangs of a new profession are perhaps sharper in America, because America has far more university psychology departments, more students, more practitioners, and more research contributions in journals than and other country (see Clark, 1960). Parenthetically, the vigor of academic psychology is in part a function of the degree of community

---

for practicing psychologists in 1945; Kentucky, in 1948; Virginia, in 1950; Georgia, in 1951; Minnesota, in 1951; and a number of other states are considering similar action. On the other hand, there has been some systematic opposition at the professional level. The American Medical Association (Gerty *et al.*, 1952) opposes licensure for psychologists but recommends certification in line with existing state laws, feeling that no clinical psychologist should practice psychotherapy without working in close cooperation with a psychiatrist. Again, the National Committee for Mental Hygiene approves the child-guidance-clinic pattern in which a psychiatrist is the director of the clinic in general, though the psychologist may direct on special occasions.

To say that there are some powerful organizations of this kind aligned against the emergence of the psychological profession, and that entrenched conservatism automatically digs in against it, is, however, in the perspective of history, not very impressive. It was in the face of similar opposition that dentists acquired their independent status, and surgeons developed out of barbers. The basic fact is that the technical and logical unity of the science is on the side of the psychologist.

application. For, in countries where psychology has been kept closely tied to philosophy and to a purely academic atmosphere, the departments have remained small, poorly supported, and narrow and conservative in interest, for example, limited to concern with sensory processes and perception. The success of the practicing psychologist in the community has brought to university psychology departments growth, growth problems, and an enrichment of research fields. With this observation, let us turn to the clinician's education.

QUALIFICATIONS AND TRAINING IN THE UNIVERSITY SETTING

With the above well-defined professional opportunities and the vast community demand, it might seem that the educational direction for clinical psychology would also be well defined. But, throughout the period of most rapid growth, in the past twenty years, the nature of training has remained hotly debated, to the point at which one might say that the greatest threat to the acceptance of the practicing psychologist comes from psychologists themselves.

The first phase of this internal conflict began with a constructive attack on traditional academic psychological training by a number of active and insightful clinical psychologists. Shakow (1942, 1949) and Thorne (1945), for example, made penetrating analyses of the requirements of clinical education. Thorne called for reconstruction of the academic curriculum, remarking that "American psychology has been a laboratory rather than a clinical science," and adding, "It takes many years to make a competent physician and there is no reason to believe that competency in clinical psychology is any more easily achieved."

Both Thorne, in his original editorial at the inauguration of the *Journal of Clinical Psychology*, and Shakow, in his several contributions to the training program, recognized, first, that clinical psychologists must first adopt swift defense measures, for themselves and for the public, against the swarm of opportunists and charlatans aware of the popular demand for treatment. This defense must be a high standard of approved professional qualification, for, as Thorne said, "clinical phychology has the responsibility of being the chief immediate representative of what psychology can do for society," and, as Shakow added, "unless psychology can provide adequately trained personnel, other disciplines, which recognize both the need and the responsibilities, will take over."

Shakow and others actually practicing in the field advocated, therefore,

. . . a broadening of the psychological curriculum; an orientation to diagnosis, therapy, and research; the introduction of medical courses covering physiology, particular aspects of anatomy, the autonomic nervous system, and endocrinology, followed by an internship . . . in an atmosphere permeated with psychology of a living kind [Shakow, 1942].

At that time, there was some disagreement as to whether full specialization should come before or after the level of the master's degree. Those who emphasize that clinical skill is an art, in which many with the ordinary Ph.D. doctorate would be hopelessly incompetent, rather than a science, argued for earlier specialization, while those who stressed the need for a sound general scientific background favored late specialization. Lowell Kelly (1947) probably expressed the opinion of most competent psychologists when he asserted that "the clinical psychologist is first a psychologist and then a clinician," and this has been commonly accepted since by most discussants. The issue is tied in with the debate as to whether the doctorate for the clinical psychologist should be the Ph.D. or, as has recently been advocated in a few universities, a doctorate of psychology that is very specifically shaped for the general psychological practitioner in those fields common to clinical and to all applied psychology.

Again we encounter a plexus of interdependent issues. The fact is that many individuals are capable of performing at a high level of technical skill, for example, in handling children, who do not have the intellectual interests to grasp issues in pure science. On the other hand, ability to conduct or understand research is related to ability in pure science. Consequently, the advocate of a high standard of general psychological education for clinicians is in general also bidding for research orientation and for the restriction of clinical training to students of higher mental caliber.

However, there is more to the selection and training of clinical psychologists than meeting the purely academic requirements, no matter how they are shaped (APA, Education and Training Board, 1953). Time was when the clinical division of psychology tended to attract a disproportionate number of people with their own emotional-adjustment problems. The boot is now on the other foot. It is recognized that clinical work makes onerous demands on the emotional resources of even the most stable and mature natures. The internship, as well as the vigilance of instructors, tends to eliminate individuals who might get along quite well in the relatively protected academic life, and are good Ph.D. material, but who lack the warmth and stability that, as Kelly and Fiske's (1952) research shows, is associated with clinical success. However, the argument that the satisfactions and demands of the clinical life make demands on additional qualities in the realm of personality is no longer used as an excuse for clinicians being accepted for practice with lower academic qualifications. While a "grandfather clause" may permit certification for continuing practice of those experienced persons who stopped academically with an M.A. or a diploma, it seems universally agreed now that the clinician in future must have a doctorate, and the only issue concerns the emphasis in training, or even the title, to be associated with this six to eight years of university and hospital education.

For, whereas the clinicians originally attacked the standard academic training, some academicians are now attacking the inadequacy of the clinician's training, pointing out that it contains too much "rule-of-thumb" practical instruction in testing and the art of therapy, together with inadequate grounding in scientific principles and research methods. In the recent Clark Committee's report to the APA, this resulted in a proposal to issue two distinct degrees, the Ph.D. and the doctor-of-psychology degree, or, respectively, degrees "pure" and "applied" psychology. On the other hand, the Boulder and Miami conferences on *Professional Preparation of Clinical Psychologists* (see Roe *et al.*, 1959) presented many more sophisticated viewpoints, which suggest that the solution is not so simple. In the first place, among some academicians who appear more concerned to get rid of the clinical psychologist than to see that he is well trained, there is a quaintly old-fashioned assumption that the center of scientific psychology lies in brass instrumental exercises in perception and learning, especially with rats. If the pie is to be cut in such a way that some pieces must fall off the plate, then, as a leading clinician has pointed out, the analysis of the most complex human behavior is not the expendable piece. Rather might many rat studies be relegated to a Ph.D. in zoology, and others to physiology. On grounds of centrality of subject matter, clinical psychology certainly cannot be legislated out of the Ph.D.! On the different grounds of "applied" versus "pure" orientation, however, the matter deserves further discussion.

If one takes medicine as a model, social experience may argue for a split of the academic-researcher and practitioner degrees, for the skills of a general practitioner are needed in emergencies, and he must be as well drilled to the best practical action as is a soldier. Three considerations throw doubt on this model: (1) The nature of the psychologists's practice does not have life-and-death urgency at any hour of day and night as in general medicine. (2) As a young science, psychology is likely to be transformed almost out of recognition, as in therapeutic procedures in less than a generation by the progress of research. The practitioner who is not also research trained and oriented is going to get badly out of touch, obsolete, and ineffective in his very practice. (3) Medicine is to some extent regretting its own model.

The typical M.D. qualification has produced practitioners notoriously incapable of directing or following research. Medical schools are in many places aiming at a new, hybrid type, and their faculties consist of researchers to some extent engaged in practice. The argument of some academic researchers for following the medical pattern could boomerang upon themselves, disqualifying them as academic men because they lack the fuller experience of practice. For it is, first, evident, from the very small research output among clinical psychologists, that their teachers have not made the Ph.D. degree the research-oriented experience they claim it to be. Second, the experience of medicine that basic research is enriched by contact with many phenomena met in practice argues not for splitting clinical from academic psychology but for educating the Simon-pure academic teacher by requiring that he have some clinical experience.

The clinical psychologist must, of course, have his year of internship. But is this not properly viewed as the equivalent of the year's internship in rat husbandry, in construction of electronic apparatus, or of apprentice-ship on the computer, which Ph.D's in other fields must necessarily ob-tain? Intrinsically, there is no reason why one should be less rich in scientific experience than the other. They are merely different fields of specialization within the Ph.D.

Finally, whatever else it may be, the movement in a minority of pedants to segregate the clinical psychologist is an anachronism. Had it been made forty years ago, when psychoanalytic and Adlerian and Jungian inspirations reigned supreme, and psychology could show little scientific progress outside the cognitive realm, it would have made immediate sense and could merely have been charged with a lack of penetration and decent optimism in seeing future developments. Today, with the integration of clinical and experimental personality theory, and the devel-opment of objective diagnostic methods, the attempt to dislocate clinical psychology from the main body of psychology is completely out of phase. (See Chapters 5 and 17.) Far from being the slogan of reformers, it is merely the death cry from the last beleaguered citadel of those who have obstinately refused to recognize the broadening of scientific methods and models beyond those of the vintage of Pavlov and Wundt.

What this battlefield most needs is a healing of unnecessary wounds suf-fered in a wrong structuring of the issues. If clinical psychology is properly viewed as one of several possible specializations in psychology, each with its equivalent of an internship, and if we recognize that the nature and phase of development of psychology are so different from medicine that we have to take a new model for a new profession, namely, the research-oriented practitioner, then it is necessary for academic psy-chologists to draw the clinician back into the fold, sympathetically recog-nizing his special difficulties—as well as the need for some self-reform. These possibilities we will take up in the next section.

Meanwhile, assuming that psychologists themselves solve this problem of university qualification, by a Ph.D. or psychological doctorate degree requiring essentially the same number of years of post-high school educa-tion as for the M.D., there will still remain problems on some other flanks.

One cropping up increasingly in the writings of psychologists concerns the need for greater control by psychologists of the internship conditions in hospitals and clinics in the administrative charge of psychiatrists. The ideal solution from the standpoint of the clinician's academic colleagues, along the lines of compromise indicated above, is not going to be possible without freedom of psychologists to prescribe the internship training of their own. Secondly, there is the problem that clinical psychology is only one section, though the largest, of a general training for applied psychology. If all are primarily to be trained as psychologists, and if most require some understanding of a clinical approach, then various aspects of industrial and educational psychological practice must surely be regarded as late specializations, requiring some extra training as is arranged for specialties in medicine.

PROSPECTIVE DEVELOPMENTS IN CLINICAL PRACTICE AND THE NEED FOR RESEARCH-ORIENTED TRAINING

The argument above that the clinical psychologist needs to be primarily a psychologist, earning the Ph.D. by competence in basic science and by a trained orientation to research, rests on (1) the fact that psychology is a young science, likely to change its practice considerably after the individual "qualifies," and (2) a change in our society that affects the image of the practitioner in *all* applied fields, namely, the fact that research is becoming "big business," invalidating the old and admittedly comfortable view of a practitioner who "qualifies" and "settles down to practice."

The difficult task of the academic teacher is not finished when the clinical student goes through the research exercise of preparing a thesis. Frequently, he has had to wean the clinical student, more than others, from some image of a crystal-gazing seer, and other values remote from those of a scientist. And now, beyond these, he needs to stimulate an interest in keeping permanently in touch with research. Some of the acerbity of the academic criticism (sometimes misdirected) and rejection of clinicians arises from the record of past clinical psychologists. To the basic scientific psychologist, they are seen as taking all (they readily out-earn the academic) and contributing nothing, for their record of research publication has been calculated as less than one article per clinician per lifetime. What is perhaps more damning is that a great number of practitioners are failing the public by using obsolete methods, averaging ten years behind current research findings. The primary solution to this is reading in good research journals and books, together with keeping a hand, on no matter how small a scale, in some kind of research. A secondary solution is more short retraining programs and workshops, by professional groups, universities, and test constructers.

Setting down irretrievably, in a textbook with at least a decade's life, what one thinks the future will bring is a game with the odds perilously stacked against one. Yet it behooves us to anticipate those developments to which a forward-looking clinician should be giving attention. First and most certain, with the increasing government support of the anti-poverty programs and help for the culturally deprived, for the mental retarded, in job retraining and rehabilitation, and in solving the adjustment problems of the aged, there will be a continuation of expanding job opportunities for clinical psychologists.

The developments in the subject itself may perhaps be best considered under (1) diagnosis, (2) therapy, and (3) the community organization of services. The largest evident transition in the first is from *ad hoc* tests—a gadgetry focal to pathology—to tests that derive from general personality theory and link the abnormal with the general dynamics of the normal personality. The rapid growth in the multivariate experimental study of personality (Eysenck, 1961; Guilford, 1961; Cattell, 1957; Cattell and Scheier, 1961) is producing a body of knowledge and interlocking principles the clinician has not previously had available, and for lack of which he has had to rest temporarily on more intuitively, qualitatively based clinical systems, as in psychoanalysis. In particular, more clinicians are perceiving that the factor-analytic approach is really a method for doing with a greater breadth of observation, and with computer recording and analysis, what the clinician has always sought to do with his own unaided memory. To use these new source-trait concepts, he does not need to learn factor analysis, but only to understand the emerging psychological concepts, and to recognize the very significant differences of profile on these factored tests (questionnaire, as in the HSPQ or 16 P.F.) arising among various types of neuroses and psychoses in relation to normals (Cattell and Scheier, 1961; Rickels and Cattell, 1965).

The present decade is likely also to see striking advances in pharmacological control, if not in positive therapy, which may alter the appearance of our mental hospitals and of private practice. In regard to more specific therapies, the reader may wish to follow the prospects described by Berger (1962), Bierer (1962), and Mullen and Rosenbaum (1962) on group therapy; Hilgard and Hilgard (1962) on hypnosis; Lebo (1956) on play therapy; Corsini (1945) on prison therapy; Adler (1963) on new Adlerian developments; Hall (1962) on dream-diagnostic therapy; Rogers (1960) on nondirective methods; Deniker (1963) on chemotherapy; Lorand (1963) on modifications in classical psychoanalysis, and Fleming (1962) on its demands; Kogan (1960) on new functions of social work; Allensmith and Goetals (1962) on the role of schools in mental health; Gilliland (1962) on music therapy; Moreno (1963) on group psychodrama; Mowrer (1960) and Tweedie (1963) on the integration with religion; McCann (1962) on the role of the churches; Nunnally (1961), Mandelbrote (1959), and Hann (1959) on the community attitudes to mental health and community organization; and Black (1959) on workshop therapy—as well as the chapters below that cover these topics.   Incidentally, it is interesting to compare these with somewhat different developments abroad, in Russia, as covered by Field (1960).

A marked increase is occurring in this decade also in a truly scientific and methodologically sophisticated attack on the genetics of mental illness (Böök, 1960; Kallmann et al., 1961).   Apart from the need for more exact methods and measurements, there is a need to educate the clinician to recognize that an understanding of genetics not only is preventive—in a eugenic sense—but also can offer valuable guidance in therapeutic steps. For example, some personality factors, for example, in the O-A Battery (Cattell et al., 1955), are far more genetically determined than others (Cattell, Kristy, and Stice, 1957), and the recognition that some factors can "do duty" for others in the adjustment process will guide the therapist not to waste his time on the immovable, but to use the patient's resources in the best way.

The impulse given to clinical psychology from anthropology is now assuming a new direction from the basic research (Meredith, 1965; Tsujioka and Cattell, 1965; Rummel, 1965) that has introduced precise measurements and new concepts to the previous rather cloudy discussions of culture patterns.   The findings by Scheier (Cattell and Scheier, 1961) of quite remarkable differences in anxiety level among major cultures, and by Tsujioka (1965) of striking differences in introversion level, at once offer new research approaches to the etiology of neurosis and suggest differences necessary in therapy in different countries.

However, the direction in which the present writer would be most inclined to predict radical advances is that in which the traditionally-trained clinician might at first be least inclined to look, namely, in the introduction of clear mathematical models and consequent ability to enlist computer aids.   With the crystallization of concepts about well-replicated personality factor structures, in ratings, questionnaires, and objective tests (Cattell et al., 1955) and the demonstration that specification equations work quite well in predicting almost any kind of clinical criterion from the new factor-measurement instruments (Cattell and Eber, 1965), all kinds of diagnoses, prognoses, and decisions on therapeutic steps can be given the greater objectivity and exactitude that a computer technician attached to the clinic can supply.   The present rough linear model may not be the final answer, as Meehl (1950) and Kahn (1960) suggest, but at least it can already give help beyond the clinician's subjective estimates, and can be improved. For example, in what has been called *Adjustment Process Analysis,* Cattell and Scheier (1961) have shown how matrix multiplication on computers can be applied to understanding the progress of the individual clinical case in terms of repeated measures on basic personality and motivation source-trait factors. Models from game theory also have promise in understanding the individual maladjustment and relearning procedure. Finally, in what has been called the "dynamic calculus," the new objective measures of drive tension level, as in the *Motivation Analysis Test* (Horn *et al.,* 1964), offer the beginnings of a "quantitative psychoanalysis" of symptom motivation structure.

It is characteristic of the above-mentioned lag that the education of the clinical psychologist in personality theory, with a few notable exceptions such as the texts of Dreger (1961), Hall and Lindzey (1957), Bischof (1964), Eysenck (1961), Guilford (1959), Sells (1962), and a few others, has failed to bring out the practical importance of the new personality theories based on factored measurement and experiment to the clinical psychologist. Here are the equivalents of the doctor's clinical thermometer, EKG, X-ray, and blood tests, which make all the difference between working with merely hopeful intuitions and working with clear theory tied to quantitative observations.

At present, the clinician is taught diagnosis and therapy in distinct courses, but the advent of new analytical instruments and rapid computing services as sketched above will mean that the same test devices that are used for diagnosis will be used in repeated applications during therapy, for example, by P-technique, to guide the tactics of therapy and evaluate its progress. Eber (1964), Swenson (1964), and a number of others have pioneered sufficiently in linking computers to producing immediate test scoring, diagnosis, and report writing to demonstrate how substantially the case load of a clinician can be expanded, with an increase rather than a decrease in his individual effectiveness (Cattell, 1965). If the clinician is to avail himself of these computer possibilities (physically provided easily on a private phone line), his education has obviously to be more centered on basic science and its accompanying mathematics, as has been advocated above. In so moving, he need not fear that he will lose his clinical role, for clinical medicine is also moving in the direction of utilizing more information provided by technicians, and keeping the totality in view by calling in the synthesizing power of the computer.

In this rapid glance over possible directions of clinical development, the question of the relationship between the community as a whole and the clinical practitioner requires momentary but nonetheless emphatic consideration. In the ebullient state that has recently prevailed among young clinicians, claims with distinctly extravagant implications have sometimes been made. The clinician, it is said, is going not only to save individuals from psychopathological difficulties but also to rescue the entire community from impoverishment, delinquency, psychological invalidism, absenteeism, hostility, hate, and war—to mention only a few of the claims. That psychological research will revolutionize the aims and techniques of public welfare work and of the statesmen, in the fullness of time, no one can doubt. But the clinician needs to demonstrate his capacity to handle tolerably complex models for the individual, and to produce measurable therapeutic change in him, before he has the right to claim influence in these still more complex areas.

SUMMARY

The "meaning" of clinical psychology—its range, its purpose within society, its methods and practitioners—is becoming sufficiently crystallized to be quite clear to all those who are now connected with it. What is not so certain is whether this concept will become realized in living. Can we struggle free from the encumbering pressures of older professions? Can we hold a steady course through the ferment of historical and cultural currents toward the significant, rounded role the development of psychology as a science indicates? Can the clinical psychologist acquire the bedside manner of the medical man—all the skills and organizational concerns of practice—without forgetting that, more than any other practitioner, he needs to keep a firm grip on the mane of research, and to maintain the knowledge and the viewpoint of a researcher? These are the critical questions, the issues that only time can settle.

Meanwhile, we need to watch our compass in relation to three main bearings. First, clinical psychology must now aim at the level of academic and professional qualification of a doctorate with internship, decidedly above those nondescript backgrounds that sufficed for the first wave of applied psychologists in the field. This is true as well of those applied fields in education and industrial psychology that also demand essential clinical skills. Second, though this may be demanding something new of human nature, clinical psychology should not be content to imitate the medical practitioner but must turn out a practitioner who is also at heart a researcher, familiar with, even if he cannot very actively participate in, the trends of recent research. For considerable developments of new techniques are likely in the near future in pharmacology, anthropological-cultural approaches, neurophysiology, genetics, behavior therapy, and especially a skilled psychometric use, aided by computers, of more searching and valid personality and motivation measurements. Only the practitioner able to read and assimilate research consequences on his own, beyond his formal training period, will be able to avail himself of these advances as they affect analytical power of diagnosis and evaluation of therapeutic tactics. Third, clinical psychology must attend to the social and ethical aspects of a growing profession, completing the licensing of practicing psychologists, avoiding what is merely fashionable, rejecting the grandiose, the expedient, the impractical or the perverted, but holding firmly to long-term aims indicated by the true natures of psychology and society.

REFERENCES

ADLER, A. 1963. Adlerian psychotherapy and recent trends. *J. indiv. Psychol.*, 19, 55–60.

ALLENSMITH, W., and GOETHALS, G. W. 1962. *The role of schools in mental health.* New York: Basic Books.

AMERICAN PSYCHIATRIC ASSOCIATION, COMMITTEE ON CLINICAL PSYCHOLOGY OF THE GROUP FOR ADVANCEMENT OF PSYCHIATRY. 1949. *The relation of clinical psychology to psychiatry,* Report No. 10. (July.)

AMERICAN PSYCHOLOGICAL ASSOCIATION. 1953, 1963. *Ethical standards of psychologists.* Washington, D.C.: The Association. *Amer. Psychologist.*

AMERICAN PSYCHOLOGICAL ASSOCIATION, AD HOC COMMITTEE ON RELATIONS BETWEEN PSYCHOLOGY AND THE MEDICAL PROFESSION. 1952. Psychology and its relationships with other professions. *Amer. Psychologist*, 7, 145–52.

AMERICAN PSYCHOLOGICAL ASSOCIATION, EDUCATION AND TRAINING BOARD. 1953. Doctoral training programs in clinical psychology and in counseling psychology. *Amer. Psychologist*, 8, 245.

BACHRACH, A. J. (ed.). 1962. *Experimental foundations of clinical psychology.* New York: Basic Books.

BERGER, M. M. 1962. An overview of group psychotherapy: Its past, present and future development. *Int. J. Group Psychother.*, 13, 287–94.

BIERER, J. 1962. Great Britain's therapeutic social clubs. *Ment. Hosp.*, 13, 203–7.

BISCHOF, L. J. 1964. *Interpreting personality theories.* New York: Harper & Row.

BLACK, B. J. 1959. The protected workshop in the rehabilitation of the mentally ill. *Psychiat. Quart. Suppl.*, 33, 107–18.

BLAU, T. H. 1959. *Private practice in clinical psychology.* New York: Appleton-Century-Crofts.

BÖÖK, JAN A. 1960. Genetical etiology in mental illness. *Milbank Mem. Fund Quart.*, 38, 193–212.

BROTEMARKLE, R. A. 1947. Fifty years of clinical psychology: Clinical psychology, 1896–1946. *J. consult. Psychol.*, 11, 1–4.

Bulletin of the Psychologists Interested in the Advancement of Psychotherapy. 1964 (November). Chicago: Northwestern Univer. Medical School.

CATTELL, R. B. 1932. Psychologist or medical man? *Schoolmaster,* September 8, pp. 330–32.

CATTELL, R. B. 1957. *Personality and motivation structure and measurement.* New York: Harcourt, Brace & World.

CATTELL, R. B. 1964. *The automated cookbook: Part I.* Los Angeles: American Psychological Association.

CATTELL, R. B., et al. 1955. *The O-A (Objective-Analytic) Personality Factor Battery.* Champaign, Ill.: Institute for Personality and Ability Testing.

CATTELL, R. B., and EBER, H. J. 1965. *The Sixteen Personality Factor Questionnaire.* (3d ed.). Champaign, Ill.: Institute for Personality and Ability Testing.

CATTELL, R. B., KRISTY, N., and STICE, G. F. 1957. Nature-nurture ratios for eleven primary personality factors in objective tests. *J. abnorm. soc. Psychol.,* 54, 143–59.

CATTELL, R. B., and SCHEIER, I. H. 1961. *The meaning and measurement of anxiety and neuroticism.* New York: Ronald Press.

CLARK, K. E. 1957. *America's psychologists: A survey of a growing profession.* Washington, D.C.: American Psychological Association.

CORSINI, R. 1945. The functions of the prison psychologist. *J. consult. Psychol.,* 9, 101–4.

DENIKER, P. 1963. Psychopharmacologie et psychopathologie. *Bull. Psychol.* (Paris), 16, 826–54.

DREGER, R. M. 1961. *Fundamentals of personality.* New York: Lippincott.

EBER, H. 1964. 16 P.F. computer analysis and narrative reporting. Champaign, Ill.: Institute for Personality and Ability Testing.

ECCLES, J. 1965. The synapse. *Sci. Amer.,* 212, 56–69.

EYSENCK, H. J. 1958. *Sense and nonsense in psychology.* Baltimore: Penguin Books.

EYSENCK, H. J. 1961. *Handbook of abnormal psychology: An experimental approach.* New York: Basic Books.

FIELD, M. 1960. Approaches to mental illness in Soviet society: Some comparisons and conjectures. *Soc. Probl.,* 7, 277–97.

FLEMING, J. 1961. What analytic work requires of an analyst: A job analysis. *J. Amer. Psychoanal. Assn.,* 9, 719–29.

FORD, D. H., and URBAN, H. B. 1963. *Systems of psychotherapy.* New York: Wiley.

FREUD, S. 1927. *The future of lay-analyses.* New York: Brentano.

GERTY, F. J., HOLLOWAY, J. W., JR., and MACKAY, R. P. 1952. Licensure or certification of clinical psychologists. *J. Amer. med. Assn.,* 148, 272–73.

GILLILAND, E. G. 1962. Progress in music therapy. *Rehabil. Lit.,* 23, 298–306.

GREGG, A. 1948. The profession of psychology as seen by a Doctor of Medicine. *Amer. Psychologist,* 3, 397–401.

GUILFORD, J. P. 1959. *Personality.* New York: McGraw-Hill.

HALL, C. 1962. *A manual for classifying activities in dreams.* Miami, Fla.: Instit. Dream. Res.

HALL, C. S., and LINDZEY, G. 1957. *Theories of personality.* New York: Wiley.

HALL, MARGARET E.   1949.   Current employment requirements for school psychologists. *Amer. Psychologist*, 4, 519–25.

HANN, P.   Attitudes about mental health.   1959. *Ment. Hyg.*, 43, 351–57.

HEISER, K. F.   1945.   Certification of psychologists in Connecticut. *Psychol. Bull.*, 42, 624–30.

HILGARD, J. R., and HILGARD, E. R.   1962.   Developmental interactive aspects of hypnosis: Some illustrative cases. *Genet. psychol. Monogr.*, 66, 143–78.

HORN, J., CATTELL, R. B., SWEENEY, A. B., and RADCLIFFE, J.   1964. *The Motivation Analysis Test.*   Champaign, Ill.: Institute for Personality and Ability Testing.

KAHN, M. W.   1960.   Clinical and statistical prediction revisited. *J. clin. Psychol.* 16, 115–18.

KALLMANN, F. J., PASAMANICK, B., and HIRSCH, J.   1961.   Genetics of mental disease: A symposium 1960. *Amer. J. Orthopsychiat.*, 31, 445–80.

KELLY, E. L.   Clinical psychology.   1949.   In W. DENNIS (ed.), *Current trends in psychology.*   Pittsburgh: Univer. of Pittsburgh Press.

KELLY, E. L., and FISKE, D. W.   1952. *The prediction of performance in clinical psychology.*   Ann Arbor: Univer. of Michigan Press.

KERN, R. A.   1951.   Improvement of professional relations in hospitals. *Vet. Adm. Informat. Bull.*, 10–17, 3–7.

KLETT, S., and SEWALL, Y.   1961.   Automatic data processing of patients records. *Ment. Hosp.*, 12, 26–28.

KOGAN, L. (ed.).   1960. *Social science theory and social work research.*   New York: National Association of Social Workers.

LEBO, D.   1956.   Age and suitability for non-directive play therapy. *J. genet. Psychol.*, 89, 231–38.

LERNER, J.   1963.   The role of the psychologist in the disability evaluation of emotional and intellectual impairments under the social security act. *Amer. Psychol.*, 18, 252–56.

LORAND, S.   1963.   Modifications in classical psychoanalysis. *Psychoanal. Quart.*, 32, 192–204.

McCANN, R. V.   1962. *The churches and mental health.*   New York: Basic Books.

McCARY, J. L.   1956. *Psychology of personality: Six modern approaches.*   New York: Logos.

McGUIRE, C.   1962.   Cultural and social factors in mental health. *Rev. educ. Res.*, 32, 455–63.

MANDELBROTE, B.   1959.   Development of comprehensive psychiatric services around the mental hospital. *Ment. Hyg.*, 43, 368–77.

MASSERMAN, J. H. (ed.).   1962. *Current psychiatric therapies.*   New York: Grune & Stratton.

MEEHL, P.   1950.   Configural scoring. *J. consult. Psychol.*, 14, 165–71.

MENNINGER FOUNDATION.   1961. *Interdisciplinary research on work and mental health: A point of view and a method.*   Topeka, Kan.: Menninger Foundation.

MENNINGER, K. A.   1947.   Psychology and psychiatry. *Amer. Psychologist*, 2, 139–40.

MEREDITH, G. M. 1965. Observations on the acculturation of sansei Japanese Americans in Hawaii. *Psychologia*, in press.

MERRITT, H. H. 1963. Recent advances in neurology significant to psychiatry. *Amer. J. Psychiat.*, **120**, 455–57.

MILLER, J. G. 1948. The mutual dependency of professional training in psychology and psychiatry. *Amer. J. Psychiat.*, **105**, 116–23.

MORENO, L. L. 1963. The actual trends in group psychotherapy. *Group Psychother.*, **16**, 1–7.

MOWRER, O. H. 1960. "Sin": The lesser of two evils. *Amer. Psychologist*, **15**, 301–4.

MULLAN, H., and ROSENBAUM, M. 1962. *Group psychotherapy: Theory and practice.* New York: Free Press.

NUNNALLY, J., and KITTROSS, J. M. 1958. Public attitudes toward mental health professions. *Amer. Psychologist*, **13**, 589–94.

NUNNALLY, J. C., JR. 1961. *Popular conceptions of mental health: Their development and change.* New York: Holt, Rinehart, & Winston.

PENNINGTON, L. A. 1953. The role of clinical psychology in interdisciplinary conflict. *Vet. Adm. Informat. Bull.*, **10–40**, 12–14.

RACHMAN, S. 1963. Introduction to behavior therapy. *Behav. Res. Ther.*, **1**, 3–15.

RAIMY, V. C. (ed.). 1950. *Training in clinical psychology.* New York: Prentice-Hall.

RICKELS, K., and CATTELL, R. B. 1965. The clinical factor validity and trueness of the IPAT verbal and objective batteries for anxiety and regression. *J. clin. Psychol.*, in Press.

ROE, ANNE (chm.). 1949. Training needs of psychologists in practice. *Amer. Psychologist*, **4**, 407–9.

ROE, ANNE, GUSTAD, J., MOORE, B., ROSS, S., and SKODAK, M. 1959. *Graduate education in psychology.* Washington, D.C.: American Psychological Association.

ROGERS, C. R. 1960. *A therapist's view of personal goals.* Wallingford, Pa.: Pendel Hill.

RUMMEL, R. 1964. Dimensions of conflict behavior within and between nations. Mimeographed ms. distributed from Department of Political Science, Yale Univer., New Haven, Conn.

SCHOENFELD, C. G. 1962. Three fallacious attacks upon psychoanalysis as science. *Psychoanal. & Psychoanal. Rev.*, **49**, 35–47.

SELLS, S. B. 1962. *Essentials of psychology.* New York: Ronald.

SHAKOW, D. 1942. The training of the clinical psychologist. *J. consult. Psychol.*, **6**, 277–88.

SHAKOW, D. 1949. Psychology and psychiatry: A dialogue. *Amer. J. Orthopsychiat.*, **19**, 191–208, 381–96.

STORROW, H. A. 1960. The measurement of outcome in psychotherapy. *AMA Arch. gen. Psychiat.*, **2**, 142–46.

SWENSON, W. M. 1964. *Automated personality description with the MMPI.* Los Angeles: American Psychological Association.

THORNE, F. C. 1945. The field of clinical psychology, past present and future. *J. clin. Psychol.*, 1, 1–120.

THORNE, F. C. 1947. The clinical method in science. *Amer. Psychologist*, **2**, 159–66.

TROW, W. C. 1950. Survey of psychological service centers. *Amer. Psychologist*, **5**, 412–21.

TSUJIOKA, B., and CATTELL, R. B. 1965. A cross-cultural comparison of second-stratum questionnaire personality factor structures—anxiety and extraversion—in America and Japan. *J. soc. Psychol.*, **65**, 205–19.

TWEEDIE, D. F. 1963. *The Christian and the couch.* Grand Rapids, Mich.: Baker Books.

VERNON, W. H. 1946. Some professional problems of the consulting psychologist. *J. consult. Psychol.*, **10**, 136–43.

WHIPPLE, G. M. 1910. *Manual of mental and physical tests: A book of directions compiled with special reference to the experimental study of school children in the laboratory or classroom.* Baltimore, Md.: Warwick & York.

WOLPE, J. 1961. The prognosis in unpsychoanalyzed recovery from neurosis. *Amer. J. Psychiat.*, **118**, 35–39.

WOLPE, J. 1963. Psychotherapy: The non-scientific heritage and the new science. *Behav. Res. Ther.*, **1**, 23–28.

YERKES, R. M. (ed.). 1921. Psychological examining in the United States army. Washington, D.C.: U.S. Government Printing Office.

I

CLINICAL METHODS

2

The Clinical Interview
and the Case Record

Irwin A. Berg *

Virtually everyone has employed the interview as a means of under-standing, motivating, or evaluating human behavior. Relatively few, however, have mastered the interview as a technique and tool chiefly because the concept of the interview is exceedingly broad. Bingham, Moore, and Gustad (1959, p. 3) offer the following definition: "An inter-view is a conversation directed to a definite purpose other than satisfac-tion in the conversation itself." With this definition in mind, it is obvious that part of the daily interpersonal activities of people in business, in-dustry, and any of the professions are clearly interviewing activities. The setting may be formal, as in a courtroom, psychologist's office, or confes-sional box; or it may be informal and take place on a street corner, door-step, or bus. But in every case, whether the interviewer is a salesman, public opinion pollster, psychologist, or factory supervisor, purposeful communication is involved.

A number of quite different techniques may be used when interviewing, varying with the purpose and training of the interviewer. The lawyer, for example, will often direct the entire course of an interview, frequently asking highly specific questions to which only a "yes" or "no" answer is allowed. At the other extreme is the nondirective interview (see Chapter 18) in which the interviewee may discuss anything in whatever way he desires. In some interviews, as in psychotherapeutic sessions, consider-able care may be taken to put the interviewee at his ease. In other cases stress may be employed, as in some police interviews, with the deliberate

* Irwin A. Berg, Ph.D. (University of Michigan), Professor of Psychology and Dean of the College of Arts and Sciences, Louisiana State University.

aim of making the interviewee uncomfortable. Thus many people of
varied training use many interviewing methods with a variety of purposes
in mind. Further, the interview takes place in a wide range of settings.
Small wonder, then, that the usefulness of the interview will be great, nil,
or even negative, depending upon who does the interviewing and the
purpose he has in mind.

THE RELIABILITY AND VALIDITY OF THE INTERVIEW

Interview Reliability. Researchers have been studying the reliability of
the interview for a number of decades and obtaining results which were
viewed with delight in some cases and with jaundiced eye in others. In
one of the older studies, for example, Rice (1929) analyzed data obtained
from 12 male interviewers who interviewed 2,000 destitute men and concluded that the political and social biases of the interviewers directly influenced the results. One of the interviewers, for example, reported that
the downfall of most human derelicts was caused by liquor; this interviewer, however, was a convinced prohibitionist. Another interviewer
was a Socialist, and he found the industrial system was the chief cause of
the unfortunate condition of these men. Similarly, when Hollingworth
(1923) had 12 sales managers interview and rate 57 job applicants, he
found the interview-based ratings to be notoriously unreliable. The
applicant who was sometimes rated number 1 by one sales manager received various ratings all the way down to 57, the lowest position, when
rated by the others. No applicant was rated in highly reliable fashion.
Carey, Berg, and Van Dusen (1951) found that ratings of employee
satisfaction interviews made by persons trained and others who were untrained in interviewing methods had reliability coefficients in the neighborhood of .65 to .70. The untrained groups were as reliable in their
judgments as the trained group, presumably because the rating task was
carefully defined and specific response categories were used. Under some
conditions, training in interviewing may even be a handicap. Wedell
and Smith (1951), for example, found that experienced interviewers were
less consistent in appraising attitudes than relatively inexperienced interviewers. In a study of the success of students in clinical psychology
training programs, Kelly and Fiske (1950) also found that experienced
interviewers were more variable in their predictions than those with less
training. Interaction patterns in test-retest interviews a week apart,
however, are quite stable as shown by Saslow, Matarazzo, Phillips, and
Matarazzo (1957). Also, acceptable reliability has been found for two
interviewers who independently interviewed 20 patients on the same
day (Matarazzo, Saslow, and Guze, 1956). Ulrich and Trumbo (1965)
reviewed a series of selection interview studies and found reports of inter-

view reliability coefficients ranging from —.20 to .97 for various characteristics. Excellent discussions of factors which affect the interview and the psychotherapeutic process from the standpoint of the research investigator are to be found in Matarazzo (1962) and in Strupp (1962).

All things considered, the interview is acceptably reliable when reasonable aims are set and a skilled person does the interviewing. As an example of reasonable aims, the carefully executed research by Hunt, Wittson, and Hunt (1953) is quite instructive. In a study of the reliability of psychiatric diagnosis based upon interviews and other data, they found that there was 93.7 per cent agreement between the precommissioning station and the hospital when the initial diagnosis for 794 naval enlisted men was "unsuitable for service." With slightly greater specificity of diagnosis such as "psychosis," "psychoneurosis," or "character disorder," the percentage of agreement, although still fairly high, dropped to 54.1 per cent. However, when a specific category such as "schizophrenia," "anxiety state," or "hysteria" was employed, the level of agreement between precommissioning station and hospital fell to 32.6 per cent. Thus interview reliability may be high or low, depending upon the level and specificity of appraisal demanded. Hovland and Wonderlic (1939), for example, obtained a reliability coefficient of .70 for a patterned interview technique designed to predict general industrial success. Similarly, Rundquist (1947) found .87 reliability in a study of 1,359 officers interviewed and evaluated for their ability to deal with people. These are quite satisfactory levels of reliability; yet had agreement on specific characteristics been demanded, the reliability would certainly have been much lower.

Interview Validity. When appropriately used by skilled persons, the interview is valid as well as reliable. As was true of reliability studies, general ratings or evaluations based upon interviews are typically more valid than specific ones, as shown in Deemer and Rafferty's (1949) study of pilot training success. Ample support for this statement is found in a number of other researches. Thus, when Barber, Rigby, and Napoli (1962) used "level of wellness" as a broad predictor variable, the clinical interview was found to be quite valid in a study of severely disturbed children. During World War II, for example, brief psychiatric interviews lasting only two to ten minutes were often used for screening and for reassignment purposes. Yet even such brief interviews can have quite satisfactory validity, as demonstrated by Wittson and Hunt (1951) and their co-workers. In a study of 944 seamen who were interviewed and classified as to severity of symptomatology, these writers found that the relationship between the interview-based ratings and subsequent NP discharges was convincingly close, as shown in Table 2–1.

Table 2–1. Incidence of Subsequent Neuropsychiatric Discharges Among Men Interviewed and Classified as to Severity of Symptomatology *

Classification	Number of Cases	Subsequent NP Discharges	
		Number	Per Cent
Mild	527	34	6.5
Moderate	367	74	20.2
Severe	38	34	89.7

* Reprinted by permission of the authors and *The American Journal of Psychiatry,* publishers.

Curiously, patients are sometimes inaccurate when reporting factual information during an interview; yet they will at the same time be completely candid in laying bare their innermost feelings and anxieties. Factual data may be omitted or misrepresented for a variety of reasons. The patient may be genuinely confused, a product of his emotional disturbance, or, in other cases, the factual information may represent something so emotionally tormenting to him that he cannot discuss it. A female patient, for example, denied ever having been married although records were later discovered which showed she had been married, very unhappily, for nearly two years. Similarly, another patient actually wrote out a list of his family members and left out a brother whom he loathed. Such behavior is highly revealing and immensely useful to the clinician in forming hypotheses with respect to the patient's dynamics. But it is essential that factual information not be taken routinely as valid. Such data should be checked. As Weiss and Davis (1960) have emphasized, one must never assume the validity of purportedly factual information.

It is not a far step from the "oral-emergency" type of intelligence test to the interview situation. Hence it is not surprising that a skilled interviewer can assess intelligence at a rather high level of validity. Using a standardized interview, Snedden (1930) found that his estimates of intelligence based upon interviews correlated .82 with the scores of written intelligence tests. In a similar study, Hanna (1950) found that his assessment of intelligence obtained from interviews correlated .71 with the American Council on Education Psychological Examination and .66 with the Ohio State University Psychological Test. Since scores on the two intelligence tests correlated .77 with each other, the estimates of intelligence obtained from the interviews cannot be regarded as significantly poorer than those obtained from the two tests.

Accordingly, it may be said with confidence that the interview can be highly reliable and valid when used appropriately by skilled persons. Indeed, agreement may be perfect when only extreme cases are considered, as in Newman, Bobbitt, and Cameron's (1946) study of officer candidate evaluation. On the other hand, the interview may add little or nothing, as Tupes (1950) showed, when specific personality traits must be evaluated by various interviewing methods. Where the task is ill-defined and the interviewer is unfamiliar with what he is assessing, or where a highly specific judgmental category is demanded, reliability and validity are low. But where the required judgment is broad and the interviewer is skilled in his task, highly reliable and highly valid results are obtained.

CONDUCTING THE INTERVIEW

Basically, the interview is a communicative process; like any psychological test, it is a means of gathering information about a patient or client.[1] Yet a number of clinicians, particularly the younger ones, experience a feeling of helplessness when faced with the prospect of conducting an interview unaided and without the support of psychological test cards or answer sheets. This feeling of inadequacy is often transmitted to the interviewee who, in turn, reacts to the situation either by clamlike silence, replying in monosyllables, or by noisy aggression directed at the interviewer. A few experiences with a taciturn patient or with a patient who shouts in stentorian tones that the psychologist "doesn't know what the devil he's doing" will reinforce the original feelings of inadequacy felt by the interviewer. As a result, he will sometimes retreat into the comparative comfort of test devices, using them as a shield between himself and the patient. He may even give vent to a series of freely offered rationalizations that he can "get more out of a Rorschach, TAT, or MMPI, than any interview will ever give." If he is a close observer and also asks a few pertinent interview questions, he may be right; however, in such cases he really is not depending upon test data alone. Nor should he, as will be seen later in this chapter, for, while the interview can be a splendid clinical tool, the maximum knowledge about a patient is obtained when the interview data are joined with test information.

Unfortunately, the typical clinician rarely has time to apply many clinical tools to every patient he sees. He must reserve his more elaborate approaches for those persons whose condition requires it, and even here he may occasionally have to compromise because of time. It is at this point that the interview is most valuable. Competently conducted by a clinically astute psychologist, the interview can supply nearly as much

[1] As used by psychologists, the terms *patient, client,* or *subject* are approximately equivalent. Hospitalized persons are typically referred to as "patients," while psychological counselors often call the people who consult them in their offices "clients." Psychoanalysts and test administrators usually refer to the persons analyzed or tested as "subjects." There is considerable overlap, for each of the three terms may be applied to the same person by various members of a professional staff.

information in considerably less time than tests alone. Further, the interview will indicate what tests can be used most profitably for an individual patient, thereby avoiding the use of an unnecessarily long test battery. It should be noted that the paper-pencil types of tests are not free from this limitation, for the better ones require profile analysis or individual item inspection. Thus time is not really saved.

The reason for this oft-encountered, slavish dependence upon tests, with attendant neglect of the interview, appears to lie in a lack of training. One does not become a good clinician on a sink-or-swim basis, nor does one reach highest competency in interviewing on such a basis either. The best clinical interviewers typically saw their first patients in a carefully structured situation. Under supervision, they gathered objective social history data from patients known to be cooperative, or administered tests which permitted some casual conversation. Gradually, as the supervisory reins were loosened and as they successfully handled less highly structured situations, the trainee clinicians reached the point where they could handle diagnostic or therapeutic interviews effectively.

The Physical Setting of the Interview. As indicated earlier, an interview may take place anywhere. Any clinician of some experience can relate instances when he was stopped on the street, in some public building, or called to the telephone by a troubled client or patient. He had no choice but to conduct an informal interview on the spot and then arrange for a later office appointment, once some temporary relief for the client had been given. But such interviews under public conditions should be avoided save when the subject is in obviously dire straits. At other times the interview must be held under semipublic conditions, as at the patient's bedside in a ward. Usually a screen can be appropriately arranged, and a fairly satisfactory interview can be held if the interviewer takes pains to behave as if the situation were natural and keeps his attention closely on the patient.

The best interviewing conditions are characterized by privacy, freedom from interruption, and some control of both inside and outside sounds. The general appearance of the room should suggest comfort and yet have a professional flavor about it. The right balance can be achieved only after observation of the patient's and one's own responses. One psychotherapist who saw most of his patients in the evening, for example, wryly remarked that he had gone too far in the direction of comfort when he recently installed a pair of lounging chairs in his office, for usually either he or the patient fell asleep in them. In the same vein, the cluttered desk or engaging objects in the border of the visual field are often an undetected source of distraction for both interviewer and subject. It was some time before the present writer realized that the piles of research data sheets on his littered desk occasionally got him more interested in the research than in the interviewee's problems.

At times, objects in the interviewing room may threaten the client instead of merely distracting him. Upon one occasion a book entitled *Men Against Madness* inadvertently left near the patient's elbow provoked a half-hour weeping spell, during which the patient could only waggle the book and cry out that he was going mad. Of course, the weeping might have occurred anyway; however, the first ten minutes of the interview had gone normally enough, before the book was noticed. For some reason, modern paintings with their bold splashes of color occasionally produce similar emotional outbursts in some patients. A number of psychological counselors, however, do not feel that this is necessarily bad. Indeed, many of them believe that the degree and area of maladjustment may thereby be more readily identified. Thus they sometimes purposely include such materials in their interviewing rooms, with the intention of introducing a mild degree of stress for susceptible patients. They may even call the patient's attention to the object and ask him to comment on it, using his responses as one would use any projective technique. But it should be emphasized that these are experienced clinicians who are fully capable of appraising and handling the behavior elicited by such situations. The clinician of lesser skill and knowledge must shun such unorthodoxy until his experience with many patients has carefully defined the limits of his capacities for him.

Rapport in the Interview. The basic task in any clinical interview is the perception of a perception. That is, the psychologist must perceive the way the patient perceives himself and his problems. Accordingly, the psychologist is concerned not as much with the accuracy of the patient's statements as with understanding *why* the patient made the statements, in other words, with perceiving the patient's perceptual frame. Conversely, the patient seeks to grasp what conception the interviewer has of his own role. The patient, in turn, strives to perceive the perception the interviewer has of himself. Hence, the paranoid patient may guardedly spar with the clinician because he suspects that the clinician is a spy, and he is seeking evidence that the interviewer also sees himself in this role. The overly dependent freshman girl, on the other hand, may expect the interviewer to be a father surrogate and trustingly request him to tell her exactly what to do. An interchange of attitudes occurs and produces an atmosphere characteristic of the social situation represented by the particular interview. When this atmosphere is permissive, reasonably harmonious, and characterized by mutual interest, the interviewing relationship is described as *en rapport or,* more commonly but somewhat tautologically, as having "good rapport established." This does not mean that interviewer and interviewee are necessarily fond of one another and that the course of the interview is serene. That is a common misconception. Indeed, as Watson (1951, p. 95) has noted, even resentment and anger may co-exist with rapport. The effectiveness of rapport thus does not depend upon mutual liking as much as upon mutual confidence, respect, and permissiveness in the sense that anything may be uttered without fear of criticism or consequences.

Obviously, if rapport is not established, little can be accomplished in an interview. One may wrench factual information as birth date, home address, etc., from the patient, but he will not do him any good. If such conditions persist, there is no alternative but to refer the patient to another clinician. However, this happens very rarely, almost never if care is exercised to observe the precautions described below.

While not all the communication in an interview is at the verbal level, most of it is; hence it is essential that the interviewer use words which are understood by the subject. Burtt (1948, p. 679) describes a survey in which it was found that four-fifths of the people in the South thought that "voluptuous" meant large or bulky, while two-thirds of the people surveyed in the Midwest thought "sonorous" meant sleep-producing. Use of words which the interviewee does not recognize or misunderstands will seriously hamper communication. In other instances, communication will be hampered because the interviewer communicates what he means well enough, but also his own disapproval or embarrassment. As Kinsey, Pomeroy, and Martin (1948) have stated, "Euphemisms should not be used as substitutes for franker terms." Masturbation should not be designated as "touching yourself" nor sexual intercourse as "relations with others." Such phrases are anathema to the good clinician. His questions, comments, and restatements are couched in clear terms and expressed candidly in such an honest manner that the interviewee fully realizes that his behavior is accepted without censure.

In addition to the words used, the way in which they are uttered is also extremely important. The hesitating or whispered inquiry may suggest to the patient that the topic under discussion is nasty and cannot be talked about except in the manner of small boys telling dirty stories in an alley. As a result, the patient is made to feel ill at ease, at the very least, and sometimes as if he were an outcast on trial. The other extreme occurs when the interviewer momentarily forgets that the interviewee may have strong, even overwhelming, guilt feelings about the incidents he is relating. If too loud a tone is used or if the candor of the interviewer cannotes something akin to enthusiasm, the interviewee may shrink from further discussion because his guilt feelings are reinforced, since he cannot feel as emancipated about his own actions as the clinician does. The best approach is for the interviewer to speak slowly in a calm, matter-of-fact way, and in a friendly, accepting manner.

Two other factors concerning the ease and rapidity with which rapport is established are worthy of note. One concerns the general social impact of the clinician and the other his cultural frame of reference. The former is composed chiefly of the motor habits, physique, manner of dress, etc., all of which suggest a secondary role in addition to the professional role of the clinician. The latter is the product of the attitudes, value systems, etc., which are peculiar to the subcultural patterns found in the socioeconomic group in which the interviewer grew up.

About the only way one can become aware of his social impact in an interviewing situation is by closely observing the reactions of the interviewees in the early stages of the interview. The physically large man may note that his size threatens some patients; hence he will have to avoid standing close to such patients, since proximity emphasizes the threat. The maternal, comfortable-appearing woman may find rapport easy to establish with certain dependent patients, but terminating the interviews may be unusually difficult. She will need to acquire interview "weaning" techniques to encourage self-reliance in such cases. Another problem is found in the energetic, rather tense clinician who communicates his tension to the patient, making him feel uncomfortable. Many such clinicians unwittingly prod the patient by indicating acceptance of a statement with a quick "yes, yes" or an explosive "umm-hm." While no serious harm is done, the effectiveness of the interview is interfered with and considerable time is often wasted.

In similar manner, the interviewer may be unaware of the determining influence by his own cultural background. Thus the patient of lower socioeconomic class background may describe premarital sex experiences which were tantamount to rape, or he may describe literal bouts of fisticuffs with his wife. The clinician may see in such revelations signs of overwhelming guilt, when, actually, the patient has no such feelings; for such behavior was tolerated, perhaps was even commonplace in his subcultural group. Or the clinician may think it significant, even suggestive of psychopathy, that there appears to be no guilt when, to the clinician, there should be. Similarly, the clinician may fail to attach any significance to incidents which may involve masturbation, for example, while to the patient such acts indicate perversion. Once the clinician understands his own reference frame and is able to perceive that of his patient as well, there is no real problem. He learns to distinguish between his own subcultural biases and those of the patient.

A perennial problem of great professional importance is the legal status of the information received by a psychologist concerning a patient. Any material imparted in confidence to a member of the clergy or to a physician is legally regarded in most states as a privileged communication. That is, persons in those professions cannot be forced to testify in court with regard to such information. While some states do not have statutory provision for privileged communication, the right to hold confidential a parishioner's or patient's utterances is accorded by custom to clergymen and physicians. Illinois has no such law, for example; however, when a Chicago psychiatrist refused to testify concerning one of his patients, the court upheld his position, as reported in Guttmacher and Weihofen (1952, p. 270). As yet, psychologists have not had an adequate legal test case which would determine the status of information imparted to them in confidence. Rapport is ultimately involved in this problem, for no patient would speak freely if it were established that his test scores and private statements could be publicly proclaimed from the witness stand by his psychologist. All such material is properly a privileged communication, and there can be only one position the psychologist will adopt: *He will keep the patient's confidence.* Failure to do otherwise will seriously, if not completely, block his professional usefulness. Berg (1954) has a discussion of the significance and implications of this problem.

Significance of Nonverbal Behavior in the Interview. Studies of interviewing methods customarily place primary emphasis upon *what* is said and pay little attention to *how* it is said. The other behavior which accompanies patients' utterances is even more roundly ignored, yet some of the most revealing information is often obtained from such peripheral observations, as Yacorzynski (1951, pp. 419 f.) has stated. At close range the anxiety-ridden patient will often be observed to grasp and fiddle with small objects in sharp, strained gestures (Berg, 1954). At a distance of 100 feet or more, one can recognize the characteristic shuffle and mask-like stare of a Parkinson's disease patient, or the limp arm and dragging foot of a brain-damaged hemiplegiac. In addition to the clinical fact observed, such observations should indicate what one is to expect in the interview. Many sufferers from Parkinson's disease are highly irritable and must be handled gently and with tender forbearance. The patient with motor cortex injury may also have cortical speech area damage. Further, he has been converted from a vigorous, active person to a near-helpless invalid. The clinician should be prepared, in such cases, for slurred, thick speech and evidences of agitated depression and self-pity. Deep understanding and friendly encouragement during the interview can mark the first step in the rehabilitation of such patients.

During the actual interview, much more detailed observation is possible and, of course, hypotheses of greater clinical value may be formulated. The very act of entering the room, for example, often tells much. The breezy, energetic entrance of the hypomanic is a striking contrast to the slow, hesitant entry of the depressed patient; both are quite different from the careful scrutiny of the surroundings given by the paranoid interviewee as he surveys the room. Clinically, one may anticipate that the elated or hypomanic patient will give a certain amount of misinformation, because he replies before hearing all of the question and because his attention span is short. The depressed patient is easily exhausted; and as White-horn (1944, p. 199) has noted, he may answer "yes" or "no" to any question simply to be spared further effort. In the same way, the paranoid interviewee can be something of a trial because of his carefully guarded replies.

Many other nonverbal behavior items provide valuable clinical hypotheses. The typical hypomanic, as a case in point, smiles quickly and infectiously, bears himself erect, speaks rapidly, and is restless, often squirming in his chair or rising and moving about the room. If he smiles at all, the depressed patient does so in a forced, sardonic fashion, and his general posture is one of dejection. His speech is slow, often labored to the point where more than a one-word reply seems painful to him. The paranoid patient often has a furtive, searching manner. Even when rapport is fairly well established, he usually talks in conspiratorial tones, leaning forward with narrowed eyes and occasionally glancing over his shoulder. Similarly, the manner in which level of affect or emotional involvement is displayed can be clinically quite revealing. A schizo-phrenic murderer, for example, described his crime in a dull, uninterested manner—almost as if someone else had done it. By contrast, a psychopath who was caught in the act of murder also described his crime as if someone else had committed it, but his narrative was quite lively and interesting. Neither gave any indication of obvious remorse or personal concern, al-though the psychopath periodically cursed his victim for "having started it all." Neurotic patients, to consider another group, show quite varied overt expressions of emotional state. Some appear tense and fidgety; others seem weary and exhausted. Some have tics and nervous, flickering smiles, while others are grim and tight-lipped. Some appear guilt-ridden and talk shamefacedly with averted eyes, while others speak with indigna-tion of the way people have used them, gazing expectantly at the clinician for signs of commiseration. Whatever form it may take, such overt be-havior reflects the inner emotional disturbance and tells something of its nature. Clinical hypotheses may thereby be formulated and later verified from such data. Davitz (1964) has an excellent and detailed dis-cussion of nonverbal factors and their significance in a clinical setting.

General Observations on Interviewing Technique. Before any inter-view is started, the clinician must answer the question "What is this interview to accomplish?" A therapeutic interview, for example, has different goals and is conducted differently from a personal, social history interview. Once the ultimate goal of the particular interview is clear, the clinician should, of course, note any additional material brought forth and which may bear upon the patient's problem. But he must first settle upon the purpose of the interview at hand to avoid being sidetracked and wasting time.

After the goal of the interview is settled, material may appear which, although incidental to the purpose of the present interview, may be fully as valuable as the more directly pertinent material. Ebaugh (1948, p. 5) gives leads which were developed by Garrett (1942) for recognizing such clues to significant information. The following is a modification of their points:

1. *Association of ideas.* The patient, for example, mentions his inability to get along with his boss in the same paragraph that he mentions his feelings toward his father.
2. *Shifts in conversation.* The material discussed may have been too painful or the patient may be seeking to relate the topic of conversation to himself.
3. *Recurrent explanations or references.* Unconscious conflict may be expressed by such "theme songs."
4. *Inconsistencies and gaps.* The patient has difficulty in saying certain things because of guilt, hostility, ambivalence, etc.
5. *Defense mechanisms.* Digressions, rationalizations, projections, and the like often indicate the general area and true nature of the conflict.
6. *Word choice.* Expletive and explosive sounds and ego words, such as "I," "me," and "mine," or emphatic words, such as "you," "we," and "us," may often relate to the problem, as Berg (1958) has reported.

Occasionally, after talking freely, the patient may remain silent for a time, with the result that the clinician feels impelled to fill the gap with some remark. Actually, silence can substantially advance the progress of the interview; for as a study by Tindall and Robinson (1947) showed, the greatest single effect of such pauses may be a clarification in the interview situation. It behooves the clinician to restrain his impatience to fill such conversational voids and to learn to use them as a useful technique.

Another problem of minor concern to the clinician is whether to take notes during the interview. In some situations, of course, there is no alternative; for birth dates, addresses, previous illnesses, etc., must be recorded on the spot. Indeed, if no record is made of such factual data, the patient may ask why such information is requested when it is not being written down. But when the patient is discussing an emotionally traumatic experience or laying bare his innermost feelings, the question arises whether note-taking does not arouse insecurities on the part of the patient and cause him to speak less freely. Actually, if rapport has been established, patients do not seem to find note-taking a threat. The clinician should explain the purpose of the notes and permit the patient to read them if he wishes. Rogers (1942, p. 243) suggests that some statement as this be made: "I hope you won't mind if I jot down the things we say. I like to study them afterward to see what we've accomplished."

Some writers, Rogers among them, suggest that very full notes be taken, including statements of both interviewer and interviewee. While there is considerable value in extensive notes, the present writer holds firmly the opinion that only brief notes or none at all should be taken during the interview. Admittedly this is a personal predilection; however, many of the highly significant behavioral observations such as facial expression, meaningful gestures, and the like are missed by the interviewer when busily scribbling with downcast face. Furthermore, when the patient gushes with emotional outpourings, the clinician often feels harried in the attempt "to get it all down," giving more attention to the notes than to the patient. With experience, one can learn to organize the interview content so that notes can be recorded after the patient has departed and few or none taken during the interview itself.

Some practitioners have advocated the use of phonographic recording apparatus in place of notes. Where the interview record must be as complete as possible, as for research purposes, such recording machines are exceedingly useful. But the recordings are in no sense a substitute for notes recorded by the interviewer himself. Where the notes can be read in 2 to 3 minutes, the interview playback of an hour's conversation will, of course, require a full hour. A typescript of the recorded interview can be read in 15 to 20 minutes; however an experienced typist will require 5 or more hours for typing it up from the disk or tape recording. Furthermore, the typist will spend about a half-hour of the clinician's time in asking him about unclear passages in the recording. One gets all of the wheat in such complete records, but one gets all of the chaff too, and in such abundance that most of the kernels are hidden. Significantly, many research centers which use complete interview transcripts also use conventional notes as well.

Closing the Interview. Usually the clinician has only a limited amount of time for a given interview, and this period cannot be extended without seriously disrupting his schedule. Yet an occasional patient may be expressing himself freely or perhaps be at the point of tears at the time when the interview should ordinarily be closed. The wise clinician maintains a 10- or 15-minute "buffer" period between patients, chiefly to jot down or review case notes but also to accommodate the occasional patient who cannot be sent away in an emotional turmoil. Ordinarily, there is no particular problem in closing an interview if a few precautions are taken. The patient should be told at the beginning of the interview how much time is available. This can be put gracefully, for example: "We'll have three-quarters of an hour to ourselves today." Similarly, near the end of the interview, a remark may be made such as: "Let's plan to go into that more thoroughly at our next meeting, if you wish. You see, we have only a couple of minutes left." Or the clinician may casually begin to summarize what has transpired during the current interview and discuss arrangements for the next one. If there is to be no second interview, one can frankly remark to the patient that, while he must close the present interview, he has enjoyed his chat with him. Rogers (1942) offers a number of practical examples of handling similar situations in a natural manner.

TYPES OF CLINICAL INTERVIEWS

In this section the common forms of clinical interviews will be briefly discussed. Nothing will be said specifically about the psychotherapeutic interview, for this area is dealt with in Part IV, "Treatment Approaches." Of course, virtually everything that has already been said has a direct bearing upon the manner of conducting such interviews and, for that matter, upon any clinical interview. Indeed, none of the interview types described below are mutually exclusive insofar as technique or approach are concerned. Their differences are in terms of purpose or goal, and because of these differences, special problems may arise.

The Intake or Admission Interview. The purpose of the intake or admission interview is, as Watson (1951, p. 88) put it, "usually concerned with clarification of the patient's presenting complaints, the steps he has taken previously to resolve his difficulties, and his expectancies in regard to what may be done for him." Ordinarily a psychiatric social worker conducts this interview; however, upon occasion, the psychologist, one of the physicians, or a psychiatric nurse may serve as intake interviewer. The basic question to be dealt with is *Why is the patient here?*, that is, what does he say is the matter with him? Important but secondary questions involve information about previous hospitalization, the names of his doctors, what the patient expects from treatment, his availability for treatment, and the like. Blau (1959) offers a sound discussion of factors involved in the initial contact with a patient.

Although typically brief, the intake or admission interview is extremely important in conserving the time of other professional staff members and in sparing the clinic or hospital from occasional embarrassing or awkward situations. The patient may in some instances desire treatment which a particular clinic may not be prepared to give. Certain hospitals, for example, do not handle alcoholic or narcotic addition cases; thus the patient can be at once referred to an appropriate institution, saving time for the examining psychiatrist, psychologist, the various attendants, and for the patient himself. Similarly, the awkward consequences of an overly casual admission procedure can be voided by a well-planned interview. Hospital staff members can relate many anecdotes of relatives who were mistaken for the patient himself, of surgical patients who were given diagnostic psychiatric interviews, or of salesmen who were escorted to a room and confronted with Rorschach cards. A careful intake interview will guard against such mistakes. It should be noted that every patient will not be able to state coherently what the nature of his troubles may be. But even inchoate replies can be highly revealing, and the astute intake interviewer can report significant aspects of the patient's behavior which he may not reveal again for some time or which may be missed by later examiners.

Ordinarily, the diagnostic and treatment sessions which come at some time after the intake interview are carried out by another staff person. This does not mean, however, that therapy begins later. The formal label of "psychotherapy," it is true, is given to the later procedures, but real therapy, in the sense of the patient's attitudes and his motivation to get well, begins at the time of the patient's admittance. It is no exaggeration to assert that a bungled intake interview can prolong treatment while an effective one can shorten it.

The Personal and Social History Interview. In many hospitals and clinics the intake or admission interview is followed immediately by the personal and social history interview. The same person, usually a psychiatric social worker, commonly conducts both interviews, often at one sitting. Sources of information other than the patient himself are, of course, utilized when completing a personal and social history report. Frequently the patient does not remember or cannot for other reasons communicate material which may have a bearing upon his problem. Thus information from friends and relatives and from hospital, military, and other records is also used for the history. But whatever the sources of information, the purpose of the personal and social history report is to gather information which will be helpful in diagnosing and treating the patient's disorder. Frequent job changes, for example, may be evidence of a more general instability. The adult schizophrenic who showed marked apathy and withdrawal symptoms as a preschool child is probably more severely afflicted than patients whose symptoms appeared more recently. Neurotic symptoms which appeared after the divorce of parents may have different etiology than similar symptoms which appeared after a head injury. In such and many other ways the personal and social history is of considerable and sometimes critical importance.

In most instances a standardized form or social history guide of some sort is used. (See pages 55–58 for an example). There are advantages in using a standardized printed form, as Louttit (1934) has noted, in that pertinent information will not be skipped; however, as he also notes, a rigid dependency upon the form may ensue. Certain obvious information may not be recorded because the form does not call for it or details which are unimportant for a particular case may be set down in time-wasting abundance. Obviously the common sense of the interviewer is the answer to such problems.

The typical information obtained in a personal and social history includes material on the patient's early life, with particular attention paid to family relationships and general environment. Also included are data on the patient's educational and vocational history, neuropathic traits, his habits and recreations, as well as other material. Much of this information can be obtained only by direct questioning. Some patients are threatened by situations which require specific answers, and they may show panic reactions of varying degrees. Others will lie, perhaps because they cannot remember and do not wish to say so, but more often because painful memories are awakened of jail sentences, of desertions, of previous hospitalizations, or the like. Many patients, of course, are truthful, but only in their cultural fashion. For example, the lad who pumped gasoline and washed cars at the corner filling station may report his work experience as "auto mechanic." In lower socioeconomic groups it is not uncommon thus to exaggerate the importance of jobs. Similarly, a patient may report "lots of times I could have murdered my sisters" when all he means is that they had an occasional minor spat.

It is in this area that the skill of the interviewer is brought out. While much of the information requested is factual, the manner in which the patient communicates his facts may be quite misleading. A female patient remarked, "Once my father fingered me with a cop." Further questioning revealed that her statement had nothing to do with sexual manipulation, as the interviewer first thought, but rather that the father had reported a theft committed by the patient to the police—that is, pointed the accusing finger. The remark was highly significant in terms of a parent-child relationship, but not in the way originally supposed. Jargon, exaggeration, special uses of common words or kidding may lead the unwary or unskilled interviewer to a false impression. Further questioning usually clears up the confusion.

The fact that an occasional patient will lie about his personal-social history, even about trivial matters, is sometimes irritating or disheartening to the newcomer to the interviewing situation. As noted earlier in this chapter in discussing the validity of the interview, such falsification is not a reflection upon the interviewer's skill or comportment but rather upon the reason why the patient is being interviewed. He *is* a patient. He may be confused, a psychopath, or something else; but he is sick. This may seem like unnecessary emphasis; yet every clinician should be prepared to ward off feelings of indignation or humiliation which may arise when he learns that virtually every fact he so laborously recorded, from age and address to family history and vocation, is false. This happens with extreme rarity, of course; but it happens to almost every clinician sooner or later. When it does, and if one is taken in, a little self-directed humor helps restore a sense of proportion. Then a firm resolution to check other information sources can turn the experience to one's advantage.

The Screening or Diagnostic Interview. The purpose of the screening or diagnostic interview is to assist the clinician in his attempts to understand the patient. If the level of diagnostic understanding required is merely a separation of the fit from the unfit, as in military neuropsychiatric examinations, the interview task is one of *screening*. That is, after a brief interview the interviewee may be adjudged fit for specific duties, such as a regular military assignment, or he may be referred for prolonged observation and extended psychological testing. Occasionally, limited or trial duty may be recommended as an alternative to regular duty or psychiatric observation. Upon other occasions the diagnostic task is highly specific, and a detailed level of understanding is required. This may involve a diagnostic label as categorized as "paranoid schizophrenia" and a description of personality dynamics. In the latter case, primary dependence is not placed upon the interview alone, for psychological tests play a most important role in such detailed diagnostic procedures.

As indicated in this chapter, the brief neuropsychiatric interview can be highly valid if conducted by a skilled examiner and if a broad diagnostic judgment only, as fit or unfit for duty, is required. A typical procedure is described (1954) in the U.S. Naval Psychiatric unit operations. The examinations typically last only two to five minutes and are conducted in privacy. The recruit is usually unclothed, since previous studies have shown that psychological defenses break down under such mildly stressful conditions and less resistance to questioning is encountered. The questions are rapid and direct, and behavior which accompanies the replies is closely observed. Thus the question "What have you done since you left school?" may be accompanied by obvious signs of tension, such as postural shifts, blinking, or stiffening of muscles, although the reply may be, "I worked in grocery stores." This would be a signal for further questioning about just what the interviewee did after working hours, etc. Such queries might be followed by questions such as "What trouble have you had with the police?" or "Tell me about the worst jam you were ever in." Few if any of the questions are stated so that only a "yes" or "no" answer can be given. Some of the questions may be leading and brutally direct as "When was the last time you masturbated?" Others may be more subtle, as when an interviewee who is suspected of truancy and delinquency is asked "What sort of things did you like to do with your gang when you were a kid?"

Certain questions have been called "projective" in that they permit the interviewee to handle them in terms of his personal dynamics. Examples of such questions used by Naval Neuropsychiatric examiners are "If you could have three wishes granted, what would you wish for?" or "Who would you take with you if you had to spend the rest of your life on a desert island with one person?" Emotional maturity, dependency needs, socialization, etc., may be reflected in the replies.

While the examination progresses, the interviewer observes the interviewee's behavior as well as noting the content of his answers. Thus thighs pressed together, a mincing walk, and fluttery feminine gestures in a male should lead the interviewer to suspect and investigate the possibility of homosexuality. The bubbling, enthusiastic replies and exaggerated gestures in another interviewee should lead the interviewer to hypothesize tentatively a manic condition and seek further evidence. Similarly, as Wittson et al. (1943) noted, the psychopath often gives evidence of his deviation by his utter impersonality or even belligerence toward the interviewer.

Ordinarily, brief neuropsychiatric interviews are not oriented toward future psychotherapeutic activity because most of the interviewees have no need for therapy. However it is not difficult to adapt the procedures of brief interviews so that those who seem to be in need of treatment are rendered more receptive to the idea. Thus an interviewee may indicate that he has often desired help, yet he feels he is not "crazy." A frank explanation about the forms of psychological assistance available, and reassurance that most people receiving such aid are not "crazy" can allay some of his anxieties. In other cases the interviewee may assert half-belligerently and half-questioningly, after describing some of his fears, that the clinician probably thinks that he (the patient) "ought to have his head looked at by a nut doctor." In such situations, the clinician may remark that all of us have worries and that such worries do not mean we are ready for a hospital. The clinician may note further that it often helps people to talk over a personal problem with a trained person. Then he may inquire whether the interviewee has ever thought of talking over his feelings with a psychological counselor. Such an approach is non-threatening and often provides a bridge for later treatment.

Even the normal person may be aided in the brief interview situation.

The present writer, for example, was told by a young man that his doctor had told him not to bite his nails because it was a sign that he was a neurotic. Just how the doctor put his original statement is impossible to say; however, it is true that nail-biting was at one time regarded as a psychopathological symptom. But as Pennington (1945) and his co-worker Mearin (1944) have shown, one out of every four or five young adults bite their nails and nearly half of the youngsters at age 13 or 14 do likewise. Accordingly, it was reasonable to present these facts and thereby reassure the interviewee. Closson and Hildreth (1944) did something of the same order under controlled conditions in a study of 1,000 Navy selectees. Certain subjects were given advice concerning any personality "weak spots" which were discovered during a brief interview. The advice was designed to prepare the subject for Naval adjustment problems which might result from his "weak spots." The subjects who were given such advice made a better adjustment than those in a control group who were not advised. Thus even a brief interview can, and probably should, have therapeutic value for the interviewee.

Pre- and Posttesting Interviews. A psychological test is a behavior sample; and as such, it is only as valid as the conditions under which the test is administered. Many of the errors in IQ or personality diagnoses which are occasionally reported are due to a mechanical handling of the tests. The subject appears for testing, the tests are administered, scored, and a report written in stereotyped phrases. Then it is later learned that an obvious error was made, one which would never have occurred if 10 or 15 minutes had been devoted to pre- and posttesting interviews. The purpose of such interviews is to guard against such errors and also to gather additional, clinically useful information. In some situations the posttesting interview is also used to transmit certain test results to the patient.

In the pretesting interview the clinician seeks to estimate the patient's condition relative to the tests to be used. This goes beyond the obvious checking for confused states or evidence of apprehension concerning the tests which the patient may exhibit. At least a gross estimate of the patient's sensory-motor adequacy should be made. More than a few patients have earned very low scores on performance tests because they were nearly blind, a handicap unnoticed by the test administrator. The same thing has happened to patients with hearing difficulties. Patients with minor muscular handicaps, however, are often a problem because they have learned to conceal their condition by means of a number of adaptive habits. Unless a specific check is made, patients with minor paralyses or with missing fingers are doomed to earn misleading, low scores on performance tests. Careful observation of the patient and a question or two during the pretest period will eliminate most such sources of difficulties.

Some patients have never taken psychological tests before. For them, a few minutes of explanation will make the task at hand clear, calm any fears, and render the results more accurate. Other patients are disoriented; and unless the purpose of the testing period is to assess the extent of confusion, testing had best be postponed. A few questions concerning time and place will indicate whether the patient is sufficiently oriented to proceed with the task at hand. Occasionally a patient is physically ill and performs poorly on tests for that reason. Indeed some of the cases where a patient first earned an IQ of 80 and then on a retest earned an IQ of 130 are due to the interference resulting from a migraine headache or the searing aches of influenza. Direct questions should be asked cautiously where illness is suspected, for the hypochondriacal patient will promptly, even enthusiastically, recount his symptoms, often misleading the clinician. However, if it is kept in mind that the genuinely physically ill person is typically listless and disinterested in elaborating his symptoms while the neurotic usually is interested and rather animated when describing his ailments, the clinician will not have too much difficulty in distinguishing between the two.

In the posttesting interview the clinician is in a position to examine hypotheses which he has formulated during the pretesting period and by observation of the patient's behavior during the test administration. If personality dynamics are being explored, for example, the clinician may have noticed that the patient showed signs of distress when dealing with aspects of the test which represented or reminded him of male figures. The clinician can then check hypotheses that some of the patient's difficulties are related to his father or other authoritarian figures or, perhaps, to homosexuality. In other cases the posttesting interview can serve as a check on the validity of the test. Thus a seven-year-old boy who seemed alertly bright during the pretesting interview earned an IQ of 72 when tested. Because of the unexpected poor performance, the clinician questioned the boy about his feelings about the test, to which the boy replied "You asked dumb questions and I gave you dumb answers." His IQ was later found to be 149. Thus, revealing hypotheses concerning personality dynamics, test validity, or probable achievement level can be verified or rejected by skillful use of the posttesting interview.

In some special situations the usual posttesting interview is concluded by interpreting test results to the subject. The present writer views with strong disfavor the transmitting of precise percentiles, IQ's, or standard scores to subjects because of mistakes in meaning which arise. In general, some broad descriptive scheme is to be preferred, such as *below average* for scores below the 26th percentile, *average* for percentiles 26–75, *above average* for percentiles 76–90, and *superior* or *very superior* for percentiles 91 or above. However, when special circumstances make it essential that precise test scores be supplied, the precautions mentioned below will be of material aid in avoiding confusion. A common source of error lies in the failure to make norm groups clear. That is, a scholastic aptitude score which falls at the 90th percentile for the general population will be the 50th percentile on college norms. This can give an unwarranted feeling of confidence to a prospective college student if he confuses the norm populations. Occasionally a percentile score is taken to mean an IQ, with the result that the subject's ego is bruised and the tests as well as the psychologist are indignantly rejected as useless. Careful phrasing of the test interpretation will prevent such confusions, many of which have caused tests to be unfairly criticized in the public press. One other area of difficulty may be noted. Subjects often think of interest test scores as measures of aptitude or achievement. While there is some relationship between the two, the correlation is only moderate, rarely exceeding .40 at best. Accordingly, some pains should be taken to emphasize that a high score on the Kuder Preference Record mechanical scale reflects interest in mechanical activities but is certainly no guarantee of high mechanical aptitude. Berg (1956) offers a discussion of sources of confusion in test score interpretation.

The Introduction to Therapy Interview. The typical patient with a psychological disturbance is often understandably apprehensive when he presents himself for treatment. Of course, if he is in an acute manic state or otherwise confused, he is not ready for interview approaches, since ancillary procedures such as sedation, rest, or other treatment may have to be instituted first. But if adjudged ready for therapeutic interview sessions by the professional staff, the patient usually wonders what will be done to him, for he had heard frightening stories about restraint and shock treatment which, if false or grossly exaggerated, render him uneasy, to say the least. Accordingly, the purpose of the introduction to therapy interview is to explain to the patient what can be done and how it can be done. Particular attention is paid to what is expected in the way of cooperation from the patient. This last aspect is most important; for if only one factor were to be named which was of greatest significance in determining the outcome of psychotherapeutic effort, it would have to be the *patient's motivation to get well.* Some patients cling to their illnesses like a drowning man to a floating spar; neither the type of treatment nor skill of therapist will avail until the patient himself desires to get well.

Much of the introduction to therapy interview resembles what Rogers calls "structuring" except that the interviewer plays a more active role in that he evaluates or interprets what the patient is saying or doing. Also, unlike nondirective interview structuring, such therapy introduction interviews are usually held in groups. But whatever the precise arrangements may be, the end goal is the same: the patient is made to feel that the therapist genuinely desires to help him and that he can and will help him. Further, the patient understands what he himself is expected to contribute to the treatment situation. Finally, the patient's desire to get well is encouraged and strengthened by every feasible method.

Many patients, of course, are not uncomfortable at the prospect of psychotherapy. On the contrary, they may even have the notion that after one or two interviews, the therapist will straighten out all their problems, as though it were necessary only to push some button or to utter some magical incantation. Other patients are defiant, suddenly expressing a "try to make me get better" attitude. In all such cases the clinician must candidly acknowledge that therapy takes time and that nothing can be done for the person who does not want help. If the patient is chagrined or surprised by such statements, it will save him from more severe disappointment later, when in the midst of a therapeutic program. Indeed, such honesty in the introductory interview may spell the difference between ultimate success and failure.

An occasional patient may appear genuinely puzzled as to why he is being interviewed in preparation for therapy, since he is aware of no problem. Chronic alcoholics sometimes express this reaction by remarking caustically: "Sure I take a drink now and then. So do you and so do my relatives. Does that mean I'm a mental case?" In other instances the patient has been tricked by relatives or friends into appearing at a clinic or a hospital under the pretense that he is to have a medical check-up. Obviously, a slip-up has occurred during the intake interview or at some other point in the admissions procedure. No patient should be hoodwinked into treatment, for therapeutic efforts are thereby foredoomed to failure. In desperation, relatives do occasionally try to "sneak" a patient into needed therapy. In all such cases the relatives should gently but firmly be told that nothing can be done unless the patient wishes to come for therapeutic interviews and fully understands why.

Interviewing Friends and Relatives of the Patient. Friends and relatives can help or hinder a patient's recovery. Hence they are often interviewed in order to determine their attitudes toward the patient and to show them how they can assist the patient in getting well. To do this the clinician must also understand the patient's attitudes toward the people in question. The patient may benefit from visits made by some persons, while others may disturb him and cause a setback in his progress. Thus the purpose in interviewing friends and relatives is to evaluate what benefit or harm may accrue from their visits with the patient and to help them adjust to having a person close to them placed under treatment. In addition, such interviews usually provide information which is valuable for understanding the kind of stresses the patient has been under, the people he lived with, and his relationships with them. Ordinary interview procedures are usually adequate when dealing with relatives; however, in the case of children, particular care should be taken to ensure that the child understands what is expected of him. Yarrow (1960) has a number of suggestions useful for the clinician when interviewing children.

Some relatives are frankly relieved to have the patient removed from their presence. The domestic upheaval resulting from the patient's behavior which led to his hospitalization has now ceased, so the relatives feel well rid of a problem. No matter how circumspect such visitors are, the patient will sense their attitudes and his recovery will usually be delayed. For obvious reasons it is not easy to change such attitudes on the part of relatives who have found the patient's behavior a source of strain. A useful approach is one in which the clinician explains to the relative that it would be best if he would not visit the patient for a while but should instead visit the clinician for a regular report on the patient's progress. The clinician indicates that he understands the relative's attitude toward the patient, but adds that the relative can, in turn, understand how the patient will feel should his attitude be communicated to the patient in some way. This explanation usually makes the relative mildly defensive and thereby helps to pave the way for attitude change. In later visits with the clinician, the relative realizes that the patient's behavior, which was so upsetting, was but a symptom of the illness and that with recovery such behavior will no longer be a problem. Then, as the relative receives additional reports on the patient's progress, he typically becomes more personally interested in the patient. When he later actually visits the patient, he is able to observe the changes himself and is heartened by them. Once such relatives become interested in the patient, the attitude change is fairly rapid and their visits are likely to be helpful to the patient.

In other cases relatives are extremely solicitous, sometimes badgering the clinician daily for information on the patient's progress and when he can return home. Such concern is understandable; however, it should be noted that in some instances the reaction is not as much a worry about the patient as a feeling of shame or guilt or both about his illness. That is, the relative is really worried about what the neighbors think about having the son, father, daughter, or sister under treatment; or the source of worry may be guilt feelings about the way the patient was treated at home before hospitalization. Thus, there is a desire to atone or "make it up to him." At other times the hospitalized patient is the family bread-winner, or the financial drain of treatment is so heavy that the relatives desperately need relief from the burden of mounting bills. No matter what the source of oversolicitude, the clinician should offer sympathetic understanding to the relative. The real cause of worry should be frankly discussed, whether it be feelings of shame about imagined scorn from neighbors, feelings of guilt, or worry about money. With catharsis and reassurance, the oversolicitousness can be relieved to some degree. Gradually, it can be channeled into ways by which the patient can be aided.

Friends and relatives should be given some help as to how they should conduct themselves during visits with the patient and how they should behave when he is home on a trial visit—or for that matter, when he is discharged. In general, the visitors should be encouraged to treat the patient as naturally as possible. Questions about details of improvement should not be indulged, nor should they be avoided either. It is natural that a relative should ask a patient some questions as "How are you feeling today?" But specific questions about what was done and how it was done may be upsetting. Hostile relatives may ignore the patient when he goes home on a trial visit, while solicitous ones may smother him with attention, sometimes reinforcing his illness. Neither approach, of course, is desirable. Accordingly, the relatives should be informed of what things the patient can do and how he should be regarded. In general, natural treatment with activities which are shared by patient and relative alike are best. Thus, if dishes are to be washed or the garage painted, let the patient actually participate, not merely watch or do it alone. With acceptance thus demonstrated, not just talked about, the patient will be speeded on the road to recovery.

The Exit or Termination Interview. At the close of treatment, it is customary to have a final interview with the patient before he is discharged. This interview is usually a summary of what the staff or the therapist thinks is important for the patient to know; hence its purpose is to facilitate the patient's transition from the treatment situation to being on his own. For the nonhospitalized or outpatient this final interview often is centered about a review of problems which the patient has met since treatment began and which he has dealt with realistically. The patient is led to realize that he will meet other similar difficulties, but that he now has proved himself capable of handling them. It is also pointed out that the patient will at times desire to return to his therapist for help when faced with a severe conflict. He is told that while it is always possible for him to see the therapist if conditions make it imperative for him to do so, he is assured that he himself can now manage his problems. Since the patient is considered to need therapy no longer, he very likely will make a successful adjustment; however, the feeling that he is not completely cast off, should he need help later, is strengthening and supportive to him.

Much the same approach is used with hospitalized patients in preparing them for the transition from hospital to home. Some additional time is spent in drawing out the patient relative to conditions and problems he will encounter on the "outside." The recovered manic patient, for example, will need to understand that exciting activities may hyperstimulate him dangerously. The involutional melancholic person who is in remission is reminded that he needs to be kept occupied and that activities, particularly those of a service type such as church or social welfare work, are of direct benefit to him. Upon the recommendation of the hospital staff, the attitudes of the patient toward his friends and relatives are reviewed, and suggestions are drawn from the patient as to how he can avoid difficulty. Since members of the family have often been previously interviewed with regard to their attitudes toward the patient, a basis for cooperation which can enhance the benefits of previous treatment is established.

In some instances a large portion of the discharge interview is devoted to encouraging the patient to regard his mental illness in the same light as a physical disease. This is a wholesome attitude, of course; however, when the patient is encouraged to volunteer information publicly about his breakdown, there is danger that he will be shunned by members of society who are less enlightened than the hospital employees. Needless frustration and danger of a second breakdown can be avoided if the regrettable fact is kept in mind that many persons on the "outside" view the recovered mental patient with distrust and discomfit. The present writer knows of a number of cases where neuropsychiatric casualties were encouraged (and in some instances given practice) to tell people: "I had some tough luck during the war. You know how it is, one guy gets hit by a bullet, another gets hit by pneumonia. Well, I got hit by a psychosis" (or by an anxiety state, combat fatigue, etc.). To the present writer's certain knowledge, at least a dozen veterans of our various wars were denied jobs when they cheerfully mentioned this item of their personal history to a prospective employer.[2] It is a sad but true fact that many who compose the general public are medievally benighted in their attitudes toward

---

[2] A statement by Karl Menninger is significant in this context. He states, "In the first place, the patient who finally decides to seek the help of a psychiatrist does so in the face of an undeniable social stigmatization." Then, later on the same page, "Compare the situation of an employee who requests time for the medical treatment of heart symptoms with that of an employee who requests time for a visit to a psychiatrist!" Page 196 in K. Menninger, A guide for psychiatric case study, *Bull. Menninger Clinic*, 1950, *14*, 192–201.

mental illness. Thus there is no point in requiring the patient to set himself up as a target.

The motivation behind the idea of pushing the patient to disclose information about his mental disturbance is that public attitudes will be changed. It is sometimes pointed out, in this connection, that the U.S. Public Health Service was able to change attitudes toward syphilis from an unmentionable word to something that should be routinely tested for. Such efforts deserve highest commendation; however, their success was not achieved by having syphilitics inform the public of the fact of their disease. Mental hygiene associations and public health agencies should properly carry the fight against foolish fears and misconceptions concerning mental disorder.

From the patient's standpoint, a sensible approach is first to teach him that a mental illness is no more to be ashamed of than physical illness. He will receive strong reinforcement in this attitude from the hospital staff. Later, when he is receptive and the time is opportune, he can be told that many people do not understand emotional disorders, hence some care should be exercised in just how the hospitalization is explained to "outsiders." Most patients who are on the brink of recovery fully recognize this and are eager for advice on how to handle such situations. A practical recommendation is to have the patient, when he is questioned about his hospital stay, reply candidly and simply, "I had some problems that were temporarily too much for me and I went to get help with them." If he is pressed further, he can add, "Yes, I feel fine now that those worries are gone." He should speak in a straightforward manner and without apology. Anyone can see the wisdom of this approach if he has had to comfort a distraught ex-patient who has been treated like a pariah after he freely volunteered details of his "schizophrenic psychosis" or some other psychiatric disorder.

THE CLINICAL CASE RECORD

Four types of general information are included in the clinical case record:[3] (1) *historical,* or personal-social history data; (2) *quantitative,* or psychological test and measurement data; (3) *impressionistic,* or information derived from behavioral observations; and (4) *the treatment record,* or material concerning medical and psychiatric treatment of the patient. The records are kept in a file folder, usually in chronological order, with the most recent reports on top. A case summary of one or two pages is

[3] A comprehensive discussion of the methods of psychological appraisal and the reports appropriate for inclusion in a clinical case record will be found in T. W. Richards, *Modern Clinical Psychology* (New York: McGraw-Hill Book Co., Inc., 1946), pp. 20–225, and in N. D. Sunberg and Leona E. Tyler, *Clinical Psychology* (New York: Appleton-Century-Crofts, 1962).

usually placed on the very top. For a long-hospitalized patient there may be several summaries which were prepared at various intervals. Other documents are typically included, such as correspondence about the patient, military service papers, etc. These other records are often kept separate from the types of information described above, although inserted in the same file folder. The record itself may vary in thickness from a small fraction of an inch to several inches, requiring two or more folders in some instances. This record is regarded as a legally confidential document, and as such it is kept under conditions of security in a locked room, locked filing cabinets, or both. In some institutions the security safeguards may include steel vaults, fireproof rooms and cabinets, as well as a continuous listing of everyone who has ever examined the folder.

The group of documents in the case record, if unevaluated, is appropriately referred to as a *case history*. When interpretations, diagnoses, or prognoses are made on the basis of such materials, the record is then referred to as a *case study*, as Traxler (1945, p. 284) has noted. Thus when the various reports from doctors, psychologists, nurses, social workers, etc., are used as a guide for treatment, the case history progresses to a case study. The folder itself is usually referred to simply as the *case record* or the *clinical folder*. The logic behind the case study is that the explanation for the patient's present behavior lies in his past. Since it is axiomatic that all behavior is caused, the man of today, whatever his mental and physical condition may be, can be understood and aided on the basis of what has happened to the man of yesterday and yesteryear. Obviously it is impossible to know everything that has happened to a given individual, nor is it important to learn every such fact since much material would be irrelevant or of minor significance insofar as his present disorder is concerned. Thus a compromise must be reached by reserving the more complete "case workups" (i.e., fairly complete social histories, psychological test results, etc.) for the most seriously ill patients. The choice is one of desperation, for the shortage of professional staff leaves no alternative. A complete personal-social history report may take a social worker a full day to prepare—several days if he must personally visit the home environment. An experienced clinical psychologist can test and write reports for two patients a day if he uses only the barest minimum of essential tests. More elaborate diagnostic testing will limit him to three or four patients per week. The same barrier to complete case records exists to the same or even to a greater extent for all the professional specialties. The psychiatrist, upon whom medical responsibility for treatment falls, would not have time to read complete case records for all patients even if they were available. He must depend largely upon the case summary to guide him in the majority of instances, reading the details of case reports only for problem patients who are responding poorly to treatment. Whatever his personal wishes, he can do nothing else in the typical clinical setting.

In some hospitals and clinics the patient or one of his friends or relatives fills out a series of forms, which provide details of the patient's personal-social background. This procedure saves time but loses the opportunity for significant behavioral observations which a professional person could make. An interesting departure from the usual procedures for gathering systematic case history data is a method, sometimes called "dynamic" or "projective," which is oriented to psychoanalytic theory. During the first interview, the patient is encouraged to talk about his early history, to describe his home, family, playmates, and the like. The underlying assumption is that whatever aspects of the patient's past life were important to him will appear in some form as the interview unfolds. He may reveal signs of obvious tension when he mentions his mother, for example, or he may talk exclusively of her, or he may not mention her at all. With additional interviews, a sizeable body of personal-social history data is gathered; but more important, the significance of the material will appear as well. The usual purpose of the therapeutic interview is thus fulfilled, but the additional questions elicit information needed for a personal-social history report, which may be separately prepared.

The Personal-social History. The following outline for the standard recording of a psychiatric case record is sufficiently complete for most purposes. Ordinarily much time would be required for filling it out; however Wells and Ruesch, who prepared the outline for their *Mental Examiners Handbook* (1945), provide a simple "cue sheet" which saves considerable time. The presence of a finding is indicated by checking or circling the appropriate number under each heading. When supplemental information is desirable, a word or phrase may be added to augment the record. Thus under *Birth and Diseases,* the eighth item, "Head injury" may be checked and some explanatory phrase added such as "accidentally shot in forehead by older brother." Similarly, identifying information such as name, address, age, etc., may be extended to include previous addresses, name of the referring physician, etc.

The nature of the quantitative and impressionistic information included in the case record will not be reviewed here, for such material is covered elsewhere in the present volume. Chapters 3, 4, and 5, among others, give a number of illustrations of how test and other quantitative data are used for furthering clinical understanding of the patient. The section on nonverbal behavior in the interview, page 36 in the present chapter, contains numerous examples of the variety and uses of impressionistic information.

STANDARD RECORDING OF PSYCHIATRIC CASE STUDY [4]

Name_____ Date_____

Address_____ Age _____

_____ Sex M F

CHILDHOOD HISTORY

This section includes the period from birth to the age of 16. Findings checked here should not be rechecked under Adult History.

Birth and Diseases

1. Premature birth
2. Instrumental or operative birth
3. Malformations (cleft palate, spina bifida, etc.)
4. Birth injuries
5. Congenital mental deficiency
6. Allergic diseases (asthma, eczema, urticaria)
7. Nervous diseases (myopathies, poliomyelitis, Little's disease)
8. Head injury
9. Loss of consciousness (fainting, coma)
10. Convulsions
11. Accidents

Home, Parents and Environment

1. Adopted child or one stepparent
2. Raised in foster home or orphanage
3. Only child
4. Sheltered childhood
5. Dissension at home
6. Broken home (one parent left before age 16)
7. Strict mother
8. Strict father
9. Rejection by father
10. Rejection by mother
11. Overprotective father
12. Overprotective mother
13. Dominant father
14. Dominant mother
15. Death of parent before age 16
16. Bicultural background (parents speak different language)
17. Intimate contact with diseased persons
18. Unfavorable social environment (slum, substandard, or delinquency neighborhood)
19. Premature sex experiences (intercourse before 16, assault, witness to coitus)
20. Excessive parental ambition for child

Neuropathic Traits

1. Minor neuropathic traits (nail-biting, thumb-sucking)
2. Nervous breakdown (depression, states of excitement)
3. Persistent fears
4. Persistent nightmares
5. Persistent obsessions
6. Persistent compulsions
7. Tics, stammering, stuttering
8. Behavior problems (truancy, fights, disciplinary problems)
9. Antisocial behavior (criminal assault, stealing)
10. Enuresis beyond 3 years
11. Emotional overractions, sudden outbursts (temper tantrums)

[4] From F. L. Wells and J. Ruesch, *Mental Examiners' Handbook* (2d ed.; New York: The Psychological Corporation, 1945), pp. 5–11. Reprinted by permission of the author and The Psychological Corporation.

Personality
1. Difficulties with other children
2. Difficulties at school
3. Sibling rivalry
4. Shy, withdrawn
5. Extreme day-dreaming
6. Cruelty
7. Fights and aggressiveness
8. Hyperactivity

Educational History
1. Started school late (after 7)
2. Less than eighth grade education
3. Repeated grades

ADULT HISTORY

This section includes the period from age 16 up to the time of the examination. Items referring to events which occurred in childhood should not be marked in this section; however, if signs or symptoms carry over into adulthood, they should be checked.

Diseases
1. Head injury (one or more)
2. Nervous disease (poliomyelitis, multiple sclerosis, neurosyphilis, etc.)
3. Convulsive disorder
4. Migraine
5. Major functional psychosis (schizophrenia, manic-depressive psychosis)
6. Major operations (2 or more)
7. Minor operations (3 or more)
8. Accidents
9. Fractures (2 or more)
10. Industrial poisoning
11. Venereal infection
12. Cardiovascular disease
13. Respiratory disease
14. Endocrine disease
15. Rheumatic disease
16. Gastrointestinal disease
17. Allergic disease

Gynecological-Obstetrical History
1. Two or more gynecological operations
2. Two or more obstetrical operations
3. Spontaneous or operative abortions
4. Premature or stillborn children
5. Persistent dysmenorrhea
6. Periods of amenorrhea
7. Sterility
8. Menopausal syndrome

Environment, Home and Social Status
1. Living alone
2. Unfavorable environment (slum or substandard housing)
3. Change of residence (more than 3 changes in last 3 years)
4. Conflict with the law (arrests, sentences)
5. Conduct disorder

Occupational History (last 3 years)
1. More unemployed than employed
2. More than 6 jobs
3. More than 3 occupations
4. Known to social agencies
5. Last job held terminated within 6 months
6. Military Service—type of discharge

Habits

1. Tobacco abuse (more than 20 cigarettes, 5 cigars, 10 pipes daily)
2. Drug abuse
3. Coffee abuse (more than 5 cups in one session or more than 3 occasions daily)
4. Alcoholism (more than 1 qt. whiskey, or 20 bottles beer, or 5 bottles wine per week)
5. Abstainer
6. Occasional drunkenness only (little alcohol consumption in between)
7. Low alcohol tolerance, emotional manifestations after 2 drinks of whiskey, strong liquor or its equivalent
8. Injured while drunk
9. Injured in fight

Sex

1. Impotence or ejaculatio praecox
2. Frigidity
3. Coitus interruptus
4. Sexual promiscuity after 25
5. Persistent masturbation after 25
6. Regular extramarital relations
7. "Unhappy" sex experiences
8. Homosexuality
9. Other perversions
10. First intercourse before 16
11. Divorce or separation

Neuropathic Traits and Symptoms

1. Nervous breakdown (depressions, states of panic and excitement, catatonic episodes)
2. Easily upset
3. Easily tired
4. Anxiety attacks
5. Anxiety tension (muscular tension with agitation and "nervousness
6. Nightmares
7. Fears or phobias
8. Obsessive thoughts and compulsions
9. Mood swings
10. Transitory affective disturbances
11. Speech disturbances (stammering, stuttering)
12. Tics
13. Metapsychic interests (mindreading, hypnotism, astrology, etc.)

Interests

1. No interests
2. Gambling
3. Radio, newspapers only

Religion

1. Atheist or no religion
2. Member of small sect
3. Change of religion

FAMILY HISTORY

Note diseases occurring in own sibling, parents, siblings of parents, and grandparents.

Diseases

1. Suicide
2. CNS disease
3. Mental disease
4. Mental deficiency
5. Nervousness
6. Nervous breakdown
7. Heart attacks
8. High blood pressure
9. Sterility
10. Convulsions
11. Fainting
12. Chronic invalidism
13. Malformations
14. Allergic diseases
15. Crime
16. Alcoholism
17. Venereal disease
18. Tuberculosis
19. Accidents, war casualties
20. Neoplasms

PRESENT SYMPTOMS AND COMPLAINTS

Mark the outstanding symptoms and complaints at the time of the examination. Do not include symptoms and complaints which occurred only in the past.

Feelings

1. Feelings of apprehension
2. Feelings of isolation
3. Feelings of guilt
4. Lack of guilt feelings after misbehavior

5. Feelings of inadequacy and insecurity
6. Fear of losing love objects
7. General unhappiness
8. Mourning

Physical Symptoms

1. Poor health
2. General nervousness
3. Fatigue
4. Weakness
5. Sleeplessness
6. Crying spells
7. Sweating
8. Trembling
9. Flushes
10. Vomiting
11. Diarrhea
12. Extreme constipation
13. Poor appetite
14. Anorexia
15. Hyperexia
16. Urinary frequency

17. Enuresis
18. Impotence-frigidity
19. Headache
20. Dizziness
21. Loss of consciousness
22. Convulsions
23. Diffuse aches and pains
24. Paraesthesias, itching
25. Breathlessness
26. Smothering
27. Paralysis
28. Low back pain
29. Difficulties of expression (speech)
30. Gritting teeth, clenching fists

Ideas and Content of Thought

1. Disappointment about failure
2. Intellectual inefficiency
3. Self-accusation and condemnation
4. Ideas of persecution

5. Ideas of reference
6. Excessive self-observation
7. Doubts and inability to make decisions
8. Fears

Body Regions Involved

1. Head
2. Face
3. Mouth
4. Neck
5. Chest
6. Abdomen

7. Genitalia
8. Anus
9. Arms and hands
10. Legs and feet
11. Pelvis
12. Diffuse

System Involved

1. Motor system
2. Somatic sensory system
3. Smell and taste
4. Vision
5. Hearing
6. Skin
7. Respiratory tract
8. Circulatory system

9. Gastrointestinal tract
10. Urinary tract
11. Joints and bones
12. Sex apparatus
13. Equilibrium and vestibular apparatus
14. Diffuse

The Treatment Record. The treatment record provides an account of what was done for the patient and how he responded. This is the most important purpose of the record, for it marks the milestones of the patient's progress or signalizes the lack of it. In addition, this record, along with the other information in the clinical folder, is a useful source of research data. By surveying a wide variety of case records, significant clinical hypotheses will arise concerning which patients improved with what treatment. Such hypotheses can then be verified or rejected later by carefully controlled studies.

Accordingly, among the materials included in the clinical folder is a continuous record of all treatment received by the patient. For a nonhospitalized or outpatient, this record may consist only of brief therapeutic interview notes and, perhaps, the findings cf a physical examination. By contrast, the treatment record of a patient who has been hospitalized for a long time will typically be both lengthy and diverse in content. Thus the results and recommendations of a physical examination will be reported and, later in the record, the action taken will be noted, such as performance of a needed tonsillectomy, treatment for anemia, fitting the patient with glasses, or whatever the medical recommendations called for. Any physical illness which the patient may have had while hospitalized will be listed in the folder. The doctor's orders, nurse's notes, medicines given, etc., which concern the patient's physical and, of course, his mental illness, are also included. In many hospitals behavior rating sheets are filled out by all persons, such as attendants, nurse's aides, occupational therapists, manual arts teachers, and others who are in regular contact with the patient. These rating forms are often inserted directly into the folder, and for good reason, since the best evidence of improvement for the slow-to-recover patient is commonly found in such ratings. Anyone may observe the marked behavioral changes which often follow treatment by shock therapy or prefrontal lobotomy, but the gradual modification of behavior which may be associated with group therapy sessions or other rehabilitative effort will be most clearly revealed to those who are in daily contact with the patient.

A large portion of the treatment record is composed of the interview notes prepared by the psychotherapist. Since a given patient may have as many as twenty or even more therapeutic interviews, these notes may achieve formidable bulk. As Sarbin (1940) has observed, three general forms of notes may be found in case records: (1) the one-phrase or one-line digest, (2) attempts at complete reproduction, and (3) selection and interpretation of the interview material. While possibly better than no notes at all, the one-line digest is virtually useless because of its brevity. Attempts at complete reproduction, on the other hand, are impractical because of the difficulty in getting everything down and because the clinically significant material is buried beneath a mountain of verbiage. It is interesting to observe in this connection that when complete photographic transcripts of interviews are made for research purposes, the usual selective and interpretive summary may be written up and filed along with the complete transcript.

In the article referred to previously, Sarbin emphasizes that the functions of any interview records are well served by the "selection and interpretation" approach. To summarize Sarbin's points, it may be stated that good interview notes enable the therapist to review previous interviews and assess progress in therapy. Should a transfer to another therapist be necessary, the notes will acquaint the second therapist with the significant details of the case. A similar objective is reached in that the notes will inform the supervisor of the activities of his staff and also permit him to follow the progress of interns in training. Finally, in addition to research uses, the interview notes are protection against misinterpretation and misquotation. This last is of grave importance, for it is not uncommon that a patient may assert, for example, "My psychologist told me to get a divorce," when the psychologist said no such thing. Thus particular attention should be paid to any instructions given to the patient when writing up the notes.

The following excerpt is taken from the notes recorded for the second interview with Carl Ignotus, a young man aged 20, who had been referred by his physician to a mental health clinic. Carl had come, as he put it, "for help in understanding myself and in finding the right job." The first interview was devoted to an account of previous jobs (11 jobs in 15 months) which Carl had held, and his experiences with a brutal father who had been divorced by Carl's mother two years before. In the days between the first and second interview, several psychological tests were administered. A summary of these findings are presented in a sample clinical report at the end of the present chapter. The excerpt immediately following represents notes which cover the first 15 minutes or so of the second interview, which lasted an hour altogether. There is nothing unusual about the notes. They are intended only to condense the significant material which appeared in the interview.

Carl remarked that he was puzzled that his mother would be interested in dating other men in view of her unhappy experiences with Carl's father prior to their divorce two years ago. He said that he worried about his mother when she was out on dates, and he was unable to sleep. He added that the lack of sleep did not matter, as he was kept awake by his asthma attacks anyway. When asked about other attacks of asthma and the circumstances associated with them, Carl mentioned some of his "worst times." One of these instances was particularly terrifying to him because he was all alone and his mother was more than two hours overdue from a shopping trip. Carl appeared to be unaware of his dependence upon his mother and the possible relationship between his attacks of asthma and his mother's absence. This area was to be explored later.[5]

The Clinical Report. Perhaps the weakest link of communication between clinical psychologists and members of other professional groups is the clinical report. All too frequently clinical reports are unnecessarily long, and, what is worse, crammed with jargon like "color shock, scatter," and a host of similar phrases which are meaningless to the nonpsychologist. As Foster (1951, p. 195) remarks, with some asperity: "The psychologist should be able to report the results of his work without wind and water." The difficulty is chiefly that many psychologists do not have the reader in mind nor do they organize their reports for him. In their excellent work on report writing, Hammond and Allen (1953, p. 9) assert that only three steps are involved in adapting the report for the reader: "(1) studying the reader; (2) planning the report to fit the reader's needs; and (3) writing so that the reader can quickly and accurately comprehend the correct meaning." A psychiatrist wants information from the clinical report different from that wanted by the vocational counselor, and the teacher of exceptional children needs information different from that required by either of the other two. There is no single report which fits the needs of all possible users.

To be of maximum service, the clinical report must, therefore, be organized with the needs of those who will use it kept firmly in mind. Hammond and Allen (1953, p. 41) list three stages in this organization process: "(1) determining the material to be included in the report; (2) selecting or developing the most effective plan for presenting this material; and (3) executing the plan." This means that certain data will be omitted, some treated lightly, and some will be fully covered, depending upon the needs of the person using the report. Thus a psychiatrist will usually desire details of personality dynamics, while the vocational counselor will prefer to have an elaboration of the patient's interests and aptitudes. The teacher of exceptional children, on the other hand, may be primarily interested in ability to learn. All three would be interested, but in different degrees, in other findings, such as indications of organic brain damage or evidence of sensorimotor handicaps. The vocational counselor, for example, might wish to know details of the extent and type of color blindness, while the psychiatrist's or the teacher's interest would not ordinarily go beyond the existence of the fact alone.

The following clinical report is one prepared at the request of a psy-

---

[5] Permission to publish these reports is extended by the author to The Ronald Press Company. Ordinarily, identifying information such as place and date of birth, home and business addresses, referral sources, etc., are included at the top of the report or case outline.

chiatrist. It concerns the case of Carl Ignotus, the young man whose interview case note excerpt was presented earlier in the present chapter. The report follows the general pattern recommended by Hammond and Allen, and it is a regular "working" report, not a model. Its aim is to tell the psychiatrist briefly what the psychologist has learned about the patient thus far, thereby providing the psychiatrist with information which will assist him in formulating the treatment program. Thus, the report is short and concise, for as Foster (1951, p. 195) asserts, "Actually, it is the rare report which requires more than one typewritten page." No space is wasted on remote possibilities or idle speculations concerning the test findings. Further, when the evidence is clear, the fact is so stated without any protective screen of circumlocution, such as "it seems possible that . . ." Particular attention is called to the absence of technical details in the report. Nothing is said of the high F plus %, the 17 M (12 good M), the shift to rare details when Rorschach card VI was encountered, the sharply elevated neurotic triad of the MMPI with Pt at 81, Sc at 73, etc. Such details are unnecessary for the report. They satisfy nobody, for the psychiatrist is exasperated by such padding and jargon, while another psychologist would want to see the test protocols and scores for himself. The soundest procedure is to leave out such distractors.

After reading the report below, the psychiatrist had a 20-minute interview with the patient and approved the recommendations in the report. He assigned the patient to a psychologist for individual interviews and requested a progress report before the patient was enrolled for group therapy sessions.

Psychological Report on Carl Ignotus [6]

Tests Administered. Wechsler-Bellevue, ACE Psychological, MMPI, Rorschach.

Summary: This patient was referred for psychiatric help because of asthma attacks, which seem to appear only when he is emotionally disturbed, and because of extreme indecisiveness in choosing a career. During the past fifteen months he has held eleven jobs, chiefly clerical in nature, two of them lasting only one day. Although twenty years old, the patient speaks of his mother and his friends in the manner of a child of ten, referring to his mother as "Mommy" or "Moms." The only friends he mentioned were women about his mother's age, and whom he called "auntie." When asked about other friends and about reasons for leaving his various jobs, he replied that he had no other close friends and that he had left most of the jobs because his asthma was aggravated due to dust. He remarked that on several jobs the people were "nasty and crude" to him. Throughout the interview, the patient revealed signs of tension, such as twisting his handkerchief, wiping perspiration from his hands and neck, speaking in a tremulous voice at times, etc.

The patient is of superior intelligence (IQ 128); his best scores were earned on test items which dealt with verbal or linguistic aspects of intelligence, while

[6] *Ibid.*

his scores on performance or quantitative items were only slightly above average for college populations. Intellectually he is capable of doing college work at an above-average level. However, the personality test data indicate that emotional disturbances overwhelm the patient and interfere with his effective functioning in most social situations, academic and otherwise. This is not true of his behavior in concrete, nonpersonal situations. Essentially, the patient is a withdrawn person, quite egocentric, compulsive, and anxious. There is strong evidence that he is incapable of relating himself to other persons and that he is threatened by problems which must be handled with or through other people. His anxieties seem to center about sex; however, there are no indications of homosexuality. His method of dealing with his anxieties appears to be either avoidance by incapacitating himself (asthma) or occupying himself with fussy details, such as being precisely on time, combing his hair just so, etc. While outwardly dependent upon his mother, the patient's dependence is of an egocentric, demanding kind in which the mother (or mother-equivalent "aunties") is used as a shield between him and the rest of the social world.

Prognosis and Recommendations. In view of the patient's strong motivation to improve and his intellectual adequacy, it is likely that he will respond quite favorably to a short series (4 or 5) of individual interviews which are first cathartic and then interpretive. Group therapy sessions are recommended after the individual interviews. The patient's verbal and intellectual competence should enable him to do well in the group sessions, permitting him eventually to relate himself to other people without being engulfed in an emotional upheaval. There may be some difficulty if the patient is pressed with interpretations too early or too rapidly during the individual interviews, for he may withdraw from the situation, probably by illness.

SUMMARY

The interview is the most widely used clinical tool for supplying or receiving information and for influencing behavior. If employed by a trained person, the interview has a high degree of validity and reliability for broad clinical judgments. While interviews may be conducted anywhere, the best conditions are those characterized by privacy, freedom from interruption, and a general atmosphere of calmness. Under such conditions, if the clinician is also able to communicate a warm acceptance of the patient, rapport will be established firmly and the interview can be carried on effectively. During the interview, certain nonverbal behavior on the part of the patient has useful diagnostic value. The patient's gait, expression, posture, etc., commonly offer explanatory hypotheses concerning his area of maladjustment. Similarly, the rate of speech, topics which are avoided, digressions, and word choice supply numerous clues which help the clinician in understanding the patient's difficulties.

While certain general techniques apply to any interview situation, the purposes of different interviews vary considerably; hence special problems may arise. Thus the intake or admission interview is chiefly concerned with the patient's presenting complaints, while the personal and social history interview aims at gathering background data which may have a bearing upon the complaints. The screening or diagnostic interview, by contrast, seeks to arrive at a judgment concerning the patient's condition. Interviews are also held prior to and after psychological test administration, and as a means of introducing a patient to therapy. In other cases the interview is used to assist friends and relatives in their dealings with the patient. Finally, when the patient is ready for discharge, an exit or termination interview is conducted to facilitate the patient's transition from hospital to home.

Interview findings, along with other material, are customarily filed in a clinical folder or case record. Four types of information are included in the case record: (1) *historical,* or background data on the patient's past life; (2) *quantitative,* or test and measurement results; (3) *impressionistic,* or nonverbal behavior, as gestures, posture, etc.; and (4) *the treatment record,* or data on medical treatment, psychiatric interview notes, and the like. The logic behind such records is that the explanation for the patient's present behavior will be found in the past and that any improvement or lack of it will be reflected in the accounts of treatment in the clinical folder.

REFERENCES

Anonymous. 1954. *Psychiatric unit operational procedures.* (Rev. ed.) Prepared under ONR contract 7 onr–45011 with Northwestern Univer. Neuropsychiatric Branch, Bureau of Medicine, U.S. Navy.

Barber, W. H., Rigby, Marilyn K., and Napoli, J. G. 1962. The clinical interview revisited. *J. clin. Psychol.,* 18, 282–86.

Berg, I. A. 1954. Ideomotor response set: Symbolic sexual gestures in the counseling interview. *J. counsel. Psychol.,* 1, 180–83.

Berg, I. A. 1954. The use of human subjects in psychological research. *Amer. Psychologist,* 9, 108–11.

Berg, I. A. 1956. Test score interpretation and client confusion. *Personnel & Guid. J.,* 34, 576–78.

Berg, I. A. 1958. Word choice in the interview and personal adjustment. *J. counsel. Psychol.,* 5, 130–35.

Bingham, W. V., Moore, B. V., and Gustad, J. W. 1959. *How to interview.* (4th ed.) New York: Harper & Row.

Blau, T. H. 1959. *Private practice in clinical psychology.* New York: Appleton-Century-Crofts.

Burtt, H. E. 1948. *Applied psychology.* New York: Prentice-Hall.

Carey, J. F., Berg, I. A., and Van Dusen, A. C. 1951. Reliability of ratings of employee satisfaction based on written interview records. *J. appl. Psychol.,* 35, 252–55.

Closson, J. H., and Hildreth, H. M. 1944. Experiment in psychotherapy during selection examination. *Nav. med. Bull.,* 43, 39–43.

DAVITZ, J. R. (ed.). 1964. *The communication of emotional meaning.* New York: McGraw-Hill.

DEEMER, W. L., and RAFFERTY, J. A. 1949. Experimental validation of the psychiatric interview for prediction of success in pilot training. *J. aviat. Med.,* **20,** 238–50.

EBAUGH, F. G. 1948. Evaluation of interviewing technics and principles of psychotherapy for the general practitioner. *J. Omaha midwest clin. Soc.,* **9,** 1–7.

FOSTER, A. 1951. Writing psychological reports. *J. clin. Psychol.,* **7,** 195.

GARRETT, A. 1942. *Interviewing: Its principles and methods.* New York: Family Welfare Association.

GUTTMACHER, M. S., and WEIHOFFEN, H. 1952. *Psychiatry and the law.* New York: Norton.

HAMMOND, K. R., and ALLEN, J. M. 1953. *Writing clinical reports.* New York: Prentice-Hall.

HANNA, J. V. 1950. Estimating intelligence by interview. *Educ. psychol. Measmt.,* **10,** 420–30.

HOLLINGWORTH, H. L. 1923. *Judging human character.* New York: Appleton-Century-Crofts.

HOVLAND, C. I., and WONDERLIC, E. F. 1939. Prediction of industrial success from a standardized interview. *J. appl. Psychol.,* **23,** 537–46.

HUNT, W. A., WITTSON, C. L., and HUNT, EDNA B. 1953. A theoretical and practical analysis of the diagnostic process. In P. H. HOCH and J. ZUBIN (ed.), *Current problems in psychiatric diagnosis.* New York: Grune & Stratton.

KELLY, E. L., and FISKE, D. W. 1950. The prediction of success in the VA training program in clinical psychology. *Amer. Psychologist,* **5,** 395–406.

KINSEY, A. C., POMEROY, W. B., and MARTIN, C. E. 1948. *Sexual behavior in the human male.* Philadelphia: W. B. Saunders.

LOUTTIT, C. M. 1934. A blank for history taking in psychological clinics. *J. appl. Psychol.,* **18,** 737–48.

MATARAZZO, J. D. 1962. Prescribed behavior therapy: Suggestions from interview research. In A. J. BACHRACH (ed.), *Experimental foundations of clinical psychology.* New York: Basic Books. Pp. 471–509.

MATARAZZO, J. D., SASLOW, G., and GUZE, S. B. 1956. Stability of interaction patterns during interviews: A replication. *J. consult. Psychol.,* **20,** 267–74.

NEWMAN, S. H., BOBBITT, J. M., and CAMERON, D. C. 1946. The reliability of the interview method in an officer candidate evaluation program. *Amer. Psychologist,* **1,** 103–9.

PENNINGTON, L. A. 1945. The incidence of nail-biting among adults. *Amer. J. Psychiat.,* **102,** 241–44.

PENNINGTON, L. A., and MEARIN, R. J. 1944. The frequency and significance of a movement mannerism for the military psychiatrist. *Amer. J. Psychiat.,* **100,** 628–32.

RICE, S. A. 1929. Contagious bias in the interview: A methodological note. *Amer. J. Sociol.,* **35,** 420–23.

RICHARDS, T. W. 1946. *Modern clinical psychology.* New York: McGraw-Hill.

ROGERS, C. R. 1942. *Counseling and psychotherapy.* Boston: Houghton Mifflin.

RUNDQUIST, E. A. 1947. Development of an interview for selection purposes. In G. A. KELLY (ed.), *New methods in applied psychology.* College Park: Univer. of Maryland Press. Pp. 90–95.

SARBIN, T. R. 1940. The case record in psychological counseling. *J. appl. Psychol.,* 24, 184–97.

SASLOW, G., MATARAZZO, J. D., PHILLIPS, JEANNE S., and MATARAZZO, RUTH G., 1957. Test-retest stability of interaction patterns during interviews conducted one week apart. *J. abnorm. soc. Psychol.,* 54, 295–302.

SNEDDEN, D. 1930. Measuring general intelligence by interview. *Psychol. Clinic,* 19, 131–34.

STRUPP, H. H. 1962. Patient-doctor relationships: Psychotherapist in the therapeutic process. In A. J. BACHRACH (ed.), *Experimental foundations of clinical psychology.* New York: Basic Books. Pp. 576–615.

TINDALL, R. H., and ROBINSON, F. P. 1947. The use of silence as a technique in counseling. *J. clin. Psychol.,* 3, 136–41.

TRAXLER, A. E. 1945. *Techniques of guidance.* New York: Harper & Row.

TUPES, E. C. 1950. An evaluation of ratings of personality traits on the basis of unstructured assessment interviews. *Psychol. Monogr.,* 64, No. 317.

ULRICH, L., and TRUMBO, D. 1965. The selection interview since 1949. *Psychol. Bull.,* 63, 100–116.

WATSON, R. I. 1951. *The clinical method in psychology.* New York: Harper & Row.

WEDELL, C., and SMITH, K. V. 1951. Consistency of interview methods in appraisal of attitudes. *J. appl. Psychol.,* 35, 392–96.

WEISS, D. J., and DAVIS, R. V. 1960. An objective validation of factual interview data. *J. appl. Psychol.,* 44, 381–85.

WELLS, F. L., and RUESCH, J. 1945. *Mental examiners' handbook.* (Rev. ed.) New York: Psychological Corporation.

WHITEHORN, J. C. 1944. Guide to interviewing and personality study. *AMA Arch. Neurol. Psychiat.,* 52, 197–216.

WITTSON, C. L., HARRIS, H. I., HUNT, W. A., SOLOMON, P. S., and JACKSON, M. M. 1943. The neuropsychiatric selection of recruits. *Amer. J. Psychiat.,* 99, 639–50.

WITTSON, C. L., and HUNT, W. A. 1951. The predictive value of the brief psychiatric interview. *Amer. J. Psychiat.,* 107, 582–85.

WITTSON, C. L., HUNT, W. A., and STEVENSON, IRIS. 1946. A followup study of neuropsychiatric screening. *J. abnorm. soc. Psychol.,* 41, 79–82.

YACORZYNSKI, G. K. 1951. *Medical psychology: A basis for psychiatry and clinical psychology.* New York: Ronald.

YARROW, L. J. 1960. Interviewing children. In P. MUSSEN (ed.), *Handbook of research methods in child development.* New York: Wiley.

3

Intelligence Testing
and Clinical Practice

ANN MAGARET GARNER [*]

Clinical practice, like other aspects of the broad field of psychology, reflects the changes both in behavioral science and in the society which supports it. The past decade has seen profound changes in the emphases and methods of psychological research, in the breadth and insistence of social need, and in the growth and definition of clinical psychology as a professional (Joint Commission on Mental Illness and Health, 1961; Shakow, 1965). Inevitably, these developments influence the details of clinical practice. The clinical psychologist today is modifying his approaches, revising his techniques, scrutinizing his results, sharpening his interpretations, and re-evaluating his role in the light of social and professional change. This is nowhere more clear than in the area of intelligence testing.

At one time, the diagnosis of general intelligence constituted the principal function of many psychologists employed in guidance centers, clinics, and agencies. Often the "batteries" of diagnostic instruments used in initial contacts with clients contained a number of intelligence scales. The clinician's main responsibility was then the selection of the technique appropriate to the "abilities" being appraised, its skillful application, and its accurate interpretation. Three recent developments have altered this approach markedly.

For one thing, clinical psychologists are becoming increasingly interested in psychotherapy as their major function, and correspondingly less

* Ann Magaret Garner, Ph.D. (Stanford University), Professor of Psychology, University of Nebraska.

involved in psychodiagnosis (Albee, 1963; Kelly, 1961; Shakow, 1965). This shift stems in large part from a complex pattern of social need, inter-professional association, and personal role definition. Undoubtedly, however, recent research which questions the predictive efficiency of a variety of techniques of appraisal (Meehl, 1960) serves also to discourage clinicians from their diagnostic task.

For another thing, the concept of "intelligence," at least in its traditional sense, has been called into question. It seems inevitable that not only are our intelligence scales bound to undergo redefinition and revision (McNemar, 1964), but also our notions of the fluid, developing nature of what we call "intelligence," and its relation to specific patterns of life experience, will change as well (Hunt, 1961).

Finally, an increasing body of research continues to confirm our conviction that the score yielded by contemporary instruments for measuring intelligence is the product of a profusion of past and present factors, ranging from stable cultural patterns of motivation to temporary situational effects. It is clear also that such factors as these lower the predictive efficiency of our scores, and contribute to our uncertainty as to what "intelligence" *is*. While these matters have been known and specified since the beginning of the testing movement, still their reiteration and emphasis today make it tempting for the busy, half-hearted, or ill-prepared diagnostician to discredit his instruments—and even his task—altogether.

We shall see later that, far from rejecting intelligence appraisal as part of his task, the clinician needs rather to take into account as many as possible of the aspects of the client's behavior, his past experiences, his present tensions, his group identifications, the clinical setting, and the examiner's own attitudes in selecting and applying his techniques and in interpreting their results. More aspects of the clinician's task have been subjected to inquiry and research than ever before; and his responsibility for the critical understanding of this research and its applicability to a particular case is greater than it has ever been.

In the midst of this uncertainty and change in the area of intelligence testing, however, the clinician's guiding philosophy must remain constant. Insofar as he accepts the diagnostic task as part of his responsibility—and it is the assumption of this chapter that individual appraisal is an essential function of the clinical psychologist—his goal is the understanding of his client as a unique individual. Such an ambitious goal cannot be achieved by the use of any one method. The qualified clinician brings to his job skills in the administration and interpretation of many specific techniques, as well as expertness in observing and comprehending human behavior. His flexibility in using these qualities in ways appropriate to the needs of his clients determines the success with which the clinician achieves his diagnostic goal.

Intelligence testing is only one of many methods for understanding clients, and its results have only limited meaning when considered alone. Like any other means of appraisal, an intelligence scale is most productive if it is used in conjunction with interview material (see Chapter 2), with scores on other tests (see Chapter 5), with performance on projective instruments (see Chapter 4), and with general observations of the patient's behavior. Isolated from a more extensive study of the client, or applied inappropriately, an intelligence measure, no matter how accurate, will yield incomplete or distorted results.

Early Development of Intelligence Tests. Intelligence tests are the product of two trends in the history of psychology. One was the increasing interest in individual differences, which resulted from the wide diffusion of the evolutionary point of view during the latter half of the nineteenth century. The other was the growing concern with the practical educational problem of classifying and placing children in school. These two trends converged, as we shall see, in the work of Binet, and led to the construction of a scale which became the model for later intelligence tests.

The evolutionary doctrine, developed first in biological science, was influential also in the allied field of psychology. The problem of the origin of differences between species brought into focus the related problem of identifying differences among individuals. Because the nineteenth-century experimental psychologists dealt principally with the topics of sense physiology and rote learning, and directed their studies toward narrowly restricted activities of their laboratory subjects, the identification of individual differences in performance was likewise limited to uncomplicated tasks. The English scholar Sir Francis Galton, for example, early obtained data regarding individual differences in discriminating between weights, in distinguishing tones of different pitches, in reaction time, pain sensitivity, and imagery, on the questionable assumption that these abilities were related to general intelligence.

Late in the nineteenth century, the American psychologist Cattell, one of Wundt's students, applied similar tests to a group of college freshmen. Other psychologists and psychiatrists—Kraepelin, Oehrn, Münsterberg, and Jastrow, to mention only a few—developed simple tests to reveal individual differences in response. The approaches of these men resembled one another in selecting simple sensory-motor tasks and restricted performances to demonstrate differences among individuals.

Toward the close of the century Alfred Binet raised a serious objection to this general approach. He argued that the behavior which reflects general intelligence is behavior involving complex functions, rather than sensory or motor tasks. The development of Binet's point of view may be traced through a series of papers published between 1895 and 1902, in which he recorded his fruitless search for single measures related to general intelligence, and his careful observations of complex behavior, and revealed his growing sophistication regarding methods of classifying persons in intelligence, and his unswerving insistence upon psychology as a study of the individual.

Binet's efforts gained impetus from the increasingly recognized need for a system of classifying school children according to levels of ability. In 1904 the French Ministry of Public Instruction appointed a commission to study criteria for the placement of retarded children in a special school. This appointment constituted for Binet and his colleague Simon a challenge which they met by the publication, in 1905, of a scale for the measurement of intelligence. This first scale was built on principles which still underlie many of our modern measuring instruments.

The 30 items comprising the 1905 scale, arranged in order of difficulty, included tests of judgment, comprehension, and reasoning, as well as simple sensory tasks. These items were standardized on children with average grade placement in primary schools, and on children considered subnormal. Results for an individual child could therefore be stated in terms of the number of years he fell behind or advanced beyond the norm for his age. Three years later, in 1908, a revision of the scale was published, containing additional items and locating the items at age levels on the basis of further empirical test. In this revision an item was considered appropriate to a given age if from 50 to 90 per cent of a group of normal children succeeded with it. Comparisons made between teachers' ratings of children's ability and test scores in terms of age suggested that the scale had validity as a measure of school apitude.

The publication of the Binet-Simon scales was greeted enthusiastically by workers elsewhere who faced the same need for classifying school children according to general intelligence. In this country the interest in child psychology, and the practical problem of administering training schools for the intellectually retarded, had already prepared the way for a favorable reception of Binet's work. Translations of the scale by Goddard, condensations and revisions by Kuhlmann, inclusion of the items in Whipple's manual of mental and physical tests, and the ready acceptance of the age-scale principle by Terman reflected this interest. By the time a second revision of the Binet-Simon scale was published by its authors (1911), the "mental testing movement" was already under way.[1]

The history of intelligence testing from this point on is a history of additional revisions of the original scale, of wider and wider use of the measures, and of variations in the techniques of test construction and scoring. It is a history of upward and downward extensions of intelli-

[1] For a detailed review of the early history of intelligence testing, see J. Peterson, *Early Conceptions and Tests of Intelligence* (Yonkers: World Book Co., 1925).

gence scales to cover ages from infancy to later maturity, and of the development and general application of group testing procedures. The publication of the Stanford and Kuhlmann revisions of the Binet scales, and the introduction of the intelligence quotient as a measure of rate of intellectual development, are both important milestones. So also are the construction of point scales and the use of factorial analysis in the selection and weighting of items. These significant gains were made, however, against a background of continual controversy, among lay and professional persons alike, over the meaning, the importance, and the determinants of intelligence test scores.

The story of the development of techniques for measuring intelligence has special meaning for the clinical psychologist. On the one hand, the extension of test methods in schools, social agencies, and clinics testifies to the usefulness of intelligence scales as diagnostic instruments. Today, the clinician has at his disposal a large number of test methods, and a large body of published research information concerning them, to assist him in the appraisal of intelligence. As the number of available techniques increases, however, so also does the clinician's responsibility for critically evaluating the research related to the techniques, and for ultimately selecting appropriate instruments and utilizing them in appropriate ways.

On the other hand, controversy over the use and abuse of tests, ending either in enthusiastic overevaluation or downright denunciation of all intelligence measures, recurs today as it has over the years since the testing movement began. The psychologist's increasing awareness of his social responsibility in the use of intelligence tests has led to a number of studies of the social consequences of the widespread use of ability measures (Berdie, 1965; Brim, 1965; Goslin, 1963). Most of these studies are still under way; but it is plain from the initial findings that there exists, among lay and professional persons alike, conflicting attitudes, misinterpretations, justifiable criticism of test procedures, and understandable concern over the methods and scope of collecting and communicating test results. The sensitive clinician must necessarily be concerned with the impact of his procedures upon society at large, as well as with the immediate obligations which he assumes toward his client. Both aspects of his task have engaged the continuing efforts of the American Psychological Association, and both have been specified, publicly and repeatedly, in the Association's statements concerning professional ethics (1953).

Significance of Intelligence Tests in Clinical Diagnosis. In many clinical settings today, the routine "battery" of diagnostic devices has given way to procedures selected to answer particular questions raised about the client. For many children and adults who seek the services of a clinical psychologist, the question of general ability as measured by an intelligence scale is irrelevant. In fact, there are just two general circumstances under which the use of an intelligence scale would be considered necessary and appropriate: (1) when the client's reaction to relatively structured problems should be observed: and (2) when the question raised about the client is one which involves behavior known to be related to scores on our present intelligence scales.

INTELLIGENCE TESTS AS STRUCTURED TASKS. Participation in intelligence testing often calls forth from the client certain reactions not easily observed with other techniques. For example, the administration of an individual intelligence test places the person in a close relationship with the examiner; we shall see later that the social give-and-take in this situation may provide important clues to the person's unique personality structure. To some extent, of course, this is true of many interpersonal diagnostic or therapeutic situations. Intelligence scales, however, typically present the client with highly structured, organized tasks, and demand from him structured, organized responses. People who seem diffuse and scattered in freer situations may perform quite differently in more restricted settings. Differences such as these constitute significant observational material for the diagnostician.

By its emphasis on the "intellectual" aspects of behavior, an intelligence scale may also provide a useful framework for observation. Most people today are "test-wise," in the sense that they bring to a diagnostic session certain expectations and preconceptions about intelligence testing (Brim, 1965). In this situation, some persons may welcome an opportunity to display their efficiency, while others may be, for a variety of reasons, particularly threatened by such tasks. In either case, the differences in approach, in motivation, and in character of defense against threat are important to the clinician.

Specific personal or emotional material, however, is usually kept at a minimum in intelligence tests. Consequently, the patient should find the content of the tasks relatively bland and unthreatening, in contrast to the stimulus materials of some personality tests. The extent to which a person still perceives the intelligence items in personalized ways, or finds the content disturbing, provides further important information for the diagnostician. Most important, however, intelligence tests commonly require the client to solve novel problems through thinking or reasoning. The steps through which he goes in problem-solving, his verbalized habits of thinking and reasoning, and his tendency to check upon or ignore the accuracy of his replies furnish a picture of the patient's typical approach to a primarily intellectual situation.

TEST SCORES AS DIAGNOSTIC AIDS. Scores on intelligence measures may help clarify many problems which arise when the clinician attempts to understand his client. It is apparent, however, that such scores can be helpful only in areas where stable relationships have been identified between intelligence test results and performance in life situations. Research on these measures has supplied more dependable descriptions of these relationships for some kinds of behavior than for others. For example, we know more about the relationship between IQ score and school success than between IQ score and susceptibility to behavior disorder. We know less about the relationships between IQ and marital happiness than between IQ and certain forms of brain disease. And perhaps most significantly, we are better able to state these relationships for groups of subjects than for the particular person who comes to the clinician's office.

One common clinical problem which requires the inclusion of intelligence appraisal among the techniques employed is illustrated by the child who is referred for school failure, and is described by his teachers as dull. School failure may be the result of slowness in development. It may also be an expression of many other difficulties, such as illness, poor vision or hearing, inadequate instruction in the earlier grades, cultural deprivation, an unfriendly school atmosphere, anxiety over achievement, or preoccupation with problems at home. The position of measured intelligence among the factors contributing to school failure is indicated by the low positive correlations, averaging about .50, which are consistently obtained between intelligence test scores and marks in school.

The clinical psychologist trying to understand a case of school failure ordinarily begins with an intelligence appraisal. In this way he can check on the hypothesis of intellectual retardation as one explanation of the child's difficulties, and make some predictions regarding later school progress. But whatever the test results, the clinician's use of intelligence measures still does not absolve him from examining with equal care the other possible factors contributing to school failure in this particular child.

Under any circumstances where the efficiency of learning or the ease of adapting to a new situation is important, the clinician may find that intelligence test scores help him to understand his client's behavior. Indeed, the relationship between learning capacity and what the tests measure is one of the more stable correlations to be found in the research literature; and the life situations in which learning is required are, of course, many. In estimating the ease of rehabilitation of physically handicapped persons, for example, or in evaluating the probable success of children in foster homes or special schools, or of delinquent persons on parole, the diagnostician may use intelligence measures as one source of information. Some clinicians find test scores helpful in evaluating the course of convulsive or brain-damaged patients. Recent attempts to cast intellectual functioning within the mold of ego theory suggest that general patterns of dealing with stress and frustration may also be related to

IQ scores. It has been indicated, for example, that coping mechanisms may be related to IQ acceleration, and that defense mechanisms may be related to IQ deceleration over a time span from early adolescence to middle adulthood (Haan, 1963). Should such research findings prevail, the range and variety of life situations to which the clinician might predict from intelligence test scores would be immensely widened.

The impressions about his client which the clinical psychologist obtains from intelligence scores often dictate his selection of further techniques of appraisal, and his interpretation of their results. Some methods for the evaluation of personality, for example, are appropriate only to persons of certain levels of performance on intelligence scales. More important, however, there are some sorts of response which are expected of persons of restricted intellectual functioning, but which carry—often ominously—other significance when made by more intelligent clients. The accurate interpretation of a wide range of diagnostic methods requires the framework of a general intelligence measure.

The choice of type of therapy to be used in cases of behavior disorder may also depend upon a diagnosis of general intelligence. Contemporary psychotherapy (Cameron and Magaret, 1951; Magaret, 1950; Miller, 1964; Murray, 1962) is essentially a learning process through which the person comes to understand and accept his attitudes as his own, and reorganizes them to suit the demands of his culture as well as his personal, private needs. The thoroughness with which he masters this learning problem—the extent to which psychotherapy is successful—is determined largely by his acquired and preferred patterns of self-justification and defense. It is determined to no small degree, however, by the general adaptability to unfamiliar situations which is measured by intelligence scales. The person whose flexibility is limited by severe intellectual immaturity can no more be expected to achieve insight into the relationships in his own behavior than can the retarded child be expected to grasp school subject matter too difficult for him.

We have said that general intelligence is by no means singularly crucial information in the clinician's understanding of his client. The relationships established between intelligence test scores and behavior in life situations are diversified. They are never close enough to permit the clinical psychologist to ignore other factors in making his diagnoses. Even when the prime consideration seems to be the measurement of general intelligence, the psychologist faces a difficult task. The choice of an appropriate group of tests, the process of administering the items, the interpretation and reporting of test scores, and the evaluating of his client's reactions in the interpersonal test situation still require of him a competence and understanding that go far beyond mere technical skill.

THE CLINICAL PSYCHOLOGIST'S CHOICE OF INSTRUMENT

The first task of the psychologist in making a diagnosis of general intelligence is the selection of a group of instruments appropriate for his patient's needs. To be able to do this, the clinician must be familiar not only with the wide variety of available intelligence scales, but also with many other factors affecting the responses made to them—the patient's age and educational background, the ease with which he uses language, his possible physical handicaps, and his ability to work under time pressure. The diagnostician rarely finds that one measuring instrument alone provides a rich and dependable enough sample of behavior to permit him to describe his patient's general intelligence.

The clinician's procedure in diagnosing general intelligence is that of obtaining samples of his patient's behavior under carefully controlled conditions, and then comparing the patient's responses with those of a well-defined group of persons who have been examined under the same conditions. A sample of behavior obtained in this way is called a *test*. Tests are conventionally arranged in a *scale* according to some principle of organization. Binet, as we have seen, placed his tests along a scale in order of their appropriateness to increasing chronological age levels. A scale yields a *score*, expressed either as the total number of items passed, or as some derivative of the total, such as a standard score, a percentile rank, or an intelligence quotient. Although the score is a quantitative expression of general intelligence, it cannot be considered a statement of the absolute amount of intelligence which the patient possesses. It is rather an indication of the position he would occupy in a specified group of persons upon whom the tests were originally standardized.

The appropriateness of a measuring instrument for a particular patient, therefore, depends upon the degree of resemblance between the patient and the members of the standardization group. An intelligence scale standardized on children, for example, is, strictly speaking, inapplicable to an adult patient. An intelligence scale standardized on English-speaking persons is not a fair measure for the patient with a foreign background or a special language handicap. A scale standardized on a largely urban, middle-class population will do an injustice to patients from rural or lower-class environments (Eells, *et al.*, 1951). Timed tests requiring rapid manual manipulation, standardized on physically normal subjects, are inappropriate for the patient who has a motor disability. Considerations such as these help determine the clinician's choice of tests, and they usually require that he employ more than one measuring instrument in the appraisal of general intelligence.

If the psychologist's first responsibility is the selection of a suitable measuring device, a second no less important task is the choice of scales which are reliable and valid. *Reliability* is a term which refers to several different procedures for appraising the consistency or dependability of test scores. It may describe the results of an analysis of responses to the various items of a scale at a single testing (*coefficient of internal consistency*). It may describe instead the degree of agreement between two forms of the same scale given at the same time (*coefficient of equivalence*). Or it may describe the extent to which the scale yields stable results upon repeated administration (*coefficient of stability*).

Measures of reliability are commonly expressed in correlation coefficients. When these indices are high, the clinician is justified in trusting the consistency or stability of the scores he obtains for a patient. However, his choice of a limiting value for the reliability coefficient, below which he rejects a measure as unreliable, must finally be a matter for his own judgment. In making his decision, the diagnostician must weigh such matters as the use to which he will put the scores, the degree of precision with which he wishes to predict later performance, and the relative emphasis upon group or individual behavior.

The clinician who is not aware of the need for interpreting and critically evaluating the reliability of the instruments he uses opens himself to serious error in understanding his patient's general intelligence. Let us suppose that he uses the 1937 Stanford-Binet scale and makes a series of measures of intelligence on the same patient over a period of years. He notes an unsystematic variation from year to year of five or six IQ points. This is the expected variation for his measure, within the limits of reliability for the Stanford-Binet IQ. Unless he realizes this, however, the psychologist may attempt unjustifiably to explain, in terms of his patient's possible instability or deterioration, a change which is only an expected characteristic of a fallible instrument.

An equally important and common error occurs when the clinical psychologist, in evaluating the results of repeated testing of the same group of patients, misinterprets the phenomenon of statistical regression as changes in the patients' level of intelligence. Or suppose the diagnostician attempts to evaluate psychiatric disorder on the basis of a pattern of subtest scores obtained on the Wechsler-Bellevue adult intelligence scale. Unless he takes into consideration the reliability of these scores, he may again attribute to his patient's responses a capriciousness which is, rather, the result of the characteristics of the instrument he is using.

The clinical psychologist is concerned not only with the reliability of his instruments but also with the *validity*—with the extent to which the scales measure what they purport to measure. The fact that an instrument is christened an intelligence scale by its author is no guarantee that it is a valid measure of general intelligence. Its validity is a product of the methods used in the selection, composition, and standardization of its constituent items; and it is to be appraised according to the type of inference which the diagnostician wishes to make from its scores (American Psychological Association, 1954). In most cases, however, the analysis of the validity of a scale involves a correlation between the scale and a *criterion* measure. In the case of intelligence scales, the definition of a criterion measure is no easy task.

The number of current definitions of general intelligence is almost as great as the number of psychologists currently writing on the topic. The definitions range from general accounts of adaptive behavior or specific descriptions of ability patterns to precise statements of interrelationships among statistically isolated factors. Some definitions seem to imply the existence of a "real" intelligence or potential capacity which may be unmeasurable; others stop at the level of behavioral description. Some writers argue for a fixed, predetermined capacity, while others are impressed with the recent evidence for a developmental concept of intelligence, which changes over time in accordance with life experiences (Hunt, 1961). Some definitions specify motivational and personality variables as part of general intelligence; others retain an exclusively "intellectual" emphasis. The qualified clinician is responsible for knowing the definitions underlying his scales and for evaluating the criteria of validity which these definitions provide.

We have already seen that two criteria of validity used by Binet in constructing his scales were a systematic increase in the number of items passed with increasing age, and the correspondence between test scores and teachers' ratings of intelligence. Some of our contemporary intelligence measures depend in part upon the same criteria. Others add to these such criteria as school success or normal distribution of scores within a random population. As more and more intelligence scales are published, correlations of newly devised scales with results from older, presumably valid, measures may provide evidence of validity. The degree of agreement between test scores and these criteria determines the confidence which the clinical psychologist can place in the validity of his instrument.

The clinician who overlooks the necessity for evaluating the validity of his instrument is open to serious errors of interpretation. He will be puzzled at the failure of a newly acquired scale to yield results comparable to his old familiar ones. He may find himself unable to interpret the meaning of repeated scores obtained from the same patient, if he has used different scales at different times. He may expect his instruments to do more than they were built to do—as when he uses an intelligence scale as an index to psychiatric diagnosis, for example.

The reliability and validity of measuring instruments, as well as their appropriateness to the patient, are important considerations for the diagnostician. No less important, however, are the clinician's decision to use individual or group measures and his selection of verbal rather than performance scales. In these matters, as in all parts of the clinical job, the problems presented by a particular patient dictate the psychologist's choices. We shall have an opportunity to examine these points more concretely in the examples of current intelligence tests which follow.

Kinds of Intelligence Tests. Let us suppose that the clinical psychologist considers possible intellectual retardation as one of many hypotheses to account for school failure in a child. In his first contacts with this child he finds no such special factors as physical handicap, motor disability, or language difficulty, which would immediately eliminate certain kinds of tests from his consideration. He must then choose, from the group and individual measures of intelligence available for this age level, those instruments which meet the accepted standards of reliability and validity. Since group intelligence scales are often routinely administered in school systems, the clinician often gets the results of such tests as part of the child's school record. He is rarely satisfied, however, with the rough classifications of general intelligence made under the quick but impersonal conditions of classroom testing. He is more likely to select for his measure instead an individual intelligence scale which, although more time consuming, affords him an opportunity to make behavior observations of the child.

Some of the scales which the clinician has at his disposal are classified as verbal and others as performance. *Verbal* scales require of the client the understanding and use of language. *Performance* scales, on the other hand, require that the person respond by doing something other than talking, and they may rule language out of the situation altogether by providing pantomimed instructions. The decision to administer one type of scale rather than the other may seem at first to rest largely upon the ease with which the patient uses language. We shall see, however, that even in children without language handicaps the relationships between a verbal and a performance measure of intelligence may be unexpectedly low. These two kinds of scales, both called "intelligence scales," appear in some cases to measure quite different kinds of behavior. Accordingly, the clinical psychologist ordinarily uses both varieties in an appraisal of general intelligence.

The number of published instruments which seek to evaluate intelligence is very large; each year sees the development of new approaches or the extension of old methods. Review of even a sizable sampling of such techniques is impossible in the present chapter.[2] Accordingly, in what follows, four rather widely used individual intelligence scales will provide examples of the problems of constructing, administering, and interpreting intelligence tests in clinical practice.

THE THIRD (1960) REVISION OF THE STANFORD-BINET INTELLIGENCE SCALE (FORM L–M). This scale is the most recent product of an unbroken line of research beginning with the early work of Binet. We have seen that Binet's notions were applied in this country by a number of investigators, among them Terman in the 1916 Stanford-Binet scales. The 1916 scale was revised in 1937, and is now available in its third form (Terman and Merrill, 1960). This third revision, made up of the most satisfactory subtests from the 1937 form, represents a careful attempt to meet the limitations which time had shown to be part of the 1937 scale while still preserving the many strengths and advantages of Binet-type testing.

The responses of 4,498 subjects, ranging in age between 2½ and 18 years, constitute the basis for the selection of items in the L–M form. The items are located on the scale according to the principle, originally developed by Binet, of suitability to a given age level. When this principle of arrangement is used, the number of tests passed can be converted to months of age. The total intelligence score obtained in this way is called the *mental age* (MA). If the child in our earlier example achieved a mental age score of seven years on this scale, he would be considered equivalent in this performance to the normal seven-year-olds on whom the scale was standardized.

Originally, in the 1916 and 1937 Stanford-Binet revisions, the ratio of mental-age score to the child's chronological age (CA) was computed, which yielded the well-known and widely accepted *intelligence quotient* (IQ). Such conventional IQ's, however, showed different variability at different age levels in the 1937 revision. Consequently, the L–M IQ is a *deviation* IQ, based on calculations by Pinneau (1961), and representing a standard score from a distribution whose mean is 100 and whose standard deviation is 16. In most cases, the deviation IQ differs only slightly from the conventional IQ; but the use of standard scores does mean that L–M IQ's are now directly comparable from one age level to another.

Careful selection of the standardization group for the 1937 revision, plus avoidance of special selective factors in choice of items for the 1960

[2] For critical reviews of current intelligence scales, the reader is referred to a source widely used by practicing clinical psychologists, the Mental Measurements Yearbooks (Buros, 1953, 1961). Reviews of research and new developments in the field of intelligence testing may be found in the various volumes of the *Annual Review of Psychology* (Farnsworth and McNemar, 1950–1965), and in *Progress in Clinical Psychology* (Harris, 1952).

revision, make the Stanford-Binet scale applicable to a wide range of children and adolescents in the American population. While it was originally assumed that development as measured by Stanford-Binet score extends to age 16, recent studies indicate that scores may well increase beyond this age (Bayley, 1955; Bradway and Thompson, 1962; Bradway et al., 1958). Consequently, IQ tables for the 1960 revision include ages 17 and 18. If it is assumed that mental age as measured by the scale neither increases nor decreases systematically with chronological age after age 18, measures can also be obtained for adult subjects on this scale.

The concept of intelligence underlying the scales is that of general intellectual ability, which is sampled by way of items requiring many sorts of behavior. No assumption is made that separate successes or failures have particular meaning, nor that analysis of "profiles" or "patterns" of response can be made. A factorial analysis of the 1937 scale by McNemar (1942) demonstrated the presence of a single common factor, with some evidence of group factors at certain age levels. The 1937 scale, from which the 1960 items are taken, yielded reliability coefficients, depending upon the method of computation, of from .85 to .98 (Pinneau, 1961). Validity of the scale is indicated in a number of ways: the percentage of standardization subjects succeeding with individual items increases systematically with increasing age; the various revisions of the scales agree closely with one another; the mean correlation of individual items with total score in the L–M form is .66.

To the casual observer watching a skilled examiner administer the 1937 Stanford-Binet to an individual child, it appears as if the child and the examiner were engaged in an informal conversation, punctuated by brief intervals of structured play. The child taking the tests, if he is being examined by an experienced psychologist, often accepts the items as games. He must identify objects by name or according to use, construct sentences, and repeat numbers. He must replace objects in a form board, copy designs, solve arithmetic problems, recognize absurdities, and interpret proverbs. He participates in a variety of tasks representing the kinds of complex samples of behavior which Binet early insisted were the only genuine correlates of general intelligence.

The 1937 revision, like the 1916 Stanford-Binet scale, has been generally adopted by clinical psychologists in spite of criticisms directed toward the inevitable imperfections of its standardization (McNemar, 1942) and toward the principle of age-scale construction. There are many reasons for this wide acceptance. We have seen that the measures originally appeared at a time when the intelligence testing movement was gaining momentum. Their demonstrated validity and reliability justified the clinician's confidence in his results. The variety of items provided the attentive examiner with endless opportunities for behavioral observations of his client. The test materials interested the child sufficiently to enlist his best efforts. Most significantly, the large amount of research published on both instruments guaranteed the clinician the necessary context within which to interpret and evaluate his results (Harris, 1952). The 1937 Stanford-Binet scale demands time, training, and skill for its administration and interpretation, but it yields a dependable and profitable return. It is highly probable that the derived 1960 scale will prove equally popular, although many research programs may prefer to continue with the 1937 revision in the interests of consistency of procedure.

THE ARTHUR POINT SCALE OF PERFORMANCE TESTS (1943, 1947). This is an instrument which, as contrasted with the Stanford-Binet, elicits non-verbal responses from the child. Fourteen different tests, including 12 form boards from other scales, the Porteus maze test (1950), and the Kohs block designs (1923), were restandardized on a group of 1,100 school children to comprise the Arthur scale. Two forms of the scale are available, although Form I has been more widely used, both in clinical practice and in research, than Form II. The scale is applicable to children aged 6 through 15 years, but the most valid and reliable scores are obtained for children between the ages of 7 and 13. Those tests which discriminate one age level from the next most sharply are given the greatest weight in the total score, which is expressed in terms of points. By converting the points to age equivalents, the clinician can calculate and interpret both mental age scores and IQ's in the conventional manner.

A performance scale of this sort provides the diagnostician with a framework within which to observe the patient which is different from that furnished by the Stanford-Binet. The child taking the Arthur tests is confronted by a variety of concrete tasks which demand both speed and accuracy of performance. His approach to the problems, his response to time pressure, his reactions to an obviously wrong solution, his hesitancies, and his blockings are all open to the clinician's observation. This performance scale and others like it serve as shock absorbers for some shy and fearful children to whom the direct question-and-answer method of a verbal scale is personally threatening. The Arthur scale in modified form is useful also in examining children with auditory and language handicaps whose intelligence might be seriously underestimated by a more verbal measure.

The clinical psychologist ordinarily uses both verbal and performance measures in studying his client. If we compare the results obtained when the Stanford-Binet and Arthur scales are applied to the same persons, the reason for this practice becomes clear. Correlations between 1916 Stanford-Binet IQ's and Arthur I IQ's range from .50 to .75; the correlation between the 1937 Stanford-Binet IQ and Arthur II IQ was .73 in one study of normal school children. There seems to be a tendency for the Arthur

II to yield lower IQ's than does the Stanford-Binet with average and bright subjects. When individual IQ's obtained on the Stanford-Binet and Arthur scales are compared with one another, there are some startling discrepancies between the two instruments. Such discrepancies always send the clinician first to a study of the statistical properties of his scale. Here there is the possibility that differences in standardization may account for the differences in scores. Often, however, these discrepancies suggest new lines of investigation for the clinician to follow in studying his patient. It is for this reason that the Arthur scale is considered a supplement to, rather than a substitute for, the Stanford-Binet in the careful appraisal of general intelligence.

Individual tests of the sort which comprise the Arthur scale are sometimes used separately in the study of intelligence. For example, the *Porteus Maze test* (1950), which consists of a graded series of paper-and-pencil mazes, yields its own MA and IQ scores, although these are not directly comparable to Stanford-Binet IQ's of either the conventional or deviation type. Although many studies show widely different correlations between Binet and maze scores, varying around an r of .60, in no sense can one be substituted for the other. Some clinicians find observations of the child's approach to the maze task—his foresight, his planning, his impulsiveness—particularly useful in helping them to understand him.

Although not part of the Arthur scale, the *Draw-A-Man test,* first standardized by Goodenough (1926) and recently revised and extended by Harris, (1964), illustrates another individual performance test. This instrument capitalizes on the relationship between children's drawings and the level of their development. The child is asked to make a picture of a man (and a woman); his drawing is then scored for many different details, and the score converted to an age expression. Considerable evidence is now available to suggest that there is a substantial relationship between Draw-A-Man scores and scores on other intelligence scales; and that, in some instances, qualitative aspects of the drawings may give the clinician further insight into his client's behavior.

THE WECHSLER ADULT INTELLIGENCE SCALE (WAIS) (WECHSLER, 1958). For many years, the clinical psychologist appraising general intelligence by means of an individual scale was forced to rely upon such measures as the Stanford-Binet and the Arthur, even in examining adult patients to whom the tests were not strictly applicable. He was able to make estimates of adult intelligence only by going beyond the age groups on which the scales were standardized, and by assuming that average adult mental age neither increased nor decreased after a given point. However, with the publication in 1939 of the Wechsler-Bellevue Adult Intelligence Scale (W–B) (Wechsler, 1944), the clinician gained an instrument standardized on an adult population. The critical need for an individual measure of adult intelligence was indicated by the immediate and enthusiastic adoption of the scale in clinics and hospitals dealing with adults, the extensive use of special revisions of the test in the armed services, and the publication of a second form in 1946 (Wechsler, 1946). The tests were restandardized in 1955, and the scale redesignated the Wechsler Adult Intelligence Scale (WAIS). This scale remains today the most widely used individual scale for the appraisal of adult intelligence.

The WAIS rests upon the observation that mean scores on many of the tasks used as intelligence tests decline in later maturity. Consequently, a score on this scale is defined in terms of the adult's position among standardization subjects of his own age, rather than in terms of 15- or 18-year-old subjects, as in the Arthur and the Stanford-Binet scales. Over two thousand persons, ranging in age from 16 through 75 years, constitute the standardization group of this scale.

Two special characteristics of this instrument demand the clinical psychologist's close consideration. In the first place, of the 11 tests constituting the scale, 6 are verbal items (information, comprehension, similarities, arithmetic reasoning, digit repetition, and vocabulary) and 5 are performance (picture completion, picture arrangement, block designs, object assembly, and digit-symbol substitution). The measure is therefore both a verbal and a performance scale, and independent estimates of verbal and performance quotients can be obtained by the application of this single instrument. Since the raw scores on the 11 "subtests are converted to standard scores, the relative ease and difficulty with which the subject handles different kinds of tasks can be easily evaluated—a fact which has led, as we shall see, to extensive research on the significance of individual patterns of subtest scores.

A second characteristic of the scale is the procedure for deriving and therefore interpreting the IQ. The method differs from that to which clinical psychologists have become accustomed. The total standard scores—verbal, performance, and full-scale—are distributed separately for different adult age groups, and the value of the IQ assigned according to the obtained distribution. In the WAIS, the test scores are equated against a set mean IQ of 100, with a standard deviation of 15. Thus, the WAIS IQ is a *deviation quotient*, calculated in terms of deviation from the mean. This procedure, which we have described earlier in the chapter, preceded the conversion of Stanford-Binet IQ's to deviation IQ's. Both methods have the decided advantage of comparing the client with standardization subjects of his own age.

Since its publication, the WAIS has been studied extensively (Guertin, et al., 1962). As might be expected, the values of its reliability coefficients differ, depending upon the methods and subjects used. Split-half reliabilities calculated from the standardization population indicate a range of reliability coefficients from .97 in the case of full-scale IQ's to .60 in the case of individual subtests in restricted age ranges (Wechsler, 1958). Some test-retest reliabilities for the WAIS are reported to be as high as .96. Validity as measured by way of comparisons of WAIS scores with those yielded by other intelligence scales shows a range of coefficients also. Relationships between WAIS and Wechsler-Bellevue performance indicate correlations of .89 for verbal quotients, .44 for performance quotients, and .77 for full-scale IQ's. One study reports a correlation between WAIS and 1937 Stanford-Binet results of .85; another with Raven Progressive Matrices of .72; another with the Shipley-Hartford in the high seventies; still another with certain parts of the Ammons scale ranging from .36 to .84, depending upon the range of talent.

Like all intelligence scales, the WAIS has certain limitations to which attention should be directed. For example, unless the clinician understands the unique derivation of the IQ score and its dependence upon adult standardization groups, he may be at a loss to explain occasional disagreements between WAIS and other scores of intelligence. Against such a limitation the clinician must balance many advantages: the obvious appropriateness of the instrument to adult subjects, the attractiveness of the items for mature persons, the possibility of obtaining both performance and verbal quotients, and the demonstrated validity and reliability of the scale. His final selection depends upon what he expects the scale to reveal about his particular client.

WECHSLER INTELLIGENCE SCALE FOR CHILDREN (WISC) (WECHSLER, 1949). The usefulness and popularity of the special features of the Wechsler-Bellevue scale led to an extension of its principles to the field of children's intelligence testing. The Wechsler Intelligence Scale for Children (WISC), published in 1949, embodies essentially the same principles as do the Wechsler-Bellevue and the WAIS scales for adults. It was carefully standardized on 2,200 children, and is appropriate to children between the ages of 5 and 15 years. The children's scale consists of five verbal tests (information, comprehension, arithmetic, similarities, and vocabulary), and five performance tests (picture completion, picture arrangement, block designs, object assembly, and coding or mazes). The performance, verbal, and full-scale quotients are derived separately for each age, and, like the adult deviation quotients, express the position of a child within his own age group.

The reliability of the WISC has been studied in the standardization group by means of coefficients of internal consistency. The obtained values range from .86 to .96 for the various scales and age groups. Corresponding coefficients for individual subtests range from .59 (comprehension) to .91 (vocabulary) at different levels. The validity of the scale is reflected mainly in numerous studies of the agreement between results obtained on the WISC and other measures of intelligence in children (Littell, 1960). Within a white American school population, WISC and Stanford-Binet scores are significantly related; correlations are predominantly within the .80's. The WISC full-scale IQ's correlate highest with Stanford-Binet scores, verbal quotients next, and performance quotients lowest. At several ages it appears that WISC scores tend to be lower than Stanford-Binet results for children within the upper and middle ranges; WISC scores, on the other hand, are higher than Stanford-Binet scores for retarded children. Correlations between WISC and Arthur IQ's range from .71 to .80; here there is an appreciable tendency for the Arthur to correlate higher with the WISC performance than with the WISC verbal scale.

Many clinicians have greeted the WISC warmly and have come to depend heavily upon it. The ease with which both performance and verbal quotients can be obtained at one testing session undoubtedly contributes to the wide acceptance of the scale. Judging from one study of fifth-grade children, the WISC takes 12 minutes less than the Stanford-Binet to administer, and samples a greater variety of reactions. There is some feeling—but as yet no definite evidence—that the performance materials are particularly attractive to children, and therefore elicit their best efforts. For some clinicians, however, these advantages are somewhat offset by the fact that the norms may not be applicable to children of different cultural and socioeconomic status, and that the WISC is relatively insensitive to differences among mentally retarded children, and among children with mental ages below five or six years. Here again, in selecting his instruments the clinician must weigh the relative importance of validity, reliability, appropriateness, and familiarity of his measures for the particular child he is studying.

Short Scales. The administration of any individual intelligence scale is a time-consuming process. Particularly when many different procedures are used to study a single client, the clinician would welcome a shortcut to the reliable appraisal of general intelligence. The Stanford-Binet L–M scale, for example, can be abbreviated to three-quarters of the testing time if only certain tests are given. The WAIS subtests can be rearranged and shortened in an almost endless variety of patterns, as can those from the WISC. If, however, an abbreviated sample of test items is to be substituted for the full scale, then the correlation between the short form and the complete scale must be carefully evaluated.

Abbreviating the Stanford-Binet scales, for example, seems to yield rather lower IQ's on the average than application of the full scale, although the difference between means for full-scale as compared with abbreviated-scale IQ's is not statistically significant. Many possible combinations of WAIS subtests have been correlated with WAIS full-scale scores by Maxwell (1957). Correlations range around .90. The accuracy of the abbreviated scales is increased with the number of subtests included; and a combination of both verbal and performance subtests provides a better predictor of full-scale scores than either sort used separately. Studies of WISC short forms yield appreciably lower correlations with full-scale score, ranging from .55 to .88 on different populations (Littell, 1960).

An abbreviated scale, of course, will never afford the clinician as adequate a sample of behavior as will the full scale. On the other hand, there are many clinical situations in which a rough or approximate determination of a client's standing is all that is necessary. Under such circumstances, the use of an abbreviated scale frees the time of both subject and examiner for detailed studies of other areas of behavior which may be more significant. As in all aspects of clinical practice, here also the approach must be suited to the particular questions the clinical psychologist is trying to answer.

INTERPRETATION OF RESULTS

What the clinical psychologist hopes to get from the results of his intelligence appraisal varies as much with the clinician as with the instruments he chooses and the person he examines. At one extreme is the conservative psychologist who operates as statistical analyst. He accepts obtained scores as his only data, interpreting and predicting from them as if they were the products of an impersonal machine. At the other extreme is the incautious clinician who operates as impulsive speculator. He goes far beyond the scores validated as intelligence measures to make personality assays and psychiatric diagnoses. It is obvious that both competence in statistical analysis and impartial, skilled observation of the client are required for adequate interpretation of intelligence test results. Neither can be ignored and neither overemphasized if the clinical psychologist is to succeed with his diagnostic job.

Statistical Considerations. An increasing number of psychologists today are beginning to question the usefulness and propriety of considering "intelligence" a dimension of human behavior which may be scaled and measured in conventional ways. Assuredly there are many problems in this approach (Hunt, 1961, McNemar, 1964), most of which have been recognized since the early days of intelligence testing. One of the main difficulties is the temptation—particularly strong in persons not versed in statistical procedures—to think of "intelligence" as a fixed, predetermined entity, and of "The IQ" as its invariable index. However, until such objections as these have stimulated the development of alternative ways of understanding the client, the clinician today must depend upon the instruments at his disposal, with their underlying assumptions of dimensionality. Simply because of the nature of their construction and their statistical properties, these instruments yield certain sorts of information about the client. We shall consider three aspects of test interpretation which reflect mainly the properties of our instruments as measuring devices: (1) the classification of scores, (2) analysis of individual items or subtests, and (3) stability of scores over time.

CLASSIFICATION OF SCORES. Let us suppose that in a case of school failure the child achieves on the Stanford-Binet scale an IQ of 80 and on the Arthur scale an IQ of 106. The clinician may interpret these scores strictly as indicators of the position the child occupies in the respective standardization groups. It is possible to classify IQ scores according to the frequency with which they occur in the standardization population and to describe a particular range of IQ scores by a label, such as "borderline," "average," or 'superior." The clinical psychologist using this means of test interpretation would describe our case of school failure as "low average" on the Stanford-Binet and "average" on the Arthur scale. The clinician is also justified in stating, on the basis of the frequency of particular IQ scores in the standardization population, that the child falls in the lower 9 per cent of the group on the Stanford-Binet and in the middle 50 per cent of the group on the Arthur scale. If he stops at this point, however, he has discharged only his minimal responsibility as statistical analyst. He has contributed virtually nothing to the understanding of this particular child who is faced with his own unique problems of school adjustment.

The properties of these two tests furnish still other methods of interpreting the results. Suppose that the Stanford-Binet mental age for the child we are considering is six years and six months, close to the average for first-graders, but that he has been placed in the third grade, where he competes daily with children two years above him in mental-age score. The clinician immediately suspects that the child may not have achieved sufficient intellectual maturity to be able to succeed at third-grade work.

Some clinicians may go further, and estimate that the child's adult mental age may be such that advanced education, if contemplated, would present difficulties which even strong interest and intense effort could not surmount. We shall see later, however, that such predictive statements are based upon a number of assumptions regarding development which are being called into question; consequently, scores on these instruments are by no means perfect predictors of future behavior. Moreover, intelligence ratings, however accurate, are by no means the only predictors of school success. The diagnostician needs also to consider the child's scores on educational achievement tests, his physical maturity, his own feelings about the classroom competition, and the demands made upon him by his parents and his teachers.

The mental-age score which corresponds to the child's IQ on the Arthur scale is eight years and six months, at the mean for third-graders. In interpreting this score the clinician wonders whether perhaps the child can compete more successfully with his classmates on concrete performance tasks than in situations requiring verbal responses. Again, this question cannot be answered without information regarding the school curriculum, the opportunities offered for manual activity, the child's interest in such tasks, the prestige attached to them, and the hopes and expectations of his parents and his teacher.

The difference between the scores obtained by the child on two separate measures of intelligence—the Stanford-Binet and the Arthur—presents a special problem in interpretation. The easiest solution to this problem would be the simple statement that the child's performance ability is higher than his verbal ability. An interpretation of this kind, however, is no more than a process of labeling, and taken by itself contributes as little to the understanding of the child as does the classification "average" or "low average."

As we have already seen, results obtained on different intelligence scales may differ from one another largely because of differences in the statistical properties of the two measures. The concepts of IQ underlying the Stanford-Binet, Arthur, and WISC scales are by no means identical; and their numerical values may well differ from one another for the same patient. In such cases as these, a performance-verbal difference in score is actually the *expected* result rather than any indicator of unusual discrepancies among abilities in the same child. A striking example of this point is to be found in the analysis of performance-verbal differences on the WISC (Seashore, 1951). The standardization group for this scale showed median differences between performance and verbal quotients of 8 points; in one-third of the cases the difference was greater than 12 or 13 IQ points.

An even more thoroughgoing investigation of this phenomenon is available for the WAIS (Field, 1960), suggesting that within the standardization group for this scale, obtained distributions of difference scores between verbal and performance IQ's extend beyond the point of statistical significance determined by the standard error of measurement. For example, a verbal-performance discrepancy of 25 points occurs once in every hundred subjects in the standardization population; while a verbal-performance discrepancy of 13 points occurs only once in a hundred times by chance, due to errors of measurement. It has been suggested that the clinician make a distinction between the "abnormality" of the performance-verbal discrepancy, in terms of its occurrence in a known proportion of a normative population, and the "reliability" of the discrepancy, in terms of the known range of differences attributable to errors of measurement. Again it is clear that the statistical properties of the scales must be taken into account in the interpretation of results.

Even allowing for the expected—occasionally wide—discrepancy between performance and verbal scores in the same patient, there remain instances of sizable discrepancies which may relate to other aspects of the child's behavior. Differences between verbal and performance measures have been investigated in a variety of contexts. Unfortunately for the clinical psychologist who hopes for an unequivocal answer, the results of research on this question are conflicting. The factors which have been related to differences between verbal and performance IQ's include such diverse ones as language disability, educational limitations, mixed cerebral dominance, concrete or abstract approaches to tasks, temporary emotional upset, delinquency, neurotic trends, gross behavior disorder, and organic deterioration. This large array of variables is discouraging in that it provides no simple explanation for the discrepancy between verbal and performance scores in a particular case. It is, however, encouraging in that it goes far beyond a mere label to furnish the clinical psychologist with promising leads for further study of his patient.

ANALYSIS OF INDIVIDUAL ITEMS OR SUBTESTS. Another problem in interpretation arises when the clinician examines his patient's scores on the individual items which make up a particular intelligence scale. On an age scale such as the Stanford-Binet, this can be done only roughly, since the tests were originally selected and located empirically, according to the criterion of age, and no attempt was made to sample exactly the same kinds of behavior at all age levels. One series of studies (Magaret and Thompson, 1950, Thompson and Magaret, 1947) has utilized the factor loadings of the various Stanford-Binet tests as a basis for classification. The results suggest that, as contrasted with normal and superior subjects, mentally defective patients do poorly on items which are heavily weighted with the first, general factor. It appears also that, contrary to popular opinion, mentally defective patients are not superior in rote memory items, although they may have special success with items involving manual manipulation of test materials. Attempts to categorize Stanford-Binet items in this way are infrequent, however.

Instead of analyzing the pattern of successes and failures on single tests of an age scale, therefore, the clinical psychologist is more likely to note the range of age levels over which the patient must be examined in order to complete the testing. This range, which may be considered an indicator of unevenness of performance, is called *scatter*. The assumption underlying this measure is that the "normal" subject should systematically fail a greater and greater proportion of tests as he goes up the scale. This assumption itself, of course, implies constant motivation and perfectly organized behavior on the part of the subject, and a perfect location of items on the same with respect to difficulty. Neither implication is necessarily or even probably true.

In evaluating the significance of scatter for his client, consequently, the clinician is again confronted by a variety of research results. Certain factors inherent in the construction of the Stanford-Binet scale—item unreliability, low intercorrelations among items, intervals between successive age levels, for example—may be responsible for scatter even in the absence of any clinically significant variability in the subject's response (Terman and Merrill, 1960). The diagnostician who is not aware of the many limitations to the use of scatter as a diagnostic sign is in danger of making unwarranted statements about his patient's performance. On the other hand, all we know about the organization and manifestation of what we call intelligence in the individual would lead us to expect differences between individuals in the distribution of successes and failures on the various test items. Like the discrepancy between verbal and performance scores, Stanford-Binet tests scatter may provide a valuable guidepost to further study of the individual.

In contrast to the age scale, a point scale such as the Arthur, the WAIS, or the WISC provides the clinical psychologist with a more exact framework within which to examine the interest variability of his client's performance. Each test, regarded as a separate unit, is administered to every subject. Since scores on the single tests can be directly compared with one another, the clinician has at hand an individual pattern of test scores from which to make his diagnoses. The analysis of these patterns of subtest scores has become so significant and so controversial a problem for the clinical psychologist that it deserves our special consideration.

For many years prior to the systematic use of differential successes and failures on intelligence tests as diagnostic indicators, clinicians had been using informal cues obtained in the testing situation as grounds for suspecting emotional disturbance or behavior disorder. These cues, when they could be identified and communicated, where usually derived from common sense, from a few vivid cases included in the clinician's personal experience with patients, or from rough parallels between descriptions of psychiatric syndromes and the kinds of behavior required on intelligence tests. Intellectually retarded clients were presumed to do better on rote memory and performance tests, for example, than on more abstract, verbal items. Difficulty with tests of immediate recall, especially in patients who scored high on vocabulary or other tests of remote learning, was considered suggestive of deterioration. This accumulation of clinical folklore—

some of it fact, some of it fiction—led to organized investigations of the relation of subtest scores to other aspects of client behavior.

Research on subtest analysis began with the use of single tests. The Kohs Block Design Test (1923), for example, which is now incorporated as one test on the Arthur scale, seemed to yield characteristic scores when applied to children with mixed handedness, to problem children, and to adult brain-injured patients. Revisions of the test permitted a more qualitative analysis of the patient's responses, and even gave support to a throughgoing theoretical interpretation of behavior disorder in terms of abstract and concrete abilities (Goldstein and Sheerer, 1941). Similar studies of other isolated tests—for example, the Porteus maze (1950), the Healy Picture Completion Test (Hanfmann, 1939), and various memory scales—served to translate clinical impressions into more precise statements of obtained relationships.

The publication of the Wechsler-Bellevue Adult Intelligence Scale, we have seen, stimulated and directed further research on patterns of subtest scores by providing the diagnostician with a scale of ten comparable subtests. The clinician in administering this scale obtains a profile of scores which shows, as relatively high and low points, the intra-individual variability in test scores for a particular patient. The question then arises as to the diagnostic significance which shall be attached to any wide deviations in subtest scores from the client's general level of performance. Does a relatively low score on digit repetition signify brain damage or temporary distractibility? Is a comparatively low score on the block designs test suggestive of emotional disturbance? Does a high information score coupled with a low comprehension score indicate the combination of good orientation with behavior disorganization, which is characteristic of a schizophrenic disorder?

In answering such questions as these, the clinician may rely upon his own impressions or upon conclusions drawn from inspection of the content of the tests. He may also use his own rough estimates of what a "typical" psychiatric patient might do with the tests, or generalize from results obtained from tests similar to those on the Wechsler-Bellevue scale. He may depend upon published "rules of thumb" for interpreting subtest deviations (Rapaport, 1946, Wechsler, 1944, 1958), which, although not always based upon reported research, still represent the fruits of wide clinical experience with the scale. He is on much surer ground, however, if he seeks the answers to his questions in the increasingly numerous reports of systematic research on pattern analysis.

On the basis of present research (Rabin, 1945, Rabin and Guertin, 1951, Watson, 1945), the most justifiable conclusion which the diagnostician can draw regarding the significance of subtest profiles is that the results are so contradictory as to demand extreme caution in labeling patients on this basis. The great majority of studies on Wechsler-Bellevue subtests yield negative, conflicting, or questionable results.

The clinical psychologist who hopes to use subtest analysis as one route to the understanding of his client will be puzzled at his inability to do so unless he appreciates some of the reasons for the disagreement among these studies. When separate subtests are used as independent measures, their reliability and validity must be evaluated, just as in the case of complete intelligence scales. The split-half reliabilities of the WAIS subtests range from .60 to .96, those of the Wechsler-Bellevue from .62 to .90, the latter based on test-retest methods. The correlations of the various subtests with the full scale also differ from one another. This differential reliability and validity may well contribute to the contradictory research results. We must remember, also, that correlation with other measures of intelligence has been used to demonstrate the validity of the total Wechsler scales. It is not surprising that scales constructed and validated as measures of general intelligence should fail to yield clear-cut psychiatric diagnoses as well.

The information which the clinician needs about a particular subject who has taken the WAIS, moreover, is not always the same as that which is provided by the research results. In his consideration of the client's profile, the clinical psychologist tries to balance high and low points, and to come to some conclusion about the pattern taken as a whole—a difficult procedure to handle statistically with groups of subjects in research investigations. Furthermore, even if reliable differences between group means are obtained in research studies, the overlapping between groups is ordinarily great enough to make the application of the diagnostic signs to an individual client hazardous. An additional difficulty is introduced by the nature of the criterion which is assumed to underlie this effort: the use of subtest analysis to predict the diagnostic decisions of psychiatrists or psychologists is probably less helpful to our understanding of human behavior than the use of some other frame of reference for our predictions. In any case, it would appear that, as in the case of scatter and of differences between performance and verbal quotients, the analysis of patterns of subtest scores has its most promising application in indicating the direction which further study of the client should take.

STABILITY OF SCORES OVER TIME. The clinician who has a series of intelligence scores available for his client is often confronted with the problem of interpreting what appear to be fluctuations in capacity over time. We have already seen that changes must be considered in light of the known reliability of the particular measure being used. On the other hand, recent advances in our knowledge of the growth rates of those forms of behavior sampled by intelligence scales must be borne in mind if the clinician is to understand the meaning of trends in intelligence test scores. In neither case, of course, is the concept of the fixed IQ accepted; rather, inquiry is directed toward the identification of the many factors which may determine changes in score.

As subjects in longitudinal studies of development arrive at their adult years, evidence accrues which provides a more accurate description of the curve of intellectual growth. In general, it appears from a number of these studies (Bayley, 1955, Honzik, et al., 1948, Sontag, et al., 1958) that scores increase over a longer time period than was formerly believed. Results on Stanford-Binet retests after 10- and 25-year intervals reported by Bradway, Thompson, and Cravens, (1958, 1962) indicate significant increases in IQ's between adolescence and adulthood—a finding which led, as we have seen, to an alteration in the IQ tables for the 1960 Stanford-Binet scale. WAIS test performance increases at least until age 25 to 30 (Guertin, et al., 1962) and may be resistant to age effects even later, depending upon the particular skills sampled.

A number of factors have been identified which may contribute to a continued increase in test scores over a long period of time. Pinneau (1961) suggests that initial brightness is significantly related to rate and time of increase in score with age; the Fels studies (Sontag, et al., 1958) suggest that certain attitudinal or personality variables may be related to increases in IQ; and Hunt (1961) argues convincingly that the nature of the child's encounters with his environment is central in the development of what we call intelligence. In any case, it is plain that shifts in obtained scores with time are to be expected, and that the responsible clinician has many leads to follow in determining the reasons for such shifts in a particular case.

A special problem related to the stability of intelligence test scores with time is found in the appraisal of deterioration, particularly among elderly persons, and among patients suffering from convulsive states, brain damage, or schizophrenic disorder. Although psychiatric and psychometric definitions of deterioration differ markedly in the kinds of behavior which they describe, they all include the implication that the deteriorated person has undergone some decline in intellectual efficiency from an earlier level of performance. This loss in efficiency is not necessarily a permanent one; the deterioration measured by the clinical psychologist may be either reversible or irreversible, depending upon the factors presumed to cause it.

The most straightforward appraisal of intellectual deterioration requires a series of measures of general intelligence made on the same patient over a period of years. If a systematic decline in test scores occurs, the clinician is justified in suspecting intellectual deterioration. We have already seen that in an accurate interpretation of a series of measures, the psychologist must take into account the reliability of his instrument, the probable error of his test scores, and the phenomenon of statistical regression. If, however, he is to understand deterioration as anything more than a measurable shift in test score, he cannot overlook such important influences as the particular incidents in the life history of his patient, conspicuous environmental changes, cumulative practice effects in taking repeated tests, and possible limitations in the patient's opportunities for learning.

Results of repeated intelligence examinations over a long period of time are rarely available for a patient. Ordinarily the question of possible intellectual deterioration is raised during a single contact with the patient, and the psychologist is forced to infer from the patient's present test performance his probable level of intellectual functioning in the past. A common but inexact procedure is to gauge the previous intelligence level from reports of past school success and vocational achievement, as these are recorded in the case history, and then to compare this estimate with the scores obtained from the present testing. The obvious limitations of such a method have led to the development of more specialized techniques for the diagnosis of intellectual deterioration.[3]

The appraisal of deterioration on the basis of one contact with the subject rests upon an assumption which, like many of the postulates underlying clinical measures, was derived originally from informal cues obtained by the clinician in his dealings with patients. It was early noted that older patients and those known to be suffering from deteriorative disorders seemed to have unusual difficulty with tests of immediate memory or of judgment, as contrasted with their success on tasks depending upon more remote learning. As we have already seen, more carefully controlled studies of changes in scores in later maturity indicated that efficiency on tests such as those of vocabulary and general information seemed to decline less rapidly with age than efficiency on tests of immediate memory, arithmetic reasoning, or block designs. Accordingly, the difference between scores on tests of past learning and those on tests requiring new learning or adjustment to unfamiliar situations was taken to be a possible indicator of intellectual deterioration. The assumption that changes characteristic of later maturity are characteristic also of deterioration in behavior disorder has been questioned by several writers. However, it still remains the guiding principle in the psychometric diagnosis of intellectual deficit.

An application of this principle is seen in the use of the WAIS subtest scores in measuring deterioration. It is clear from the performance of the standardization groups for this scale that scores on some of the tests— for example, digit repetition, arithmetic, digit-symbol substitution—decline more sharply with age than do others, for example vocabulary, information, or comprehension. A comparison between scores on the

[3] A critical summary of the problems involved here is to be found in Anastasi, 1961.

tests which hold up with age and those which decrease with age has therefore been proposed as a measure of deterioration for a particular patient. Critical appraisals of this method are few, although there is some evidence that it does not yield results which agree closely with more specialized tests of deterioration (Garfield & Fey, 1948, Margaret & Simpson, 1948). Two investigators were able to obtain both pre-morbid and present performance of patients on intelligence scales, and to compare scores on the Wechsler-Bellevue and other indices of deterioration with the discrepancies between the two testings (Canter, 1951, Rappaport & Webb, 1950). Results of these studies are, however, not clearcut in either confirming or questioning the validity of the deterioration indices.

The Shipley-Hartford Scale for Measuring Intellectual Impairment (1940) measures deterioration in terms of a discrepancy between scores on tests of vocabulary and scores on tests requiring the patient to abstract a principle of arrangement from a series of items. Scores on both kinds of tests are converted to age, and the ratio of vocabulary to abstraction age—called the conceptual quotient (CQ)—provides a single index of intellectual deficit. Studies of this measure suggest that, as compared with control and psychoneurotic subjects, patients diagnosed as schizophrenic or brain-damaged, as well as older subjects, achieve lower CQ's. Reported reliabilities for vocabulary, abstraction, and total scores range from .87 to .92. The Shipley-Hartford scale, although limited by its standardization on children and young adults only, and by its inappropriateness for intellectually retarded patients, has the advantage of providing a self-administering measure of deterioration.

Although the statistical properties of the instruments thus provide a basis for a wide range of test interpretations, still the clinician's job involves more than even these varied analyses of test scores. It goes beyond the classification of scores, the analyses of scatter, of interscale discrepancies, and of subtest profiles, and the appraisal of score changes over time. Each additional analysis is an occasion for the clinician to follow new leads in the understanding of his client's behavior. If he were to stop with test interpretation, however, the psychologist would forfeit a significant opportunity. His client's general behavior in the interpersonal test situation is as important as the test scores in helping the clinician to obtain an understanding of the individual.

Characteristics of the Interpersonal Testing Situation. The testing situation constitutes for the patient a complex interpersonal relationship. In some ways, this relationship is rigidly structured by the strict procedures of an individual test. In other ways, it resembles a clinical interview in its free and unstructured character. The use which the patient makes of this complex situation must be understood and reported by any clinical psychologist whose role is to be more than that of a competent psychometrician. If the patient's responses to test items are taken as samples of behavior from which to generalize, so also are his reactions during the test hour taken to be indicators of his characteristic behavior in other environments.

The patient brings to the solution of any test items his own typical approach to problems, his own habits of reasoning, and his patterns of motivation in interpersonal situations, as well as whatever abilities are relevant to the particular tests he confronts. His success or failure with the test items is the product of this total constellation of personality, motivational, and intellectual factors. Indeed, these ingredients of test performance can seldom if ever be separately teased out and evaluated individually. It is always a question whether a patient's failure on a test is to be assigned more to deficiencies in the patient's intellectual skills and talents, or more to his individual motivational pattern.[4] Consequently, the clinical psychologist must be particularly sensitive to cues related to motivational and emotional factors in his patient's behavior if he is to make a just appraisal of general intelligence. We may consider these interpersonal aspects of the appraisal process under three headings: (1) individual and personalized approaches, (2) expectations and motivation, and (3) special cultural considerations.

INDIVIDUAL AND PERSONALIZED APPROACHES. Early in the development of intelligence scales, Terman pointed out that the administration of an individual intelligence test was similar in many ways to the carrying out of a controlled experiment. We have already seen that in obtaining an intelligence score the clinical psychologist is in effect comparing his client with a standardization group previously examined under the same conditions as those to which the patient is subjected. If the conditions are not the same, he cannot make the comparison. At the moment when he is administering an individual test item, the clinician must play a role like that of the impersonal laboratory experimenter who cannot depart from a set procedure without altering his final results to an indeterminate degree.

This adherence to standardized procedures also guarantees the clinician a uniform background against which to observe his patient. For all patients being examined, the testing conditions, the test materials, the time restrictions, and even the words used by the psychologist must be the same. Yet in spite of this uniformity, the impressive thing about the responses obtained in such a controlled situation is their variability from person to person. These individual differences appear not only in test scores, but also in the patient's approach to the task, his dependence on

---

[4] A useful paradigm for the analysis of the variables affecting test performance is to be found in Goslin (1963), following a model presented by McClelland (1958).

the examiner, his method of problem solution, the persistence of his effort, his tolerance of time pressure, and the defenses he offers for failure. Standardized test procedures, far from producing stereotyped behavior, rather tend to emphasize individual variations among patients.

The clinician who confines his observations to the characteristic behavior of his patient in responding to test instructions still cannot help wondering about the reasons for this behavior and speculating as to what his patient might do in other similar situations. A case in point is the person who explains his failure on a test item by the statement, "It's my fault. I'm not much good at this stuff, or at anything, I guess." Such a comment may suggest several interpretations to the psychologist. It may be no more than a chance, insignificant remark; or it may be an intropunitive defense, a bid for reassurance, or a generalized passive acceptance of defeat which is typical for this particular patient. If it is a defense, the clinical psychologist faces the further question of its relation to early parental training in guilt, and its possible predictive value with respect to later difficulties with persons in authority. Certainly this patient is showing a different reaction from one who meets the same frustration with calm acceptance, sullen withdrawal, ridicule of the test, or hostility toward the clinician. Unquestionably he differs also in important ways from the patient who does not even recognize that he has failed the test.

Reactions to success on the test are as significant as reactions to failure. The patient may solicit praise for a good performance, either subtly or directly; he may accept it with indifference, with pleasure, or with embarrassment; he may reject it as unwelcome or undeserved. Praise may stimulate the patient to a better performance, inhibit him by increasing his tension and anxiety, or provide him with a reason for relaxing his best efforts. Some patients set so high a standard of performance for themselves that commendation from the clinician is unimportant to them.

The patient's method of solving a particular test problem provides a basis for the observation of more circumscribed behavior. A question on the comprehension test of the Wechsler-Bellevue scale, for example, requires the patient to explain how he would find his way out of a forest. It leads to such diverse answers as "By the sun"; "I'd use my watch as a compass"; "I've never lived near a forest"; "North, south, east, west. The sun because it shines so bright." These responses represent, of course, different degrees of success in solving the problem. But they also represent a diversity in choice of words, in completeness of expression, in concreteness of response, and in organization of thinking which ranges, in these examples, from the expected answer of the average adult to the statement of a seriously disorganized schizophrenic patient.

The block designs test, also part of the Wechsler scale, affords another illustration of the variety of the attacks made by different clients on an individual test item. In putting the blocks together to form a pattern which is depicted on a card, one patient will attempt to reproduce the design as a whole, while another will methodically analyze the picture and with the blocks build up the pattern piece by piece. One person may work hurriedly and inquire repeatedly how much time he has, while another may work calmly and insist upon completing the design even though the time limit has already been passed. Some patients are unable to tell whether or not their finished pattern is the same as that in the picture; some become preoccupied with one part of the design and repeat it in stereotyped fashion; some comment upon and even become anxious over the fact that the colors of the blocks do not match exactly the colors on the model card. We have already seen that these reactions have been used not only as the basis for scoring a test of this sort, but also as a basis for the qualitative analysis of general patient behavior.

Other individual test items, and other aspects of the patient's responses during the testing hour, provide innumerable opportunities for the observation of behavior.[5] The alert and experienced clinical psychologist will watch for and record such reactions. He will view the total, complex test situation as a significant sample of individual behavior and formulate from it a variety of hypotheses to assist him in understanding his patient. Moreover, he will not stop with this, but will go on to interpret and evaluate what the patient does and says when not involved in taking the tests but when conversing informally with the clinician.

The content of a test item or a casual remark from the clinician may be the starting point for a conversation. It may then become obvious that the patient has been preoccupied with topics quite remote from the restricted and highly structured test items. In other words, the tests have been serving more as stimuli for the patient's associations and projections than as controlled experimental procedures. A patient may respond to the question "Why are laws necessary?" for example, with "They aren't," and proceed to express with vigor his hostility toward the law, his own infractions of rules and regulations, his feelings about those infractions, and his antagonism toward authority in general. Another patient may say anxiously, as the clinician moves the parts of the performance test across the table toward him, "The blocks jumped at me," and go on to reveal fears and delusional ideas which he had not previously communicated.

The diagnostician takes advantage of such interruptions as these when they occur—and they occur when they are important to the client—as

[5] For a discussion of behavior reports based on children's responses to the 1937 Stanford-Binet Scale, see R. Pintner, A. Dragositz, and R. Kushner, Supplementary guide for the revised Stanford-Binet Scale (Form L), *Appl. Psychol. Monogr.*, 1944, No. 3. For a similar discussion based on WAIS responses, see Wechsler, 1958, Chapter 11.

opportunities for understanding better the individual with whom he is working. He may not hesitate to sacrifice the exact and orderly administration of test items, and therefore the validity of test scores, to informal interviewing which may ultimately yield richer results (see Chapter 2). Of course if he does this he must not overlook the fact that any test results obtained under such conditions are open to serious question and do not deserve the weight he would give them if the tests had been administered in the standardized way. But the psychologist is no clinician who ignores opportunities for interview and discussion with his patient, and prefers test scores, however precise, to a fuller understanding of the individual.

EXPECTATIONS AND MOTIVATION. Persons who participate in intelligence testing as examinees bring to this social situation a number of anticipations and expectations. We have seen (Brim, 1965) that there are many people who question the usefulness of intelligence measures, and who feel that the testing situation is threatening, mysterious, or inconsequential. Such misconceptions will certainly influence the nature of the relationship between examiner and subject; and this in turn may well affect not only the performance and hence the score of the subject, but the efficiency and sensitivity of the clinician as well.

One of the commonest phenomena in the testing situation is the client's development of anxiety over his achievement. The careful studies of Sarason and his associates (1960) on the variable of "test anxiety" in elementary school children indicate the pervasiveness of effects of this attitude upon test scores. Persistent negative relationships between intensity of test anxiety and success in a variety of problem-solving situations suggest that anxiety may operate to lower scores on tests of intelligence. That this effect is also present in older subjects, this time studied on the WAIS, is clear from an experimental study by Sarason and Minard (1962); and that it extends to distrustful attitudes as well has been suggested by still other studies (Wiener, 1957). It should be noted, however, that in general it is the client's pervasive, habitual attitudes which are implicated in his test performance, rather than temporarily induced states (Nichols, 1959).[6]

In a larger sense, what is being argued here is that the response elicited by the clinician who administers an intelligence test item is that response with the highest behavior potential in a particular situation. It is not necessarily the most "correct" response. A multiplicity of factors, of which anxiety and distrust are only two illustrations, may determine the response which is made. Under other circumstances, a patient may feel that a reply will jeopardize his position in some way, and he may not respond at all. These matters have been studied within this framework by Thorpe and Mahrer (1959), who suggest that the client might, under

[6] An analysis of these factors is to be found in Anastasi (1961).

certain circumstances, be invited to give a number of responses to a test item, and then be scored only on his *best* answer.

That the clinician may be affected in his attitudes and performance by the interaction with the client is also clear. While much of the recent evidence on these points comes from studies of the social psychology of the psychological experiment (Rosenthal, 1964), we have seen that test situations bear marked similarities to standard experimental procedures. It is to be expected, therefore, that the involvement of the clinician with particular aspects of his client's performance will induce changes in that performance. One experimental study, indeed, suggests that examiners respond differently to "warm" clients and to "cold" ones (Masling, 1959); and that these differences are expressed not only in generally reinforcing comments to the client, but also in greater leniency of grading and hence higher test scores.

SPECIAL CULTURAL CONSIDERATIONS. In the last analysis, we have said, the interpretation of a test result depends upon the comparison of the client's response with those made by members of the group of persons upon whom the test was standardized. It is a truism of test construction and interpretation, as mentioned above, that the client must be similar to the members of the standardization group on a variety of important variables in order for the test to be appropriate to him. These requirements are obvious when we consider such variables as age, sex, and language; they are less obvious when we consider the more subtle dimensions of socioeconomic level, educational advantage, and minority group membership.

The question of "fairness" of intelligence tests for persons of different cultural or class affiliations is a complex and knotty one. As one writer puts it (McNemar, 1964), the scores of underprivileged persons may be useful indices of their *immediate* functioning, even though these same scores may be attenuated by social or economic conditions which one would hope to see improved. Culturally "unfair" tests, as another writer puts it (Deutsch, *et al.*, 1964), may predict culturally "unfair" criteria, but still these criteria may be exceedingly important. On the other hand, efforts to construct "culturally fair" tests proceed; indeed, many of the changes in item placement on the 1960 Stanford-Binet scales may be considered attempts to align test content with the sort of cultural context, in home and school, in which children of the sixties are growing up.

The clinician is necessarily concerned with evaluating, if possible, the effects of cultural deprivation, lack of privilege, or minority group status upon the performance of his client. In this situation he can find considerable assistance from an analysis of the problem made by Deutsch and his associates (1964). These authors point out, for example, that there are many characteristics of minority group children which affect their test performance, in addition to the obvious lack of appropriate standardization subjects in many of our commonly used instruments. Such children are probably less verbal, more fearful, less self-confident, less motivated by achievement, more likely to be bilingual, and less likely to be exposed to intellectually stimulating materials than are other youngsters. It is clear that all these differences may have some effect upon their test performance, and that the responsible clinician must be sensitive to these effects.

SUMMARY

Intelligence testing in modern clinical psychology, we have seen, is more than the automatic administration of routine test procedures. It begins with a judicious choice of instruments, suited to the patient and constructed to yield valid and reliable results. It requires not only precise knowledge of the characteristics of intelligence scales, but also skill in interpreting test results that are expressed in a variety of ways. It demands an ability to evaluate the results of highly controversial research, and to advance hypotheses to account for a patient's behavior which go beyond unproductive labeling, but stop short of unfounded speculation. The clinician, in diagnosing general intelligence, plays the dual role of a proficient laboratory experimenter and the impartial, understanding observer of human behavior.

But however expertly it may be performed, intelligence testing is still only one of many diagnostic tools which the clinical psychologist must use, and general intelligence is only one of many aspects of patient behavior which he must study. The test in the hands of a competent clinician raises more questions than it answers; it points out more areas for further study than any single kind of diagnostic technique can encompass. When, therefore, the limits of intelligence testing have been reached for a given patient, the responsible clinician must continue his investigation by whatever other methods he has at his disposal. The psychologist who restricts himself to one approach can produce little more than a caricature of his patient. It is only by a skillful variation of his diagnostic procedures that the clinician finally arrives at a full and faithful portrayal of the unique individual.

REFERENCES

ALBEE, G. W. 1963. American psychology in the sixties. *Amer. Psychologist*, 18, 90–95.

AMERICAN PSYCHOLOGICAL ASSOCIATION. 1953. *Ethical standards of psychologists*. Washington, D.C.: American Psychological Association.

AMERICAN PSYCHOLOGICAL ASSOCIATION, COMMITTEE ON TEST STANDARDS. 1954. Technical recommendations for psychological tests and diagnostic techniques. *Psychol. Bull.*, **51**, No. 2, Part II.

ANASTASI, ANNE. 1961. *Psychological Testing.* (2d ed.) New York: Macmillan.

ARTHUR, GRACE. 1943. *A point scale of performance tests.* Vol. I. *Clinical manual.* New York: Commonwealth Fund.

ARTHUR, GRACE. 1947. *A point scale of performance tests. Revised Form II. Clinical manual.* New York: Psychological Corporation.

BAYLEY, NANCY. 1955. On the growth of intelligence. *Amer. Psychologist,* **10**, 805–10.

BERDIE, R. F. 1965. The ad hoc committee on social impact of psychological assessment. *Amer. Psychologist,* **20**, 143–46.

BINET, A. 1898. La mesure en psychologie individuelle. *Revue philos.,* **46**, 113–23.

BINET, A., and SIMON, T. 1905. L'application des méthodes nouvelles au diagnostic du niveau intellectuel chez enfants normaux et anormaux d'hospice et d'école primaire. *Année psychol.,* **11**, 245–366.

BINET, A., and SIMON, T. 1908. Le développement de l'intelligence chez les enfants. *Année psychol.,* **14**, 1–94.

BINET, A., and SIMON, T. 1911. La mesure du developpement de l'intelligence chez les jeunes enfants. *Bulletin de la Société libre pour l'Etude psychologique de l'Enfant.*

BRADWAY, K. P., and THOMPSON, C. W. 1962. Intelligence at adulthood: A twenty-five year follow-up. *J. educ. Psychol.,* **53**, 1–14.

BRADWAY, K. P., THOMPSON, C. W., and CRAVENS, R. B. 1958. Preschool IQs after twenty-five years. *J. educ. Psychol.,* **49**, 278–81.

BRIM, L. G. 1965. American attitudes toward intelligence tests. *Amer. Psychologist,* **20**, 125–30.

BUROS, O. K. 1953. *The fourth mental measurements yearbook.* Highland Park, N.J.: Gryphon.

BUROS, O. K. (ed.). 1961. *Tests in print.* Highland Park, N.J.: Gryphon.

CAMERON, N., and MAGARET, ANN. 1951. *Behavior pathology.* Boston: Houghton Mifflin.

CANTER, A. H. 1951. Direct and indirect measures of psychological deficit in multiple sclerosis. *J. gen. Psychol.,* **44**, 3–26, 27–50.

DEUTSCH, M., FISHMAN, J. A., KOGAN, L., NORTH, R., and WHITMAN, M. 1964. Guidelines for testing minority group children. *J. soc. Issues,* **22**, No. 2, (Suppl.), 127–45.

EELLS, K., DAVIS, A., HAVIGHURST, R. J., HERRICK, V. E., and TYLER, R. 1951. *Intelligence and cultural differences.* Chicago: Univer. of Chicago Press.

FARNSWORTH, P. R., and McNEMAR, Q. (eds.). 1950–65. *Annual review of psychology.* Stanford, Calif.: Annual Reviews. Vols. I–XVI.

FIELD, J. G. 1960. Two types of tables for use with Wechsler's intelligence scales. *J. clin. Psychol.,* **16**, 3–7.

GARFIELD, S. L., and FEY, W. F. 1948. The Wechsler-Bellevue and Shipley-

Hartford scales as measures of mental impairment. *J. consult. Psychol.,* **12,** 259–64.

GOLDSTEIN, K., and SHEERER, M. 1941. Abstract and concrete behavior: An experimental study with special tests. *Psychol. Monogr.,* **33,** No. 239.

GOODENOUGH, FLORENCE. 1926. *Measurement of intelligence by drawings.* New York: Harcourt, Brace & World.

GOSLIN, D. A. 1963. *The search for ability: Standardized testing in social perspective.* New York: Russell Sage Foundation.

GUERTIN, W. H., RABIN, A. I., FRANK, G. H., and LADD, C. E. 1962. Research with the Wechsler intelligence scales for adults: 1955–60. *Psychol. Bull.,* **59,** 1–26.

HAAN, N. 1963. Proposed model of ego functioning: Copying and defense mechanism in relationship to IQ change. *Psychol. Monogr.,* **77,** No. 8 (Whole No. 571), 1–23.

HANFMANN, E. 1939. Thought disturbances in schizophrenia as revealed by performance in a picture completion test. *J. abnorm. soc. Psychol.,* **34,** 134–50.

HARRIS, D. 1952. Intellective functions: Children. In D. BROWER and L. E. ABT (eds.), *Progress in clinical psychology.* New York: Grune & Stratton.

HARRIS, D. B. 1964. *Children's drawings as measures of intellectual maturity: A revision and extension of the Goodenough Draw-A-Man test.* New York: Harcourt, Brace & World.

HONZIK, M. P., MACFARLANE, J. W., and ALLEN, L. 1948. The stability of mental test performance between two and eighteen years. *J. exper. Educ.,* **17,** 309–24.

HUNT, J. McV. 1961. *Intelligence and experience.* New York: Ronald.

JOINT COMMISSION ON MENTAL ILLNESS AND HEALTH. 1961. *Action for mental health.* New York: Basic Books.

KELLY, E. L. 1961. Clinical psychology—1960: Report of survey findings. *APA Div. clin. Psychol. Newsletter,* **14,** No. 1, 1–11.

KOHS, S. C. 1923. *Intelligence measurement: A psychological and statistical study based upon the block-design tests.* New York: Macmillan.

LITTELL, W. M. 1960. The Wechsler Intelligence Scale for Children: Review of a decade of research. *Psychol. Bull.,* **57,** 132–56.

McCLELLAND, D. C. 1958. Issues in the identification of talent. In D. C. McCLELLAND, A. L. BALDWIN, URIE BRONFENBRENNER, and F. L. STRODTBECK, *Talent and society.* Princeton, N.J.: Van Nostrand. Pp. 1–29.

McNEMAR, Q. 1942. *The revision of the Stanford-Binet Scale.* Boston: Houghton Mifflin.

McNEMAR, Q. 1964. Lost: Our intelligence? Why? *Amer. Psychologist,* **19,** 871–82.

MAGARET, ANN. 1950. Generalization in successful psychotherapy. *J. consult. Psychol.,* **14,** 64–70.

MAGARET, ANN, and SIMPSON, M. 1948. A comparison of two measures of deterioration in psychotics. *J. consult. Psychol.,* **12,** 265–70.

MAGARET, ANN, and THOMPSON, C. W. 1950. Differential test responses of normal, superior and mentally defective subjects. *J. abnorm. soc. Psychol.*, **45**, 163–67.

MASLING, J. Effects of warm and cold interaction on administration and scoring of an intelligence test. 1959. *J. consult. Psychol.*, **23**, 336–41.

MAXWELL, E. 1957. Validities of abbreviated WAIS scales. *J. consult. Psychol.*, **21**, 121–26.

MEEHL, P. E. 1960. The cognitive activity of the clinician. *Amer. Psychologist*, **15**, 19–27.

MILLER, N. E. 1964. Some implications of modern behavior theory for personality change and psychotherapy. In P. WORCHEL and D. BYRNE (eds.), *Personality change.* New York: Wiley.

MURRAY, E. J. 1962. Direct analysis from the viewpoint of learning theory. *J. abnorm. soc. Psychol.*, **26**, 226–31.

NICHOLS, R. C. 1959. The effect of ego involvement and success experience on intelligence test scores. *J. consult. Psychol.*, **23**, 92.

PINNEAU, S. R. 1961. *Changes in intelligence quotient: Infancy to maturity.* Boston: Houghton Mifflin.

PORTEUS, S. D. 1950. *The Porteus maze test and intelligence.* Palo Alto, Calif.: Pacific Books.

RABIN, A. I. 1945. The use of the Wechsler-Bellevue scales with normal and abnormal persons. *Psychol. Bull.*, **42**, 410–22.

RABIN, A. I., and GUERTIN, W. H. 1951. Research with the Wechsler-Bellevue test: 1945–1950. *Psychol. Bull.*, **48**, 211–48.

RAPAPORT, D. 1946. *Diagnostic psychological testing.* Chicago: Year Book Medical Publishers.

RAPPAPORT, S. R., and WEBB, W. B. 1950. An attempt to study intellectual deterioration by pre-morbid and psychotic testing. *J. consult. Psychol.*, **14**, 95–98.

ROSENTHAL, R. 1964. Experimenter outcome-orientation and the results of the psychological experiment. *Psychol. Bull.*, **61**, 405–13.

SARASON, I. G., and MINARD, J. 1962. Test anxiety, experimental instructions, and the Wechsler Adult Intelligence Scale. *J. educ. Psychol.*, **53**, No. 6, 299–302.

SARASON, S. B., *et al.* 1960. Anxiety in elementary school children. New York: Wiley.

SEASHORE, H. G. 1951. Differences between verbal and performance IQs on the Wechsler Intelligence Scale for Children. *J. consult. Psychol.*, **15**, 62–67.

SHAKOW, D. 1965. Seventeen years later: Clinical psychology in the light of the 1947 committee on training in clinical psychology report. *Amer. Psychologist*, **20**, 353–62.

SHIPLEY, W. C. 1940. A self-administering scale for measuring intellectual impairment and deterioration. *J. Psychol.*, **9**, 371–77.

SONTAG, L. W., BAKER, C. T., and NELSON, V. L. 1958. Mental growth and personality development: A longitudinal study. *Monogr. soc. res. in Child Developm.*, **23**, No. 2, 68

TERMAN, L. M., and MERRILL, M. A. 1937. *Measuring intelligence.* Boston: Houghton Mifflin.

TERMAN, L. M., and MERRILL, M. A. 1960. *Stanford-Binet intelligence scale (manual for third revision): Form L–M.* Boston: Houghton Mifflin.

THOMPSON, C. W., and MAGARET, ANN. 1947. Differential test responses of normals and mental defectives. *J. abnorm. soc. Psychol.,* 42, 285–93.

THORP, T. R., and MAHRER, A. R. 1959. Predicting potential intelligence. *J. clin. Psychol.,* 15, 286–88.

WATSON, R. I. 1946. The use of the Wechsler-Bellevue scales: A supplement. *Psychol. Bull.,* 43, 61–68.

WECHSLER, D. 1944. *The measurement of adult intelligence.* Baltimore: Williams & Wilkins.

WECHSLER, D. 1946. *The Wechsler-Bellevue Intelligence Scale, Form II.* New York: Psychological Corporation.

WECHSLER, D. 1949. *The Wechsler Intelligence Scale for Children.* New York: Psychological Corporation.

WECHSLER, D. 1958. *The measurement and appraisal of adult intelligence.* Baltimore: Williams & Wilkins.

WIENER, G. 1957. The effect of distrust on some aspects of intelligence test behavior. *J. consult. Psychol.,* 21, 127–30.

4

Projective Techniques

JULES D. HOLZBERG [*]

Projective techniques represent one of two major approaches to the assessment of personality. Psychometrics has been significantly involved with personality assessment. Its historical origins lie in the study of individual differences and the consequent development of psychometric techniques designed to quantify various dimensions of human behavior. Perhaps the most significant of these was the development of intelligence tests, which probably was the very first successful application of this tradition to the study of significant human behavior. The psychometric orientation also led to the development of instruments for the measurement of a variety of other aspects of human behavior including aptitudes, skills, attitudes, interests, and personality. Thus, out of the efforts of psychometricians, there emerged various types of objective personality instruments in the form of questionnaires or rating scales characterized by quantitative measurement, objectivity, reliability, and specifications of the variables of behavior being measured.

These characteristics were quite in contrast to those of projective techniques which have tended to ignore precise measurement because of an interest in description rather than measurement (Symonds, 1949); to have little concern about the reliability problem because of what was felt to be an overstressing of the importance of reliability (McClelland, 1957); to be uninterested in the precise specification of variables being measured because of the conviction that each subject should define his own variables.

Psychometrics, with its emphasis on personality questionnaires and rating scales, and the clinical orientation, with its interest in the various projective techniques, represented two somewhat diverse approaches to

[*] Jules D. Holzberg, Ph.D. (New York University), Director of Research, Connecticut Valley Hospital, and Professor of Psychology, Wesleyan University.

the assessment of personality that have more often than not occasioned periods of bitterness between the advocates of each, often with little recognition that these may be two complimentary methods of assessing human personality, each method having certain advantages not possessed by the other.

While projective techniques have had a wide range of application in a variety of fields concerned with the study of human behavior, their most extensive and intensive application has been in the study of the personalities of individuals in the clinical situation, where they have been used to assist in formulating the psychodiagnostic picture and the therapeutic plan of the individual patient. While these methods have become the cornerstone of the study of the patient for assessing clinical diagnosis and therapeutic potential, they have been utilized extensively in personality research, including anthropological investigations (Lindzey, 1961). Holzberg (1963) has recently suggested that, because projective testing and psychotherapy have certain common processes, projective techniques may be useful in preparing the subject for his role in psychotherapy.

Controversy has surrounded these methods almost from their inception and it would be difficult to deny that they are still a focus of considerable disagreement. While the issues underlying the controversy have varied from time to time, the honest intellectual differences have been clouded by the flamboyant misuse of these methods by some of their advocates as well as by substantial ignorance of their rationale by opponents.

It seems appropriate to begin our discussion of projective techniques by examining the influences that have played a role in stimulating interest on the part of clinical psychologists in projective techniques. Most students of these methods would acknowledge that psychoanalytic theory was probably one of the most important factors influencing the application of projective techniques to the clinical situation. One of the signal contributions of psychoanalysis was its emphasis on the role of unconscious motivation in human behavior and the differing levels of awareness at which motives can operate, that is, conscious, preconscious, and unconscious. One of the prime characteristics of projective techniques has been their purported sensitivity to motivation of which the subject was unaware and their ability to penetrate to levels of unawareness that had hitherto not been possible with other assessment devices.

Another important development influencing the application of projective techniques was the revolt within psychology against the use of molecular units of behavior. While this protest was in part rooted in psychoanalysis, this "holistic" emphasis had independent origins in organismic psychology. This theoretical orientation emphasized that no aspect of an individual could be fully understood without taking into consideration all other aspects of the functioning personality. To a great extent, this orientation compelled many clinical psychologists to look with disfavor upon such personality assessment instruments as questionnaires and rating scales since these tended to assess relatively isolated aspects of the personality without regard for their interaction, patterning, and hierarchy of importance. Projective techniques have often been described by their advocates as "holistic," precisely because of their presumed ability to "pull" for more molar units of behavior and to delineate the dynamic interplay of those variables that were relevant to the specific individual under study. Those very qualities that led the "holistic" psychologist to adopt projective techniques also led to criticisms from the psychometric psychologist who viewed these qualities as leading to imprecise and nonobjective assessment.

A further impetus to the application of projective techniques came from those psychologists with a phenomenological orientation, which emphasized the importance of understanding the individual through his perception of his subjectively experienced world. To the phenomenologist, projective techniques provided a means of approaching the subjective or phenomenal world of the subject as he experienced it, in terms that were defined by the subject and not by the variables specified by the test constructor (Frank, 1939). The latter issue has been important to the phenomenologist who feels that each person perceives his world in categories that are relevant to his own personality. Objective personality questionnaires and rating scales have therefore been criticized for providing a set of a priori categories whereas projective methods such as the Thematic Apperception Test permits the subject to define the categories pertinent to the subject's own personality. Kelly's (1955) theory of personal constructs is a major systematic theoretical attempt dealing with this issue. He would feel that projective techniques do not go far enough in permitting the subject to define his own categories. To the extent that any method, such as the Rorschach, has an a priori scoring system, one may find validity for Kelly's position. Furthermore, to the extent that one's theory of personality determines projective test interpretation, it is evident that such theory explicitly defines the categories of behavior analysis and their hierarchy of significance for the subject.

Another influence should be noted. The surge of interest in projective methods coincided with the growth of psychotherapy of all types as a method of intervention in psychopathology. The most important tool for most psychotherapies is the clinical interview which is also a basic method for personality assessment. The professional trained to use the interview is accustomed to dealing with complex and multiform data and to interpret such data, not primarily by resort to psychometric norms, but by clinical sensitivity and theoretical sophistication residing in the interviewer. To such professionals, techniques such as the Rorschach and the

Thematic Apperception Test were seen as yielding data similar in complexity to those procured in the interview and requiring for their interpretation the same clinical skills used in interpreting interview data. To some, projective techniques possessed one advantage over the interview: they provided a more standard set of stimuli, although as we shall see, it may be difficult to insist that any stimulus can be the same to all subjects. It should be noted that some interviewers have not accepted these techniques because they feel it introduces an artificial barrier between subject and examiner and thus interferes with the interpersonal interaction.

Shneidman (1965) has suggested that projective techniques served as a focus of protest against a movement in psychology whose approach was dehumanizing the individual. He has described psychology, particularly American psychology, as oriented to a "tough-minded" approach that fractionates the person in order to implement a model of scientific precision. A more "humanistic" psychology concerned with the totality of the human being, seen "compassionately and practically," found projective methods compatible with this orientation. It is Shneidman's concern that projective techniques will lose their historical and real raison d'être if they become wedded to psychology's preoccupation with precise measurement and computer technology. This is the concern of a humanistic psychologist!

While projective techniques have appealed to the philosophical and theoretical orientations of many clinical psychologists, they have certainly not been fully accepted by all clinical psychologists and certainly not by psychology in general. For the most part, their critics have utilized the accepted standards of psychometrics and have correctly indicated the ways in which projective techniques have failed to meet these criteria. In doing so, they have ignored the admonitions of the advocates who have insisted that these methods were not psychometric in their origin nor in their application and that new criteria of the adequacy of these methods must be developed outside of psychometrics. Projective techniques have been criticized for the following: their data are too complex for analysis; they have not been adequately standardized in the sense of having adequate norms; they have not attained appropriate standards of objectivity, reliability, and validity. It is probably true that where considerable work has been done in evaluating these methods, as in the Rorschach, results have often been far from consistent. Attempts have been made to make certain of these methods more objective, but, according to the advocates, at a cost to their clinical contribution. In fact, some projective technique advocates would insist that they are truly the "objective" psychologists because of their primary concern with the "object" of study, that is, the subject, rather than with scores (Kelly, 1955). It has been possible to demonstrate one or another type of reliability with many of these methods

(Holzberg, 1960), but the critical problem of validity still remains a challenge (Harris, 1960).

Another major source of criticism has been from psychological theorists who feel that projective methods were not related to psychological theory current at the time of their emergence (Thurstone, 1948) and some would feel that this is true even at the present time. Interpretations of projective data have often been within the framework of psychoanalytic theory, the tenents of which are still resisted by significant segments of American psychology. This has tended to isolate advocates of projective techniques from psychologists generally since there has often been a semantic problem introduced in communication between those for and against projective methods.

At a more practical level, there have been criticisms directed at a number of the projective methods, particularly the Rorschach and the Thematic Apperception Test, because of the high cost of time involved in procuring and analyzing data from an individual subject. To this should be added the criticism of some that what is needed is more clinical observations of a subject's behavior that would not require an interpretive process between test data and actual behavior. To the psychologist who views projective methods as yielding information about covert aspects of personality, such a criticism has been rejected because it fails to understand the essential purpose of these methods. In this context, it should be noted that Frank (1939), who was the first to systematically conceptualize the nature of projective techniques, did not offer these devices as a substitute for "quantitative statistical procedures" but more as a way of compensating for the deficiencies of more objective instruments.

In summary, it may be possible to categorize psychologists according to their attitudes toward projective methods as follows: those who object to all of these methods for any or all of the reasons noted earlier; those who object to certain projective methods but endorse others; those who accept all projective methods as a necessary component of the methodology of personality study.

THE DEFINITION OF PROJECTIVE TECHNIQUES

Most proposed definitions of projective techniques have attempted to differentiate them from objective personality questionnaires and rating scales. It will become self-evident in this discussion how complex this definitional problem is.

One of the critical problems in definition has been the meaning of "projective" and the psychological process from which this term derives, projection. The similarity in sound and overlapping of meanings of these two words have contributed to the problem of definition. The concept of projection developed in psychoanalytic theory as a construct to explain one particular mode of dealing with distressing anxiety. While Freud's first use of the term is not entirely clear, it was described in detail by Freud in the now famous Schreber case (Freud, 1911). It is in his detailed account of this particular case that Freud developed the idea that "internal perceptions" can be replaced by "external perceptions" such that the subject rejects impulses within himself and attributes these very same impulses to persons in his surrounding environment. Thus, the internal perception stemming from unacceptable latent homosexual strivings in Schreber's "I love him" is altered and becomes another internal perception, "I hate him," through the defense of reaction formation. This perception is similarly unacceptable and must be disowned. It is at this point in the defensive process that the internal perception becomes transformed through projection into the external perception "He hates me," which is the paranoid interpersonal posture. By use of projection, the individual denies the presence within himself of obnoxious impulses such that they are not recognized as being a part of himself, but rather of others. While originally designated by Freud as a basic mechanism operating in the condition of paranoia, he recognized that this process of defending against objectionable impulses can occur in other conditions as well as in everyday behavior of normal people. Thus, Freud stated: "For when we refer the causes of certain sensations to the external world, instead of looking for them (as we do in the case of others) inside ourselves, this normal proceeding, too, deserves to be called projection" (1911, p. 66). Freud suggests here another definition of "projection," namely a process whereby a person simply "extends" psychological qualities outward.

Others have advanced the thesis that there may be different types of projection that need to be identified. Murray (1933), whose Thematic Apperception Test is today one of the most widely used of the projective methods, has tried to distinguish between supplementary and complementary projection. By supplementary projection, Murray means the attribution of an individual's own qualities directly upon another, whereas in complementary projection, the individual perceives others in such a way as to make their motives congruent with his own impulses. In the former, the individual does not recognize that which he has projected, whereas in the latter, he perceives his own impulses and experiences the environment as being congruent with these. More recently, Murray (1951) has described contrast projection in which the person tends to experience others as being more dissimilar to him than they are in reality.

Bellak (1950) has also attempted to differentiate various types of projection. He suggests that the term "apperceptive distortion" be used as a generic description of which the concept of projection would be simply one type of distortion. Included in this concept of apperceptive distortion are a number of behavioral mechanisms identified as projection, inverted projection, simple projection, sensitization, and externalization. He would reserve the term "projection" for the defense mechanism actually used in paranoia. This would represent the greatest degree of distortion in which the individual's objectionable impulses must be thoroughly denied to the self and are eventually attributed to others in his environment. It is Bellak's interpretation that this behavioral process could be recognized by the individual only after intensive psychotherapy. His other categories of apperceptive distortion should also be briefly mentioned because some of them have relevance to the definition of projective techniques. Inverted projection is a behavioral response usually characterized as the defense of reaction formation. In this maneuver, the individual inverts his true feelings such that he does not recognize them, but on the contrary displays behavior which is just the opposite in order to deceive himself as well as others. Simple projection is described by Bellak as the essentially normal phenomenon of the individual perceiving his environment as a function of his contemporary inner feelings. This would be exemplified by the depressed person observing that others around him seem unhappy. Sensitization is the tendency of a person to have a state of heightened awareness to aspects of his environment which are pertinent to his inner emotional states. Externalization is used by Bellak to describe the process by which the person consciously attributes to others those qualities which are descriptive of himself. This is sometimes observed in a subject who, in making up a story to the Thematic Apperception Test, is quite aware of the fact that he is describing one or more characters in a way that is descriptive of himself.

From a summary point of view, the term "projection" seems to have been utilized to describe essentially two types of behavioral response. One of these, the defense mechanism of projection as it is used in psychoanalysis, is the process whereby an individual, to preserve his own security and integrity, is compelled to deny certain impulses within himself and attributes these very same impulses to others. The other sense in which the term "projection" has been used is when motives and personality organization are deemed to influence perception and judgment. Dissatisfaction with the label is to be seen in the use of other terms, for example, apperceptive distortions (Bellak, 1950), misperceptive or dynaceptive tests (Cattell, 1957), imaginative productions (White, 1944), personologic methods (Shneidman, 1965), etc.

It is of interest to indicate the way in which these techniques of clinical assessment came to be labeled as "projective techniques." Until quite recently, it was agreed that Frank (1939) originated this label to designate a class of instruments which up to that time had not been categorized.

More recently, Lindzey (1961) has suggested that the origin of the term more appropriately should be credited to Murray (1938) who in his volume *Explorations in Personality* used the term "projection" test. In spite of this, Frank must be acknowledged as having had the greatest influence in the adoption of "projective techniques" as a generic concept encompassing the class of instruments with which we are concerned.

Because of the influence of Frank in conceptualizing this whole movement, it seems important to give some attention to his thinking at that time. Frank examined these methods from a holistic background and saw such instruments yielding information about the individuality of a person, about the nature of the social and private world as it is experienced by the individual, and about the social psychological field in which the subject operates. He was thus led to conclude that projective methods are a necessary approach to the assessment of personality because they yield data that define these very dimensions. Throughout his paper, the emphasis is on the "private world" of the individual, a world that cannot be assessed by standardized, objective instruments of personality measurement but that require techniques that give the individual free play, particularly for his imaginative processes. He was also concerned with the need for techniques that reveal the latent or covert dimensions of personality. He suggested that projective techniques are particularly sensitive to those domains of the personality that are unknown to the individual or about which the individual is reluctant to speak because of the distress associated with such revelation. He saw projective techniques as providing the individual with a "field" that permits him to organize his experiences by dealing with objects or materials that have relatively limited structure and minimum cultural definition. In this way, the individual "projects" onto the field the nature of his "private world" of feelings and meanings. It was important to Frank that the true projective method must permit the subject to respond in terms of his own categories of meanings and feelings, as opposed to the priori categories in personality questionnaires and rating scales. The projective technique should provide the opportunity for the individual to leave the imprint of his personal meanings and experiences upon the material presented.

Lindzey (1961) has observed that Frank never intended that his description of the process involved in the projective method be interpreted as projection in the classical Freudian sense. Rather, he was describing the process whereby the individual simply reveals the nature of his personality by being given the opportunity to manipulate a field that he is free to interpret in whatever way is appropriate to his personal meanings and feelings.

After this brief historical interlude, we now return to the task of defining a projective technique. We are indebted to Lindzey (1961) who has most recently offered a set of distinguishing criteria that seem most appropriate in defining the nature of projective techniques so that they may be distinguished from objective personality instruments. Lindzey suggests two sets of criteria, one primary and the other secondary. His primary criteria are:

1. *Sensitivity to unconscious dimensions of the personality.* Projective techniques are primarily designed to make accessible those aspects of the self that are unknown to the individual. It is clearly evident that this attribute of the projective technique does not lie directly in the test itself but is much more a designation of the purpose for which the test is used.

2. *The multiplicity of responses permitted the subject.* Generally speaking, projective techniques do not restrict the subject to some a priori limited number of responses but, on the contrary, permit the subject to determine what responses he will make. The typical questionnaire provides the subject with a fixed number of alternative responses from which he may select one or perhaps rank the alternatives. In the projective technique, the subject determines the alternatives available to him.

3. *Multidimensionality.* Most of the projective techniques, as we have indicated earlier, do not specify an a priori list of dimensions that the tests measure. Even in the Rorschach, where scoring categories have been traditionally used, certain of these categories will be interpreted because of their pertinence in one subject, but these same categories will be ignored as irrelevant in another subject.

4. *The subject's lack of awareness of the purpose of the test.* A common characteristic of the projective technique is that the subject usually does not possess a full comprehension of the way in which his responses will be utilized and interpreted. Even in the Rorschach Test, where many subjects are sometimes explicitly aware of the significance of the content of their associations, they will not realize that the far more important interpretations are based on the formal, noncontent aspects of responses.

5. *The quantity and complexity of the response data elicited.* Many projective techniques, such as the Rorschach and the Thematic Apperception Test, provide data that are both quantitatively large and complex—an important reason why quantification, even if it were desirable, is so difficult.

Lindzey's secondary criteria, which do not apply as universally as his primary ones, are:

1. *The stimulus ambiguity of the projective technique.* This criterion is present in varying degrees with the different projective methods. Thus, the typical sentence completion test is often less ambiguous as a stimulus

than the Rorschach. However, even within a single test, certain stimuli may be more ambiguous than others. Thus, among the Thematic Apperception Test cards, certain of the cards are clearly more ambiguous in terms of clear identification of objects in the picture, the sex of the human beings, their actions, etc.

2. *Appropriateness for holistic analysis.* Projective techniques, for the most part, require that the assessment of personality must be based on the integration of various aspects of the personality leading to a pattern or profile rather than a final result represented by a total score. It seems appropriate here to indicate that the appropriateness of this approach to personality has even influenced the way in which certain objective personality questionnaires are actually used in clinical practice. For instance, the Minnesota Multiphasic Personality Inventory, while yielding a series of discrete measures on a variety of personality dimensions, is often interpreted in a similar fashion to a projective technique by an interpreter attempting to integrate the discrete series of scores into some kind of profile or pattern. Thus, it seems evident that appropriateness for holistic analysis seems less a product of the test itself than of the method of interpretation that one wishes to employ.

3. *The ability to evoke fantasy responses from the subject.* This criterion recognizes that many, but not all, of projective techniques encourage the subject to use his imaginative processes in bringing about a response to the task.

4. *The absence of a right or wrong status for responses.* As is often explicit in the instructions to the projective technique, there is no correct or incorrect response, only a response characteristic of the individual.

While it is evident that not all projective techniques meet all of the criteria listed by Lindzey, and that several of the criteria can be applied as well to nonprojective techniques, it is evident that many more projective techniques than objective personality instruments fit these criteria. In summary, it is appropriate to quote Lindzey's (1961) definition of a projective technique:

A projective technique is an instrument that is considered especially sensitive to covert or unconscious aspects of behavior, it permits or encourages a wide variety of subject responses, is highly multidimensional, and it evokes unusually rich or profuse response data with a minimum of subject awareness concerning the purpose of the test. Further, it is very often true that the stimulus material presented by the projective test is ambiguous, interpreters of the test depend upon holistic analysis, the test evokes fantasy responses, and there are no correct or incorrect responses to the test. [P. 45.]

This definition does not deny that all psychological instruments of assessment are designed to reveal attributes of the self, but projective techniques are that category of psychological instruments that meet the above criteria in terms of the quality of stimulus, the nature of the response, and the method of interpretation.

PSYCHOLOGICAL THEORY AND PROJECTIVE TECHNIQUES

There have been three diverse attitudes with regard to the relationship between psychological theory and projective techniques. One attitude is that projective techniques are essentially unrelated and foreign to any established psychological theory. A second attitude is that psychological theory is insufficient to the task of explaining the rationale of projective techniques and that these techniques must create their own theoretical substructure. The third attitude insists that projective techniques and psychological theory are interrelated, although the prime limitation is the absence of a unifying theory of behavior competent to explain the diversity and complexity of human behavior.

Learning Theory. It is inevitable, with the dominant role that learning theory has played in American psychology, that projective techniques should be examined from this theoretical viewpoint, although it is clear from our earlier discussion that this theory in no significant way contributed to the development of the projective technique movement. In fact, some of the most ardent critics of projective techniques have been psychologists identified with learning theory.

Auld (1954), in an interesting attempt to relate learning theory concepts (habit strength, generalization, conflict) to the TAT, begins with the need to identify and distinguish three situations: origin situation, test situation, and criterion situation. "Emotional habits" provide the linkage between these three situations in that those habits originally learned in the origin situation emerge in the test situation and determine behavior in the criterion situation. Thus, Auld sees the role of the psychologist using projective techniques as that of determining the nature of the emotional habits in the projective test situation which will reveal the specific habits learned in the origin situation. Where these have been identified, the psychologist can then make predictions as to how these habits will be manifested in the criterion situation. He utilizes the learning theory concept of generalization to explain the fact that the extent to which the emotional habits learned in the origin situation appear in the test situation, to this extent can predictions be made to the criterion situation. To be able to make effective predictions, the psychologist must identify the strength of the habit and the degree of conflict (approach versus avoidance) engendered by that habit.

Another learning theorist, Atkinson (1958), has attempted to relate motivational theory to projective techniques, more specifically to the Thematic Apperception Test. Atkinson's formulation states that the TAT provides many cues that serve to arouse a variety of motives. These motives, when activated by TAT stimuli, lead the subject to make responses that have evolved from earlier experiences where these motives have been aroused. There have been other attempts to relate learning theory to projective techniques, one of the most detailed being the papers by Goss and Brownell (1957) and Brownell and Goss (1957). For the reader interested in this particular area, the review of these two papers will be very rewarding.

Perception Theory. Since perception is involved in every projective technique, it would seem desirable to attempt to relate the psychology of perception and projective methods. With the demonstration of the effects of psychological needs upon perceptual processes, there has been an attempt to bridge this aspect of psychological theory and projective methods. Abt (1950) attempted to develop what he calls a "projective psychology" because of the lack of a pertinent psychological theory for projective techniques. It is of interest that a nonclinical psychologist (Bruner, 1948) has denied that projective techniques needed its own theoretical substructure. He felt that a general theory of perception, once elaborated, would be the bridge between projective methods and general psychology. While Abt's formulations are too vague to permit specific application to projective methods, they do emphasize the important role of perception in projective techniques. In developing the concept of selectivity of perception, he offers the rationale that the individual, in responding to stimuli, does so on the basis of both internal and external factors. Essentially, external factors are the autochthonous factors that have been the focus of interest of Gestalt psychologists, and are concerned with the objective factors in the stimulus. To the user of projective tests, the internal factors are of greater relevance, for these are the factors that principally play a role in the selectivity of perception. Abt suggests while internal and external factors operate in perception, their respective roles vary as a function of the degree of structure of the stimulus. As one diminishes the degree of structure in the stimulus, internal factors play a more dominant role in perception.

A series of investigations that have attempted to relate perceptual theory and projective techniques have been conducted. On the basis of these, Eriksen (1954) has advanced the thesis that projective techniques are predominantly perceptual devices and, like perception, are subject to the motivations operating in the subject. He concludes that what is needed in projective testing is more normative material which could serve as a criterion of the degree of ambiguity of projective stimuli. The presumption is that greater structure would reduce variance across subjects. Consequently, norms that defined typical responses can be used as a measure of stimulus structure. More recent work by Murstein (1963) is of significance in delineating the degree of structure or ambiguity required in a test stimulus such as the TAT in order to procure those responses from which the psychologist can draw inferences regarding the individual dynamics of the subject. Eriksen further feels that there is still too little known regarding the types and levels of motives that are elicited in response to projective stimuli. He questions whether only unconscious needs are being expressed in projective tests and he can indicate from research on perception that motives of all degrees of awareness operate in perception.

It should be noted that it was a psychoanalyst who made a functional contribution to clinical interpretation by developing a rationale for Rorschach responses based on perception and association (Rapaport *et al.*, 1946). Rapaport saw these two processes as central to the emergence of a response. It was his thesis that the Rorschach stimulus evokes "a perceptual organizing process" which has continuity with perception in everyday life. The initial, vague perception of the stimulus stimulates an association process in order that an appropriate content be proposed. Thus, in order for an effective response to be made, there must not only be an intact perceptual process and association process, but both must be functionally integrated. Deviant, bizarre, or original responses can be interpreted in terms of the adequacy of the two processes and their effective "cogwheeling."

While there have been these attempts in relating perception theory and projective techniques, it is evident that no comprehensive perceptual theory is as yet available that can serve as the sole theoretical basis for projective methods.

Psychoanalytic Theory. As one would anticipate from our discussion of the developmental history of projective techniques, there has been a prolific literature attempting to relate psychoanalytic theory to projective techniques. Rapaport was among the very first psychoanalytic theorists who attempted to bridge these two areas (Rapaport *et al.*, 1946). While he cautioned against precipitously and uncritically using psychoanalytic theory in understanding projective techniques, he nevertheless was firmly committed to the belief that this theoretical system had much to contribute to the understanding of these methods (Rapaport, 1952). In contrast to other attempts to relate psychoanalytic theory to projective methods, it was Rapaport's belief that the newer ego psychology rather than the "instinct" psychology of psychoanalysis held the greater promise in this attempt to relate these two areas. Rapaport had been involved in the development of a psychoanalytic theory of thinking that he felt would be an important theoretical tool in illuminating the nature of the interviewing process between projective stimulus and the subject's response. Unfortunately, he died before he was able to carry his theoretical formulations to their conclusion, but what he did is a monumental record of accomplishment in theory building that has not been fully recognized in American psychology for he, like projective techniques, was caught in the emotional response to psychoanalytic theory.

One of Rapaport's significant contributions was his differentiation of two types of cognitive processes, that is, the application of known concepts or "fixed tools of thought" and the formation of concepts or "process of thought" (1952). This led him to stress the importance of the structure of a test inasmuch as the more highly structured tests, for example, the Wechsler Intelligence Scale, were seen by him as yielding information on "fixed tools of thought" while the less structured tests, for example, the Rorschach, yielded information about the "process of thought." The conceptual breadth of a person like Rapaport is seen in the extent to which he attempted to integrate structured and unstructured tests, rather than engaging in a polemic as to which type of technique was superior to the other. He even extended the application of the concept of projection by indicating that stylistic characteristics of the subject, while unknown to the subject, can be reflected in well-structured tests such as an intelligence test.

Another contribution of Rapaport (1952) was his attempt to understand the meaning of the variations among subjects in their "conscious experience" of the perceptions that they describe on the Rorschach. He carefully describes what has been observed by every clinician: some subjects describe their percepts as if these were real objects; some offer an easy and popular response with the conviction that they are creating something unusual; still others report physiological phenomena that they experience in concurrence with their perceptions. Rapaport offered the conclusion that these differences in performance are intimately related to two psychoanalytic phenomena: reality testing and constriction of inner experiences.

Schafer (1954) has probably made the most significant functional contribution in his attempt to relate psychoanalytic theory to projective techniques. His formulations have unquestionably had great impact on the practicing clinician. In his very significant book *Psychoanalytic Interpretation in Rorschach Testing: Theory and Application,* Schafer applied the psychoanalytic concepts of transference and countertransference to the projective technique situation. These two concepts emerged from observations in psychoanalytic therapy. Irrational attitudes on the part of both patient (transference) and therapist (countertransference) influence their perceptions of each other and affect their behavior in the therapy situation. According to Schafer, a similar process goes on in the testing situation, so that the attempt to obtain *absolute* examiner objectivity is difficult, if not impossible. Consequently, the tester must come to learn the nature of the circumstances under which his objectivity tends to be diminished in order that he may take into consideration how this affects the subject's test performance and the examiner's interpretations. The examiner in his testing role brings into the test situation certain attitudes that are a function of the particular role of the clinical psychologist in the setting in which he is operating, and that are also a function of the clinician's personality. With regard to the role of the clinical psychologist, Schafer emphasizes a problem of identity in that the clinical psychologist often has confusion concerning his professional role, confusion that emerges out of a sense of inferiority to other professionals, particularly psychiatrists. Furthermore, partly as a function of his role, partly as a function of his personality, the tester enters into the test situation with a set of expectations from the subject, just as the subject surely enters the test situation with a set of expectations about the psychologist and the examination. Schafer has sensitively delineated certain role dimensions of the examiner that are present to varying degrees in different examiners. To the extent that the psychologist is an observer of the patient's conscious and unconscious processes, he is operating with a voyeuristic attitude. Inasmuch as the psychologist must control the testing situation in order for the testing to be accomplished, he must assume an autocratic role. Since the clinical psychologist uses his training and knowledge to draw significant psychological conclusions, he plays an oracular role. Last, but by no means least, since testing usually occurs in the context of a patient suffering and needing help, the psychologist functions in a saintly role. It is Schafer's thesis that these role demands influence the attitudes of the tester and his expectations from the patient. Where the patient's extent and manner of responding run counter to these expectations, the tester may unknowingly behave in ways that will distort the subject's responses and their interpretation.

While these role performances are seen by Schafer as implicit in the clinical testing situation and therefore imposed on all clinical testers, although to varying degrees, he does identify certain idiosyncratic personality attributes of the tester that may operate to affect the responses of subjects to the test situation. He lists a number of relevant personality types among clinicians: the tester with a weak sense of personal identity; the inhibited or withdrawn tester; the dependent tester; the highly intellectualized and constricted tester; the sadistic tester; and the masochistic tester. These are but some of the personality types that are found among testers—as well as among therapists of all disciplines—and that influence the subject's perception of the testing situation.

Schafer then lists aspects of the subject that play a role in determining his response to the test situation: Where projective tests, such as the Rorschach, are utilized, there is a threat to the subject's personal privacy; the patient, by professional definition, cannot control the interpersonal relationship in the testing situation; he may fear being confronted through the test with objectionable aspects of his own personality; he may be threatened by the encouragement to regress to more immature psychic levels in order to produce responses; he can be frightened by the freedom offered by the projective test situation, as in the case of the Rorschach, where the patient is given almost complete freedom to respond in any way he wishes.

Schafer further indicates that responses will reveal various kinds of defensive reactions as they are characteristic of the subject's personality. The most common defenses encountered in the Rorschach are projection, isolation, intellectualization, compulsive perfectionism, repression, denial, reaction formation, counterphobic defense, masochistic strategies, ingratiating maneuvers, and rebellious operations. Schafer indicates how the Rorschach can be analyzed so as to lead to understanding of the subject's characteristic defensive style.

One further contribution of Schafer should be indicated in his attempt to relate psychoanalytic theory to projective techniques. Drawing upon Freud's concepts of primary and secondary process, Schafer has developed a very interesting formulation that attempts to explain the response process occurring in the patient. The most primitive level of psychic organization, where there is no concern for the demands of reality, constitutes the primary process. Secondary process functioning occurs where the child in his development becomes not only aware of reality but attempts to constructively adapt to its demands. Schafer has attempted to illuminate the response process, particularly in the Rorschach, using these concepts. When the examiner introduces the subject to the testing situation, he deliberately encourages, particularly with a technique like the Rorschach, the patient to engage in free fantasy (primary process) but with a careful testing of reality (secondary process), that is, also to justify his responses. To the extent that the subject operates principally under the influence of free fantasy, to this extent may one say that the primary process is dominant. To the extent that testing of reality is predominant in the subject's responses, to this extent may one speak of the secondary process as being dominant. It is Schafer's thesis that subjects show marked individual differences in the extent to which these two processes predominate, and that the same individual may vary from time to time in terms of the dominant process. If one conceptualizes primary process functioning as being more regressed than that of secondary process functioning, Schafer's formulation takes on significant meaning. He has applied the concept of "regression in the service of the ego" (Kris, 1952) to explain the capacity of an individual to retreat to a more regressed mode of functioning in order to serve the function of adaptation. Furthermore, Schafer sees the projective test situation as one that invites the subject to "regress in the service of the ego" and that individuals differ in terms of the degree to which they can engage in this process. Some subjects can only function in the Rorschach test situation by simply describing the blots very concretely, implying there is some inability or unwillingness to regress. Others may engage in very imaginative activity, and permit themselves to play intrapsychically so as to produce spontaneous and creative responses that can be justified. This would represent adaptive "regression in the service of the ego." Others may regress very readily, but begin to produce content that is bizarre and reflective of deep unconscous conflicts, responses that may themselves be distressing to the subject. This would constitute an inability to control the regressive process and is likely to be present in an individual whose ego is significantly impaired.

It is evident that Schafer has meaningfully attempted to integrate a number of aspects of psychoanalytic theory into the rationale of projective techniques. While it is true that he has not attempted to relate systematically all of psychoanalytic theory, this need hardly be a serious criticism at this stage of development. Rather, one might look upon Schafer's work as one in a series of early steps in relating psychoanalytic theory to projective methods. It is important to emphasize once again that Schafer's analysis is not only a conceptual contribution, but one that has actually enriched the interpretive process in projective testing.

In summary, the following can be stated as the significant contributions of Schafer to the understanding of the projective testing experience. He has emphasized the need to analyze the total testing situation in order to determine how it affects the subject's responses. This means understanding the expectations and anxieties that the subject brings to the testing situation as well as the motives, attitudes, and general theoretical orientation brought by the examiner. He has delineated different levels of psychological functioning and the importance of the individual's ability to regress adaptively in order to meet the demands of the projective test situation. He has indicated the typical modes of defense of the subject that can affect the way he responds to test stimuli. While this inevitably complicates the process of interpretation, it nevertheless provides an additional means for determining the kind of defensive structure brought to the testing by the subject. Finally, his emphasis on the phenomenon of identity and the roles imposed upon tester and subject are significant contributions. Central to all these is his concern with conscious and unconscious motivation operating in both subject and tester, and how operations similar to transference and countertransference operate in the test situation. It is his conclusion that these factors either can result in distortions of the subject's responses and their interpretation or, if used with clinical acumen, can lead to more sensitive understanding of the subject's personality.

Holt (1954) has also examined the relationship between psychoanalytic theory and the Rorschach, particularly as it pertains to the interpretation of content. His analysis in part parallels that of Schafer's. He indicates that the Rorschach is specially adapted to elicit both primary process content (more primitive mental content appropriate to the psychological world of infancy and psychosis) and secondary process content (mental content depicting the more logical and controlled psychological activity appropriate to the more mature adult). He has developed a scoring system for the Rorschach assessment of these levels of psychological functioning (Holt and Havel, 1960). He also elaborates the thesis that the Rorschach provides information on the extent to which the subject is capable of identifying with other people. A highly novel suggestion regarding the Rorschach is Holt's attempt to introduce the psychonanalytic concept of the neutralization of sexual and aggressive energy. Psychoanalytic theory indicates that the fixed energy of the organism is originally invested in the sexual and aggressive drives. To the extent that this energy can be neutralized of its sexual and aggressive content, to this extent is energy more freely available to serve other personality functions. Holt indicates that the Rorschach provides data as to the availability of such neutral energy. This concept bears a relationship to contemporary thinking in psychoanalysis having to do with the conflict-free ego.

Holt (1961), applying psychoanalytic theory, grapples with the relationship of fantasy and projective techniques, an issue needing clarification inasmuch as many projective devices require fantasy activity on the part of the subject. He examines the similarities and differences between daydreams and TAT stories. His listing of differences is of significant interest and includes the roles of motives and defenses, quality of consciousness, affective involvement, spontaneity, self-relevance, etc. It is evident that Holt feels that the relationship between fantasy and projective responses needs further elaboration.

It should be noted that there have been other attempts to apply psychological theory to projective methods. Among these are Deutsch's (1954) theoretical formulation of the relevance of field theory for projective methods, Hanfmann's (1952) attempt to integrate these fields on the basis of organismic theory, Holt's (1954) formulations of the relevance of Murray's personology to projective methods, and Murstein's (1959) attempt to deal with adaptation-level theory as it pertains to projective testing. Surely, there will be other attempts at integrations between psychological theory and projective methods, and these should be actively encouraged, not only by the academic theorist, but by the clinician using projective methods. While it is difficult to imagine a single comprehensive theory of human behavior, attempts at understanding the projective technique as a stimulus, the test situation, the interviewing processes that produce the response, and the interpretations of responses are all of value to both the academic theorist and the clinical practitioner.

For the most part, theorists attempting to relate psychoanalytic theory and projective techniques have limited themselves to Freudian theory and its more recent developments in ego psychology. Klopfer (1954) has discussed the relationship between Jungian psychoanalytic ego psychology and the Rorschach technique. This remains one of the rare attempts to relate other psychoanalytic theories to these methods and points to an unexplored area that is of potential significance.

INTERPRETATION OF RESPONSES

Lindzey (1961) has made a significant contribution in delineating a series of assumptions that are involved in the interpretation of responses to projective techniques. While by no means complete, they can serve as an introduction to the important process of interpretation. Obviously, interpretation is a highly complex process precisely because it depends on the clinical skills and theoretical sophistication of the interpreter. Lindzey's catalogue of assumptions follows.

1. To the extent that the subject is confronted with a stimulus that permits a variable response, to this extent will the response be characteristic of the subject. These characteristics of the subject will have varying degrees of subject awareness.

2. The particular responses may be a function of the motives of the individual or may be a product of the individual's defensive organization or, as is often most likely, a combination of both. It is a probable clinical fact that rarely is a motive, particularly an unconscious one, expressed without being filtered through the individual's defenses.

3. Not only are the responses determined by motives and by the individual's defensive organization, but they are also affected by temporary emotional states (e.g., Clark, 1952), the nature of the subject's cognitive abilities (e.g., Webb and Hilden, 1953), verbal productivity (e.g., Lindzey and Goldberg, 1953), the autochthonous qualities of the stimulus (e.g., Siipola, 1950), the type of response set brought to the test by the subject (e.g., Cronbach, 1946), etc. The meaning of the testing situation and par-

ticularly its purpose as it is understood by the subject will determine or affect the nature of the subject's response. The way in which the subject defines the test situation will be influenced by factors such as the nature of the relationship between subject and tester, the identity of the examiner (e.g., Baughman, 1951), the personality of the examiner (e.g., Bellak, 1944), his or her sex (e.g., Clark, 1952), the nature of the physical setting in which the testing occurs (e.g., Weisskopf, 1950), antecedent events preceding the testing situation, prior experience with test situations, the nature of the instructions (e.g., Henry and Rotter, 1956), administration in a group or solitary setting (e.g., Kimble, 1945), presence of the examiner (e.g., Bernstein, 1956), etc. The nature of the social groups in which the subject holds membership and the social values emanating from such membership will determine the subject's definition of the test situation.

4. The responses of the subject in the test situation indicate behavior tendencies in the subject. Whether a behavior tendency may be overtly acted out will depend upon a number of factors, including the subject's internalized values concerning such behavior, the acceptability of such behavior in the particular social situation, etc.

5. The failure of the subject to present a response that is characteristic of other subjects' responses to a particular test stimulus may indicate the significance of this omitted response tendency in the subject's everyday life. Responses that do not differentiate the subject from others are of less significance. Responses that are consistent from test stimulus to test stimulus may reflect important dimensions of the personality, although responses that differ markedly from those that a subject has made in similar situations may also be significant. Interindividual as well as intra-individual deviance is considered of interpretive significance.

6. Responses to the test situation that are not appropriate to the stimulus, for example, idiosyncratic, are more likely to indicate significant dimensions of the subject. Test responses of the subject that are essentially primitive, nonlogical, or bizarre (presumably reflecting primary process content) are more likely to point up significant aspects of the individual than responses that are more rational.

Lindzey recognizes important elements that would be absent if we were to consider the above a complete list of assumptions. These missing elements pertain to differentiating direct, as opposed to symbolic, manifestations of motives; identifying the latent meaning of symbolic responses; differentiating motives that are unconscious from motives of which the subject is aware; determining when a motive will be publicly expressed; identifying responses that reflect more enduring qualities from those that indicate transient states; differentiating motives from defenses. These problems in interpretation indicate that no automatic rule-of-thumb is available for interpreting projective test data, although there have been courageous attempts to justify a "cookbook" approach to interpretation (Meehl, 1954). Such attempts ignore the purpose of projective methods in clinical study, that is, the formulation of a sensitive and dynamic picture of the individual personality, and, moreover, create the danger of the interpreter using "cookbooks" as "dreambooks" (Rapaport, 1950). Holzberg (1957) has dealt with the complexity of the clinical method and why "cookbook" approaches seem inapplicable to the task of such sensitive personality analysis, considering Schafer's (1954) admonition that a test "cannot do its own thinking." Both Tomkins (1947) and Holzberg (1957) have indicated that the time-honored canons of inference and scientific method can be applied to projective test data.

VARIETIES OF PROJECTIVE TECHNIQUES

What follows are descriptions of different projective techniques that have been developed and have been applied in clinical and research situations. While it is not feasible to detail here all of the techniques that would meet the criteria noted earlier, an attempt has been made below to list those techniques that have had relatively active usage and about which there is adequate literature to which the student might be directed.

Lindzey (1959) has delineated the various recommended categories for sorting projective techniques. Certain classifications have distinguished among projective methods on the basis of the nature of the test materials, for example, degree of structure, sensory modality involved, etc. Some sortings have emphasized the way in which the particular technique was developed, for example, theory-derived tests, empirically derived tests, etc. Other classification schemes have attempted to sort projective techniques according to the way in which the test is interpreted, for example, analysis of content, analysis of formal or scorable responses, etc. Other systems have sorted these tests according to their purpose, for example, assessment of motives, psychiatric diagnosis, etc. Some classifications have suggested that the tests might be differentiated in terms of the method of administration, for example, group method, individual method, etc. Finally, some have suggested that the techniques can be sorted on the basis of the type of response that the test elicits from the subject, for example, associations, drawings, completions, etc. It is Lindzey's conclusion that it is this latter type of classification that is the most meaningful because it is more descriptive of the psychological processes that are brought into play by these methods. He therefore suggests the following five categories of projective techniques based on the type of response that is elicited from the subject: association techniques (e.g., Rorschach), construction, techniques (e.g., Thematic Apperception Test), completion techniques (e.g., Sentence Completions), choice or order techniques (e.g., Szondi), and expressive techniques (e.g., Draw-A-Person). It is very evident that even this meaningful classification provides considerable overlap. Therefore, our descriptions of the various techniques that follow are not grouped according to any particular set of criteria, but rather are presented in terms of their active usage in clinical and research situations. What follows is designed to give the beginning student of projective techniques an overview of the broad range of techniques that fall into the category of projective methods.[1]

The Rorschach Test. Probably the most widely used projective technique in the clinical situation is the Rorschach. It was developed by Rorschach (1942) as a way of studying personality through an "experiment in perception." It consists of ten plates that are reproductions of symmetrical inkblots. Half of the blots are achromatic on a white background. The remaining five cards utilize color, with two of these including gray and black along with other colors while the remaining three are multicolored with gray and black elements practically nonexistent. Each card is presented individually to the subject in a standardized order that was originally designated by Rorschach and the subject is asked to state what he sees or what the blots look like or suggest. There are two phases to the administration of the test. During the first phase, the tester records verbatim the subject's responses and his reaction time in giving the first response to each card. He will also usually record the total time taken by the subject on each card. It has become traditional to indicate the position of the card for each response and the amount of rotation of the card that the subject has engaged in. During the second phase, the subject is presented each card once again, his previous responses are read back to him, and he is discreetly asked to point out the areas to which he was responding and to describe as fully as possible what characteristics of the areas influenced him in offering the response that he did.

No projective technique illustrates the multidimensional quality described earlier than does the Rorschach. While the scoring of the Rorschach for the beginner seems rather complicated, each score is rooted in a theoretical rationale. While it is a fact that there have been a number of different scoring schemes that have been advanced, Rickers-Ovsiankina (1960) listing at least eight, the overlaps between these systems are more basic than their differences. Thus, all of these systems of scoring require that each response be scored for its location (where in the blot the subject saw his response), determinant (what characteristic of the blot influenced

[1] In preparing these descriptions, the author utilized Buros (1953, 1959), Lindzey (1961), and Shneidman (1966).

the subject's response), and the content (what the subject actually reported). This general scoring system provides answers to the where-why-what answers. It is not possible to detail all of the scoring categories used in the Rorschach, even those that are agreed upon by different scoring systems. Briefly, however, the scoring of location is to determine the extent to which the subject is responding to the whole blot (W) or to some major (D) or minor aspect of the blot (Dd). If the subject reverses the figure and ground and responds to the white space rather than to the gray, black, or colored portion of the blot, this is also scored (S). In scoring for determinants, the response is scored in terms of whether the form (F) of the blot is essential, whether there was some indication of movement that suggested this phenomenon to the subject, whether variations in the blackness (C'), texture (c) or shading (K) influenced the response, or whether the response was essentially determined by the color (C). Form responses are typically scored in terms of whether the form is appropriate $(F+)$ or inappropriate $(F-)$ and movement responses are usually categorized in terms of whether it is a human figure (M), an animal figure (FM) or some inanimate object (m) that is seen in movement. Often there are combinations of determinants, most frequently form and color, and the extent to which one is more dominant (FC, CF) is reflected in the scoring. Scoring for content is quite simple, and it is most usual to indicate whether the response is that of a human (H), animal (A), object (obj), anatomy (At), sex (Sex), blood (Bl), etc. A number of scoring systems also score for the extent to which a response is popular (P) for which certain norms are available, and the extent to which they are considered original (O), the latter obviously not based on any formal norms but on the experience of the examiner. It is usually scored as original if the response does not occur more frequently than once in a hundred records. The scores are summed for the entire record and, together with the number of responses (R) and the reaction time (RT) to each card, are presented in what is called a psychogram which is essentially a summary of the individual scores and certain ratios derived from them $(M:C, W:M)$.

Many psychologists begin the interpretive process with the psychogram, developing certain propositions about the individual concerned from it, and then content and sequence analyses (examining the order in which the responses are presented on each card) are utilized to test the propositions initially established and to enrich the interpretation by the further development of new hypotheses about the subject. It is apparent that this is not a technique that can be routinely administered in a "cookbook" fashion but requires a sophisticated personality theorist to weave together the various scores and the qualitative content of the record in order to emerge with a picture of the personality. Although responses are scored, the attempt is to conceptualize the total configuration.

Primarily, the instrument yields information regarding the intellectual functioning and the affective life of the subject. While there are some who have suggested that the Rorschach may be a more sensitive indicator of a subject's intellectual functioning than the standard intelligence test, clinical practice generally sees the Rorschach as supplementing the formal description of intelligence yielded by standard intelligence tests but not displacing these important measures of intellectual capability. Thus, the Rorschach would be used to yield information on the subject's level of reality testing, abstracting ability, the logicalness of his thinking processes, the extent to which intellectual abilities are being used in a constructive manner, the degree of conventionality of the person's thinking, etc.

With regard to the subject's affective life, which is probably the more important contribution of the Rorschach, it will yield such information on the adequacy of emotional control, spontaneity, lability, introspectiveness, anxiety and its control, defensive organization, the presence of anxiety and the content in which it is aroused.

There have been differing reports on the reliability and the validity of the Rorschach, and it is evident that there is disagreement as to where the Rorschach stands in meeting the traditional psychometric tests in this area. For the interested student, discussions on the validity and reliability of the Rorschach can be found in chapters by Harris (1960) and Holzberg (1960).

For the student interested in the Rorschach, the most important references are those of Klopfer (Klopfer et al., 1954) and Beck (1945, 1952, 1961), each of which approaches the scoring and interpretation of the Rorschach from a somewhat different orientation. Beck has stressed a more normative approach while Klopfer's approach is more phenomenalistic. Both have unquestionably influenced current practice with the Rorschach on the American scene. The original volume on the Rorschach by the author himself (Rorschach, 1942) still remains one of the significant readings in the Rorschach literature and should not be ignored by the student. At a more advanced level, the work of Schafer (1954) attempting the interpretation of the Rorschach within a psychoanalytic frame of reference remains one of the most important contributions. Harrower and Steiner (1945) have developed a group administration technique for the Rorschach, but there is serious question whether individual and group administration yield the same results. For a somewhat original approach to the Rorschach, Piotrowski (1957) is of interest. For a scathing criticism of the Rorschach in particular, and projective methods in general, the reader is referred to Eysenck (1959). For the student who wishes to use the Rorschach in research, probably Cronbach's (1949) contribution is as relevant today as it was when first published.

Holtzman Inkblot Technique. This inkblot technique (Holtzman *et. al.,* 1961) is an attempt to produce a device that will yield the rich and complex data of the Rorschach within the context of the statistical precision associated with psychometric tests. The authors desired to develop an inkblot technique that would be more reliable, more objective, longer, and more controlled in administration and scoring than the Rorschach. They also felt the need for an equivalent form for retesting and have thus prepared two parallel forms of 45 inkblots each.

The subject reports with one percept for each card, after which there is a specific inquiry. The subject's responses can be scored for 22 variables. Included among these are reaction time, location, space, movement, shape, color, populars, and integration. Scoring for form involves a differentiation between definitiveness and appropriateness of the form. There are content scores for pathognomic verbalization, hostility, anxiety, and barrier and penetration, as well as the usual content categories of human, animal, and anatomy.

Thematic Apperception Test. There seems little question but that the Thematic Apperception Test (Murray, 1943), like the Rorschach, is one of the most widely used of all projective methods. It was designed specifically to stimulate fantasy. It consists of a series of 30 achromatic pictures, usually with one or two people represented, with specific cards being recommended by the author depending on whether the subject is an adult or a child, and whether male or female. Twenty-nine of the 30 cards are pictures that vary in content and have considerable range of ambiguity. The thirtieth card is a blank white card. In actual clinical practice, the specific cards and their number are selected by the psychologist, partly on the basis of what cards research and prior experience have demonstrated to have greater yield in terms of the psychological content desired.

Each card selected is presented to the subject individually (although there have been many modifications of the test for group use) and he is told to make up a story from the picture in terms of these four elements: what is going on in the picture; what the characters are doing, thinking, and feeling; what antecedent events were occurring prior to the scene in the picture; and the outcome of the story. The subject's responses are recorded as nearly verbatim as possible.

In contrast to the Rorschach, there is little standardization of scoring of stories for clinical use. Over twenty methods for interpreting TAT material have been advanced (Shneidman, 1951), although Shneidman indicates that there are certain common steps in the clinical interpretative analysis. Murray (1943) originally suggested an analysis based upon identifying the central figure in a story, specifying the needs operating in this figure, and delineating presses or environmental demands that were impinging upon this figure. To a very great extent, this method, with modifications, is probably the basic method of analysis used in the clinical situation.

For purposes of research, there have been a number of objective methods developed for assessing variables in the test. Some of these have been in the nature content variables (achievement, dependency, aggression, etc.) while other systems of analysis have been based more on formal qualities in the subject's responses (verbal productivity, the ratio of various parts of speech, etc.).

In comparison to the Rorschach, it has been stated that the TAT describes the content of personality while the Rorschach deals with its formal structure. This is essentially correct, but fails to recognize that differentiation between content and structure in the study of human personality is at best an abstraction and that, in actual fact, both instruments tap both domains of personality functioning. As a general principle, it can be stated that the TAT is more likely to be used for assessing motives and conflict areas. The Rorschach is more likely to be utilized to determine personality organization, affective life, anxiety, and reality testing.

There are a number of books that deal with this technique (Bellak, 1954; Henry, 1956; Stein, 1955; Tomkins, 1947) and the interested student will find these of considerable interest. As with Rorschach's own volume, Murray's original manual for this test (1943) probably remains a basic must for the student interested in developing competence in this technique.

Make-A-Picture Story Test. This technique (Shneidman, 1948, 1960) is closely related to the TAT. Instead of a ready-made picture, the subject is given a series of human and animal figures and a series of miniature theatrical backgrounds and is requested to select figures to populate each background. When he has done this, he is asked to create a story as he would for a TAT picture. The test materials consist of 22 background scenes, for example, a living room, bathroom, street, cave, attic, desert, medical, cemetery, etc., and 67 figures of male and female adults, children, animals, etc., appropriately scaled. The figures are in various poses and have different facial expressions. The backgrounds are presented one at a time while all 67 figures are available to the subject. The aim of the author is to investigate the "psycho-social aspects of fantasy production." It originally was developed as a method to study schizophrenic fantasy (Shneidman, 1948). His scoring categories bear upon the problem of interpersonal relationships. These deal with such questions as the number of figures used, the number of times the same figure was used, the actual figures selected, the activity and interaction of the figures, their meaning, etc. The content of the stories are usually interpreted in the manner of TAT stories.

Children's Apperception Test. This is a TAT-like instrument, designed for children between 3 and 10 years of age (Bellak, 1954). They contain animal figures because it is assumed that children will more readily identify with animals than with humans. The 10 pictures were drawn to elicit material relevant to common problem areas faced by children, such as oral conflicts, sibling rivalry, perception of parents, oedipal problems, and general drives and modes of responding to the world.

A supplement to this test, consisting of 10 additional animal scenes, was designed to probe problems of a more transitory nature, such as fears in play situations, interpersonal problems in the classroom, fantasies about being an adult, oral themes, reactions to physical handicaps, competitiveness with others, body image ideas, fears of physical illness, bathroom reactions, and fantasies about pregnancy. Interpretation is primarily qualitative and clinical.

Blacky Pictures. This ingenious technique consists of twelve cartoons depicting various experiences of a dog named Blacky (Blum, 1949, 1950). In addition to Blacky, there are three other characters, mamma, pappa, and Tippy. Neither Blacky nor Tippy are identified by sex or age, and thus the technique can be used for either men or women, children or adults. For male subjects, Blacky is introduced as a "he" and for females as a "she." The twelve cartoons were drawn to elicit responses bearing on 12 significant variables derived from psychoanalytic theory and dealing with either a stage of psychosexual development or an object relationship characteristic of such a stage: oral eroticism, oral sadism, expulsiveness, anal retentiveness, oedipal intensity, masturbation guilt, castration anxiety (penis envy), positive identification, sibling rivalry, guilt feeling, positive ego ideal, and love object (narcissistic or anaclitic). This is one of the very few projective methods that emerged out of a specific theoretical orientation, in this case psychoanalysis. It was the author's claim that the use of animals rather than humans would make responding to the task, considering the variables involved, much less stressful and remote and thus stimulate fantasy production.

The test is administered in several stages. In the first stage, the subject is asked to create a story for each cartoon as in the TAT except for special introductory remarks that structure each picture, for example, "Here is Blacky and his (her) mamma." When all the stories are completed, the subject is asked a number of standard questions, many of them in multiple choice form. These questions elicit specific information about each of the cartoons. After this, the subject is asked to sort the cartoons into the ones he likes and the ones he does not like, and then finally to select the single cartoon he likes most and the one he likes least. As with any projective technique, any spontaneous remarks or behavior elicited from the subject during the testing is recorded.

The test is primarily interpreted qualitatively, although it is possible to develop some degree of quantification by rating each variable as strong or weak. More recently, Blue (1956) has developed a defense preference inquiry, a slight modification of the test, in which the subject is asked to choose alternative responses for each card. Blum offers evidence that the subject's responses can be scored in order to determine the strength of various mechanisms of defense such as projection, reaction formation, regression, and avoidance.

The technique has had wide usage both in research as well as in the clinical setting. It is obviously a technique that will be more acceptable to the examiner with a strong psychoanalytic orientation.

Auditory Apperceptive Techniques. While auditory stimuli have not had very general use, they remain a still unexplored area for the development of projective methods. Shakow and Rosenzweig (1940) modified Skinner's (1936) Verbal Summator which was a record disc consisting of various vowel combinations. Subjects are instructed that the record consists of the speech of a man and are asked to identify what the man is saying. It has, however, had very little usage beyond the specific setting in which it was developed.

One technique in this general area developed by Stone (1950) consists of five 45 rpm records on which have been recorded a number of sounds, for example, wind storm, fog horn, typewriter, etc. There are 10 sets of three sounds each. The subject is asked to make up a story as with the TAT, using each set of three sounds, telling what led up to the sounds, what is happening, and how the story ends. Some norms are provided for order of sounds, description of sounds, length of stories, characters named, situations, and outcomes.

Davids and Murray (1955 developed an auditory apperception technique in which they present incoherent material on a record, material felt to be relevant to eight aspects of personality: pessimism, distrust, anxiety, resentment, egocentricity, optimism, trust, and sociocentricity. The subject is presented with much more material than can possibly be retained and is asked to recall what he can and to indicate which of his recalls he considers the major and which the minor ideas. Scores are obtained for the eight personality variables by computing the proportion of material relevant to each variable recalled.

While all of these techniques have apparently had limited clinical and research usage, they have been applied with some degree of success to individuals who are not able to use visual thematic material, that is, the blind or those who will not or cannot respond to visual stimuli.

Rosenzweig Picture Frustration Study. This test is designed to assess one specific area of behavior, that is, the subject's reaction to frustration conceptualized within the author's frustration theory. This is a paper-and-pencil technique (Rosenzweig, 1945, 1949) in which the subject responds to 24 cartoon-like drawings depicting two persons in an interaction. The test stimuli were selected to represent ego-blocking and super ego-blocking. A frustrating verbalization is directed from one person to the other in each drawing. The subject is asked to provide a response for the individual in the drawing who has been frustrated, by writing the first reply that comes to his mind after seeing the picture in the booklet in which the drawings are presented.

The subject's responses can be scored for a number of variables descriptive of the subject's characteristic manner of dealing with frustration. There are scoring samples provided by the author for the scoring of the direction of the response (extrapunitive, intrapunitive, impunitive). An extrapunitive response is one in which resentment is directed toward the frustrator, for example, "You should be more careful." An intrapunitive response is one in which the resentment is directed toward the self, for example, "It was stupid of me." An impunitive response is one in which the subject minimizes the frustration in the situation, for example, "It really isn't very important." The responses are also scored for the type of reaction (obstacle-dominant, ego-defensive, need-persistive). An obstacle-dominant response is one in which the frustrated object is emphasized in the response. An ego-defensive response is one in which attention is focused on the protection of the thwarted individual. A need-persistive response is one in which the solution of the frustrating problem is paramount.

These two categories (direction and type of response) can be combined and thus yield nine possible variables in which each direction of response is combined with each type of response, for example, extrapunitive-need persistive, intrapunitive-obstacle dominant, etc. The subject's responses are totaled in each of the general and specific categories so that it is possible to derive an overall score that indicates the tendency of the subject to use each mode of response. The test also provides for a popular score, the Group Conformity Rating, which indicates capacity for conformity with conventional behavior under stress.

The interpretation of the subject's performance is based upon the scores of the variables although it is not conformity with conventional behavior under stress.

The interpretation of the subject's performance is based upon the scores of the variables although it is not unusual in the clinical situation to utilize the qualitative content of the specific responses made. It has been Rosenzweig's suggestion that the test taps behavior that is not necessarily unconscious, but, rather, in the realm of what a neutral observer would report. While it has had usage in the clinical situation, it has also been extensively used in research, particularly where the concern has been with the variable of aggressive reaction to frustration. The test has been adapted for use with children, and can be administered readily in a group situation.

Sentence Completion Technique. This technique consists of a number of sentence stems or stubs (e.g.: "I lose ambition when . . ." "Harry was upset when . . .") and the subject is asked to add additional words to these in order to make a complete sentence. The test may be administered in a group where subjects are presented the incomplete sentences on a sheet, or it may be administered individually when the stem or stub is read to the subject and he is asked to respond orally. It is usual to instruct the subject to respond as rapidly as possible since many clinicians feel that this yields more revealing information about the subject.

There have been a number of published completion techniques, the most prominent of which are those by Rotter and Rafferty (1950) and Sacks and Levy (1950). In the former test, which consists of 40 items, the subject's responses are scored for the thematic characteristics of the completions in order to yield a total score of maladjustment. The technique developed by Sacks consists of 60 items that presumably yield information on 15 personality variables. Each personality variable is tapped by four stems designed to yield information on the following: attitude toward mother, father, family unit; attitudes toward women and toward heterosexual relations; attitudes toward friends, superiors at work or school, people supervised, colleagues at work or school, fears, guilt feelings; attitudes toward own abilities, the past and the future, and personal goals. Sentence completion tests have been tailor-made for specific clinical and research uses.

Like the TAT, the sentence completion technique is utilized primarily to assess content (motives, attitudes, conflicts, etc.) rather than the structure of personality. Many clinicians have the impression that this technique is different from the TAT in that it tends to provide content information at a somewhat more conscious level. One variation in the technique that has been developed is the use of first or third persons in the stems or stubs. The rationale advanced for this is that the third person stems are perhaps more capable of assessing more covert aspects of the subject's personality.

There is no single source to which the interested reader may be referred, but there are a book and a number of chapters from three other books that are relevant to this instrument. The book is by Rohde (1957) and the chapters are by Bell (1948), Rotter (1951), and Sacks and Levy (1950).

Insight Test. This is an interesting story completion technique (Sargent, 1953) consisting of a description of 15 commonplace human situations, presenting problems involving parents, friends, etc. The ambiguity of the stimuli is sought by minimal description of the situations and the people involved. The subject is asked to describe what the central character did, and why he did it, and how he felt. The subject is given the idea that the test measures his understanding of others. This type of test consists of more complex stimulus material than the sentence completion test and requires a lengthier and more complex response. The situations tap areas such as family adjustments, religion, attitudes toward the opposite sex, vocational feelings, etc. One of these situations is as follows: "A young man gets the impression that others are discussing him. On several occasions he thinks the conversation has stopped or the subject changed when he entered the room. (a) What did he do and why? (b) How did he feel?" The test's purpose is to determine the nature of the individual's insight into others, both at the affective and cognitive levels. The responses can be analyzed on a formal level in three areas: type of emotional expressions used, various expressions, and the type of conflict solution. Content analyses such as those done on TAT material can also be utilized. A major emphasis of the author is on assessment of the relation between affect and coping and defense mechanisms. She has developed three major scores: affect (A), defense (D) and malignancy (M). She places particular emphasis on the ratio between affect and defense scores (A/D).

Despert Fables. The technique has been developed by Despert (1949) who translated them into English from French, in which they were originally published. The test consists of 10 short ancedotes, each leading to a problem posed for the subject. The stories are read to the child who is requested to solve the problem. The stories are designed to permit evaluation of such areas as castration fears, possessiveness, weaning complex, etc.

An example of one such story that deals with separation anxiety is as follows:

"A daddy and mommy bird and their little baby bird are sleeping in a nest on a branch of a tree. All of a sudden a big wind comes along and shakes the tree, and the nest falls to the ground. The three birds wake up abruptly. The daddy flies to a pine tree, the mother to another pine tree. What is the little bird going to do? He already knows how to fly."

Word Association Test. This test consists of a list of words read to the subject one at a time, with the subject being invited to respond with the very first word that occurs to him. The examiner will usually record not only the subject's response but also his reaction time. The two lists of words that have had considerable usage are those by Kent and Rosanoff (1910a, 1910b) and by Rapaport *et al.* (1946). Very often, word association lists are tailor-made to elicit information specific to certain variables. Responses can be compared to norms that determine whether they are idiosyncratic. The test may be scored according to specific motives implicit in the stimulus words or the responses, for example, sex, aggression, etc. The important clinical application has been in interpreting the subject's associations qualitatively. In addition to interpreting the responses, the examiner will often consider deviations in reaction time since such deviations are taken to reflect disturbance in the area represented by the stimulus word. Rapaport, in developing his word association technique, delineated four aspects for interpretation (Rapaport *et al.*, 1946): close reactions (the subject repeats the stimulus word or defines the word); distant reactions (the subject's response bears little relationship to the stimulus); content disturbances (the subject may indicate unfamiliarity with the word, may misunderstand it, etc.); disturbances in productions of responses (the subject fails to respond or is abnormally delayed). He suggests that the list be administered twice with the subject being encouraged to give the same word as he did the first time.

The best-known usage of the word association technique has been in association with various physiological measures that record the subject's respiration, galvanic skin response, etc., as they occur in response to the stimulus word. Lie detector techniques often are based on the combination of word association performance and accompanying physiological responses. The word association technique has been described by Bell (1948), Rapaport, Schafer, and Gill (1946), and Rotter (1951).

Szondi Test. This easily administered technique consists of 48 photographs of faces of mental patients in European hospitals in the following eight diagnostic categories: homosexuality, sadism, epilepsy, hysteria, catatonic schizophrenia, paranoid schizophrenia, manic depression (depressed), and manic depression (manic). There are 6 photographs in each of the categories. The photographs are presented in a prescribed order in sets of 8, 1 photograph for each diagnostic category. The subject is asked to select 2 photographs he likes the most and the 2 he dislikes the most. He will thus have selected a total of 12 photographs liked the most and 12 disliked the most. It has been recommended by Deri (1949) that the test be administered at least on six different occasions, with at least a day between each testing, and ideally there should be about 10 administrations. The test is scored by merely tallying the subject's likes and dislikes according to the diagnostic category into which they fall.

The rationale of the test is that each of the diagnostic categories represent a different area of tension or drive state, with two categories representing a vector. The vectors and their drives are: S-Vector (sexual) which includes sadistic and homosexual drives; P-Vector (paroxysmal-surprise) which includes the epileptic and hysterical factor; Sch-Vector (self) which includes the catatonic and paranoid factors; C-Vector which includes the depressive and manic factors. Deri has slightly modified this rationale by talking of "need-systems," with each factor representing a need. She believes that the Szondi should be a good measure of tensions and discharges in these need-systems. The basic assumption is that the psychopathological dynamics in the members of each diagnostic category are communicated to and perceived by the subject through the photographs. Choices made by the subject are presumed to be a result of satiation or tension in the various need-systems and to reflect the dynamic processes of sexuality and aggression, cycles of control and discharge, ego structure and function, and object relationships. Where the subject tends to like pictures representing a particular category, the interpretation is that there is tension in this area and that the individual accepts the basic drive and identifies with this dimension. This is likely to be expressed publicly. Where the individual tends to pile up scores of dislike in a particular category the interpretation is that the subject denies or is unable to accept this drive or set of feelings associated with this area. This is likely to be inhibited or repressed behavior. Where the subject tends to build up both positive and negative scores in a specific area, the interpretation is that conflict or ambivalence is present in the particular area. Where the subject does not indicate either like or dislike in a particular area, the interpretation is that this area does not operate as an area of tension. The interpretation is complex since it involves not only the selection and rejection of factors, but also the interplay of need-systems. The theoretical basis for the test seems to be a combination of psychoanalytic and Lewinian topological and vector psychology.

As indicated earlier, it is recommended that the test be repeated at least six times in order to determine which factors remain constant and which are more variable. In this way, the interpreter can establish which responses of the subject are reflective of more momentary states and which are more basic. It has been suggested that the Szondi is especially valuable for demonstrating changes in personality. Deri has suggested using the photographs as stimuli to telling stories, although no verbal responses are normally required.

Although the test emerged out of a hereditary theoretical rationale regarding the effects of recessive genes upon behavior (the test was designed by Szondi to measure unconscious traits associated with recessive genes), the test can be used without any relevance to this theoretical formulation.

Tomkins-Horn Picture Arrangement Test. This technique (Tomkins, 1957, 1959) consists of 25 plates, each of which contains three line drawings that portray the same figure involved in three different but related activities. The authors attempted to sample four areas of psychological functioning: social orientation, optimism-pessimism, level of functioning, and work attitudes. As with the picture arrangement subtest of the Wechsler Adult Intelligence Scale, the subject is asked to indicate the order "which makes the best sense" and to write a statement for each of the three pictures as to what is going on in the drawings. The authors have done extensive work in developing objective methods for dealing with the various arrangements that have been selected by subjects, while the statements describing the situation are interpreted more at a qualitative level.

An interesting premise of this technique is that only those responses that occur with sufficient rarity can be interested. Patterns are used in interpretation only if they can be readily interpreted. Thus, they present a series of patterns that occur in less than five per cent of normal subjects and have a priori significance. In interpreting the results of a given subject, only those response patterns are used that are relatively rare among normals and that have a priori meaning, and are compared with responses of abnormal subjects. They also have conformity keys indicating popular tendencies in responses, but essentially ignore the interpretation of these popular responses. They attach special significance to the drawing placed last in the sequence on any given plate. They have done considerable normative work which has made it possible for them to identify those sequences that are observed infrequently. In fact, this is one of the few projective techniques that has many of the features of a psychometric test, for example, objective scoring, and norms for identifying rare patterns and for classifying subjects in terms of resemblance to abnormal groups.

Four Picture Test. This technique (Van Lennep, 1951) uses four subtly colored pictures, representing different social situations, which are presented at one time to the subject and he is asked to incorporate them into one story. Each picture is vaguely drawn, so that forms and faces are indistinct. Picture I represents being together with one other person (a room with two persons talking across a long table), Picture II being personally alone (a bedroom), Picture III being socially alone (a street scene with a single figure under a lamppost), and Picture IV being together with many others in a group (a tennis match, with observers). The four pictures are put before the subject so as to make a square and the subject is asked to produce one story in which the four pictures are integrated. He is free to use any sequence in the development of a story and may often be asked to make up several integrated stories. Stories may be oral or written. The author claims that better results are obtained if the pictures are withdrawn after a minute or two. Interpretation is essentially through an analysis of the content of the stories (conflicts and themes) as well as through a formal analysis. The latter is accomplished through study of the order and span of combination and number of pictures used. These data may be used to assess the level and manner of intellectual functioning, his organizational ability, flexibility, etc. An interesting basis for interpretation is the time dimension of the fantasy—lack of coherent time in schizophrenics, successive (after each other) time sequences in the stories of depressives, future time emphasis in hysterics, etc. A novel basis for interpretation is the nature of causality in connecting the pictures, for example, making each event the result of the preceding event or making each event a function of a goal to be reached by the performer.

The rationale of the test is that the stories told by the subject reflect the subject's general attitudes toward life, its values and moral standards, his feelings about himself, and the nature of his interpersonal relationships. It differs from the TAT in that it stresses social interaction, is more ambiguous, and requires that the pictures be organized into a sequence. It has been suggested that the FPT has richer possibilities for formal analysis while the TAT provides more personal content.

Kahn Test of Symbol Arrangement. This test (Kahn, 1955), designed to yield a sample of symbolizing behavior, consists of 16 small plastic objects, for example, dogs, hearts, butterflies, anchor, stars, and circle. The subject is shown a strip of felt, divided into 15 numbered parts. He is asked to arrange the objects five times. On the first and second trials, he is asked to arrange the objects in any order he wishes. On the third trial, he is asked to arrange the objects as he did on the second trial (from memory). On the fourth trial, he arranges the objects from "highly liked" to "highly disliked." On the fifth trial, he again arranges them in any way he likes.

After each trial, the subject is asked to name the objects, give reasons for his arrangements and for his likings and dislikings, and free associate to the symbolic meaning of each object. These verbalizations are categorized as to level of symbolization and serve as the basis for the major score —the symbol pattern. After the five trials, he is asked to group the objects into eight categories: Love, Hate, Bad, Good, Living, Dead, Small, and

Large. Kahn (1956, 1957) has developed a scoring system that he feels yields objective criteria about unconscious symbolization processes.

Role Construct Repertory Test. This test (Kelly, 1955) is aimed at role constructs. Methodologically, the test is an application of the familiar concept-formation test procedure. It uses as "objects" those persons with whom the subject has had to deal in his daily living. Instead of sorting blocks or objects, the subject sorts people. Unlike the traditional concept-formation test, the test is concerned with how the particular items are dealt with, not merely the level of abstraction involved. It is concerned with the subject's relations to particular people.

The subject is given a *Role Title List* usually in written form. He is asked to respond to the list by designating by name the personal identities of the people in his own realm of experience who fit the role titles, for example, "a teacher you liked," "your wife or girl friend," "your mother," "the most intelligent person whom you know personally," etc. He may be asked to write his responses within rectangular spaces on a single blank form.

Following the completion of the responses to the Role Title List, the examiner selects three people designated for three roles by the subject and asks, "In what important way are two of them alike but different from the third?" He then instructs the subject to do the same for a variety of other combinations of three people. These provide information about the constructs used by the subject to describe interpersonal relationships.

The results can be subjected to formal as well as clinical analysis. The number of constructs gives information on the subject's role construction system. Constructs that are repeated on different figures can be considered as evidence of permeability of constructs. The number of figures to which the construct is applied suggests the range of permeability. Permeability is an indication of the availability of a construct for meeting varied life situations. Other analyses are in terms of fields of permeability, contrasting constructs, unique figures, and superficial and vague constructs.

Draw-A-Person Test. Goodenough (1926), prior to the projective technique movement, developed criteria for the scoring of the drawing of the human figure by children for purposes of intellectual measurement. She very early realized, and reported, the degree of variability in the quality of drawings from individual to individual, even with the same level of intelligence. Her own observations, as well as those of clinical psychologists using the technique as a measure of intelligence, soon identified the technique as potentially capable of illuminating certain aspects of personality. In its broader sense, the interpretation of this technique rests very heavily on self theory and body image theory (Schilder, 1935). Its theoretical rationale has been most explicitly formulated by Machover (1948) as a method to assess "impulses, anxieties, conflicts, and compensations" in the subject.

The administration is remarkably simple. The subject is asked to draw a whole person. Neither sex, age, dress, or attitude is specified. After the completion of this first part of the test, he is then asked to draw a person of the opposite sex. The subject is usually provided with a pencil that has an eraser and a white sheet of paper of standard size (8½ x 11 in.). In the clinical situation, the subject's performance is carefully observed and any verbal statements or other relevant behaviors are noted. The interpretation uses not only the finished product of the drawings of the subject, but any comments as well as unusual behaviors displayed during the performance on the task. Some clinicians use a standard inquiry at the conclusion of the drawing of both figures, asking a number of questions in order to procure more information that may be relevant in the personality analysis.

Both the content of the picture as well as the quality of productions are used in the analysis. Content issues pertain to the areas of the body with which the subject seems to be having difficulty, areas omitted, whether the subject shows impaired performance in drawing one sex fiigure as opposed to the other, etc. Formal characteristics analyzed are those having to do with the size of the drawing, where it is placed on the page, the line emphasis, erasures, etc. Formal artistic training is usually not considered a bar to the use of this technique on the presumption that any creative product is a reflection of its creator.

There have been no specific interpretive rules developed that have been used generally in clinical practice. Although simple to administer, its interpretation is complex. The clinician analyzes the drawing and its associated material in terms of some clinical and theoretical understanding of self theory and body image theory. The basic assumption is that the subject's experience with his own body results in symbolic investments in different parts of the human figure drawn. For the interested student, Machover's book (1948) is a good introduction. She discusses each body part in terms of its symbolic, unconscious meaning, for example, use of buttons and dependency, hair emphasis and virility, etc. It is evident that symbolic interpretations must take account of both the sex of the subject and the sex of the drawing, as well as questioning the absolute and universal meaning of symbols. Hammer's volume (1958) provides one of the more systematic discussions of drawings as projective techniques. Figure 4–1 presents drawings produced by deviant subjects.

Fig. 4-1. Draw-a-Person Test. Upper left—chronic undifferentiated schizophrenic, sixty-three-year-old man, IQ 113; upper right—narcissistic character disorder, forty-year-old woman, IQ 137; lower left—adjustment reaction of adolescence with depressive features, fifteen-year-old boy, IQ 110; lower right—brain syndrome, sixty-three-year-old man, IQ 101.

House-Tree-Person Technique. With this technique (Buck, 1948a, 1948b, 1949), the subject is requested to draw a house, a tree, and a person on separate sheets of paper. While the subject is drawing, the examiner observes the subject's sequence, behavior, tempo, etc. After all of the drawings are completed, the examiner carries out an extensive interview. Buck selected these three items for his technique because of their universal familiarity and their ability to stimulate free verbalizations. He has advanced the idea that each drawing is a "self-portrait" and that the drawings may be interpreted in terms of their personal significance for the subject.

Bender Visual Motor Gestalt Test. This test was formally introduced by Bender (1946) as a method to study visual-motor coordination. The test originally developed out of Gestalt Perception Psychology and consists of nine geometrical figures composed of circles, lines, or dots, each figure on a separate card, which is presented to the subject one at a time. He is asked to make a copy of each figure. Some examiners ask the subject to draw from memory as many figures as they can remember.

The rationale of the test is embedded in both Gestalt and psychoanalytic psychology. Gestalt psychology postulates a biological principle that influences the perceptual experience in terms of a trend toward completion and reorganization. It further assumes that destructive forces in the personality will introduce characteristic distortions of patterns. Bender (1938) offers evidence of how reproductions of the figures are distorted in various psychopathological conditions. Hutt and Briskin (1960) have applied psychoanalytic principles, particularly the psychology of symbolism, to the reproductions, for example, phallic interpretations of pointed objects and circles, etc. It has also been interpreted in terms of the formal characteristics used in the Draw-A-Person Test, for example, heaviness of line, erasures, planning ability in the use of space, etc. Pascal and Suttell (1951) have developed an objective scoring system for research applications. Figure 4–2 consists of drawings made by deviant subjects.

Finger Painting. Napoli (1946, 1947, 1951) stimulated interest in the technique of finger painting as a diagnostic as well as therapeutic device. The subject is given a wet piece of paper and is permitted to select whatever colors of paint he wants. The instructions are "to cover the whole sheet of paper and to go off the sides of the paper." Throughout the subject's performance as well as during the cleanup period, he is encouraged to verbalize regarding the painting experience or the "finished product." There are very few guides to interpretation that have been developed. Most commonly, interpretation is based on the analysis of the motor behavior, paint preference, formal and symbolic characteristics of the painting, and the subject's verbalizations. It has often been used as an accompaniment to psychotherapy where a series of such unstructured paintings are collected in order to assess the progress of treatment. It is one of the least structured of projective techniques and comes closest

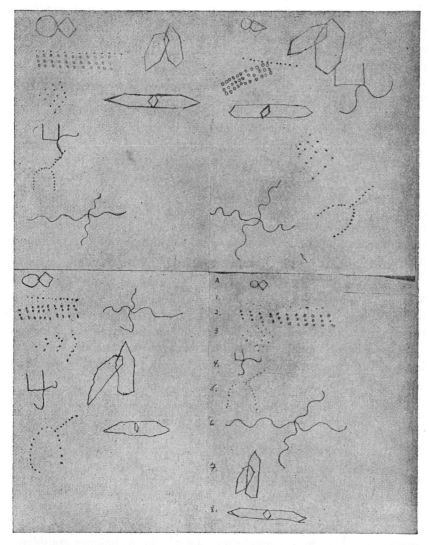

Fig. 4–2. Bender Visual Motor Gestalt Test. Upper left—Adolescent adjustment reaction, fifteen-year-old girl, IQ 112; upper right—epileptic, seventeen-year-old girl, IQ 90; lower left—chronic brain syndrome, sixty-four-year-old woman, IQ 103; lower right—narcissistic character disorder, forty-year-old woman, IQ 137.

to "free association" on a graphic-motor level. It is adaptable to group or individual administration.

World Test. This technique (Bolgar and Fischer, 1947; Buhler and Kelley, 1941; Lowenfield, 1939) consists of a large number of small objects

(150 or more) such as houses, people, soldiers, automobiles, and trees. It is quite unstructured and permissive. The subject is invited to do whatever he likes with these objects, and to use as many as he cares to—"Now you may play." The examiner discusses the final constructions with the subject, making inquiry about the events, their meanings, etc., accompanying the world building activity.

Interpretation is essentially qualitative. Analysis is in terms of choice and number of objects, variety of objects chosen, amount of space used, and spontaneous verbalizations. Buhler *et al.* (1951) has identified five types of symptom worlds produced by subjects: aggression, where killing and accidents take place; empty, where few objects are utilized in a relatively sparse and unpopulated world; closed, where various types of enclosures are used; chaotic, where the pieces do not seem to have any coherent integration; and rigid, where the subject's productions are over-symmetrical. Buhler feels that two or more symptom worlds is diagnostic of psychopathology.

Psychodrama. This method of assessing personality originated with Moreno (1946) who has used it both as a therapeutic as well as a diagnostic device. There are many variations that have been used but in all the subject is requested to act out publicly some personally significant experience or interaction. In some instances, the subject may select the incident to be presented, while in others he may be assigned a particular role in a particular drama. The subject may interact with other objects, or he may play-act with people who have been trained to present a somewhat standard stimulus situation and who are described by Moreno as "auxiliary egos." This method permits the individual to act out his wishes, conflicts, and fantasies.

The interpretation of the subject's behavior is almost entirely qualitative with little objective criteria for the interpreter. The manner in which the subject acts out his role is compared to the performance of other subjects. Sometimes the subject is asked to create an imaginary person and to build a relationship. The observer notes the kind of relationship constructed and how he communicates. Of all the techniques considered here, it provides observation of social interactional behavior that is closer to real-life behavior than any of the other projective methods. Moreno feels that the spontaneity of psychodrama is of importance in uncovering and understanding conflicts and how they are dealt with.

SUMMARY

Interest in projective methods emerged from a dissatisfaction with psychometric methods of personality measurement and from a search for methods more compatible with the clinical stress on holism, phenomenology, unconscious processes, and content more compatible with that of the clinical interview. Projective techniques have been criticized for failing to meet psychometric standards of objectivity, reliability, validity, and specification of variables being studied and for operating outside the realm of contemporary psychological theory. An attempt has been made in the present chapter to define projective techniques in terms of the stimulus properties, the nature of the responses elicited, and the method of interpretation applied. Contributing to confusion in the definition of projective techniques has been the fact that "projective" is a broader conception than "projection" as the latter is used in psychoanalytic theory. The relationship between projective methods and psychological theory has been examined and the relevance of learning theory, perception theory, and psychoanalytic theory considered within this context. It is evident that it has been psychoanalytic theory that has made substantive contributions to the understanding of the elicitation of responses and their interpretation. Fundamental assumptions in the interpretation of projective test data have been outlined, although the process of interpretation admittedly still remains complex. Finally, various projective methods have been described in terms of their theoretical rationale, systems of administration and scoring, and practical applications.

REFERENCES

ABT, L. E. 1950. A theory of projective psychology. In L. E. ABT and L. BELLAK (eds.), *Projective psychology: Clinical approaches to the total personality.* New York: Knopf.

ABT, L. E. and BELLAK, L. (eds.). 1950. *Projective psychology: Clinical approaches to the total personality.* New York: Knopf.

ANDERSON, H. H., and ANDERSON, G. L. (eds.). 1951. *An introduction to projective techniques.* New York: Prentice-Hall.

ATKINSON, J. W. (ed.). 1958. *Motives in fantasy, action, and society.* Princeton, N. J.: Van Nostrand.

AULD, F. 1954. Contributions of behavior theory to projective techniques. *J. proj. Tech.,* **18**, 421–26.

BAUGHMAN, E. E. 1951. Rorschach scores as a function of examiner differences. *J. proj. Tech.,* **15**, 243–49.

BECK, S. J. 1945. *Rorschach's test.* Vol. II. *A variety of personality pictures.* New York: Grune & Stratton.

BECK, S. J. 1952. *Rorschach's test.* Vol. III. *Advances in interpretation.* New York: Grune & Stratton.

BECK, S. J., BECK, A. G., LEVITT, E. E., and MOLISH, H. B. 1961. *Rorschach's test I: Basic processes.* (3d rev. ed.) New York: Grune & Stratton.

BELL, J. E. 1948. *Projective techniques: A dynamic approach to the study of personality.* New York: Longmans, Green.

BELLAK, L. 1944. The concept of projection: An experimental investigation and study of the concept. *Psychiatry*, **7**, 353–70.

BELLAK, L. 1950. On the problems of the concept of projection. In L. E. ABT and L. BELLAK (eds.), *Projective psychology: Clinical approaches to the total personality.* New York: Knopf.

BELLAK, L. 1954. *The Thematic Apperception Test and the Children's Apperception Test in clinical use.* New York: Grune & Stratton.

BENDER, L. 1938. *A visual motor gestalt test and its clinical use.* Research Monograph No. 3. New York: American Orthopsychiatric Association.

BENDER, L. 1946. *Instructions for the use of the Visual Motor Gestalt Test.* New York: American Orthopsychiatric Association.

BERNSTEIN, L. 1956. The examiner as inhibiting factor in clinical testing. *J. consult. Psychol.*, **20**, 287–90.

BLUM, G. S. 1949. A study of the psychoanalytic theory of psychosexual development. *Genet. Psychol. Monogr.*, **39**, 3–99.

BLUM, G. S. 1950. *The Blacky Pictures: Manual of instructions.* New York: Psychological Corporation.

BLUM, G. S. 1956. Defense preferences in four countries. *J. proj. Tech.*, **20**, 33–41.

BOLGAR, H., and FISCHER, L. K. 1947. Personality projection in the World Test. *Am. J. Orthopsychiat.*, **17**, 117–28.

BROWNELL, M. H., and GOSS, A. E. 1957. Stimulus-response analysis of inferences from projective test behavior. *J. Pers.*, **25**, 525–38.

BRUNER, J. S. 1948. Perceptual theory and the Rorschach test. *J. Pers.*, **17**, 157–68.

BUCK, J. N. 1948a. The H-T-P test. *J. clin. Psychol.*, **4**, 151–59.

BUCK, J. N. 1948b. The H-T-P technique: A qualitative and quantitative scoring manual. Part I. *J. clin. Psychol.*, **4**, 319–96.

BUCK, J. N. 1949. The H-T-P technique: A qualitative and quantitative scoring manual. Part II. *J. clin. Psychol.*, **5**, 37–76.

BUHLER, C., and KELLEY, G. 1941. *The World Test: A measurement of emotional disturbance.* New York: Psychological Corporation.

BUHLER, C., LUMRY, G. K., and CARROL, H. S. 1951. World Test standardization studies. *J. Child Psychiat.*, **2**, 1–81.

BUROS, O. K. 1953. *The fourth mental measurements yearbook.* Highland Park, N.J.: Gryphon.

BUROS, O. K. 1959. *The fifth mental measurements yearbook.* Highland Park, N.J.: Gryphon.

CATTELL, R. B. 1957. *Personality and motivation structure and measurement.* New York: Harcourt, Brace & World.

CLARK, R. A. 1952. The projective measurement of experimentally induced levels of sexual motivation. *J. exp. Psychol.*, **44**, 391–99.

CRONBACH, L. J. 1946. Response sets and test validity. *Educ. Psychol. Measmt.*, **6**, 475–94.

CRONBACH, L. J. 1949. Statistical methods applied to Rorschach scores: A review. *Psychol. Bull.*, **46**, 393–429.

DAVIDS, A., and MURRAY, H. A. 1955. Preliminary appraisal of an auditory projective technique for studying personality and cognition. *Am. J. Ortho-psychiat.*, **25**, 543–54.

DERI, S. 1949. *Introduction to the Szondi test: Theory and practice.* New York: Grune & Stratton.

DESPERT, L. J. 1949. Dreams in children of preschool age. *Psychoanal. Study Child*, **34**, 141–80.

DEUTSCH, M. 1954. Field theory and projective techniques. *J. proj. Tech.*, **18**, 427–34.

ERIKSEN, C. W. 1954. Needs in perception and projective techniques. *J. proj. Tech.*, **18**, 435–40.

EYSENCK, H. J. 1959. Personality tests: 1950–1955. In G. W. T. H. FLEM-ING, *Recent progress in psychology.* Vol. III. London: Churchill.

FRANK, L. K. 1939. Projective methods for the study of personality. *J. Psychol.*, **8**, 389–413.

FRANK, L. K. 1948. *Projective methods.* Springfield, Ill.: Charles C Thomas.

FREUD, S. 1911. Psychoanalytic notes on an autobiographical account of a case of paranoia (*dementia paranoides*). In J. STRACHEY (ed.), *The complete psychological works of Sigmund Freud.* Vol. XII. London: Hogarth, 1958.

GOODENOUGH, F. L. 1926. *Measurement of intelligence by drawings.* New York: Harcourt, Brace & World.

GOSS, A. E., and BROWNELL, M. H. 1957. Stimulus-response concepts and principles applied to projective test behavior. *J. Pers.*, **25**, 505–23.

HAMMER, E. F. (ed.). 1958. *The clinical application of projective drawings.* Springfield, Ill.: Charles C Thomas.

HANFMANN, E. 1952. William Stern on "Projective Techniques." *J. Pers.*, **21**, 1–21.

HARRIS, J. G. 1960. Validity: The search for a constant in a universe of variables. In M. A. RICKERS-OVSIANKINA (ed.), *Rorschach psychology.* New York: Wiley.

HARROWER, M. R., and STEINER, M. E. 1945. *Large-scale Rorschach techniques.* Springfield, Ill.: Charles C Thomas.

HENRY, E., and ROTTER, J. B. 1956. Situational influence on Rorschach responses. *J. consult. Psychol.*, **20**, 457–62.

HENRY, W. E. 1956. *The analysis of fantasy: The Thematic Apperception Technique in the study of personality.* New York: Wiley.

HOLT, R. R. 1954. Implications of some contemporary personality theories for Rorschach rationale. In B. KLOPFER, M. D. AINSWORTH, W. G. KLOPFER, and R. R. HOLT, *Developments in the Rorschach technique.* Vol. I. *Technique and theory.* New York: Harcourt, Brace & World.

HOLT, R. R. 1961. The nature of TAT stories as cognitive products: A psychoanalytic approach. In J. KAGAN and G. LESSER (eds.), *Contemporary issues in thematic apperceptive methods.* Springfield, Ill.: Charles C Thomas.

HOLT, R. R., and HAVEL, J. 1960. A method for assessing primary and secondary process in the Rorschach. In M. A. RICKERS-OVSIANKINA (ed.), *Rorschach psychology.* New York: Wiley.

HOLTZMAN, W. H., THORPE, J. S., SWARTZ, J. D., and HERRON, E. W. 1961.

Inkblot perception and personality: Holtzman inkblot technique. Austin, Texas: Univer. of Texas Press.

HOLZBERG, J. D. 1957. The clinical and scientific methods: Synthesis or antithesis? *J. proj. Tech.*, **21**, 227–42.

HOLZBERG, J. D. 1960. Reliability re-examined. In M. A. RICKERS-OVSIANKINA (ed.), *Rorschach psychology*. New York: Wiley.

HOLZBERG, J. D. 1963. Projective techniques and resistance to change in psychotherapy as viewed through a communications model. *J. proj. Tech.*, **27**, 430–35.

HUTT, M. L., and BRISKIN, G. J. 1960. *The clinical use of the revised Bender-Gestalt test.* New York: Grune & Stratton.

KAHN, T. C. 1955. Personality projection on culturally structured symbols. *J. proj. Tech.*, **19**, 431–42.

KAHN, T. C. 1956. Test of Symbol Arrangement: Administration and scoring. *Percept. mot. Skills Monogr. Suppl.*, **6**, No. 4.

KAHN, T. C. 1957. The Kahn Test of Symbol Arrangement: Clinical manual. *Percept. mot. Skills Monogr. Suppl.*, **7**, No. 1.

KELLY, G. A. 1955. *The psychology of personal constructs.* New York: Norton.

KENT, G. H., and ROSANOFF, A. J. 1910a. A study of association in insanity. *Am. J. Insanity*, **67**, 317–90.

KENT, G. H., and ROSANOFF, A. J. 1910b. A study of association in insanity. *Am. J. Insanity*, **67**, 37–96.

KIMBLE, G. A. 1945. Social influence on Rorschach records. *J. abnorm. soc. Psychol.*, **40**, 89–93.

KLOPFER, B. 1954. Rorschach hypotheses and ego psychology. In B. KLOPFER, M. D. AINSWORTH, W. G. KLOPFER, and R. HOLT, *Developments in the Rorschach technique.* Vol. I. *Technique and theory.* New York: Harcourt, Brace & World.

KLOPFER, B., AINSWORTH, M. D., KLOPFER, W. G., and HOLT, R. R. 1954. *Developments in the Rorschach technique.* Vol. I. *Technique and theory.* New York: Harcourt, Brace & World.

KRIS, E. 1952. *Psychoanalytic explorations in art.* New York: International Universities Press.

LINDZEY, G. 1959. On the classification of projective techniques. *Psychol. Bull.*, **56**, 158–68.

LINDZEY, G. 1961. *Projective techniques and cross cultural research.* New York: Appleton-Century-Crofts.

LINDZEY, G., and GOLDBERG, M. 1953. Motivational differences between male and female as measured by the Thematic Apperception Test. *J. Pers.*, **22**, 101–17.

LOWENFELD, M. 1939. The world pictures of children: A method of recording and studying them. *Brit. J. Med. Psychol.*, **18**, 65–101.

McCLELLAND, D. C. 1957. Toward a science of personality psychology. In DAVID and VON BRACKEN (eds.), *Perspectives in personality theory.* London: Tavistock.

MACHOVER, K. 1948. *Personality projection in the drawing of the human figure.* Springfield, Ill.: Charles C Thomas.

MEEHL, P. E. 1954. *Clinical versus statistical prediction.* Minneapolis: Univer. of Minnesota Press.

MORENO, J. L. 1946. *Psychodrama.* New York: Beacon House.

MURRAY, H. A. 1933. The effect of fear upon estimates of the maliciousness of other personalities. *J. soc. Psychol.,* 4, 310–39.

MURRAY, H. A. 1938. *Explorations in personality.* New York: Oxford.

MURRAY, H. A. 1943. *Thematic Apperception Test manual.* Cambridge, Mass.: Harvard Univer. Press.

MURRAY, H. A. 1951. Foreword. In H. H. ANDERSON and G. L. ANDERSON (eds.), *An introduction to projective techniques.* Englewood Cliffs, N.J.: Prentice-Hall.

MURSTEIN, B. I. 1959. A conceptual model of projective techniques applied to stimulus variations with thematic techniques. *J. consult. Psychol.,* 23, 3–14.

MURSTEIN, B. I. 1963. *Theory and research in projective techniques (emphasizing the TAT).* New York: Wiley.

NAPOLI, P. J. 1946. Finger-painting and personality diagnosis. *Genet. Psychol. Monogr.,* 34, 129–230.

NAPOLI, P. J. 1947. Interpretative aspects of finger-painting. *J. Psychol.,* 23, 93–132.

NAPOLI, P. J. 1951. Finger painting. In H. H. ANDERSON and G. L. ANDERSON (eds.), *An introduction to projective techniques.* Englewood Cliffs, N.J.: Prentice-Hall.

PASCAL, G. R., and SUTTELL, B. J. 1951. *The Bender-Gestalt test.* New York: Grune & Stratton.

PIOTROWSKI, Z. A. 1957. *Perceptanalysis.* New York: Macmillan.

RAPAPORT, D. 1950. The theoretical implications of diagnostic testing procedures. *Int. Cong. Psychiat. Reports,* 2, 241–71.

RAPAPORT, D. 1952. Projective techniques and the theory of thinking. *J. proj. Tech.,* 16, 269–75.

RAPAPORT, D., GILL, M., and SCHAFER, R. 1946. *Diagnostic psychological testing: The theory, statistical evaluation and diagnostic application of a battery of tests.* Chicago: Year Book Publishers.

RICKERS-OVSIANKINA, M. A. 1960. *Rorschach psychology.* New York: Wiley.

ROHDE, A. R. 1957. *Sentence completion method: Its diagnostic and clinical application to mental disorders.* New York: Ronald.

RORSCHACH, H. 1942. *Psychodiagnostics: A diagnostic test based on perception.* (4th ed.) New York: Grune & Stratton. (Originally published in 1921).

ROSENZWEIG, S. 1945. The picture-association method and its application in a study of reactions to frustration. *J. Pers.,* 14, 3–23.

ROSENZWEIG, S. 1949. *Psychodiagnosis.* New York: Grune & Stratton.

ROTTER, J. B. 1951. Word association and completion methods. In H. H. ANDERSON, and G. L. ANDERSON (eds.), *An introduction to project techniques.* Englewood Cliffs, N.J.: Prentice-Hall.

ROTTER, J. B., and RAFFERTY, J. E.   1950.   *Manual for the Rotter Incomplete Sentences Blank, College Form.*   New York: Psychological Corporation.

SACKS, J. M., and LEVY, S.   1950.   The sentence completion test.   In L. E. ABT and L. BELLAK (eds.), *Projective psychology: Clinical approaches to the total personality.*   New York: Knopf.

SARGENT, H. D.   1953.   *The insight test: A verbal projective test for personality study.*   New York: Grune & Stratton.

SCHAFER, R.   1954.   *Psychoanalytic interpretation in Rorschach testing: Theory and application.*   New York: Grune & Stratton.

SCHILDER, P.   1935.   *The image and appearance of the human body.*   Psyche Monograph, No. 4.   London: Routledge & Kegan Paul.

SHAKOW, D., and ROSENZWEIG, S.   1940.   The use of the Tautophone ("Verbal Summator") as an auditory apperceptive test for the study of personality.   *Charact. & Pers.*, 8, 216–26.

SHNEIDMAN, E. S.   1948.   Schizophrenia and the MAPS test: A study of certain formal psychosocial aspects of fantasy production in schizophrenia as revealed by performance on the Make a Picture Story (MAPS) test.   *Genet. Psychol. Monogr.*, 38, 145–224.

SHNEIDMAN, E. S.   1951.   *Thematic test analysis.*   New York: Grune & Stratton.

SHNEIDMAN, E. S.   1960.   The MAPS test with children.   In A. I. RABIN and M. R. HAWORTH (eds.), *Projective techniques with children.*   New York: Grune & Stratton.

SHNEIDMAN, E. S.   Projective techniques in America.   In B. WOLMAN (ed.), *Handbook of clinical psychology.*   New York: McGraw-Hill, in press.

SIIPOLA, E. M.   1950.   The influence of color on reactions to ink blots.   *J. Pers.*, 18, 358–82.

SKINNER, B. F.   1936.   The Verbal Summator and a method for the study of latent speech.   *J. Psychol.*, 2, 71–107.

STEIN, M. I.   1955.   *The Thematic Apperception Test: An introductory manual for its clinical use with adults.*   (Rev. ed.)   Cambridge, Mass.: Addison-Wesley.

STONE, D. R.   1950.   A recorded auditory apperception test as a new projective technique.   *J. Psychol.*, 29, 349–53.

SYMONDS, P. M.   1949.   *Adolescent fantasy: An investigation of the picture-story method of personality study.*   New York: Columbia Univer. Press.

THURSTONE, L. L.   1948.   The Rorschach in psychological science.   *J. abnorm. soc. Psychol.*, 43, 471–75.

TOMKINS, S. S.   1947.   *The Thematic Apperception Test.*   New York: Grune & Stratton.

TOMKINS, S. S.   1957.   *The Tomkins-Horn Picture Arrangement Test.*   New York: Springer.

TOMKINS, S. S.   1959.   *PAT interpretation.*   New York: Springer.

VAN LENNEP, D. J.   1951.   The Four-Picture Test.   In H. H. ANDERSON and G. L. ANDERSON (eds.), *An introduction to projective techniques.*   Englewood Cliffs, N.J.: Prentice-Hall.

WEBB, W. B., and HILDEN, A. H.   1953.   Verbal and intellectual ability as factors in projective-test results.   *J. proj. Tech.*, 17, 102–3.

WEISSKOPF, E. A. 1950. An experimental study of the effect of brightness and ambiguity on projection in the Thematic Apperception Test. *J. Psychol.*, 29, 407–16.

WHITE, R. W. 1944. Interpretation of imaginative productions. In J. McV. HUNT (ed.), *Personality and the behavior disorders.* New York: Ronald.

5

Objective Personality Tests and Computer Processing of Personality Test Data

RALPH MASON DREGER [*]

In the *Mental Measurements Yearbooks* (e.g., Buros, 1959) and *Tests in Print* (Buros, 1961), many hundreds of tests are listed, and those listed are not all that have been published. Undoubtedly, many hundreds more have not been published. Indeed, to paraphrase an ancient apothegm, "Of the making of many tests there is no end."

The existence of this huge volume of tests, however, most of them classifiable in some manner as psychological tests, does not mean that psychologists, even clinical psychologists, utilize a large number of tests in their work. Sundberg (1961), in one of the best surveys ever made of the use of tests in clinical installations, undergirded what is fairly evident to the discerning observer—that psychologists use relatively few measurement instruments. The range of the number of tests used by various *agencies* was from 5 to 82, and the median was 26. Emphasis is placed on "agencies," for it is not uncommon for individual psychologists to develop a canon (more formally called a "test battery") of only five or six tests. And some few lean on one or two instruments almost exclusively. While it may be contended that it is the clinician himself who is important, not the tests, the weight of evidence appears to rest with tests used appropriately as compared with unaided clinical judgment (Meehl, 1954; Taft, 1959),

[*] Ralph Mason Dreger, Ph.D. (University of Southern California), Professor of Psychology, Louisiana State University.

154

dissenting voices to the contrary (Holt, 1958; McHugh *et al.*, 1959) notwithstanding.

It is, then, the purpose of this chapter to provide the clinical psychologist or prospective clinician a rational guide through one major portion of the vast mass of so-called objective personality tests, so that he can choose wisely among them, and, for what has become increasingly imperative for scientific usage of objective tests in the present era, can utilize effectively the automated techniques developed in recent years in connection with some of the more prominent measuring instruments.

Some degree of objectivity obtains in all tests, and even the most objective test is not free from subjectivity. Ideally, though, an objective test, lying along the continuum from subjectivity to objectivity, yields the same set of scores to anyone who follows the rules prescribed for that test. In practice, the rules may be inadequate, and the test itself or the administrator or scorer may not conform to the rules. If, however, agreement obtains among those who are trained to follow the rules pertaining to a specific test, the test may be regarded as objective: The higher the degree of agreement, the greater the objectivity of the personality test.

Personality is assumed here to be a broad construct (Dreger, 1962): "Personality consists of the organized functions of the individual." These functions may include the operations of DNA molecules, the passage of a nerve impulse, the flexing of a set of muscles, a sense of "organ inferiority" (Adler), a dynamic trait of *"tough-mindedness,"* and the role of "big businessman." Hence, any measure of any of these personality functions is a "personality test," including tests of physiological and psychophysical functions, intelligence and aptitude, achievement, temperament, interests, values, attitudes, and interpersonal relations. For continuity with common usage, however, temperament is considered here to be equivalent to "personality," and, as in the previous edition of this text (Berdie, 1954), interests and values are treated separately. In addition, some attention is paid to (roughly) psychophysiological and psychomotor measures.

GENERAL CONSIDERATIONS RELATED TO CONSTRUCTION AND USAGE OF OBJECTIVE TESTS

For persons referred by self or others to him, the psychological clinician is expected to answer definite questions. Beyond the specific referral question or questions, however, are other professional considerations. The psychologist, who of all persons must be aware of the total personality even when dealing directly with only part of it, is less than a psychologist if he is not concerned about the whole person. It almost goes without saying that he must answer the referral question if it is within his power to do so. But, whatever the source of referral, while the psychologist is evaluating the person before him, that person is *his* patient or examinee, and his responsibility for that particular period is not only to the referral source but also to the person. It may be, and often is, the case that the psychologist sees far more to a person's problems than the referral question implies. It is his duty to pursue, then, whatever his professional judgment dictates.

It is at this point that objective personality tests enter. Only one set of controlled observations among others, these tests are nevertheless the best means available to shorten the observational task required if the psychologist is going to be a "compleat clinician." He uses these tests, and now the automated techniques recently made available, to increase his observational powers, to speed up the observational process, and thus to free himself for the task of judgment required when the results of all his observations are in.

Assume that the clinical psychologist has had an adequate background in statistics. That is, he has learned the rationale and techniques of both sampling and descriptive statistics, which are employed in the construction of psychological tests, and he has a knowledge of the assumptions and limitations of these statistics when applied to the refractory data of personality. Building on such a foundation, the psychologist adds a more specialized knowledge of test theory (Gulliksen, 1950) whereby he comes to grips with the mathematical equations embodied in test scores, the types of errors involved in obtaining these scores, what reliabilities and validities pertain to tests of various lengths and to the statistical populations on the basis of which his tests are standardized, the relative values of different methods of scoring and standardizing test scores, how items (questions or statements) may best be selected to maximize the value of a test, and what relation psychological tests have to the body of psychological theory (Loevinger, 1957). The psychologist has need, further, of practical application of theory to specific types of tests and representative tests (Freeman, 1962). It is scarcely conceivable that a psychologist who uses objective tests at all (and now even projective tests) can avoid tests that have been factor-analyzed. Consequently, he requires at least a nodding acquaintance with factor analysis [1] (Harman, 1960).

What the issues are in the measurement of personality (Messick and Foss, 1962) and especially in the field of concern here, objective personality tests (Bass and Berg, 1959), must be more or less familiar to the clinician in order for him to select his tests and interpret their results. Issues relating to the "faking" of tests are well known to the intelligent layman. But subtler issues like "response sets" or styles are not evident even to the psychologist unless he is cognizant of the research literature revealing them, response styles such as *acquiescence* and *social desirability*, and deviation patterns according to the *deviation hypothesis*. At this place, the battles of the giants over these and other response styles and the ingenious methods devised to deal with them need not be described. It is only necessary to point out that issues like these may, and in many cases are, involved in the tests a psychologist chooses for his tools.

Problems both greater and smaller than those appertaining to personality tests themselves cannot be disregarded by the clinical psychologist, even if all he is going to do is "give a test." The values of the social class to which the test constructer and test administrator belong (in all likelihood the same class) affect the choices of items, the wording or other construction of items, and the atmosphere of the assessment situation. The person of the examiner in the assessment situation, the interaction of his temperament with that of the examinee, the meaning of the situation to the examiner and examinee, the condition of the examinee physically and psychologically, and the interactions of test stimuli, examiner, and examinee are among the factors to be considered after a test or battery of tests has been decided upon. And finally, the biases of the examiner himself toward certain of his instruments, his preferences for, and experience with, administration and interpretation of one battery or another of tests, are important variables in what by now should be recognized as a complex of variables in choice, administration, and interpretation of objective personality tests.

After consideration of all these prior concerns, the psychologist is ready for the use of his objective tests. Then, whether the clinician has administered a test himself or has had it administered by an assistant, whether it has been given individually or in a group, whether it has been scored by hand or by machine, and whether the psychologist has examined the profile of scores from its subtests (if it has these) or has read the print-out of interpretation from a computer, the clinical psychologist is, at the last, confronted with the professional process of weighing the objective personality test data in the scales with the other observations he or someone else has made, to answer the referral question or questions and to assess the personality, in a broad or limited fashion as required by the circumstances.

MAJOR AREAS OF PERSONALITY MEASURED BY REPRESENTATIVE OBJECTIVE TESTS

According to the definition of personality given above, all objective measures ranging from blood tests to sociograms and family relations tests could be incorporated in this section. However, the measurement of intelligence is so vast a realm in itself that Chapter 3 is devoted exclusively to this one main area of personality assessment. Major emphasis is placed here on temperament tests, those usually called "personality tests."

In order to broaden the clinician's armamentarium, Table 5-1 has been constructed to provide a ready reference on tests available for different ages, conditions, and personality functions of persons whom the clinician may be called upon to examine in a variety of settings. Intellectual tests are listed for completeness of batteries. On the other hand, educational tests are omitted even though the clinician often makes use of such instruments as the *Metropolitan Achievement Tests,* the *Stanford Achievement Tests,* the *Iowa Tests of Educational Development,* and the *Gray Oral Reading Test.* For these latter tests, which have to be excluded for space considerations, Buros' textbooks (1959, 1961) may be consulted. In the classifications of the table, as well as in the text, there is no intent to polychotomize into rigid classes. An intelligence test yields temperament data, as a temperament test yields intellectual estimates, and both may give psychophysiological information. Only the major classification of a test is used.

Every clinician who has wide experience and knowledge of test literature would compile a somewhat different list. In this case, the surveys of actual frequencies of use and a search of the literature for extensively researched instruments have been combined with fairly broad experience and consultation as to the needs of clinicians. A rather heavy weighting may be noticeable in favor of tests for children. Not only personal experience but also contacts with psychologists from all parts of this country and other countries reveal that one major lacuna in the training and experience of clinicians is child evaluation (and therapy also; see Chapters 6, 7, 10, 11 and 21 especially, in this text). A list of publishers or suppliers appears at the end of the test listing.

PSYCHOPHYSIOLOGICAL AND PSYCHOMOTOR MEASURES

Identifying psychological correlates of physical or physiological functions has been a goal of psychology at least since J. McKeen Cattell sought to discriminate intellectual capacity by psychophysical measures, and found almost no correlation between intellectual abilities and reaction times. More recently, however, greater success seems to have attended efforts to establish relations between physiological and temperamental measures.

Measurement of blood pressure, for example, has been well standardized for many years. As McGinn and his associates (1964) have pointed out, psychologists seem to have lost this interest in relating personality (more accurately, temperament) variables to blood pressure since about

1930. Yet the evidence suggests that there are relations worth exploiting. Temporary changes in blood pressure seem to be associated with identifiable psychological experiences, going up with belief one has told a lie, with dreams, jazz-type music, threatening interview content, hypnotic reproduction of parachute jumps, combat conditions, and natural disaster conditions, and going down with belief one has told the truth and listening to classical music. Some evidence appears to support differential reactions to fear (or anxiety) and to anger situations, with rises in systolic pressure and lesser increases in diastolic pressure for fear, and greater diastolic increases for anger. Less sure results obtain for relating specific temperament patterns to normal or hypertensive conditions.

Some of the hypothesized correlations between physiological and psychological states of psychosomatic medicine have not been substantiated, and doubt remains for physiological measures of anxiety (Martin, 1961). Nevertheless, despite the overselling of "lie detectors," with a consequent negative public reaction, physiological measurements have appeal as one form of objective personality testing.

Closely allied with the foregoing are psychophysical and psychomotor measurements. The latter have been explored from a research viewpoint most adequately by Fleishman and his associates (Fleishman, 1954; Fleishman and Hempel, 1954). Factor analysis of a large number of psychomotor tasks reveals such abilities as two kinds of psychomotor coordination, one emphasizing fine, sensitive adjustments, the other grosser movements, as well as factors of wrist-finger speed, eye-hand coordination, postural discrimination by which precise bodily adjustments can be made without visual clues, and control of continual adjustments relative to a continuously moving object. Testing of these and other psychomotor abilities is of interest to the clinical psychologist for research purposes. But, from an applied standpoint, these tests have relation to "organicity" as discussed below.

In one major series of researches (Eysenck et al., 1957), a very definite relation has been shown between traditional psychophysical measures and emotional disturbance. Perceptual processes including eye adaptation and accommodation have proved to be generally most efficient for clinically normal persons, less efficient for psychoneurotics, and least so for psychotics.

MEASURES OF "ORGANICITY"

One of the most frequent requests the psychologist receives is to determine "organicity," especially in children. What is asked for is the determination of the presence or absence of lesions in the brain that may or may not contribute to emotional, intellectual, or social problems. "Or-

Table 5–1. Objective Diagnostic Tests of Value to the Clinical Psychologist

Name of Test	Publisher or Supplier*	Range of Usefulness†	Clinical or Descriptive Comment
Psychophysiological and psychomotor			
Eysenck Perceptual Tests	—	Adults	Battery of perceptual tests (Eysenck et al., 1957) distinguishing normals, neurotics, and psychotics from one another.
Halstead's Neuropsychological Test Battery	‡	Child–adult	Not strictly "objective test," but impossible to omit. Halstead (1947) and Reitan (1955, 1959), battery deviser and reviser, in forefront of brain-damage detection.
Memory-for-Designs Test (Graham-Kendall)	Specialists	CA 8.5–adult	Standard instrument for assessing brain damage. May be used as screening device, helpful in differentiating functional and organic.
Objective-Analytic Personality Test Batteries (O-A)	IPAT	CA 11–adult	See text.
Visual-Motor Gestalt Test (Bender-Gestalt)	Ortho	CA 4–adult	Standardized by Hain (1964) and Pascal and Suttell (1951), widely used for discriminating brain-damaged from normal; may indicate visual-motor maturation.
Visual Retention Test, Revised (Benton)	PC	CA 9–adult	Standard instrument for assessing brain damage. (Like Graham-Kendall, q.v.)
Intelligence			
Arthur Adaptation of the Leiter International Performance Scale	Stoelting	CA 2–12	Pantomime administration. Highly clinically useful for hearing, speech, language handicap, etc., child, despite some standardization lacks.
Arthur Point Scale of Performance Tests	PC	CA 4½–adult	Essentially performance-type, some verbal directions; IQ comparable to, but may differ widely from, Binet.

* See list of test publishers and suppliers below.
† Range of Usefulness" means the range for which standardization obtains. By cautious extrapolation, the clinician may utilize tests beyond this range, but he must recognize that objectivity diminishes sharply outside the standardization.
‡ See also the discussion in L. S. Kogan, Chapter 23 of this book, and articles on methods and issues of factor analysis relating to objective personality tests (Becker, 1960; Cattell, 1961; Holtzman, 1962; Peterson, 1965; and Wittenborn, 1961).

Table 5–1. (Continued)

Name of Test	Publisher or Supplier	Range of Usefulness	Clinical or Descriptive Comment
Cattell Infant Intelligence Scale	PC	CA 3–30 months	Avowed purpose: to extend Binet scales downward. Though only yielding an (equivalent) IQ, test more in keeping with psychometric standards than Gesell Developmental Schedules.
Columbia Mental Maturity Scale	Harcourt	CA 3–12	Yields IQ comparable to Binet. Child may not catch on to principle, so complete failure may not mean lack of general intelligence. Helps with verbally handicapped.
Easel Age Scale	CTB	CA 4–8–6+	Free painting of child scored objectively for EAQ, comparable to IQ. One of most painless tests to administer. Well-standardized, though statistics not entirely adequate.
Goodenough-Harris Drawing Test	Harcourt	CA 3–15	Successor to Goodenough Draw-a-Man; better standardized; stresses objective IQ scoring, not clinical interpretation.
Guilford-Zimmerman Aptitude Survey	Sheridan	High school–adult	Factors verbal comprehension, numerical operations, perceptual speed, spatial orientation, spatial visualization, and mechanical knowledge. Insufficient external validation.
Kent Series of Emergency Scales (E-G-Y)	PC	CA 5–14	Three overlapping scales. Fair standardization. Quick estimate of Binet-type IQ; intended by Kent as preliminary measure, but respectable correlations with Binet and Wechsler Verbal.
Raven Progressive Matrices	PC	CA 5–65	IQ based on British norms, performance-type, some verbal directions, which need slight altering to American vocabulary, good nonverbal test, almost universally interesting.
Stanford-Binet Intelligence Scale Form L-M	Houghton	CA 2–adult	See Garner (Chapter 3).

Table 5–1. (Continued)

Name of Test	Publisher or Supplier	Range of Usefulness	Clinical or Descriptive Comment
Vineland Social Maturity Scale	ETB	CA 0–25+	Yields Social Quotient somewhat comparable to IQ, derived from knowledgeable informant. Sometimes only measure possible if examinee untestable; useful mainly for young children. Only fair standardization.
Wechsler Adult Intelligence Scale (WAIS)	PC	CA 16–adult	See Garner (Chapter 3).
Wechsler-Bellevue Adult Intelligence Scales, Forms I & II	PC	CA 10–adult	See Garner (Chapter 3). Though older, may be preferable in that normally takes less time than WAIS and overlaps WISC better.
Wechsler Intelligence Scale for Children (WISC)	PC	CA 5–15	See Garner (Chapter 3).
Temperament			
Alcadd Test	WPS	Adult alcoholics	For use with known alcoholics to determine practical questions of degree of drinking, patterns, etc. Good reliability and validity for population (cf. Manson Evaluation).
Anderson Incomplete Stories	Anderson	Older elementary	Series A—six stories; Series B—five stories. Used in extensive cross-cultural research by author. High reliability; theme analysis, with norms showing distinct cross-national differences.
A-S Reaction Study	Houghton	College–adult	Time-tried measure of dominance (ascendance) and submission in men and women.
Children's Personality Questionnaire (CPQ)	IPAT	CA 8–12	See text.
Despert Fables	Peixotto	Grades 1–8	Peixotto (1956) norms in frequency tables. Revealing of parent and sibling attitudes of child by story-completion technique. Needs cross-validation.

Table 5–1. (Continued)

Name of Test	Publisher or Supplier	Range of Usefulness	Clinical or Descriptive Comment
Early School Personality Questionnaire (ESPQ)	IPAT	CA 6–8	See text.
Guilford-Martin Inventory of Factors GAMIN	Sheridan	Grade 10–adult	See text.
Guilford-Martin Personnel Inventory	Sheridan	Grade 10–adult	See text.
Guilford-Zimmerman Temperament Survey	Sheridan	Grades 9–16, adult	See text.
High School Personality Questionnaire (HSPQ)	IPAT	CA 12–18	See text.
Holtzman Inkblot Technique (HIT)	Holtzman	Preschool–adult	See text.
How Well Do You Know Yourself?	EAC	High school–adult	Yields 19 factor scores: irritability, practicality, punctuality, etc. Fair standardization, but not validated by independent studies. Limited use thus far suggests promise.
Inventory of Factors STDCR	Sheridan	High school–adult	See text.
Michigan Picture Test	SRA	Grades 3–9	Promising, well-standardized, scored in dynamic terms. Though it is one of best objectively scored projectives, clinician uses qualitatively more than quantitatively.
Mooney Problem Check List	PC	Jr. high school–college	Direct solicitation of problems—perhaps one of best ways to find out what problems individual really has; skeleton norms, so not strictly "objective test"; widely used in initiating counseling.
Perceptual Reaction Test (PRT)	Berg		See Holzberg, Chapter 4.
Rosenzweig Picture-Frustration Study (P-F) (children, adult)	Rosenzweig	CA 4–13, adult	Scores for need reactions, direction of aggression, and group conformity. Interesting, transparent to high-intelligence adults; not well correlated with other important data; internal consistency questionable.

163

Table 5–1. (Continued)

Name of Test	Publisher or Supplier	Range of Usefulness	Clinical or Descriptive Comment
Rotter Incomplete Sentences	PC	College	Fair degree of differentiation between adjusted and maladjusted. Combination quantitative and qualitative analysis for familial attitudes, social and sexual attitudes, general attitudes, and character traits.
Sixteen Personality Factor Questionnaire (16 P-F)	IPAT	CA 16–adult	See text.
Structured Doll Play Test (SDP)	Test	CA 2–6	Intended hopefully for use through CA 11. Provides structured situations for eliciting psychological maturity-immaturity, peer choice, and parent choice. Needs better standardization, but best-standardized of type.
Temperament-abnormal			
Behavioral Classification Project Items (BCP)	BCP	CA 6–13+	See text.
Behavior Rating Scales	Burdock	CA 1–14, adult	Graduated series of behaviors indicating disturbance; use professional or subprofessional raters on ward, at work, in school.
Color Pyramid Test	Huber	Grade K–adult	Widely used in Germany for discrimination among psychiatric syndromes, and somewhat in this country for traits of normals. Nonverbal. Promising.
Diagnostic Check List for Behavior of Disturbed Children	Rimland	CA 3–7	Differentiates autistic and childhood schizophrenia and both from normal child. Most serious of all attempts to identify autistic children.
Hospital Adjustment Scale	Consulting	Adult patients	Yields scores (probably not independent): communication and interpersonal relations, care of self and social responsibility, work activities and recreation, as well as efficiency in work and social relations.
Inpatient Multidimensional Psychiatric Scale	Consulting	Adult patients	Brief measure of 10 psychiatric syndromes, factor-analytically supported.

Table 5–1. (Continued)

Name of Test	Publisher or Supplier	Range of Usefulness	Clinical or Descriptive Comment
In-School Screening of Children with Emotional Handicaps	ETS	Grades K–12	Experimental edition available for research. Well standardized. Uses self, peer, teacher evaluations. Excellent for community mental health survey.
IPAT Anxiety Scale	IPAT	High school–adult	See text.
Kahn Test of Symbol Arrangement (KTSA)	Specialists	Child–adult	Performance test, relatively well standardized; differentiates brain damage, functional disorders, and normals, reveals psychodynamics, developmental levels.
Manson Evaluation	WPS	Adults	General adjustment scale for screening purposes, used in conjunction with Alcadd Test for identifying alcoholics.
Minnesota Multiphasic Personality Inventory (MMPI)	PC	Grades 9–12, adults	See text.
Wittenborn Psychiatric Rating Scales	PC	Adult patients	Nine clusters of "descriptive diagnoses" related to, but more sharply defined than, Krepelinian or American Hospital diagnoses; probably too many scales, considering intercorrelations.
Interests			
How Well Do You Know Your Interests?	EAC	Grade 13–adult	Must use with caution because 120 items yield 53 scores, yet ease of administration and scoring, and "factorial validity" satisfactory for cautious clinician.
Kuder Preference Record—O & V	SRA	Grade 9–adult	See Berdie (1954).
Strong Vocational Interest Blank for Men	Consulting	CA 17–adult	See Berdie (1954).
Vocational Preference Inventory	Holland	Adults	See footnote 5, page 177.
Attitudes and values			
Fels Parent Behavior Rating Scales	Fels	Parents	Require home visitation; most adequate attempt to quantify (30 scales) parent behavior and home environment.

165

Table 5–1. (Continued)

Name of Test	Publisher or Supplier	Range of Usefulness	Clinical or Descriptive Comment
K-D Proneness Scale and Check List	Harcourt	Grades 7–12, CA 7+	Two instruments—one for child, one for teacher to predict delinquency. Must be used with great caution because of standardization difficulties; nevertheless, one of very few, and possibly best of, such instruments.
Purpose in Life Test	Crumbaugh	Adults	See text.
Study of Values (Allport-Vernon-Lindzey)	Houghton	Grade 13–adult	Spranger's types: theoretical, economic, aesthetic, social, political, religious. Useful for comparing (sometimes fakable) conscious attitudes with normative groups. See Fig. 5–2.

Test Publishers and Suppliers

Abbreviation	Name
Anderson	Dr. Harold H. Anderson, Department of Psychology, Michigan State University, East Lansing, Michigan.
BCP	Behavioral Classification Project, Department of Psychology, Louisiana State University, Baton Rouge, La.
Berg	Dr. Irwin A. Berg, Department of Psychology, Louisiana State University, Baton Rouge, La.
Burdock	Dr. E. I. Burdock, New York, N.Y.
Consulting	Consulting Psychologists Press, Palo Alto, Calif.
CTB	California Test Bureau, Los Angeles, Calif.
Crumbaugh, J. C.	Dr. J. C. Crumbaugh, Columbus, Ga.
EAC	Executive Analysis Corporation, New York, N.Y.
ETB	Educational Test Bureau, Educational Publishers, Nashville, Tenn.; Minneapolis, Minn.; Philadelphia, Pa.
ETS	Educational Testing Service, New York, N.Y.
Fels	Fels Research Institute, Yellow Springs, Ohio
Harcourt	Harcourt, Brace & World Test Department, Atlanta, Ga.
Holland	Dr. John L. Holland, National Merit Scholarship Corp., Evanston, Ill.
Holtzman	Dr. Wayne H. Holtzman, Department of Psychology, University of Texas, Austin, Tex.
Houghton	Houghton Mifflin Company, New York, N.Y.; Atlanta, Ga.
Huber	Hans Huber, Bern, Switzerland
IPAT	Institute for Personality and Ability Testing, Champaign, Ill.
Ortho	American Orthopsychiatric Association, New York, N.Y.
PC	The Psychological Corporation, New York, N.Y.
Peixotto	Dr. Helen E. Peixotto, Child Center, Catholic University of America, Washington, D.C.
Rimland	Dr. Bernard E. Rimland, U.S. Naval Personnel Research Laboratory, San Diego, Calif.
Rosenzweig	Dr. Saul Rosenzweig, Department of Psychology, Washington University, St. Louis, Miss.
Sheridan	Sheridan Supply Co., Beverly Hills, Calif.
Specialists	Psychological Test Specialists, Missoula, Mont.
SRA	Science Research Associates, Chicago, Ill.
CHS	C. H. Stoelting Co., Chicago, Ill.
Test	Test Developments, Burlingame, Calif.
WPS	Western Psychological Services, Beverly Hills, Calif.

ganicity" may be diffuse, as in some toxic conditions and cerebral palsies, or it may be localized as a cortical or subcortical lesion in one or both hemispheres or in one lobe or in the cerebellum, or in any combination of all these areas. Obviously, therefore, "organicity's" name is legion. Evidence seems conflicting as to whether, especially in reference to the cerebral cortex, "organicity" is a more or less unitary reaction of the organism, as one might expect from Lashley's principle of "equipotentiality" and Goldstein's ideas of concrete and abstract attitudes, or the individual's "organicity" is more or less specific to the loci of his lesions.

In recent research, the swing has been away from a unitary concept of brain damage to a multifaceted or multidimensional concept (Haynes & Sells, 1963). Yet testing for "organicity" has in most instances appeared to follow the unitary paradigm. The influence of the Bender-Gestalt Test (see Visual-Motor Gestalt Test in Table 5–1) has perhaps been overwhelming here. For there can scarcely be any doubt that by far the majority of clinical psychologists who test for "organicity" at all employ the Bender-Gestalt as their first instrument. And it is just about as certain that qualitative aspects and "global judgments," rather than any of the objective methods of scoring the Bender, have accounted for the major "hits" psychologists have made in identifying the presence of "organicity." [2]

For gross detection of brain damage, it must be admitted that the unquantified use of the Bender and sometimes human figure drawings have sufficed for the clinician. Emphasis here is on the clinician, however, for "global judgments" depend more on the experienced clinician than on the identifiable characteristics of the instrument. When attempts to quantify the Bender or Rorschach (Haynes & Sells, 1963) for more adequate objectification have been made, they have met with only indifferent success. Other tests that have been devised (see Table 5–1) for gross detection of brain damage have proved somewhat more adequate psychometrically, though whether more efficient practically is not clear at this time.

In the vanguard of the multifaceted approach to "organicity," Reitan (1955, 1959) has proceeded on the assumption that different types of brain injury or dysfunction are associated with different psychological reactions. Making use of a battery of tests constructed by Halstead (1947), with several additional instruments, Reitan has been able to detect general and specific "organicity" with greater success than any other. Strangely, although some few psychologists have sought to learn Reitan's methods,

[2] One of the ironies of clinical history is that two of the psychologist's major tools—the *Rorschach*, far and away the most widely used of all, and the *Bender*—were devised by psychiatrists with little psychometric skill, then taken over by psychologists, presumably psychometric experts, who utilize these tests, as far as one can tell, primarily in a qualitative or psychiatric way in their clinical work.

and though he has published extensively, the large majority of clinical psychologists have continued to use the less efficient and less precise global methods.

TEMPERAMENT INVENTORIES

The instruments considered in this section are often called "personality tests" or "personality inventories," though it is evident that "personality" as defined scientifically refers to more than is measured by these inventories. Only the major instruments or those most widely researched in recent years are covered in this discussion. Others are described briefly in Table 5–1; for clinical use, some of these may be more important than those detailed here.

The Minnesota Multiphasic Personality Inventory (MMPI). If a few of the most popularly investigated inventories are excluded from consideration, the MMPI has had more research done with and on it than all other objective temperament tests put together.

At the outset, an original pool of items intended both for broad temperament ("personality") coverage and for inclusion of neuropsychiatric conditions was administered to clinically diagnosed neuropsychiatric patients in the University of Minnesota Hospitals and to an experimentally comparable group of normal persons visiting relatives in the hospitals. Those items empirically discriminating among the various psychiatric groupings and between the psychiatric patients and normals were scaled for normalcy-abnormalcy on each of nine scales representing major syndromes of disorder. One additional scale (Si) was subsequently utilized to help make up the profile (see Fig. 5–1) and is employed routinely in MMPI analysis, though its basis of inclusion (like the Mf scale) is different from that of the others. Subsequently, over 200 scales have been developed for use with the 550 items.

Study of the profile in Fig. 5–1 gives some basic understanding of the MMPI. The ordinate scale consists of standard scores, T or Tc (T-corrected), generally representing lack of pathognomy at the lower end and increasing psychiatric difficulty at the upper end. Numbers printed within the body of the scale refer to the raw numbers of items an individual may indorse on the individual scales, or, in the case of "corrected" scales raw numbers plus the correction factor (e.g., Hs + .5K). The line drawn at the T-score of 50 identifies the mean of the normal standardizing Minnesota group on each of the MMPI scales. Lines drawn at 30 and 70 enclose approximately two-thirds of the scores of the normal reference group. What scores below 30 signify is almost anybody's guess. But scores close to and beyond 70 represent approaches to, or achievement of, abnormality. The baseline of the profile identifies the scales usually

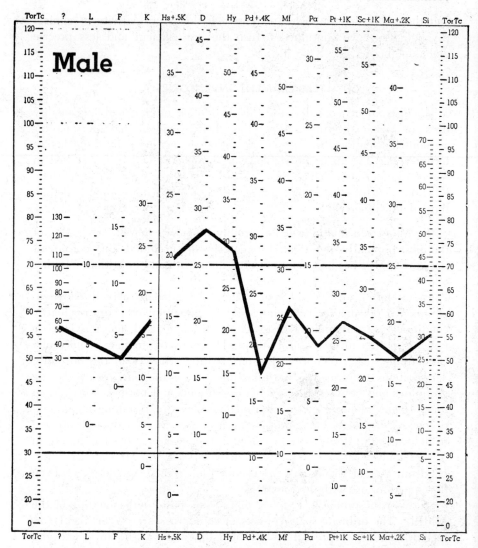

Fig. 5–1. MMPI profile of a young man whose symptoms and complaints suggested psychoneurosis. (Reprinted by permission granted by The Psychological Corporation, New York, publishers of the Profile Chart.)

scored for an individual.[3] To the left of the vertical line in the chart are the so-called validity scales, which are intended to overcome some of the difficulties to which inventories of this nature are subject.

[3] A profile identification code has been worked out so that comparisons may be made from one individual to a standard "case." Such a code appears like this:

49'8523—'1 5:3:13

The most succinct explanation of this coding is found in Hathaway & Monachesi (1961).

Since this is not a textbook in abnormal psychology, extended description of the substantive scales is not called for. Hs is the hypochondriasis scale. D is the depression scale. When elevated together with Hy, the hysteria scale (neurotic somatic complaints), these scales and Hy form the so-called neurotic triad, a situation demonstrated in Fig. 5–1. Standing somewhat by itself is the Pd or psychopathic deviate scale. Though the term *psychopath* has fallen into disrepute in recent years, the usage here seems clear-cut enough, that is, as disregard for the accepted mores, a seeming inability to profit from punishing experiences as manifested by repetition of the same difficulties, and at least partial affective lacks in respect to others (see Chapter 14).

As indicated above, the Mf, masculinity-femininity, scale is different from the others. It distinguishes between the sexes generally speaking, but, because of peculiarities in its construction, it is not at all clear that it performs the task it was designed to do, to reveal sexual inversions. For one thing, many of the items are quite transparent to intelligent persons. And, with men of upper-social-class origin, many of the "feminine" items are characteristic of the class, so the scale in part measures culture patterns more than masculinity-femininity. At least, the pathognomonic character of a high score is diluted.

Sometimes called the "psychotic tetrad," the next four scales, Pa or *Paranoia*, Pt or *Psychasthenia*, Sc or *Schizophrenia*, and Ma or *Hypomania*, form patterns in combinations with one another indicative of the (usually) more serious disturbances. In psychoanalytic terminology, elevated scores here suggest more deeply regressed disturbance. *Psychasthenia* is also a term that has gone out of use except in special cases like this one. It refers to obsessive-compulsive features combined with phobic and guilt reactions, and, withal, an emotional detachment from one's own problems.

The last scale on the profile, Si, *Social Inversion*, really covers both social introversion and social extroversion as well as emotional involvement with people. It is based on a Jungian rationale and the work of the Guilfords (see the section on the Guilford scales, below), and, from both this foundation and other rational considerations, it cannot be considered as a clinical scale as are most of the others. However, if the deviation hypothesis holds (Berg, 1961), deviation from known norms on the Si scale may well indicate abnormality in a psychopathological sense.

What does the MMPI accomplish? Grossly (Dahlstrom and Walsh, 1960; Hathaway and Monachesi, 1961; Welsh and Dahlstrom, 1956), the MMPI has been found suitable for screening and selection purposes, for delineating symptom states like degree of accessibility, malingering, overt anxiety, and depression, for determining the kind and amount of impulse control an individual has, including delinquency and criminality tendencies, for differentiating among diagnostic groups, and for assessing treatment possibilities, relevant treatment variables, and success of treatment.

Theoretical interpretations of empirical findings on the MMPI have not been lacking. Factor analysis has, for example, been utilized to uncover the underlying "dimensions" accounting for performance on the MMPI. Special problems like the built-in correlation resulting from scoring the same items for different scales confuse the factor-analytic picture. But ordinarily two interpretable factors (Welsh, 1965) have arisen, an "A" factor, which appears to be an ego-strength dimension, and an "R" factor seemingly related to introversion-extroversion. Kassebaum, Couch, and Slater (1959) by a special matrix operation on MMPI data appear to have solved one of the long-standing differences between Freudian and Jungian psychology as to the nature of introversion and extroversion.

Edwards (1964) summarizes a long series of studies that appear to demonstrate that psychopathological responses on the MMPI are strongly associated with social undesirability, as determined independently, and that "good" traits as measured especially by nonclinical scales are similarly associated with social desirability. Edwards thinks it is possible to develop scales of neutral social-desirability value, thus sharpening scales to measure what they purport to measure. Although objections can be—and, one can be sure, have been!—raised to Edwards' work, the following theoretical question haunts the user of the MMPI: "Just what am I measuring, what the scale is supposed to measure or some set of response styles?" However, from a clinician's viewpoint all is not lost, in respect to social desirability at least, for it is important to a clinician to know, first, whether his examinee knows what is socially desirable and, second, whether he cares. Comparison in this case, as in the use of any other test, with external criteria is, or ought to be, standard practice.

The Guilford Series of Inventories. All of the Guilford scales listed in Table 5–1, including the *Aptitude Survey* and the *Inventory of Factors STDCR*, were derived by factor analysis, utilizing an internal consistency criterion. In the temperament realm, increasing use has been made of the *Guilford-Zimmerman Temperament Survey* (GZTS) to the exclusion of inventories like *GAMIN* and *STDCR*, which it partly replaces. These inventories are unlike the MMPI in being primarily measures of temperament *traits* rather than, as in the case of the initial scales of the MMPI, indicators of psychiatric *syndromes*.

What the GZTS attempts to measure in the personality may be seen best by reference to Table 5–2. Warning must be given here that the names bestowed on factor-derived traits may be misleading, as even summaries like the ones in the table may be. Only an examination of the items that identify the trait, a knowledge of the population on which measurements were taken for the factor analysis, and an understanding of the

Table 5–2. Traits Measured by the Guilford-Zimmerman Temperament Survey

Trait Name	Summary Description
General Activity	Energetic, rapid, efficient movement versus deliberate, tired, inefficient movement
Restraint	Serious-minded persistence versus impulsive carefreeness
Ascendance	Dominant, persuasive leadership quality versus hesitant, avoiding submissiveness
Sociability	Seeking social activities and having friends versus avoiding social activities
Emotional Stability	Even, cheerful composure versus fluctuating moods and depressive outlook
Objectivity	"Thick-skinned" versus self-centered hypersensitivity
Friendliness	Agreeableness versus belligerence
Thoughtfulness	Reflective introspectiveness versus extroversion
Personal Relations	Faith in people and social institutions versus fault-finding criticalness
Masculinity	Masculine, hard-boiled emotional control versus feminine, sympathetic emotional expressiveness

methods by which the factors were derived can yield basic and scientific meaning to the factor traits.[4]

Not a great deal of research, comparatively speaking, has been done with the *Aptitude Survey*, but a fairly large volume of research (cf. Jackson, 1961) has accumulated in connection with the *Temperament Survey*. There have been criticisms of its construction, in that no outside criteria were utilized against which to validate the separate scales, in that there is a general bias toward selection of positive poles of the scales, and in that the reliabilities reported for the individual scales (ranging from .75 to .85) are not high enough for use with individuals or even in applied group settings. These objections, together with the fact that the GZTS, like other such inventories, is subject to response sets and fakability (Voas, 1958), certainly must be kept in mind if the clinician is to employ this instrument. And yet, as research results have been reported across the years, the conviction becomes almost inescapable that the test as a whole is valid and useful in industry and schools (e.g., Jackson, 1961; Khan, 1962; Watley and Martin, 1962), and clinicians, it must be remembered, work extensively in these settings.

The evidence for the usefulness of the GZTS in clinical installations is not as clear, possibly because clinicians working in these settings have not

---

[4] Further meaning of these traits can be garnered from factor analysis of the matrix of first-order factors (e.g., Bendig and Meyer, 1963).

availed themselves of its potentialities. Sundberg's (1961) survey of hospitals and institutions, clinics, and counseling centers reveals that none of the Guilford temperament inventories, several of which have been in existence for many years, are included in the list of 62 tests mentioned as used by 10 per cent or more of the sample agencies.

Cattell's Personality Factor Tests.   Covering the widest range of personality phenomena, the widest assortment of assessment methods, and the widest range of ages, Cattell's tests have likewise amassed an impressive array of research literature.   (Consult Table 5–1 for the most prominent of these tests.)   The basic patterns of these tests are best described in *Personality and Motivation Structure and Measurement* (Cattell, 1957).

Cattell divides the data of personality into L-data, Q-data, and T-data. The first, L-data, refers to life record, *in situ* or criterion variables, "real life" situations that may be sampled more or less objectively.   Q-data are questionnaire variables, either introspective responses without specific behavior validation or questionnaire responses behaviorally cross-validated.   The latter type is more properly classified, Cattell asserts, with T-data or objective test variables.   This use of "objective test" is stricter than the one we employ in this chapter; Cattell refers to situations in which, when responses are measured, the respondent does not know their personological meaning.

Life record variables are, as Cattell maintains, the most neglected of the three sources of data.   Since these data are often difficult to assess validly and reliably, emphasis on these is not great here.   But it should be recognized that, insofar as these data can be quantified and scored reliably, they fall within the purview of this chapter.

Q-data are represented in the Cattell system by the "personality questionnaires."   These begin at present with the *Early School Personality Questionnaire;* "at present" in this case signifies that it is known that a *Pre-school Personality Questionnaire* is in the making.   Proceeding through the *Children's Personality Questionnaire*, the *High School Personality Questionnaire*, and the *16 P-F Questionnaire*, these scales extend measurement of temperamental-social variables into adulthood.   In addition to this series, the Cattell questionnaires include one that attempts to assess intelligence in a "cultural fair" way, two anxiety tests, and a neuroticism scale.

Considerably greater use has been made of the *16 P-F Questionnaire* and more research has been done with it than with the other tests.   What this test purports to measure may be judged from Table 5–3.   Note once again that names may mislead.   Some likenesses may be observed between Guilford's factortraits and Cattell's; undoubtedly some of these traits are

Table 5–3. Traits Measured by the Sixteen Personality Factor Questionnaire

---

A. **Reserved,** detached, critical, cool (Sizothymia, previously Schizothymia) versus **Outgoing,** warm-hearted, easygoing, participating (Affectothymia, previously Cyclothymia)

B. **Less intelligent,** concrete-thinking (Low scholastic mental capacity) versus **More intelligent,** abstract-thinking, bright (High scholastic mental capacity)

C. **Affected by feelings,** emotionally less stable, easily upset (Low ego strength) versus **Emotionally stable,** faces reality, calm, mature (High ego strength)

E. **Humble,** mild, accommodating, conforming (Submissiveness) versus **Assertive,** independent, aggressive, stubborn (Dominance)

F. **Sober,** prudent, serious, taciturn (Desurgency) versus **Happy-go-lucky,** impulsively lively, gay, enthusiastic (Surgency)

G. **Expedient,** evades rules, feels few obligations (Low superego strength) versus **Conscientious,** persevering, staid, rule-bound (High superego strength)

H. **Shy,** restrained, diffident, timid (Threctia) versus **Venturesome,** socially bold, uninhibited, spontaneous (Parmia)

I. **Tough-minded,** self-reliant, realistic, no-nonsense (Harria) versus **Tender-minded,** dependent, overprotected, sensitive (Premsia)

L. **Trusting,** adaptable, free of jealousy, easy to get on with (Alaxia) versus **Suspicious,** opinionated, hard to fool (Protension)

M. **Practical,** careful, conventional, regulated by external realities, proper (Praxernia) versus **Imaginative,** wrapped up in inner urgencies, careless of practical matters, Bohemian (Autia)

N. **Forthright,** natural, artless, sentimental (Artlessness) versus **Shrewd,** calculating, worldly, penetrating (Shrewdness)

O. **Placid,** self-assured, confident, serene (Untroubled adequacy) versus **Apprehensive,** worrying, depressive, troubled (Guilt proneness)

Q1. **Conservative,** respecting established ideas, tolerant of traditional difficulties (Conservatism) versus **Experimenting,** critical, liberal, analytical, freethinking (Radicalism)

Q2. **Group-dependent,** a "joiner" and sound follower (Group adherence) versus **Self-sufficient,** prefers own decisions, resourceful (Self-sufficiency)

Q3. **Undisciplined,** self-conflicting, careless of protocol, follows own urges (Low integration) versus **Controlled,** socially precise, following self image, compulsive (High self-concept control)

Q4. **Relaxed,** tranquil, torpid, unfrustrated (Low ergic tension) versus **Tense,** frustrated, driven, overwrought (High ergic tension)

---

the same, but the problem of identifying factors from one set of investigations to another is not by any means as easily solved as by obtaining verbal similarities. It is obvious also that some factors may be the same from set to set even though named differently (especially considering Cattell's idiosyncratic terminology).

More than twice as many factors as are named and measured in the *16*

P-F Questionnaire have been described by Cattell and his associates, for example, "Fantasy Tendency," "Psychotic Tendency (Psychoticism)," "Commention vs. Abcultion" (an acceptance of social values versus a rejection of such values). In the anxiety realm (Cattell and Scheier, 1961), although Cattell finds several first-order [5] factors, which may be called "anxiety measures," a second-order factor, F(Q)11, seems to measure "general anxiety." From some of the most extensive empirical research efforts in psychological history, two questionnaire measures of anxiety have been developed—the *IPAT Anxiety Scale* and the *8-Parallel Form Anxiety Battery*. Another anxiety battery classifies with T-data tests described below. Cattell has distinguished anxiety and anxieties as components of neuroticism, and a special scale, the *Neuroticism Scale Questionnaire* (NSQ), has been devised to measure six dimensions contributing to the clinical patterns of neuroticism.

T-data ("objective test data") replicate the findings in the other media with many variations that may depend on lack of correlation among personality functions or on errors of measurement from one medium to another. The *Objective Analytic Personality Test Batteries* and the *O-A Anxiety Battery* have been assembled to sample objectively measurable behavior for assessment of a large number of factors, some of which also appear from analyzing questionnaire data. The developers of these batteries warn that the component tests are not as simply administered as questionnaires, take more time to administer (ordinarily) than projectives, and require greater skill and knowledge, especially of test construction and psychological theory. But these tests measure behavior rather than self-assessments, yield reliable scoring, and assess fundamental dimensions of temperament.

The Cattell tests may be strongly criticized for the low reliabilities of the individual factor scales, for some possible gaps in the total personality coverage, for the release of tests before they have been sufficiently standardized, and for the use of chance samples of standardization, in addition to the usual objections to the questionnaire techniques on which many of the tests rely. In a kind of freewheeling way, however, Cattell and his numerous cohorts have gone ahead and empirically demonstrated the validities of even some apparently unreliable scales, have shown significant test profile differences among occupational and psychiatric groupings, have shown almost boundless energy and imagination in undertaking vast research programs opening up new areas of test construction and use, and have kept a running dialog between psychometrics and personality test-

[5] "First-order" refers to the results of a factor analysis of the original intercorrelations among test scores. When the factors themselves are intercorrelated, a second-order factor matrix results. Even third-order factors may be extracted from intercorrelations of second-order factors. Oblique rather than orthogonal factors are assumed in both cases.

ing. If these immense labors issued only in a modicum of practical clinical results, these would still be worthwhile for clinicians to consider. In actuality, however, a number of clinics and hospitals have been putting the Cattell series of tests to work; the psychological literature is only beginning to reflect this trend.

Other Temperament Tests. Table 5–1 lists other useful tests than the ones it is possible to describe here. For special purposes or for considerations like availability of a certain test or budget restrictions, some other tests may very well serve better. Among those that have had considerable use or research are *Edwards Personal Preference Schedule* and the *Kahn Test of Symbol Arrangement* (L'Abate and Craddick, 1965). This latter is a performance-type test that has proved fairly successful as a test of "organicity," of schizophrenia, and possibly of character disorders, as well as for identifying maladjusted children and different cultural thought patterns.

VOCATIONAL INTEREST INVENTORIES

For some reason, in recent years, clinical psychologists appear to have lost interest in interest inventories. It is even more the case today than when Berdie wrote, in the Second Edition of this text, "Tests of this type are more often found in the vocational counseling center than in the psychological clinic" (Berdie, 1954, p. 177). Counseling psychology and guidance counseling have burgeoned in the meantime and have expanded their vocational specializations, while clinical psychology, except in some areas, has moved away from what was at one time a major pursuit of some clinical psychologists, "clinical vocational counseling" (Darley, 1941). Nevertheless, clinicians should know something about testing in this field if for no other reason than to know how to make appropriate referrals.

The two most well-known inventories have been described adequately in Berdie (1954) and in a number of general-psychology texts: the *Strong Vocational Interest Blank* and the *Kuder Preference Record.* Other somewhat older inventories are treated in the *Mental Measurements Yearbooks.* Two newer inventories among others have come to the attention of counselors, both of which show promise—the *Minnesota Vocational Interest Inventory* (Clark, 1961) and the *Holland Vocational Preference Inventory* (Holland, 1962).[6] And an entirely different type, the *Geist Picture Interest Inventory* (Geist, 1963), has appeared.

Research has concentrated for some time, on, first, making the older

[6] The *Holland Vocational Preference Inventory* is, strictly speaking, not a vocational interest inventory at all. It uses occupational titles to arrive at temperament variables projectively. It is included among interest inventories because it *is* a vocational-choice instrument and it does distinguish among occupational groupings.

inventories more valid for the purposes they are intended to serve, in part by checking the responses made by many different occupational groups to sharpen the occupational keys and diminish "faking" and in part by long-term follow-up to determine the stability of occupational choices as expressed indirectly on the inventories. A second major area of research has sought temperament ("personality") and other correlates of vocational interests (Holland, 1962). Self concepts, intellectual abilities, achievement goals, psychological adjustment status, and motivational patterns at least show definite relations to interests expressed on the various inventories. As a sample of such correlations, a factor analysis of the *Kuder Preference Record* (KPR) together with the *Primary Mental Abilities* test battery and the *Guilford-Zimmerman Temperament Survey* was made by Bendig and Meyer (1963). One second-order factor linked most of the KPR scales with some intellectual traits, and another factor related interests and temperament. In the first, not surprisingly, a positive relation is shown between literary interests and general intelligence, and, in the second, a negative relation is seen between mechanical and scientific interests on the one hand and social activity as measured by the GZTS on the other.

The implications of the research just briefly touched upon here are extensive. Most projective techniques and many objective temperament scales described above are devised to approach certain areas of the personality obliquely. On the basis the results of many years of correlational research, it is now possible to utilize interest inventories as another avenue of approach. Temperament patterns and self concepts at the least can be assessed indirectly. It is obvious from the literature that clinicians by and large have not found this means of indirectly revealing temperament patterns.

ATTITUDES, VALUES, AND ROLES

Again, for completeness of coverage, the measurement of attitudes and values needs attention in a clinical psychology text. In reality, many of the temperament tests and projectives (see Holzberg, Chapter 4, in this text) assess both attitudes toward people and institutions and the basic values an individual holds. Ordinarily, these are indirectly and qualitatively assessed, however. A more direct and objective means of measuring values is found in the Allport-Vernon-Lindzey *Study of Values*. Somehow, despite a foundation in a personality typology not acceptable to American psychologists generally, this self-report instrument has continued to hold up in research and practice surprisingly well. At one time, *A Study of Values* was used as an interest inventory, but it has become almost exclusively regarded as an indicator of general values rather than occupational interests. Figure 5–2 gives a profile of a patient, with the six "types" of men represented as scales, against the normative distributions of which the patient is implicitly compared.

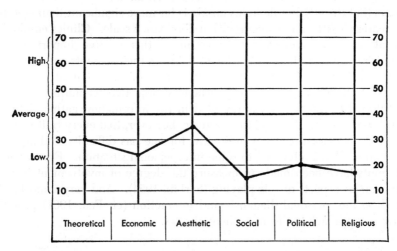

Fig. 5–2. The profile of values earned by a psychiatric male patient, aged thirty. (Profile chart reprinted with permission granted by The Houghton Mifflin Company, publishers of the Allport-Vernon-Lindzey *Study of Values,* rev. ed., 1951.)

Another test of the value systems of individuals is called the *Purpose in Life Test* (PIL) (Crumbaugh and Maholick, 1964). This test is mentioned, even though it has not come into general use, because, predicated on an existential value system, the PIL seeks to measure the "existential frustration" arising from failure to fulfil the "will to meaning." This frustration is the essence of the "noogenic neurosis," which Frankl maintains accounts for about 55 per cent of the present-day clinical case load. Whether or not other clinicians would accept such a high proportion—different theorists tend to find their case loads conforming to their expectations—a clinician need not be an existentialist to recognize a goodly number of his cases whose difficulties are directly related to the meaninglessness they feel in their lives. Any serious attempt—as is the PIL—to assess objectively this sense of purposelessness is a welcome addition to a scarcely-furnished niche in the clinician's cupboard.

Ever since Thurstone and Chave (1929) proved that "Attitudes can be measured," there have been refinements of theory (Torgerson, 1958) and practice in attitude measurement. So many different attitude scales have been devised, no attempt is made here to detail any of them. Buros' *Yearbooks* can be consulted for such attempts as Remer's *Generalized*

Attitude Scales, and Cook and Selltic (1964), for attitude measurement by other means than self-reports.

Roles played by the individual may be more important than some temperament traits. Such an obvious fact is seen immediately when one considers that the child's role in his family is far more significant than whether he scores slightly above average on a dominance scale. Clinics employing social workers have explicitly recognized this relative importance by requiring a thorough investigation of the roles their patients enact. Quantification of roles, however, has lagged far behind that related to other areas of the personality. No satisfactory objective technique has been developed to assess roles as revealed in the information gathered by interview methods. It is well to recognize, however, that every trait-measuring test also measures roles indirectly, for one has difficulty finding traits that do not have reference to some interpersonal situation. Furthermore, attempts have been made to measure the degree of involvement in roles and similar aspects of role playing (Sarbin, 1954). And very importantly, work in interpersonal diagnosis and interaction (cf. Foa, 1961) provides a rough approach to the assessment of roles.

TEST PROFILE ANALYSIS

When a test yields many scores, as most of the temperament, interest, and values tests do, the problem arises of interpreting these many scores for an individual or individuals. Analysis of scales or scores in relation to one another has come to be known as "profile analysis." Usually, scale scores for a group of persons on a particular test are reduced to standard scores to make them comparable, then, either in actuality or by mathematical symbolization, the scale points of each individual are connected by straight lines to form a profile (as in Figure 5–1), and the profiles of all persons are compared with one another.

Profile analysis may be carried out by visual inspection. Generally, however, profile similarities cannot be detected in this crude way. It is thus necessary to employ mathematical methods of analyzing profiles to determine whether or not any regularities are present and, if so, what they are. Many and complicated are the difficulties attending such analyses (Cattell, 1957; Nunnally, 1962), a discussion of which lies beyond the scope of this chapter. It is sufficient to say that methods of analysis must take account of the three major elements of information provided by a test's profiles of a group's scores: First is the *shape* of the profile, whether, for instance, it is nearly a flat line across the chart or is full of peaks and depressions, is like a saw or a dromedary, and so forth. Second is the *level;* that is, no matter what the shape, where does the profile line lie in respect to the mean of all scores—generally crossing the mean line, generally above it, or generally below it? Two profiles of almost exactly the same shape but different levels can be indicative of two very different kinds of personalities. Third, the *dispersion* or *emphasis* must be taken into account, the amount of scatter of individual scores on any scale.

Different methods of analysis have been employed to set up clusters of individuals for diagnostic purposes. One method (Cattell, 1949, 1957), a combination of correlational and cluster analysis, was used to determine "types" of children among normal and clinical groups measured by the Behavioral Classification Project (BCP) items (Dreger, 1964; Dreger *et al.*, 1964). From profiles of 32 children on nine factors, five clusters of children emerged classifying all but one of them. These groups or "types" of children (with the number in each case in parentheses) are denominated as follows:

1. Relatively Mature, Semi-Sociable Egocentricity (4)
2. Relatively Immature, Non-Sociable Semi-Surgent Egocentricity (9)
3. Sociable Anxiety (5)
4. Semi-Sociable, Non-Anxious, Desurgent Retardation (6)
5. Egocentric, Anti-Social Aggressiveness (7)

Names of clusters may be just as misleading as names of factors. Yet the fact that 31 out of 32 of these children were grouped into five fairly distinct categories, with some psychological meaningfulness attaching to the categories, suggests the usefulness of profile analysis of objective tests to clinical psychology. In the next section, machine processing of profiles is described; basically, all that this processing amounts to is making profile analysis more efficient.

COMPUTER PROCESSING OF PERSONALITY TEST DATA

Virtually all of the tests on which factor analyses or other complicated statistics have been prepared can be regarded as subjects of computer processing. For, in recent years, many statistical analyses have been accomplished by digital computers. In a sense, then, computer processing of personality test data has been going on for a relatively long time. However, the title of this section has come to have a specialized meaning within only the last year or so prior to this writing. It has come to mean the machine processing of multiscore tests in such a manner as to yield descriptions of personality (primarily temperament) printed out by a computer. If at first blush this simple definition of computer processing of personality test data does not seem remarkable, be assured that it is not only remarkable; it is revolutionary.

As with other revolutions, this one has its prehistory. At least three movements besides the vital technical developments of computing itself can be discerned in the background of what we now know as computer processing of personality test data. Cybernetics had influenced psychologists in general personality theorizing and in learning theory in particular to try to simulate human processes. A symposium held at the Educational Testing Service and Princeton University (Tomkins and Messick, 1963) described simulation work either actually done or seriously contemplated in perception, cognition, affect, problem solving, memory, motivation, attitudes, neurosis, and overt behavior. Added to this first influence, computer simulation of personality, was a second, a fairly long-term, but more recently rapidly growing, attempt to automatize interpretations of the two most widely used objective tests, the MMPI and 16 P-F tests. In 1955, Meehl, in his Midwestern Psychological Association presidential address (Meehl, 1956), entitled "Wanted—a Good Cookbook," stressed the need for, and gave some evidence supporting the validity of, an actuarial method of making personality descriptions from MMPI profiles. By "actuarial" in this case is meant the explicit formulation of rules relating to specified test scores on the basis of empirical evidence, by which an individual may be described in standard terms. Meehl maintained that, if test results can be automated into standard descriptions in this way, the clinical psychologist, who is less efficient in this activity than a computer, could be freed to do the creative job he really should be doing. Since Meehl's address was delivered, not only have scales on the MMPI multiplied until it is impossible for any clinician to take the time to score more than a fraction of these, but the rules relating even the first MMPI scales (Fig. 5–1) have grown so complex no clinician can keep them all in mind when interpreting the usual MMPI profile. A parallel development has taken place in the multiplication of profiles identifying occupational and psychiatric groups on the 16 P-F.

A third influence on the development of computer processing of personality test data has been the surge of interest in attempting to derive an adequate classification of children's emotional disorders by means of behavioral descriptions. Dissatisfaction among the increasing number of clinical psychologists working with children with the nosology implied in the manual provided by the American Psychiatric Association has generated independent efforts in at least half a dozen centers to establish a nosology based on what parents or knowledgeable others actually observe the child doing. But, when one gets behind clinical generalizations like "has strong oedipal leanings," "is passively dependent," "shows poor reality orientation," and so forth, to observable behaviors, the number of items that must be used to describe a child's relevant activities, combinations of which will give personality descriptions, increases to an extent that only computers can handle the many thousands of interrelations involved.

So much of what has been done in the way of processing personality test data by computers has been done so recently that most of it has not been published as of the time of this writing. Accordingly, Table 5–4 has been prepared to give an overview of the field without recourse in most instances to formal bibliographic citation. Some published references have been included either of a general nature (Borko, 1962; Cooley and Lohnes, 1962) or of a more specific nature referring to particular tests (Holtzman *et al.*, 1961; Kleinmuntz, 1963a, b; Marks and Seeman, 1963). One (Thomas *et al.*, 1964) is included with misgivings, for it seems that the massive labors of computers and printer have generated little usable information on Rorschach location categories on a highly selected sample of the population. The various papers mentioned otherwise contain actual computer programs for handling test data, printouts of results of such programs, or descriptions of programs and their results.

Computer interpretations are now available for the MMPI, the *California Personality Inventory,* and the 16 P-F (see Table 5–4), in experi-

Table 5–4. Automated Programs for Processing Personality Test Data

Author	Program or Paper or Text Describing Program	Source of Information
H. Borko	*Computer applications in the behavioral sciences*	See references.
W. W. Cooley & R. R. Lohnes	*Multivariate procedures for the behavioral sciences*	See references.
R. B. Darlington	Programs useful in item analysis and test construction, for the Control Data 1604 computer	University of Minnesota
B. Denton	A computer simulation of human concept learning	Information Processing Rep. No. 11, University of Texas
R. M. Dreger	Printout of BCP factor scores	Behavioral Classification Project, Louisiana State University
H. W. Eber	Computer reporting of 16 PF data	Paper, SEPA, 1965
J. C. Finney	Programmed interpretation of MMPI and CPI	Paper, American Psychiatric Assn, 1965
R. D. Fowler	The automated cookbook	Paper, SEPA, 1965
D. R. Gorham	The development of a computer scoring system for inkblot responses	Paper, Inter-American Congr. of Psych., 1964
R. E. Graetz	Research utilization of patient data computer files in clinical drug studies	Paper, Western Sec., Operations Res. Soc. of Amer., 1964
W. H. Holtzman et al.	*Inkblot perception and personality*	See references.

Table 5–4. *(Continued)*

Author	Program or Paper or Text Describing Program	Source of Information
Institute for Personality and Ability Testing	Announcing a new digital computer scoring service for the 16 PF	IPAT News No. 18, Champaign, Ill.
Institute for Personality and Ability Testing	Computer-assembled narrative reports from IPAT's 16 PF Personality Factor Questionnaire	IPAT
International Business Machines Co.	MMPI computer analysis and interpretation of results for psychological tests. IBM 1620 system, # 02.0.022	IBM Program Distribution Center, N.Y.
B. Kleinmuntz	MMPI decision rules for the identification of college maladjustment: A digital computer approach	See references.
P. A. Marks	MMPI Report	University of Kansas Medical Center
P. A. Marks & W. Seeman	*Actuarial description of abnormal personality*	See references.
Mayo Clinic	Symposium on automation techniques in personality assessment	Staff Proceedings, Mayo Clinic, Jan. 31, 1962
E. C. Moseley & D. R. Gorham	Holtzman Inkblot Technique Dictionary in English, and Computer Method for Evaluating Inkblot Techniques	Veterans Administration, Perry Point, Md.
J. A. Starkweather	Computest: A computer language for individual testing	Paper, APA, 1964
W. M. Swenson & J. S. Pearson	Automated personality description with the MMPI	Paper, APA, 1964
Caroline B. Thomas et al.	*An index of Rorschach responses*	See references.
D. J. Veldman	Computer Programs and Dataprocessing Procedures for the Computer Analysis of Personality Projects	University of Texas

mental form only in several cases. The printout of one set of scores and a "Personality Description" from the MMPI is seen in Table 5–5. At the University of Alabama, a smoother narrative report has been developed, one that reads nearly the same as a written report by a live clinician (see Fowler, Table 5–4).

A somewhat different printout comes from computer scoring of the Holtzman Inkblot Technique (HIT) (see Gorham, Table 5–4). Up to

Table 5–5. Printout of a Psychological Report of an MMPI Record Analyzed by a Computer

UNIVERSITY OF KANSAS MEDICAL CENTER
MMPI REPORT
(EXPERIMENTAL FORM)

NAME

PROFILE CODE 2 (2–7)

SEX M AGE 28 O/I CP NO 1 DATE 2/2/65 REFERRED BY P. A. MARKS MD DEPT PSY ROOM 100 PSY. NO. 11

SCALE	L	F	K	HS	D	HY	PD	MF	PA	PT	SC	MA	SI	ES	LB	A	R	AT
RAW SC.	6	3	24	0	21	22	20	35	10	9	6	17	27	53	15	9	23	4
RAW SC. +K	6	3	24	12	21	22	30	35	10	33	30	22	27	53	15	9	23	4
T-SCORE	57	48	69	52	60	60	76	78	55	71	65	63	52	64	75	46	66	66

ABNORMAL PROFILE   3 T-SCORES ABOVE 70   WELSH CODE ***547'8932–610/.
UNCLASSIFIABLE BY ATLAS CODE
CHECK ITEMS 133, 139

PERSONALITY DESCRIPTION

TENDS TO GIVE SOCIALLY APPROVED ANSWERS REGARDING SELF-CONTROL AND MORAL VALUES
TENDS TO MINIMIZE OR SMOOTH OVER FAULTS IN SELF, FAMILY, AND CIRCUMSTANCES (K)
NUMBER OF PHYSICAL SYMPTOMS AND CONCERN ABOUT BODILY FUNCTIONS FAIRLY TYPICAL FOR CLINIC PATIENTS
MILDLY DEPRESSED OR PESSIMISTIC (D)
PROBABLY SENSITIVE AND IDEALISTIC WITH HIGH ESTHETIC, CULTURAL, AND ARTISTIC INTERESTS
RESPECTS OPINIONS OF OTHERS WITHOUT UNDUE SENSITIVITY
TENDS TOWARD ABSTRACT INTERESTS SUCH AS SCIENCE, PHILOSOPHY, AND RELIGION
PATIENT IS AWARE OF AND CONCERNED ABOUT ASOCIAL ATTITUDES AND EMOTIONAL IMPULSES BUT UNABLE TO CONTROL THEM.
PROBABLY ENERGETIC AND ENTHUSIASTIC. VARIED INTERESTS
HAS CAPACITY TO MAINTAIN ADEQUATE SOCIAL RELATIONSHIPS
RECOMMEND PSYCHIATRIC CONSULTATION

six words may be used by an examinee in describing each inkblot. The computer takes these words from punched cards, scores them for the 16 variables used for categorizing responses, then prints out scores, a list of words used more than once, and a list of words not contained in a stored "dictionary" of about 7,000 words, which account for most of the words ever used to describe the HIT inkblots.

These samples of computer processing of personality test data may whet the appetite of the empirically-minded clinician, but may cause cold chills in the one who sees computers supplanting clinicians. The issues are certainly more than academic and should be explored (Finney, 1965; Holtzman, 1960; Kleinmuntz, 1963). But no one supposes that the physicist has been supplanted by the cyclotron or even the computer, which he uses extensively, or that the physician would trade his modern laboratory techniques for the old-fashioned examination of a lady's arm thrust through a hole in a curtain. Highly trained and broadly experienced clinicians are essential to writing programs for computer analyses. And, when the computer has performed its work—far more efficiently than the clinician can do it—just as much training and experience are required to utilize the output. Computer processing of objective personality test data requires, in the final analysis, greater professional competence in the clinical psychologist than unaided, intuitive methods of analysis demand.

SUMMARY

This chapter endeavors to acquaint prospective clinical psychologists, as well as the practicing clinician, with major objective personality tests and their professional use. As a professional person, the clinical psychologist uses such tests only to sharpen his observation of the total person referred to him by self or others. To use these tests for professional judgments, he must have theoretical and statistical background and knowledge of societal and small-group dynamics.

Objective tests include psychophysiological, psychophysical, and psychomotor measures that reveal personality characteristics and distinguish between normal and disturbed persons. "Organicity" tests, though usually predicated on a unitary concept of brain damage, need to reveal specificities of brain-lesion conditions.

The most widely used clinically of objective temperament tests, the MMPI, partly because of its validity scales and defined populations standardization, has proved useful in many settings. "Response styles" with the MMPI and other tests may account for some of the test performance. Both Guilford's inventories and Cattell's tests, defining factor traits rather than psychiatric syndromes, have been widely accepted—the former less in clinical situations than their potentialities warrant. Cattell's scales, for most ages and personality phenomena, include the 16 P-F, for 16 personality factors, and other scales for normal, anxiety, and neurotic dimensions beyond the 16.

Vocational interest inventories, of which the *Strong* and *Kuder* are the best known, reveal obliquely many intellectual and temperamental patterns, making them useful for indirect assessment of noninterest characteristics.

General value patterns and "existential frustration" are assessed, respectively, by the typologically based *Study of Values* and the *Purpose in Life Test*. Despite the clinical and theoretical importance of roles, these have not received as careful objective measurement as other personality areas.

Many objective tests yield profiles of scores. Mathematical treatment, "profile analysis," taking account of shape, level, and dispersion of profiles, can result in psychologically meaningful clusters of individuals, as shown by the BCP.

Computer processing of personality test data provides, much more efficiently than can unaided clinical judgment, profile analysis with printout of an individual's test-revealed characteristics. Computer simulation of personality test data, automation of MMPI and 16 P-F interpretive rules applications, and interrelating of the multiplicity of children's problem behaviors have helped generate computer processing of tests including even one inkblot test (HIT). These new developments in test analysis call for even greater professional competence in the clinical psychologist than was called for in premachine days.

REFERENCES

Bass, B. M., and Berg, I. A. (eds.). 1959. *Objective approaches to personality assessment.* Princeton, N.J.: Van Nostrand.

Becker, W. C. 1960. The matching of behavior rating and questionnaire personality factors. *Psychol. Bull.,* **57**, 201–12.

Bendig, A. W., and Meyer, W. J. 1963. The factorial structure of the scales of the Primary Mental Abilities, Guilford-Zimmerman Temperament Survey, and Kuder Preference Record. *J. gen. Psychol.,* **68**, 195–201.

Berdie, R. F. 1954. Interest and personality measurement. In L. A. Pennington and I. A. Berg (eds.), *An introduction to clinical psychology.* (2d ed.) New York: Ronald.

Berg, I. A. 1961. Measuring deviant behavior by means of deviant response sets. In I. A. Berg and B. M. Bass (eds.), *Conformity and deviation.* New York: Harper.

Borko, H. 1962. *Computer applications in the behavioral sciences.* Englewood Cliffs, N.J.: Prentice-Hall.

Buros, O. K. (ed.). 1959. *Fifth mental measurements yearbook.* Highland Park, N.J.: Gryphon.

Buros, O. K. (ed.). 1961. *Tests in print: A comprehensive bibliography of tests for use in education, psychology, and industry.* Highland Park, N.J.: Gryphon.

Cattell, R. B. 1949. r_p and other coefficients of pattern similarity. *Psychometrika*, pp. 279–98.

Cattell, R. B. 1957. *Personality and motivation structure and measurement.* New York: Harcourt, Brace & World.

Cattell, R. B. 1961. Theory of situational, instrument, second order, and refraction factors in personality structure research. *Psychol. Bull.*, **58**, 169–74.

Cattell, R. B. and Scheier, I. H. 1961. *The meaning and measurement of neuroticism and anxiety.* New York: Ronald.

Clark, K. E. 1961. *Vocational interests of non-professional men.* Minneapolis: Univer. of Minnesota Press.

Cook, S. W., and Selltic, Claire. 1964. A multiple-indicator approach to attitude measurement. *Psychol. Bull.*, **62**, 36–55.

Cooley, W. W., and Lohnes, P. R. 1962. *Multivariate procedures for the behavioral sciences.* New York: Wiley.

Crumbaugh, J. C., and Maholick, L. T. 1964. An experimental study of existentialism: The psychometric approach to Frankl's concept of *noogenic* neurosis. *J. clin. Psychol.*, **20**, 200–207.

Dahlstrom, W. G., and Welsh, G. S. 1960. *An MMPI handbook: A guide to use in clinical practice and research.* Minneapolis: Univer. of Minnesota Press.

Darley, J. G. 1941. *Clinical aspects and interpretation of the Strong Vocational Interest Blank.* New York: Psychological Corp.

Dreger, R. M. 1962. *Fundamentals of personality: A functional psychology of personality.* Philadelphia: Lippincott.

Dreger, R. M. 1964. A progress report on a factor analytic approach to classification in child psychiatry. *Psychiat. Res. Rpt. 18*, Nov.

Dreger, R. M., Reid, M. P., Lewis, P. M., Overlade, D. C., Rich, T. A., Taffel, C., Miller, K. S., and Flemming, E .L. 1964. Behavioral Classification Project. *J. consult. Psychol.*, **28**, 1–13.

Edwards, A. L. 1964. Social desirability and performance on the MMPI. *Psychometrika*, **29**, 295–308.

Eysenck, H. J., Granger, O. W., and Brengelmann, J. C. 1957. *Perceptual processes and mental illness.* New York: Basic Books.

Finney, J. C. 1965. Methodological problems encountered in a programmed composition of psychological test reports. Paper read at Southeastern Psychological Association, Atlanta, April, 1965.

Fleishman, E. A. 1954. A factorial study of psychomotor abilities. *Res. Bull.* AFPTRC-TR-54-15.

Fleishman, E. A., and Hempel, W. E., Jr. 1954. Factorial analysis of complex psychomotor performance. *Res. Bull.*, AFPTRC-TR-54-12.

Foa, U. G. 1961. Convergences in the analysis of the structure of interpersonal behavior. *Psychol. Rev.*, **68**, 341–53.

Freeman, F. S. 1962. *Theory and practice of psychological testing.* (3d ed.) New York: Holt, Rinehart, & Winston.

GEIST, H. 1963. Work satisfaction and scores on a picture interest inventory. *J. appl. Psychol.*, **47**, 369–73.

GULLIKSEN, H. 1950. *Theory of mental tests.* New York: Wiley.

HAIN, J. D. 1964. The Bender-Gestalt Test: A scoring method for identifying brain damage. *J. consult. Psychol.*, **28**, 34–40.

HALSTEAD, W. C. 1947. *Brain and intelligence: A quantitative study of the frontal lobes.* Chicago: Univer. of Chicago Press.

HARMAN, H. H. 1960. *Modern factor analysis.* Chicago: Univer. of Chicago Press.

HATHAWAY, S. R., and MONACHESI, E. D. 1961. *An atlas of juvenile MMPI profiles.* Minneapolis: Univer. of Minnesota Press.

HAYNES, J. R., and SELLS, S. B. 1963. Assessment of organic brain damage by psychological tests. *Psychol. Bull.*, **60**, 316–25.

HOLLAND, J. L. 1962. Some explorations of theory of vocational choice: I. One and two year longitudinal studies. *Psychol. Monogr.*, **76**, No. 26 (Whole No. 545).

HOLT, R. R. 1958. Clinical and statistical prediction: A reformulation and some new data. *J. abnorm. soc. Psychol.*, **56**, 1–12.

HOLTZMAN, W. H. 1962. Methodological issues in *P* technique. *Psychol. Bull.*, **59**, 248–56.

HOLTZMAN, W. H. 1960. Can the computer supplant the clinician? *J. clin. Psychol.*, **16**, 119–22.

HOLTZMAN, W. H., THORPE, J. S., SWARTZ, J. D., and HERRON, E. W. 1961. *Inkblot perception and personality: Holtzman Inkblot Technique.* Austin: Univer. of Texas Press.

JACKSON, J. M. 1961. The stability of Guilford-Zimmerman personality measures. *J. appl. Psychol.*, **45**, 431–34.

KASSEBAUM, G. G., COUCH, A., and SLATER, P. 1959. The factorial dimensions of the MMPI. *J. consult. Psychol.*, **23**, 226–36.

KHAN, LILLIAN. 1962. Factor analysis of certain aptitude and personality variables. *Indian J. Psychol.*, **37**, 27–38. (*Psychol. Abstr.*, **37**:6716.)

KLEINMUNTZ, B. 1963a. MMPI decision rules for the identification of college maladjustment: A digital computer approach. *Psychol. Monogr.*, **77**, No. 14 (Whole No. 577).

KLEINMUNTZ, B. 1963b. Profile analysis revisited: A heuristic approach. *J. counsel. Psychol.*, **10**, 315–21.

L'ABATE, L., and CRADDICK, R. A. 1965. The Kahn Test of Symbol Arrangement (KTSA): A critical review. *J. clin. Psychol.*, **21**, 115–35.

LOEVINGER, JANE. 1957. Objective tests as instruments of psychological theory. *Psychol. Reports, Monogr. Suppl. 9*, **3**, 635–94.

McGINN, N. F., HARBURG, E., JULIUS, S., and McLEOD, J. M. 1964. Psychological correlates of blood pressure. *Psychol. Bull.*, **61**, 209–19.

McHUGH, R. B., and APOSTOLAKOS, P. C. 1959. Methodology for the comparison of clinical with actuarial prediction. *Psychol. Bull.*, **56**, 301–8.

MARKS, P. A., and SEEMAN, W. 1963. *Actuarial description of abnormal personality: An atlas for use with the MMPI.* Baltimore: Williams & Wilkins.

MARTIN, B. 1961. The assessment of anxiety by physiological behavioral measures. *Psychol. Bull.*, **58**, 234–55.

MEEHL, P. E.   1954.   *Clinical vs. statistical prediction.*   Minneapolis: Univer. of Minnesota Press.

MEEHL, P. E.   1956.   Wanted—a good cookbook.   *Amer. Psychol.,* 11, 263–72.

MESSICK, S., and ROSS, J. (eds.).   1962.   *Measurement in personality and cognition.*   New York: Wiley.

NUNNALLY, J.   1962.   The analysis of profile data.   *Psychol. Bull.,* 59, 311–19.

PASCAL, G. R., and SUTTELL, BARBARA J.   1951.   *The Bender-Gestalt Test: Its quantification and validity for adults.*   New York: Grune & Stratton.

PEIXOTTO, HELEN E.   1956.   Reliability of the Despert Fables, a story completion projective test for children.   *J. clin. Psychol.,* 12, 75–78.

PETERSON, D. R.   1965.   Scope and generality of verbally defined personality factors.   *Psychol. Rev.,* 72, 48–59.

REITAN, R. M.   1955.   An investigation of the validity of Halstead's measures of biological intelligence.   *AMA Arch. Neurol. Psychiat.,* 73, 28–35.

REITAN, R. M.   1959.   The effects of brain lesions on adaptive abilities in human beings.   Unpublished paper, Indiana Univer. Medical Center, Indianapolis.

SARBIN, T. R.   1954.   Role theory.   In GARDNER LINDZEY (ed.), *Handbook of social psychology.   Vol. I.   Theory and method.*   Cambridge, Mass.: Addison-Wesley.

Sixteen Personality Factor Questionnaire.   1957.   Champaign, Ill.: IPAT.

SUNDBERG, N. D.   1961.   The practice of psychological testing in clinical services in the United States.   *Amer. Psychol.,* 16, 79–83.

TAFT, R.   1959.   Multiple methods of personality assessment.   *Psychol. Bull.,* 56, 333–52.

THOMAS, CAROLINE B., ROSS, D. C., and FREED, ELLEN S.   1964.   *An index of Rorschach responses: Studies on the psychological characteristics of medical students—I.*   Baltimore: Johns Hopkins Press.

THURSTONE, L. L., and CHAVE, E. J.   1929.   *The measurement of attitude: A psychophysical method and some experiments with a scale for measuring attitude toward the church.*   Chicago: Univer. of Chicago Press.

TOMKINS, S. S., and MESSICK, S. (eds.).   1963.   *Computer simulation of personality: Frontier of psychological theory.*   New York: Wiley.

TORGERSON, W. S.   1958.   *Theory and methods of scaling.*   New York: Wiley.

VOAS, R. B.   1958.   Relationships among three types of response sets.   *USN Sch. Aviat. Med. proj. Rep.,* Proj. No. NM 16 01 11, Sub. 1, No. 15.

WATLEY, D. J., and MARTIN, H. T.   1962.   Prediction of academic success in a college of business administration.   *Personnel Guid. J.,* 41, 147–54.

WELSH, G. S.   1965.   MMPI profiles and factor scales A and R.   *J. clin. Psychol.,* 21, 43–47.

WELSH, G. S., and DAHLSTROM, W. G. (eds.).   1956.   *Basic readings on the MMPI in psychology and medicine.*   Minneapolis: Univer. of Minnesota Press.

WITTENBORN, J. R.   1961.   Contributions and current status of Q methodology.   *Psychol. Bull.,* 58, 132–42.

II

THE PROBLEM APPROACH
IN THE CLINIC

6

Problems of Childhood
and Adolescence

BOYD R. MCCANDLESS AND RICHARD DAVID YOUNG [*]

THE PRESENT STATE OF KNOWLEDGE

Society demands that the behavior problems of children be dealt with by the teacher, social worker, clinical, and school psychologist, counseling and guidance worker, psychiatrist, and other professionally trained persons. Such professional people work more through knowledge gained in their personal experience than on the basis of full and adequate data. While many research data are available, they are scattered, fragmented, and often conceptually unclear as well as methodologically defective. It is a truism to say that only when more integrated and technically sound research programs are conducted, coupled with the development of a more adequate science of personality stemming from these programs, can clinical problems be handled with maximum effectiveness. More important, only then can educational and training programs be efficiently designed to prevent the development of the behavior problems so prevalent today.

Personal Norms. Our current knowledge of the problems of childhood and adolescence comes principally from the following four sources. The most often used knowledge in working with children and their families comes from the *personal norms* of an experienced clinician. In the hustle and bustle of clinical practice with mothers, fathers, and children of all

[*] Boyd R. McCandless, Ph.D. (University of Iowa), Director, University Schools Clinic Complex, and Richard David Young, Ph.D. (University of Washington), Assistant Professor of Psychology, both of the Indiana University.

backgrounds and ages, the clinician learns what to do and what not to do. If he is reasonably intelligent and sensitive, his practice serves as a continuously operating "laboratory" which provides him with hypotheses and informal experimentation. The chief difficulty with this state of affairs is that such knowledge, practically and scientifically, is almost impossible to communicate to others. This has led many, experts and laymen, to say that the social welfare professions are more art than science. The well-known annual volumes of *The Psychoanalytic Study of the Child* always contain a number of articles attempting to communicate clinical experimental phenomenon.

The Clinical Census.   The second source of knowledge is the *census,* where the problems met in the clinic are categorized or classified. While there is no one accepted system of classification, as Kanner (1957) has indicated, the categorizations currently in use provide students and professional workers with a general notion of what to expect from day to day. Within clinical circles, there has been an increased resistance to the use of classification, and authorities such as Menninger (1955) and Rogers (1951) have asked that all "labeling" be stopped.   Problems associated with classification systems of behavior problems have been detailed by Szasz (1957) and Zigler and Phillips (1961).   While a census has no explanatory value, it can provide hypotheses to be tested by empirical research.   An example of the potential fruitfulness of this source can be seen in the development of interest in early infantile autism since 1943 (Eisenberg and Kanner, 1956).

Case Histories.   The third source of information is the *case history approach* and its modifications, such as the anecdotal record.   This approach is useful as a training tool and plays an important role in communications among co-workers and workers from different disciplines.   Those who work with behavior problems are becoming increasingly aware of the difficulty in attempting to use in any rigorous way the complex and subjective data provided in the usual case history.   Examples of this method, vividly used, are found in Redl and Wineman (1951), Riese (1963), and Erikson (1963).   Even the most sophisticated reader can be intrigued by such works.   There is, however, always the danger of misunderstanding between authors and readers.   Riese, for example, may mean one thing, the reader understand another.   Finally, in the scientific sense, the case history approach provides no explanation.

During the last few years there has been a noticeable increase in the single case study approach by those interested in behavior modification (Williams, 1959; Bentler, 1962).   These studies concentrate on one or two major variables, thus reducing the complexity of the data.   They carefully define their procedures and measures so that replication is possible.

Despite the rigorousness of the procedures and reporting, the impossibility of generalizing from a single case to other cases imposes a problem upon these reports and their authors. From either type of case report, however, the research worker may form multiple new hypotheses, and the practitioner may immediately consider modifications in his clinical techniques.

Experimental data provide the fourth source of current knowledge. Here, studies are subject to one of three different criticisms: first, there are experiments which have direct "face validity": they deal with problems as seen in a clinic or by the practitioner. From the practical viewpoint they seem meaningful and useful. In terms of scientific method, however, they present difficulties in defining independent, intervening, and dependent variables. An example of such a study is provided by Miller and Baruch (1950) who used allergic (mostly those with asthma and hay fever) as experimental subjects and children referred for other behavior difficulties as control subjects. Parent interview data, office observations, teacher-provided data, and the content of play sessions constituted the methods of study. The authors maintain that their hypotheses (i.e., allergic children show less overt hostility than nonallergics) was supported. They proceeded to make a psychoanalytic analogue between allergy and suppression of hostility, and implicitly concluded that play therapy, providing opportunity for elicitation and interpretation of hostility, alleviates the allergic condition. Flaws in the observational methods, opportunities for experimental contamination (the investigators, for example, knew the group to which each child belonged), and failure to report reliability of the observations all serve to make the clinical worker reserved in his acceptance of their results and conclusions. The study, nonetheless, has great practical appeal.

On the other hand, a study by Gewirtz and Baer (1958) may be considered by some as "impractical" by virtue of its failure to provide data pertaining directly to clinical problems. These investigators hypothesized that deprivation and satiation of social reinforcement would enhance the effectiveness of the reinforcement in the order: deprivation > nondeprivation > satiation. The verbal approval (social reinforcement) of the experimenter was made contingent upon one response of a two-response game. The effectiveness of approval as a reinforcer was considered to be indicated by a change in the relative response from a baseline level. First- and second-grade students were assigned to one of three experiment conditions upon being taken from their classroom: (1) deprivation—the child remained alone in the experimental room for 20 minutes prior to playing the game; (2) nondeprivation—the children played the game immediately upon their arrival at the experimental room; and (3) satiation—under this treatment the subject was exposed to 20 minutes of drawing and cutting out designs while the experimenter praised him and admired his work prior to playing the game. The results indicated that approval functioned as an effective reinforcer under all conditions, but was most effective after deprivation and least effective after satiation. The authors conclude that deprivation and satiation operations have an effect on a child's social drives similar to their effects on primary drives. The authors attempt no practical applications. The experiment is a rigorous empirical investigation, which may not be directly applicable to clinical problems but has important implications. For example, Bandura and Walters (1963) learning theory approach to personality development and behavior modification relies heavily on social reinforcement. This type of research is also relevant to Ferster's (1961) theoretical model of the development of autism in which the role of social reinforcement is a central issue.

Third, some experiments may be criticized for not being linked to an existing theory of human behavior (e.g., not being relevant to psychoanalytic or behavior theory). This, some contend, limits the usefulness of an experiment. Despite its obvious appealing analogue to human behavior, the brilliant work of Harlow (1958) and his colleagues on "mother love" in monkeys is subject to this criticism. The usefulness of an experiment to our understanding of a problem cannot be judged solely by the immediate pragmatic value of the results.

The basic argument involved between the first approach to experimental data and the latter two approaches seems to center around the adage, "You can't reduce life to the laboratory." This argument, of course, is more likely to be stressed by the applied worker than by the experimentalist. Indeed, the former's emphasis upon the issue may in part be due to the frustration engendered by this strongly felt need for information on the vital, pressing, practical problems he faces every day. Each year, more and more technically competent research is being reported in the area of childhood behavior problems. One may not be able to "reduce life to the laboratory," but with a solid knowledge of experimental techniques plus a little imagination and ingenuity, the problems of childhood and adolescence *are* subject to experimental investigation.

Reasons for the unsatisfactory state of current knowledge are easy to find: first, professional workers with children have been slow to develop the experimental-theoretical approach as contrasted with the normative. Students too often have not been rigorously trained in the philosophy of science and research methodology. The results in professional workers who produce research of an inferior quality and who cannot effectively evaluate and/or integrate the research findings of others. As a corollary of the above, there are few centers whose chief function is research work with children. Despite the fact that there are many schools and many children, most school administrators, with justification, maintain that their first task is education. From their point of view (the authors do not agree with them, but understand their point of view), research is a luxury and interferes with regular classroom schedules. Adequately trained professional workers are few and the number of children with problems is so great that research suffers because of service demands. The pressure for service on workers who are trained to understand personal-social dynamics is so great that their (perhaps more profitable) research work tends to be pushed aside. The authors of this chapter can testify to this. Additionally, any research with children is difficult. More patience is needed with the child as a subject than, for example, with the white rat or the college sophomore. The establishment of rapport with a preschool child requires much time and unusual personal skills. It is almost impossible to gather data by groups with children younger than the fourth-grade level. Many types of research require the mother and father to serve as subjects. Getting mothers as subjects is time consuming, tact demanding, and expensive; but getting fathers as subjects is almost impossible. With clinical studies, the concepts involved are often complex, making it difficult to formulate experimental approaches and to produce clear-cut research designs in such ways that significant conclusions are eventually reached. The research worker in the area of child adjustment has not been especially well paid, although completely relevant data are not available. Finally, and, perhaps least important, research in child development has traditionally attracted a higher proportion of women scientists than have other psychological areas. Practically speaking, it is more difficult for a woman to do research and lead a normal life than it is for a man. Women, due to marriage and motherhood, are more likely to be in and out of a career. This produces a lack of continuity which interferes with research. In summary, as a function of all these factors, the clinician has more *problems* than he has facts. With such limitations in mind, attention can be turned to a consideration of clinical problems commonly encountered in practice with children and adolescents.

TYPICAL PROBLEMS ENCOUNTERED AT THE VARIOUS AGE LEVELS

Most students have some idea of the nature of the behaviors described as adult psychopathology. Too many, however, believe that the problems of childhood and adolescence are simpler versions or precursors of the adult condition. The emotional and behavioral disorders of childhood differ in many significant ways from the adult disorders, and *the younger the child the more marked are the differences.* As a simple illustration, let us contrast the initial picture presented by an adult client with that of a child client. The adult will verbalize his feelings of extreme anxiety, discomfort, fear, or emotional upheaval. He will be at least partially aware that his behavior is abnormal, or at least disrupting, and that he wants to alleviate his suffering. He will actively seek the help of a professional worker, and he will be motivated to cooperate in his treatment. The child, on the other hand, will almost never seek out treatment of his own accord. Instead, he will be brought to the clinic by his parents or a representative of society. When asked what his problem is, he will almost certainly see no problem whatsoever. His motivation for behavioral change will be low, either because he does not believe there is anything wrong or he is too frightened of what may happen if there is a change. Beyond the obvious differences such as those just mentioned, there is the additional factor that the child's interpersonal relations and psychological processes are constantly changing and being developed; thus, they do not have the durability and consistency which typify the adult.

There are at least four important aspects of interpersonal situation with which the normal child must cope which can lead to the establishment of behavior problems. The first is the very long period of psychological and biological dependency which characterizes childhood. Childhood, adolescence, maturity, and old age can all be partially delineated by the quantity and quality of a person's dependency upon others. The complete dependency of early childhood, as well as our culturally defined adolescent struggle for independence, provides patent situations for the learning of normal and abnormal behavior.

Second, the interpersonal relationships of the child are much more *variable* than those of the adult. This is partially due to the rapidly developing and frequently changing psychological processes of the child. Every parent has been amazed at the rapidity with which his child can genuinely "swear life-long allegiance" to a new friend only to form a new, equally deep affiliation the next month. A third aspect of these relationships which is significant is that of the child's *social role*. The concept that "children should be seen and not heard" may no longer be fashionable; but other social roles, less succinctly communicated, nonetheless shape the child's behavior. The role played by the one-year-old in his world is quite different from that required during the preschool period or again during preadolescence. We are, of course, observing a markedly different organism at each of these ages, both in terms of psychological and biological development.

Finally, the child is extremely *vulnerable* to both inner and outer stresses. The abrupt disorganization of behavior as a result of stresses can be seen in the outburst of temper and crying that occurs when a young child is told he must leave a friend's birthday party early. Just as quickly as the temper tantrum started, however, it stops when an appropriate substitute for the party is provided. Much of the normal socialization process of the child is devoted to developing adequate self-control and inhibitory behaviors when confronted with various stresses.

The First Two Years. During this stage of his development, the child moves almost entirely behind the *aegis* of parents and/or nursemaids, older siblings, baby-sitters, grandparents, roomers-in, and so on. His problems, other than those directly traceable to physical causes such as contagious diseases or physical-neurological-glandular incapacity are usually a product of the family situation. Perhaps the most lethal behavior disorder of babyhood, fortunately decreasing in its incidence, is marasmus. This literal wasting away of the child appears to occur only when the infant is shifted from a reasonably constant and adequately affective family climate to a protracted hospital routine, or is early placed for long periods on one of the relatively rare "institutional wards" in an outmoded foundling home. This, then, appears to be a disorder of isolation that stems from the lack of sufficient stimulation to maintain life. Workers such as Goldfarb (1955), Levy (1947), and Spitz (1954) have directly or indirectly documented this ailment of isolation, although aspects of these studies have been questioned on points of scientific method (Pinneau, 1955; or Casler, 1961). Our best conclusion is that marasmus seems not to occur when mothers or their stimulating and affectionate surrogates are present in the environment.

Second in seriousness and first in frequency come the difficulties of training. Feeding is usually considered the most important of the training areas. Infant feeding practices have passed through a full cycle in the last four or five decades. From the depersonalized, highly scheduled regime prescribed in the early behaviorist paradigm for child care, United States mothers have returned to less regimented feeding schedules and to more permissive and accepting methods of dealing with their infants. These practices are derived most recently from the psychoanalytic orientations and, more remotely, from the way grandmothers or great-grandmothers of the present parent generation handled their babies. One of the most useful, anxiety-allaying sourcebooks for infant care, illustrative of this swing of the pendulum, is the popular book by Spock (1957). It presents a modified psychoanalytic approach to baby care, altered to fit the author's wide experience with mothers, fathers, and their infants. Every clinical worker should be familiar with Spock's book as well as the Federal Security Agency pamphlets (Faegne, 1951; Faegne and Chandler, 1945). For parent-child problems within the normal range, these provide a sensible basis for counseling and guidance.

To return to problems of training during infancy, child psychology specialists seldom have anything to do with how parents interact with their children except when extreme difficulties arise. Advice on feeding, bathing, napping, toileting, and other routine practices is ordinarily given by the family physician, general practitioner, family pediatrician, or experienced relatives. Parents are often affected, of course, by lectures on child development, high school or college courses on the topic, advice given by mothers and mothers-in-law, and most significantly their own rearings, need systems, and their previous experiences with other children. The orientation of our culture is such that few problems exhibited by children under two years of age are referred for psychiatric and psychological services. This is one of the several reasons why the fund of soundly based research information at this level is so small. As a basis for counseling parents, nonetheless, the clinician should possess information about infant development so he may answer questions on such subjects as "brightness-dullness" and "normality." He must also know the repertoire of facts about the wide range of individual differences subsumed by these areas. He needs to know children and parents according to the developmental and research literature, as well as in a practical sense. Such training equips him to recognize typical parent-child conflicts, developmental problems, and areas of difficulty involving goal-seeking behavior. He should also know, in a work-a-day fashion, something about the typical frustrations and satisfactions which the parent of an infant or runabout child encounters.

CHILDREN'S PROBLEMS AND PARENTAL REACTIONS

Many of the so-called problems which arise, such as the runabout child's destructiveness and parental concern about sleeping, eating, toilet training, and thumb-sucking, are due to inadequate parental information more than parental "maladjustment." The more severe, nonphysiological disturbances, however, often appear to be related to parental tension. Examples of such disturbances are: serious and persistent under- or overeating, extreme withdrawal, soiling and smearing of considerable intensity and for long duration, frequent and severe nightmares or night terrors, some problems of night wakefulness, intense and prolonged fear of parental desertion or of strangers. Parental reactions related to such problems may include rejection, overexpectation, overprotection, or overcontrol of the child. In the case of a parental reaction of rejection, the rejection may spring from many sources in the parent's personality or life history, as well as the current situation. Examples include the immature and dependent parent who rejects responsibility in general, and for whom the addition of responsibility in the form of a child is intensely anxiety evoking. The child may have been initially unwanted, or the rejection may be one phase of a maternal postpartum depression. Other parental problems encountered in relation to the child's difficulties may include exaggerated anxiety for any one of several reasons over infant handling, including such factors as parental compulsive cleanliness, overinsistence on food intake, paternal resentment of the infant's pre-emption of the mother's time, parental conflict over methods of rearing, extreme over-stimulation of the infant, and many others. Other infant behavior problems may arise from easily ascertainable errors on the part of the parent, such as indecisiveness about nap and bedtime, or their insistence on consumption of a food the child dislikes. Such problems can ordinarily be managed by re-education and anxiety-allaying counseling.

The Factor of Culture. Our culture excuses parents from much of their responsibility for early childhood difficulties by such devices as humor and folklore. Examples are: cartoons showing unshaven fathers pacing in the dawn with squalling infants, parental panic when confronted with their newborn child, frustration with the destructive and unreasonable runabout-aged child, the eternal problem of drinks of water during the night, reassurances that "you're always more nervous with your first," and so on. Such folklore perhaps serves as an "escape hatch" that helps parents avoid facing the fact that very early childhood behavior problems cannot be other than the parents' responsibility (except in cases of birth damage, organic difficulty, and so on, where competent medical help should be sought as a first step). But the normal child sees almost no one other than his parents—hence his problems are *their* problems, and they must carry the responsibility.

Reviews of the recent literature (Heinstein, 1963; Caldwell, 1964) summarize the scattered research material. The conclusion is about as follows: if the parent honestly believes he is doing the "right thing" (the thing that is typical of the local community socioeconomic group to which he belongs) then—regardless of whether this is breast, bottle, or cup feeding; scheduled or unscheduled feeding; permissive or highly controlled handling—his infant is likely to go through his first two years without serious trouble. The most "modern" advice is to apply, with common sense, the general principles of human learning interpreted according to what children are able to do at specified ages.

Problems of the Preschool Years (Ages Two to Six). This age span has been selected because it covers the period between infancy and admission to school. It is not surprising that many of the problems mentioned previously, except for marasmus, are found among preschool children. Since parents progressively hold their growing children more responsible for their own acts, the training problems faced during this period are seen as more serious and dramatic. The preschool child is also more mobile in the community. Parental anxiety about how his child is affecting and being judged by others may produce and aggravate problems. Matters of discipline and control also enter the picture more forcibly than at the early age levels. The problems of infancy that persist during this span of years are thus likely to be more clear-cut and seen as more severe. Generally speaking, the principles that apply to the infant also apply to the two- to six-year-old child.

Problems also arise from the following two parental expectations: (1) that the child will begin to assume "sensible" (reasonable from an adult's point of view) control over his behavior, and (2) that the child will reflect favorably on the parents in his dealings with other adults and children. Parents, without thinking of the child's view of the matter, want him to accept adult values and standards. Problems associated with the first of these factors concern such things as destruction of property and equipment, failure to assume ordinary precautions for the maintenance of life and limb, refusal to restrain aggression within reasonable limits, and disobedience. Problems relating to the second parental overexpectation include such things as poor manners, masturbation, enuresis (bedwetting), thumb-sucking, shyness with relatively unfamiliar adults and children, obvious fears, peculiarities of behavior such as tics, stuttering, and other defiant patterns of behavior.

The significance of these problems lies first in how they affect the parent and second, in how they affect the child's safety. As far as destructiveness is concerned, any preschool child possesses the potential to destroy. He breaks up or tears things apart because he wants to "see what is inside," because he has not learned that things cannot be replaced, because he has not been taught more constructive or rewarding ways of handling equipment, or possibly because he wants to "get even" with his parents for something that, from his point of view, is ill-defined and vague. Because of his parents' reactions, he may have learned to use destructiveness as a tool to "master" and "control" them.

To the small child, his personal safety is of no concern. If he wants to get to the other side of the street, he dashes across. He thinks no more of the fact that his life cannot be restored than he does about the toy truck he has smashed. To panic him by extreme parental apprehension (logically correct from the parents' point of view) may be as destructive as to give him no training at all; in the first case, he may "freeze" in a danger situation because he does not know how to handle it—he is too anxious; in the second, he is simply heedless.

In dealing with such problems, the clinical worker should help the parents to reduce their blind fear, but not their realistic concern about their child's safety. The child must be helped by example (words do not always work very well at this age) to understand the possible consequences of reckless behavior, but at the same time he must be free enough to think, within his limits, so as to behave flexibly and adaptively in the fact of danger. In other words, he must develop enough concern so that he is cautious, but not paralyzed by fear.

Aggressivity in Children. Different parents regard their children's aggressive behavior in different ways. One parent may say, "Under *no* circumstances will I tolerate a child who spits!" Another parent may be so tolerant as to state, "I must say, I *will* defend myself when my child starts hitting me with his heavy building blocks." Most of the problem with the so-called "aggressive" or "negativistic" period of early childhood seems to be due to the parents imputing contrariness to behavior patterns which have much less emotional than developmental importance. A sensible general rule-of-thumb is that children often seem to need to express aggression sufficiently violent that it worries their parents. Such aggression, of course, cannot be so extreme that it severely hurts the one who receives it (i.e., runabout children cannot strike their baby brothers or sisters with sticks, nor bite them so they are injured). Generally, we work with young children so that they learn first to hit with their fists, or to slap, rather than strike with blocks and sticks. They must learn not to kick while wearing heavy shoes. They may be verbally abusive within limits, but should not bite.

This gradual learning of milder and less damaging, culturally acceptable aggression must be quietly and consistently taught (or shaped). Some parents will punish their children violently for aggressive behavior, then feel guilty and "make it up to the aggressive child" with so many indulgences that, in actuality, they reinforce his violent behavior. From the child's viewpoint, in such a case, he has mastered not only the child or person to whom he has been aggressive, but his parents as well. He may also model further aggressive behavior on his parent's behavior (e.g., Sears *et al.*, 1957; Bandura and Walters, 1963).

Nonaggressive children, primarily boys, can create as much parental overconcern as their overly aggressive siblings. Our culture begins sextyped appropriate play during these preschool years and the boy who is afraid to aggress against his peers may be establishing the "mama's boy" behavior patterns seen in later years as well as paternal rejection as a "sissy."

Obedience. Parents have as wide a range of restrictions about obedience as they have about aggression. Some parents accept "sassing" and moderate disobedience calmly. Others are threatened and immediately retaliate, treating the child as unpleasantly as they consider he has treated them. Some sensible compromise based on the parents' attempt to see what is reasonable from the child's point of view, yet with which they can also live, usually results in a workable relationship in the home. If the parent has given a five-minute warning that dinner is "about ready," and has followed it by "Now it's here—Come and eat!" he has a reasonable right to expect that the child will come to the table. The normal preschool child will either come or accept being brought to the table without thinking he has been unjustly treated. On the other hand if, without warning, he is told "Get to the table this second!" he may ignore, rebel, or react with violence if he is forcibly brought to the table. He sees no logic to the parents' "request." In other words, parental fairness is usually followed by the child's fairness. If the parent has considered the child's viewpoint, the child eventually learns to consider and appreciate the parent's viewpoint. There are exceptions to such a rule-of-thumb, of course: if the child has had an unusually trying day, if he is coming down with an illness, or if he is extremely tired (among any one of a number of things), the parent must keep this fact in mind. The child has not had enough experience to do so. The parent must be careful, however, not to establish a condition under which disobedience is permissible. Many an *enfant terrible* has developed from the simple "I don't have to—I don't feel well."

Learning good manners—a great source of conflict between children and parents—follows much the same learning pattern. If we look at the relations between adults (including teachers) and children, we are forced to conclude that adults are unconscionably rude to children. Children may adopt their parents' (or teachers') manners, particularly when the home is a relatively "free" one, to "get back" at their parents, or simply due to modeling and imitation behavior.

Masturbation and Toilet Training. Young children of both sexes usually masturbate at some time. The child has none of the guilt reactions to this behavior that his parents or teachers have. The first step that should be taken with the masturbating child is to see that he has no inflammations or irritations and, particularly with boys, that their clothes fit moderately loosely. After such a check, ignoring the behavior seems to be the most effective procedure: the general pressure of society is such that it will go away without the parent getting emotionally involved. When the parent is extremely upset by masturbation (which United States parents tend to be), it is as likely that the problem is as much the parent's as it is the child's, and the child may use it as an attention-getting device, or consolidate it as a satisfying piece of personal behavior.

Enuresis (bed-wetting, but also daytime incontinence) is another preschool and early school age problem that causes much tension between parents and their children, particularly their boys. It is likely, judging from the author's clinical experience, that bed-wetting among perfectly "normal" children occurs much more frequently and last much longer (well into the school years) than the normative literature indicates. The literature is usually based on parents' reports, which are biased by the fact that in our culture bed-wetting is a "bad thing." There is no clear knowledge about the psychological meaning of prolonged bed-wetting (for example, up into the ninth or tenth year, particularly for boys). The most popular clinical guess fits with psychoanalytic theory; it is a way of "getting even" with parents (particularly mothers who, among other things, ordinarily handle the laundry).

Parents who have trained their children with reasonable consistency and calmness seldom meet the problem. If it persists well into the elementary school years, the child should (as in all cases involving physical symptoms) be checked by a competent physician. If there is nothing wrong organically, the clinician has at least three options: (1) He may choose to work closely with the physician, reinforcing the usual sensible recommendations that the parents relax, that late evening fluids be restricted, that the child be trained to use an alarm clock to awaken him, and so on. (2) If the bed-wetting has no symbolic meaning to the child (i.e., if he is not using it as a method of "revenge" on his parents), certain types of conditioning device may be successfully employed. Typically, these close a circuit at the first sign of dampness and awaken him unceremoniously by the abrupt ringing of a bell. These devices seem to work well and without troublesome side effects for many children. (3) The child may be recommended for individual or group therapy when other techniques do not work. His failure to respond to other methods of "drying him up" probably means that there are emotional and/or family problems associated with the behavior and, as they are alleviated, the bed-wetting will also disappear. Most clinicians recommend that the parents also enter into the therapeutic-counseling relationship, a position which the present writers hold. It is usually easier to obtain cooperation from the mother than the father, although, at least some research exists (Hetherington and Brackbill, 1963) that suggests that the father is at least as much, if not more, a contributing factor than the mother in such personal (i.e., nonpublic) problems as elimination training. The much higher frequency of enuresis in boys suggests that further clinical research must pay closer attention to separation of specific practices as applied to boys or girls.

It should be added that most normal and sensibly toilet-trained children begin to sleep dry sometime between two and about three and one-half years of age and that they soon thereafter voluntarily reject diapers (it has been mentioned that these data are "soft," in that mothers are likely to give false answers because of the high value placed on continence in our culture).

Thumb-Sucking. The previous section has extended beyond the preschool years, to which we shall now return to discuss thumb-sucking. Kanner (1944) amusingly points out that thumb-sucking was considered more a virtue than a symptom of personal disturbance until the present century, when psychoanalysis linked it with infant and childhood sexuality, orthodontists came on the scene and made much to-do about its effect on the child's tooth and jaw alignment, and concepts of sanitation (i.e., the "dirty old thumb will get germs in you") became prevalent throughout all segments of United States society. Previously, the general opinion was that "the thumb-sucking baby is the placid baby."

The evidence about its effect on tooth-jaw conformation is not clear, but what there is suggests that no permanent damage is done unless the child continues persistently, vigorously, and with much mechanical pressure to suck his thumb until after the eruption of the permanent teeth. Some authors (Miller and Baruch, 1950) consider it a sign of "oral personality"; Honzik and McKee (1962, and personal correspondence) report data suggesting that, if anything, persistently thumb-sucking little girls grow up to be more "womanly" than nonthumb-suckers, and that at late adolescence there is no personality difference between boys who have and have not sucked their thumbs. Honzik also found the highest proportion of persistent thumb-sucking among the children of parents who were most highly educated and were rated as most happily married. It seems to occur most when the child is fatigued, hungry, or lonely and insecure as a means of anxiety reduction (Palermo, 1956) and perhaps (Sears and Wise, 1950) when he has been permissively fed by breast or bottle rather than by cup. The data included in this last study are not statistically significant, however. Recently Baer (1962) has demonstrated effective laboratory control of thumb-sucking by withdrawal and representation of a rewarding event.

In other words, thumb-sucking may or may not be a behavior problem, and it may or may not indicate other emotional maladjustment. The chances are that it does not. The best advice to parents seems to be: discourage it mildly in early infancy, that is, by gently removing the child's thumb from his mouth. If it persists, forget about it (which is difficult, since everyone from the milkman on to grandmother is likely to comment about it with disapproval). In fact, cultural pressure against it is so great that one child known to the present authors, during her post-tonsillectomy awakening from anaesthesia, screamed in terror, "They've cut off my thumbs!" Even on a hospital cart on her way to the operating table, the nurse had chided her with "Does it taste good?" and "Aren't you afraid you'll suck it off?" and the anaesthetist had commented in similar fashion as he fitted the anaesthetic mask into place.

The cultural pressure is, in the long run, the best agent for eliminating thumb-sucking, and does not involve the parent in prolonged or intense conflict with his child. The kindergartner is soon "broken from" the habit by his peers and, ordinarily, will drop the mannerism soon after entering school except for brief periods when he may use his thumb as a device to help him get to sleep—a device that seems relatively harmless from any point of view.

SOCIAL AND EMOTIONAL ADJUSTMENT

Public shyness which continues over long periods of time may result from too much pressure by the parents to socialize the child before he is ready; or by inconsistent demands made on the child in social situations with adults (a given behavior is acceptable when the guests are of the parents' generation, or drink cocktails; but unacceptable when grandma and the great aunts are present, or the guests are, for example, strongly opposed to a cocktail or a cigarette); or when the child is given little if any exposure to social situations that include adults.

Modeling and teaching—when the child has reached the age to understand the teaching—seem the most effective ways to help the child learn poise. Remedial measures, and we are speaking from clinical experience rather than solid data, seem to be: first, accept the shyness as one of the child's natural characteristics; give him plenty of time when in new surroundings to understand the situation by allowing him simply to sit in the parent's lap while he gets his bearings; when he is old enough, teach him by role playing how to answer the doorbell and telephone, to accept an introduction, to respond to a direct question with a short answer; then transfer his role playing to actual situations which include familiar and friendly adults, so structured that this success will generalize to situations with unfamiliar adults.

Social Withdrawal, Fears, and Phobias. Continued and intense withdrawal from social situations following a few weeks in kindergarten or first grade should be regarded more seriously. The authors recommend that the parents or teacher call in an outside consultant for advice as to further retraining which may involve individual or group therapy counseling. A good example of effective classroom treatment of severe isolate behavior can be seen in the report of Allen *et al.* (1964).

Fears within the "normal" range can usually be handled by patient teaching and by modeling. The principle that "what is understood, we no longer fear" holds, within sensible limits. For illustrative research see Levy and McCandless (1952) and London and Peterson (1964). Parents can take many constructive steps in dealing with their children's fears: for example, fear of dogs is very common with young children. To help his child with this fear, the average parent buys a puppy. But puppies bounce, scratch, nip, and have teeth like needles; in other words, they are not likely to help the fear. What is needed is a tired, somnolent, old dog that has had a long and wearing life with children. Many children are terrified by fire and police sirens, or even the whistles of trains. A trip, accompanied by parents, to the fire station, the depot, or the police station can be helpful, and the present authors have found officials in such situations understanding and cooperative. The child can be helped to recover from a nightmare by parental soothing and brief lying down beside him in bed (not carried to such a point that the child demands to sleep nightly with the parent). The common fear of darkness can be helped by a soft night light or by giving the child his own flashlight. Fear of lightning and thunder may be reduced by explanation, although it is best to prevent it by parent modeling.

Normal fears, however, can move into phobias, which are best defined as persistent, violent, and single, but more usually multiple, fears. When such a point is reached, expert outside-the-family or schoolroom help should be sought.

We understand the theory of tics and other compulsive behaviors little better than we do a theory of thumb-sucking (thumb-sucking probably differs from a tic in that it gives the child direct comfort, whereas such tics as exaggerated blinking, stuttering, and so on do not appear to produce comfort). Many children "headbang" or rock heavily before going to sleep, upon awakening in the night, or after morning awakening and before they are removed from their cribs or beds. Psychoanalysts have made much of this but have provided more speculation than data. There seems to be a greater frequency both of headbanging and rocking for boys than girls and either behavior (except for the type of headbanging that bruises or wounds) may be regarded as comfort giving. These behaviors usually disappear as the child moves into the upper preschool years and are perhaps best ignored unless they are extremely exaggerated in form, when advice should be sought. Compulsive eyeblinking, pulling out hair such that bald patches result, or eating paint and dirt consistently should be checked medically. If no explanation comes from this check, parent-child relations should be explored more deeply, preferably in family-type therapy counseling with emphatic effort being made to include the father.

One of the most violent tics in the present authors' experience was a nine-year-old girl's extremely conspicuous, violent hitching and hunching motion of the head, neck, shoulders, and torso. After many hours of play therapy, the child suddenly burst out with the statement, "This is how the car made me do when we had the wreck!" In this wreck, a baby sister had been killed. The girl in treatment had been markedly jealous of her infant rival. Following the statement quoted above, and after repeated dramatization in play of the girl's belief that the mother had loved the baby better than her, and that she herself had killed the baby (children believe in "magic"), the tic disappeared completely.

Many will disagree, but the present authors regard stuttering as a tic. There are many theories of stuttering, ranging from the psychoanalytic point of view that it is one of many possible signs of oral aggression through to the learning "self-reflexive" theory of Johnson (1961). Johnson believes that stuttering can almost invariably be prevented by parental patience and lack of overconcern with the stammering, repetitive speech that typifies preschool children, particularly boys. Persistent, conspicuous stuttering should always be treated with speech-hearing therapists who, as a group, work closely with medicine, psychology, education, and social work. This and other related problems are discussed in Chapter 11.

THE OLDER CHILD

Problems of the School Years and Adolescence. The routine problems of feeding, sleeping, toilet, and basic habit training which are so conspicuous in the first five years of life become less frequent and intense during the elementary, junior, and senior high school years. The problems that exist are often a function of parents' failure to realize that "all children are like that"; that is, for parents, children's manners never become perfect, wraps are never hung up, little boys continue to break things and track in dirt, ears are not properly washed, the child gets average rather than superior grades, girls *live* in the bathroom, and so on. When these matters loom very large for either parent, family life may become so filled with conflict that it becomes a nightmare for the child *and* his parents. The child will steadily disassociate himself from the family until, by the time he is an adolescent, he is a stranger to his parents and possibly to his brothers and sisters.

Other parents overprotect their children or almost seem to be afraid to set the limits necessary for the child's security and safety. For the child (and the parent) to be happy enough that they remain friends during the long mutual lifespan that characterizes the United States culture, children must be "set free" by stages. Parents do not succeed equally well in this setting-free process, and the clinician sees the most conspicuous failures and/or their children.

The Sex Role. The literature on sex role identification and identification, in the sense of developing a conscience, is so voluminous that it cannot be discussed here except in outline form. Illustrative references are McCandless (1960) and Mussen and Distler (1950).

Briefly, the child develops an appropriate sex role (he is a male, and happy about this state of affairs; or she is a female, and happy about it) and a moderately flexible but affective conscience—a set of socially acceptable, *personal* controls—when the following family conditions are met:

1. The parent of the same sex is seen by the child as possessing appropriate sex-type power.
2. The same sex parent gives more love and positive reward than rejection and punishment.
3. The same sex parent provides an example of behavior that is socially acceptable, within reasonably broad limits.
4. The family is relatively free from conflict.
5. The child feels affection and respect for *both* parents. These conditions, of course, can be met by foster parents, other family or community personnel, and so on.

The role of an adequate home life and good parent-child relations in producing good child adjustment has been demonstrated repeatedly in the practice of every clinical worker and is also well documented by research (e.g., Cass, 1952a, b; Becker *et al.*, 1959; Peterson, *et al.*, 1959; Payne and Mussen, 1956; Mussen and Distler, 1959; Schoeppe, *et al.*, 1953; and more recent studies). Cass suggests that the more the parent is aware of and informed about her child (the more significant portions of her studies dealt with mothers and their adolescent daughters), and the less stringent the control she exercised, the more closely the girl modeled on her mother; that is, in very general terms, the happier the girl was with her young womanhood. Data for boys pointing in the same direction are included in the other studies listed above. It seems quite clear that knowledge about their children, sympathy and understanding of the children, and moderate techniques of control help the children to grow into successful adults (and to escape the clinician). For example, in discussing how boys and girls solve their major developmental problems (appropriate sex identification, adequate achievement in school, freedom from law-breaking, independence, and so on), Schoeppe *et al.* (1953) say, "Doggedly reappearing is the fact that children whose parents exercised severe control in their formative years were hindered in these accomplishments (p. 49). These authors go on to say that such an atmosphere stifles the development of a "positive, self-directing, confident self concept" and results in an "inner feeling of guilt about impulsivity which in turn [impedes] mature emotional reactivity." Girls, they somewhat needlessly add, should be treated differently from boys.

During the school years there is an ever increasing extra-familial influence upon the child—the peer group. This is particularly noticeable and important when the child moves from the democratic spirit of elementary school to the highly complex social stratification of high school. As the child grows older and into his teens, the group's power to influence behavior reaches, and in certain areas surpasses, that of the family (Coleman, 1961; Rosen, 1955). Perhaps the most relevant and significant aspect of peer influences upon behavior problems of the age group comes about when low status is assigned the child by his peers. Lippitt and Gold (1959) note that teachers differ in their response to high- versus low-status children. The negatively evaluated child becomes aware of his status and this has a marked influence upon his self-concept (Ausubel *et al.*, 1952; Horowitz, 1962; Rosen *et al.*, 1960). Campbell and Yarrow (1961) have reported that children's reputations (high or low status) are actually more stable over time than their behavior patterns. More importantly, changes in reputation actually drew out of the children behavior which was in accordance with the expectation based upon reputation (Polansky *et al.*, 1950). This can lead to a vicious circle of frustration and anxiety in which the expectation of peers has a built-in self-reinforcing and maintaining schedule. The tremendous importance of the peer group in establishing and modifying values and attitudes in delinquent youths has been reviewed by Cohen (1955) and Sykes and Matza (1957).

The current model for behavior difficulties in the elementary school and adolescent years does not differ much from the classical concept of the child who attacks as contrasted with the child who withdraws, although such a dichotomy is often more apparent than real. "Attackers" are the youngsters who get into conduct trouble in the classroom, who cannot be controlled by their parents, and who often run afoul of the police. Traditionally, we refer to them as delinquent or delinquent prone. When their behavior is extreme, the term *sociopath* or *psychopath* is often applied to them. Professionally, we have been singularly ineffective in dealing with them in face-to-face counseling situations, although there seems to be some room for optimism in the steadily growing disciplines of group and family therapy (McCord and McCord, 1964; Ackerman, 1961).

Such children may and do come from every social class and ethnic group, although the rate of severe acting-out appears to be greater in lower socioeconomic groups. Membership in ethnic minority groups which have carried a strong cultural heritage and a tradition of education as a means of upward social mobility (e.g., youngsters from the Jewish religion or from Japanese and Chinese origin) tend to have a lower rate of delinquency. The problems of such children are undoubtedly due to a complex interaction of social-familial-personal factors. A summary of finding on social class differences in children's behavior and personality characteristics can be found in McCandless (1960).

School Dropouts. About 33 per cent of United States school children fail to finish high school (U.S. Bureau of the Census, 1960). Actually, the term "high school dropout" almost deserves a category of disorder of its own. Hathaway and Monachesi (1963) have reported that high school dropouts tend to occur among children who, when seen as ninth graders, were: (1) of low IQ, (2) disliked school and were doing poorly, (3) children of farmers and day laborers, or (4) who came from broken homes. The neurotic and/or socially introverted adolescent was much more likely to be a "drop out" than to become delinquent. Havighurst *et al.* (1962) present very similar results. In an increasingly technological and automated society, the dropout is ill equipped to earn a livelihood. Such youngsters meet increasing frustration, since United States society as now constituted offers them few constructive channels by which to reach mature and secure independence. This combination of poor personal adjustment to the demands of the school environment and a few pathways to self-sufficiency is deeply—almost hopelessly—frustrating. This frustration, added to the increased biological and social drives of adolescence, is frequently turned *against* society in ways destructive to both society and the child. Hathaway and Monachesi (1963) and Coleman (1961) suggest that the school systems might make a significant advance in handling these problems by changing from their rigid, conformist approach to education to offering opportunities for constructive self-expression by the rebellious, excitement-loving students.

The second extreme of the present model, the withdrawing child, is probably less well understood and certainly not as well recognized as the acting-out child. He is, however, seen in psychological clinics more frequently as an initial reference, whereas the attacking child may be first handled by a social authority agent, such as a truant officer, a policeman, or probation worker. Frequently the withdrawn child is labeled as schizoid, socially introverted, and/or neurotic. In contrast to their rebellious peers, they are very often inarticulate and find it extremely difficult to approach or maintain any consistent social relationships. They tend to be rejected by peers ("He's a deadhead") and family ("John won't want to go with us, he prefers to stay at home") and overlooked by their teachers ("Half the time I don't even know when he's in class"). The withdrawn child frequently finds school a painful experience because of the rough give-and-take social interactions between peers and the frequent reprimands which hurt him. A large proportion of them escape the frustration and resentment by dropping out of school.

The "adolescent depressive" seems to occur more frequently now than previously; he is, essentially, the young person who does not ask the classic question "How do I get to where I am going?" but seems to ask instead "Why am I going anywhere?" One of his major characteristics is that of school underachievement, an area that has been seriously neglected by clinical psychology, psychiatry, and social work, but a type of maladjustment that deserves the closest attention by all the professions devoted to human welfare. Hathaway and Monachesi (1963) found that high intelligence test scores and good grades were particularly character- istic of adolescents who had a carefree attitude toward life and a *marked absence* of depression.

Kimball (1952), some years ago, working with an intellectually and socially superior group of adolescent boys found from her data that serious underachievement was one of the ways her subjects had available to them to punish their parents, particularly their fathers. The clinical experience of the present authors leads them to similar hypotheses. Payne and Farquhar (1962) find evidence suggesting that a negative "mirror self concept" goes with underachievement; that is, the child who believes that others think ill of him (in this study, the "others" were teachers) thinks ill of himself and reflects this poor opinion in his school achievement.

Payne and Farquhar also find some evidence that, for overachieving high school boys, their overall pattern of adjustment is to a degree fem- inine, while the overachieving girl is somewhat masculine. This has implications for high school dropouts. Havighurst *et al.* (1962) suggest that male dropouts are aggressive, female dropouts passive. The impli- cations of these two studies, while most tentative, are intriguing. Anxiety and depression, arising from conflicts outside of the school environment, produce interference with attention, concentration, and often a reported inability to maintain a sustained interest in anything. Learning diffi- culties are many times the first sign of early undetected behavior prob- lems, particularly in the preadolescent.

Boy's bodies (e.g., Staffieri, 1965) also seem to play a role in their ad- justment, including the way they are regarded by their classmates. From the ages of four and five on through college, broad-shouldered, narrow- hipped males are overwhelmingly viewed favorably (regardless of the body build of the viewer); fat, barrel-bodied boys are viewed as having almost entirely undesirable social traits; while very lean boys are seen as shy, withdrawing, weak, and so on. The effect of such social regard on the self-concepts of boys, adolescents, and young men must be quite marked. Similar data are not clear, or have not been gathered for girls.

During this age period, sex becomes a pressing problem and sexual exploration occurs. The range of "acceptable" sexual behavior for pre- adolescents and adolescents differs widely from one socioeconomic and ethnic group to another. In all groups, however, effeminacy may become a nightmare for the boy just as masculinity is for the girl. The "double- standard" of sexual behavior is established in United States society early in the teen years; "sexual promiscuity" or sexual delinquency is a term applied almost exclusively to the girl. Unfortunately, girls who have at- tempted to resolve their conflicting feelings through sexual delinquency have received much less professional attention than the group deserves. What few data we have (e.g., Vincent, 1961) suggest that such girls are deeply disturbed, and that the sexually acting-out girl is less important as a sociolegal concept than as a symptom of deep personal maladjustment which Vincent, at least, links to inadequate mother-daughter emotional relationships.

Experimentation with homosexual, voyeuristic, and exhibitionistic behaviors at this age is much more common than is generally recognized. For example, Kinsey reporting for boys and men (Kinsey *et al.*, 1948) finds that about half of the older males and two-thirds of the preadolescent boys reported homosexual activity of some kind during their preadolescent years. An occasional behavior of the type mentioned above is probably of little significance and is best handled by ignoring it or reassuring the parents and child. However, if undue anxiety is present or if the behaviors threaten to become established behavior patterns, professional treatment should be offered. The boy or girl who is struggling toward an appropriate sex-role identification needs help just as certainly as he does if he is a fire-setter, an underachiever, or a school dropout.

Before closing this section on clinical problems, the authors feel that some mention should be made of childhood schizophrenia. We agree that there is a sizable number of children who present extremely unusual developmental and behavioral characteristics. Within recent years, these children have been increasingly labeled as childhood schizophrenics. But, as Rumke pointed out, "all that is queer is not schizophrenic." The symptoms of the childhood disorder are much different from those of the adult (delusions are absent and hallucinations are very unusual). In fact, the only similarity seems to be the social withdrawal of the patient and the "bizarre" (meaning we do not understand them) qualities of some of his behavior. An interesting point frequently overlooked is that the childhood disorder usually occurs before age four and practically never after five, whereas the adult disorder does not show an onset until well after puberty. If the psychotic behavior is the same, one would expect some continuity of frequency and time of onset of the behavior pattern. Furthermore, there are relatively few cases reported longitudinally where the child schizophrenic ultimately develops the symptom patterns of the adult disorder, and this number is probably not any larger than one would expect from any group, knowing the base rates for the adult disorder. Add to this the fact that the overlapping and frequently indistinguishable behavior patterns of the schizophrenic child, the organically brain-damaged, and the developmentally retarded are such that differential diagnosis is extremely unreliable. Any rigorous attempt to differentiate among the assumed subcategories within the schizophrenic syndrome (for a description see Mahler *et al.*, 1959) leads to even greater chaos. The term "childhood schizophrenia" has not described any useful syndrome of behaviors. At best, it has merely pointed to a group of extremely heterogeneous and severe deviations from normal behavior. Simultaneously, it has lead to confusion in clinical reference and a great deal of premature speculation about etiological factors. By far the best description of the clinical syndrome is Kanner's (1957) who called it infantile autism. The authors of this chapter contend that the use of the term "childhood schizophrenia" is not warranted and leads more to confusion than to clarity.

BASIC PREMISES FOR DIAGNOSIS AND THERAPY

It is maintained here that the clinician's first step is to gain and use knowledge about the environment within which the child lives. This includes a detailed awareness of (1) the characteristics and mores of children of this age in general, (2) of children of the same general age and socioeconomic class as the child in question, and (3) of children who are his age and who are functioning in the particular school and community environment to which he belongs. The clinician's formal training and continuous professional reading will provide him with normative information and specific examples about the first two attributes. An example of this type of information is the excellent study of MacFarlane *et al.* (1954) which covers the behavior problems of normal children from 21 months to 14 years of age. For the third, he must gather his own data. These can be obtained from two major sources, the school and the child/ family, in the following ways.

Sociometry. Sociometric data from the classroom are available in many modern schools. If not available, they can be gathered without difficulty. Taken together with qualitative materials such as those provided by "Guess Who" material, they quickly yield clinically useful leads as to how the child stands in his classroom, the types of persons accepting and rejecting him, and his status with children of the opposite sex. In other words, an important sociometric map of the child's strong and weak points and general acceptance status, based upon his peer group, is provided. This material is especially effective for the school psychologist, who may have some acquaintance with the individual personalities in the room or class, but should be requested routinely by agencies outside of the school that are working with the child. The data can give the clinician an idea of the duration of the social response to the child when the sociograms have been collected systematically. Peers are frequently the best judges of one another's behaviors and it may be that marked changes in the social status of a child are one of our simplest warning signals of the early development of behavioral problems. Bronfenbrenner (1945) and Thompson (1960) describe the many principles operative in gathering and handling socio-metric and "Guess Who" data.

The School as Data Source. The school also provides information pertaining to academic standing, adequacy of participation in extracurricular activities, and the like. It is necessary to know the breadth of a child's activities and participation as well as the adequacy of them. The child who concentrates in one activity differs from the child who participates in "everything." Generally speaking, the personality mechanisms of the underachiever are different from those of the overachiever. Rosen and D'Andrade (1959) studied high-need-for-achievement boys versus low-need-for-achievement boys, matched for intelligence, and found consistent differences between the two groups on a series of ingenious experimental procedures. They conclude that the superior performance of the high-need group was not due to intelligence but, rather, to greater self-reliance and more enjoyment of competitive activities. Intellectual competence, of course, plays an important role in the school adjustment, although perhaps less so than is assumed by many teachers and psychologists.

Test Data. Where school information is lacking, more detailed testing, such as individual intelligence tests and diagnostic instruments for specific academic skills, should be administered. There are two types of tests which are of special importance. The *achievement tests* which are designed to assess the effect of instruction or training. Within this group tests of reading and arithmetic (e.g., the Wide Range Achievement Test) are of clinical interest. The second type is the *aptitude test,* which is assumed to reflect the cumulative influence of the experiences of daily life rather than specific training material. There is a wide assortment of well-standardized tests of both types.

The clinical significance of testing is illustrated in the case of a 15-year-old youngster classed as mentally defective by a group intelligence test who was found to be deaf but of superior intelligence on an individual performance examination. A hearing aid, some special remedial reading teaching, and an emphasis on the development of shop skills produced in one year's time a boy who, although no academic wizard, could read at the fourth-grade level and was self-supporting in a skilled trade. Such dramatically successful instances are, of course, few.

Information from Teachers. The teacher is a valuable source of information about the behavior of her students. With grade-school-age clients, the teacher often spends more hours per day in close contact with the child than anyone else, including the parents. Every clinical case should include at least a brief evaluation of the student by his teacher. In most cases, it also helps to know about the personality and the expectations held by the teacher. Teacher expectations of having difficulty with certain children are often confirmed by youngsters with behavior problems; her behavior toward the child may lead him to behave in accordance with her prediction.

Despite their overall utility, teacher evaluation must be used with caution. For example, in the Hathaway and Monachesi study (1963), teachers could not successfully predict delinquency in girls because they did not expect such behavior from girls, particularly those from higher socioeconomic homes. Rather marked differences in teacher approval and disapproval have been reported for boys and girls (Meyer and Thompson, 1956). The differences should not be ignored, for they may provide important information concerning the teacher-child interaction which can assist in the diagnosis and treatment of the problem behavior. Many modern schools maintain cumulative records which should be carefully studied, both for the quantitative data contained therein and for the "critical incidents" frequently reported by teachers and others who have worked with the child. Many noneducational specialists who work with children (including clinical and school psychologists) and who write such reports for the record, as well as convey them directly to educators, do not know how to communicate meaningfully with teachers. This skill in communication is essential.

The Child and Family as Information Sources. The second major source of data is obtained from the child/family. We have divided this section into three aspects: the child, the family, and the social milieu. This division is made for convenience; when dealing with a specific case, the data must be integrated.

The most important single source of information is *always* the child. There is absolutely no substitute for observation and interviews with him. The clinician must know how the child looks at his problems, his world, his own behavior, and that of others. How does he perceive his school and his ability to cope with it? How does he view his social group? What does he think of his teachers? From his viewpoint, are they failing him or "doing right" by him? What is his thinking about his parents, his siblings, his less immediate relatives? What makes him angry, or frightened, or restless? The gaining of that picture and the correction of the child's unrealistic and maladaptive responses to it are, of course, the essences of therapy. Yarrow (1960) has provided an excellent review of the literature dealing with interviewing children. Observation of the child in his class and social group, when possible, is helpful in establishing an effective therapy program.

Diagnostic interviewing with children is frequently a very time-consuming activity as the child is not able to verbalize his view of the world as systematically and logically as the adult. In an attempt to obtain the same kind of information but with greater speed, psychologists have developed and utilized a number of personality tests. Some school systems administer personality tests and the results are available to the teachers, counselors, psychologists, and other agencies when parental permission for release is obtained. These personality inventories are usually of the paper-and-pencil variety. They are primarily valuable as a group screening device. Their use, if the gross score is considered precisely predictive for the single case, is at best limited and may be positively dangerous. Considerable skepticism should therefore be exercised by the clinician when using data from currently available paper-and-pencil tests. As far as projective techniques are concerned, the average worker in the field is well versed in administration, scoring, and interpretation. He is likely, however, to be less well versed in his knowledge of the range of responses within the normal population. Owing to naïveté concerning scientific method and the philosophy of science, the clinician may use these results with a confidence and even dogmatism quite unjustified by the available evidence (Murstein, 1963). Clinicians continue to use projective techniques, but such use is justifiable only if scientific caution is exercised. The indiscriminate and profuse use, accordingly, is to be avoided.

Stress in Children and Adults. The disorders of adulthood and childhood differ in several important ways and which are relevant to both interviewing and testing since most testing and interviewing techniques are predicated upon the adult models of psychopathology. When the interpersonal relationships among adults are disturbed, the behaviors tend to become more and more rigid over time. For example, the hypochondriacal person who is concerned with headaches, low-back pain, etc., tends to become increasingly concerned about his body over time. Whenever the patient finds himself in a stressful situation, the pattern of hypochondriacal complaint is repeated. The child, on the other hand, fluctuates greatly in his adaption to stressful situations. Over time, for example, a child may change from a rigid compulsive behavior pattern to an uncommunicative withdrawn one to a delinquent behavior response. The children's reactions will be relatively unstable and will change in behavioral form as well as direction.

With the possible exception of some of the behaviors labeled as psychotic, all psychopathologies are responsive to changes in the social milieu. It is commonly assumed that the adult patient is less responsive than the child. This apparent difference in the disorders may explain why in the majority of the adult disorders, the reorganization of behavior, "recoverability," appears to be much slower than for children disorders.

In summary, we have found that disorders of childhood are less stable, less durable, less consistant, and more recoverable than those of the adult. All of these variables should be carefully considered in working with diagnostic tests and interviews.

Over the last decade there has been an ever increasing awareness by clinical personnel that the child must be viewed within the context of the family. The theoretical writings of Eric Erikson and the clinical writings of Ackerman have been particularly influential. The individual behavior patterns within a family do not operate independently; they are initiated, maintained, and extinguished, at least partially, by the responses of other family members. For example, Bateson *et al.* (1956) have presented a model for the development of psychopathology based upon mother-child interactions in which the child is placed, by the mother, in an unfavorable discrimination situation and in which he is punished, irrespective of his response. They have called this situation the "double-bind" and have attempted to apply it to the development of schizophrenia. In order for the clinician to understand the family milieu in which the child client must operate, an interview with both parents is essential. A short interview simultaneously with all family members, when the client is over five years of age, provides an excellent opportunity to observe intrafamilial interactions, but should be conducted only by skillful professionals.

It has been recognized for some time that conflicts within the family can affect the adaptation of the child to the extrafamilial environment. The intellectually superior son, for example, of a domineering, overachieving, and highly successful physician, could not form close interpersonal peer relations; he was weak and passive, but he successfully aggressed against his father with repeated school failures and minor acts of delinquency which were socially embarrassing to the father. In such cases it seems most appropriate to deal first with the interpersonal levels of interaction between father and son, instead of jumping to the so-called intrapsychic conflict which is assumed by some to be causally related to these problems.

Extrafamilial conflict and pressure upon the child can also produce behavior disorders and intensify minor problems within the family. Over 30 years ago, in an attempt to show the reciprocity between behavior development and social forces, Alfred Adler pointed out the psychological damage to the child of stultifying poverty. His insight was ignored by all but a few. With the notable exception of the social worker, professionals who have dealt with childhood problems have rarely left their offices to see what the child's world is really like. The profound poverty of a Harlem or an Appalachia, the frequently open crime and terror in sections of our urban communities, the subtle as well as the evident discrimination against a wide range of ethnic and religious groups—these and many other extrafamilial and extra-"psychic" forces are powerful molders of a child's behavior. They contribute significantly to problems of childhood and adolescence. We do not have the techniques for protecting the child from the harmful aspects of these forces. The forces will not go away by themselves; yet we cannot continue to ignore them and treat the child as though they did not exist.

The Need for an Organizational Framework. In order for the information collected from the school and from the child/family to be intelligible, the clinician should have a reasonably coherent framework around which to organize his hypotheses and plan of treatment. As has been indicated earlier in this chapter, the latitude in the choice of a framework is wide. Choice is probably best made in terms of the climate of the installation in which the clinician works, the nature of his training, and the persons with whom he communicates his findings. Within these broad general guidelines, the clinician must learn to prepare his hypotheses and attendant tests of the hypotheses in a direct and observable manner. The history of the attempt to understand childhood disorders is filled with unreported or vaguely presented hypotheses. Real progress in the field has been made only when professionals have been explicit in their formulations and, as a consequence, have been willing to be wrong. Clinicians, as well as research workers, must adopt the empirical research attitude.

The utilization of various avenues in the collection of information relative to the individual child and his problem prior to diagnosis and treatment may seem unreasonable to some. Dissenters from this view may be exemplified by Rogers (1951), whose statements here deserve careful attention. Rogers believes that the collection of voluminous diagnostic and "steering" types of information casts the clinician in the role of a "problem solver"—the one who, for the client, knows all the answers. Certainly, where the collection of such material leads the clinical worker to disregard the problem as well as the child's view of the situation, such data gathering is to be decried. The majority of workers in the field, however, endorse the principles supporting the manifold approach suggested in this chapter. The viewpoint underlying this careful study of the child is in general similar to that held by those subscribing to the common-sense psychiatry of the late Adolf Meyer (1950) and as currently illustrated by Leo Kanner (1957). Recent books by Bandura and Walters (1963) and Bijou and Baer (1961, 1965) offer learning theory systems of social and personality development which may become useful in providing a framework for organization of the collected data.

The present authors look upon the collection of data as the basic step in the protoscientific method. As such, it is the best approximation to a clinical problem which can be reached by the modern clinical worker handicapped as he is by the lack of definitive information and well-established, empirically derived relationships. In the absence of reliable knowledge, the clinician must fortify himself with all the information he can possibly garner relative to the child with a problem. As Sullivan (1947) would have said, such information helps the clinician and his patient mutually to reach full communication and consensual validation. It is not, however, an end point and professionals must strive to avoid normative and idiographic stagnation.

Before summarizing this chapter, we believe it is important to take note of a new and rapidly increasing area of clinical concentration—prevention of behavior disorders in children. Caplan (1964) has suggested a model for preventative psychiatry which has three levels. *Primary prevention* involves lowering the number of new cases of a given disorder by counteracting the conditions which produce the disorder. This program does not prevent a particular person from developing the disorder; rather it reduces the base rate for the entire population being worked with. *Secondary prevention* reduces the "prevalence" of a given disorder at a given time by shortening the length of time the problem remains present in existing cases. This can be done by early diagnosis, efficient referral to the proper professional, and effective treatment. *Tertiary prevention* aims at reducing the residual defect after the behavior disorder has been treated. If considered on the individual level, this is rehabilitation. It is obvious from what has been written previously in this chapter that we do not as yet have the knowledge necessary to put Caplan's model into effect, but there are interesting beginnings, as is evident in the contribution of 16 research workers in Caplan (1961).

SUMMARY

The purpose of this chapter has been to set forth, in detail appropriate to the space allotted, the service pressures exerted upon the specialist in the child behavior clinic who functions professionally in terms of: (1) the current limitations in man's accurate knowledge of children's problems; (2) his training and chosen reference frame; (3) "best guesses" formulated from the collection and study of all available data; and (4) his accumulated knowledge consequent to years of practical experience. Those problems having high incidence of referrals to the clinician have been described and, in turn, related to the aforementioned four highly significant determinants of clinical function. Those problems characteristically found in early infancy and childhood, in the age span from two to six years, and during the school and adolescent years have been indicated. The basic premises for diagnosis and therapy, as a unitary function performed by the clinical psychologist, are noted. The ever present need for greater refinement and extension in our knowledge of child problems, both at the experimental and applied levels, can best be satisfied by recourse to the rigors of the scientific method.

REFERENCES

ACKERMAN, N. W.   1958.   *The psychodynamics of family life.*   New York: Basic Books.

ALLEN, K. EILEEN, HART, BETTY M., BUELL, JOAN S., HARRIS, FLORENCE R., and WOFF, M. M.   1964.   Effects of social reinforcement on isolate behavior of a nursery school child.   *Child Develpm.,* 35, 511–18.

AUSUBEL, D. P., SCHIFF, H. M., and GASSER, E. B.   1952.   A preliminary study of developmental trends in socioempathy: Accuracy of perception of own and others' status.   *Child Develpm.,* 23, 111–28.

BAER, D. M.   1962.   Laboratory control of thumbsucking by withdrawal and representation of reinforcement.   *J. exp. Analysis exp. Behav.,* 5, 525–28.

BANDURA, A., and WALTERS, R. H.   1963.   *Social learning and personality development.*   New York: Holt, Rinehart & Winston.

BATESON, G., JACKSON, D. D., HALEY, J., and WEAKLAND, J.   1956.   The genesis of mental disorders and social deviance—toward a theory of schizophrenia.   *Behavioral Sci.,* 1, 251–64.

BECKER, W. C., PETERSON, D. R., HELLMER, L. A., SHUMAKER, D. J., and QUAY, H. C.   1959.   Factors in parental behavior and personality as related to problem behavior in children.   *J. consult. Psychol.,* 23, 107–18.

BENTLER, P. M.   1962.   An infant's phobia treated with reciprocal inhibition therapy.   *J. Child Psychol. Psychiat.,* 2, 185–89.

BIJOU, S. W., and BAER, D. M.   1961 and 1965.   *Child development: a systematic and empirical theory.*   Vols. I–II.   New York: Appleton-Century-Crofts.

BRONFENBRENNER, U.   1945.   The measurement of sociometric status, structure, and development.   *Sociometric Monogr.,* No. 6.

CALDWELL, BETTYE M.   1964.   The effects of infant care.   In M. HOFFMAN and L. HOFFMAN (eds.), *Review of child development research.*   New York: Russell Sage Foundation.   Pp. 9–88.

CAMPBELL, J. D., and YARROW, M. R.   1958.   Personal and situational variables in adaptation to change.   *J. of soc. Issues,* 14, 29–46.

CAPLAN, G. (ed.).   1961.   Prevention of mental disorders in children.   New York: Basic Books.

CAPLAN, G.   1964.   Principles of preventive psychiatry.   New York: Basic Books.

CASLER, L.   1961.   Maternal deprivation: a critical review of the literature.   *Monogr. Soc. Res. Child Develpm.,* 26, No. 2.

COHEN, A. K.   *Delinquent boys.*   New York: Free Press, 1955.

COLEMAN, J. S.   *The adolescent society.*   New York: Free Press, 1961.

EISENBERG, L., and KANNER, L.   1956.   Early infantile autism, 1943–1955.   *Amer. J. Orthopsychiat.,* 26, 556–66.

ERIKSON, E. 1963. *Childhood and society.* (2d ed.) New York: Norton.

FAEGNE, M. L. 1951. *Infant care.* Washington, D.C.: Federal Security Agency, Children's Bureau, Publ. No. 8.

FAEGNE, M. L., and CHANDLER, CAROLINE. 1945. *Your child from one to six.* Washington, D.C.: Federal Security Agency, Children's Bureau, Publ. No. 30.

FERSTER, C. B. 1961. Positive reinforcement and behavioral deficits of autistic children. *Child Develpm.,* 32, 437–56.

GEWIRTZ, J., and BAER, D. M. 1958. Deprivation and satiation of social reinforcers as drive conditions. *J. abnorm. soc. Psychol.,* 57, 165–72.

GOLDFARB, W. 1955. Emotional and intellectual consequences of psychological deprivation in infancy: A revaluation. In P. H. HOCH and J. ZUBIN (eds.), *Psychopathology of childhood.* New York: Grune & Stratton. Pp. 105–11.

HARLOW, H. 1958. The nature of love. *Amer. Psychologist,* 13, 673–85.

HATHAWAY, S. R., and MONACHESI, E. D. 1963. *Adolescent personality and behavior: MMPI patterns of normal, delinquent, dropout, and other outcomes.* Minneapolis: Univer. of Minnesota Press.

HAVIGHURST, R. J., BOWMAN, P. H., LIDDLE, G. P., MATTHEWS, C., and PIERCE, J. V. 1962. *Growing up in River City.* New York: Wiley.

HEINSTEIN, M. I. 1963. Behavioral correlates of breast-bottle regimes under varying parent-infant relationships. *Monogr. Soc. Res. Child Develpm.,* 28, No. 4.

HETHERINGTON, E. M., and BRACKBILL, Y. 1963. Etiology and covariation of obstinacy, orderliness, and parsimony in young children. *Child Develpm.,* 34, 919–43.

HONZIK, MARJORIE P., and McKEE, J. P. 1962. The sex differences in thumbsucking. *Gen. Pediatrics,* 61, 726–32.

HOROWITZ, FRANCES D. 1962. The relationship of anxiety, self-concept, and sociometric status among fourth, fifth, and sixth grade children. *J. abnorm. soc. Psychol.,* 65, 121–214.

JOHNSON, W. 1961. *Stuttering and what you can do about it.* Minneapolis: Univer. of Minnesota Press.

KANNER, L. 1944. Behavior disorders in childhood. In J. McV. HUNT (ed.), *Personality and the behavior disorders.* Vol. II. New York: Ronald.

KANNER, L. 1957. *Child psychiatry.* (3d ed.) Springfield, Ill.: Charles C Thomas.

KIMBALL, BARBARA. 1952. The sentence completion technique in a study of scholastic underachievement. *J. consult. Psychol.,* 16, 353–58.

KINSEY, A. C., POMEROY, W. B., and MARTIN, C. E. 1948. *Sexual behavior in the human male.* Philadelphia: Saunders.

LEVY, L., and McCANDLESS, B. 1952. Expectancy of punishment as a function of type of differentiation in original learning. *J. abnorm. soc. Psychol.,* 47, 520–25.

LIPPITT, R., and GOLD, M. 1959. Classroom social structure as a mental health problem. *J. soc. Issues,* 15, 40–49.

McCandless, B. R. 1960. *Children and adolescents: Behavior and development.* New York: Holt, Rinehart, & Winston.

McCord, W., and McCord, Joan. 1964. *The psychopath: An essay on the criminal mind.* New York: Van Nostrand.

MacFarlane, Jean W., Allen, Lucile, and Honzik, Marjorie P. *A developmental study of the behavior problems of normal children between twenty-one months and fourteen years.* Los Angeles: The Univer. of California Publications in Child Development, 1954, Vol. 2.

Mahler, Margaret, Furer, N., and Settlage, C. F. 1959. Severe emotional disturbances in childhood: Psychosis. In S. Arieti (ed.), *American Handbook of Psychiatry,* Vol. I. New York: Basic Books. Pp. 816–39.

Menninger, K. 1955. The practice of psychiatry. *Dig. Neurol. Psychiat.,* **23,** 101.

Meyer, A. 1950–52. The collected papers of Adolf Meyer (E. E. Winters, general ed.). Baltimore: Johns Hopkins Univer. Press.

Meyer, W. J., and Thompson, G. G. 1956. Sex differences in the distribution of teacher approval and disapproval among sixth-grade children. *J. educ. Psychol.,* **47,** 385–96.

Miller, H., and Baruch, D. W. 1950. A study of allergic children. *Amer. J. Orthopsychiat.,* **20,** 506–19.

Murstein, B. I. 1963. *Theory and research in projective techniques* (emphasizing the TAT). New York: Wiley.

Mussen, P. H., and Distler, L. 1959. Masculinity, identification, and father-son relationships. *J. abnorm. soc. Psychol.,* **59,** 350–56.

Palermo, D. S. 1956. Thumbsucking: A learned response. *Pediatrics,* **17,** 392–99.

Payne, D. E., and Farquhar, W. 1962. The dimensions of an objective measure of academic self-concept. *J. educ. Psychol.,* **53,** 187–92.

Payne, D. E., and Mussen, P. H. 1956. Parent-child relations and father identification among adolescent boys. *J. abnorm. soc. Psychol.,* **52,** 358–62.

Peterson, D. R., Becker, W. C., Hellmer, L. A., Shumaker, D. J., and Quay, H. C. 1959. Parental attitudes and child adjustment. *Child Develpm.,* **30,** 119–30.

Peterson, D. R., and London, P. 1964. Neobehavioristic psychotherapy: Quasihypnotic suggestion and multiple reinforcement in the treatment of a case of postinfantile dyscopresis. *Psychol. Rec.,* **14,** 469–74.

Pinneau, S. 1955. The infantile disorders of hospitalism and anaclitic depression. *Psychol. Bull.,* **52,** 429–52.

Polansky, N., Lippitt, R., and Redl, F. 1950. An investigation of behavioral contagion in groups. *Hum. Relat.,* **3,** 319–48.

Redl, F., and Wineman, D. 1951. *Children who hate: The disorganization and breakdown of behavior control.* New York: Free Press.

Riese, Hertha. 1963. *Heal the hurt child.* Chicago: Univer. of Chicago Press.

Rogers, C. 1951. *Client-centered therapy.* Boston: Houghton Mifflin.

Rosen, B. C. 1955. Conflicting group membership: A study of parent-peer-group cross pressures. *Amer. sociol. Rev.,* **20,** 155–61.

ROSEN, B. C., and D'ANDRADE, R. 1959. The psychosocial origins of achievement motivation. *Sociometry,* **22,** 185–217.

ROSEN, S., LEVINGER, G., and LIPPITT, R. 1960. Desired change in self and others as a function of resource ownership. *Hum. Relat.,* **13,** 187–93.

SCHOEPPE, AILEEN, HAGGARD, E. A., and HAVIGHURST, R. J. 1953. Some factors affecting sixteen year olds' success in five developmental tasks. *J. abnorm. soc. Psychol.,* **48,** 42–52.

SEARS, R. R., MACCOBY, ELEANOR E., and LEVIN, H. 1957. *Patterns of child rearing.* New York: Harper & Row.

SEARS, R. R., and WISE, G. W. 1950. Relation of cup-feeding in infancy to thumbsucking and the oral drive. *Amer. J. Orthopsychiat.,* **20,** 123–38.

SPITZ, R. A. 1954. Unhappy and fatal outcomes of emotional deprivation and stress in infancy. In T. GOLDSTON (ed.), *Beyond the germ theory.* Health Education Council. Pp. 120–31.

SPOCK, B. M. 1950. *The pocket book of baby and child care.* New York: Pocket Books.

STAFFIERI, J. R. 1965. *A study of social stereotype of body image in children.* Unpublished doctoral dissertation, Indiana University.

SULLIVAN, H. S. 1947. *Conceptions of modern psychiatry.* Washington, D.C.: William Alanson White Psychiatric Foundation.

SYKES, G. M., and MATZA, D. 1957. Techniques of neutralization: A theory of delinquency. *Amer. sociol. Rev.,* **22,** 665–70.

SZASZ, T. 1957. The problem of psychiatric nosology: A contribution to a situational analysis of psychiatric operations. *Amer. J. Psychiat.,* **114,** 405–13.

THOMPSON, G. G. 1960. Children's Groups. In P. MUSSEN (ed.), *Handbook of research methods in child development.* New York: Wiley.

VINCENT, C. E. 1961. *Unmarried mothers.* New York: Free Press.

WILLIAMS, C. D. 1959. Case report: The elimination of tantrum behavior by extinction procedures. *J. abnorm. soc. Psychol.,* **59,** 269.

YARROW, L. J. 1960. Interviewing children. In P. MUSSEN (ed.), *Handbook of research methods in child development.* New York: Wiley.

ZIGLER, E., and PHILLIPS, L. 1961. Psychiatric diagnosis: A critique. *J. abnorm. soc. Psychol.,* **63,** 607–18.

7

Mental and Educational Retardation

WALTER L. WILKINS *

Since most biologists and other scientists now accept as inevitable, at least for the immediately foreseeable future, the existence of a substantial number of mentally retarded persons, the psychological study of the potentialities and deficiencies of persons so afflicted becomes even more compelling than it was when nineteenth-century theorists in eugenics had some ambitions of eliminating the socially less efficient members of society by selective breeding. Society has always had the problem of the person who could not manage his affairs with ordinary prudence, sometimes because of particular deficiencies in conduct and sometimes because of general lack of aptitude for learning the prudential aspects of living. As society becomes more highly urban, more organized, and more technical, the adjustment problems of persons of markedly limited ability became more difficult. Careful study of the behavior of the retarded becomes necessary to permit planning that may effectively maximize the probability of their getting along in daily living and leading reasonably happy and useful existences.

The interest in the study of the deviate in intelligence has come from many sources. Dynamic psychiatry fostered attitudes that emphasize regarding all patients as individual persons with real problems and as deserving of professional respect. Better systems of classification of deviates have been constantly sought, even though no system for classifying retardates is fully accurate. The most important scientific advance that

---

* Walter L. Wilkins, Ph.D. (Northwestern University), Scientific Director, U.S. Navy Medical Neuropsychiatric Research Unit, San Diego.

focussed attention on problems of the retarded was the extensive introduction of intelligence tests. One of the primary purposes of Alfred Binet's original test was the identification of children who could not profit sufficiently from the ordinary classroom routines, and his scale was almost immediately translated and adapted for various languages and cultures. While intelligence tests are now more widely used in industrial, military, and ordinary scholastic situations than with the retarded, their wide introduction can be at least partially attributed to the practical information they provided concerning the relative development of intellectual functions in those who are intellectually slow.

A more recent intensification of interest in both research on and teaching of the mentally retarded comes from the personal interest of President Kennedy, whose familial situation, as well as the concern he felt about all aspects of mental health, galvanized public action (U.S. Department of Health, Education, and Welfare, 1963).

THE PROBLEM

The President's Panel on Mental Retardation, of the Department of Health, Education, and Welfare, set up by President Kennedy, estimates that, out of a 1960 population of 179 million in the United States, there were 5.4 million mentally retarded persons and that the 1970 population, of approximately 214 million, should show about 6.4 million. Put another way, about 126,000 infants born each year in the United States will turn out to be mentally retarded. Of these infants, 4,200 will be severely retarded—unable even to guard themselves against common dangers—12,600 will never learn to read or reckon, and about 110,000 might well be in some measure self-sufficient but will need very special help and training for even a chance to be such. The number of persons in residence in state institutions for the mentally retarded is approximately 160,000 (Yannet, 1964), and there are usually more men than women. Sir Aubrey Lewis reports that, for England and Wales, the proportion of men to women will be 4:3. He also calls attention to a prevalence, for the general population, of .8 to 1.0 per cent—but, for children under age 18, a prevalence of 3.0 to 3.5 per cent (Lewis, 1960).

But the true number of mental retardates can be estimated in only the crudest fashion (Dingman and Tarjan, 1960), not only because of the difficulties in definition but also because of ordinary problems of counting. There is little doubt that one segment of the retarded population represents the lower end of the normal distribution curve of intelligence and another segment represents an excess number beyond what might be expected from the extrapolation of that curve—and presumably consists of persons who suffer from demonstrable neurological disease that prevents the development of expression of whatever intellectual capabilities they might have been endowed with.

Despite the size of this population needing a range of clinical services—medical, educational, social, rehabilitative, as well as psychological—there are presently far too few practitioners attracted to the field and even too few training opportunities and situations where graduate students in psychology might broaden their clinical competences and insights by testing, training, and treating the mentally retarded and counseling their parents and relatives (who make up almost 10 per cent of the population). They might make dramatic advances in care and treatment possible through their research skills and their zeal, because mental retardation, in its causes and its consequences, is one of the most poorly understood of all the conditions that prevent human beings from living a full, responsible, and rewarding life.

While the scientific study and the individual clinical appraisal of the mentally retarded person have been of interest to psychologists for many decades, from Binet's concern in developing a simple, usable method of identification of the retarded in France—a concern that persists to this day (Kohler, 1957)—the study of the retarded has had less appeal for psychologists than the ever popular neurotics, the ever baffling antisocial personalities, or the omnipresent normals (McCoull and Slupinski, 1957). So there are few psychologists working directly with the mentally retarded (Gibson, 1964), and legislatures have even had to direct state universities, as in California, to initiate doctoral programs in the field of exceptional children.

DEFINITION AND CLASSIFICATION

Definition is difficult because developmentally retarded individuals do not constitute a homogeneous group any more than do certain other atypical groups identified by a single name, such as those described in Chapters 10 through 14. And, as the term covers many problems, the conditions have many predisposing and precipitating situations, and these all require a variety of approaches and skills. As the literature reviews stimulated by recent federal laws demonstrate, mental retardation is a challenging problem in neurology, and so many medical conditions, from molecular changes in some cells to brain bases of intelligence, can be involved; it is a problem in psychiatry, as so many maladaptive behaviors can result; it is a problem in psychology, as the child's learning, his maturation, and, indeed, the whole range of his adaptive behavior are affected; it is a challenge of a most fundamental sort in sociology and education. "Defect is not a biological entity, or indeed a psychological or pathological entity, but rather a congeries of morbid conditions" (Lewis, 1960).

As the collection of highly accurate statistics would help to clarify the problems and to focus research and therapeutic efforts, a number of different ways to count cases have been developed. Davitz and Lorge (1964) proposed a multidimensional system of definition encompassing six diagnostic categories: etiology; intelligence including the common MA and IQ and symbolic and performance test intelligence plus general education attainment and specific abilities; maturation, with ratings for self-help, motor development, and socialization; psychological and social status, with emphasis on activity level as well as degree of emotional disturbance and social adjustment; physical status, with attention to handicaps of sensory, motor, or speech functioning; and prognosis, which might range from deterioration to complete reversibility of retarded functioning. All these are arranged to facilitate coding as well as collection of data beyond the bare demographic facts.

The basic definitions at the present time, however, are those of the American Association of Mental Deficiency (Heber, 1959), which regards mental retardation as "subaverage general intellectual functioning which originates during the developmental period and is associated with impairment in adaptive behavior." The *medical* classification distinguishes eight varieties, as diseases and conditions due to (1) infection, (2) intoxication, (3) trauma or physical agent, (4) disorder of metabolism, growth, or nutrition, (5) new growths, (6) prenatal influences, (7) uncertain cause with structural reactions manifest, and, finally, (8) uncertain cause with functional reaction present.

The *behavioral* classification of the Association describes retardation in terms of both measured intelligence, with levels from V to I defined by standard deviations (SD) below the mean on common intelligence tests, and adaptive behavior, with levels from IV to I, involving mild impairment down to profound, defined by observation or by such norms as are provided by the Vineland Social Maturity Scale or the Cain-Levine Social Competency Scale.

Since the heart of the definition relates to subaverage intellectual functioning, the psychologist needs to know what is meant by intellectual functioning and how far below average "subaverage" might be for practical purposes. The present state of the art in measuring general intelligence is reviewed in Chapter 3, but in general one can say that psychologists testing a child suspected of being retarded will ordinarily use some instrument of a global sort that will allow an objective assessment of the child's development as compared with children of his age (and general cultural background), but will, of course, need more than an IQ.

The Heber *Manual*, in a two-page 1961 modification, indicates that retardation will be considered *profound* if the person tests five or more standard deviations below the mean in intelligence or comes up with an IQ of less than 25. It is considered *severe* if the person tests 4 to 5 SD below the mean, with an IQ of 25 to 39; it is *moderately severe* if 3 to 4 SD units below the mean with an IQ of 40 to 55. Retardation is considered *mild* with an IQ from 55 to 69; and *borderline* if 1 to 2 SD below the mean with an IQ of 70 to 84.

The Heber definitions encompass more than measured intelligence. Adaptive behavior, a composite term to cover all aspects of adaptation to one's environment, intellectual, affective, motor, motivational, and social, may be largely dependent on the same sorts of development as is measured intelligence, but in a fair proportion of retarded children there will be a noticeable discrepancy between how they behave and how they test. The *mild* retardation again represents a deviation of at least one SD; the *moderate,* at least 2; the *severe,* at least 3; and the *profound,* at least 4 SD below the average.

In the basic *Manual,* the child is also rated for manifest evidence of impairment or nonimpairment in some supplementary categories—for such personal-social factors as cultural conformity, interpersonal relations, and responsiveness, and such sensory-motor factors as skills in the motor, auditory, visual, and speech areas.

Regardless of how one classifies the mentally retarded, the degree of severity of the retardation is quite important, as the difficulty of managing a child or a program is roughly proportionate to the severity of the handicap. The profoundly retarded, level I on intelligence and on adaptive behavior, once called "idiots," are those whose intelligence level is so low that even under optimal conditions they will require custodial care. Individuals this severely handicapped commonly have physical, sensory and motor defects (Benton, 1964; Carter, 1965); they comprise .1 per cent of all births (Masland, 1963).

Less profoundly retarded persons, represented by levels II and III in intelligence as well as in adaptive behavior are widely described in state laws as trainable mentally retarded (TMR). They comprise about .25 to .5 per cent of the population (Dingman and Tarjan, 1960). Academic sorts of classroom instruction benefit them hardly at all, but the improvement in their happiness, their self-sufficiency in simple household tasks, and their management is noteworthy in good TMR programs.

The mildly retarded, including levels IV and V on the intelligence measures and level IV in adaptive behavior, comprise at least 2.5 per cent of the population and are called in state laws the "educable mentally retarded" (EMR). They can profit from classroom instruction, especially if it is adapted to their levels of learning ability, and they generally may be expected to become citizens in the community, with jobs sufficiently good to allow them to support themselves and their families. Under the old British Mental Deficiency Act of 1913, a feebleminded person was defined as being incapable of benefiting from ordinary school instruction, requiring some supervision for his own protection, and being able to compete economically with his fellows only under optimal conditions. The educable mentally retarded are such (Rychlak and Wade, 1963).

There have been some criticisms of the Heber definitions. To include people only 1 SD below the mean in intelligence seems inappropriate to many clinicians. Although any thorough survey of an average hospital for mental defectives will turn up some patients with IQ's above 80, it is unlikely that this fact should result in assuming that all persons with IQ's in the low 80's are mentally deficient. Castell and Mittler (1965) found that almost one-fourth of the patients in their survey of British subnormality hospitals had dull-normal IQ's, but they concluded that the subnormality of intelligence, at least in England, should run 2 SD below the mean on intelligence tests and should never be applied to less than 1.4 SD below the mean.

The acceptance by the AAMD of the social-competence criterion represents a considerable change in attitudes on what retardation involves. Only a few decades ago, the irreversibility of deficiency was so taken for granted that, if a child of low IQ improved, it was assumed that the initial testing had been erroneous, or at least that the diagnosis of deficiency had been arrived at prematurely. The more sanguine view of retardation now obtaining assumes that the educable mentally retarded may be capable of marked improvement, and, indeed, several studies of the later careers of persons who spent considerable time in special classes in the common schools have indicated that they hold down jobs that, while not demanding a great deal in the way of abstract intelligence, do demand persistence and some "gumption," and that they make reasonably good citizens and neighbors. Lady Wootton has sharply criticized the social-competence definition of retardation, however, because she feels that such competence may be more closely related to social class and opportunity than to capability (1959). There are, in fact, a good many persons of intelligence represented by IQ's, say, in the 80's who may behave quite stupidly, when one considers the social consequences of their behavior.

No one seriously advocates any more, if indeed anyone ever did, the use of a single criterion, especially IQ, to identify the retarded. But careful study of the Heber *Manual* reveals that the primary emphasis on social competence is quite balanced with careful assessment by medical, psychometric, and other methods. After all, as Penrose points out, mental deficiency is a problem not only of social ineptitude but also of scholastic inefficiency. Psychologists, physicians, and administrators of schools continue to depend on intelligence-test results for guidance in the daily clinical and administrative judgments that must be made, with parental collaboration hopefully, in individual cases. An IQ may be by itself a poor base for prediction of social adjustment, considering all the intangibles that might go into such a prediction, but the IQ or some equivalent, especially if it is fleshed out with a comprehensive inventory of the individual's present and prospective abilities, is useful in the prediction of certain aspects of living, especially such a basic matter as how well the common school subjects might be mastered. In their therapeutic zeal, some clinicians, limited in practice with the retarded, have seemed to suggest that the measurement of intelligence, or at least the clinical use of intelligence-test results, has outlived its usefulness, but its uncritical use and naive misinterpretation are what need to be outlawed (Sarason, 1959).

PSYCHOLOGICAL ASSESSMENT THROUGH TESTS

The purposes of testing a retarded child will be much the same as the purposes in any sort of psychodiagnosis in which the clinical psychologist engages. Provision of objective information relevant to accurate identification of the disease certainly is first, since accurate treatment is related to accurate diagnosis. But, since accurate diagnosis of the mentally retarded is not as frequently achieved as it might be, the clinician will often have to be satisfied with a pertinent description of the assets and shortcomings within the child and of the significant factors in his environment. One purpose of this description should be to provide a realistic basis for placement, whether this be institutional or not, educational or trainable, or vocational—and for planning (Stull, 1961). The inventory and evaluation of assets and liabilities will judge the child as objectively as possible in comparison with his peers of life age, if possible—but with some objective standard of development, if life age is inappropriate (Benton, 1964).

The assessment of the individual must in every case include coverage of a number of aspects of development: medical examination to establish the cause of retardation, if such can be determined, to assess the extent of sensory, motor, and other disabilities, and to judge the need for medical treatment; psychometric assessment to determine the level of maturation and specific abilities and disabilities; study of personality factors to estimate the need for therapy as well as assets for such; study of social maturation, peer adjustment, and possible social factors in eventual job adjustment; and educational evaluation to determine the degree of retardation and any specific disabilities to be overcome through remedial work.

General Ability. The assessment of general intelligence is one of the clinical psychologist's oldest and best competences. The Stanford-Binet and the Wechsler Intelligence Scale for Children (WISC) are still the standard instruments, even though they have some shortcomings in use with retardates (Baumeister, 1964). The Robinsons (1965) believe the time-tested Stanford-Binet, in its 1960 edition, to be still the best. It is attractive to children, easy to use with preschool-age children, and can give instructive results at a somewhat lower level of abilities than can the WISC. Most clinicians working with retardates will wish to supplement the findings from these global types of appraisal of intellectual functioning, not only to follow up the clinical clues gained from observing the child and to corroborate or refute clinical hunches from the examination or from the child's history but also to extend the range of appraised abilities beyond those tapped by the Stanford-Binet.

For young children, the two 1961 Bayley scales for infants and preschool children can be recommended and also the Harris-Goodenough Test of Psychological Maturity—the familiar "Draw-a-Man." Most psychologists working in pediatric hospitals or with very young children can also make good use of the Gesell materials (Fishler *et al.*, 1965), and Gilliland's Northwestern University Tests, even when these are used informally or fortuitously.

Special Abilities. The Stanford-Binet is commonly assumed to be heavily weighted with items dependent on language for directions and for response, and this may be a desirable feature in its use with the mentally retarded, or it may be undesirable, depending on the case and the purpose of testing. In any event, the abilities of most significance, because of their crucial place as tools for further learning, are speech and reading. Because three out of four institutionalized mentally deficient persons are also defective in speech development, it is sometimes assumed that severe speech disorder is almost diagnostic of intellectual retardation. Yet the two need not go together. A child who is extremely slow in developing recognizable speech and whose present speech abilities make him difficult to test will be initially suspected by the psychologist of being generally handicapped in most intellectual functions. And it is even possible for a child of average intelligence who has a severe deficiency in speech to appear mentally deficient. Because of this, the help of a speech pathologist or a psychologist with special training in the area of speech rehabilitation is needed not only for the diagnosis of the specific problems of the child but also for help in the actual therapeutic management (see Chapter 11). A psychologist not working closely with a speech expert should make extensive use of clinical instruments that do not demand a variety of verbal responses from the subject. The routine performance tests are standard clinical tools in such appraisals, but such instruments as the Peabody are also useful.

The most important of the tool subjects is reading, and Kirk (1962) has demonstrated that persons of rather retarded general mental development can be taught to read with surprisingly good results. Although school systems with progressive programs for the retarded have suggestive academic expectancy charts for general and reading expectations, the psychologist can use a rough guide when he expects a reading level approximately indicated by the child's MA. In general, a child of age seven to nine with a mental age of four to six will not yet have begun to read, unless in a very unusual situation, but should be in an intensive educational program emphasizing reading readiness. Children of age nine to eleven with a mental age of six to seven should have begun with preprimers, primers, and simple books. When an MA of seven to eight and one-half is reached, the child should be reading primary books and developing word-recognition methods. If the child reaches levels above this in MA, he can be taught to read third- to fifth-grade books, and to use some of the elementary reference books everyone needs to use, such as the telephone book, parts of newspapers, and road maps.

Two tests recently introduced to the psychologist's armamentarium are quite useful in assessing these areas. The Illinois Test of Psycholinguistic Abilities (McCarthy and Kirk, 1963) has substantial utility. Its nine subtests provide a profile that not only gives the examining clinician a good bit of information about the differential maturation of language functions but also can help to distinguish brain-injured from emotionally disturbed children (Bateman, 1965).

The Peabody Picture Vocabulary Test (Dunn, 1959), which correlates nicely with the Stanford-Binet (.76 for educable mentally retarded and .66 for trainable mentally retarded), is attractive to children and takes less time than the Stanford-Binet, even though it is a good deal longer than the older Ammons Full Range Picture Vocabulary Test. It provides the examiner with a measure of the vocabulary development of the child and useful information about the range of concepts the child possesses. Both of these tests are valuable in contributing to the greater refinement of diagnosis and remedial treatment called for by O'Connor and Hermelin (1963), and to achievement of the goals described by Spreen (1965).

The desire to broaden the range of testing of the abilities of the retardate has resulted in more than these recent advances in the assessment of vocabulary development and general language abilities (Bateman, 1964). Since perceptual and motor abilities are so apt to be involved in the case of the retardate, and the IQ is a poor guide to deficiencies of such sorts, it is wise to include, where possible, some appraisal of developmental levels in such areas. The Frostig Developmental Test of Visual

Perception provides a handy means of appraising details of the maturation of perceptual functions (Maslow, Frostig, Lefever, and Wittlesey, 1964). The Lincoln-Oseretsky scale, adapted by William Sloan (1955) for use with retardates, has useful norms for determining the comparative level of motor development.

As the basic Heber definition of mental retardation indicates, there should be some appraisal of the social maturity of the child. Doll's Vineland Social Maturity Scale, a list of 117 items of habitual social activity, was designed to provide a normative basis on which the retardate's social competences could be fairly compared with those of children of equal life age. The instrument is scored by checking the presence or absence of each behavior listed and summing to obtain a social age. By comparison of this sum with a life age, a social quotient is obtained. In clinical practice, a social quotient of below 70 associated with an intelligence quotient of below 70 suggests a rather broad picture of deficiency and the need for special educational provisions. The Gesell battery has also included, as part of developmental assessment of the preschool child, some social norms.

A more recent instrument is the Cain-Levine Social Competency Scale (1963), which is quite useful for trainable mentally retarded children ages five to thirteen, or for an IQ range of 25 to 59. It consists of four subscales—self-help, initiative, social skills, and communication—which sum for a total social-competence score.

Another instrument designed to help in the rating of a child of trainable levels is the T.M.R. Performance Profile for the Severely and Moderately Retarded (DiNola, Kaminsky, and Sternfeld, 1963). This is a longer and more detailed instrument than the Vineland or the Cain-Levine and provides, in a sense, a checklist for the clinician who wishes to make a thorough inventory of all varieties of tasks for which a retarded child might be assessable. Included are behaviors subsumed under (1) social behavior, including self-control, personality, group participation, and social amenities; (2) self-care, including grooming, eating, clothing, and safety; (3) communication, including listening as well as talking and reading; (4) basic knowledge, including knowledge of common identifications, numbers, and social facts; (5) practical skills, including tools, chores, household items, and readiness for work; and (6) body usage, including coordination, health habits, eye-hand coordination, and general physical fitness.

Peer nomination and sociometric devices, so useful in identifying cases needing clinical attention among normal children and adults, have also been used with the retarded. While it is easy to watch on a school playground to see who is chosen last, it is more systematic to use a standard device. Johnson studied the peer relations of mentally retarded children who were in regular school classrooms and found that they were more isolated and more rejected than children of average intelligence. This suggested that the retarded child may be very effectively segregated while in a normal classroom. Not all retarded children who are in regular classrooms or in special classrooms in regular schools are isolated on a sociometric instrument, but the majority are (Johnson in Cruickshank and Johnson, 1958). In addition to having other handicaps, the retarded are poor at developing human relationships. And they hardly ever initiate a game or other social interaction—so they are not choosers to begin with, and then they frequently wind up unchosen.

Personality Factors. For the assessment of personality factors in the mentally retarded, the routine inventories of the pencil-and-paper variety are even less useful than they are with the physically handicapped (see Chapter 10). Not only are valid norms for the retarded not available generally, but the marginal or lower levels of intelligence and of literacy make the interpretations the subject might put on the meaning of the items unpredictable. For much the same reasons that group tests of intelligence are suspect at borderline or lower levels, namely, poor discriminative power and inadequate understanding of the directions and of the items, the pencil-and-paper inventory is almost without clinical value. For this reason, there was at one time considerable effort to determine how the retarded typically responded to the Rorschach plates, the TAT, the Mosaic, and other instruments. Molish's review (1958) will carry the student beyond the extent of Chapter 4 to considerations of the utility of the Rorschach and the other instruments with the retarded. Whenever these instruments provide clinical cues that may alert the clinician to the possibility of brain damage, emotional deprivation, or other significant aspects of developmental deprivation, they are valuable. The recent evidence on their limited validity probably contraindicates their routine use, however. This is not to suggest that personality is a less important factor in the retarded than in the normal, for it is just as important (Earl, 1961; Edgerton and Sabagh, 1962).

Mentally retarded children and youths are not equally deficient in all directions. Many of them can learn to work with concrete materials and objects better than they can learn to handle abstract ideas or symbolic aspects of thinking. In general, they can be expected to learn of symbolic materials about as much as their mental age might suggest, but many can do much better than this, while many are much poorer. They seem to do appreciably better on subtests that call for responses depending on extended educational or life experience—a phenomenon that has suggested to some educators that the educational program for the retarded might well last longer than that for his normal-IQ peer.

A little experience testing the retarded will reveal that the pattern of successes and failures they have in the Binet or the Wechsler, and in other tests used for comparisons, will differ from those of children of the same mental age but with higher IQ's. And the spontaneous language, so rich in meaning for the psychologist who utilizes minimal cues in testing children, will also be different—and generally sparser. There is also a lack of autocritical ability in the mentally retarded (the student should recall Alfred Binet's original threefold definition of intelligence); for instance, in tests, they do not often say "don't know" in response to items they are uninformed about, as do brighter children. They frequently give an answer although it may be an inappropriate one. For such reasons, the interpretation of intelligence-test results, not only of the general ability tests but also of the supplementary special tests of sensory, linguistic, perceptual, and social maturation, even of such a relatively simple test as the Harris-Goodenough Draw-a-Man, must be made on the basis of considerable experience with the retarded, and more clinical training facilities should provide the student with opportunity for such.

EDUCATIONAL DEVELOPMENT

The chief task of children in the developmental years is acquiring the skills, attitudes, and information necessary for leading a useful and happy life. For the mentally deficient, teaching of the common school subjects must be done without pressure and tensions. Even simple manual skills are more easily developed when pressure for quick achievement or for school grades is de-emphasized. Social adjustment is jeopardized when the slow child is required to face up to academic standards beyond his current capabilities. And the effect on mental health is worth noting. A retarded child sitting daily in a classroom where he does not quite understand much of what is going on is frustrated, and that frustration acts as a barrier to further learning. Special adaptations of the curricular materials and of the teaching methods are necessary, and many state and city school systems have recently developed a variety of materials both apposite and challenging to the child (Study Commission, 1965). The clinician, with his special background, is frequently helpful in the school system because he can tailor a course of study to each exceptional child.

He may also act as consultant to the curriculum authorities in their planning for such children. Each child above the severely retarded level must be trained to take some part in the world's work and even to make himself as economically self-sufficient as possible. Beyond this, he should lead an adequate social and recreational life. Specific goals to be thought of as typifying the attainment of a sixteen-year-old mentally retarded child were outlined by Martens in 1950 and are still valid:

1. The knowledge and disposition to keep physically well in order to enjoy life at its maximum
2. An ease and a joy in social relationships that help him to make friends and to participate in social and civil experiences
3. An ability to plan and to choose leisure activities wisely
4. An ability to live as a contributing member of a family and a neighborhood group, and later to maintain his own home as head of a family
5. The ability to earn as much of the necessities of life as possible
6. The knowledge and ability to spend his salary wisely

Another statement, reinforcing Martens' goals, is that of Synder (in Hellmuth, 1964), who stresses that the focus of the program for the elementary school should be on self-realization through familiarity and self-identification with the environment, on socialization to increase the possibility of relating to others, on attaining facility in handling problems of daily living through use of the environment and one's own skills, and on developing "responsibility through living and serving in the community in as productive a way as possible." After there has been some development of sensory-motor awareness and better modes of communication, the child is encouraged in such traits as finishing what he has started. Then socialization with peers and stabilization of classroom behaviors make possible the introduction of academic materials and simple handwork. And finally, knowledge of the immediate environment, some mastery of common branches of learning, and further growing can lead to individual responsibility (Erickson, 1965).

It hardly needs to be noted that these goals are similar to the goals for all children and that their attainment should be proportionate to the resources and opportunities for the child, all of which should be maximized. As the majority of educable mentally retarded children under modern programs may be expected to leave special classes and become ordinary citizens, the main objective of social adjustment must be complete social independence (Windle, 1962). The emphasis on happiness is proper for both trainable and educable children. In fact, the long-time motto of the Vineland School in New Jersey, where so many psychological techniques for studying the retarded were first tried and developed—the first English Binet, the Porteus Mazes, and Doll's Scale—was "Happiness first; all else follows."

Realistic academic expectancies are more difficult to come by than some persons think. There is the general difficulty of predicting human behavior at all and the complications resulting from teachers who may be good or bad, inspiring or not, dedicated or not. Without doubt, great gains in speech and in social controls can be ensured for the trainable mentally retarded, and most of Martens' goals can be approached. The specific of classroom instruction for the retarded, reviewed by Johnson (1958), by Kirk (1958, 1962), and by Cain and Levine (1963), should be familiar to the practicing psychologist. Many state departments of education, through their programs for the EMR and TMR, have suggested some realistic expectancies—not as norms for teachers or as guides to parents but as framework for studying the likely accomplishments of the individual child. The child with an IQ roughly below 60 may in general be expected to achieve most of the goals of second grade by the time he reaches age fourteen to sixteen. The child with an IQ under 70 but 60 or above should reach such goals by age eleven to thirteen and by age fifteen or sixteen be at a fourth-grade level.

Academic expectancy charts can sometimes be used by the psychologist to help clarify teachers' notions of what an individual child, with his particular pattern of assets and handicaps, might be expected to attain. To help parents in their often confused search for more accurate expectations, there are a number of good pamphlets such as *Your Mentally Handicapped Child* (1964).

Children of school age but of mental development such that they will not profit from ordinary classroom instruction until they are eight, nine, or ten years of age can profit from much that the school can do for them in the way of preschool activities. Experiences that can foster the development of physical and mental health and self-help skills such as those listed in the TMR checklists, for handling clothing, eating, housekeeping activities, bathroom routines, imaginative and creative activities, for learning to get along with peers, for developing language and speech and acquaintanceship with numbers and some quantitative abstractions, are discussed by Kirk (Stevens and Heber).[1] Children mature enough to master some reading and arithmetic are, of course, provided with challenging experiences involving these tools but need specific provision for experiences in practical arts (Wiggin, 1961) and can profit from direct teaching of skills and insights important in social adjustment. There is, however, a determinable level below which a child will in all probability not profit from formal schooling to an extent comparable to the efforts that must be put into it by himself, his parents, his peers, and his teachers. The decision to place a child in an EMR situation should be reached by the parents, school administrators, a physician when indicated, and a school psychologist. Each of those routinely involved in these decisions has something important to contribute to the decision: the parent, from long years of training and living with the child; the administrator, from his knowledge of the demands of the school and of society; and the psychologist, because of his objective and thorough assay of the child's potentialities. Criteria for such placement are suggested in Robinson (1965) and, more briefly, in a small handbook for school psychologists pub-

[1] This edited volume by H. A. Stevens and R. Heber is entitled *Mental Retardation: A review of research*; Chicago, the University of Chicago Press, 1964. Its 500 pages provide the reader with authoritative summaries on recent advances and pinpoint areas in need of continued research concentration.—L.A.P. (ed.).

lished by the California Association of School Psychologists and Psychometrists (Swanson, 1965).

A rather large number of schoolchildren come to the attention of the psychologist because of specific disabilities. The largest proportion of these are children who, for one reason or another, have difficulty in learning to read, but there are also others, who fall behind and fail in arithmetic, spelling, or handwriting. As these skills are the tools with which one learns about the social heritage and the world about him, through social studies, science, and literature, children with such difficulties face a situation that may affect not only academic adjustment but also general adjustment to peers, to parents, to siblings, and to themselves. Some children require special remedial educational provisions because of too much absence on account of sickliness, too frequent change of schools, poor previous schooling, or the cultural deprivation found in some urban subcultures. Specific disabilities are detectable in progressive schools through the instruments routinely used as diagnostic tests in arithmetic, reading, or language arts. Other disabilities involve physiological or psychological abnormalities that make efficient learning difficult or even impossible without special help by trained therapists. Specific sensory handicaps may cause failure. This is so axiomatic that the school psychologist has every child referred to him for specific learning difficulties checked for visual and aural acuity. Faulty muscular control may be involved in reversals in word recognition or in writing. Emotional factors are related to learning difficulties and to school phobia and may not be ignored. The diagnosis and treatment of the psychotic child whose behavior may simulate that of the mentally retarded child is referred to in Chapter 13, and Rimland (1964) has developed some new hypotheses concerning the autistic child.

Finally, it should be remembered that the retarded child learns slowly and with difficulty. Snyder suggests that his partial insights and his impaired functioning may affect his perceptions of the environment including the learning environment of the classroom; these perceptions may be limited and different and may arouse fear. His poorer memory abilities may require more drill—or better drill. And, since he is poor at analyzing new situations, his teachers must keep things simple for him. Concept formation is difficult, as performance on the Wechsler Similarities Test demonstrates. Psychologists familiar with the behavioral manifestations of brain damage on test and other performance—the distractibility and the perseverations—will see these behaviors in a good many retarded children.

The mentally retarded, both boys and girls, are also retarded in sex development (Mosier, Grossman, and Dingman, 1962). The greater the degree of mental deficiency, the greater the retardation in development of secondary sexual characteristics. Moreover, while the severely retarded or trainable retarded rarely develop any strong interest in the opposite sex, the educable retarded may. Says Snyder, "because adolescents may use sexual promiscuity as a weapon of revolt, sex offenses make up a sizable proportion of delinquent behavior in retardates. In retarded girls, particularly, but also among boys, it often occurs among those who have a need for affection and acceptance" (Hellmuth, 1964).

Adjustment in Family and Community. The family situation in which the retardate finds himself is highly relevant to whether he makes any sort of adequate adjustment. A wide variety of environmental conditions affect adjustment (McCandless in Stevens and Heber, 1964; Wakefield, 1964), but the family is most potent. Familial attitudes toward a retarded child have been shown to be different from attitudes toward a normal child. Such attitudes are culturally conditioned too. The adjustment of the released patient when he returns to his family is illustrative. Families of low-social-status patients are less likely to regard them as retarded and more likely to assume that they can play some useful adult role. The emotional acceptance of a retarded child is frequently less severe a problem with parents who are emotionally mature and financially able (Erickson, 1965).

Another key point in the life of the retarded child is faced when he reaches a school-leaving age and faces the challenge of an entry into the world of work. Most occupations open to the retarded fall into the category of laboring, unskilled service-type jobs. Whereas, in general, it seems that children classified as *educable* while in special classes can be expected to have some job success and those classified as *trainable* tend not to have such expectations, recent experience with occupational training centers and sheltered workshops suggests that persons of IQ 40 to 60 might be successfully placed (Fraenkel, 1961). Vocational adjustment cannot be predicted from measured intelligence alone—the organized use of abilities is a better predictor, and level of conceptual ability will suggest probable level of employment (Heber, 1963). Fortunately, attitudes of many employers toward hiring of the handicapped are positive (Phelps, 1963).

Effective planning for a wise program for the retarded child requires, as indicated above, the wholehearted cooperation of parents as well as of school authorities and teachers, but it also must include the community. Parents' councils for the retarded exist in a great many communities, and the National Association for Retarded Children, since 1950, has grown to a major source of help and coordination through its local units, which support clinics, nursery classes, recreation, religious education, job placement, day-care centers, and sheltered workshops, and, through these and other activities, aids with referral and almost any feature of community contact. Its newspaper, *Children Limited,* provides timely descriptions of new programs.

THERAPY

A consensus of mental hygienists would probably include in any list of emotional needs requiring satisfaction such items as a feeling of security, a feeling of belonging, affection, discipline and order, recreation, and a sense of one's own worth and of one's place in the universe. The mentally retarded child has these emotional needs just as the normal child does. No doubt, most of them should be satisfied within the family circle for the child who does not need institutionalization, but the school and the church can certainly play a more vital role in filling the emotional needs of the retarded than they have. The presence of a handicapping condition always puts a strain on parent-child relations (Sarason, 1959), and the school and church, through counselors, can bring real emotional resources to the help of parent and child (Hoffman, 1965). The mentally retarded child may easily develop misinterpretations of his handicap. If borderline or anywhere near it, he can recognize the facts not only that he is apt to be chosen last in free play situations but also that the other children seem to outstrip him easily in just about everything he attempts. This realization may lead him to regard himself as unworthy—and, in fact, he may be so charged by elders or peers—and to infer that this unworthiness is a result of his being bad in some way. He may also feel that the demands put upon him by parents and teachers, in their well-meaning attempts to help him, are harsh, and he may thus interpret such efforts as rejection of him. The personality of the child may consequently be conditioned by conscious or unconscious factors in his partial and perhaps faulty perception of the world around him. So a realizable goal of therapeutic effort with the retarded would be to prevent as far as possible and to ameliorate the results of such perceptions.

Despite the fact that educable mildly retarded children can demonstrate quite impressive gains in both cognitive and social areas (Clarke, Clarke, and Reiman, 1958), the applications of specific psychotherapeutic techniques to children of limited IQ has often been disappointing (Albini and Dinitz, 1965; D. C. Beier in Stevens and Heber, 1964).

About one-fourth to one-third of children who are mentally retarded display prominent psychiatric problems but present these problems in ways that are baffling to the therapist. Often the therapy must address itself to the emotional plight of the child rather than be focussed on the retardation (Sternlicht, 1965).

In some situations, therapy must inevitably involve some radical change of environment. Whenever adequate medical attention to the needs of the patient is required, the child must be in hospital. A fair proportion of the populations in state colonies and hospitals are made up of such persons. No home could provide the stability of routine or the medical care the child needs.

Other things being equal, it is always desirable to keep a handicapped child in his own family circle. But a penalty is frequently paid for keeping a mentally retarded child in the home. When behavior is worse because of parental attitudes, when parental affection is unwholesome, when parents' attitudes cause conflict, when the child can develop little loyalty to the family or is terribly insecure or rejected, and when parental attitudes seem rigid and unchangeable, or when the child just stands a better chance of care and affection away from home, placement should be seriously considered. Many retardates are quite affectionate and lovable—Down's syndrome children being a ready example—and the decision for institutionalization is always a complex one.

Recent attempts to modify behavior in mentally retarded children by means of operant conditioning have been highly encouraging (Bijou, 1963; Birnbrauer, Bijou, Wolf, and Kidder, 1965), and Edgar Doll, developer of the Vineland scale and a long-time leader in the scientific study of the retarded, has expressed the hope that operant conditioning will be a most valuable adjunct in work with both the educable and the trainable mentally retarded (in Hellmuth, 1964). For a further discussion, see Chapter 21.

An excellent group of textbooks (Earl, 1961; Hutt and Gibby, 1965; Jordan, 1961; Masland, Sarason, and Gladwin, 1958; Sarason, 1959), of handbooks (Cruickshank and Johnson, 1958; Ellis, 1963; Stevens and Heber, 1964), of readings (Rothstein, 1961), of proceedings of experimental congresses (Øster, 1964), and of major experimental studies (Johnson and Blake, 1960; Kirk, 1958), testify to the increasing importance of the field of mental retardation. Leo Kanner (1964) has written a brief but learned history of the study of the retarded.

SUMMARY

The aim of the clinical study of the retarded child is the careful and systematic inventory of his assets and disabilities—intellectual, scholastic, emotional, social, ethical—to help plan the full exploitation of his potentialities, including compensating for the disabilities, so that he may lead as full, productive, well rounded, and happy a life as his endowment can possibly permit.

REFERENCES

ALBINI, J. L., and DINITZ, S. 1965. Psychotherapy with disturbed and defective children: An evaluation of changes in behavior and attitudes. *Amer. J. ment. Def.*, 69(4), 560–67.

BATEMAN, BARBARA. 1964. Learning disabilities—yesterday, today, and tomorrow. *Except. Child.*, 31(4), 167–77.

BATEMAN, BARBARA, 1965. The role of the ITPA in differential diagnosis and program planning for mentally retarded. *Amer. J. Orthopsychiat.*, 35(3), 465–72.

BAUMEISTER, A. A. 1964. Use of the WISC with mental retardates: A review. *Amer. J. ment. Def.*, 69(2), 183–94.

BENTON, A. L. 1964. Psychological evaluation and differential diagnosis. In H. A. STEVENS and R. HEBER (eds.) *Mental retardation.* Chicago: Univer. of Chicago Press. Pp. 16–56.

BIJOU, S. W. 1963. Theory and research in mental (developmental) retardation. *Psychol. Rec.*, 13, 95–110.

BIRNBRAUER, J. S., BIJOU, S. W., WOLF, M. M., and KIDDER, J. D. 1965. Programmed instruction in the classroom. In L. P. ULLMAN and L. KRASNER (eds.), *Case studies in behavior modification.* New York: Holt, Rinehart, & Winston.

CAIN, L. F., and LEVINE, S. 1963. The mentally retarded. *Rev. Educ. Res.* 33(1), 62–82.

CAIN, L. F., LEVINE, S., and ELZEY, F. F. 1963. *Manual for the Cain-Levine social competency scale.* Palo Alto, Calif.: Consulting Psychologists Press.

CARTER, C. H. (ed.). 1965. *Medical aspects of mental retardation.* Springfield, Ill.: Charles C Thomas.

CASTELL, J. H. F., and MITTLER, P. J. 1965. Intelligence of patients in subnormality hospitals: A survey of admissions in 1961. *British J. Psychiat.*, 111, 219–225.

CLARKE, A. D. B., CLARKE, A. M., and REIMAN, S. 1958. Cognitive and social changes in the feebleminded: Three further studies. *British J. Psychol.*, 49(2), 144–57.

CRUICKSHANK, W. M., and JOHNSON, G. O. (eds.). 1958. *Education of exceptional children and youth.* Englewood Cliffs, N.J.: Prentice-Hall.

DAVITZ, J. R., DAVITZ, L. J., and LORGE, I. 1964. *Terminology and concepts in mental retardation.* New York: Teachers College, Bureau of Publications, Columbia University.

DINGMAN, H. F., and TARJAN, G. 1960. Mental retardation and the normal distribution curve. *Amer. J. ment. Def.*, 64(6), 991–94.

DINOLA, A. J., KAMINSKY, B. P., and STERNFELD, A. E. 1965. *T.M.R. performance profile for the severely and moderately retarded.* (2d ed.) Ridgefield, N.J.: Reporting Service for Exceptional Children.

DUNN, L. M. 1959. *Peabody picture vocabulary test.* Minneapolis: American Guidance Service.

EARL, C. J. C. 1961. *Subnormal personalities: Their clinical investigation and assessment.* Baltimore: Williams & Wilkins.

EDGERTON, R. B., and SABAGH, G. 1962. From mortification to aggrandizement: Changing self-concepts in the careers of the mentally retarded. *Psychiatry, 25*, 263–72.

ELLIS, N. R. (ed.). 1963. *Handbook of mental deficiency.* New York: McGraw-Hill.

ERICKSON, M. J. 1965. *The mentally retarded child in the classroom.* New York: Macmillan.

FISHLER, K., GRALIKER, BETTY V., and KOCH, R. 1965. The predictability of intelligence with Gesell Developmental Scales in mentally retarded infants and young children. *Amer. J. ment. Def.*, **69**, 515–25.

FRAENKEL, W. A. 1961. *The mentally retarded and their vocational rehabilitation: A resource handbook.* New York: National Association for Retarded Children.

GIBSON, D. 1964. Psychology in mental retardation: Past and present. *Amer. Psychologist*, **19**(5), 339–41.

HEBER, R. 1959. A manual on terminology and classification in mental retardation. *Amer. J. ment. Def.*, **64**(2), 1–11.

HEBER, R. (ed.). 1965. Special problems in vocational rehabilitation of the mentally retarded. U.S. Department of Health, Education, and Welfare, Vocational Rehabilitation Administration, Rehabilitation Service Series No. 65–16.

HELLMUTH, J. (ed.). 1964. *The special child in century 21.* Seattle: Special Child Publications of the Seguin School.

HOFFMAN, J. L. 1965. Mental retardation, religious values, and psychiatric universals. *Amer. J. Psychiat.*, **121**(9), 885–89.

HUTT, M. L., and GIBBY, R. G. 1965. *The mentally retarded child: Development, education, and treatment.* Boston: Allyn & Bacon.

JOHNSON, G. O., and BLAKE, KATHRYN A. 1960. *Learning performance of retarded and normal children.* Syracuse: Syracuse Univer. Press.

JORDAN, T. E. 1961. *The mentally retarded.* Columbus; Ohio: Charles E. Merrill.

KANNER, L. 1964. *A history of the care and study of the mentally retarded.* Springfield, Ill.: Charles C Thomas.

KIRK, S. A. 1958. *Early education of the mentally retarded.* Urbana: Univer. of Illinois Press.

KIRK, S. A. 1962. *Educating exceptional children.* Boston: Houghton Mifflin.

KOHLER, C. 1957. *L'Enfant Arrière dans sa Famille.* Paris: Centre D'Activités Pédagogiques.

KURTZ, R. A. 1965. Comparative evaluations of suspected retardates. *Amer. J. Dis. Child.*, **109**, 58–65.

LEWIS, A. 1960. The study of defect. *Amer. J. Psychiat.*, **117**, 289–304.

McCARTHY, J. J., and KIRK, S. A. 1963. *The construction, standardization, and statistical characteristics of the Illinois Test of Psycholinguistic Abilities.* Madison, Wis.: Photo Press.

McCOULL, G., and SLUPINSKI, L. 1957. The role of the clinical psychologist in a mental deficiency hospital. *Ment. Health*, **16**(2), 52–57.

MARTENS, ELISE H. 1950. *Curriculum adjustments for the mentally retarded.* U.S. Office of Education, Federal Security Agency, Bulletin No. 2. Washington, D.C.: Government Printing Office.

MASLAND, R. L. Mental retardation. 1963. In M. FISHBEIN (ed.), *Birth defects.* Philadelphia: Lippincott.

MASLAND, R. L., SARASON, S. B., and GLADWIN, T. 1958. *Mental subnormality: Biological, psychological and cultural factors.* New York: Basic Books.

MASLOW, PHYLLIS, FROSTIG, MARIANNE, LEFEVER, D. W., and WHITTLESEY, J. R. B. 1964. The Marianne Frostig Developmental Test of Visual Perception, 1963 Standardization. *Perceptual and Motor Skills,* 19, 463–99.

MOLISH, H. B. 1958. Contributions of projective tests to problems of psychological diagnosis in mental deficiency. *Amer. J. ment. Def.,* 63(2), 282–93.

MOSIER, H. D., GROSSMAN, H. J., and DINGMAN, H. F. 1962. Secondary sex development in mentally deficient individuals. *Child Develpm.,* 33, 273–86.

O'CONNOR, N., and HERMELIN, B. 1963. *Speech and thought in severe subnormality.* New York: Macmillan.

OSTER, J. (ed.). 1964. *Proceedings International Copenhagen Congress on the Scientific Study of Mental Retardation.* 2 vols. Copenhagen: Statens Andssvageforsorg.

PENROSE, L. S. 1963. *The biology of mental defect.* (3d ed.) New York: Grune & Stratton.

PHELPS, W. R. 1963. Attitudes related to the employment of the mentally retarded. M.A. thesis, Marshal University, August, 1963.

RIMLAND, B. 1964. *Infantile autism.* New York: Appleton-Century-Crofts.

ROBINSON, H. B., and ROBINSON, N. M. 1965. *The mentally retarded child: A psychological approach.* New York: McGraw-Hill

ROTHSTEIN, J. H. (ed.). 1961. *Mental retardation: Readings and resources.* New York: Holt, Rinehart & Winston.

RYCHLAK, J. F., and WADE, IONA. 1963. American usage of the terms "educable" vs. "trainable" mental retardates. *J. ment. Subnormality,* 9(2), 70–75.

SARASON, S. B. 1959. *Psychological problems in mental deficiency.* (3d ed.) New York: Harper & Row.

SLOAN, W. 1955. The Lincoln-Oseretsky motor development scale. *Genet. Psychol. Monogr.,* 51, 183–252.

SPREEN, O. 1965. Language functions in mental retardation: A review. I. Language development, types of retardation, and intelligence level. *Amer. J. ment. Def.,* 69(4), 482–94.

STERNLICHT, M. 1965. Psychotherapeutic techniques with the mentally retarded: A review and critque. *Psychiatric Quart.,* 39(1), 84–90.

STUDY COMMISSION ON MENTAL RETARDATION. 1965. *The undeveloped resource: A plan for the mentally retarded in California.* Sacramento: The Commission.

STULL, C. E. 1961. Psychological diagnoses. *Amer. J. ment. Def.,* 65(6), 696–98.

SWANSON, L. W. (ed.). 1964. *Evaluation and placement of mentally retarded children.* Monterey: California Association of School Psychologists and Psychometrists.

U.S. DEPARTMENT OF HEALTH, EDUCATION, AND WELFARE. 1963. *Proceed-*

ings White House Conference on Mental Retardation. Washington, D.C.: Government Printing Office.

WAKEFIELD, R. A. 1964. An investigation of the family backgrounds of educable mentally retarded children in special classes. *Except. Child.*, 31(3), 143–46.

WINDLE, C. 1962. Prognosis of mental subnormals. Monograph Supplement, *Amer. J. ment. Def.*, 66(5),

WOOTTON, BARBARA. 1959. *Social science and social pathology.* London: G. Allen.

YANNET, H. 1964. Mental retardation. In W. E. NELSON (ed.), *Textbook of Pediatrics.* (8th ed.) Philadelphia: Saunders.

Your mentally handicapped child. 1964. London: National Association for Mental Health.

8

Psychosexual and Marital Problems

ALBERT ELLIS *

Although many of the problems discussed in the present section of this book—such as problems relating to mental and educational retardation, psychosomatic ailments, physical handicaps, brain damage, psychoneurosis, psychosis, and psychopathy—are hardly rare in our society, they cannot be said to be ubiquitous. The problems to be discussed in this chapter, however—sex and marriage problems—are so common that it might indeed be contended that any individual in our culture who does not personally encounter them during his life is not a normal person. The following points about these problems can accordingly be set forth at once:

1. They virtually never exist in their own right, but are invariably connected with the individual's total behavior or "personality."
2. They are never exclusively *individual* problems, but are intimately related to the mores, customs, and laws of the culture in which the person resides.
3. They are not attributable *either* to physiological, inherited, sexual-amative "instincts" (drives) or to social conditioning or learning, but are causally connected with *both* hereditary *and* environmental, physiological *and* psychological factors.
4. They are not, as yet, fully understandable in terms of any one orthodox theory of personality whether it be Freudian, neo-

* Albert Ellis, Ph.D. (Columbia University), Director, Institute for Rational Living, Inc., and Private Practice of Psychotherapy, Marriage and Family Counseling, New York City.

Freudian, or anti-Freudian. Sexual and marital problems indeed can best be understood in the light of a heterodox, cross-cultural, fact-centered view.

PSYCHOSEXUAL PROBLEMS OF INFANCY

One of Freud's (1962–1964) notable contributions to science was his insistence that human sexuality normally predates puberty and that infants usually display distinct manifestations of sexual activity. Not content with postulating infant sexuality, Freud and his followers have also insisted that all normal infants go through several specific pregenital and genital phases, including the oral and anal stages, and that these are succeeded by later phallic and genital steps in childhood sexuality. Although most authorities appear to agree with the Freudians that oral and anal activities are important in infant behavior, much controversy presently exists as to (1) whether they are as important as the Freudians insist, (2) whether they are truly sexual stages, and (3) whether the oral-anal-phallic-genital progression is as rigid as Freudian literature states or implies. Granting that some infants are significantly affected by their oral and anal experiences and that fixations on these levels of behavior leading to subsequent emotional disturbances may sometimes occur, it may still be held that much of the infant activity the Freudians call sexual is, in fact, sensual, and that it only occasionally becomes sufficiently significant in the child's life to serve as a focal point for later severe maladjustment. Thus far, undisputed factual evidence in this connection is too sparse to merit broad or dogmatic generalizations. Clinical observations on certain psychosexual and psychoamative problems of infancy are more readily available. A selected few of these will now be discussed.

Infant Autoerotism. Masturbation has been found to exist in very young children (H. Ellis, 1936; Stekel, 1961), and, according to Kinsey *et al.* (1948), orgasm has been observed in boys as young as five months of age. Except where it is indicative of some local genital irritation or some general emotional disturbance, infant masturbation is well within the range of normal behavior, and leads to no unfortunate results. No corrective action or emphasis on the part of the parents is usually indicated, and when such overemphasis is given to infant autoerotism, it often indicates disturbance on the part of the parents rather than the child.

Infant Seduction. Some parents, particularly mothers with their sons, consciously or unconsciously act out their own psychosexual desires, shortcomings, and disturbances with their infant children, and may directly or indirectly make sexual overtures to these children. Although it has never been established that such forms of sexual seduction produce uniformly harmful results, many clinical histories have been reported which trace childhood or adult sexual aberrations back to prior infant seduction (Freud, 1962–1964).

PSYCHOSEXUAL PROBLEMS OF CHILDHOOD

According to orthodox Freudian theory, children pass through an Oedipus (or an Electra) complex between their third and sixth years, fall in love and want to have sexual relations with the other-sex parent during this period, and have to resolve this "complex" before they may go on to attain sexual maturity. Findings and discussions in this connection would appear to indicate that this theory has only limited applicability. Not *all* children seem to be specifically attracted to their other sex parent; many who are so attracted easily work through these attractions; Oedipal feelings vary widely from culture to culture, and from family to family within a given culture; and many serious emotional disturbances of childhood and adulthood seem to have little or no connection with early Oedipal attachments (Wedge, 1952). Orthodox Freudian theory also posits a so-called *latency period,* between children's sixth and twelfth years, when they presumably retreat from sexuality because of their anxieties, guilt, and Oedipal difficulties. It has been found by Kinsey *et al.* (1948), however, that all boys at all ages in our culture display specific overt sexual activity; and anthropologists such as Malinowski (1961) and Mead (1960) have reported that no latency period exists among the children of peoples raised in other cultures. It is probable that much of the so-called latency period, when it does exist, is chimerical in that children in our society have much more freedom of action in school, sports, companionship, and other activities than they have during their first six years, and therefore they tend to engage in relatively fewer sexual acts even when, often, they engage in absolutely more. Moreover, although the sexual behavior of infants and children is usually easily observable by adults, that of older children is not. The chances are, accordingly, that even in our own society much sexual "latency" is more mythical than real.

Sex Education. Perhaps the main childhood sex problem in our culture is that of the child's obtaining an adequate sex education. That young children have considerable sexual awareness and curiosity is clearly shown in studies by Conn (1940) and in unpublished findings by Kinsey and his associates. A considerable literature has appeared which endeavors to explain how parents and teachers should approach sex education. Many of these articles and books, however, are somewhat biased by their author's views of sex. In general, most problems in sex education are problems of parents rather than of children; and the clinical psychologist can properly treat them as such. Parents who cannot give children adequate education should themselves be educated and treated so that they may eventually be able to do so; or else they should not be encouraged to give pertinent information, but should have it objectively imparted to their children by a psychologist, marriage counselor, physician, teacher, or other individual who is sufficiently unbiased as well as scientifically trained in this area.

PSYCHOSEXUAL PROBLEMS OF ADOLESCENCE

Adolescence in our culture is normally a time of sexual and amative tension largely because of our tremendous emphasis upon sexual repression and amative competitiveness. Several of the most frequently encountered psychosexual problems of adolescence will now be discussed.

Adolescent Autoerotism. As has been known for at least a century, and as recent researchers have reaffirmed, the great majority of adolescent boys and a large minority of adolescent girls masturbate. After many years of violent interdictions against masturbation, modern thinking, particularly as shown by Dearborn (1961) in a masterful survey of the subject, has come to the realization that masturbation by adolescents (and adults) is normal, that in itself it is harmless, and that it serves a useful and salutory function for young boys and girls. But even so, because of a marked cultural lag in this connection, youngsters severely disturbed by their masturbatory desire or acts continually appear in clinics and in psychologists' offices. These cases can usually be handled easily if the psychologist has objective attitudes toward masturbation and if he does not hesitate to make these attitudes clear to the client.

Adolescent Homosexuality. Young people, literally by the millions, have become emotionally attached temporarily to members of their own sex (homoeroticism) or engage in overt sexual relations with those of the same sex (homosexuality). Kinsey *et al.* (1948, 1953) find that 37 per cent of all males have some overt homosexual experience to the point of orgasm between adolescence and old age. Most homosexual affairs of adolescents run their courses and give way to exclusively heterosexual behavior. Consequently, Freud assumed that adolescent homosexuality was a natural phase of human behavior. Recent findings (Pomeroy, 1958; Ruitenbeek, 1963), however, indicate that homosexuality may occur before, concurrently with, or after heterosexual behavior, and that there are by no means any set age-periods of homosexual or heterosexual behavior among individuals in our culture.

In connection with adolescent masturbation and homosexuality, the case of John may be cited. John, a 17-year-old athlete, came to see the psychologist because he was afraid of becoming homosexual and because his hair was falling out as a result, he thought, of his masturbation. Referral to a dermatologist showed that John had a mild neurodermatitis of the scalp. This quickly cleared when properly treated; there was no permanent hair loss. John came from a religious, unusually puritanical family, and had rigorously refrained from going out with girls whom he was afraid even to touch. He started masturbating at the age of 13, forced himself to stop for a time, but then became obsessed with the idea of doing it. The more he controlled the desire, the more obsessed he became. Finally, at the age of 16, he met another boy his age who induced him to engage in one homosexual act, which he enjoyed. He refrained from repeating this, only again to become obsessively concerned about his becoming homosexual. When he developed the itching scalp and noticed some of his hair falling out, he became certain that this was the result of his sex thoughts and his masturbating. He thought he might be going crazy. When, in the course of several counseling sessions, John was led to understand the source of his disturbance, and was informed that both masturbation and occasional homosexual acts might occur within the normal range of adolescent behavior, and when he was released from some of his groundless sexual fears and encouraged to go out with girls, his symptoms vanished and he began to acquire a much better conception of himself. Coincidentally, his athletic prowess also showed a remarkable improvement.

Adolescent Crushes. These infatuations or love affairs may be heterosexually or homosexually oriented; and, contrary to the frequently encountered statements and implications in some texts, the great majority of these attachments, as shown in studies by A. Ellis (1949, 1950, 1962b) are heterosexual. It has also been found that, when engaged in by college-age adolescents, crushes and loves are not necessarily all-out, uncontrollable emotions, but tend, rather, to be profound and powerful feelings over which the lovers maintain a considerable degree of ego-protective control and to which they do not too often become compulsively subservient. Nonetheless, adolescent crushes can be a serious problem to many young people and can represent one of the normal hazards of growing up in a highly competitive culture like our own.

PSYCHOSEXUAL PROBLEMS OF THE YOUNG ADULT

Young adulthood brings with it many individual and social psychosexual problems; and some evidence exists which indicates that problems of sex, love, and marriage are often more important to young adults in our culture than are almost all their other problems combined (Ellis and Fuller, 1950). Whereas clinical psychologists have for many years done marriage counseling, they are now increasingly being called upon to consider many premarital problems as well.

Premarital Sex Relations. By convention these relationships are banned by our mores as well as by some of our statutes (Kling, 1965). It is not surprising, however, that investigators such as Davis (1929), Dickinson and Beam (1934), and Ehrmann (1960), Finger (1947), Ford and Beach (1960), Kinsey *et al.* (1953), Hamilton (1929), Kirkendall (1961), and Reiss (1960) have found a relatively high incidence in the population samples studied. One major reason for confusion in this connection is found in the contradictory attitudes toward sex shown in our folklore and mass media. As the present writer has reported in *The Folklore of Sex* (A. Ellis, 1961), our magazines, "best sellers," newspapers, radio and television shows, film and stage productions, popular songs, and anecdotes do not ordinarily promote any one consistent sex attitude, but almost invariably, directly or indirectly, voice the view that sex is nasty and tasty, a vicious and delicious business. In consequence the average American is, consciously or unconsciously, almost completely muddled and confused in his sex views, feelings, and acts.

Although theories on premarital sex relations are many, the actual facts, other than the fact that they have always existed, still do, and will likely continue to exist, appear to be few. One other point that seems to be fairly well established by the Kinsey studies on the human male and female is that for both sexes those individuals who have premarital sex relations tend to obtain organisms more easily and frequently after marriage than those who are premaritally celibate. While debate on the ethics of premarital sex activity continues to rage (A. Ellis, 1963a, 1963d, 1965a; Guyon, 1963; Reiss, 1960; Stokes, 1962), unmarried young people are faced with the practical issue of remaining or not remaining continent; and no adequate solution for most or all of them has by any means as yet been forthcoming. Certain it is that much more thought must be given to the entire problem as well as to the individual case before any social solution can be found.

Choice of a Marital Partner. Marriage, as many sociologists have indicated for the last few decades, has largely become an affectional and companionable relationship instead of the basically socioeconomic relation it once was (Folsom, 1961; Winch, 1963). Hence, choice of a marriage partner has become increasingly difficult, and prospective mates, in increasing numbers, have found it advisable to arrange for premarital counseling. Modern courtship, moreover, still tends to be something of a superromantic, unrealistic, sex-teasing affair which does as much to obscure as to highlight each couple's basic potentialities for compatibility in marriage (A. Ellis, 1962b). Again, the more we learn about human behavior, the more we find that the roles the couples publicly enact for themselves, as well as for others, are largely defenses rather than the underlying patterns and traits most likely to come to the surface in a long-term marital relationship. Premarital counseling sessions, therefore, in the course of which the counselor may help couples understand themselves and each other, may be quite valuable and can ward off potentially unhappy marriages. Related to this are the so-called marriage prediction tests devised by psychologists and sociologists (Adams, 1950; Burgess and Cottrell, 1939; Burgess and Wallin, 1953; Locke, 1951; Terman, 1938). These scales, purporting to help in marital selection, are as yet poorly standardized, superficial, and fallible. The psychologist who engages in marriage counseling is accordingly cautious in using these tests as bases for prediction.

An illustrative instance of premarital counseling may be seen in the case of Paul and Martha, who came for counseling because, although engaged for over a year, Paul kept putting off the marriage date and could not say, even in a general way, when he wanted to set it. First Paul and Martha were seen separately by the counselor, then together. In the course of the individual sessions it was soon found that while Martha was a reasonably well-adjusted person, Paul was an anxiety neurotic of many years standing who could never make up his mind about any important matter, including where to live, for whom to work, or whether to buy a car. He was a deep-seated neurosis stemming from his belief that it was catastrophic for him to make any serious mistake—a belief that was partially instilled by his adoring mother, who never let him make decisions for himself. Paul and Martha were both apprised of this fact and of the necessity for Paul's undergoing psychotherapy prior to marriage. Martha saw this immediately and decided that she would break the engagement unless Paul entered psychotherapy. With typical neurotic indecision, Paul could not make up his mind and the engagement was broken. Martha subsequently married a much less neurotic partner.

MARITAL PROBLEMS

The clinical psychologist is inevitably confronted with a host of marriage and family problems for which he will be unequipped unless his training includes a wide knowledge of sociological and anthropological as well as psychological and sexological findings. A vast literature on the sociology of the family now exists; and although it is impossible to review even a small sample of this literature within the confines of the present chapter, it must be noted that any clinical psychologist who attempts to diagnose or treat human beings with marriage problems should be well acquainted with several modern classics in this area, including works by Cavan (1963), Kephart (1961), Murdock (1949), and Winch (1963).

Specific sex problems of marriage—including problems of the honeymoon, of sex arousal and satisfaction, and of birth control—are also numerous. Various of these problems are considered in detail in sex manuals, many of which, however, like Van de Velde's (1960) widely sold book, are ultraromantic, moralistic, factually outdated, and unreliable. The clinician must accordingly be well acquainted with the best and most down-to-earth literature in this area, including such books as those by Clark (1961), A. Ellis (1965b), Hegeler (1964), Hirsch (1961), Kelly (1961), the Kronhausens (1964), and Street (1962).

Marriage Counseling. The most serious and most prevalent marriage and family problem of this generation is marital breakup, or the contemplation of separation or divorce. One of the relatively newer techniques, developed to cope with this problem, is marriage and family counseling. Although this form of counseling goes far beyond the consideration of divorce problems alone, the fact remains that most couples who seek marriage counseling are already in serious difficulties. They come for help in ascertaining why they are in trouble and what, if anything, can be done about it. It is found that cases of marriage breakdown result from such facts as: (1) unrealistic ideals and goals in marriage; (2) selection of marriage partners, often based on neurotic choice; (3) deep-seated incompatibilities between the partners; (4) ignorance with regard to certain vital aspects of marriage, especially sex activities; and (5) serious and long-standing emotional disturbances in one or both marriage partners. It is the function of the marriage counselor not to tell couples whether or not to get a divorce but to help them to perceive clearly the underlying sources of their marriage difficulties, to understand themselves and their mates, and to work out their own best solutions on a realistic rather than on an overemotional or neurotic basis (A. Ellis, 1962a; Ellis and Harper, 1961a, 1961b; Mudd and Goodwin, 1961). When well done, marriage counseling becomes at least a process of intensive brief psychotherapy. Often it develops into intensive psychotherapy, for one or both of the spouses, on a more lengthy basis. The clinical psychologist who attempts marriage counseling should accordingly be trained and experienced in methods of depth-centered psychotherapy (see Part IV), even though he may not necessarily use these approaches in every case he sees.

An illustrative case of marriage counseling is that of the Madderts, who were seen together for seven sessions of highly active-directive rational-emotive psychotherapy. Although they had only been married for a few months, Mr. Maddert was very much confused as to whether he wanted to be married at all and Mrs. Maddert was terribly upset because he did not seem to love her and because she could not face the thought of his possibly leaving her. Because of their mutual state of upset, they were rarely having sex relations, were getting more and more angry at each other, and could hardly discuss anything without Mrs. Maddert's immediately breaking into tears.

In rational-emotive counseling or psychotherapy, psychoanalytic and nondirective methods are eschewed and the counselee is quickly shown what is the philosophical source or the basic irrational idea behind his symptoms; and his self-defeating philosophy of life is vigorously questioned and challenged by the therapist from the first session onward (A. Ellis, 1957, 1962a, 1963c; Ellis and Harper, 1961a, 1961b). In this case, Mrs. Maddert was first shown that she defined herself as worthless if she were not absolutely, securely loved; and that unless she clearly saw the sentences she was telling herself in this regard, and unless she vehemently counterattacked and changed them, she had no chance of being happily married with just about any husband, and certainly not with her own indecisive mate. Although she at first insisted that her spouse's indecisive behavior was badly affecting her, the therapist would have none of this notion, but kept insisting (in spite of her tears and her whining) that humans are not upset by others, but only by the nonsense they tell themselves *about* these others' poor behavior. He forcefully stuck to the realistic fact that she must see and uproot her own nonsense and accept herself as a valuable person and a potentially happy individual *whether or not* her husband fully accepted her. Then, and then only, he firmly maintained, would she be able to live unanxiously with this, or any other, husband.

Fortunately, Mrs. Maddert was quickly able to see that she, and not her husband, was her own worst enemy; and she made a tremendous effort unblamefully to accept herself as emotionally disturbed and to try to change her catastrophizing philosophy. Within a few weeks, she was remarkably calm, even though her husband was still indecisive and was able to contemplate the fact that if they finally did have to be divorced that would be too bad, but it would not be absolutely dreadful. As she calmed down, Mr. Maddert lost his guilt over upsetting her and was able to give some time and energy to thinking about his own problem of indecision. He was helped by the therapist to see that he viewed himself as worthless if there was even a slight possibility that he would be unachieving in his marriage, in his work, or in any other important area of his life. When he saw that this was so, and began to fight hard to accept himself even if he were not perfectly achieving, he was then able to realize that it was not truly his marriage but the possibility of his failing at his job as an accountant that had driven him into a state of panic, and that his marital indecisiveness had been something of a smoke-screen to prevent him from admitting how worried about his work he actually was. He, like his wife, kept questioning and challenging his central value of liking himself only when he could impress others with his business success; and a few weeks later, he too was remarkably calm and decisive. It was then ascertained that the Madderts really did care deeply for each other, that they were quite sexually and nonsexually compatible, and that their negative interactions had stemmed from each one's individual disturbances and decreased to near-zero as these ameliorated. In a situation where long-winded psychoanalytic interpretation of the past or passive-reflective concentration on the present might well have side-tracked the counselees from the main issues, and perhaps even done harm, the counselor's highly intrusive philosophic depropagandizing swiftly paid off—as it frequently does in this active-directive, rational-emotive method of psychotherapy.

PSYCHOSEXUAL PROBLEMS OF ADULTHOOD

The causes and treatment of all the psychosexual problems of adulthood cannot be adequately analyzed in a single chapter. Several of the major and more common problems can, however, be considered.

Autoerotism. Not only children and adolescents, but many adults, both married and unmarried, masturbate. Indeed, males who never do so seem to be rare; and unmarried females who never masturbate are clearly in the minority. As Taylor (1933) showed long ago, and as Kinsey *et al.* (1948, 1953) have verified, complete "sublimation" of sexuality in human beings, especially males, is almost impossible; and when other sexual outlets are blocked, as they often are in our culture, masturbation is a logical result. It may almost be dogmatically stated that autoerotism, when the individual does not erroneously *think* he is being harmed by it, is one of the most beneficial and least harmful sex acts know to humanity. It does not, in itself, cause physical or emotional disorders; it is not an "immature" mode of sex activity; it does not mitigate against sex adjustment in marriage; it is not a sexual "perversion"; it is almost impossible to engage in it excessively; and it does not normally lead to social or sexual seclusiveness (A. Ellis, 1963b, 1965b, 1965d; Kinsey *et al.* 1948, 1953). Indeed, there is considerable evidence to indicate that an individual's not masturbating, when he has no other sex outlets, may be psychologically and psychosomatically debilitating. Although autoerotism may result in such sequelae as nervousness, seclusiveness, and premature ejaculation in the male or relative frigidity in the female, it is not masturbation itself but neurotic worry, ideation, and fantasy, sometimes accompanying it, that lead to such disturbances. Masturbation alone should ordinarily not be psychologically treated; but masturbators, if and when they exhibit general personality disturbances, or if they have false ideas regarding autoerotism, should sometimes be seen psychotherapeutically.

Frigidity and Impotence. Marriage counselors and clinical psychologists often see individuals who consider themselves sexually inadequate. The most prevalent kinds of sexual inadequacy are the inability of the male to achieve or to sustain erection and the inability of the female to achieve satisfactory orgasm. Actually, both impotence and frigidity are less common than is often supposed, because false ideas of the "normal" lasting power of the average male and the vaginal sensitivity of the average female are woefully prevalent in our society. The average American male, as Kinsey and his associates have shown, has an intromission period of from two to five minutes; and the average American female is quite sensitive clitorally but relatively insensitive vaginally (A. Ellis, 1962b, 1963a, 1963d, 1965b; Kinsey, et al., 1948, 1953; Masters and Johnson, 1962, 1963). Unfortunately, many writers have erroneously stated or implied that the "normal" and "mature" male must be able to carry on active copulation for a half-hour or more and that the "normal" and "mature" woman must be able to achieve orgasm merely by penile-vaginal intercourse. In reality, literally millions of "normal" males and females will never be able to attain these unrealistic sex goals, are therefore traumatized, and are made to believe that they are sexually inadequate.

Modern findings show that, when they are labially and clitorally stimulated in a consistent, proper manner, females can usually achieve orgasm almost as quickly as males. Armed with such findings as these, and having the courage and frankness to draw the logical conclusions from them, the clinical psychologist or marriage counselor will find it not too difficult to dispel many of his clients' mistaken notions regarding frigidity and impotence and to help them overcome their difficulties. When serious instances of either of these sex disorders exist—that is, when females can obtain a satisfactory orgasm under virtually no circumstances or when males cannot achieve erection or genuinely suffer from premature ejaculation—organic pathology must first be eliminated before it is assumed that the difficulty is of psychogenic origin. In the majority of cases, however, both impotence and frigidity appear to be psychologically caused, and are intimately related to various kinds and degrees of anxiety, fear, guilt, and inadequacy feelings. In consequence, the treatment of frigidity and impotence is similar to the treatment of those with other types of neurotic symptoms (See Part IV, "Treatment Approaches") and involves intensive (although not necessarily prolonged) psychotherapy. The following case report is illustrative.

Mr. Dewar came for psychotherapy with the complaint that he had no difficulty in achieving an erection, but that many times as soon as he started copulation his erection would subside. Mrs. Dewar, who was first seen in connection with her husband's problem, complained that she only occasionally enjoyed sex relations with him. Mr. Dewar was referred to a urologist, who reported that he had no organic involvements or deficiencies. Mrs. Dewar was referred to a gynecologist, who reported that she, free from organic pathology, had unnecessarily severe and probably psychogenic menstrual pains. She was fitted with a diaphragm. Mr. Dewar was seen regularly, once each week, for psychotherapy, and it was soon determined that he was a most inadequate person generally who could not assert himself effectively on the job, with his friends, or in any other life situation. His difficulties were largely traceable to his shame over the behavior of his thoroughly inadequate and unsuccessful father, whom he believed he was doomed to emulate; and over his allowing himself to be completely dominated by an aggressive, talented, and quite successful brother, with whom he felt he could never compete. In addition he believed that a woman could be sexually satisfied only by penile-vaginal intercourse, that such intercourse had to occur nightly, and that he was a total loss as a lover and as a person if he did not continually give his wife an orgasm in that manner. When, in the course of psychotherapy, he was helped to understand that he evaluated himself only in terms of having a successful power struggle with others, to prove thereby how "good" he was, and when he began to change this irrational idea and to go for the joy (rather than the pronounced achievement) of marital relations, he began to be able to focus on *what* he was doing instead of *how* he was doing sexually, and his competence greatly increased. Moreover, he was also able to accept the fact, which the counselor forcefully brought to his attention, that noncoital as well as coital methods of sexual satisfaction exist and that nightly intercourse is not a necessary demand of married life nor a requisite for male sex adequacy, he became more relaxed and less anxious about his sexual and nonsexual relations. After 12 sessions, he became fully potent.

Mrs. Dewar, who was also seen once a week, at first was quite resistant to psychotherapy, and would evasively say that everything was going along fine and that she had no difficulties. At the fifth session she admitted that she kept having sex dreams about men other than her husband. At the eighth session she confessed, with great self-recrimination and anxiety, that she had sex relations with one of her uncles when she was 16 years old. She was apologetic for not bringing out this information sooner, and said she felt much better now that she had revealed it. However, her frigidity and her menstrual pains still continued unabated. Finally, at the fifteenth session, she confessed that she had been holding

back information again, and that what really concerned her was that, at
the age of 13, she had had sex relations with several boys, including her
brother, and that each time she now had sex relations with her husband
the memory of what she had done in the past recurred to her and she
"just didn't want to have anything to do with sex." When she made this
confession, the therapist showed her that there was no reason why she
had to be guilty about her past incestuous relations, since she had engaged in them when she was very young and it is hardly unusual for
girls of 13 to be as promiscuous as she was—especially when, as in her
case, they find that granting males sex favors is an excellent way of getting these males to like them. Even though she had been technically
wrong or mistaken for doing what she had done, she was, the therapist
held, a fallible human who could only expect to make a good number
of mistakes during her life; and blaming herself for these mistakes would
hardly help her make fewer of them in the future. Moreover, by turning
off all her sexuality at the remembrance of her past "sins," she was punishing her husband as much as herself—and *that* was hardly cricket.
When Mrs. Dewar was able to work through much of her guilt in connection with her past sex episodes, and to accept herself as a valuable
person even though she had conducted herself foolishly during her early
teens, she began to have regular orgasmic satisfaction, and her menstrual
pains lessened considerably.

Homosexuality. Older authorities, such as Havelock Ellis (1936), were
convinced that this condition was genetically or constitutionally caused.
And certain modern investigators (Kallman, 1952; Wolfenden, 1957) still
stress direct or indirect constitutional predispositions in at least some
cases of homosexuality. Most workers, however, emphasize the influence
of psychological, environmental, or conditioning factors (Allen 1951;
Bieber *et al.*, 1962; Cory, 1963, 1964; Ruitenbeek, 1963). This writer has
shown, in a study of human hermaphrodites, that no matter what the
physiological and hormonal makeup of the individual, direct constitutional factors are likely to influence only the *power* but not the *direction*
of the sex drive (A. Ellis, 1945). This means that both homosexuality and
heterosexuality are learned reactions, although the urge of men and
women to have some form of sexual release is partly innate. It is necessary in this connection to distinguish between those who are mainly or
exclusively homosexual and those who occasionally engage in homosexual
acts—especially since, as Kinsey *et al.* (1948) have shown, some 37 per
cent of American males at one time or another exhibits some kind of
homosexual behavior while only 4 per cent is exclusively homosexual.
The present writer (1965a) maintains that while sporadic homosexuality

is not necessarily indicative of neurosis, *exclusive* homosexuals are usually emotionally disturbed. They generally fall into one of four categories:

1. Those who have a sexual fixation on members of their own sex— from which they cannot escape
2. Those who have a phobia in regard to members of the other sex which prevents them from having satisfactory heterosexual relations
3. Those who have an obsession about members of their own sex which drives them toward homosexual acts or an obsessive interest in assuming the normal role of members of the other sex
4. Those who have a compulsion toward having exclusively homosexual relationships

Since fixations, phobias, obsessions, and compulsions are neurotic or psychotic symptoms (regardless of their contents), it is difficult to see how any exclusive homosexual can be anything other than, in some degree, disturbed.

As to why individuals in our culture become exclusively homosexual, there have recently been found scores of reasons, rather than the few causes often emphasized by earlier writers. Some of the major causes for an individual's exclusive homosexuality are as follows:

1. His being raised by a parent to assume the role of the other sex
2. His failure, for a number of reasons, to succeed in his own-sex role
3. His identification with a strong parent of the other sex, particularly when his own-sex parent is weak
4. His incestuous attachment to his other-sex parent, with consequent guilt about having sex relations with any members of the opposite sex
5. His hostility toward or fear of members of the other sex
6. His underlying puritanism and guilt about heterosexual relations
7. The many difficulties in achieving satisfactory heterosexual relations in this society
8. His being able more easily to find love and approval from members of his own sex
9. His experiencing early homosexual satisfactions, and his tendency to become neurotically fixated on immature levels of behavior
10. His specific or general psychological problems and disturbances, of which his homosexual activities may be mere symptoms

Many psychotherapists, particularly orthodox Freudians, contend that homosexuals cannot be "cured" but can only be "adjusted" to and made more comfortable with their inversion. Other clinicians (Allen, 1951; A. Ellis, 1965a; Robertiello, 1961) stoutly hold that homosexuals can be "cured" and quote cases in support of their claims. Clinical evidence seems to show that if the cure is realistically defined in terms of the homosexual's giving up his exclusive desire for relations with members of his own sex, it is not too difficult to treat him successfully—provided, however, that he wants to be treated. An illustrative case may be quoted in this connection.

Georgie was a very hostile boy of 28, who was exceptionally bright and who managed to keep a high school teaching job in spite of the fact that he had sex relations with several of his own pupils. He was highly promiscuous and would commonly pick up a young boy for the night, blackmail or physically force him to do things that the boy hardly wanted to do, and then laugh at his distress, and sometimes even beat him up before letting him go. He liked his rough and tumble "gay" life and only came to therapy because he got in trouble with the police, who forced him to come while he was on probation.

At first, Georgie refused to do any work at psychotherapy, as he was only waiting for his probationary term to end, and looked forward to returning to his old pattern of homosexuality. The therapist kept actively showing him, however, that he was acting like an idiot and that, by spending his whole life trying to put other people down, he was actually achieving little pleasure for himself and was seriously defeating his own end. Moreover, the therapist insisted, if Georgie had such a need violently to humiliate others, he must have been playing the seesaw technique: chimerically putting himself "up" at the expense of putting them "down." This meant that he probably despised himself, underneath, and that was his particular method of "one-upmanship."

The therapist ruthlessly kept showing Georgie what a little baby he was: how he demanded that the world revolve around him, that he grandiosely have things his own way, and that he never be in the slightest way frustrated—as by girls, who might *ultimately* give him the sex and love he wanted to get from them, but who would *first* make him earn these rewards by acting nicely to them. While determinedly uncovering and attacking Georgie's childish philosophy of life, the therapist clearly indicated that he had no personal hostility toward Georgie *himself,* and was in fact attacking his ideas because he wanted to help him *be* himself, rather than remain a weakling who had falsely to perfume himself with hostile "strength." The therapist also, finally, got Georgie to admit that he had largely chosen his physically violent way of homosexual life because he thereby could avoid risking what he would really have liked most to do: try to be an outstanding college professor, instead of the second-rate high school teacher that he was.

On many occasions, the therapist was pretty certain that he would never get anywhere with Georgie. But unlike his patients—whose sickness largely consisted of their easily giving up and avoiding life responsibilities when the going got rough—he kept persisting in revealing and vehemently counterpropagandizing Georgie's irrational self-verbalizations about the world's owing him a living and his needing to cover up his seeming intellectual weakness with physical "strength"; and eventually the counterattack paid off. By the thirty-second session, Georgie was seriously beginning to question his way of life and to admit its inherently self-defeating aspects; and by the fortieth session of individual and twelfth session of group therapy, he started dating girls for the first time in his life and soon lost almost all interest in boys. A year after therapy ended, he married, was quite kind to his wife—and began to go for his Ph.D. in literature, preparatory to becoming a college teacher. The active-directive method of rational-emotive psychotherapy, even with this most difficult kind of a patient, eventually won out where more passive psychotherapeutic techniques would have probably failed.

Hypersexuality. Many in our culture believe that they, or others they know, are "oversexed," but there is rarely any sound reason for such a belief. Occasionally, as in the condition called *priapism*, a male is unable to lose his erection, or individuals may have insatiable sex desire (*satyriasis* in the male, *nymphomania* in the female). Such ailments, when they actually exist, are likely to be caused by physical irritations, anomalies, or diseases, and should be treated by medical specialists. Most cases of so-called satyriasis or nymphomania, however, are misnamed in that they exist in those merely having strong sex drives, and who find their urges inconvenient to their lower-sexed mates or out of keeping with their own notions of sexual "normality." Also, some women become "nymphomaniacs" in that they keep seeking orgasmic release which, usually because of their own emotional disturbances, they never achieve. Excessive sexual activity, however, is almost impossible for any person, inasmuch as the sex desires automatically become quiescent when the individual has had the number of climaxes sufficient and proper to satisfy his needs. Excessive sex drive, if and when it actually exists, may indicate a physiological or hormonal dysfunction, or it may suggest a personality maladjustment, often of the obsessive-compulsive type (Ellis and Sagarin, 1964).

Sex Aberrations and Perversions. Virtually all so-called perversions, aberrations, or deviations are "perverse" or "abnormal" by virtue of social as opposed to biological criteria. In fact, as this writer (1962b, 1963a, 1965d) has shown, notions of sexual "abnormality"—whether based on statistical, hygienic, biological, or moral concepts—are, in the last analysis, derived from the values of the society in which they are held. "Normal" sex activities are those which are approved in a given culture—those which society has made, declared, legislated, or otherwise caused to be viewed as "normal." From an objective standpoint, virtually all so-called perversions are "normal" in that they are practiced, without any harmful effects, by many animal species and by certain primitive and civilized peoples. Thus, "perverse" acts like oral-genital relations, peeping (voyeurism), sadism and masochism, incest, exhibitionism, and homosexuality are widely practiced and socially accepted in some parts of the world. When they are thus culturally accepted, they are usually harmless.

From a psychological standpoint, sex acts may logically be said to be "perverse" or "abnormal" when they are engaged in exclusively, fixatedly (as a fetish), obsessively, or compulsively. Any human act, for that matter, which may be performed successfully and pleasurably in many different ways, but which is arbitrarily, fearfully, and neurotically restricted to one circumscribed outlet, may be psychologically viewed as abnormal or perverted. Thus, an individual who will eat only one food, or will eat only at midnight, or will blow his nose only when he has gone through an involved and seemingly senseless ritual is to some extent emotionally disturbed. Most sex acts which are commonly called "perverted" or "abnormal" in our culture, however, are misnamed. At the same time, many persons, such as those who are predominantly or exclusively homosexual, or exhibitionistic, or sadistic in their sex outlets, are emotionally disturbed and hence "perverted" or aberrant. These individuals, if they desire professional help, can be psychotherapeutically treated in much the same manner as other emotionally maladjusted persons whose symptoms are largely nonsexual.

Sex Offenses.   Sex offenders are those who commit acts that are banned by law.   As several modern writers have noted, if all our sex statutes were strictly enforced, some 95 per cent of American males would be sex offenders at some time during their lives.   Many of these statutes are, of course, not enforced; yet each year tens of thousands of males and females are arrested for sex offenses.   Many of these are seen by clinical psychologists for diagnostic or therapeutic purposes.   Although convicted sex offenders are commonly considered overimpulsive, fiendish criminals, actual researchers have shown this assumption to be false (Abrahamsen, 1950; Ellis and Brancale, 1956; Tappan, 1950).   Intensive psychological and psychiatric studies of several hundred convicted sex offenders seen at the New Jersey Diagnostic Center showed that the majority were rather innocuous, inadequate, passive, and minor offenders; that only a small percentage of them used force or duress upon their victims; that only about 3 per cent could be legitimately classed as "psychopaths" while the majority were mildly or severely neurotic; that most of these convicted sex offenders were sexually inhibited and constricted rather than overimpulsive and oversexed; and that high percentages of severe emotional immaturity, underlying hostility, subnormal intelligence, and alcoholism were present among them.   Sex offenders are not hopelessly incurable in all or most instances. Reports of their successful treatment have been published by several psychotherapists, including Karpman (1960), London and Caprio (1950), and Rosen (1964).

THE TREATMENT OF THOSE WITH PSYCHOSEXUAL
AND MARITAL PROBLEMS

Because psychosexual and marital problems never exist in isolation, but only as problems of human individuals, and because human beings must be realistically viewed from the vantage of their total personalities, the effective treatment of those with psychosexual and marital problems is synonymous with the effective treatment of individuals with general personality problems. Consequently, clinical sexology or marriage counseling, considered as professions, should not be restricted to physicians, social workers, and sociologists, but should be practiced by clinical psychologists as well—and practiced not merely as separate skills in their own right but as integral parts of general psychotherapy. The present writer's judgment is that no one should engage in sex, marriage, or family counseling unless he is well versed and experienced in at least one technique of intensive psychotherapy. This conclusion is drawn from an extensive experience in which it has been consistently found that from 60 to 80 per cent of the clients coming for marriage counseling and sex problems are never likely to find a solution to their problems unless they accept some form of (brief or prolonged) intensive psychotherapy. Inasmuch as treatment approaches are discussed in Part IV of this volume, these will not be discussed in detail at this point. Certain specific comments, however, can be made here regarding the type of person who should normally interview and treat those with specific psychosexual and marital problems.

As this writer has elsewhere noted (A. Ellis, 1965a), persons who question, diagnose, and treat the sexually and maritally disturbed should fulfill the following requirements:

1. They should be professional people who have had adequate training, including supervised clinical experience, in one of the psychological disciplines, such as clinical psychology, psychiatry, or psychiatric social work.
2. They should have distinctly objective sex attitudes and be free from rigidity, orthodoxy, and moralism.
3. They should have had a reasonably active sexual-amative life themselves and have no serious problems in this area.
4. They should have, in addition to their knowledge of the science of human behavior, a specialized knowledge of the historical, sociological, and anthropological views of sex, love, marriage, and family relations.

5. They should be emotionally stable, nonhostile persons who are able to gain and maintain rapport with difficult, negativistic, or uncommunicative respondents.
6. They should be unafraid of sexual topics and should be able to discuss them without embarrassment in down-to-earth language.
7. They should, even if they are mainly doing interrogation for diagnostic purposes, preferably have training and skill in psychotherapy, and be well prepared to handle traumatic material or emotional upsets that may be ventilated during or as a result of the interview procedure (see Chapter 2).

SUMMARY

The clinical psychologist, if he is to help human beings with psychosexual and marital problems, would best have a wide range of information in psychological, sociological, anthropological, sexological, and allied areas, an unusual degree of objectivity and courage in facing sexual facts that are often unrealistically ignored in our culture and that are moralistically treated upon occasion even in professional literature. He should be free from theoretical orthodoxies and from personal rigidities, and be able to view each client as a unique individual who, in spite of his being reared in a somewhat unified cultural milieu, and in spite of his having acquired many socially inculcated attitudes and prejudices, rarely if ever falls into neatly niched "types" or characterologies. He should be solidly trained in diagnostic methods, hypothesis formation, and its attendant problem-solving implications, and he should be well grounded as well as experienced in psychotherapy. Psychosexual treatment and marriage counseling inevitably and significantly involve the imparting of relevant information to the client with a consequent relinquishment of needless, ignorance-grounded anxiety and guilt. But psychosexual and marital counseling, when adequately performed, also involves the treatment of the client's general personality problems—without which treatment any solution of specific psychosexual and marital difficulties is most likely to be partial, superficial, and temporary.

REFERENCES

[ABRAHAMSEN, D.] 1950. *Report on study of 102 sex offenders at Sing Sing Prison.* Utica, N.Y.: State Hospitals Press.

ADAMS, C. R. 1950. Evaluating marriage prediction tests. *Marriage Fam. Living,* 12, 55–56.

ALLEN, C. 1951. *The sexual perversions and abnormalities.* London: Oxford Univer. Press.

BIEBER, I., *et al.* 1962. *Homosexuality.* New York: Basic Books.

BURGESS, E. W., and COTTRELL, L. S. 1939. *Predicting success or failure in marriage.* New York: Prentice-Hall.

BURGESS, E. W., and WALLIN, P. 1953. *Engagement and marriage.* Philadelphia: Lippincott.

CAVAN, RUTH S. 1963. *The American family.* New York: Crowell.

CLARK, LEMON. 1961. *The enjoyment of love in marriage.* New York: Cress.

CONN, J. H. 1940. Sexual curiosity of children. *Amer. J. Dis. Child.,* **60,** 1110–19.

CORY, D. W. 1963. *The homosexual in America.* New York: Paperback Library.

CORY, D. W. 1964. *The lesbian in America.* New York: Citadel.

DAVIS, KATHERINE B. 1929. *Factors in the sex life of 2200 women.* New York: Harper & Row.

DEARBORN, L. W. 1961. Autoerotism. In A. ELLIS and E. ABARBANEL (eds.), *The encyclopedia of sexual behavior.* New York: Hawthorn Books.

DICKINSON, R. L., and BEAM, L. 1934. *The single woman.* Baltimore: Williams & Wilkins.

EHRMANN, W. W. 1960. *Premarital dating behavior.* New York: Holt, Rinehart & Winston.

ELLIS, A. 1945. The sexual psychology of human hermaphrodites. *Psychosom. Med.,* **7,** 108–25.

ELLIS, A. 1949. Some significant correlates of love and family behavior. *J. soc. Psychol.,* **30,** 3–16.

ELLIS, A. 1950. Love and family relationships of American college girls. *Amer. J. Sociol.,* **55,** 550–58.

ELLIS, A. 1957. *How to live with a neurotic.* New York: Crown Publishers.

ELLIS, A. 1961. *The folklore of sex.* (Rev. ed.) New York: Grove Press.

ELLIS, A. 1962a. *Reason and emotion in psychotherapy.* New York: Lyle Stuart.

ELLIS, A. 1962b. *The American sexual tragedy.* (Rev. ed.) New York: Lyle Stuart and Grove Press.

ELLIS, A. 1963a. *If this be sexual heresy . . .* New York: Lyle Stuart.

ELLIS, A. 1963b. *Sex and the single man.* New York: Lyle Stuart.

ELLIS, A. 1963c. *The origins and the development of the incest taboo.* New York: Lyle Stuart.

ELLIS, A. 1963d. *The intelligent woman's guide to man-hunting.* New York: Lyle Stuart.

ELLIS, A. 1965a. *Homosexuality: Its causes and cure.* New York: Lyle Stuart.

ELLIS, A. 1965b. *The art and science of love.* New York: Lyle Stuart.

ELLIS, A. 1965c. *The case for sexual liberty.* Tucson: Seymour Press.

ELLIS, A. 1965d. *Sex without guilt.* (Rev. ed.) New York: Lyle Stuart and Grove Press.

ELLIS, A., and BRANCALE, R. 1956. *The psychology of sex offenders.* Springfield, Ill.: Charles C Thomas.

ELLIS, A., and FULLER, E. W. 1950. The sex, love, and marriage questions of senior nursing students. *J. soc. Psychol.,* **31,** 209–16.

ELLIS, A., and HARPER, ROBERT A. 1961a. *Creative marriage.* New York: Lyle Stuart.

ELLIS, A., and HARPER, R. A. 1961b. *A guide to rational living.* Englewood Cliffs, N.J.: Prentice-Hall.

ELLIS, A., and SAGARIN, E. 1964. *Nymphomania: A study of the oversexed woman.* New York: Gilbert Press.

ELLIS, H. 1936. *Studies in the psychology of sex.* New York: Random House.

FINGER, F. W. 1947. Sex beliefs and practices among male college students. *J. abnorm. soc. Psychol.*, 42, 57–67.

FOLSOM, J. K. 1961. The sexual and affectional functions of the family. In A. ELLIS and A. ABARBANEL (eds.), *The encyclopedia of sexual behavior.* New York: Hawthorn Books.

FORD, C. S., and BEACH, F. A. 1961. *Patterns of sexual behavior.* New York: Ace Books.

FREUD, S. 1962–64. *Collected papers.* New York: Collier Publishers.

GUYON, R. 1963. *A case for sexual freedom.* Hollywood: France' International Publications.

HAMILTON, G. V. 1929. *A research in marriage.* New York: Albert and Charles Boni.

HEGELER, INGE, and HEGELER, STEN. 1964. *An ABZ of love.* New York: Medical Press.

HIRSCH, E. W. 1961. *The power to love.* New York: Pyramid Books

KALLMAN, F. J. 1952. Comparative study on the genetic aspects of male homosexuality. *J. nerv. ment. Dis.*, 115, 283–98.

KARPMAN, B. 1960. *The sexual offender and his offenses.* New York: Julian Press.

KELLY, G. L. 1961. *Sexual feeling in married men and women.* New York: Permabooks.

KEPHART, WILLIAM M. 1961. *The family, society and the individual.* Boston: Houghton Mifflin.

KINSEY, A. C., POMEROY, W. B., and MARTIN, C. E. 1948. *Sexual behavior in the human male.* Philadelphia: Saunders.

KINSEY, A. C., POMEROY, W. B., MARTIN, C. E., and GEHARD, P. H. 1953. *Sexual behavior in the human female.* Philadelphia: Saunders.

KIRKENDALL, L. A. 1961. *Premarital intercourse and interpersonal relationships.* New York: Julian Press.

KLING, S. G. 1965. *Sexual behavior and the law.* New York: Bernard Geis Associates.

KRONHAUSEN, P., and KRONHAUSEN, E. 1964. *The sexually responsive woman.* New York: Grove Press.

LOCKE, H. 1951. *Predicting adjustment in marriage.* New York: Holt, Rinehart & Winston.

LONDON, L. S., and CAPRIO, F. S. 1950. *Sexual deviations.* Washington, D.C.: Linacre Press.

MALINOWSKI, B. 1961. *The sexual life of savages in Northwestern Melanesia.* New York: Harvest Books.

MASTERS, W. H.   The sexual response cycle of the human female.   I.   Gross anatomic considerations.   *West. J. Surg. Obst. & Gynec.*, 1960, **68**, 57–72.

MASTERS, W. H., and JOHNSON, V. E.   The sexual response cycle of the human female.   III.   The clitoris: anatomic and clinical considerations.   *West. J. Surg. Obst. & Gynec.*, 1962, **70**, 248–257.

MASTERS, W. H., and JOHNSON, V. E.   1963.   The sexual response cycle of the human male.   I.   Gross anatomic considerations.   *Western J. Surg. Obstetrics & Gynecol.*, **71**, 85–95.

MEAD, MARGARET.   1960.   *From the south seas.*   New York: New American Library.

MUDD, EMILY, and GOODWIN, HILDA M.   1961.   Marriage counseling.   In A. ELLIS and A. ABARBANEL (eds.), *The encyclopedia of sexual behavior.*   New York: Hawthorn Books.

MURDOCK, G. P.   1949.   *Social structure.*   New York: Macmillan.

POMEROY, W. B.   1958.   Paper delivered at the annual meeting of the Mattachine Society, Sept. 8, 1958.

REISS, I. L.   1960.   *Premarital sexual standards in America.*   New York: Free Press.

ROBERTIELLO, C.   1961.   *Voyage from Lesbos.*   New York: Avon Books.

ROSEN, I.   1964.   *The pathology and treatment of sexual deviation.*   Fair Lawn, N.J.: Oxford Univer. Press.

RUITENBEEK, H. M. (ed.).   1963.   *The problem of homosexuality in modern society.*   New York: Dutton.

STEKEL, W.   *Auto-erotism.*   New York: Evergreen Books, 1961.

STOKES, W. R.   1962.   Our changing sex ethics.   *Marriage Fam. Living*, **24**, 269–72.

STREET, R.   1962.   *Modern sex techniques.*   New York: Lancer Books.

TAPPAN, P. W.   1950.   *The habitual sex offender.*   Trenton, N.J.: Commission on the Habitual Sex Offender.

TAYLOR, W. S.   1933.   A critique of sublimation in males.   *Genet. Psychol. Monogr.*, **13**, 1–115.

TERMAN, L. M.   1938.   *Psychological factors in marital happiness.*   New York: McGraw-Hill.

VAN DE VELDE, T. H.   1960.   *Ideal marriage.*   New York: Random House.

WEDGE, B. M.   1952.   Occurrence of psychosis among Okinawans in Hawaii.   *Amer. J. Psychiat.*, **109**, 255–61.

WINCH, R. F.   1963.   *The modern family.*   New York: Holt, Rinehart & Winston.

[WOLFENDEN, J.]   1957.   *Report of the committee on homosexual offenses and prostitution.*   London: Her Majesty's Stationery Office.

9

Psychosomatic Phenomena

GEORGE SASLOW AND JOSEPH D. MATARAZZO *

THE CONCEPT: EARLY VIEWS

Long before the term *psychosomatic* was used, there was much anecdotal and empirical evidence that a sick individual's thinking, feeling,
and doing had significant relation to his illness.   Thus, the famous seven-
teenth-century physician Sydenham noticed that, by thinking for half an
hour of his great toe, he could always bring on an attack of gout.   Margetts (1950) points out that the word itself first occurred in early nineteenth-century German psychiatric literature.   Examination of the
pertinent medical publications led Stainbrook (1952) to the conclusion
that, despite the early use of *psychosomatic,* the general attitude of nineteenth-century medicine to the relationship of mind and body in disease
is most aptly described by the term *somatopsychic medicine.*   Thus, important medical figures considered all insanity the result of respiration,
circulation, and colon.   Accordingly, they made appropriate physiological
observations, and, as Stainbrook puts it, recognized the physiopathology
they studied as the cause of the psychopathology in which they were interested.   Contemporaneously, other attitudes were also apparent.   Tuke
(1872) spoke of excitomotor acts without conscious ideation in explanation
of sleepwalking; Creighton (1886) stated that "as a result of the unex-
pressed emotion of anxiety . . . , the grief unrelieved by tears . . . , the
mind . . . with all such repressions or want of expression by the usual
channels—is apt to take a peculiar revenge or to find a peculiar outlet by
discharging itself unconsciously upon the glandular system."   In still

* George Saslow, Ph.D. (New York University), M.D. (Harvard University), Professor of Psychiatry, and Joseph D. Matarazzo, Ph.D. (Northwestern University),
Professor of Medical Psychology, both of the University of Oregon Medical School.

other circles, some disorders were viewed in a more comprehensive manner than in terms of bodily changes causing mental changes or vice versa.
For example, Knight (1890) described the three necessary determinants
of asthma as "the neurotic habit," "a morbid condition somewhere in the
respiratory tract . . . ," and "the exciting factor, which may be atmos-
pheric, digestive, mental or other remote irritatives which act reflectively
on bronchial tubes."

Even before the present century, experimental and clinical observations of the relations between stressful life situations (or symbols thereof)
and physiological (including emotional) responses were numerous. These
observations, however, were of variable quality, dramatic and unique,
incompletely described, limited to single instances, unsystematic, or
simply not reproducible by other workers. Examples from many sources
referred to by Stainbrook are Bichat's impression of the high frequency of
heart, lung, and stomach disorder among Parisians during the French
Revolution; Cooper's impressions that carcinoma of the rectum ensued
upon mental distress and that grief or anxiety of mind was one of the
most frequent causes of breast cancer, with a confidently postulated series
of intermediate pathophysiological and anatomical changes that he did
not study or demonstrate; the famous observations of Beaumont upon
the stomach of Alexis St. Martin; Mosso and associates' observations of
vasoconstriction in response to sounds and other stimuli during sleep and
hypnosis, and of variations in skin temperature with changes in thought
and feeling; studies on the psychogalvanic reflexes; studies by the German
psychophysiologists of relations between blood pressure and emotions;
Campbell's comment upon the deaths of patients with angina pectoris at
times of violent anger; the sudden arrest of menstruation in the women of
a town that was the scene of a severe earthquake; the production of
cutaneous blisters and other cutaneous lesions by hypnotic suggestion;
Trousseau's attack of asthma when he detected a servant's thievery. As
might be suspected from so great a variety and quantity of observations,
explanatory hypotheses were also numerous and variable with regard to
quality and evidential support.

Although not acknowledged as such at the time, or since for that matter, the systematic studies of Pavlov on the *conditioned response*, near
the turn of the century, provided this evidence. As Pavlov said, on the
occasion of accepting his Nobel Prize, in 1904, "experiments with psy-
chical stimulation prove to be exact, but miniature, models of the experiments with physiological stimulations by the same substances. Thus,
with regard to the work of the salivary glands, psychology occupies a
place close to that of physiology" (1957, p. 143). Pavlov's major contribution to psychosomatic medicine was the careful and repeated laboratory
demonstration that symbolic representation of a stimulus can be substi-

tuted for the actual stimulus to an inborn physiological mechanism. Although unrecognized by clinicians for many decades, Pavlov's work was the first experimental demonstration that symbols of events (thoughts in the human, as was later demonstrated) could produce physiological changes as dramatic as those produced by natural stimuli acting along the same physiological pathways.

It is illuminating to note that, as the nineteenth century ended and the twentieth began, Putnam (1899) rated "a thorough preliminary course in psychology . . . as following closely on chemistry and physics as a preparation for the work of a general (medical) practitioner," and Barker (1906) urged that general practitioners should master psychotherapy. Freud was working out major aspects of his psychotherapeutic technique and theory of personality development, but no one had yet utilized information obtained about a patient's life situations by Freud's free association method or by other interview methods to place the patient in a situation that was meaningful and stressful and so to study systematically life situations involving physiological-response sequences. This was to come later, in the work of Wolff and Wolf and their associates.

1900–1950

While Freud himself did not explore systematically the field of psychosomatic medicine, his free association technique made available unusually detailed observations of a patient's life experiences, thinking, feeling, overt and covert physiological responses, and behavior, over years of time. It was not long before psychoanalysts who had been trained by him or his pupils, and who also had a special interest in particular medical disorders, began to study intensively the relations of these factors to one or another specific medical disorder (asthma, duodenal ulcer, migraine, hypertension, etc.). Deutsch is known to have done so since 1922 and has published a book describing his procedure (1949). Dunbar (1935) collected some 2,000 different examples from the entire history of medicine of clinically observed, recurring combinations of personalities, situations, emotions, and bodily functions. Saul (1944) summarized, through 1941, the clinical psychoanalytic observations of relationships between emotional tension and the functions of various organs and organ systems. Alexander and French (1948) published a series of papers based on the psychoanalytic study of patients suffering from chronic disturbances of the vegetative organs ("vegetative responses to disturbed emotional states"). In the works referred to above, experimental observations of the organ responses at the time of the psychoanalytic interviews are rare. Instead, the responses are linked causally to unconscious "nuclear conflicts" as defined in the Freudian psychoanalytic framework, for example, between denied and repressed oral-receptive and oral-aggressive tendencies in duodenal ulcer.

Still another kind of activity that helped develop the concept of psychosomatic medicine was the experimental work of Cannon (1915) in the early twentieth century. His experiments demonstrated the feasibility of studying the physiological changes undergone by intact mammals in situations so stressful as to provoke responses labeled "emotional." They made evident the wide range of bodily adjustments that occur in the enraged or fearful animal, and became the basis of our knowledge of the physiological responses associated with emotion. His hypothesis of the autonomic system as an emergency response system influenced physiologists, psychologists, psychiatrists, and other physicians so profoundly that Cobb (1952) regards modern psychosomatic medicine as having begun with Cannon.

Subsequent to Cannon's work, the greatest contributions to psychosomatic medicine appear to have been made by Wolff and collaborators at the New York Hospital (Cornell Medical College), in a series of studies dating from 1939. The methods used are described, in general, by Wolff (1950) in his concluding remarks to the 1949 meeting of the Association for Research in Nervous and Mental Disease (devoted to the topic *Life Stress and Bodily Disease*). They are described in detail in the numerous special studies reported upon and referred to in the same volume. Broadly speaking, a given subject was studied by a variety of methods (appraisal of his behavior, verbal descriptions of life experiences in therapeutic interviews, fluctuations in his illness in relation to life events or subject's behavior, etc.) until enough was known to warrant planned short-term experiments. In these experiments, indicators of the function of an organ or system relevant to a symptom or disease in the given subject were measured and recorded by suitable physiological and biochemical procedures. Following a control period of relative relaxation and security, an event (symbolized by the clinician-interviewer's words) suspected of disturbing the subject was abruptly introduced verbally into an ongoing interview. If significant changes were then observed in the patient's measured organ or system functions at this time and not during discussions of other, more neutral topics, and if these subsided when the patient-subject was successfully reassured, it was inferred that the event (usually a conflict-evoking one) and symbols thereof were regularly linked to the bodily changes. In this manner were studied such diseases, processes, and responses as epilepsy, diabetes, glaucoma, hay fever, stomach ulcer, ulcerative colitis, essential hypertension, hives, Raynaud's disease, migraine and other headaches, serum antibody titers, body heat regulation, dyspnea, secretion of bronchial mucus, colonic and gastric functions, backache, cardiac function and circulatory efficiency, and bladder function. These experiments were merely a modern variant of Pavlov's classic demonstrations on dogs fifty years earlier.

In many of Wolff's investigations, it was demonstrated that alterations in physiological processes and responses, and episodic fluctuations in studied aspects of various disorders, occurred in close and regular relation to particular kinds of life events and symbols thereof, and that such life events were meaningfully related to the longitudinal life experience of the subject. Holmes *et al.* (1950) demonstrated also, in the case of nasal hyperfunction and hay fever, that the altered nasal functions induced by exposure of a sensitive subject to allergenic pollen in adequate dosage were in *no way different* from those induced by exposure of the same subject to a symbol of a conflict-evoking life situation, and that the two types of stimuli—allergenic pollen and symbol of stressful event— could summate, with resultant hay fever symptoms. Other similar demonstrations of summative effects of quite diverse stimuli are scattered throughout Wolff's publications. Such experiments with human subjects clearly should be thought of as modern extensions of Pavlov's earlier experiments with dogs.

After Cannon's main work had been done, important new observations enlarged our concepts of the organism's response to stress. He had studied emergency responses, lasting for minutes only, wasteful and dangerous if maintained. Extending this work, Selye and co-workers (1953) have demonstrated that the mammal responds to continued or repeated nonspecific stress (severe exercise, oxygen deprivation, cold, surgical injury, "nervous strain," toxic substances, enforced immobilization, intense sonic stimulation) by activation of the anterior pituitary in some manner unknown. This discharges adrenocorticotrophic hormone (ACTH) into the blood stream, with subsequent increased production of adrenocortical hormones. The whole process is slow to start and long lasting, and can be associated with disorders analogous to human hypertension, peptic ulcer, rheumatoid arthritis, and various other chronic medical conditions. A number of studies on man have confirmed major parts of Selye's work. For example, Gray *et al.* (1951) showed that repeatedly injected ACTH was associated in man with the gastric responses related to ulcer.

As Wolff's group accumulated data on the responses of organs and systems in the manner described above, their point of view shifted to focus upon the entire constellation of feelings, "attitudes" (defined operationally), and bodily changes that a subject experiences and exhibits in reaction to stress, as in the studies of Graham (1950) on hives and of Grace, Wolf, and Wolff (1951) on bowel function.

It became apparent also, from such studies as those of Flynn *et al.* (1950) on identical twins, one hypertensive and one normotensive, that the "*stock*" (Wolff's term for genetic, constitutional, or congenital factors in an individual's functioning) may be a variable of major importance. This was implied in certain other investigations such as those on "susceptible" individuals with hay fever but was here studied deliberately as such. The demonstrated importance of "stock" in the human subject is congruent with its role in animal experiments such as those discussed by Scott (1950) and Scott and Marston (1950). Scott (1944) also notes that, in his animal studies, genetically produced differences in behavior that are unimportant under ordinary circumstances may in particular stress situations result in all-or-none differences: Genetic factors may thus be extremely important in special cases.

1950–Present

The start of the second half of the twentieth century saw research in psychosomatic medicine become more sophisticated. Lacey (1959) has written an excellent review of psychosomatic phenomena during interviews, to which the reader is referred. Several illustrative studies of psychosomatic phenomena not treated in his review can be summarized. Mahl (1949, 1950, 1952) studied the relationship between fear and the secretion of HCL in the stomach of dog, monkey, and man. He confirmed Cannon's earlier observation that *acute* fear ("emergency reaction") was associated with a decrease in HCL secretion but, consistent with his hypothesis that in certain psychosomatic stomach conditions chronic stress produces an increase in HCL secretion, he found such *increases* in all three species under *prolonged* or chronic stress. His several studies show how scientific hypotheses can be generated from careful clinical observation, tested rigorously in controlled animal studies through extreme ranges of pertinent variables, and then the results re-examined in natural and laboratory experiments using humans.

Mahl's experiments did not produce ulcer. This step was taken by Sawrey and Weisz (1956) and Sawrey, Conger, and Turrell (1956), who, in a series of ingenious and now classic experiments, studied the effects on stomach lesions in rats under various combinations of psychological and physiological treatments. They successfully produced stomach ulcers in their rats but demonstrated that lesion formation was a complex function of numerous pertinent variables such as conflict, hunger, thirst, and shock. No lesions were produced by hunger and thirst without shock, by shock and thirst alone, by thirst alone, or by shock alone. The most stomach lesions (in 76 per cent of their large group of animals) occurred with the combination of hunger plus shock plus conflict. Thus conflict per se was shown to contribute significantly to ulcer formation; hunger and shock also contributed significantly, but only in interaction; and thirst did not contribute significantly. In a subsequent study, Conger, Sawrey, and Turrell (1958) demonstrated that animals stressed alone had less resistance to stomach ulceration than did animals stressed in a "social" situation with other animals. This research, in marked contrast to the primarily clinical, psychoanalytic, observations of the previous generation, demonstrated the dangers of a single-factor hypothesis for explaining ulcer or similar disease, and the necessity of carrying on experiments that make possible the examination of multiple relevant factors under controlled laboratory conditions.

The importance of this last point is underscored in the research by Brady and associates on "executive" monkeys. Their experiments, summarized in Brady (1964), utilized two monkeys in tandem, one (the "executive") of which was solely in control of avoidance of shock for both animals. "Executive" monkeys, required to perform this avoidance response for periods of six hours on and six hours off, died of ulcers in striking numbers. The control animal in each pair, although receiving the same electric-shock experience, did not develop ulcers. Subsequent studies varied the time on the avoidance task from a 6–6 hour schedule to various other combinations of stress and rest (18 hours of stress, 6 hours of rest; or 30 minutes of stress followed by 30 minutes of rest; and other combinations). None of the "executive" monkeys under these other schedules, even the presumably more stressful ones, developed ulcers. The investigators explained this paradoxical finding by additional experiments, which showed that the periods of stress often decreased the secretion of HCL, and that the abnormally high levels of secretion occurred several hours after the beginning of the rest interval that intervened between periods of stress. This type of highly relevant temporal sequence (not yet replicated) could not have been isolated, or even conceived, by any of the kinds of purely or mainly *clinical* observation that characterized the earlier work in ulcer etiology.

Another example of the need to isolate pertinent variables in psychosomatic phenomena, and to examine them over a wide range, is illustrated in the replication of the Lacey and Smith study of heart rate conditioning by Weiland *et al.* (1963). Lacey *et al.* (1954, 1955) had concluded that a conditioned heart rate response to certain words ("cow") could *generalize* to other stimuli (other rural words) meaningfully related to this UCS. Wieland *et al.* confirmed these results but demonstrated that they were highly dependent on the intensity of shock used as the UCS; that is, 5 ma of shock did not give the effect, whereas 10 ma replicated the findings of Lacey and Smith.

That research as sophisticated as the above can be carried out even in man under natural conditions was demonstrated by Mirsky (1958), who, studying psychological, physiological, and social determinants in the predisposition and precipitation of duodenal ulcer in man, showed that a number of ulcers beyond chance expectation appeared during Army basic training in young inductees who at the beginning of basic training had the highest levels of serum pepsinogen levels but no evidence of ulcer. Mirsky concluded (p. 310), "Those who insist that the development of duodenal ulcer is determined solely by 'organic' factors are as fallacious as those who claim that 'psychic' factors are sole determinants."

Experiments such as the above were being conducted in this country at the same time that Russian investigators were developing ingenious methods for studying conditioned interoceptive responses in man. A review of this research is given by Razran (1961, 1965). Studying humans in seemingly well-controlled experiments, the Russian investigators have succeeded in conditioning such responses as the urge to void a full bladder, etc. They also have published considerable evidence for semantic generalization in man, namely, that these internal responses conditioned initially to a specific word could be generalized to a variety of other words or concepts similar to it. The Russian work deserves careful study because of its own intrinsic worth, the new methods employed, its relevance to the problems in this chapter, and because it appears hardly known outside the Soviet Union.

Little of this Russian extension of Pavlovian methods to the intact human appears to be under way in the United States. Rather, in response to advances in clinical and experimental endocrinology, American research has become interested in exploring the interrelationships between psychosocial and endocrine factors in behavior. Examples are studies of Sachar et al. (1963) and C. T. Wolff et al. (1964). In the study by Sachar et al., schizophrenic patients, at times of high degrees of anxiety and depression, showed marked elevations in urinary 17-hydroxycorticosteroid excretion—as high as two to three times normal. In the studies of C. T. Wolff et al., urinary 17-hydroxycorticosteroid levels were measured during the period of sustained stress (the impending death of their child) in 31 parents of children suffering from fatal illnesses. Clinical methods of assessing the effectiveness with which a parent coped with ("defended against") the threat of the loss of a child were shown to have a suitable degree of reliability. From such a clinical assessment, the investigators made predictions of the mean urinary 17-hydroxycorticoid excretion rate of the parents. These predicted endocrine values were made independent of the actual endocrine data. The actually measured excretion rates were found to correlate significantly with the predicted rates. Thus, these observations relate inferred attitudinal state (during periods of sustained stress), on the one hand, and excretion rate of complex endocrine substances, on the other.

That periods of sustained stress may be associated with all manner of minor and major illnesses (medical, surgical, psychiatric, neurological, infectious, etc.) is suggested by the observations of Hinkle and Wolff (1957) and Hinkle and Plummer (1952). In a longitudinal study of some 3,000 individuals over periods ranging up to 20 years, they observed that there were marked inequalities in the distributions of illnesses among these individuals, with a small percentage of the subjects contributing most of the episodes of illness for the entire group. The episodes of illness in any one individual occurred in clusters, generally involved *multiple* bodily systems (including disorders of mood, thought, and behavior), and included both minor and major illnesses of any involved system. The investigators, finding that these clusters of illnesses occurred in relation to definable life stress as perceived by each individual, concluded that "illness is a state of the total organism."

Independent confirmation of one aspect of this conclusion was presented by Matarazzo, Matarazzo, and Saslow (1961), who, studying medical and psychiatric patients, found a high degree of correlation (Pearson r values around .60) between numbers of medical and psychiatric symptoms in both groups. They concluded that "the high positive correlation found in the present study between the number of medical and psychiatric symptoms tends to confirm the Hinkle and Wolff observation that the state of health or illness is a condition of the organism as a whole, and that when the organism is under stress, it is likely to reflect this stress by symptoms of malfunction in a number of areas."

That the earlier narrow conception of psychosomatic medicine must be extended even farther is indicated by animal experiments on a wide variety of illnesses (virus infection, carcinosarcoma, whole-body irradiation, etc.) that, according to a review by Ader and Friedman (1964), may be related in part to early experiential and current environmental stress. These new but potentially unusually significant experimental observations will need careful cross-validation.

OVERVIEW

It should be clear that the research since 1950 reviewed in this last section emphasizes the complexity of the relationships among external events; an individual's perception of them; the complex neurological, biochemical, endocrine, and physiological events; and the behavioral responses observable by others. Nevertheless, H. Wolff's general formulation of 1950 is still pertinent (Wolff, 1950). He pointed out in that summation that the need to be part of a group is one of man's strongest drives. It follows that cultural pressures and goals do much to further or block inherent or deep-rooted individual potentialities that are based on stock, temperament, growth, development, and life experiences—at times when the individual is exposed to conflict-evoking situations. He notes that identical physiological response patterns and their related disease syndromes exhibit themselves in cultural settings in which quite *different* social pressures are being exerted. He juxtaposes in this respect the pressure on the young American male toward emancipation from parental authority and the pressure on the young Japanese male to assume a lifelong burden of filial piety, submissiveness, obligation, and debt to his parents. He considers such observations to support the view that it is not the *particular* pressures or goals (whether in regard to parents, power, possessions, work, etc.) that constitute stress for an individual in a given society, but the conflicts engendered in him as a cultural participant.

Wolff's conclusion is essentially the same as that reached by Green (1948) in his search for a cross-culturally valid formulation of the causes of personality conflict: that neither early life conditioning nor the unique goals of a given culture are the source of personality conflict, but that the cultural causes of personality conflict can be explained in terms of the extent to which the members of any given cultural system embody roles, goals, and self conceptions that are internally inconsistent. In most cases, the inconsistency is found in a chronological context: at different stages in the life history, mutually contradictory roles to be enacted, and goals to be striven for, receive cultural sanction. Or, roles and goals that are supposed to be fulfilled at the same time are mutually contradictory. Green's formulation holds for native cultures with economic, political, and philosophic bases radically different from our own, and whether much dominated by western influences or relatively little. The simpler cultures restrict the range of roles and goals available to any individual; modern technological, especially urban, society extends and diversifies them indefinitely. A significant aspect of Green's formulation is that those individuals who exhibit personality conflict are not regarded as "abnormal," as physiologically inadequate, or as culture deviates (they may, in some cultures, be the statistical norm). Mead (1947) also points out the common tendency to regard culture as something outside the individual rather than as a principal element in his development, and emphasizes that it is probably impossible to separate conceptually patterns of pathophysiological responses from the culturally determined conflict areas of a given individual.

The work of Selye and the cultural considerations just mentioned indicate that pathophysiological responses and their related medical disorders may follow upon quite nonspecific types of stress, and also upon a great variety of specific situations acting via a common pathway such as the pituitary-adrenal axis with diverse end results. If we give weight to the possibility that stress may act nonspecifically, we shall not be surprised that Wolff formulates his conclusion concerning the relation between pathophysiological responses and the situations that evoke them in terms of broadly stated "protective reaction patterns," which have diverse and multiple determinants as well as variable components (such as increased blood pressure alone, rapid heart alone, or both together, in similar stressful situations). Wolff has never attempted to categorize the types of culturally patterned (learned) drives that are most often incompatible, or the frequency with which specified incompatible pairs evoke particular pathophysiological responses, nor has anyone ever enumerated the learned drives in our culture in such a way as to achieve wide consensus. On the other hand, psychoanalytic investigators of these matters have often reported more specific relationships between conflicting learned drives and pathophysiological responses.

Definitive comparative evaluation of the body of conclusions reached by the psychoanalytic students of psychosomatic medicine on the basis of their chiefly clinical data, and by H. Wolff and associates, and by experimenters since 1950 on the basis of their chiefly experimental data is not possible. The investigative methods of H. Wolff *et al.* lean heavily upon well-standardized biochemical, physiological, and similar procedures, utilize interview and human experimentation skills that depend on psychotherapeutic principles derived from Freud, and are described in relatively simple operational language. Questions may be raised about the representativeness of the subjects studied, and the omission of types of control experiments that, if performed, would strengthen the conclusions reached. The work has tended, with only a few exceptions, to neglect unconscious processes, particularly unconscious cues and drives, although this has been less true in recent years. Psychoanalytic critics have implied that cues, drives, and responses of which a subject (in such experiments as Wolff's) is consciously aware are irrelevant or even misleading; that unconscious cues, drives, and responses are a priori most relevant to these problems; and that only through the application of special procedures and concepts can one define the pertinent unconscious factors, which then will be found to be highly specific. However, the observations of Wolff and Wolf on the famous gastrostomy subject Tom support the view that the stress most significant or most threatening (as defined by stated criteria usually based on knowledge of the life history) to the individual at the time of the experimental measurements is the one most relevant to changes in the stomach or in any part of the organism, whether the stress constellation is conscious or unconscious (Wolff and Wolf, 1947; Wolf and Glass, 1950). Since important life difficulties are often inaccessible to the subject's awareness, the degree of awareness of the subject must be taken into account in all such observations and experiments, but the basic significance of the situation to the individual is likely to be a more useful variable than the degree of inaccessibility.

Until the early 1950's, the psychoanalytic investigations of psychosomatic problems had been almost entirely of a clinical observational kind. When combined with measurements of organ function, the measurements and the interview productions to be related to them have often been made hours or even days apart. The convincing demonstrations in various of H. Wolff's studies with humans and of Brady's earlier summarized studies with monkeys, which show that marked changes in such organ functions can be a matter of minutes or delayed by hours, probably render invalid many attempted correlations of interview material, behavior, etc., with organ-function measures when intervals of days or weeks separate the two sets of data. Another major problem in such research involves the heavy reliance, still customary and perhaps necessary, on data from interviews. All such interview-derived data tend to be highly unreliable. A critical review of research utilizing the interview has been published by J. Matarazzo (1965); the reader is referred especially to the section describing the research of Raines and Rohrer.

CURRENT VIEW: COMPREHENSIVE MEDICINE

At this point in time, it is apparent that the early concept of "psychosomatic medicine" as the "relationship between mind and body" in well-defined but quite restricted diseases (e.g., ulcer or hypertension) has proved too narrow. A view consonant with recent work in the field is well presented by Stewart Wolf (1963). His thesis is that (1) many diseases including stomach ulcer, hemolytic anemia, diabetes, infection, etc., represent simply *too much* or *too little* of essentially normal adaptive reactions (e.g., "the patient with hemolytic anemia differs from you and me not in the fact that he is destroying red cells but in the fact that he is destroying them more rapidly than we are"); (2) regulation of these reactions is often achieved through cyclic variations in the homeostatic systems; (3) wide swings in a cycle may constitute the evidences of disease (the hypertensive patient has often had a history of *hypotensive* episodes in youth); and thus (4) modifications in these wide swings to a point of equilibrium between health and disease may be achieved through influences on the regulatory processes from the higher centers of the central nervous system.

We would extend his thesis to include the obvious fact that the higher activity of the central nervous system is intimately dependent on the external environment (physical, social, and interpersonal). Within this broad framework of organism-environment relationships, the illustrative recent research results presented above are not so surprising. Not many examples are available of pathophysiological responses and related medical disorders looked at in terms of the numerous relevant factors. One such is the hypothesis concerning essential hypertension presented by Saslow *et al.* (1950), according to which the existing data compel us to consider a number of factors (genetic, renal, endocrine, mechanical, personal-adjustment, cultural, etc.) as of partial etiological relevance, but no one appears alone to be either necessary or sufficient. A more recent example is that of Grant (1959), which deals with celiac disease in the same comprehensive manner. The concepts of S. Wolf and Selye and the observations of Hinkle and Wolff increase markedly the kinds of "bodily disorders" that may be related to personal adjustment. If we now take the further step of enlarging our concept of bodily disorder beyond that of the pathophysiological and pathoanatomical responses to a defined stress situation (whether this stressor be infectious agent, allergenic substance, nonspecific oxygen deprivation, cold, X-radiation, interpersonal event, or symbolic danger) so as to include those personal adjustments or behaviors of the sick individual that determine that life with any given pattern of altered bodily functions and structures will or will not be optimal, we find ourselves considering so large an array of personality-bodily disorder relationships that it is coextensive with all illness. It is difficult not to take this step when we consider that the life of a particular patient with a supposedly "simple" and "easily cured" disorder such as pneumococcal pneumonia may depend not so much on our medical knowledge, in a narrow sense, as on whether he is a Christian Scientist or becomes delirious and suicidal when he has a high fever. Many physicians have, in fact, taken this step, and regard tuberculosis, for example, as a disorder as much of the personality as of the lungs (or other anatomical site).

It is no longer easy, then, to delimit a class of disorders as "psychosomatic." It seems more appropriate to deal with a variety of personality-illness relationships, and to specify the relevant factors in each relationship. That this is actually the procedure practiced by students who were at first interested in a narrower concept of "psychosomatic medicine" is shown by the wide range of topics presented in the volume *Life Stress and Bodily Disease* edited by H. Wolff (1950), by the range of problems included as "case histories in psychosomatic medicine" by Miles, Cobb, and Shands (1952) (e.g., a child's reaction to adenoidectomy, impulsive behavior in a crippled boy, convalescence in a patient with permanent neurological disability, hysteria with pseudoneurological paralysis, duodenal ulcer, etc.), and by the presentation by Saslow (1952) of a number of kinds of personality-illness relationships for which no good class name even exists.

Current practice and concept, then, especially as articulated by Stewart

Wolff (1963) make "psychosomatic medicine" synonymous with medicine viewed in such a way that all the major factors relevant to any illness are defined in relation to each other in any given individual. How can this practice and concept of comprehensive medicine be formulated?

ILLNESS VIEWED COMPREHENSIVELY

Halliday (1941–43) attempted to develop a viewpoint of medicine sufficiently comprehensive to include such diverse etiological agents as infectious micro-organisms and cultural symbols, and to be congruent with his unusually wide range of medical experiences. But he gave insufficient consideration to emotions, behavior, and learning theory—without which a satisfactory unitary conceptual framework was not possible. Dollard and Miller (1950), interested chiefly in behavior, attempted to integrate the contributions of learning theory, psychoanalytic experience, and sociocultural observations into a unified view of human behavior—based wherever possible on available experimental data. They were not concerned with the problem of how human behavior fits into a general framework of disease. Guze, Matarazzo, and Saslow (1953) attempted to develop a conception of illness that would be applicable to all kinds of medical problems (including the behavior or psychiatric disorders as well as the conventionally labeled "psychosomatic" disorders), would take into account the areas not dealt with by Halliday or by Dollard and Miller, and would be based on available clinical, observational, and experimental data. They found it possible to develop such a formulation, provided the construct "emotion" were defined operationally and used appropriately. Emotion was defined as a drive state of the organism, specified in terms of the antecedent environmental conditions and the measurable physiological changes, gross behavior, verbal reports, etc., manifested by the organism in consequence of these conditions. So defined, pathophysiological responses associated with emotion are not "caused by" emotion: They represent the very physiological changes at least part of which constitutes the drive state. In those instances in which physiological responses cannot be measured, emotion is defined operationally in terms of the conditions of the experiment or clinical observations. Since drive states, by definition in this conception, impel the organism to actions that are drive-reducing, emotion (as defined above) may be considered to cause adjustive or drive-reducing behavior such as avoidance, withdrawal, repression, or going to a doctor. Their formulation is best illustrated in the accompanying diagram (Fig. 9–1). In terms, then, of this diagram, a comprehensive approach to illness may be stated as follows:

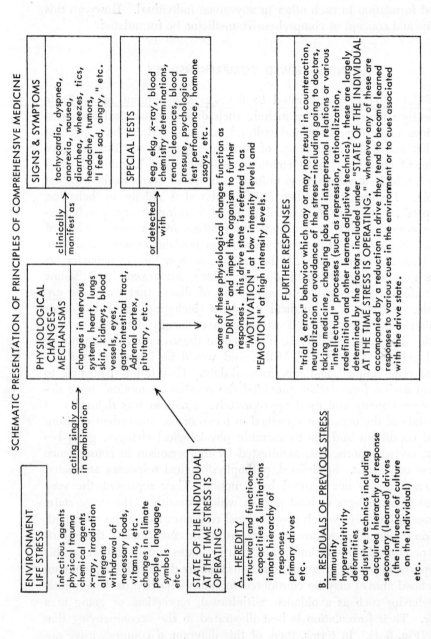

Fig. 9–1. A diagrammatic presentation of a comprehensive approach to illness. (Reprinted with permission from the *Journal of Clinical Psychology,* 1953, **9,** 127–36.)

Environmental stresses, acting singly or in combination, take on significance in terms of the individual's state at the time they are encountered. The individual's "state" represents the sum total of his previous life experiences as well as his genetic capacities and limitations. In response to the life stresses imposed upon the individual, various physiological changes take place.

These physiological changes can be inferred from the following: The patient's subjective complaints or symptoms, the various signs which examination of him will reveal, the results of special laboratory tests and procedures, and his subsequent behavioral responses. That aspect of the altered physiology which induces further behavioral responses is what is referred to as motivation, emotion, or drive state. It should be emphasized that the drive state is indistinguishable from the physiological changes and can only be defined in terms of cues, symptoms, signs, results of special tests, and behavior. In operational terms, this is nothing more than anchoring a construct at both the antecedent and consequent ends.

As a result of the drive state, "trial and error" behavior ensues which is largely determined by the various factors included under "state of the individual at the time stress is operating." That is to say, an individual's hereditary capacities and limitations, innate hierarchy of responses and primary drives, modified by personal and cultural experience, will determine his behavior. Thus the individual's characteristic adjustive techniques and learned secondary drives will manifest themselves in his further responses. These may include going to doctors, taking medicine, changing jobs and interpersonal relations, or various "intellectual" processes (such as repression, distortion, rationalization, redefinition, etc.). Such behavior may or may not result in counteraction, neutralization, or avoidance of the initiating stress. Whenever new responses are accompanied by a reduction in drive, they tend to become learned responses to various cues in the environment or to cues associated with the drive state.

Although the behavior of all patients can be understood and described with reference to the same conceptual framework, the importance of a patient's behavior, however, will vary from case to case. In some, the behavioral responses of consulting the physician once or a few times will be the only ones of significance and no further attention will be paid to this area. An example of this is the patient with uncomplicated pneumococcal pneumonia who comes to his doctor and is successfully treated. On the other hand, if a patient with pneumonia becomes delirious, his subsequent behavior may be of great importance and may sometimes be the immediate cause of death (through suicide or other self-destructive acts). In yet another situation, a patient with pneumonia may refuse to consult a physician because of fear, religious beliefs, etc., and thus deprive himself of adequate medical care—a reaction that may result in prolonged illness and even death. For a number of patients with vague, moderately disabling symptoms, repeated consulting of a physician can become a technique of short-term drive reduction. In the traditionally labeled psychiatric disorders (neurotic or psychotic) behavior responses, such as these, always assume a prominent position (Guze, Matarazzo, and Saslow, 1953, p. 135).[1]

This formulation permits comprehensive consideration of the nature and treatment of any illness, and a way of looking at psychotherapy that is congruent with other medical treatment. Recently, a "psychiatric" ward in a general hospital designed in terms of these principles has been

[1] Reprinted with permission from the *Journal of Clinical Psychology*, 1953, 9, 127–36.

described by Saslow and Matarazzo (1962). It should be noted that the factors in the formulation are equally valid and operative in normal behavior, as is clear from Murphy's consideration of the development of personality (Murphy, 1947).

EXAMPLES OF ILLNESS VIEWED COMPREHENSIVELY

At this point, it is appropriate to consider several examples of illness in which it is apparent that the way the patient is living is so intimately related to the sickness that the two events cannot be easily separated. In each case, a brief history of the patient will be followed by a short description of some of the pertinent experimental findings. The reader is invited to apply to each case the formulation just described and shown diagrammatically in Fig. 9–1. The reader should also not consider these examples as "proof," since, in view of the difficulties with interview-derived data (Matarazzo, 1965), we offer them merely as descriptive illustrations of the manner in which the conceptual scheme shown in Fig. 9–1 can be used.

The first case is that of a Negro married woman who was forty-one years old when studied. She gave a lifelong history of abdominal discomfort associated with emotional turmoil. This symptom had become intensified over the five to six years that preceded our contact with her, and the onset of this accentuation of her complaint was dated by the patient to a violent argument with her husband during which he struck her severely over the left eye. This blow resulted in permanent visual impairment. Four years later, because of severe constipation, a gastrointestinal X-ray examination was performed and reported as negative.

She was admitted to the hospital in June of that year because of sudden gastrointestinal bleeding (including the vomiting of blood and the passage of black, tarry stools), weakness, and faintness. During this admission, a diagnosis of bleeding peptic ulcer of the duodenum was made. Following discharge from the hospital in July, she was seen at a medical-school outpatient clinic.

The patient was raised in a strict home. Her father died three years prior to her hospitalization. He had suffered from asthma and kidney disease. The patient's mother was her father's second wife. She died when the patient was six months old. Soon after the patient's mother's death, her father remarried and had four more children by his third wife. The patient was raised by this stepmother, and, since she was the oldest child in the home, the patient assumed much of the responsibility for raising the younger children.

The patient did not get on well with her stepmother, who used to beat her frequently. Her father was strict and authoritarian; all the children learned to be "seen and not heard." Any infraction of the rules was severely and promptly punished, and there was little open rebellion or hostility permitted in the household. The patient was very anxious to leave home, but her father would not permit it unless she married. She consequently married when seventeen without really loving her husband. For the first fourteen months of the marriage, they lived with the husband's family. This arrangement was unsatisfactory for the patient. She finally managed to get her own quarters, but for the next nineteen years she and her husband were almost constantly besieged by visitors from her husband's family. The patient resented this but was unable to say or do anything about it until the fight described above.

The patient regarded her marriage as a total failure. Clinically, she was described as a quiet, docile, sensitive person who is conscientious, obsessive-compulsive, unassertive, somewhat prudish, and retiring. She speaks softly and never shows strong emotion. Her husband, from her description, is loud, vulgar, uncouth. He drinks excessively, has never supported the patient, runs up debts that she feels obligated to pay, and in general shows no interest in the marriage or in the patient's welfare. Nearly all of the patient's ulcer symptoms occur in immediate temporal relation to difficulties with her husband or in relation to reminders or symbols of such difficulties. Even casual clinical inquiry reveals that she can return home from work feeling fine and be preparing a meal when she will hear her husband's key in the lock and immediately develop typical ulcer symptoms. Or if she receives a bill for some things her husband has purchased, she will experience the typical abdominal discomfort.

Despite considerable insight into the relationship between her marital discord and her symptoms, the patient was unable to alter her behavior in any way. Her characteristic adjustive technique, learned as a child, is to inhibit any overt demonstration of hostility, resentment, or aggression, although on the infrequent occasions in which she "blows her top and gets things off her chest," she doesn't have symptoms. She gets temporary and intermittent relief from diet and various medications, especially if the prescribed regimen is altered repeatedly.

The apparent relationship between such environmental stimuli as disturbed life situations and the physiological responses characteristic of duodenal ulcer that clinical studies like the above tend to clarify has been investigated experimentally. In duodenal ulcer, the characteristic physiological alterations, in addition to the presence of the ulcer, are those of gastric hyperfunction. These include increased motility of the stomach, increase in gastric blood flow, and increased production of acid. The classic studies of human gastric function are those of Wolf and Wolff (1947) on their subject Tom, who had a permanent opening into his

stomach from the abdominal wall (gastrostomy), through which the
stomach could be observed directly.

The data from one of their typical experiments are reproduced in
Fig. 9–2. It is clearly demonstrated that the stimulus of talking about

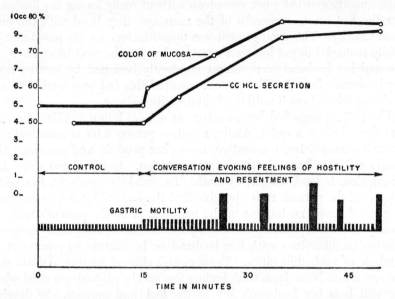

Fig. 9–2. Increased motility accompanying hyperaemia and hyperacidity
in association with hostility and resentment. (Reproduced with the permission
of Oxford University Press, publishers of S. Wolf and H. G. Wolff, *Human
gastric function: An experimental study of a man and his stomach*, 1964.)

stressful life events results in increased motility, blood flow (as indicated
by color of mucosa), and acid secretion. The subsequent studies of Mahl,
Sawrey *et al.*, and Mirsky, reviewed earlier, are experimental and clinical
refinements and elaborations of these observations by Wolf and Wolff on
the relationship between gastric malfunction and stressful experiences.

The second case is that of a twenty-nine-year-old white, married farmer
with mild, labile hypertension. He was raised by a strict "Prussian"
father, who never allowed the children to make any decisions for themselves, and an outgoing, spontaneous, emotional, "shameless" mother, who
used to embarrass him by her readiness for argument, discussions of
intimate affairs, and free criticism of others. Until the age of six or
seven, he was raised as a "mamma's boy." Because of this, he was teased
by his father and older brothers, and he began to object to his mother's
demonstrativeness. After about the age of seven, he tried hard to change
his relationship with his mother and avoided all her overt manifestations
of affection.

Ever since then, he has been trying to avoid all manifestations of strong emotions in himself and others, because any demonstration of emotion makes him feel uncomfortable and frequently will result in symptoms of tension and anxiety. Despite his unusual physical strength and development (resembling those of a heavyweight boxer), he has never had a fight. He "can't stand a scene and can't bear to be present when someone else's feelings are hurt." He accepts overburdening responsibility without any kind of remonstration and is a chronic worrier. He is neat and perfectionistic and likes routines, though at the same time he feels restless and thinks of getting out from under the heavy load he is carrying.

In the past, when tension would gradually build up, he would become moody and finally go by himself and cry for hours. This would relieve him, and he would be much better for several months. Recently, whenever he gets tense and moody, he is unable to cry and hence never gets any significant relief. As the tension mounts, he develops typical anxiety symptoms. He is shy and sensitive and does not make friends readily, is preoccupied with the impression others have of him and as a result finds it hard to make decisions. He stated that he wants "everyone to like" him.

He and his wife do not get along well for the following reasons: He is uncomfortable about his wife's overt affection and yet cannot talk to her about it or show overt affection on his part. And he cannot please her by going out more often, because getting out with people makes him uncomfortable.

Results of psychological tests indicate that the patient is extremely nonassertive and is a conforming person who "bottles up" his feelings and gives in to people rather than resisting even the most frustrating tasks. When involved in conflicts, he is uncomfortable and escapes as soon as he can. Any overt aggression is followed by guilt feelings.

In the study of this patient, no systematic observations of the relationship between specific cues and the elevated blood-pressure responses were made. Specially planned circumstances are necessary for observations of this character.

One of the major difficulties in correlating various stimuli with the physiological response of elevated blood pressure is that this response is below the level of the subject's awareness; it is an unconscious physiological response. Consequently, in clinical interviews, it is impossible to know which cues the subject responds to with hypertension. Pfeiffer and his co-workers (1950) have studied patients similar to the one just described and have shown that it is possible to define the relevant stimuli. Figures 9–3 and 9–4 are illustrative of results they have reported (1950). In these striking data can be seen not only the elevation in blood pressure but also

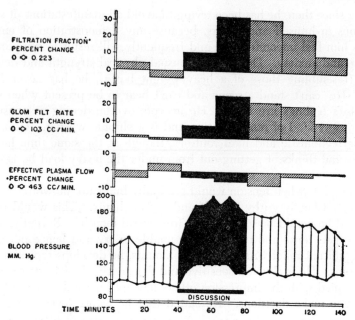

Fig. 9–3. Prolonged elevation of glomerular filtration rate with rise in filtration fraction during elevation of blood pressure during emotional stress. (Reprinted from J. B. Pfeiffer, Jr., and H. G. Wolff, Studies in renal circulation during periods of life stress and accompanying emotional reactions in subjects with and without essential hypertension: Observations on the role of neural activity in regulation of renal blood flow, *J. clin. Invest.*, 1950, **29,** 1227–42, with permission.)

the changes in renal function that are characteristic of so-called essential hypertension (Goldring, 1944). Although these observations of Pfeiffer and Wolff on hypertension and others like them are fifteen years old, a report of a recent international conference on psychophysiological aspects of cardio vascular disease edited by Saslow and Blachly (1964) concluded that essentially little new information had been added in this field.

The third case is that of a young girl with diabetes. She was first so diagnosed at the age of five. Because of some unexplained family situation, the patient lived for an entire year in the pediatric ward of a hospital, where she became a favorite of doctors, nurses, and attendants and where she was "spoiled." At the same time, she resented the fact that her family had deserted her (this was her interpretation), and, after discharge to her parents, who lived in rural Missouri, she became a serious, chronic behavior problem. She was hard to discipline and disobedient, had frequent temper outbursts, and responded to emotion-provoking situations by refusing to follow her diet and later, when she administered her own

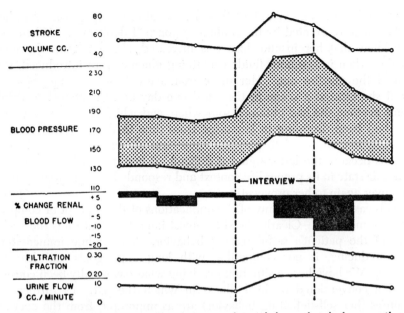

Fig. 9–4. Changes in cardiac output and renal dynamics during emotional stress. (Reprinted from J. B. Pfeiffer, Jr., and H. G. Wolff, Studies in renal circulation during periods of life stress and accompanying emotional reactions in subjects with and without essential hypertension: Observations on the role of neural activity in regulation of renal blood flow, *J. clin. Invest.*, 1950, **29**, 1227–42, with permission.)

insulin, by refusing to take her insulin regularly. There was sufficient evidence to support the idea that she frequently resorted to these self-defeating measures in order to "get back" at her family for real or imagined injustices.

She was passed around from relative to relative because of her family's bad financial status, and she quickly wore out her welcome at each new place by the inordinate demands she made on others and by her terrifying behavior if these were not promptly met. During the ten years of her illness, she was admitted to various hospitals over seventeen times because of diabetes acidosis and/or coma. Prior to most of these episodes, she had discontinued her prescribed diet and insulin, but she insisted that on a few occasions she had continued following her doctor's advice right up to the time of admission. Her most recent admission, at the age of fifteen, was precipitated by an unfortunate sexual experience to which she responded with guilt and bitterness, which led her to abandoning her diet and insulin.

While in the hospital, she was impossible to regulate. She blandly refused to cooperate with the doctors whenever she became upset, no matter for what reason. Warnings that she would die if she persisted in her behavior were greeted by the smiling response "I don't care." Whenever she knew that her insulin dose was increased, she cut down the food intake; when intravenous fluids containing glucose were introduced, she pulled the needles out. Her urine examinations defied understanding until she created a scene in the ward one day and threatened to drink some acetone she had obtained somewhere and which she later admitted she had been dropping in her urine from time to time. When seen in consultation, she tried to play the consultant off against the ward physicians because the latter found it difficult, at first, to see her precarious diabetic state in its proper life context and responded inappropriately over and over again to her provocations.

This case illustrates many of the implications of the concept of comprehensive medicine. Clearly the single most important feature is the problem of the patient's self-defeating behavior. This, while immediately drive-reducing, is not compatible with long-range goals and learned drives. We have here a situation involving what has usually been considered a conventional medical illness in which the patient's further responses (her self-defeating behavior) are as important, from the over-all clinical point of view, as the specific psychological disturbances of diabetes (see Fig. 9–1).

The relevance of the patient's further responses to her survival is obvious. In addition, the experimental data of Hinkle et al. (1950) show that some of the physiological alterations characteristic of the diabetic state are influenced directly by life situations or symbols thereof. In these studies (Figs. 9–5 and 9–6), particular attention was paid to the level of ketone bodies, which, as is clear from the figures, rose noticeably during the stress of an interview. The importance of this variable is related to the influence of the level of ketone bodies on the acid-base balance of the blood. As the level rises in diabetic acidosis, serious and ultimately fatal derangements in acid-base balance occur, and one of the major features of treatment in diabetic acidosis and coma is the attempt to correct the altered acid-base relationships and the deleterious effects that follow. In these studies, the stress was discontinued before the increase of ketone bodies reached levels of clinical importance.

It has been emphasized that an adequate approach to illness involves dealing with a number of relevant factors. In the three clinical cases just presented, this multiplicity of relevant factors was implied. For greater explicitness, we should mention additional factors that need consideration in these three diseases but that are not readily apparent from the material thus far presented. In diabetes and hypertension, there appear to be significant familial or genetic factors. In all three diseases, there are sex differences of importance, and, in hypertension, there are

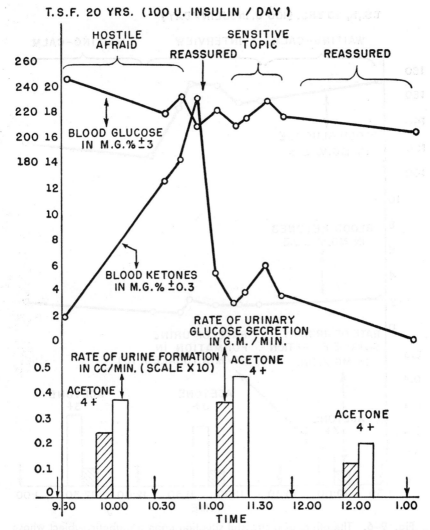

Fig. 9–5. Diagram of a control study on a diabetic subject whose initial ketone level was higher than 1.5 mg. per cent, demonstrating a relative stability of the blood ketones in the absence of specific stimuli. The fluctuations of blood glucose are relatively great. (Reprinted from L. Hinkle, G. B. Conger, and S. Wolf, Studies on diabetes mellitus: The relation of stressful life situations to the concentration of ketone bodies in the blood of diabetic and nondiabetic humans, *J. clin. Invest.*, 1950, **29**, 754–69, with permission.)

striking racial differences, as there are in diabetes. The physiological disturbances in peptic ulcer may be initiated by such stimuli as coffee, tobacco, alcohol, and highly spiced food. There appears to be a seasonal

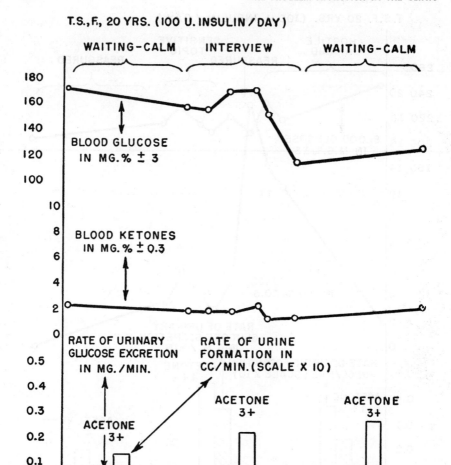

Fig. 9–6. The effect of a stressful situation upon a diabetic subject whose initial ketone level was higher than 1.5 mg. per cent. A marked rise in the ketone level is evident during stress, followed by an equally great fall with reassurance. The polyuria and glycosuria associated with the rise in blood ketones may be compared with those of the control study on the same subject shown in Fig. 9–5. (Reprinted with permission from the *Journal of Clinical Investigation*, 1950, **29,** 754–69.)

fluctuation in ulcer symptoms. Diabetes varies greatly, depending on the age of the patient at the time of onset and his nutritional state, while its course may be strikingly influenced by infections and operations. Thus, it is clear that there are many factors that are important in a comprehensive approach to disease. They are distributed among the major areas of the scheme in Fig. 9–1, and they may be of importance separately or cumulatively.

The particular examples selected in Figs. 9–2 through 9–6 were first published in 1950. Although the studies of Mirsky and Sachar on human subjects utilize more recent and more sophisticated physiological and biochemical response measures and interview-elicited data, the clarity with which these earlier cases were presented do not seem to us to have been improved upon.

THE PROBLEM OF SPECIFICITY IN PSYCHOSOMATIC MEDICINE

To refer again to the three cases just discussed, it should be pointed out that the adjustive techniques and other personality attributes of the patients are in no way to be considered representative of all patients with each of the illnesses considered. Whether specific personality patterns exist for each such disorder has been a matter of much debate. This problem of *specificity* may be stated in the form of a question: "Why is it that certain people respond to life stresses with duodenal ulcer, while others respond with elevated blood pressure, some with both, and still others with neither?" From the presentation thus far and from an analysis of Fig. 9–1, it becomes apparent that the factors that determine the specificity of the physiological response to stress are to be found in the area of the individual's state at the time of exposure to stress. Such specificity factors are multiple and may be genetic or acquired. At the present time, the relevant factors in any given physiological or behavioral response have not been completely defined, although there are a number of general theories designed to account for the facts. It should be said that, in terms of the way these theories have been propounded thus far, they are not necessarily mutually exclusive. In addition, most of the theoretical writing has not been supported by controlled observation or experiment. The theories extend from those that attribute the characteristics of specificity in each psychosomatic condition to genetic determinants (Draper *et al.*, 1944) to theories that propose early infantile and childhood experiences result in certain "nuclear constellations" that, in turn, are associated with the specific physiological responses (Alexander and French, 1948). But Alexander, who holds the latter view, also considers constitutional factors of importance. Consistent with this view, the experimental observations of Lacey and VanLehn (1952) have led them to the view that "the variety of the individual patterns [of response to ice water] found is the result of the total life experience of the individual plus physiological factors that are gene-determined."

During the past two decades, considerable controversy has developed over the issue of specific attitudes associated with specific illnesses. Freeman *et al.* (1964, pp. 557–59) published a brief but adequate review of the problem of specificity at the end of which they concluded (p. 559),

At this point hypotheses differ considerably from one study to the next so that it is difficult to arrive at substantive conclusions from this body of work as a whole. The postulated psychological characteristics differentiating people with a particular illness from those with another have varied greatly. Many of the studies have used poorly defined psychological terms and have separated groups of patients on a *post hoc* basis. Investigators have simply taken groups with different physical illnesses, and looked for whatever psychological differences they could find. Any study proceeding on this basis absolutely requires crossvalidation, and yet it is almost never performed.

CONCLUDING STATEMENT

Although many of the recent experiments on psychosomatic phenomena reviewed earlier in this chapter are superior to the clinical case reports of the period from 1930 to 1950, the authors feel that the present status of many major issues in the field called "psychosomatic medicine" must be characterized in language not unlike that used by Freeman *et al.* in the quotation above on the problem of specificity. This acute need for more solid experimental underpinning applies to such issues as the presumed effect of psychological stress on psychophysiological response; the cumulative effect of various stimuli in psychosomatic conditions; the observations of Hinkle and Wolff, and our own studies on the ecology of illness; and all of the other alleged somatophysic and psychosomatic interrelationships earlier and currently extant in the clinical and experimental literature. While the variables and recording techniques are more explicitly characterized today, no current investigator seems to have improved upon the brilliant and careful observations of Pavlov, for example, his discovery that, in a dog, the mere sight of his master could induce a profound set of gastrointestinal responses. Before further progress beyond such basic observations can be made, investigators will have to subject their methods and observations to the same seemingly tedious but necessary scientific checks as did the father of experimental psychosomatic medicine, Pavlov. Few investigators write as if they understand this necessity.

REFERENCES

ADER, R., and FRIEDMAN, S. 1964. *Psychological factors and susceptibility to disease in animals: Symposium on medical aspects of stress in the military climate.* Washington, D.C.: Walter Reed Army Institute for Research, Walter Reed Army Medical Center.

ALEXANDER, F., and FRENCH, T. M. 1948. *Studies in psychosomatic medicine: An approach to the cause and treatment of vegetative disurbances.* New York: Ronald.

BARKER, L. 1906. Some experience with the simpler methods of psychotherapy and re-education. *Amer. J. med. Sci.,* 132, 499–522.

BRADY, J. V. 1964. Behavioral stress and physiological change: A comparative approach to the experimental analysis of some psychosomatic problems. *Trans. N.Y. Acad. Sci.,* 26, 483–96.

CANNON, W. B. 1915. *Bodily changes in pain, hunger, fear and rage.* (2d ed.) New York: Appleton-Century-Crofts.

COBB, S. 1952. Introduction: Some principles and applications of psychosomatic medicine. In H. W. MILES, S. COBB, and H. C. SHANDS (eds.), *Case histories in psychosomatic medicine.* New York: Norton.

CONGER, J. J., SAWREY, W. L., and TURRELL, E. S. 1958. The role of social experience in the production of gastric ulcers in hooded rats placed in a conflict situation. *J. abnorm. soc. Psychol.,* 57, 214–20.

CREIGHTON, C. 1886. *Illustrations of unconscious memory in disease, including a theory of alternations.* London: H. K. Lewis.

DEUTSCH, F. 1949. *Applied psychoanalysis.* New York: Grune & Stratton.

DOLLARD, J., and MILLER, N. E. 1950. *Personality and psychotherapy.* New York: McGraw-Hill.

DRAPER, G., DUPERTUIS, C. W., and CAUGHEY, J. L., JR. 1944. *Human constitution in clinical medicine.* New York: Harper & Row.

DUNBAR, HELEN FLANDERS. 1935. *Emotions and bodily changes.* New York: Columbia Univer. Press.

FLYNN, J. T., KENNEDY, M. A. K., and WOLF, S. G. 1950. Essential hypertension in one of identical twins: An experimental study of cardiovascular reactions in the Y twins. In H. G. WOLFF, S. G. WOLF, and C. C. HARE (eds.), *Life stress and bodily disease: Proceedings of the Association for Research in Nervous and Mental Diseases.* Baltimore: Williams & Wilkins.

FREEMAN, EDITH H., FEINGOLD, B. F., SCHLESINGER, K., and GORMAN, F. J. 1964. Psychological variables in allergic disorders: A review. *Psychosom. Med.,* 26, 543–75.

GOLDRING, W., and CHASIS, H. 1944. *Hypertension and hypertensive disease.* New York: Commonwealth Fund.

GRACE, W. J., WOLF, S. G., and WOLFF, H. G. 1951. *The human colon: experimental study based on direct observation of four fistulous subjects.* New York: Harper & Row.

GRAHAM, D. T. 1950. The pathogenesis of hives: Experimental study of life situations, emotions, and cutaneous vascular reactions. In H. G. WOLFF, S. G. WOLFF, and C. C. HARE (eds.), *Life stress and bodily disease: Proceedings of the Association for Research in Nervous and Mental Diseases.* Baltimore: Williams & Wilkins.

GRANT, J. M. 1959. Studies on celiac disease: I. The interrelationship between gliadin, psychological factors and symptom formation. *Psychosom. Med.,* 21, 431–432.

GRAY, S. J., BENSON, J. A., JR., REIFENSTEIN, R. W., and SPIRO, H. M. 1951.

Chronic stress and peptic ulcer. I. Effect of corticotropin (ACTH) and cortisone on gastric secretion. *J. Amer. medical Assn.*, **147**, 1529–37.

GREEN, A. W. 1948. Culture, normality, and personality conflict. *Amer. Antrop.*, **50**, 225–37.

GUZE, S. B., MATARAZZO, J. D., and SASLOW, G. 1953. A formulation of principles of comprehensive medicine. *J. clin. Psychol.*, **9**, 127–36.

HALLIDAY, J. L. 1941–43. Principles of aetiology. *British J. medical Psychol.*, **19**, 367–80.

HINKLE, L., CONGER, G. B., and WOLF, S. G. 1950. Studies on diabetes mellitus: The relation of stressful life situations to the concentration of ketone bodies in the blood of diabetic and non-diabetic humans. *J. clinical Invest.*, **29**, 754–69.

HINKLE, L., and PLUMMER, N. 1952. Life stress and industrial absenteeism: The concentration of illness and absenteeism in one segment of a working population. *Industr. med. Surgery*, **21**, 365–75.

HINKLE, L. E., JR., and WOLFF, H. G. 1957. Health and the social environment: Experimental investigations. In A. H. LEIGHTON, J. A. CLAUSEN, and R. N. WILSON (eds.), *Explorations in social psychiatry.* New York: Basic Books. Pp. 105–37.

HOLMES, T. H., TREUTING, T., and WOLFF, H. G. 1950. Life situations, emotions and nasal disease: Evidence on summative effects exhibited in patients with "hay fever." In H. G. WOLFF, S. G. WOLF, and C. C. HARE (eds.), *Life stress and bodily disease: Proceedings of the Association for Research in Nervous and Mental Diseases.* Baltimore: Williams & Wilkins.

KNIGHT, F. 1890. The rational treatment of bronchial asthma. *Boston Med. Surgery J.*, **122**, 80–82.

LACEY, J. I. 1959. Psychophysiological approaches to the evaluation of psychotherapeutic process and outcome. In E. A. RUBINSTEIN and M. B. PARLOFF (eds.), *Research in psychotherapy.* Washington, D.C.: American Psychological Association. Pp. 160–208.

LACEY, J. I., and SMITH, R. L. 1954. Conditioning and generalization of unconscious anxiety. *Science*, **120**, 1045–52.

LACEY, J. I., SMITH, R. L., and GREEN, A. 1955. Use of conditioned autonomic responses in the study of anxiety. *Psychosom. Med.*, **17**, 207–17.

LACEY, J. I., and VANLEHN, R. 1952. Differential emphasis in somatic response to stress. *Psychosom. Med.*, **14**, 72–81.

MAHL, G. F. 1949. The effect of chronic fear on the gastric secretions of HCL in dogs. *Psychosom. Med.*, **11**, 30–44.

MAHL, G. F. 1950. Anxiety, HCL secretion, and peptic ulcer etiology. *Psychosom. Med.*, **12**, 140–69.

MAHL, G. F. 1952. Relationship between acute and chronic fear and the gastric acidity and blood sugar levels in *Macaca mulatta* monkeys. *Psychosom. Med.*, **14**, 182–210.

MARGETTS, E. L. 1950. The early history of the word "psychosomatic." *Canadian medical Assn J.*, **63**, 402–4.

MATARAZZO, J. D. 1965. The interview. In B. B. WOLMAN (ed.), *Handbook of clinical psychology.* New York: McGraw-Hill.

MATARAZZO, RUTH G., MATARAZZO, J. D., and SASLOW, G. 1961. The relationship between medical and psychiatric symptoms. *J. abnorm. soc. Psychol.*, 62, 55–61.

MEAD, MARGARET. 1947. The concept of culture and the psychosomatic approach. *Psychiatry*, 10, 57–76.

MILES, H. W., COBB, S., and SHANDS, H. C. 1952. *Case histories in psychosomatic medicine.* New York: Norton.

MIRSKY, I. A. 1958. Physiologic, psychologic, and social determinants in the etiology of duodenal ulcer. *Amer. J. digestive Dis.*, 3, 285–314.

MURPHY, G. 1947. *Personality: A biosocial approach to its structure and function.* New York: Harper & Row.

PAVLOV, I. P. 1957. *Experimental psychology and other essays.* New York: Philosophical Library.

PFEIFFER, J. B., JR., and WOLFF, H. G. 1950. Studies in renal circulation during periods of life stress and accompanying emotional reactions in subjects with and without essential hypertension: Observations on the role of neural activity in regulation of renal blood flow. *J. clinical Invest.*, 29, 1227–42.

PUTNAM, J. J. 1899. Not the disease only, but also the man. *Boston Med. Surgery J.*, 141, 53–57.

RAZRAN, G. 1961. The observable unconscious and the inferable conscious in current Soviet psychophysiology: Interoceptive conditioning, semantic conditioning, and the orienting reflex. *Psychol. Rev.*, 68, 81–147.

RAZRAN, G. 1965. Russian physiologists' psychology and American experimental psychology: A historical and systematic collation and a look into the future. *Psychol. Bull.*, 63, 42–64.

SACHAR, E. J., MASON, J. W., KOLMER, H. S., JR., and ARTISS, K. L. 1963. Psychoendocrine aspects of acute schizophrenic reactions. *Psychosom. Med.*, 25, 510–37.

SASLOW, G., and BLACHLY, P. H. 1964. Timberline conference on psychophysiologic aspects of cardiovascular disease. *Psychosom. Med.*, 26, 405–541.

SASLOW, G. 1952. On the concept of comprehensive medicine. *Bull. Menninger Clinic*, 16, 57–65.

SASLOW, G., GRESSEL, G. C., SHOBE, F. O., DuBOIS, P. H., and SCHROEDER, H. A. 1950. The possible etiological relevance of personality factors in arterial hypertension. In H. G. WOLFF, S. G. WOLF, and C. C. HARE (eds.), *Life stress and bodily disease: Proceedings of the Association for Research in Nervous and Mental Diseases.* Baltimore: Williams & Wilkins.

SASLOW, G., and MATARAZZO, J. D. 1962. A psychiatric service in a general hospital: A setting for social learning. *Inter. J. soc. Psychiat.*, 8, 5–18.

SAUL, L. J. 1944. Physiological effects of emotional tension. In J. McV. HUNT (ed.), *Personality and the behavior disorders.* Vol. 1. New York: Ronald.

SAWREY, W. L., CONGER, J. J., and TURRELL, E. S. 1956. An experimental investigation of the role of psychological factors in the production of gastric ulcers in rats. *J. comp. physiol. Psychol.*, 49, 457–61.

SAWREY, W. L., and WEISZ, J. D. 1956. An experimental method of producing gastric ulcers. *J. comp. physiol. Psychol.*, 49, 269–70.

SCOTT, J. P. 1944. The magnification of differences by a threshold. *Science,* 100, 569–70.

SCOTT, J. P. 1950. The relative importance of social and hereditary factors in producing disturbances in life adjustment during periods of stress in laboratory animals. In H. G. WOLFF, S. G. WOLF, and C. C. HARE (eds.), *Life stress and bodily disease: Proceedings of the Association for Research in Nervous and Mental Diseases.* Baltimore: Williams & Wilkins.

SCOTT, J. P., and MARSTON, M. V. 1950. Critical periods affecting the development of normal and maladjustive social behavior of puppies. *J. genet. Psychol.,* 77, 25–60.

SELYE, H. 1953. The general-adaptation-syndrome in its relationships to neurology, psychology, and psychopathology. In A. WEIDER (ed.), *Contributions toward medical psychology: Theory and Psychodiagnostic methods.* New York: Ronald. Pp. 234–74.

STAINBROOK, E. 1952. Psychosomatic medicine in the nineteenth century. *Psychosom. Med.,* 14, 211–27.

TUKE, D. H. 1872. *Illustrations of the influence of the mind upon the body in health and disease, designed to elucidate the action of the imagination.* London: J. & A. Churchill, Ltd.

WEILAND, W. F., STEIN, M., and HAMILTON, C. L. 1963. Intensity of the unconditional stimulus as a factor in conditioning out of awareness. *Psychosom. Med.,* 25, 124–32.

WOLF, S. G. 1963. A new view of disease. *J. Amer. Medical Assn.,* 184, 129–30.

WOLF, S. G., and GLASS, G. B. J. 1950. Correlation of conscious and unconscious conflicts with changes in gastric function and structure, and observations on the relation of the constituents of the gastric juice to the integrity of the mucous membrane. In H. G. WOLFF, S. G. WOLF, and C. C. HARE (eds.), *Life stress and bodily disease: Proceedings of the Association for Research in Nervous and Mental Diseases.* Baltimore: Williams & Wilkins.

WOLF, S. G., and WOLFF, H. G. 1947. *Human gastric function: An experimental study of a man and his stomach.* Fair Lawn, N.J.: Oxford Univer. Press.

WOLFF, C. T., FRIEDMAN, S. B., HOFER, M. A., and MASON, J. W. 1964. Relationship between psychological defenses and mean urinary 17-hydroxycorticosteroid excretion rates (parts I and II). *Psychosom. Med.,* 26, 576–609.

WOLFF, H. G. 1950. Life stress and bodily disease: A formulation. In H. G. WOLFF, S. G. WOLF, and C. C. HARE (eds.), *Life stress and bodily disease: Proceedings of the Association for Research in Nervous and Mental Diseases.* Baltimore: Williams & Wilkins.

10

The Physically Handicapped

STANLEY S. MARZOLF *

THE PROBLEM

The importance of sensory and motor function and the integrity of the entire neural apparatus for daily living is usually overlooked. However, even mild degrees of functional deficiency may unobtrusively, yet most assuredly, interfere with efficient living. Manifestly severe deficiencies in structure and impairment of function quite obviously present serious obstacles to optimal self-realization.

Incidence. The frequency of occurrence of any condition per unit of population, usually 1,000 or 100,000, is known as its incidence. Knowledge of the incidence of handicapping conditions is often a matter of interest. From a sociopolitical point of view such knowledge is helpful in making an appeal for popular and legislative support of measures designed to benefit the handicapped through research and education or rehabilitation.

Variation of incidence with time may suggest causal factors or reflect the effectiveness of preventive measures. Differential incidences related to sex, age, socioeconomic level, nature of employment, or geographic factors may give clues to etiology.

Accurate data from which incidence may be determined are hard to obtain. Some data are gotten in the decennial censuses, but many factors, not the least of which is public opposition to extensive personal inquiry, severely limit the information available. Some information is provided by state and national governmental agencies that deal with handicapped persons. The best data are provided by special surveys

* Stanley S. Marzolf, Ph.D. (The Ohio State University), Professor of Psychology and Director, The Psychological Counseling Service, Illinois State University.

made expressly for the purpose. Information about such studies is available from various bureaus of the U.S. Department of Health, Education and Welfare and in publications of the World Health Organization.

The Clinician's Problem.   Diagnosing present difficulty, predicting probable educational or vocational accomplishment, and assisting the individual toward achieving self-realization are activities in which the clinician engages. Physical handicap may call for the exercise of any or all of these functions, or be involved when some other problem is the focus of attention.

Instances where a physical handicap is not the focal problem but where it has etiological significance for some other problem occur quite frequently. Children referred because of poor social adjustment to their peers or to adults may have an unrecognized physical disability, such as poor vision or a hearing loss, which at least indirectly is a contributing factor in their behavior. Other children, referred because of educational retardation presumed to be the consequence of intellectual dullness, are often found to suffer from a visual or auditory defect that has interfered with learning. The fact that a crippling condition is so minor as to be scarcely noticeable to the casual observer cannot be taken as an indication of its insignificance for the one who has it. In vocational planning, minor defects must be recognized and considered, for they may have major importance for some jobs; the color weak individual is virtually incapacitated for tasks requiring precise color discrimination.

Children who have severe handicaps need psychological study in order that intelligent plans and procedures for their education may be followed. Older handicapped youths are confronted with an especially difficult problem of vocational choice and are particularly in need of factual knowledge concerning the abilities they have. Adults who are handicapped through war or accidental injury need considerable assistance in reorganization and rehabilitation, a process that often must have therapeutic counseling as its principal and basic element.

The psychologist's concern with physical disabilities should not be limited to his work with individuals but should include support of those social and legal measures that will reduce the incidence of the disabilities. In most cases, prevention and early detection of disabilities require public education and, in some cases, legal measures. In all cases, support for necessary research is essential. The psychologist can and should use his influence in behalf of such measures.

Necessary Knowledge and Skill.   In order to function at the highest professional level in any clinical activity, the psychologist must be familiar with the behavior limitations that may result from disability and also the physiological disabilities that may account for manifest behavior anomaly.

The clinical psychologist must, of necessity, be familiar with medical and physiological terminology if he is to be able to understand health records and medical reports. The psychologist never uses such terminology in reports to, or in conversation with, his clients, unless the client is known to be familiar with the terms. Careless and unnecessary use of technical and medical terminology, or psychological terminology for that matter, only complicates the clinical interview, and runs the chance of engendering needless fears or fostering feelings of inadequacy, or hypochondriacal glee.

When working with those in whom a handicap is severe and constitutes the central problem, it is often necessary to use special tests and techniques of testing; some attention will be paid to these matters. Counseling the severely handicapped requires adherence to the same objective, accepting attitude that must underlie all counseling, although in this situation the conditions that thwart objectivity are especially prominent.

Some clinical psychologists work in agencies that serve those with physical handicaps exclusively, but many more psychologists will encounter such persons incidentally. In such cases the principal concern is evaluating the extent to which the physical handicap has contributed to the psychological problem under consideration. Above all, the psychologist must ever be alert to the possibility of the existence of handicapping conditions that are not readily apparent. This is especially important in dealing with children. They may have visual, auditory, or motor impairment that has gone undetected. They have not had sufficient life experience to know that what they see or hear is different from the way other children see and hear. They may be unable to perform motor acts, but they are in no position to judge whether they have a neuromuscular deficit or are just stupid. Even when they are aware of differences they do not have the vocabulary with which to describe their observations. The psychologist should be alert to the possibility of physiological deficit whenever a problem of inferior performance, general or special, is noted.

There are kinds of behavior that result from organic lesions and in some cases the behavior manifestations are unnoticed by the untrained observer. Parents may not have noticed such behavior in their child or have misinterpreted it. They have never reported it to a physician, and the usual medical examinations that have been made have not been of sufficient duration for the behavior to be noted. The competent psychologist who is not too absorbed in test administration or too restricted in his observation may well be the first to note such behavior. When such symptoms are noted, neurological consultation should be sought.

PHYSIOLOGICAL AND MEDICAL ASPECTS OF DISABILITY

Visual Handicaps. It is fairly obvious that severe visual impairment is a handicap to daily living, but it is not as obvious how slight functional deficiences may affect performance. As a consequence, relatively minor visual defects are often unrecognized for what they are and deficiencies in adjustment are erroneously blamed on other factors. Any degree or kind of visual defect is likely to have consequences for adjustment, and severe handicap is a major problem of adjustment in itself.

Visual defects range from slight reduction in acuity to complete blindness (amaurosis). The many varieties can be classified as those associated with (1) defective refraction, (2) anomalies of the eye parts, and (3) dysfunction of the external ocular muscles. Selected visual defects from each of the three groups, together with others not readily classifiable, will be described below.

The meaning of visual acuity requires elaboration. Visual acuity is the minimum separation between two lines that can be detected. It is customary to express the degree of acuity as the ratio of the distance at which a test object is viewed to the distance at which it can be correctly recognized by the normal eye. Normal acuity is the ability to see a separation that subtends a visual angle of one minute. The best-known procedure for testing this is the Snellen Chart, or some modification of it. Such charts consist of lines of letters, numbers, or other objects. The size of the objects on any one line is the same, but the sizes vary from line to line, as shown in Fig. 10–1. The objects on one line are just large enough to be recognized at 20 feet by the normal eye, and the objects on other lines are such as to be recognizable at 10 feet up to 200 feet. Standard practice is to view the chart from a distance of 20 feet. At this distance the 20-foot-line test object subtends a visual angle of five minutes (½ degree). If the subject can, at 20 feet, correctly identify the objects on the 20-foot line, his vision is said to be 20/20, or normal. If, on the other hand, the subject can read only the 70-foot line (or greater), his vision is said to be 20/70.[1] Each eye may be tested separately.[2]

---

[1] Ophthalmologists often prefer to designate acuity in meters. In these units normal acuity is 6/6, and 20/70 is roughly equivalent to 6/21. Deficient acuity may be designated as a per cent of normal vision, as follows:

Snellen Notation	Visual Efficiency
20/20	100.0%
20/35	87.5
20/70	64.0
20/100	48.9
20/200	20.0

[2] For more detailed procedures in the use of a test chart, see G. M. Whipple, *Manual for mental and physical tests—simpler processes* (Baltimore: Warwick & York, 1924), Test 14: "Visual Acuity."

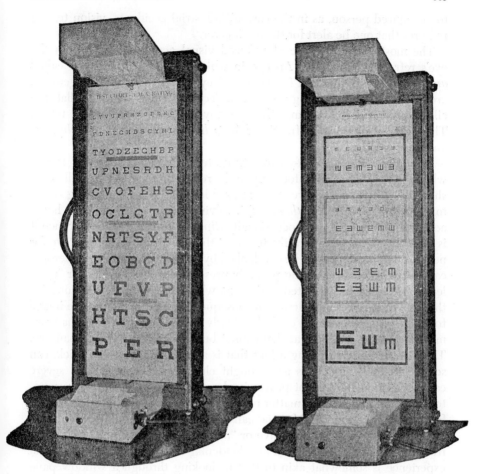

Fig. 10–1. Visual acuity test charts. (Courtesy of the National Society for the Prevention of Blindness and the Welch Allyn Company, Auburn, N.Y.)

The Keystone Telebinocular [3] and the Massachusetts Vision Test [4] have been developed for use in the schools by teachers and nurses for survey purposes. For industrial use the Ortho-Rater [5] has been developed. The psychologist who works in a situation where he does not have access to eye examination results should familiarize himself with the one of these instruments that seems most appropriate for his needs. The use of any such instrument must be limited, of course, to the discovery of the need for referral to an ophthalmologist. Where disability benefits may accrue

[3] Keystone View Company, Meadville, Pa.
[4] Welch Allyn, Inc., Auburn, N.Y.
[5] Bausch & Lomb Optical Company, Rochester, N.Y.

to an injured person, as in the case of industrial accidents, vision testing requires that one be alert for the malingerer.

The most common cause of reduced visual acuity is a defect in the eye's refractive function. An eye in which such defect exists is called *ametropic*. In the normal (*emmetropic*) eye the structural arrangements are such that when fixating a remote object the lens is relatively flat, the ciliary muscle is relaxed, and the light rays come to focus on the retina. There are four kinds of refractive defect: *hyperopia, myopia, presbyopia,* and *astigmatism.*

Hyperopia (farsightedness) sometimes termed "hypermetropia," results when the light rays fail to focus upon the retina because the eyeball is too short for the resolving power of its relaxed lens. The accompanying symptoms include eyestrain (*asthenopia*) involving pain around the eyes, headache, fatigue, vertigo, and occasionally *diplopia* (double vision). Since it is possible, at least temporarily, to adjust the lens of the hyperopic eye for near vision, the defect will be overlooked by superficial testing. Hyperopia can be corrected by wearing properly prescribed double convex or "plus" lenses.[6] Myopia (nearsightedness) exists when the eyeball is too long for the resolving power of its lens. In consequence of the disparity, the image formed by a distant object could be clearly in focus only if the retina were moved forward a bit, a feat that cannot be performed by the human eye. The myopic person, having a lens that is always relatively too thick, can see clearly only if objects are brought close to his eyes, and in severe cases even this adjustment proves inadequate. The most obvious symptoms are holding reading matter close to the eyes and failure to recognize friends at a distance. Myopia can usually be corrected by wearing glasses that have double concave or "minus" lenses. *Astigmatism* results from distortions at the corneal and lenticular surfaces. Astigmatic visual experience is somewhat akin to that of looking through a window pane in which there are imperfections and through which imperfections objects seem twisted and distorted. Cylindrical lenses worn in relation to the axis of astigmatism correct this defect in most instances. *Presbyopia* is the farsightedness of old age and results from reduced elasticity of the lens. The condition develops gradually from middle age onward and leads those in whom it is well developed to say, "There is nothing wrong with my eyes; my arms are too short," for their eyes can no longer accommodate for near vision. Ordinarily "plus" lenses are required for reading, but those who have been hyperopic usually require bifocals, which provide a correction for both far and near objects.

Accidental injury to the eye is most likely to damage its frontal surface, the cornea, and leave scar tissue. Even minor injuries may become in-

[6] The power of the lens is measured in *diopters*. A lens of 1 diopter has a focal length of 1 meter.

fected and ulcerous, a condition known as *keratitis*. Often the body's capacity for attacking infection may be reinforced to the extent that the condition will be alleviated and arrested. Sometimes surgical measures may be taken with good results, but sometimes the damage may progress to the point where the cornea becomes perforated and the eye must then be enucleated. Keratitis is manifested in a corneal opacity that if located over the pupil will, of course, obscure vision.

Perhaps the most commonly known structural disorder of the eye is the cataract, an opacity of the lens that interferes with vision. Cataracts apparently result from a variety of etiological factors, all of which have the effect of altering the physical and chemical processes in the colloid system of the lens. A cataract may develop slowly and never become particularly serious. If and when it does become serious, surgical removal is the only treatment. In older people, the entire lens must be removed and the eye fitted with a cataract lens. *Trachoma* is an infection of the conjuctiva that, if unchecked, will produce opacity of the cornea and blindness.

Most retinopathies are associated with general systemic conditions such as hypertension, kidney dysfunction, and diabetes. In some cases, for example diabetes, improved means of maintaining life has the effect of increasing the number of elderly blind. *Retinitis pigmentosa* is a chronic progressive degeneration and atrophy of the retina with a characteristic deposit of pigment. *Retrolental fibroplasia* is a congenital abnormality that, although not newly discovered, has recently become important because of the increased viability of premature infants. Some of these infants, who formerly would have died, have this condition—an opaque membrane back of the lens—and are generally blind. Occasionally the retina becomes detached from the rear surface of the eyeball, with blindness as the ultimate result. A *glioma* is a malignant tumor of the eye, which destroys its function. *Glaucoma* is a condition resulting from an increase of intraocular pressure, with subsequent deterioration of the retina and blindness. It develops principally among the middle-aged and older, without pain or warning. Its early detection is essential. *Amblyopia* is a somewhat indefinite term applied to a variety of conditions but particularly to reduced acuity resulting from toxic agents. A number of retinal and optic nerve abnormalities result in distortion of the visual field. *Tunnel vision* is reduced peripheral sensitivity of the retina and is best described as the ability to see clearly only those objects directly in front of the observer. *Central scotoma* (darkness) is a reduction of sensitivity in the central area of the retina only. *Hemianopsia* is diminished acuity of one-half of the retina.[7]

Diminution of sensitivity to different wave lengths of light results in

[7] For a classification of the causes of blindness, see Hurlin (1960).

faulty discrimination of hues and is popularly known as "color blindness."
It is more correct to speak of "color weakness," since loss of chromatic
sensitivity may exist in varying degrees from slight to severe (Murray,
1942). It is not uncommon for individuals to be unaware of the fact that
they are color weak. There are a number of tests of color vision of which
the following are examples: *Ishihara Color Perception Test,*[8] the *Dvo-
rine Pseudo-Isochromatic Plates,*[9] and the *Farnsworth-Munsell 100-Hue
Test for Color Discrimination.*[10]

The external or extrinsic eye muscles are those that move the eyeball and
control the coordinated use of the two eyes. *Squint* (cross-eyedness),
or *strabismus*, results from the failure of one or more of these eye muscles
to function properly, with the result that the axis of one eye deviates from
its normal position. Diplopia is present, but eventually the image of one
eye is suppressed and the eye may become amblyopic. Refractive correction, exercise, and surgery are the possible treatments. The cosmetic
effect of squint is a handicap in addition to its effect upon vision. The
heterophorias are defects in the coordinated use of the two eyes. They
may be corrected by the use of prism lenses, by exercises (orthoptic training), or, in extreme cases, by surgery.

Hearing Handicaps. Mild hearing loss is likely to be unrecognized, just
as is mild visual impairment, but while a severe visual handicap is virtually certain to be recognized for what it is, the behavior resulting from
a severe hearing loss is often blamed on anything but hearing defect—all
too often upon assumed low intelligence. It is probably not accidental
that two men associated with the earliest attention to the training of the
feebleminded, Itard in France and Saegert in Germany, were workers
with deaf mutes.

Evaluation of hearing loss is the task of the audiologist. The profession of audiology dates from 1945 and is related to otology, speech correction, and clinical psychology (Newby, 1964, Chap. 1). The audiologist
determines the amount and kind of hearing loss that exists, fits hearing
aids where necessary and feasible, and makes recommendations regarding
speech therapy.

Hearing loss is the degree to which sound energy must be above the
usual threshold in order to be heard. The unit of sound intensity is the
bel, so named in honor of the inventor of the telephone. Ordinarily this
unit is divided into 10 parts, each of which is a decibel. The extent to
which a given individual's threshold is above the accepted reference level,
expressed in decibels, is the degree of hearing loss. The reference level
is as nearly as possible the average threshold for a particular frequency.

[8] Chicago: C. H. Stoelting Company.
[9] Baltimore: Scientific Publishing Company.
[10] New York: Psychological Corporation.

As shown in Fig. 10–2, the threshold values vary considerably with pitch.[11]

In 1951 the American Standards Association adopted a reference level intended to serve as an audiometric zero for calibration of testing devices. In 1965 the International Standards Organization (ISO) proposed an International Standards Level for Pure-Tone Audiometers. This proposed standard differs somewhat from the 1951 American standard. The use of the new reference zero will not affect the establishment of individual thresholds nor the medicolegal definitions of degrees of hearing loss. It will permit the production of audiograms that are internationally comparable (Davis, 1965).

The medicolegal definitions mentioned above refer to degrees of loss, expressed in per cent, upon which claims for disability compensation may be based. The person whose audiogram is shown in Fig. 10–4 has a 20.5 per cent hearing loss, according to the procedure for calculating loss sponsored by the American Academy of Ophthalmology and Otolaryngology (Newby, 1964, p. 102).

The psychologist's chief concern with testing of hearing arises from the importance of discovering mild, easily overlooked, or misinterpreted hearing losses. The possibility that relatively mild acoustic insufficiency is responsible for undesirable behavior manifestations, especially in children, should not be neglected. If the results of an adequate hearing test cannot be regularly obtained, the psychologist should become sufficiently competent in the use of the audiometer to use it as a survey instrument so as to detect those in need of otological referral.

The old-time watch and whispered speech tests have been replaced by the pure-tone audiometer. For survey work in the schools or in industry, group audiometers are available whereby as many as 40 may be tested at one time. The test material consists of a series of phonographically recorded two-digit numbers or two-syllable words (spondees) spoken at decreasing loudness levels. The individual records what he hears on individual record sheets. His threshold is the loudness level at which he succeeds on half the items. Those whose threshold indicates a certain degree of loss, usually either 6 or 12 decibels, are referred for individual examination.

Individual examination may be made with the use of a pure-tone audiometer, which consists essentially of a resonant electrical circuit. This circuit may be adjusted to oscillate at various fixed frequencies so that, with the use of earphones, corresponding pitches may be heard. The intensity of the sound is varied by means of an attenuator, or volume

---

[11] The psychological concept of stimulus threshold or limen as a basis for audiology has been challenged by the Theory of Signal Detectability. Signal detection (awareness of the designated stimulus) is viewed as a problem in the testing of statistical hypotheses. See Jerger (1963) and Swets (1964).

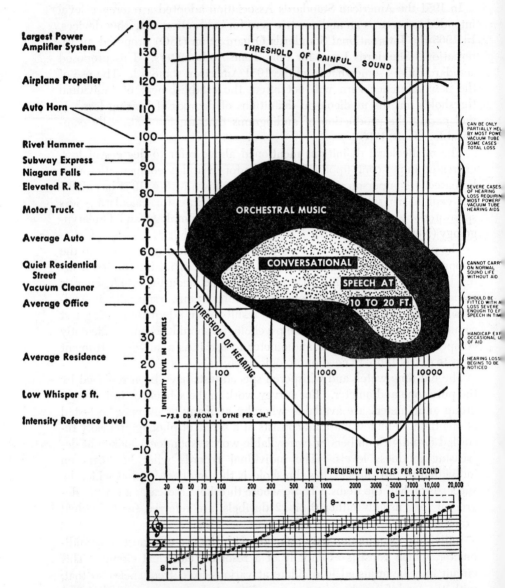

Fig. 10–2. Schematic representation of intensity and frequency characteristics of the human ear and loudness of sounds. (Reprinted with permission granted by The Maico Company, Inc., Minneapolis, Minn.)

control, calibrated in decibels. A device for testing hearing by bone conduction and for producing a masking noise for use in certain clinical procedures may also be provided with the instrument. Some instruments permit testing at frequencies at octave intervals, but others permit use of continuously variable pitches.

The "sweep-frequency" method of testing hearing may be adequate for survey purposes. It consists of setting the audiometer to correspond to a 10 or 15 decibel loss and checking the hearing at a range of frequencies. If the stimulus can be heard at all the selected pitches, the individual is said to have adequate hearing. Failure to hear at any one of the pitches is an indication of the need for more precise clinical testing.

The preparation of an audiogram, such as those shown in Fig. 10–3, 10–4, and 10–5, requires determination of the threshold at each of a number

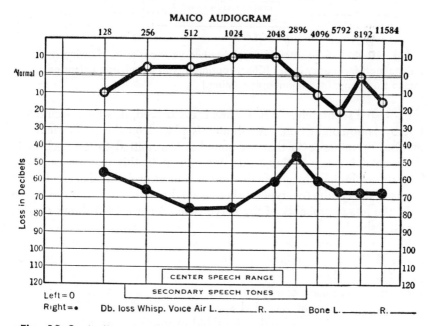

Fig. 10–3. Audiogram of a twenty-one-year-old college man who has only residual hearing in the right ear. (Chart reprinted with permission extended by The Maico Company, Inc., Minneapolis, Minn.)

of frequencies or pitches beginning at 125 cycles per second (cps). The result of such testing is a sample of the full range of hearing and does not tell precisely what the hearing is like between the frequencies tested. It is sometimes desirable to determine thresholds at various intermediate pitches. Air conduction testing is done by placing earphones over each ear so that the sound agitates the air column in the external meatus. Each

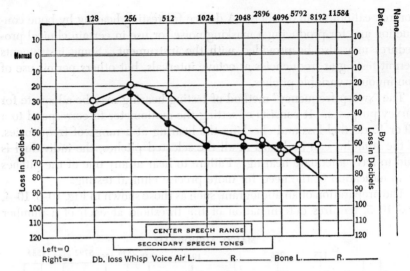

Fig. 10–4. Audiogram of an eighty-two-year-old man, showing a characteristic high-frequency loss. (Chart reprinted with permission extended by The Maico Company, Inc., Minneapolis, Minn.)

ear is tested separately. When a loss is discovered, it is then desirable to test by bone conduction. A vibrator is placed on the postauricular or mastoid prominence so that the sound is transmitted to the cochlea by the cranial bones. If thresholds determined in this manner are lower than those obtained by air conduction, it is most probable that the hearing loss is of the conductive type; if there is no difference between the thresholds, the loss is probably of the nerve type. Figure 10–5 shows conduction thresholds.

The assumption underlying pure-tone audiometry is that inferences about ability to comprehend speech may be made from knowledge of the pure-tone thresholds. Sometimes, however, a speech audiometer is used for clinical purposes, chiefly to check upon the results of the pure-tone examination. Live or recorded speech may be presented by means of controlled amplification, and a threshold of intelligibility determined. A number of tests and test records are available for this purpose (Newby, 1964, Chap. 5).

While it is important, in the interest of arresting the progress of a defect, to discover any hearing loss as early in life as possible, it is obviously impossible to use ordinary methods with children who do not yet have speech, or sufficient intellectual comprehension of the necessary instructions. To meet this problem, the conditioned galvanic skin response and other neurophysiological methods have been tried (Newby, 1964, pp. 198–201).

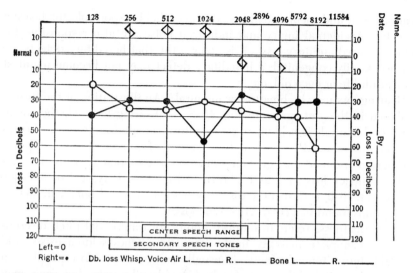

Fig. 10–5. Audiogram of a fourteen-year-old boy, showing disparity between air and bone conduction characteristic of conductive-type loss. Bone conduction thresholds are shown by arrowheads, pointing left for the left ear and right for the right ear. (Chart reprinted with permission extended by The Maico Company, Inc., Minneapolis, Minn.)

Defects of hearing may be either congenital or acquired (adventitious). Congenital defects may be hereditary. Macklin (1949), from a study of deafness in children at a school for the deaf, concluded that heredity is a more frequent cause of deafness than had been supposed. Stephens and Dolowitz (1949) reported that 62 members in a family of 319 in six generations suffered from hereditary nerve (sensori-neural) deafness in varying degrees of severity. Brill (1963) from the records of 819 deaf children concluded that the incidence of deafness due to the recessive gene is considerably greater than the incidence due to the dominant gene, and that the transmission of deafness through the genetic factor that is recessive can be expected to increase. When maternal rubella occurs during pregnancy, especially between the sixth week and the third month, deafness is likely to result (N. E. Murray, 1949).

There are many ways in which acoustic handicap may be acquired. Lancaster (1951) cited evidence to the effect that deafness appeared in epidemic form in Australia among children born in 1899, 1916, 1924, 1925, and 1938–41. He stated further that there is presumptive evidence that all of these epidemics, with the exception of that in 1916, were caused by antecedent epidemics of rubella. Glorig (1950) claimed that streptomycin and dihydrostreptomycin, if given in sufficient quantity, may cause irreversible changes in both divisions of the eighth nerve. The Rh factor, scarlet fever, and meningitis have also been held responsible for hearing defects. Accidental injury and industrial noise are also responsible for some acquired auditory loss. It is noteworthy that hereditary defects are not necessarily congenital; a hereditary defect may not become manifest until adult life or even old age.

Hearing loss may be binaural or monural. An illustration of the former is shown in the audiogram in Fig. 10–3. A hearing loss, whether monaural or binaural, is seldom if ever uniform at all frequencies. Losses may be pronounced at low, middle, or high frequencies. The type of audiogram obtained may give an indication of the etiology of the loss. A high frequency loss such as is shown in Fig. 10–4 is typical of old age, and in Fig. 10–5, is shown the disparity between air and bone conduction audiograms found in a conductive-type loss.

"Tone deafness" refers to reduced ability for differential pitch discrimination. Complete inability to descriminate pitches seldom exists, and thus the term "tone deafness" is usually inaccurate. Most people can distinguish a pitch difference of only 4 double vibrations, but some may discern a difference of less than 1 double vibration. The pitch test of the Seashore Measures of Musical Talent, Series A, for use with an unselected population, presents pairs of stimuli that differ in frequency by 17, 12, 8, 5, 4, 3, and 2 double vibrations, while Series B, for use with the more talented, presents pitch differences of 8, 5, 3, 2, and 1 double vibrations.

Auditory handicaps range in degree from minimal loss in acuity to extreme hearing loss. When auditory acuity is so poor as to be of no functional utility, the person is said to be deaf (anacusia). This degree of defect is usually a binaural loss of at least 60 decibels. Those with binaural hearing loss of from 20 to 60 decibels are said to be hard of hearing. In no case are these decibel limits to be considered as precisely definitive.

Hearing loss may be conductive or sensorineural (formerly called perceptive). The most frequent cause of the conductive type is otitis media, wherein an infection penetrates the middle ear through the eustachian tube, the resulting pressure serving in some cases to rupture the ear drum. When the external ear canal (meatus) becomes impacted with wax (cerumen), a hearing loss may exist. Sometimes the bones of the middle ear (ossicles) become ankylosed, that is, rigidly fixed together so that they cannot transmit the vibrations from the eardrum (tympanum) to the oval window (fenestra ovalis) of the cochlea. Other cases of hearing loss are due to otosclerosis, a condition existing when one of the ossicles, the stirrup (stapes), becomes ankylosed in the oval window. The perceptive type of hearing loss results from damage or maldevelopment within the cochlea or from lesions of the auditory branch of the eighth cranial nerve.

There is nothing that can be done to correct sensorineural deafness. Certain kinds of conduction loss can be alleviated by medical treatment. When otitis media occurs, it is often desirable to puncture the tympanum surgically, thus anticipating a permanently damaging rupture. Excessive cerumen in the ear canal can readily be removed. Occasionally a delicate operation known as fenestration (the Lempert or window operation) is successful in cases of oval window defect. When a hearing loss cannot be alleviated by medical treatment, it may be possible to give relief by a properly fitted aid. For greatest benefit the wearer must be trained in its use.

A diagnosis of *functional hearing loss* is made in cases where no organic basis for test responses can be found, there are unaccountable intratest and intertest discrepancies, and the obtained hearing loss is not in accord with the examinee's hearing behavior in other situations (Jerger, 1963, Chap. 3). When there is some organic basis for hearing loss but this basis in inadequate to account for obtained loss, the condition is known as an organic condition with *functional overlay*. A functional loss may be due to some as yet undiscovered organic condition or it may be psychogenic, that is, a *conversion reaction*.

Other Sensory Handicaps. Defects in sense modalities other than vision and hearing are rare. When defects in taste, smell, kinaesthesis, the static sense, and others occur, they are usually medical problems, since they are either symptoms of complex neurological disorders or components of symptom clusters (syndromes) discussed in Chapters 9 and 12.

Kinaesthetic sensitivity is necessary for maintenance of muscular tonicity and the orientation of body parts in space. Should the neural pathways in the dorsal portion of the lumbar segment of the spinal cord be injured or infected, proprioceptive impulses from receptors located in the trunk and leg muscles fail to reach the cerebral cortex. Walking becomes more and more uncoordinated; this condition may result from neurosyphilis and, if so, is known as *locomotor ataxia* or, because of the location of the lesion, *tabes* (wasting) *dorsalis*. In this condition the upright position of the body cannot be maintained with the eyes closed; the patient falls or sways—the *Romberg Sign*. Should the lesion within the dorsal portion of the spinal cord become more extensive, insensitivity to touch and pain in the lower extremities may result. Figure 10–6 is illustrative of two loci of cord lesion.

Disorders in the sense of equilibrium are occasionally encountered in association with auditory defect of the perceptive type. Infectious disease is one common cause of such symptoms as nystagmus, vertigo, gastric disturbance, pallor, perspiration, and falling toward the affected side— symptoms often observed in acute motion sickness. The nystagmic response may be entirely absent or, conversely, continuously present. In

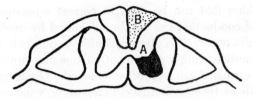

Fig. 10–6. Diagrammatic sketch of the spinal cord, showing areas involved in *anterior poliomyelitis* (A) and *tabes dorsalis* (B).

either instance precise judgment of position and body balance is difficult. Persistence of such symptoms obviously precludes success in certain highly specialized vocational activities.   One vestibular syndrome is known as *Ménière's Disease.*

Loss of sensitivity to taste and odor stimuli (*ageusia* and *anosmia,* respectively) occur occasionally.   Except for certain occupations, these deficiencies have little adjustive significance.   They are, however, of considerable import when found, along with other symptoms, to comprise diagnostic signs pointing to the locus of brain damage or tumorous growth.   The neurologist, accordingly, investigates any reported gradual or rapid loss in receptor sensitivity.

Disorders of the cutaneous senses include loss of tactual sensitivity (*anesthesia*), distorted sensitivity (*paresthesia*), and heightened sensitivity (*hyperesthesia*).   Paresthesia is frequently described by patients as the sensation of "ants crawling over the body" (*formication*).

Neuropathology.   In addition to the role played by the sense organs and their receptor structures in the initiation of adaptive acts, adjustment to the environment requires coordinated movements mediated chiefly by the nerves and skeletal muscles.   Such adaptive acts include locomotion, manipulation of objects, and speech.   The latter is subject to defects, the correction of which engages the attention of the speech correctionist.   All normal motor function, however, entails the maintenance of muscle tonus, defined as a sustained condition of mild muscular contraction, and characterized by the easy initiation of any act and by a coordination that is smooth rather than erratic.   Because faulty action of the skeletal muscles ordinarily results from agenesis, maldevelopment, or injury to the nervous system, motor disabilities are often called neuromuscular defects.   The location of the *lesion* (area of injury) within the specific segment of the nervous system accordingly determines the specific muscle groups involved, and hence the nature of the defect.   By virtue of his knowledge of the innervation of the skeletal muscles, the neurologist can thus denote the site of the lesion by a careful study of the disability and of the characteristic reflexes.   Deviations in the latter are known as neurological signs.

Neuromuscular defects may consist of reduced movement or paralysis (*akinesia*). Paralysis may exist in the form of *flaccidity* or *spasticity*. The former usually results from a spinal cord lesion that destroys innervation of the affected part so that there is muscle *hypotonus* (reduced muscle tension), flabbiness, and atrophy. Spasticity usually results from lesions in the brain that prevent reflex control of muscle tonus with consequent excessive contraction (*hypertonicity*), that is, excessive muscle tension. Because of the variable locations and extents of neurological lesions, spastic and flaccid paralyses do not necessarily involve the entire body musculature. Specific deformities, such as foot or wrist drops, drooping eyelids (*ptosis*), a paralysis of the levator muscle, and the *Argyll-Robertson pupil*, a paralysis of the iris so that the pupil accommodates for distance but not for light, as well as more extensive involvements, are often found.

In order to specify the muscle groups involved in a paralytic condition, descriptive phrases have been adopted. Damage to certain areas of the motor cortex is accompanied by *hemiplegia,* a contralateral paralysis of the body muscles. Paralysis of an arm or leg is known as *monoplegia;* a similar paralysis of both arms or of both sides of the body is known as *diplegia. Paraplegia* denotes a paralysis of both legs or of the lower trunk, while *quadraplegia* involves all four extremities. In most cases of akinesis, the vegetative functions of the body, dependent for the most part upon the autonomic innervation, are intact. Hypokinetic muscular conditions, defective motor reactions, include the partial loss of ability to coordinate movements and are well illustrated in the *ataxic* condition which results from loss of proprioceptive excitations in tabes dorsalis or from cerebellar lesions. Neuromuscular defects, therefore, are accompanied by degrees of reduced movement ranging in severity from mild hypokinesia to akinesia.

Hyperkinesis (excessive mobility) may vary from excessive movement confined to a limited number of small muscle groups to the severe convulsion that involves the entire skeletal musculature. *Tremors* are slight rhythmical movements of varying speed that are best observed when the fingers or tongue are extended. A tremor that disappears when voluntary movement is executed is known as a *rest* tremor, while one that occurs only when voluntary movement is attempted is known as an *intention* tremor. Tremors are readily observed in alcoholic states and are associated with many neurological conditions. Muscular *spasms* are energetic contractions of muscle groups larger than those involved in tremors. *Tics,* the functional counterpart of muscle spasms, are movements of restricted muscle groups such as twitching of the eyelids, mouth, or facial muscles. *Athetosis* is characterized by excessive tentacle-like writhing movements so uncoordinated that even gross voluntary movement is severely hampered. *Convulsions* or *seizures* may have both a tonic and a clonic phase. In the tonic phase there is excessive rapid-fire motor discharge so that the muscles are, for all practical purposes, in a state of continuous contraction; muscular rigidity is observed. The clonic phase is intermittent contraction and relaxation, resulting in violent jerking movements.

Injuries to the brain may manifest themselves in a variety of behavior alterations, many of which the inexperienced observer will conclude are willful perversities, but that are indeed beyond the control of the person who exhibits them. Children who are exceedingly distractible, given to emotional outbursts upon slight provocation and to splurges of somewhat eccentric activity, who find it virtually impossible to function under pressure, and who often show distortion of perceptual processes are probably brain injured. Irregularities of birth, severe febrile illness in infancy, and physical trauma are often responsible, but one is not justified in assuming that if one or more of these conditions is reported in the history, the child has cerebral pathology. The existence of such pathology may be suspected from the behavioral signs and from the history, but must be supported by complete neurological examination, which, at present, is virtually certain to include an electroencephalographic study.[12]

Adults who have functioned at a satisfactory or even high level of efficiency may suffer loss and impairment of function due to cerebral injury. The nature of the impairment depends, to some extent, upon the location of the injury, but there are a number of characteristics that are found in most brain-injured adults. Goldstein, whose interest in these problems began with a study of German soldiers injured in World War I, considers the catastrophic reaction, to the need to meet a task for which competence has been lost, as one indirect consequence of cerebral damage. More direct consequences of injury are a slowing of reactions, perseveration, difficulty either in shifting attention or in holding attention to one task, sharply reduced ability to differentiate perceptual figure from ground, and loss of ability to form abstractions. Clinical psychologists work closely with neurosurgeons in the assessment of damage resulting from head injury (Reitan, 1959). Much more work yet remains to be done in the study of these phenomena and the correlated neuropathology.

Poliomyelitis is the best known and most feared of all the crippling conditions. The first major epidemic occurred in 1916. Poliomyelitis, resulting from a virus infection that damages the cells of the anterior horn of the spinal cord (see Fig. 10–6), is characterized by a flaccid paralysis. The damage may occur at different levels of the cord and the location and extent of the damage determines the location and extent of the paralysis.

---

[12] The literature regarding brain injury in children has become quite extensive. The following are recommended for further study: Birch (1964); Doll (1952); Mac Keith and Bax, 1963; and Strauss and Lehtinen (1947).

In some instances no paralysis results; in others a limb may be crippled, while in others paralysis of the intercostal muscles necessitates living in an iron lung to produce the necessary breathing movements. Although neural destruction is irremediable, physical therapy can restore function to those muscles still possessing residual innervation. Orthopedic surgery may alleviate deformities resulting from the loss of some muscle function. During the summer of 1952 gamma globulin was used experimentally for the first time to provide temporary immunity to the virus. Widespread innoculation beginning in 1956 (oral in 1962) reduced the incidence markedly and in 1963 only 396 cases of paralytic poliomyelitis were reported (*Health, Education and Welfare Trends, 1964*).

Cerebral palsy (formerly known as Little's Disease) is one of the major causes of crippling in children, and is a name that designates a number of closely allied conditions. The most common of these is spasticity,[13] and the second condition, only slightly less frequent in occurrence, is athetosis. These two conditions account for 85 per cent of all cases. The remaining 15 per cent consist of three varieties: ataxia, tremor, and rigidity. Spasticity results from lesions in the cerebrum; athetosis, from midbrain lesions; tremors and rigidities, from lesions of the basal ganglia; and ataxia, from cerebellar lesions. Varieties associated with medullary and diffuse lesions are also recognized.

The most frequent cause of cerebral palsy is birth injury occasioned by premature, delayed, or rapid birth, abnormal presentation of the fetus, and the use of instruments. Hemorrhages, anoxia, and cyanosis may be present, and neurological damage ensues. Certain infectious diseases that occur in early infancy, as, for example, whooping cough, encephalitis, or meningitis, may leave permanent neural damage. Rh factor incompatibility may also be responsible for some cases. There is no cure for cerebral palsy, but the extent of crippling may be alleviated by physical therapy, orthopedic surgery, and the prescription of orthopedic shoes, braces, and the like. From time to time magazines report dramatic but nevertheless exaggerated promises of cure, but these claims have not been borne out.

Paralysis agitans (shaking palsy) was first described by J. P. Parkinson in 1817 and is often referred to as the *Parkinson syndrome*. There is muscular enfeeblement; the posture is stooped; the gait is slow and propulsive. Facial expression is masklike; perspiration is profuse. A marked and partially diagnostic tremor of rest is evident; this is aptly described as "pill roller's palsy" since the movements of the hands resemble rolling pills between the thumb and fingers. Numerous other neuromuscular defects are observed, among which is the cogwheel reac-

---

[13] The term "cerebral spastic palsy" has often been erroneously applied to all varieties.

tion identified by the neurologist as a disorder in the normal synergetic action of the triceps and biceps, and manifested in a slow jerky movement in extension of the arm. The condition appears to be due to lesions of the basal ganglia. True or idiopathic Parkinsonism has a gradual onset, usually in middle or late maturity. The syndrome is often a sequel to encephalitis and it also occurs in the course of a generalized cerebral arteriosclerosis, particularly in advanced age.

Paralysis may result from tumors of the brain, spinal cord, or peripheral nerves; some of these tumors can be surgically removed, following which physical therapy may restore function. Some paralysis, usually hemiplegia, may be caused by a cerebral thrombosis, hemorrhage, or embolism. Injuries to the brain or spinal cord account for still other cases of paralysis.

Epilepsy has the longest history of any illness, save perhaps malaria. The derivation of the word from the Greek, meaning "to lay hold on," reminds us of the ancient and long persistent belief in demonic possession as its cause, and frequent reference to it as the "falling sickness" indicates the sole clinical manifestation that was recognized for many centuries. The history of epilepsy is illustrative of the history of ignorance (Bunker, 1947). Berger's discovery, in 1929, of electrical manifestations of brain activity led to the development of electroencephalography as a technique for studying convulsive states. Investigations soon showed that convulsive states were associated with *dysrhythmic* neural discharges; and that many individuals who exhibited a cerebral dysrhythmia did not manifest clinical seizures of any kind. Some individuals have periods of dysrhythmic cerebral activity without overt manifestation of seizures, in other words, a subclinical seizure. The electroencephalograph may be used to locate focal cerebral lesions (see Fig. 10–7 and Glaser, 1963).

Clinical varieties of epilepsy were designated by French investigators as *grand mal, petit mal,* and *psychomotor* (epileptic equivalent, psychic seizure). Hughlings Jackson was first to describe what is now known as a *focal convulsion* or *Jacksonian* epilepsy. Psychomotor attacks are now known to be of focal origin, a lesion of the anterior temporal lobe (Brain, 1962, Chap. 22).

The grand mal seizure is the commonly recognized "epileptic fit." In some cases the individual has a premonition of the seizure, known as an *aura*. The nature of the aura differs but is usually a sensory experience. Following the aura there is a violent tonic spasm of the body musculature accompanied by loss of consciousness. The patient falls and is rigid. Because respiration is momentarily stopped, the skin becomes dusky and eventually cyanotic; because of the spasm, the saliva cannot be swallowed and "foaming at the mouth" results. The tonic rigidity may last from 10 to 30 seconds, and is followed by a clonic spasm. Such a

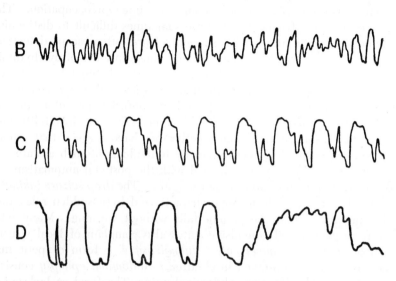

Fig. 10–7. Illustrative electroencephalographic records. Specimen A shows a normal alpha or 10-per-second rhythm. Specimen B shows a portion of the record obtained, between seizures, from a *grand mal* patient. Marked irregularity in amplitude and frequency are noted when comparison is made with A. Specimen C exhibits the double spike occasionally observed in *petit mal* seizures. This record was obtained during such an attack suffered by a white woman who sometimes experienced *grand mal* seizures as well. Specimen D shows the brain wave record of a twelve-year-old boy during and immediately after a *petit mal* seizure. (Courtesy of The Bureau of Psychological Services, Institute for Human Adjustment, University of Michigan, Ann Arbor.)

seizure usually lasts from 2 to 5 minutes. Following it there may be a period of unconsciousness, and there is almost always a period of stupor and confusion. The patient is amnesic for the seizure interval and may know that a seizure has occurred only because of postconvulsion headache, dizziness, or pain from injuries received in the fall. In some cases there is a rapid succession of seizures, each following before recovery from the preceding, a condition known as *status epilepticus*. Death frequently occurs in such episodes. Sometimes the attack is followed by the performance of *postictal*, that is, postseizure, automatisms that may be of considerable violence and are often called *epileptic frenzy*.

The typical petit mal seizure is little more than a short period of "absence" during which the individual may pause for a moment, become slightly pale, possibly stare fixedly, or show minor twitching. There is amnesia for the episode but, since it is of such short duration, the patient's experience is probably much like that of anyone who loses track of what he is doing because of a momentary inner preoccupation. The attacks occur quite frequently, and are sometimes difficult to distinguish from abortive major attacks. These mild seizures often escape detection. In children the electroencephalograph may show episodes of dysrhythmic discharge, although no convulsion is manifest. Ultimately petit mal seizures may occur. Such subclinical seizures are called *larval epilepsy.*

The psychomotor seizure is a period of confusion or automatic behavior that may last for a considerable time. Extreme irritability and violence may be exhibited. Some authorities have claimed that crimes of violence are sometimes performed by individuals in such a state. A psychomotor seizure may be confused with the postictal automatism.

There are a number of other minor seizures. The *drop seizure (akinetic* or *static)* is a rather unusual type characterized by a sudden relaxation of the muscles so that the patient falls without warning. Many who suffer from generalized convulsive states also complain of local spasms known as *myoclonic movements. Pyknolepsy* is a form of petit mal episode occasionally observed in children. *Abdominal epilepsy* consists of repeated attacks of severe abdominal pain. The focal or Jacksonian epilepsies consist of temporary spasms of body extremities, usually without loss of consciousness.

Etiologically, epilepsy is classified as *symptomatic* (secondary) or *idiopathic* (essential, cryptogenic, or primary) depending on whether the cause is known or unknown. Symptomatic epilepsy may result from congenital or acquired lesions, while idiopathic epilepsy is said to exist when no lesion can be discovered. Paroxysmal discharges of cortical neurones are present in all cases, however. Hereditary factors are doubtless responsible for some epilepsy, but the hereditary factor has generally been overrated. In 10 to 15 per cent of cases a history of epilepsy in some other member of the family, or ancestors, or collateral relatives is found (Ford, 1952).

The principal treatment for epilepsy is the use of anticonvulsant drugs, which began in 1857 with the bromides. It was not until 1912 that phenobarbital came into use. Dilantin followed in 1937 and mesantoin in 1945. Since that time a number of other pharmaceuticals have been developed, chief of which are phenurone, paradione, and tridione. The latter seems to be most effective in the control of petit mal seizures. Anticonvulsant drugs often have a synergistic effect in that two or more in combination are more effective than any one taken alone. In institutions, drugs are used in conjunction with a carefully regulated system of rest, diet, and activity—the latter being considered rather important. Psychic seizures are refractory to pharmacological treatment, although some improvement has been obtained with mesantoin and phenurone. Ketogenic (fat-laden) and dehydration diets are sometimes used, and where focal inquiry exists, surgical technique may be effective. One form of this surgery is known as a topectomy.

The *choreic* syndromes and *choreiform* movements designate a group of neuromuscular handicaps most common in children. They are of particular interest to the psychologist because the symptoms may suggest habit mannerisms or tics. The most common variety is *Sydenham's* chorea, popularly known as St. Vitus' Dance (named from a dancing mania which occurred in Germany in the Middle Ages). It occurs most frequently among girls between the ages of six and nine, and may follow rheumatic fever. Motor incoordination is exhibited by the proximal segments of the limbs, appearing suddenly, irregularly, and forcing the arm, for example, into a wide excursive arc. Emotional instability and seclusive trends may be noted. The condition normally runs its course in from one to three months. The prognosis is good.

Huntington's chorea is a serious degenerative hereditary condition that terminates in dementia, paranoidal psychotic manifestations, and eventually death. The distal segments of the limbs are characteristically observed in writhing, athetoid movements, and the gait is erratic. It appears between the ages of 35 to 50 years.

The choreic syndrome may result from congenital maldevelopment and be quite athetoid in character.

Encephalitis is literally an inflammation of the brain, presumably brought about by a virus. An epidemic broke out in Romania in 1915 and in Vienna in 1917, where it was described by von Economo. It was epidemic in this country in 1918. This form is known as Type A, to distinguish it from Type B, thought to be responsible for Japanese epidemics and possibly for outbreaks that have occurred in Australia and St. Louis, Missouri. We shall confine our discussion to Type A. The onset of encephalitis is marked by such symptoms as headache, lassitude, and vomiting. The acute phase manifests itself variously. Somnolence and stupor, extraocular palsies and diplopia occur. In other cases high fever, delirium, excitement, restlessness, and insomnia are characteristic. Occasionally the Parkinson syndrome appears during the acute phase and, in other cases, known as the fulminating, death supervenes. Two to 10 weeks is the usual duration of the acute phase.

Permanent *residua* may be observed following abatement of the acute phase, the most common of which are ocular disorders, mental retardation, difficulty in concentration, irritability, reversal of sleep rhythm.

Many patients who seem to recover may develop a chronic phase in which various sequelae appear. Among the possible sequelae are the Parkinson syndrome, convulsive phenomena, reversal of sleep rhythm, mental and personality disturbances. Personality disturbance may take the form of extreme destructiveness (Ford, 1952).

Multiple sclerosis, of unknown cause, is a progressive or remittent disease involving chiefly the white matter of the central nervous system. It is primarily a disease of adult life, with a mean age at onset of 28 years and a mean age at death of 54 years. The most common symptoms are ocular manifestations, weakness, reflex changes, and ataxia. There is no satisfactory treatment.

There are several disorders that produce crippling but are not primarily neurological. *Progressive muscular dystrophy* is a degeneration of the muscles. There is progressive weakness and wasting resulting in defective posture and gait. Those afflicted can walk well on level ground but have great difficulty in climbing stairs, or in straightening the body from a bent-over position. There are a number of forms of this condition, but the most common is the pseudohypertrophic, which usually begins in the first decade of life and affects males predominantly. The duration of the illness is from 6 to 12 years. Weakness of the intercostal muscles predisposes the sufferer to pneumonia, which is the frequent cause of death. This condition should be distinguished from muscular atrophy, a progressive wasting of the muscles that is the consequence of some disorder of the nerve supply to the muscles.

Legg-Perthes disease is one of several epiphyseal conditions, disorders of the growing portion of bones. In this disease, which occurs early in life, the head of the femur becomes dead bone, softens, and is completely destroyed. The chief treatment is removal of all weight from the affected part, usually necessitating bed rest, with traction. Later the individual may get about on crutches. Recovery usually follows in two or three years. Surgical removal of some destroyed bone may be required. Residual limitation of movement may be alleviated by physical therapy.

Tuberculosis of the bone, usually appears before the age of six. The tubercle bacillus, transported by the blood stream, attacks the spongy bone tissue and causes considerable destruction. The vertebra, small bones of the hands and feet, and the ends of the long bones are most frequently affected. Rest and occasionally surgery to remove affected tissue are the principal treatments.

Osteomyelitis, an inflammation of the bone marrow, may be either acute or chronic, and is a staphylococcus infection following trauma of the bone. The condition is extremely painful, involving heat and local tenderness. Antibiotics and surgery are the best available treatments.

PSYCHOLOGICAL ASPECTS OF PHYSICAL DISABILITY

While the clinical psychologist must have some knowledge of the physiological and medical aspects of disability in order to participate in cooperative efforts in behalf of the handicapped, it is the psychological characteristics of handicapped persons that are his chief concern and proper province. He must be as well informed as possible about the problems of daily living that are occasioned by the various kinds of disability, the effect of disability upon the development of personality and the adequacy of adjustment, and the extent to which intellectual functioning may be affected. Only general conclusions regarding these matters can be covered here, since the reader is assumed to have a background in general psychology and mental hygiene, and since some relevant topics are covered in other chapters.

Problems of the Disabled. It is difficult for the unimpaired to appreciate the difficulties of the disabled. One may easily see that the crippled cannot move about, and have some appreciation of this condition because of personal experience with a sprained ankle or a broken arm, but the meaning of congenital impairment or severe adventitious loss is another thing. The great obstacles encountered in satisfying the daily personal needs and the necessity for relinquishing goals toward which one has been working prior to injury are a combination of burdens the unimpaired have not experienced. It is difficult to appreciate how the problems of independent travel loom so large in the life of the blind and how the great difficulty in communicating is such a frustrating social handicap for the deaf. For the congenitally blind, color can have no meaning and the verbal usage of color is what Cutsforth, himself blind, considers an example of the "hypocrisy of verbalism" (Cutsforth, 1951). Tones of voice intended to convey tender affection have never been heard by the congenitally deaf. It is claimed that deafness causes more social frustration than any other disability. The development of sexual attitudes and function is often distorted, and in certain disabilities, notably the paraplegic, problems associated with sex become quite severe. (Pringle, 1964; Rainer et al., 1963; Wright, 1960).

The problems encountered by the adventitiously handicapped are somewhat different from those met by the congenitally disabled. The blinded and deafened had had past experience with space and language, respectively, which definitely minimizes certain training problems. However, the sense of frustration occasioned by the necessity for giving up vocational aspirations toward which progress has already been made may outweigh any advantages accruing from experimental background.

The degree to which the disabled may achieve adequate lives will be increased if negative opinions, common misconceptions, esthetic aversion, and false emotionalism can be replaced by sincere, objective acceptance on the part of society. In fact, it is often negative attitudes toward the handicap rather than the handicap itself that are the more serious obstacle. It is probable that maladjustment among the handicapped results more often from failure to solve the problems of social participation than from failure to clear the hurdles raised by the physical limitation itself.

Reluctance of employers to hire the handicapped presents an unnecessary obstacle that nationwide campaigns urging "Hire the Handicapped" have lessened somewhat. Opposition to the handicapped employees may exist among other employees, especially those lackadaisical workers who dislike having their meager performance outdone by physically limited workers. The usual excuses offered for reluctance to hire the handicapped must always be suspect; devious defensiveness growing out of personal insecurity is probably the major basis for such unwillingness.

Personality Characteristics of the Handicapped. It has often been claimed that particular disabilities have characteristic personality patterns associated with them. Such claims have been made for the blind, the deaf, the cerebral palsied, and the epileptic especially. While it is true that many blind persons exhibit certain characteristics known as blind-isms (Chevigny and Braverman, 1950) and that phantasy and withdrawal are common, such behavior is but a reaction to the frustrations and negative social attitudes that the blind encounter. The adjustive peculiarities of the blind are no more caused by blindness than are the adjustive peculiarities of the seeing caused by vision (Carroll, 1961; Garrett, 1952). If certain deaf persons are somewhat paranoid it should not be too surprising since negative behavior toward them has been accompanied by speech they have not been able to hear (Rainer et al., 1963). There is no clear-cut evidence to support belief in a cerebral palsy stereotype, but it has been claimed that the athetoid and spastic differ from one another (Garrett, 1952). There is no evidence for the existence of an "epileptic personality," though there may be some characteristics that are associated with some types of epilepsy (Tizard, 1962).

Some crippling conditions, particularly those resulting from head injuries, involve damage to the brain and thus changes in behavior may possibly be expected, but in general any personality characteristics that become notable after the onset of an adventitious handicap most probably can be explained in terms of the kind of personality that had been developed prior to the onset. It is the person who has the handicap and the family in which he grows up that count most, not the disability itself.

Adjustment of the Handicapped. The terms "handicapped" and "disabled" have been used interchangeably, in accord with common usage. However, it has been noted (Hamilton, 1950) that degree of disability, in physical terms, and degree of handicap may not be the same. The extent to which a given disability will prove to be a handicap depends to a large extent upon the person and his environment. In the general population it is usually true that feelings of adequacy are not correlated with more objective measures of competence. Many persons are handicapped by imagined disabilities.

In general it has been found that maladjustment is more common among the handicapped, but, as is true in most cases where statistically significant differences between two group means are found, the amount of overlap of the two groups is ignored. It has been estimated (Barker *et al.*, 1946) that 35 to 40 per cent of the handicapped are better adjusted than the nonhandicapped. During the years since this estimate was made there has been some improvement in treatment of the handicapped; the amount of overlap has probably increased. The great variation in degree of acceptable self-realization among the handicapped negates the popular conception that there is a necessary connection between the fact of physical disability and the quality of personal adjustment.

Undoubtedly the existence of a disability serves in some instances to activate compensatory behavior that may include constructive and highly valuable output. The same may be said with respect to defects that are not real but only fancied. The handicapped and nonhandicapped alike must learn to distinguish between unconsciously developed adjustive efforts and intelligently conceived substitute activities that must be undertaken whenever any kind of thwarting occurs.

Unfavorable social attitudes, already mentioned, constitute a major adjustive problem for the handicapped. The experience of peer rejection may be encountered early in life and become acute during adolescence, when peer acceptance is of especially great importance. Various explanations for such rejection have been proposed. It seems most probable that there is no one reason that is solely responsible in all cases. An any rate, the disabled do find themselves in what has been described as the marginal status of minority groups (Barker *et al.*, 1946). Jordan (1963) claims that there are noteworthy differences between minority groups and the disabled, and holds that a concept of disadvantaged group is more suitable.

It often happens that the individual with mild or less obvious handicaps has a more difficult time than the person with a severe and obvious disability. Those with mild degrees or forms of disability are so much like others that it is hard for parents, teachers, and peers to see why they can not perform adequately in all situations. The disabled person himself will have difficulty in knowing whether or not he is making unwarranted allowances to himself for genuine limitations of function.

The self concept, so important in determining the quality of adjustment, is doubtless associated with the body image, and this in turn is a reflection of the conception of one's body held by others. In slowly developing chronic conditions a marked discrepancy between the body structure and the body image may develop, and in the case of acquired disability there will be a discrepancy between the former body image and that which is new. It is clear that ambiguous perceptions of the world and of the self may easily be characteristic of the life of the disabled (Wapner, 1965).

Parental influences are especially important in determining the course of life adjustment for all, but they may be particularly important for those with congenital disabilities or disabilities acquired early in life. Parents often feel that they are in some way responsible for disabilities that are congenital and thus have guilt feelings. To assuage these guilt feelings they may overindulge and overprotect the child and thus reduce his chances for development. Other parents see their disabled child as a frustration of their hopes, an added time-consuming care, a financial burden, or a reflection upon their progenitor status, with the consequence that they rather reject the child. Such rejection may take the form of manifest neglect, but more often it leads to oversolicitous care in an effort to deny the rejection. Even where parents accept the child without reproach, unwise coddling may result in attitudes of overdependence.

Discovering parental attitudes inimical to the healthy development of personality does not conclude the psychologist's endeavors on behalf of a child. Unfavorable attitudes that are discovered very probably do explain the child's behavior. Help for the child will involve changing parental attitudes. The psychologist who maintains an objective, nonjudgmental attitude in dealing with the child often loses this objectivity when confronting the parents. It should be obvious that the attitude a parent has is a consequence of his own personality development in his own family situation. The parent who felt himself at a disadvantage with respect to his siblings may see the birth of a crippled child as a continuation of the same old pattern. The parent will see this child in comparison with nonhandicapped nieces and nephews and be resentful. The man who married someone disapproved of by his parents may feel that having a disabled child is a punishment for going against his parents' wishes. Many other possibilities growing out of the parent's relationships with their parents, their aunts and uncles, and their siblings will be found. Parents can be helped to a better understanding of themselves and a consequent better acceptance of their disabled child if the psychologist simply remembers that parents too have problems.

Parental attitudes are often influenced by close friends, or even by neighbors. These persons may be full of advice and reproach. The latter is expressed if the parents do not treat their child like the self-appointed advisers think is proper. In this situation the basic problem is why the parents are so subject to the opinions of friends and neighbors. Clearly their own self-esteem is not adequate. Once they can come to see this, and why it is so, they can proceed to sound child management. Often the most valuable thing a psychologist can do for a child is to help the parents understand and accept their own feelings. Improved acceptance of the handicapped child will follow.

Intellectual Function of the Disabled. It is not uncommon for the uninformed to express great surprise when it is found that a visually or acoustically handicapped child has superior intelligence or is intellectually gifted. While it is true that some studies have shown that the average IQ of those with handicaps is lower than that of the general population, the differences are small and there is thus considerable overlapping of the intelligence score distributions. Whatever differences exist may be accounted for by the inadequacy of the tests used. Tests that must necessarily be used to accommodate for the visual or auditory handicap may not measure certain aspects of intelligence—aspects in which the handicapped groups may not be inferior. Those who are congenitally handicapped may have been unduly overprotected and thus restricted in opportunity for development (Garrett, 1952; Stephens and Dolowitz, 1949). There is some evidence that the deaf are inferior in abstract reasoning (Oleron, 1950).

The notion that the blind develop superior acuity in other senses requires comment. Such compensatory sensory modification does not take place and, in fact, there is some evidence that cutaneous sensitivity is inferior to that of the sighted (Chevigny and Braverman, 1950). The blind can and do develop facial vision (obstacle sense), that is, an awareness of objects they approach. The nature of facial vision as perception of minimal auditory cues has been established (Supa et al., 1944). Among the deaf, lip reading (more correctly speech reading) is often well developed even without special training. For many, such skill can be acquired with training, but there are some individuals for whom it is quite difficult.

Studies of the intelligence level of the crippled have shown that, on the average, their scores are lower than those of the nondisabled. However, the most important findings of such studies is that the degree of intellectual impairment depends upon the cause of crippling. When decline of intellectual function is found, one may suspect that cerebral involvement has developed. For many years it was a common assumption that the cerebral palsied, particularly the severely handicapped, were quite dull. With the discovery that some severely handicapped cerebral palsied have superior intelligence, there was increased inclination to expect that all severely handicapped cases were potentially capable of superior accomplishment. Roughly one may say that about 25 per cent of the cerebral palsied may have average or better than average intelligence, and that about 40 to 45 per cent will be mentally defective. Clearly each case must be carefully evaluated, and furthermore it must be borne in mind that whatever level of intellectual ability is established, the adjustive usefulness of the ability will be restricted by the amount of motor impairment that exists.

The intelligence of idiopathic epileptics is no different from that of the general population. In symptomatic epilepsy it is more probable that intellectual impairment may be found. Intellectual deterioration does occur, but rarely.

Services Available for the Handicapped.   There are many ways in which the handicap of a disability can be reduced. Early detection of onset of certain ultimately disabling conditions may make it possible for medical and surgical methods to arrest or control the progress of the disorder. Once the disability exists, eyeglasses, hearing aids, prosthetic devices, and orthopedic braces may be prescribed and fitted. The resources of physical medicine, including physical therapy, will have great benefits.

Special training of various kinds is helpful. The deaf or hard-of-hearing person must be trained to use his hearing aid. Training is also necessary for the person who has been fitted with a prosthesis, although acceptance of the prosthesis is often more difficult than learning to use it. Braille reading and the use of cane or guide dog are skills that may be helpful. The acoustically handicapped can profit from training in speech reading, aural training (optimal use of residual hearing), speech correction, and, in some instances, instruction in the manual alphabet (sign language). Methods of training the partially sighted to make more efficient use of their limited vision have been markedly successful.

Special facilities and methods of instruction are becoming increasingly available for the public school education of the physically handicapped, under the name of "special education." An increasing number of states have programs for the blind, partially sighted, deaf, hard of hearing, the crippled, cardiopathic, and others. Special classes are provided where necessary, but every effort is made to avoid segregating those with disabilities from other children. Teachers specially trained for working with various kinds of handicapped and special equipment are provided, but the handicapped children associate with others in regular classes and activities as much as possible.

Occupational therapy can be of value in physical disability by improving endurance, retraining coordination, and providing prevocational exploration. The handicapped may be trained in occupations suitable for them or in the skills and methods that will prepare them for regular industrial employment. Many physically impaired can compete with the unimpaired. Those who are unable to tolerate industrial employment or become entirely independent may be employed in sheltered workshops. The most severely disabled may engage in home industries where they may work as energy permits.

Services for the disabled are provided by private, city, state, and federal agencies. Federal funds are made available to states through the Office of Vocational Rehabilitation. Many of these services are available to the war injured through the Veterans Administration. A rehabilitation center often provides or supervises vocational training, sheltered workshops, and home industries. One of the major agencies providing rehabilitation service is the Goodwill Industries, Inc. This organization has autonomous centers in over a hundred cities in the United States and Canada, and offers training in workshop facilities. The basic program is the collection of household discards, clothing, furniture, and utensils which are then renovated and sold through Goodwill stores.

Evaluating Capacities and Abilities. The education or rehabilitation of the handicapped should be planned and undertaken in accordance with the individual's assets and liabilities. Where maladjustment exists, discovery of the nature and more specific causes is necessary. Some of the information needed for these purposes can best be supplied by tests.

Tests designed for general use require integrity of the body. From the beginning of individual testing, students in training have been impressed with the importance of watching for any sensory, motor, or other organic deficiency which might lower the validity of the test score as an estimate of the trait being investigated. It is clear then that adequate testing of the disabled requires modifications which permit assessment of the individual by presenting stimuli and calling for behavior that does not involve the impaired function. Where impairment is multiple and severe, testing becomes all but impossible. Even when testing is possible, one must be alert for the effects of limitation of experience not only by the handicap, but by the parents who may have restricted opportunity for development through overprotection.

The partially sighted can be tested by the use of the Binet or the various forms of the Wechsler with slight modifications. Binet materials which are to be read by the examinee can be typed in kindergarten type. Certain performance subtests of the Wechsler-Bellevue, such as the Picture Completion, the Picture Arrangement, and the Digit Symbol will have to be omitted in many instances. There is a considerable range of visual efficiency among the partially sighted, and thus the degree of validity of results achieved on a test will vary. The Stanford Achievement Tests have been published in large type; when used, time limits are extended 50 per cent. Other tests may be prepared in large type or read to the subject if time is not a factor in the test. Work-limit tests should be used whenever possible.

Considerable attention has been given to methods for testing the blind. Irwin, in 1914, modified the newly developed Goddard-Binet. Since then extensive work has been done by Hayes who, in 1942, published the Interim Hayes-Binet Intelligence Tests for the Blind, a modification of the Terman-Merrill Revised Stanford Binet Scale. The six verbal tests of the Wechsler scale can also be used. Braille editions are available for a number of well-known group intelligence, achievement, interest, and personality tests. A number of employment and vocational tests, using modified instructions, are available. For projective purposes, three-dimensional materials, and orally presented stories and incomplete sentences may be used.

Testing of the hard of hearing does not present a particularly difficult problem when the handicap is recognized, and effort is made to speak loudly and distinctly with the examinee in a position to see the speaker's face. A desk model hearing aid is often helpful. Paper and pencil, performance, and employment tests can be used without modification.

A number of individual intelligence tests are available for use with the deaf. For children the nonverbal tests of the Merrill-Palmer Scale of Mental Tests, the Nebraska Test of Learning Aptitude, and the Ontario School Ability Tests may be used. Pantomime directions are included in the manual for the Arthur Performance Ability Scale (I). The Arthur Adaptation of the Leiter International Performance Scales and the performance subtests of the Wechsler scales may also be used. Paper and pencil tests of all kinds obviously may be used, although the content of personality tests is not always applicable. In general, there are more tests which may be used with the hard of hearing and the deaf without modification, than there are available for the blind. This must not be taken to mean that acoustic handicap is less severe; the effect of having a limitation upon linguistic communication may be profound.

Testing the crippled presents problems as varied as the nature of the crippling conditions one encounters. Many kinds of severe crippling, those involving the legs only, present no difficulty for testing. When speech or the function of the hands is involved, or when, as so frequently happens, both are impaired, testing may become so difficult as to be virtually impossible. Situations of this kind arise most frequently in cerebral palsy, where it is also true that the vagaries of function found among the brain injured are likely to be present.

The purpose of testing is not to obtain a score, but rather to get information which will be helpful for the purpose at hand, be it educational planning or rehabilitation. Any score that is obtained must, as always, be interpreted in terms of all other available information about the person. For the handicapped this means that developmental and test-related factors which may lower performance must be taken into account. Conclusions drawn may often need to be provisional and frequent re-evaluation is essential.

Testing to discover the existence and extent of cerebral dysfunction is often necessary and desirable. In the course of examining children for determining general level of intelligence, kinds of behavior may be noted which suggest neurological damage. Supplementary testing may reveal further corroborative evidence. Of the many tests and testing procedures used for this purpose perhaps the most common are the Bender Visual-Motor Gestalt and the Benton Visual Retention tests. In adults, evaluation of function subsequent to injury or severe illness may be needed to discover if there is a psychological deficit. These problems have had considerable attention and much additional work needs to be done. Especially needed is knowledge of how to adapt rehabilitative measures to the forms of dysfunction found to exist (Reitan, 1959; Taylor, 1961).

Counseling the Handicapped. There is general acceptance of the view that the aim of counseling in any situation is fostering self-realization. There is also consirerable agreement that the counselee must take the responsibility for his own growth, but there are differences of opinion about how much responsibility he may be expected to take. Doubtless the only answer we can now give is that the counselee should be expected to take as much responsibility as he possibly can and that this will vary from possibly very little at the beginning to culmination in adequate self-direction.

When our chief concern is with handicapped children, it is the parent with whom counseling may possibly be undertaken. The earlier the parents can be brought to an objective view of disability and institute adequate training the better for the ultimate personality status of the child. When working with older physically disabled, we must remember that it is not only the impaired who have suffered from parental rejection, over-protection, or domination: such influences are found in the life histories of the unimpaired also.

Visual and auditory handicaps present special problems in counseling. Most counselors have found that periods of silence are often effective and that considerable growth may occur during such periods. The effect of such silence in counseling sessions with the blind is a dubious matter however. The communication difficulties of the deaf quite obviously present considerable obstacles for counseling.

Rehabilitation counseling is directed toward assisting the disabled to reorganize their lives in accordance with an altered status. A realistic acceptance of the disability with its limitations is the ideal reorganization. There are those who surrender to the disability and become dependent, and there are others who seek to ignore it. Neither of these reactions to loss of function is realistic. The reaction to adventitious disability is undoubtedly related to the kind of personality organization that existed prior to the loss, and it is this that accounts for the wide variation in reaction to loss. It should be obvious that for those who engage in rehabilitation counseling, a realistic attitude toward disabilities is a prime essential. (See Chapter 22.)

SUMMARY

Sensory and motor impairment may be congenital or acquired. Congenital deficits present developmental problems in varying degrees depending on the nature and degree of the deficit. Undesirable parental attitudes toward the handicapped child usually constitute a major obstacle to desirable personality development. When such unfavorable attitudes do not exist, or when those that exist are altered, the child can develop into a well-adjusted individual. In fact, there is little difference in the level of adjustment of the handicapped when compared with the nonhandicapped.

Physical disability may be acquired in later life as a result of illness or injury. In such cases major occupational reorientation may be required. How well this may come about will depend on prior personality adequacy to a considerable extent.

All handicapped persons are likely to encounter negative social attitudes, which may be the biggest problem with which they must deal.

The clinical psychologist may be the one who first discovers obscure but handicapping disabilities. He may contribute important knowledge and skill to the education or rehabilitation of the manifestly handicapped. Finally, he will take responsibility for public education and social action on behalf of the handicapped.

REFERENCES

ALLEN, R. M., and JEFFERSON, T. W. (eds.). 1963. *Proceedings of the third annual professional development seminar for psychologists and rehabilitation personnel: Psychological assessment of the disabled.* Coral Gables, Fla.: Miami Univer. Press.

BARKER, R. G., WRIGHT, B. A., and GONICK, M. R. 1948. *Adjustment to physical handicap and illness: A survey of the social psychology of physique and disability.* New York: Social Science Research Council.

BAUMAN, MARY K., and HAYES, S. P. 1951. *A manual for the psychological examination of the adult blind.* New York: Psychological Corp.

BIRCH, H. G. (ed.). 1964. *Brain damage in children: the biological and social aspects.* Baltimore: Williams & Wilkins.

BRAIN, L. 1962. *Diseases of the nervous system.* (6th ed.) Fair Lawn, N.J.: Oxford Univer. Press.

BRILL, R. G. 1963. Deafness and the genetic factor. *Amer. Ann. Deaf,* 108(4), 359–73.

BUNKER, H. A. 1947. Epilepsy: a brief historical sketch. In P. H. HOCH, and R. P. KNIGHT, (eds.), *Epilepsy: Psychiatric aspects of convulsive disorders.* New York: Grune & Stratton.

CANFIELD, N. 1949. *Audiology, the science of hearing: a developing professional specialty.* Springfield, Ill.: Charles C Thomas.

CARROLL, T. J. 1961. *Blindness: What it is and what it does.* Boston: Little Brown.

CUTSFORTH, T. D. 1951. *The blind in school and society: A psychological study.* New York: American Foundation for the Blind.

DAVIS, H. 1965. International standard reference zero for pure-tone audiometry. *Trans. Amer. Acad. opthalmol. otolaryngol.,* 69, 112–18.

DAVIS, H., and SILVERMAN, S. R. (eds.). 1960. *Hearing and deafness.* New York: Holt, Rinehart, & Winston.

DI CARLO, L. M. 1964. *The deaf.* Englewood Cliffs, N.J.: Prentice-Hall.

FORD, F. R. 1952. *Diseases of the nervous system in infancy, childhood and adolescence.* (3d ed.) Springfield, Ill.: Charles C Thomas.

GARRETT, J. F. (ed.). 1952. *Psychological aspects of physical disability.* Washington, D.C.: Office of Vocational Rehabilitation.

GARRETT, J. F., and LEVINE, EDNA S. *Psychological practices with the physically handicapped.* New York: Columbia Univer. Press, 1962.

GIBBS, F. A., and STAMPS, F. W. 1958. *Epilepsy handbook.* Springfield, Ill.: Charles C Thomas.

GLASER, G. H. (ed.). 1963. *EEG and behavior.* New York: Basic Books.

GLORIG, A. 1950. The relation of streptomycin and dihydrostreptomycin to the hearing and vestibular apparatus. *J. Speech Hearing Disorders*, **15**, 124–218.

GRAHAM, M. 1960. *Social research on blindness.* New York: American Foundation for the Blind.

HAMILTON, K. W. 1950. *Counseling the handicapped in the rehabilitation process.* New York: Ronald.

HUNT, J. T. 1963. Children with crippling conditions and special health problems. *Rev. educ. Res.*, **33**, 99–108.

HURLIN, R. G. 1960. 1960 revision of the standard classification of the causes of blindness. *Sight-saving Rev.*, **30**(3), 153–56.

ISAACSON, R. L. (ed.). 1964. *Basic readings in neuropsychology.* New York: Harper & Row.

JERGER, J. (ed.). 1963. *Modern developments in audiology.* New York: Academic Press.

JORDAN, S. 1963. The disadvantaged group: A concept applicable to the handicapped. *J. Psychol.*, **55**(2), 313–22.

LANCASTER, H. O. 1951. Deafness as an epidemic disease in Australia: A note on census and institutional data. *British medical J.*, No. 4745, 1429–32.

LENNOX, W. G., and LENNOX, MARGARET A. 1960. *Epilepsy and related disorders.* Boston: Little Brown.

LERNER, J. 1963. The role of the psychologist in the disability evaluation of emotional and intellectual impairments under the Social Security Act. *Amer. Psychologist*, **18**(5), 252–56.

MACKEITH, R. and BAX, M. 1963. *Minimal cerebral dysfunction.* London: National Spastic Society Medical Education and Information Unit with Heinemann.

MACKLIN, M. T. 1949. The importance of heredity in causing congenital deafness. *Hygeia*, **27**(8), 538–39, 574–75.

MURRAY, ELSIE. 1942. Color blindness: Current tests and the scientific charting of cases. *Psychol. Bull.*, **39**, 165–72.

MURRAY, N. E. 1949. Deafness following maternal rubella. *Med. J. Australia*, **1**, 126–30.

MYKLEBUST, H. R. 1965. *The psychology of deafness: sensory deprivation, learning, and adjustment.* (2d ed.) New York: Grune & Stratton.

NATIONAL HEALTH EDUCATION COMMITTEE. 1961. *Facts on the major killing and crippling diseases in the United States today.* New York: The Committee.

NEWBY, H. A. 1964. *Audiology.* (2d ed.) New York: Appleton-Century-Crofts.

OLÉRON, P. 1950. A study of the intelligence of the deaf. *Amer. Ann. Deaf*, **95**, 179–95.

O'NEILL, J. J. 1964. *The hard of hearing.* Englewood Cliffs, N.J.: Prentice-Hall.

PENFIELD, W., and JASPER, H. 1954. *Epilepsy and the functional anatomy of the human brain.* Boston: Little Brown.

PRINGLE, M. L. K. 1964. The emotional and social adjustment of blind children. *Educ. Res.*, **6**(2), 129–38.

PUBLIC HEALTH SERVICE, U.S. DEPARTMENT OF HEALTH, EDUCATION, AND WELFARE. 1962. *Health Statistics—United States July 1959–June 1961.* Washington, D.C.: Government Printing Office.

RAINER, J. D., ALTSHULER, K. Z., KALLMAN, F. J., and DEMING, W. E. (eds.). 1963. *Family and mental health problems in deaf populations.* New York: Columbia Univer. Psychiatric Institute.

REITAN, R. M. 1959. *Effects of brain lesions in human beings.* Bloomington: Indiana Univer. Press.

SCHAPERO, M. (ed.). 1960. *Dictionary of visual science.* Philadelphia: Chilton.

STEPHENS, F. E., and DOLOWITZ, D. A. 1949. Hereditary nerve deafness. *Amer. J. hum. Genet.,* 1, 37–51.

SUPA, M., COTZIN, M., and DALLENBACH, K. M. 1944. Facial vision: The perception of obstacles by the blind. *Amer. J. Psychol.,* 57, 133–83.

SWETS, J. A. (ed.). 1964. *Signal detection and recognition by human observers: Contemporary readings.* New York: Wiley.

TAYLOR, EDITH M. 1961. *Psychological appraisal of children with cerebral defects.* Cambridge, Mass.: Harvard Univer. Press.

TIZARD, BARBARA. 1962. The personality of epileptics: A discussion of the evidence. *Psychol. Bull.,* 59, 196–210.

TOWBRIN, A. 1960. *The pathology of cerebral palsy: The causes and underlying nature of the disorder.* Springfield, Ill.: Charles C Thomas.

WAPNER, S., and WERNER, H. (eds.). 1965. *The body percept.* New York: Random House.

WRIGHT, BEATRICE A. 1960. *Physical disability: A psychological approach.* New York: Harper & Row.

NOTE: Agencies providing information and assistance for the handicapped: American Foundation for the Blind; American Hearing Society; Association for Aid of Crippled Children; Goodwill Industries of America, Inc.; Institute for the Crippled and Disabled; National Association of the Deaf; National Council on Rehabilitation; National Epilepsy League; National Foundation for Infantile Paralysis; National Multiple Sclerosis Society; National Muscular Dystrophy Association; National Society for Crippled Children and Adults, Inc.; National Society for the Prevention of Blindness; U.S. Department of Health, Education and Welfare: Public Health Service, Children's Bureau, Office of Vocational Rehabilitation; World Health Organization.

For addresses and names of additional organizations, see: Frederick G. Ruffner *et al.* (eds.). *Encyclopedia of associations.* Vol. I. *National organizations of the United States.* Vol. II, *Geographic and executive index.* (4th ed.) Detroit, Mich.: Gale Research Co., 1964. Pp. 541 ff.

11

Speech Disorders

CHARLES VAN RIPER *

The clinical psychologist will often confront individuals with speech disorders, since their incidence is relatively high and they are frequently accompanied by the kinds of emotional problems that occasion referral to the psychological clinic. Approximately 5 per cent of the school-age population (ages five to twenty-one) have serious speech defects,[1] and, although the incidence declines with age, many individuals retain their disorders throughout their lives. In our highly verbal society, deviations in speech are often severely penalized, and these penalties, together with communicative frustration, create severe problems in maladjustment. Also, since certain of the speech disorders may be produced by psychological conflicts, it is important that the psychologist should possess some of the basic information in this field.

In other chapters of this volume, speech is frequently mentioned as a diagnostic sign. The monotone that betrays the deafened, the tumbling logorrhea of the manic patient, the request of the psychiatrist for the utterance of "Methodist Episcopal" as an indicator of the extent of general paresis—all testify to the importance of abnormal speech as symptomatic of physical and emotional difficulties. Every clinical psychologist soon learns to listen to the subtler aspects of speech—the sudden changes in inflection, tempo, vibrato, or stress—which reflect his client's varying emotional reactions and offer clues to his inner state. Speech is, indeed, a tool whereby much of our therapy is accomplished and evaluated.[2]

---

* Charles Van Riper, Ph.D. (University of Iowa), Head, Department of Speech Pathology and Audiology, Western Michigan University.

[1] ASHA Committee on the Midcentury White House Conference, "Speech Disorders and Speech Correction," *Speech Hearing Disorders*, 1952, **17**, 129–37.

[2] The formal linguistic categories of grammar and syntax comprise phases of communication that are in no sense considered speech defects. The reader is referred to

Important as these considerations are, there are specific disorders of speech that every clinical psychologist will meet in his professional practice. Few of the problems dealt with in this volume will reveal the ignorance or incompetence of a therapist or diagnostician as quickly as will a speech disorder. Consider the stutterer who gives a spuriously low score on a verbal intelligence test because of his word fears, the delayed-speech case with the severe behavior problems that magically disappear as soon as he has words to express his emotions and manipulate his environment, the puzzling aphasic with his bizarre difficulties in all of the symbolic skills. These cases and many others may first be referred to the clinical psychologist, or he may be called upon to function as a member of a team that includes the speech therapist. Without some knowledge of the nature and etiology of speech disorders, he will soon find himself in difficulty and unable to function effectively as a member of the professional team.

Fortunately, a new profession, speech pathology and audiology, has developed rapidly in recent years. Modeling itself in many ways after the field of clinical psychology, it has set up standards of training and competence that enable the practicing psychologist to refer appropriate cases to its membership with confidence. In turn, psychologists may expect many referrals from these workers, since they possess sufficient background in psychology to render them sophisticated enough to recognize their limitations in such functions as psychological testing and counseling. Many of the individuals with severe speech disorders require a team approach in both diagnosis and treatment.[3]

TYPES OF SPEECH DISORDER

The disorders of speech are usually classified under the headings of (1) articulation, (2) voice, (3) rhythm, and (4) symbolization because these are the aspects of speech most often affected and because most of the abnormalities seem to fall quite naturally into these categories. An etiological classification is also sometimes used, with the speech defects divided into functional and organic groupings. *Dysarthria* and *dyslalia*,

---

Maria Lorenz and Stanley Cobb, Language behavior in psychoneurotic patients, AMA *Archneurol. Psychiat.*, 1953, **69**, 684–94; Language behavior in manic patients, *ibid.*, 1952, **67**, 763–70; and to J. C. Whitehorn and G. K. Zipf, Schizophrenic language, *ibid.*, 1943, **49**, 831–51. The projective aspect of speech is discussed in Chapter 4 of the present volume. These problems lie outside the scope of the present chapter.

[3] It should be mentioned here that there are some speech therapists, usually located in the public schools, who are certified by the state departments of special education but who are not members of the American Speech and Hearing Association and who do not possess the latter's certificate of clinical competence. A list of those in your area who are so qualified may be procured by writing the executive secretary of the American Speech and Hearing Association, in Washington, D.C.

for example, are both speech defects of articulation, and, while the pronunciation errors may be identical in a pair of cases, the former term alone is reserved for the individual with an organic disability such as cerebral palsy or aphasia. But speech is affected by so many environmental influences that we can never be certain that all or any of the abnormality is due to organic factors alone. A few individuals, to illustrate, with open clefts of the palate have been found with adequate speech due to ingenious compensatory mechanisms. Several cases with only the roots of the tongue remaining after trauma have been noted to possess intelligible speech. For these and other reasons, the symptomatic rather than the etiological classification is more often used (Van Riper, 1963).

Disorders of Articulation: Dysarthria and Dyslalia. These have a varied and inexact nomenclature including several varieties of *lisping* (laternal, interdental, nasal, occluded, and strident); *lalling,* which usually refers to the mispronunciations due to an inactive tongue tip; *baby talk* (infantile perseveration), in which the easier and earlier-acquired consonants replace the more complex and later-maturing ones; and *oral inaccuracy,* which refers to careless and slurring articulation.

Speech therapists seldom use these labels, preferring to call the disorder one of articulation and to delimit it further in terms of the type of pronunciation error involved. These errors fall within four major groups: *substitutions, omissions, distortions,* and *insertions.* They comprise the basic problems of therapy. Most articulatory speech disorders are the result of poor pedagogy on the part of parents, perceptual deficiencies, low intelligence, negativism, infantilism and emotional conflicts, organic abnormalities of the peripheral speech structure, and brain damage (Berry and Eisenson, 1956). In severe articulation disorders, the intelligibility may be so impaired as to render communication almost impossible. *Delayed speech,* usually considered a special case, since it often exhibits a marked linguistic disability in addition to the pronunciation errors, can arise from the same etiology. Its differential diagnosis from congenital aphasia is often difficult and is usually established through birth history and the presence or absence of abnormal motor development and neurological anomalies (Wood, 1964). The articulation disorders account for approximately 70 per cent of all defects of speech.

The average child does not master all of his speech sounds until the age of six, with *s, l, r, th,* and the blends being the last acquired. The milder cases (those with relatively few errors who can make the sound in isolation although not in speech) tend to overcome their pronunciation problems without formal speech therapy before the age of nine years. After this age, the incidence in terms of grade or chronological age does not seem to show much decrease without special training (Powers, 1957).

Therapy for the articulation disorders generally consists of training in auditory discrimination of the errors of substitution, omission, or distortion; phonetic training in the utterance of the correct phonemes; strengthening of the sounds in isolation; effecting a transition into meaningful speech; and making the new skills habitual. Etiological factors are attacked when still operative. Deep psychotherapy is seldom required, although some mental hygiene or release therapy often facilitates treatment (see Part IV). Public-school speech therapists usually work successfully with these cases.

Disorders of Voice (Dysphonia). These are classified according to their abnormality in terms of pitch, intensity, and timbre. Here again, the nomenclature is unsatisfactory, several terms being used for the same disorder. Some voices may be defective in one or more of these factors. The falsetto usually involves both pitch and timbre abnormalities; the individual whose habitual pitch is placed at the bottom of his normal pitch range tends to have both weak intensity and a monotone; the strident (piercingly harsh) voice may also be hypernasal. Some voice disorders may occur with concomitant articulatory deficiencies. Cleft-palate speech, for example, while characteristically nasal, is also often accompanied by lalling articulation (Morley, 1954).

Many of the disorders of voice have a psychogenic origin. Imitation, emotional stress, and faulty habits account for the majority of them. However, no voice disorder exists that cannot have either a functional or an organic cause, or both. *Aphonia,* the complete loss of voice, can be due to growths on the vocal folds, to vocal abuse and strain, or to hysteria. *Hypernasality* may be due to a soft palate of insufficient extent to close off the nasal cavity, or it can be due to identification with a parent who speaks in the same way. It, too, can be the result of a vocational pattern, as in auctioneering. *Eunchoid voice* (too high a pitch) may be due to a lack of secondary sexual development or to faulty habits of vocalization. *Hoarseness* can be due to strain resulting from utterance in the presence of strong masking noise, or it can come from paralysis or other pathology (Moore, 1957).

Therapy for the voice disorders may in some instances require the services not only of a professional speech therapist—one who holds clinical certification in the American Speech and Hearing Association— but also of the oral surgeon, the orthodontist, and the psychiatrist. Deep psychotherapy may be indicated. Therapy, once the contributing causes have been alleviated, consists in the use of various techniques for teaching a normal pitch or intensity level, or for modifying the voice quality in the direction of adequacy (Murphy, 1964). Voice therapy presents many difficult problems and should be intrusted to the expert speech therapist rather than to teachers of elocution, public speaking, or singing.

Disorders of Rhythm. Of these, stuttering (stammering) is the most frequent. There are two major diagnostic and therapeutic categories for stuttering: primary and secondary. In the first, usually found in young children, the symptoms are primarily unforced, automatic repetitions or prolongations of a sound or syllable. The child does not seem to be aware of them, nor does he react by avoidance or struggle. In the secondary stage of stuttering, avoidance and struggle do occur, and the symptomatology is often bizarre and grotesque when approach and release reactions become conditioned to the cues precipitating the blockings. The secondary stutterer shows marked fears of both words and speaking situations. Often, personality changes occur as the abnormality grows in severity and the social penalties increase (Murphy and Fitzsimmons, 1960).

The disorder usually arises early in the life of the individual, at about two to four years of age. According to Robinson (1964), if the child can be kept from developing the secondary reactions, the prognosis is favorable. The symptoms tend to disappear before puberty. Secondary stuttering does not show this characteristic. The etiology of stuttering is diverse. It may develop from the normal hesitations of a child learning to speak, especially if these are invested with parental anxiety or if they result in frustration. It may result from emotional conflicts involving speech or the organs of speech (Glauber, 1958). In a minority of cases, it may be due to a native deficiency in the ability of the individual to perform temporal patterns of movement with speech or precision (*dysphemia*) (West, 1958). Whatever the original cause or causes, the disorder seems to follow much the same course of development into the secondary stage. Therapy is difficult, and relapse is frequent.

Therapy for the primary stutterer consists largely of parental counseling seeking to remove the disruptive influence of environmental pressures, release therapy for the child, increasing his basic security, and in some instances training in desensitization to the communicative factors causing breakdown. Treatment for the secondary stutterer may involve deep psychotherapy and certainly long-term speech therapy by a competent professional speech therapist. Many of the acquired struggle and avoidance reactions may be eliminated through careful retraining. The stutterer must be taught to accept his stuttering as a problem and to modify the symptoms toward an acceptable nonfluency.

Among other disorders of rhythm, we may include cluttering (Weiss, 1964), speech broken and distorted by excessive rate; the speech in multiple sclerosis (see Chapter 10) where a curious scanning of words, syllable by syllable, occurs; and the speech of cerebral palsy, which is marked by athetoid tremors and uncoordinated gasps that interrupt the even flow of utterance (McDonald, 1964).

Disorders of Symbolization. These are all classified under the general heading of *aphasia.*. Aphasia causes a loss in the ability to send or receive meanings. All of the language functions may be involved: reading, writing, speaking, and comprehending speech, cartoons, or even a gesture. Certain of these may, of course, remain relatively untouched. Nonlanguage deviations can also occur, such as loss of memory, loss of attention and concentration, excessive preservation of responses, and loss of ability to handle abstractions or symbols of any kind (Eisenson, 1954).

There are many terms used in describing the various patterns of abnormality found in aphasia. Among those most often used today are *receptive aphasia,* difficulty in comprehending verbal or written language symbols; *expressive aphasia,* difficulty in finding the words the aphasiac wishes to utter, inability to write, calculate, or spell, and the like; *apraxia,* difficulty in executing meaningful movements; and *agnosia,* loss of the ability to recognize stimulus objects as meaningful. The cause of aphasia is injury to the brain cortex. This may be traumatic, as in the case of a shrapnel injury, or it may come from a vascular accident, the breaking of a blood vessel, or the presence of a tumor, among other similar pathological agents (Wepman, 1951).

The problem of aphasia in children presents many difficulties. In those cases in which the child had previously been speaking well but became aphasic as the result of severe illness with prolonged high fever or has suffered brain trauma as from an automobile accident, the diagnosis is readily available. However, the psychologist who works in a setting such as a child guidance clinic or in the public schools or in a children's hospital may expect to meet many children who present delayed speech and language or reading and writing difficulties that are puzzling and atypical. These are often termed the "brain-damaged" or "perceptually impaired"—labels that leave much to be desired. They have also been called "aphasoid" because of the similarity to the adult aphasic. They tend to do poorly on verbal tests of intelligence, showing marked scatter, but, even on such instruments as the WISC, their performance is often strange and inconsistent. New tests such as the Illinois Test of Psycholinguistic Abilities are being designed to define both quantitatively and qualitatively the symbolic deficits these children show. The psychologist should be alert to the possibilities of misdiagnosis if only the usual batteries of tests are administered. The differential diagnosis (Wood, 1964) should include consideration of such possibilities as (1) high-frequency hearing loss, (2) childhood schizophrenia, (3) mental retardation, (4) negativism, and (5) delayed maturation in speech and language, as well as (6) aphasia. The whole problem of aphasia, still far from being understood, needs much investigation by psychologists. For the best current review of the disorder, see the book by Schuell, Jenkins, and Jimenes-Pabon (1964).

I shall now present two case studies, which will illustrate typical problems in the field of speech pathology and illuminate the role of the psychologist in their solution.

CASE STUDY OF AN APHASIC

This report is presented in the manner of its development as well as in terms of the daily routine in the speech clinic, the better to illustrate these functions.

Dear Sir:

Dr. . . . ., our company physician, has suggested that we refer one of our clients, Mr. J., aged 35, married, no children, to you for psychological examination. Mr. J. was seriously injured in an auto accident three years ago and we, as his insurance company, wish to determine whether or not he can be freed from his present status of total disability.

As of this date, Mr. J. is neither employed nor employable, because of a brain injury resulting from the accident. It is described in the enclosed neurologist's report. The injury prevents him from all communication, either written or oral. Our company physician, however, feels that the neurologist's report is unduly pessimistic and that some measure of rehabilitation can be effected. The man impresses us as being quite intelligent, although communicatively helpless. One arm is still paralyzed. Because he is without speech, we have been unable to

secure either self-employment or outside employment for him.

What we require from you is an estimate of the extent of language loss, the amount of mental deterioration, a statement of the emotional effect of the injury with reference to his employability, a prognosis as to restoration of speech and/or writing, the type of training needed, and the approximate cost of the psychologic or speech therapy. When can you see him?

The insurance company provided us the neurologist's report based upon an examination just prior to the referral:

Expressive aphasia of three years duration due to trauma in the left frontal-parietal region. Upper right arm paralyzed. Right leg partially affected. No hemianopsia. Some mirror movement of opposite extremity when right leg is moved. Some apraxia. Electroencephalography corroborated locus of injury. No further involvement. No epileptiform spikes. Language function markedly impaired. Comprehension fair. Hyperactive reflexes. *General impression:* little possibility of improvement. Prognosis for recovery of language function definitely poor. Cranioplasty is adequate.

This was our reply:

Dear Sir:

We will be able to examine your client, Mr. J., at 2:30 P.M., Friday, June 30th, and to attempt to procure the information you desire. However, the psychological examinations of an aphasic are dependent upon many variables (rapport, fatigue, emotional state) and usually several sessions are required. We also wish to interview Mrs. J. before we see the patient. A preliminary case history and an exploratory interview are always necessary with these cases. If you can arrange to have her at the office at 9:30 A.M. on the same day, we can accept the case.

Interview with Mrs. J. Mrs. J. was an intelligent, attractive woman of thirty who prior to marriage had been a high school teacher of Latin and French. She was cooperative and easy to interview. She had tried to do some reading on aphasia in the medical literature but without too much comprehension. She brought with her the first page of a two-page medical report made by the attending physician at the time of injury. The second page had unfortunately been lost. Mrs. J. reported that the physician who had done the operation had died in the interim. The report read as follows:

Multiple fractures of the skull localized primarily in the parietal region but extending over the vault, were shown by the Roentgen examination. Convulsions proceeding from the right side were frequent. A decompression operation in the area of injury demonstrated laceration of subdural tissue. Multiple hematoma and hemorrhaging. Vessels were tied, necrotic tissue, blood clots and bone splinters were removed. Babinski reaction on right side.

The following is a summary of information provided by Mrs. J.:

The patient was a right-handed male, formerly a teacher in a small college, who had been injured in an automobile accident at the age of thirty-two. The skull had been fractured in the area of the left parietal lobe, resulting in a coma of six days' duration. The injury and subsequent operation had necessitated the removal of about 6 cc. of cortical tissue. This portion of the skull was eventually covered by a silver plate. Total loss of the power to speak resulted and was accompanied by paralysis of the right arm and leg, and a few epileptic seizures of the *grand mal* type at first, which soon gave way to minor *petit mal* episodes, finally clearing within four months. Occasional temporary paresthesias appeared and disappeared during this period.

Recovery of the ability to use the right leg in walking took place about the sixth month after the injury, and the patient became able to utter spontaneously a few words. Most of these were profane interjections, although during the past three years he did upon occasion repeat a phrase or two when his wife tried to teach him to talk. He often moved his lips as though talking to himself, but used gestures or an occasional attempt at writing to make his needs known. She claimed, however, that he could understand everything and was able to comprehend printed

although not written materials. She insisted that he was still very intelligent and felt that he could learn to talk and write again with proper
training.

With reference to personality attributes Mrs. J. reported frequent alternations of euphoria and depression, the latter accompanied by vocal-
ized sobbing. She described his former personality as introvertive, shy,
sensitive, and retiring. "His teaching and writing [Mr. J. was the author
of a textbook on foreign-language teaching and of numerous technical
articles] were his life, his hobby, and his major source of self-respect,"
she said. "That's why it's so tough on him now."

Besides the income from his disability insurance, the family had no
other resources, its savings having been used up in medical fees. Mrs. J.
had done some tutoring to augment the finances and wanted to return to
teaching. She had not done so, fearing further convulsions and because
her husband "hates to let me out of his sight." (This phrase was spoken
with evident irritation.) The insurance company had tried to get Mr. J.
interested in raising rabbits, but the project had failed after one litter
had died. "He hates all animals. All he loves is books. He sits for hours,
holding one, pretending to read. I think he does read the paper though,
judging from his eye movements." Mr. J., according to his wife, worried
over finances and disliked the sight of money.

Mrs. J. expressed her willingness to assist in the language retraining:

I'll be glad to go to every training session with him, if it will help. I doubt
whether he will ever be the same again, but any improvement should make my
life easier. I've tried hard to help him, but often I think I just make him worse.
I don't know what to do. Do you feel he really can be helped?

In reply to her query, we were cautious. We told her that it was impossible for us to give her any real assurance without examining her husband, that aphasia takes many forms, and that there were many gradations
in severity. However, we also said that some aphasics had been able to
recover remarkable amounts of language behavior through proper training
and self-help. We referred her to two articles: William Rose's "A Physician's Account of His Own Aphasia," [4] and Colonel Lawrence Bixby's
Comeback from a Brain Operation.[5] We also suggested that for comprehensive background information, she read Wepman's *Recovery from
Aphasia* (1951). Finally, in terminating the interview, we asked her to
return with her husband for his afternoon appointment. She was told
that we would want her to share in the initial interview but not in the
testing sessions. We also asked her if he could comprehend our instructions and for any behavioral signs that might indicate resistance, frustration, or catastrophic reactions on the part of the patient. She replied:

[4] *J. Speech Hearing Disorders*, 1948, **13**, 294–305.
[5] *Harpers*, 1952, **205**, 69–73.

He can understand anything if you go slow enough and don't talk too complicatedly. Give him time. Sometimes, after you ask him a question, he seems to have to say it to himself before he understands. Watch his bad arm. If it begins to lift up a little, he's getting too tense. His lower lip quivers, too. If you push him too hard he'll start to sob or laugh and then he can't stop, even when he wants to. He gets tired pretty easily so don't give him too much at one time.

Planning the Initial Interview. Here, we were faced with several problems: Should we merely try to get a general impression of the problem through interviewing and informal exploration, or should we subject him to a thorough testing program? What testing procedures were available and advisable? How should we define our role as agents of the insurance company to the client, who was probably expecting some sort of therapy program? What should be the minimal objectives of the first interview? We decided to make the interview an exploratory one in which we would try to assess the degree of expressive and receptive language loss, the patient's attitude toward his problem, and his drive toward recovery, and to prepare him for further testing. The study of the aphasic's defects is done best when the approach is flexible and when treatment is viewed as a "continuous psychological examination."

Summary of First Interview with Mr. J. Mr. and Mrs. J. were prompt for their appointment. He walked in with only a slight limp and sat down without difficulty. Speaking casually but in short sentences and with frequent pauses, I explained to him that I wanted to see what could be done to help him, and that some of the things I would ask him to do would probably be too difficult. He was assured that this would not matter, inasmuch as I was more interested in what he could do than in what he could not do. I began by testing comprehension, using such sentences as "Is this my nose?" and "Is the pencil on the book?" These were all understood. The client nodded and gestured to indicate that he could do them easily. We then asked him to follow our directions, using commands such as those described by Eisenson (1954): "Close your eyes." "Shake my hand." He was able to perform all single commands of this type as well as all those of the twofold type: "Stretch our your arm, and wave your hand." However, he failed on the first two of the threefold directions: "Put the key on the chair, shut the door, and bring me the box," so I returned to a single command in order to end this activity with a success. Mr. J. reacted to failure by looking helplessly toward his wife and shaking his head sadly.

Remembering that Henry Head had mentioned that writing one's name is easier and more automatic than any other form of spontaneous writing and that, accordingly, this skill was the last to disappear and the first to reappear, I took out a blank check and wrote my name on the line.

I then tore it up and put the pieces in the waste basket. I then asked Mr. J. to do the same. This he did, shaking his head negatively, although with great effort and poor control. He was elated over the writing performance, showing it to his wife, who seemed surprised and pleased. Then he held the paper in his teeth, tearing it apart, but keeping the signature piece. He reached in his pocket and pulled out a dollar bill. He made a motion as though to tear this, then shook his head to indicate that he knew the value of a signed check. He overlaughed when I indicated my understanding of his pantomime. Mr. J. failed in copying single words.

Emptying some pennies onto the desk, I arranged them in sequences: one penny, two pennies, three pennies, etc., then asked him to do the same. He was successful up to six, then repeated the six arrangement three more times. I observed his lips moving as he touched each pile, so I began to count aloud with him: "one, two, three, four, five, six, seven . . ." I hesitated at this point. He whispered "eight, nine, ten" quite distinctly. When I asked him to count aloud, he refused. His wife said quickly, "He just can't do that." I then gave him some cards on which were typed or written some of the commands previously used. He was able to perform all of those that he had understood orally, thus indicating his ability to comprehend visual symbols, but he failed in reading all the script commands. When he was asked to try to read the typed (printed) cards aloud, he refused, and thereafter appeared to have more trouble in comprehending them.

Mrs. J. was asked to help me demonstrate the next activity. I asked her to repeat in a whisper the word that I pronounced aloud as I pointed out and named several articles about the office. Mr. J. watched the scene closely, and it was apparent that he too was whispering or forming some of the words his wife was repeating. When Mr. J. was then asked to perform the activity, he had only two successes: "chair" and "picture," the latter sounding more like "pipper," insofar as we could hear it. On many of the others, he made little effort, merely shaking his head.

He was then told that I wished to examine his mouth. I put on a head mirror and stuck a tongue depressor in his mouth, commanding him to say "ah." This he did perfectly. No sign of paralysis was noted. I also had him repeat most of the vowels and many consonants in this way, and one word ("no"). Noticing that he was tiring, I praised him for his performance, said that I felt encouraged about the possibility of progress, and asked him if he would like to come back for more testing and trial therapy another time. At this point he became greatly excited, laughed, and uttered his first spontaneous speech: "No . . . oh . . . goddam . . . no . . . I . . . uh . . . huh . . . no . . . I mean . . ." and then began to cry, pointing to his mouth and shaking his head alternately positively and negatively. "He means 'yes, yes,'" said Mrs. J. "He wants to come back. He didn't mean to say 'no.'" Another appointment was made for him, for Monday, July 3d.

The following tentative impression was arrived at during this interview: "Intelligence adequate. Disorder primarily expressive rather than receptive. Some hysterical aphonia. Aspiration level low. Unstable. With adequate rapport and time, therapy should enable this patient to recover usable speech. Further examination and trial therapy indicated."

Subsequent Testing. Further sessions were held with Mr. J., and in these we tried to use more standardized procedures of examination, despite the objection by Wepman (1951), who holds that formal objective testing is not particularly useful in planning and carrying out therapy. "Most patients are frustrated by the tests and offer strenuous objections to them." We felt that, since Weisenberg and McBride (1938) had been able to give their subjects the intricate series of tests they describe in their monograph, our obligation to the patient and to our employer, the insurance company, necessitated an equally thorough investigation. Throughout the series of tests, we were, nonetheless, continuously alert to protect our patient against too much frustration. We constantly inserted activities in which he was successful, whenever failure occurred. We minimized the failures and magnified the successes. Our success is evident from the fact that only twice during the entire period did catastrophic reactions occur. Mr. J. enjoyed the sessions and looked forward to them.

We were never able to give any test's items in their usual order, nor was any test given completely. We followed Goldstein's dictum that a patient's pathology is not a defect in performance but is, rather, to be found in the impairment of a definite and normal procedure to solve a task. Often on the intelligence tests we had to provide several responses and ask Mr. J. to nod his head when the correct one was given, a procedure of whose dangers we were well aware. Nevertheless, with the aphasic, these tests are more likely to give spuriously low scores than the opposite.

The following general scales were administered: The Wechsler-Bellevue, the Stanford-Binet, and the Bender Gestalt. The Halstead-Wepman Aphasia Screening Test (1949) was given almost in its entirety, as was the Goldstein Stick Test (1948). Certain items from the tests used by Eisenson (1954) and by Schuell (1955) were also administered. The results are presented below.

GENERAL TESTS. Only the performance battery of the Wechsler-Bellevue was given. Mr. J. failed completely in the Digit Symbol subtest, writing the number "5" below each of the numbers. He often erased this num-

ber, but, on returning to the task, he again put down, "5." He appeared to
know that he was doing it incorrectly. On the Block Design subtest, he
had several successes; one of the more complicated patterns was mirrored
but otherwise was correct. Again he seemed to realize that his patterns
were in error, for he reshuffled the blocks and tried to rearrange them.
In the Picture Completion subtest, Mr. J. failed on the first item, pointing
to his own nose over and over again, trying to convey a meaning we were
unable to grasp. On the Object Assembly subtest, he succeeded only in
assembling the face correctly. As he did so, he felt his own eyes and
nose with his fingers while arranging the jigsaw pieces. He did remarkably well on the Picture Arrangement problems, accompanying this
activity with a constant mumbled jargon in which no word could be
identified. Throughout the performance on this battery, he tended to
react impulsively and without forethought. Much self-correction, however, was evident. No total score was computed. When the Porteus
Maze Test was administered, he failed on even the simplest patterns,
partly because of the unsteadiness of his left hand but largely because he
tended to persevere in a given direction. Mr. J.'s performance on the
Bender Gestalt Test is reproduced in Fig. 11–1 and is best characterized,
briefly, as highly perseverative and as showing deterioration to more
primitive forms, and a strong tendency toward closure. Energy output
was low, with subsequent economy of effort.

Test performance in general tended to support Mrs. J.'s testimony that
the patient had earlier reacted intelligently in all ordinary life situations,
having exhibited excellent memory for people and places, and having
been able to locate and replace a defective resistor in a table radio. Also,
he had read with pleasure such magazines as *Harper's* and *The Saturday
Review of Literature*. It was concluded that he currently showed marked
disability in symbolic functioning, especially in activities involving verbalization and abstract design. Analysis of test performance, awareness of
errors, comprehension of instructions, and data from his social history all
indicated sufficient general intelligence to make therapy advisable.

SPECIAL TESTS FOR APHASIA. The Halstead-Wepman Test was given,
although not with the items in the usual order. The results are summarized in Table 11–1. During this portion of the examination, Mr. J.'s
performance remarkably improved, with better rapport as the test proceeded. The absence of Mrs. J. seemed to ease the situation and to
facilitate language output. Mr. J. occasionally repeated a word or phrase
after the examiner during the instructions and uttered a few spontaneous
words and phrases. The testing was structured as an experience in discovery of what powers he did not know he possessed. This was accepted
by him. Results corroborated previous impressions that if he could be
given speech therapy, a marked improvement in the whole picture would

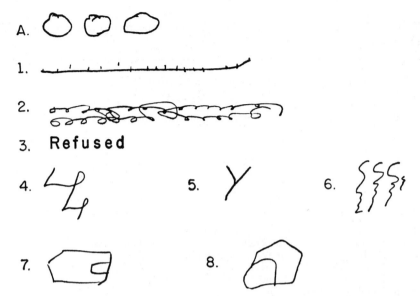

Fig. 11–1. Drawings made by the client, Mr. J., on the Bender Gestalt Test.

result. The agnosia, though present, was definitely not a major obstacle. The dysarthria, although we had no definite estimate of its severity, did not seem to be too profound, since much of the spontaneous speech was intelligible. At the same time, the apraxia appeared severe, preventing us from predicting probable success in treatment. It was apparent, however, that one retarding factor was his unwillingness to attempt speech, consequent to his defeatest attitude toward speech production. Trial speech therapy, nonetheless, seemed indicated.

The Goldstein Stick Test was next administered. This consists of stimulus figures made up of short sticks arranged in different designs of increasing complexity. The subject must copy the figures in one situation, and, in a second, he must draw them from memory. Here, Mr. J. tended to translate the abstract geometrical designs into representations of concrete objects, with the possibility that inner speech served as a vehicle for memory. Strong tendencies toward closure and perseveration, as in the Bender Gestalt Test, were noted. Little amnesia was noted in those instances in which the figures could be given meaning. Gestural language was fairly intact, perhaps to prove useful in later speech therapy. There was some indication that the apraxia was less profound in writing than in speech.

From the Weisenberg-McBride (1935) monograph we selected the Mirror Reading Test, which Mr. J. failed. We also asked him to write

Table 11–1. Summary Description of Client's Performances on the Halstead-Wepman Screening Test for Aphasia *

I. *Agnosias*
   a. Very minor defect in visual form; failed 1 of 10 items.
   b. No visual number defect.
   c. No visual letter defect.
   d. Minor alexia in silent reading; failed all items when asked to read aloud.
   e. Visual size was satisfactory.
   f. Visual color was satisfactory.
   g. Audiovisuo-kinetic function markedly defective.
   h. Auditory verbal—good performance, with delay on two items.
   i. Auditory music—good. No failures.
   j. Auditory number—failed two items.
   k. Tactile—refused.
   l. Body (topagnosia)—no failures.

II. *Apraxias*
   a. General (nonverbal)—generally good; failed one of nine items.
   b. Verbal—marked disability; failed all but two items.
   c. Writing (Agraphia)—marked disability; failed six of eight items; used left hand; used gestures to indicate he could not write.
   d. Number—refused.
   e. Calculation—refused.
   f. Construction—refused.
   g. Ideokinetic test—refused.

III. *Anomia*
   Attempted all items, but used jargon phrase "uhbugga," or "no," or "Jesus." Recognized errors after they were uttered. Became disturbed.

IV. *Dysarthria*
   Occasional substitution of "t" for "s" in word "Jesus." One burst of meaningless jabber, approximately ten syllables in length, with marked repetition.

V. *Paraphasia*
   a. Paragrammatism—not enough speech to determine.
   b. Agrammatism—not enough speech to determine.

---

* Halstead-Wepman Screening Test outline, reprinted with permission granted by The University of Chicago Press, publishers.

from dictation with his eyes closed the following words: *run, top, red,* and *book.* The first three were meaningless scribbles. The last was written "bakka." Only the first item of a sentence-completion test was filled in correctly: "I see you. Can you see ———?" He wrote the word "mme" in the blank space, saying it aloud at the same time. We were able to get him to repeat a few words after us, if he touched the object with his good hand and said it in unison on the second attempt. *Finger* was "finner," *pen* was "pen," and *shoe* was "s-soo-, no, soooo." He seemed both surprised and elated with this achievement, so we placed earphones on his head. We then dictated certain of Schuell's (1964) sentences through them, with moderate amplification, while he repeated them through a microphone attached to our own headset. A good deal of speech resulted, two samples of which follow:

Sharpen the pencil	"appen pinso"
The sun is shining	"sunny shine sunsine"

This repetitive speech was not evoked when Mr. J. could hear his own voice through a loudspeaker. He was able to count aloud to ten without error when a masking noise was fed into his earphones. No dysarthria was evident in this performance. He did not appear to realize he had spoken, and he was unable to count to ten when the earphones were removed.

Interpretatively, much of Mr. J.'s difficulty seems to reside in the monitoring of his motor output. When this is decreased or masked in such a way that the performance cannot be immediately evaluated, he does much better. A good deal of residual language remains and can be made available in either spoken or written form.

Trial Therapy. The ability of Mr. J. to speak spontaneously had been demonstrated only in sporadic instances. We felt it wise to investigate this problem further. In the final session, we initiated a program of "parallel talking," a technique used by speech therapists for retraining aphasics, delayed-speech cases, and mental retardates. This technique consists of having the therapist verbalize a running commentary on the client's voluntary behavior until its novelty has worn off and the patient has accepted it as entirely natural. Then the therapist leaves a sentence or phrase unfinished, and the client, through his need for closure, often finishes it himself. The therapist distracts the patient, ignores the voluntary utterance, and returns to his commentary as before, then repeats the process. Often, the therapist describes his own behavior in the same fashion in a form of *self-talk*. With Mr. J., we began by using self-talk, then switched to the parallel talking. It was highly successful. Mr. J. uttered not only single words but whole phrases and one additional sentence. He had gone over to the doorway, turned on the light, and then turned it off. As he had done so, we had verbalized his behavior in this way: "Get up . . . go over by door . . . ; turn on . . ." Mr. J. said, "light and tun off some more. Light a gone."

In reviewing our findings prior to the preparation of a report for the insurance company, we used Eisenson's (1949) criteria to check our estimate of Mr. J.'s prognosis. Eisenson holds that prognosis appears good for young aphasic patients whose disturbances are associated with traumatic causes, whose personalities are or have been outgoing, for whom a retraining program is started early, and who have relatively modest levels of aspiration. He considers persistent euphoria, excessively rigid and psychopathic-like personalities, and overdependence on the clinician as negative indicators. It is apparent that Mr. J. possesses a few of the favorable signs. He responded so favorably to our trial therapy and to the entire testing program that we felt speech therapy was certainly indicated. This we stated in our report to the insurance company, which promptly employed a speech therapist with whom we had a professional consultation regarding our findings. Three hourly therapy periods were provided each week for four months. At the end of this interval, Mr. J. was able to converse freely in all unemotional situations, although he occasionally groped for words. His oral reading improved markedly, although comprehension at times presented more difficulty than did silent reading. Writing and calculating remained very deficient. He is currently receiving further retraining in these areas. Mr. J. is presently employed as a part-time receptionist in a social agency. Emotionally, he has made an excellent adjustment.

CASE STUDY OF A SECONDARY STUTTERER

Miss Audrey Johnson, an eighteen-year-old stutterer, was referred to the university speech clinic by the public-school speech therapist with whom she had worked in high school. At the clinic, two diagnostic interviews were conducted that explored the nature of her speech problem. Information was sought about specific word and situational fears, the feelings and thoughts she had about herself as a stutterer, significant interpersonal relationships that might influence the severity of her problem, and the ways in which her stuttering was ego-alien or ego-syntonic. Questions were asked that were designed to assess her ego strength, level of anxiety, and motivation for change. A psychological test battery composed of the Rorschach, TAT, Bender Gestalt, and MMPI was administered by the clinic's psychologist in addition to a sentence-completion test specifically designed for stutterers. An intensive exploration of her social and problem history was conducted by the psychiatric social worker. Evaluation of these data suggested that some of the problems Miss Johnson was experiencing were related to the stormy issues that confront the late-blooming adolescent, and, as a result, it was decided to complement her speech therapy by referring her for concurrent psychotherapy. This psychotherapy was carried out in the psychological clinic of the university by a clinical psychologist.

Case-History Summary

Name: Audrey Johnson   Date of birth: January 14, 1947
Address: 9792 Bolt St.
Referred by: Fred Levy, public-school speech therapist
Reason for referral: Stuttering

OBSERVATIONS OF SPEECH BEHAVIOR:

Occasional stuttering blocks were observed. These were character-istically of very short duration (one to two seconds) and consisted of silent mouth postures with rapid tremors. At the moment of stut-tering, Audrey would look away from her listener, and she would resume eye contact only when the block had passed. Other than a brief, rapid exhalation used to terminate the fixation, the blocking itself is marked by few overt signs of struggle. No signs of discom-fort, such as blushing, were observed to follow the stuttering. In-creases in communicative stress generated by the interviewer did not result in an increase in the frequency or severity of her stuttering. Her fluent speech is rapid and uncomfortable for the listener to hear and is full of colloquialisms and pet, adolescent phrases with special meanings. She tends to jump quickly from one thought to another as if feeling rushed to finish what she is saying. She was not difficult to follow but did give the impression of seldom coming directly to the point. She cried easily and appropriately, but, at times, she continued to cry even though she had shifted away from the topic that brought on the tears.

FAMILY RELATIONSHIPS:

Father: Audrey's father is a forty-seven-year-old high school–educated factory worker. He tends to be quiet and participates little in social affairs outside the immediate family. He characteristically relates to Audrey by teasing her in a joking way. He prefers Audrey to her two younger brothers, and, in family disputes, takes her part. At times of crisis, she turns to him for assistance. In recent years, he has become critical of her stuttering, and he constantly tells her to slow down when she is talking. He is concerned about her dating and has set up strict rules about when and with whom she can date. He was very anxious when Audrey decided to go away to school. He objects to his wife's working and has made this issue a chronic source of family tension. He is described by others (not Audrey) as an impatient person. In the past several years, he has suffered from duodenal ulcers. He has no speech defect.

Mother: Mrs. Johnson is a forty-nine-year-old high school teacher with a master's degree in education. She met her husband during World War II, when he was stationed near her home. They were married in 1945. After the birth of her third child, in 1954, Mrs. Johnson returned to school, receiving her master's degree and teaching credentials in 1959. She has worked steadily since then. She is described as a verbally aggres-sive, domineering person who insists on having her own way. She is penurious and carefully scrutinizes family requests for funds. She does not express her feelings easily and tends to relate to Audrey in intellectual terms. She places no special emphasis on Audrey's stuttering and gives the impression of trying to ignore it. She sees her daughter as an emotional person who complains easily and unnecessarily. She has no speech defect.

Siblings: Don, sixteen, has been a severe behavior problem in school. He is truant, gets into fights easily, and neglects his schoolwork. He is very fond of Audrey, and she is the only family member who can control him. She frequently acts as a mediator between Don and his father. Don, in turn, is supportive of Audrey and is probably the person most aware of Audrey's feelings about her speech. Don stuttered for a brief period in the sixth grade but has no speech problem currently. Audrey was seen by the family as being responsible for Don's temporary period of nonfluency.

John, the youngest of the children, is eleven years old. He is described as quiet and shy. He has done fairly well in school and does not show any of the behavior that characterizes his older brother. He has no speech defect.

Other Significant Figures: When the Johnsons first moved to the city, they lived for a time in the home of a maternal aunt. She has always been very fond of Audrey and has singled her out for special attention. During a particular stormy period in the life of the family, Audrey was sent to live with her for several weeks. During periods of illness, the aunt moves into the Johnsons' home and cares for the children. She has no speech defect.

DEVELOPMENTAL HISTORY:

Pregnancy and birth were essentially normal. Bottle-fed. Sitting, crawling, and walking within normal limits. Toilet trained at fifteen months with some bed-wetting until age four. First word at thirteen months. Two-word phrases at fifteen months. Usual childhood diseases with no complications. Severely injured in an automobile accident at age nine. Hospitalized three weeks and confined to bed at home for four months in a body cast. No sequelae. Mother was working part time during this period and going to school. Major responsibility for care was left to the maternal aunt. Audrey missed one semester of school and felt "left out" and "alone" when she returned to the fourth grade. Peer relationships prior to this time were reported as good.

SCHOOL HISTORY:

Audrey remembers kindergarten with mixed feelings. She had two teachers. She was very fond of one and disliked the other. She remembers particularly the impatience of one teacher and having been picked up and held lovingly by the other. The first grade was uneventful. Of the second grade, she remembers being slapped by the teacher for dis-obedience. Audrey's mother came to school to discuss the matter, and the teacher denied the incident. Audrey reports that she was always afraid to get up and talk in this class. Audrey missed one semester of the fourth grade owing to injuries received in the automobile accident. The following summer, with the help of her mother, she made up the missed classes. The fifth and sixth grades are marked by her first clear memory of stuttering. At that time, she was also "nervous" with her peers. She can remember walking to school with a girl friend and stuttering. Audrey moved from her grammar school one-half year before she was to graduate. She felt upset by the move and again had feelings of being "left out" and "alone." Some scholastic problems are reported in the seventh grade. Audrey failed an arithmetic class. In the eighth grade, she received speech therapy for the first time, without result. In the tenth grade, she again received speech therapy for her stuttering. She liked both ex-periences. In high school, she had a public-speaking teacher who is remembered as an impatient, tense, and irritable man. She stuttered much more with this teacher than with any other. Since coming to the university, she has experienced academic trouble with an elementary mathematics course. This difficulty seems to be associated not with the teacher but with the class content. She enjoys her freshman public-speaking course because the teacher is warm and friendly to her.

SOCIAL DEVELOPMENT:

Audrey describes herself as having few close friends of either sex. She was never a popular girl in school. She feels she has continually been forced to break off and then re-establish new peer relationships. This has been difficult for her to do and has been the source of many personal feelings of inadequacy and self-doubt. She did not begin to date until her last year in high school. After dating several boys once or twice she "began to go steady." This relationship was broken up by the boy shortly before graduation. Her sexual experience has been minimal, limited to careful caressings. She is presently living in a dormitory at the university, and this is her first time away from home. She was homesick at first but now finds things to do on the weekends so that she will not have to return to her family. She has not dated since entering the uni-versity but would like to do so.

SPEECH HISTORY:

Neither Audrey nor her family has any clear memories of any stutter-ing prior to the fourth grade. Mrs. Johnson has suggested that Audrey began to have some difficulty with her speech shortly after the slapping incident in the second grade, but she does not remember it as stuttering.

Audrey remembers feeling reluctant to ask her mother for assistance while she was recovering from the automobile accident. This speech reluctance was more noticeable when her mother had to be interrupted from something in order to care for Audrey. Audrey felt much more at ease when her aunt was caring for her. She reports that, even now, her aunt "babies her" when she stutters. Of the fifth and sixth grades, she remembers feelings of embarrassment and shame associated with stuttering in class. At this point, she began actively to seek ways of avoiding routine classroom speech assignments; for example, questions from the teacher would be dismissed with an "I don't know," even though she knew the answer. Audrey felt that during junior high school, her speech became progressively worse as the result of the confluence of several factors: the first, the change of schools in the sixth grade; the second, the increasing tension between her parents, which culminated in threats of divorce; the third, being blamed by her father for causing her brother's speech defect. She describes this period: "I was disgusted with myself. It seemed to me that any time I wanted to say anything relatively important I would have a block."

At the present time, Audrey does not feel her speech is as severe a problem as it once was. Much of her current concern about speaking relates to her anticipatory fears of stuttering. "I never know when it's going to pop up." For this reason, she is fearful about entering teaching as a profession. Her fears about speaking in class are primarily focused on her education courses. She has a specific situational fear of the telephone. Both calling and answering are difficult for her. She has specific fears of stuttering on plosive sounds (p, b, t, d, k, g) but reports no specific word fears. Men, strangers, peers, or "relaxed" people are easier to talk to than women, friends, authority figures, or "impatient" people. Audrey does not stutter when she is angry. She feels that her stuttering will prevent her from realizing her full academic potential, and that she may continue to be misunderstood and unappreciated by other people because of it. She feels that it is unfair that she should have to continue to evaluate every relationship and speaking experience in terms of her stuttering. This thought angers her and is part of her reason for wanting therapy.

PSYCHOLOGICAL-TEST RESULTS:

The following interpretations of test data were provided by the clinic's psychologist:
Bender Gestalt.

The difficulty Audrey experiences in relating efficiently to her environment is apparent in her disorganized responses to this test. We would suspect that this person has trouble organizing the events of her life, over-reacting to some situations, and unduly inhibiting herself and restricting her behavior in others. Perceptual distortions are apparent. We suspect intense feelings of anxiety in terms of task consummation. Perseveration and response rigidity are prominent.

Draw-a-Person Test.

Andrey's sexual and social roles as revealed by the Draw-A-Person are poorly defined with little evidence of genital psychosexuality. For example, it is difficult to tell whether she sees men as feminine or women as masculine. She clearly isolates impulses and feelings from body parts to which they may be related. Thus it is possible that she is totally unaware of her stimulus value as a woman. She is probably experiencing anxiety in social relationships and may be relying on outmoded social skills to insure peer acceptance. She may also be literally "closing her eyes" to significant interpersonal cues which, if acted upon appropriately, would lead to more satisfactory adjustment.

Thematic Apperception Test.

The majority of the themes in Audrey's TAT material are replete with open and unsatisfied adolescent sexual fantasy. Again and again she conceives of herself as a lonely young girl who becomes infatuated with an attractive, charming and married Knight Errant. Despite the obvious investment that she has made in developing this technique, there are clear and overt signs that fantasy is becoming less and less satisfying as a reducer of sexual tension. For example in card 2 she dramatizes the sexual plight of the adolescent who is at once "too young and too old." In 6 GF the girl in the scene imagines that the man has approached her to pick her up. The man however, is only interested in a "match." In these stories as in the others, the outcomes are sad and she is again hurt, alone and afraid. Unquestionably her inability to achieve mature sexuality is related to a strict and punitive mother who is viewed by Audrey as quick to prejudge and punish her even though the circumstances might not warrant it. Some of the mother's influence is also seen in comments which identify story characteristics as "too smug" or "too sure of herself." Taken in the context of the other thematic material Audrey may be feeling that she is losing in her battle for independence and that the only adequate solution may lie in the total acceptance of her mother's values.

Minnesota Multiphasic Personality Inventory.

The MMPI reflects the character structures of an anxious, resentful and confused adolescent. The problems of sexual role are again highlighted by Audrey's stereotyped portrayal of herself as a "feminine" woman. That this role is not comfortable for her is seen in the suspicious and resentful way in which she approaches people. Unquestionably she feels trapped and angry in many social relationships because of the confusion which the behavior of others creates in her. She is not yet capable of recognizing that she can facilitate the satisfaction of her own needs through the manipulation of others. Further she is not aware that she relies heavily on over-learned, excessively conforming social patterns in her dealings with people. There are some tendencies toward symptom formation of a hypochondriacal kind.

Rorschach.

The Rorschach most clearly portrays the untapped psychological resources which are available to Audrey. Her form level is good and occasionally responses suggestive of superior intellectual ability are offered. We would interpret the test results as indicating that there is genuine capacity for significant emotional relationships and the ability for empathy, insight and self-acceptance. There are also signs of self-assertiveness and individuality. Some of Audrey's conflicts are conscious and are related to her inability to accept her own needs for love and affection. She tends to limit and restrict her relationships because of the frustration she feels when people are unable to accept her cold and hesitant manner. Nevertheless she probably struggles on despite feelings of anxiety and discomfort. She is however, concerned with the possibility that human contacts may be becoming too complex and frustrating to tolerate.

SUMMARY OF PSYCHOLOGICAL TESTS:

In summary, the psychological tests highlighted Audrey's lack of success in interpersonal relationships. She feels isolated, helpless, inadequate, hurt, and afraid. Her system of values is poorly structured, and her identity as a woman is confusing to her. She feels unable to rely on her own judgment to lead her to human relationships that will be more satisfying. She is very resentful of this state of affairs and is currently casting around, sometimes in an impulsive fashion, in an effort to establish some stable human contacts. She relies heavily on romantic fantasy as a solution to her sexual feelings about men. It is as if she is struggling to break out of a childlike mold and enter into a more mature, adult world. The possibility that her stuttering might come to have more significance as a symptomatic defense against feelings of failure had to be considered. Accordingly, a joint program of speech therapy and psychotherapy was considered.

Outline of Therapy. Prior to the establishment of a formal treatment program, Audrey's case was examined in detail by members of the speech-clinic staff. It was felt that much of her speech problem is relatively clear-cut; that is, many of the developmental and maintaining factors present in her history are of a kind that is typical of many other stutterers, for example, her specific phonemic and situational fears, the change in the frequency and severity of her stuttering as a function of certain relationships and feelings, the presence of avoidance behavior designed to eliminate or hide the speech blocks, and, most significant, a history of speech fear that led to her acceptance of the role of a stutterer. All of these factors suggested that speech therapy was an appropriate treatment choice.

However, some of Audrey's problems are related to areas of adolescent conflict that have not yet become an integral part of her stuttering self concept. She experiences difficulty in establishing satisfying heterosexual relationships and in developing feelings of independence from her family. She is puzzled and confused by the social adequacy of her peers. She is becoming frustrated by the intellectual demands of the university. While these problems reach into, and are touched by her stuttering, it is clear that her speech handicap is not now seriously interfering with her ability to arrive at a satisfactory solution to these issues.

Of major concern to the speech-clinic staff was the possibility that Audrey might begin to use her stuttering as a neurotic device that would hamper her psychological growth. As a consequence, it was decided that maximum therapeutic gains would probably result if she were given the opportunity to explore some of her feelings that relate to this adolescent turmoil. A joint conference was then held with the staff of the psychological clinic, and Audrey's case was again reviewed. It was decided to assign both a speech therapist and a psychotherapist to her case, and treatment was begun.

SUMMARY

The need for understanding the disorders of speech is important for the student interested in clinical psychology, since many people with those disorders are first referred to the psychologist for diagnosis and, in some instances, for treatment. In order to assist the student to become acquainted with the field of speech, the most often encountered disorders have been described in terms of their symptoms, causes, and treatment. The case reports presented should help to make clear the diagnostic and therapeutic techniques involved, as well as the significance of speech disorders for the clinical psychologist.

REFERENCES

AINSWORTH, S. 1957. Methods for Integrating Theories of Stuttering. In L. E. TRAVIS (ed.), *Handbook of Speech Pathology*. New York: Appleton-Century-Crofts.

BANGS, J. L., and FREIDINGER, A. 1950. A case of hysterical dysphonia in an adult. *J. Speech Hearing Disorders.* 15, 316–23.

BERRY, M. E., and EISENSON, J. 1956. *Speech Disorders.* New York: Appleton-Century-Crofts.

BRYNGELSON, B. 1938. Prognosis of stuttering. *J. Speech Hearing Disorders,* 3, 121–23.

DARLEY, F. C. 1964. *Diagnosis and Appraisal of Communication Disorders.* Englewood Cliffs, N.J.: Prentice-Hall.

EISENSON, J. 1949. Prognostic factors related to language rehabilitation in aphasia. *J. Speech Hearing Disorders,* 14, 262–64.

EISENSON, J. 1954. *Examining for aphasia.* New York: Psychological Corp.

GLAUBER, I. P. 1958. The psychoanalysis of stuttering. In J. EISENSON (ed.), *Stuttering: A symposium.* New York: Harper & Row.

GOLDSTEIN, K. 1948. *Language and language disturbances.* New York: Grune & Stratton.

GRANICK, L. 1947. *Aphasia: A guide to retraining.* New York: Grune & Stratton.

HALSTEAD, W. C., and WEPMAN, J. M. 1949. The Halstead-Wepman Aphasia Screening Test. *J. Speech Hearing Disorders*, 14, 9–15.

JOHNSON, W., DARLEY, F. C., and SPRIESTERSBACH, D. C. 1963. *Diagnostic methods in speech pathology*. New York: Harper & Row.

KARLIN, I. W., and STRAZZULA, M. 1952. Speech and language problems of mentally deficient children. *J. Speech Hearing Disorders*, 17, 286–94.

McDONALD, E. T. 1964. *Cerebral palsy*. Englewood Cliffs, N.J.: Prentice-Hall.

McDONALD, E. T., and BAKER, H. K. 1951. Cleft palate speech: An integration of research and clinical findings. *J. Speech Hearing Disorders*, 16, 9–20.

MORLEY, M. E. 1954. *Cleft palate and speech*. London: Livingstone.

MURPHY, A. T. 1964. *Functional voice disorders*. Englewood Cliffs, N.J.: Prentice-Hall.

MURPHY, A. T., and FITZSIMMONS, R. M. 1960. *Stuttering and personality dynamics*. New York: Ronald.

POWERS, M. H. 1957. Functional disorders of articulation: Symptomatology and etiology. In L. E. TRAVIS (ed.), *Handbook of speech pathology*. New York: Appleton-Century-Crofts.

ROBINSON, F. 1964. *Introduction to stuttering*. Englewood Cliffs, N.J.: Prentice-Hall.

SCHLANGER, B. B. 1960. A longitudinal study of speech and language development of brain-damaged mentally retarded children. *J. Speech Hearing Disorders*, 24, 354–60.

SCHUELL, H. M. 1955. Minnesota test for differential diagnosis of aphasia. (Research ed.) Minneapolis: Univer. Minnesota Printing Department.

SCHUELL, H. M., JENKINS, J. J., and JIMENES-PABON, E. 1964. *Aphasia in adults*. New York: Harper & Row.

TEMPLIN, M. C. 1957. Certain language skills in children. *Child Welfare Monogr.* No. 26. Minneapolis: Univer. of Minnesota Press.

VAN RIPER, C. 1963. *Speech correction: principles and methods*. 4th ed. Englewood Cliffs, N.J.: Prentice-Hall.

VAN RIPER, C., and IRWIN, J. V. 1958. *Voice and articulation*. Englewood Cliffs, N.J.: Prentice-Hall.

WEISENBURG, T. H., and McBRIDE, K. E. 1935. *Aphasia*. New York: Commonwealth Fund.

WEISS, D. 1964. *Cluttering*. Englewood Cliffs, N.J.: Prentice-Hall.

WEPMAN, J. M. 1951. *Recovery from aphasia*. New York: Ronald.

WEPMAN, J. M., and JONES, L. V. 1961. *Studies in aphasia: An approach to testing*. Chicago: Education-Industry Service.

WEST, R. 1958. An agnostic's speculations about stuttering. In J. EISENSON (ed.), *Stuttering: A symposium*. New York: Harper & Row. Pp. 169–222.

WEST, R., ANSBERY, M., and CARR, A. 1957. *Rehabilitation of speech*. New York: Harper & Row.

WOOD, N. 1964. *Delayed speech and language development*. Englewood Cliffs, N.J.: Prentice-Hall.

12

The Psychoneuroses

GERALD R. PASCAL *

Earlier chapters in this section dealing with the problem approach in the clinic have considered various behavior disorders that are of concern to the clinical psychologist in his daily activities. The present chapter deals with those conditions commonly called "psychoneuroses." In the 1952 diagnostic and statistical manual of the American Psychiatric Association, the psychoneuroses are classified with disorders of psychogenic origin, and, hence, are considered etiologically to be without clearly defined physical cause or structural change in the brain. "Psychoneurotic disorders" are briefly defined in this manual as follows:

The chief characteristic of these disorders is "anxiety" which may be directly felt and expressed or which may be unconsciously and automatically controlled by the utilization of various psychological defense mechanisms, (depression, conversion, displacement, etc.). In contrast to those with psychoses, patients with psychoneurotic disorders do not exhibit gross distortion or falsification of external reality, (delusions, hallucinations, illusions) and they do not present gross disorganization of the personality.[1]

The psychoneuroses, therefore, are generally differentiated from the psychoses in that they do not exhibit gross distortion of reality or disorganization of the personality. They are differentiated from the acute and chronic brain disorders in that no impairment of brain tissue is involved. Psychoneuroses are further differentiated from other mental disorders sometimes considered with the psychoneuroses. Thus, the APA statistical manual classifies under a separate rubric the *Personality Disorders*

* Gerald R. Pascal, Ph.D. (Brown University), Research Professor of Psychiatry, University of Mississippi Medical School.
[1] This quotation and Table 12–1 are reprinted with permission granted by the Committee on Nomenclature and Statistics of the American Psychiatric Association (1952, p. 31).

said to be characterized by developmental defects or pathological trends in the personality structure, with minimal subjective anxiety, and little or no sense of distress (see Chapter 14 of this book). Another main heading is given over to *Transient Situational Personality Disorders,* which classification, it is said, should be restricted to reactions that are more or less transient in character and that appear to be an accute symptom response to a situation without apparent underlying personality disturbance.

It is not feasible here to reproduce the contents of the APA statistical manual as it pertains to the psychoneuroses. The student had best consult the manual itself to obtain a clear conception of the thought and care needed to present a descriptive classificatory system sufficiently fine so as to make statistical recordings of mental disorders reasonably accurate. Although, only the specific psychoneurotic reactions are given in Table 12–1, it should be borne in mind that related reactions such as the personality disorders, personality trait disturbances, sociopathic per-

Table 12–1. Brief Characterization of the Classes of Psychoneurotic Illness *

1. Anxiety reaction: Anxiety is diffuse, unbound.
2. Dissociative reaction: The repressed impulse giving rise to anxiety is discharged through such avenues as dissociated personality, fugue states, and amnesic periods.
3. Conversion reaction: Anxiety is channeled into functional symptoms of body parts as in hysterical paralyses, blindness, aphonia, and the like.
4. Phobic reaction: Anxiety is displaced to some symbolically significant idea or situation.
5. Obsessive-compulsive reaction: Anxiety is associated with the persistence of unwanted ideas and repetitive impulses, thereby protecting the person from the pain involved in facing still more basic difficulties.
6. Depressive reaction: Anxiety is allayed by feelings of depression and statements of self-depreciation.
7. Psychoneurotic reaction; other: All reactions adjudged psychoneurotic and not elsewhere classified.

* This description is in large part based on the anxiety theory of neurosis. For further study, consult Cattell and Scheier (1961), Eysenck (1961), and Fenichel (1945).

sonality disturbances, and transient situational disorders are differentiated from them.

The reaction types given in Table 12–1 are operational in that they can be observed by the experienced examiner. Unfortunately, however, they do not often exist in a "pure" state in any one individual.[2] Thus,

2 When the so-called pure case is found, it is often designated as classical. Many times such cases become the subject matter for case reports in textbooks, the better to set forth the differences among the clinical types.

depression is a concomitant of most psychoneurotic reactions, and of many other mental disorders. Anxiety is not specific to the neuroses, but may accompany a number of mental disorders, such as psychophysiological, autonomic, and visceral disorders. Indeed, psychoneurosis itself may be part of a reaction such as acute or chronic brain disorder. Further to confound matters, psychoneuroses are sometimes not easily differentiated from the psychoses.

The reliability of psychiatric diagnoses has been the subject of at least two studies. Both are in agreement that psychiatric diagnoses are unreliable. Ash (1949) found disagreement on more than half of 52 cases as to major diagnostic category when these cases were interviewed jointly. Mehlman (1952) checked over 4,000 cases for the reliability of diagnoses and came to the conclusion that the existing classificatory system can have very little value for patient management or research. One difficulty with the present system is that it is based on symptoms. Symptoms fluctuate within an individual patient. Individual patients also tend to have symptom complexes, so that it is often difficult to ascertain which symptom predominates. Another criticism is that the present system is subjective in the sense that neither the situations under which the symptoms are observed nor the observational techniques are standardized. Whatever we may think of the present-day descriptive classificatory system, it is necessary for the clinical psychologist to familiarize himself with it so that he may communicate with his colleagues. Although some beginnings have been made toward a better, more reliable system (Lorr and Rubenstein, 1955; Overall and Gorham, 1962; Wittenborn and Holzberg, 1951), it will be some time before a satisfactory classification of the mental disorders can be achieved.

It is one job of the clinical psychologist to help diagnose the extent and nature of mental disturbance, and, as well as he can, to predict the outcome of specific treatment. Although he needs to know the psychiatric classificatory system, fortunately he is not limited to the theories or techniques that lead to such a system. The purpose of the present chapter is to show the clinical psychologist at work with specific reference to the psychoneuroses. But the work of the clinician arises directly from his theoretical orientation. Therefore, in order to understand the methods employed by him, it is necessary to present, briefly, a theoretical framework.

A FRAME OF REFERENCE

The specialty of clinical psychology is a new one, and, fortunately, it is in a relatively fluid condition. There are many hypotheses to account for the data of our field. The approach to be presented is the writer's own preference and is elsewhere more completely stated (Pascal, 1959). There are others with their own adherents, reflected in the different chapters of this volume. Yet, in spite of differences, there is a hard core compounded of solidly established fact that guides the work of all well-trained clinical psychologists.

One of these well-established facts is that a mentally ill individual shows a relative inefficiency. This relative inefficiency can be established by contrasting the patient's efficiency in meeting the demands of his environment before his illness and that which prevails during the illness. Psychological tests also provide a measure of relative efficiency, or *psychological deficit,* as we shall call it. Thus, if a man is a college graduate in business administration, and at the time of testing is unable to solve an eighth-grade arithmetic problem, then that man displays a deficit. "Psychological deficit," following Hunt and Cofer (1944), is briefly defined as a deviation from expectancy for a man of a given status. When an individual obtains a weighted score of 10 of the Vocabulary subtest of the Wechsler-Bellevue Scale, then, within probability limits, we expect him to achieve a similar weighted score on the other subtests. If he does not, then he exhibits scatter, and a deviation from expectancy that may or may not be significant.

It is this scatter which can be used as a measure of deficit on the Wechsler-Bellevue. Figure 12–1 shows what happens when an estimate of Wechsler-Bellevue scatter is plotted against a crude measure of the severity of mental illness (Pascal and Zeaman, 1949). Similar relationships can be shown between seriousness of illness and other measures of deficit such as the $F+\%$ on the Rorschach (Rapaport et. al., 1945), the Bender-Gestalt (Pascal and Suttell, 1951), and a whole host of other measures. For a detailed discussion of this matter, the student is referred to the chapter on psychological deficit by Pascal (1959). "Psychological deficit," then, can be considered a measurement term for the seriousness of mental illness. It can be thought of as a quantitative continuum; [3] it replaces the qualitative terms previously used. A number of studies show that the differences between normal, neurotic, and psychotic, in this respect, are not qualitative but quantitative (Eysenck, 1952; Pascal and Suttell, 1951).[4] Somewhere along this hypothetical continuum lie the neurotics with respect to deficit.

[3] Although "psychological deficit" can be operationally defined, it is a concept that at present has more heuristic than immediate value for the practical problems of clinical psychology. In order to describe accurately and quantitatively the deficits of mental illness, those common to all patients and peculiar to some, the concepts have to be visualized as tremendously more complex and flexible.

[4] For a different position with respect to the differentiation between psychoses and psychoneuroses see Eysenck's chapter in the *Handbook of Abnormal Psychology* (1961).

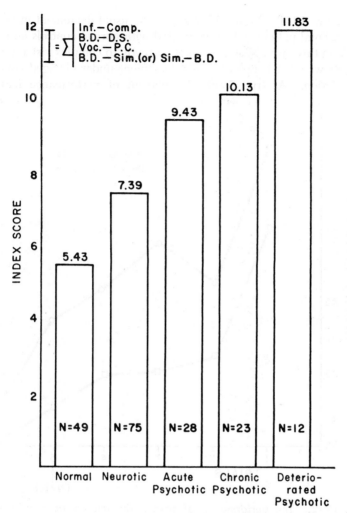

Fig. 12–1. Relationship between a Wechsler-Bellevue Index Score (of scatter) and selected psychiatric syndromes. (Reproduced by permission granted by the *American Journal of Psychiatry.*) (Pascal and Zeaman, 1949.)

There are two important aspects of psychogenic psychological deficit that we need to consider. On the one hand, it is a function of constitutional, motivational, and acquired characteristics of the individual, and on the other hand, it is reversible as contrasted to deficit that is found in organic illnesses, such as paresis. Let us take performance on a learning task as our measure of deficit. There is a substantial body of literature indicating that mental patients are impaired when contrasted with normal controls (Boring, 1913; Eysenck, 1961; Hull, 1917; Huston and Shakow, 1948). Figure 12–2 shows the usual decrement in performance of mental patients when contrasted with normal controls on a learning task, in this case learning to react correctly to complex visual patterns. It also shows what happens to this decrement under changed conditions of motivation. At trial 5, after a plateau of performance had been

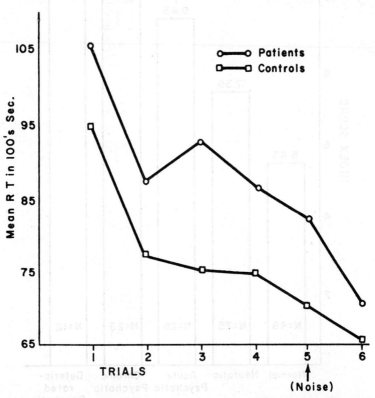

Fig. 12–2. The performance of psychiatric patients as contrasted with scores earned by normal control subjects in a simple learning task. (Reprinted by the permission of the *Journal of Personality.*) (Pascal and Swenson, 1952.)

reached, both patients and controls were subjected to white noise at an intensity level of 116 decibels above absolute threshold, introduced through earphones. The white noise stayed on until the subject responded correctly to the stimulus pattern. Under this disagreeable condition all subjects were highly motivated to react correctly, and as rapidly as possible. Figure 12–2 shows that after two trials with the white noise, the difference in performance between controls and patients is largely wiped out. In fact, there is not a significant difference between the two groups in final performance, although there had been previous to trial 5. Such results point up two things: (1) that the decrement or deficit is reversible, and (2) that altered conditions of motivation affect performance in mental patients. It is to this latter point that we shall now address ourselves.

That there is a functional relationship between deprivation of organismic needs and behavior of the organism is also a well-established fact. Rats have galloped, swum, rolled, and staggered thousands of maze miles, driven by need deprivation (McGeogh and Irion, 1951). We also generally accept the fact that there is a hierarchy of needs such that some are prepotent over others. For instance, an early study by Warden (1951) showed, with rats, the prepotency of the need for water over the need for food and sexual gratification. In the hierarchy of needs, the more basic need to the well-being of the organism, the more prepotent is motivating behavior, other things being equal (Maslow, 1943a, 1943b, 1943c; Murray, 1938).

Ungratified needs motivate behavior. The inability to gratify needs results in stress to the organism. Selye (1950) has done a good deal of work to show the effects of physiological stresses upon the organism. That the stress resulting from extreme cold, heat, lack of food, and fatigue will cause psychological deficit is fairly well accepted. What is not so commonly realized is that there is also stress resulting from the deprivation of psychological needs, which will cause psychological deficit. We are all familiar with the need to be safe and its deprivation in front-line soldiers, some of whom "crack up" as a result of this kind of stress. There are other psychological needs, such as the need to be loved, to be accepted, and so on, the absence of which causes stress that may lead to deficit (Pascal, 1959).

The diagnosis of a mental patient, therefore, needs not only to consider the extent of deficit, but also the nature of the stresses acting upon the patient. These can be obtained from case history material and from projective techniques like the Rorschach. Yet not all people under similar stresses react with similar amounts of deficit, or with any discernable deficit at all, for that matter. Some individuals under stress may get what is called "psychosomatic" illness rather than mental illness. We need, therefore, to consider a very complex variable, the resistance to mental illness, which we shall call the "X" factor.

The X factor is by definition (Pascal, 1951) inversely related to psychological deficit: the greater the resistance, the less the individual is apt to react to psychological stress with psychological deficit. It may be partially constitutional (Kallman, 1946). One can conceive of an individual as having inherited a weak neopallium as well as one can conceive of him as having inherited a weak heart, in the sense of constitutional medicine (Bauer, 1945). The X factor also must consist of learned habits, those habits acquired to satisfy needs. A study by Sipprelle (1954) shows that the X factor is partially made up of defense mechanisms, some of which increase the value of X, others that decrease it. Thus, with physical scientists, studied by Sipprelle, it was found that a narrow range of interest, ordinarily considered a sign of poor adjustment, actually contributed to the scientists' resistance to deficit. If a child, in order to satisfy security needs, learns to blame others, he will have acquired a habit that may decrease his resistance to stress, and that may, in fact, make stress more likely and thus increase deficit. A number of prognostic studies show that this tendency to blame others is an indication of a poor prognosis for the outcome of mental illness and thus, by implication, an indication of low resistance (Albee, 1950; Feldman et al., 1954; Pascal et al., 1953; Smith, 1951). Our notion of diagnosis has, therefore, to be further complicated by finding out the learned habits of the individual, those habits acquired to satisfy his physiological and psychological needs.

We may now crudely formulate our position with respect to diagnosis as follows:

$$\text{Psychological deficit } F = \frac{\text{stress}}{X} \text{ [Pascal, 1951]}$$

This formulation states that once it is decided that the patient's disorder is psychogenic, we need, in order to make a diagnosis, to know the seriousness of the disorder (the psychological deficit—P.D.), the nature of the deprivation now producing stress, and the acquired habits now being used by the patient to satisfy needs (X). Note that this position is cross-sectional and, in Lewin's sense (1936) ahistorical. Note also that the diagnosis derived from such a formulation implies the treatment. The problem, broadly speaking, is to decrease stress and increase the X factor. For detailed discussion of this approach, see Pascal (1959). This approach, diagnostically speaking, makes no reference to the categories of so-called neuroses, psychoses, and the like. By focusing attention upon the extent of deficit and its balancing mechanisms, the psychologist can be more specific in his clinical evaluations. He can determine, for instance, whether the patient is dangerous to himself and others, and hence in need of hospitalization—without reference to labeling the disorder as neurotic or psychotic. Not all conditions, it is well recognized, conform to the "either-or" dichotomy so often assumed. The stress-deficit approach avoids this artificial taxonomic construct and replaces it with a constructive, measuremental frame of reference whereby severity and resistance factors can be set forth after a detailed study of each unique individual patient.

The theoretical position broadly described above is used to focus attention upon the problems presented by each of the three patients studied by the psychologist in the manner indicated below. In each, the problems of diagnosis are resolved with little emphasis upon taxonomy but, rather, with major concern for prognosis and treatment.

NEUROSIS FOLLOWING CEREBRAL INCIDENT

The patient was a 52-year-old college graduate, an engineer. He was married, had four children, the oldest of whom was 10 years old. He had had an acute brain disorder associated with a circulatory disturbance, cardiac disease, suffering right-sided hemiplegia and aphasia. He was referred to the clinical psychologist because of a delayed recovery in the absence of neurological signs. The neuropsychiatrist's question was the extent of residual brain damage and the prognosis. At the time the patient was first seen by the clinical psychologist, he complained of inability to do simple arithmetic problems, inability to understand complicated and rapid speech, inability to understand newspaper writing, fear of crowds, fear of driving a car (which he had done previous to his stroke), difficulty with fine movements of his right leg and arm, and anesthesia in these extremities. At the time of examination, the patient was oriented for time, place, and person, and was verbal, with a good command of English. He was a bald-headed man, mesomorphic, and quite short in stature. He was compliant and seemed very anxious about his prognosis. The problem, as the psychologist saw it, was to determine how much, if any, residual brain damage existed, its nature, and the prognosis for definitive treatment.

The first task was to secure a case history, which was obtained from the patient and his wife, a harassed woman, old looking for her age and larger than the patient. The patient was an only child. His father died when he was six and he had kindly rememberances of his father. His mother he described as brutal for she whipped and dominated him. He said that he used to wish she were dead. She was ill a good deal of the time and he said that he believed it was "mostly put on" to win sympathy. As a child, the patient was small for his years; hence he did not compete successfully with boys his own age. He was, however, a good student and had the reputation for being bright. He got along well with other boys and in high school, became the manager of the baseball team. He graduated from college with good grades, went to work for a large engineering corporation, and fairly rapidly rose to an executive position.

At the age of 25 he married. His wife was a good housekeeper and took good care of him. The patient had to travel a good deal on his job, but he got along well with his wife until the birth of their first child. At that time, the patient began to suffer from ejaculatio praecox and impotence, which continued for 10 years during which period three other children were born. The patient made no effort to do anything about his condition, much to his wife's distress. The patient did not get along well with his oldest son, but tolerated his other three children. One day he and a friend were waiting to cross at a street corner. The patient remembers feeling faint and suddenly, without pain, collapsing on the street. Thereafter, he had little memory of what had happened until he awoke to realize he could not move his right side, could not speak except in simple phrases, and could not understand very well what people were saying to him. He recovered fairly rapidly from this state to the point where he could walk, talk fairly well, and read uncomplicated material, but in spite of much practice he was unable to attain anything like his former self-sufficiency and efficiency.

The first test administered to the patient was the Wechsler-Bellevue. He obtained a verbal IQ of 130 and a performance IQ of 106. This test showed no signs of irreversible deficit, but the scatter indicated fairly profound deficit, undoubtedly psychogenic in origin. Thus, the patient, in spite of professed symptoms of aphasia, showed very good verbal ability. In spite of his complaints of difficulty with simple arithmetic problems, he showed good performance on the arithmetic subtest. It was noticed that he performed better on the subtests that involved direct responses to the examiner's questions than on subtests in which he was thrust upon his own resources. For instance, he obtained a weighted score of 13 on the Picture Completion test, but only 9 on the Block Design. In addition, intratest variability was noted; that is, he failed easy items and solved more difficult ones.

However, in view of the patient's history and the psychiatrist's request, the patient was systematically examined for organic brain damage. He was tested for visual memory, visual comprehension, and visual abstraction, and these were contrasted with his performance on the same material presented by auditory rather than visual means. In similar manner, a number of cortical areas were tested for psychological function. The Wells-Ruesch manual (1945) contains a number of these tests; others are taken from Weisenberg and McBride (1935); still others, such as the double alternation test (Hunter, 1920; Hunter and Bartlett, 1948; Pascal and Jenkins, 1959) are useful in assessing the neurophysiology and the psychology of brain damage. The patient was able to read at the twelfth-grade level; yet he had protested inability to read the newspaper. He could write satisfactorily. However, he failed the simple serial subtraction test and the double alternation test, the latter being easily solved by normal ten-year-olds (Hodges, 1953).

On the basis of the foregoing tests it was quite apparent to the examiner that the patient's problem was not organic but psychogenic. The last test administered was the Rorschach. This final test was selected because the Rorschach is particularly sensitive to organic deficit and it also provides a further estimate of the extent and the nature of the deficit, supplementing the case history material in providing information about current stresses and habit patterns. The Rorschach data showed no signs of organicity. On the contrary, it clearly reflected the patient's childish dependency, especially on masculine figures of authority, his intellectual strivings, his fears, his hypochondriacal concerns, his profound feelings of masculine inadequacy and his deep-seated aggression directed against feminine figures. In the Testing of the Limits for Sex Procedure (TLS) (Pascal et al., 1950), the patient saw Card II, the whole thing, as a female sex organ at menstruation, with the white space as the center of the organ, the black as the pubic hair, and the red as the blood. (The popular response in TLS here is the lower center line as a female sex organ). The patient's response is obviously deviant and indicates clearly to the experienced examiner the patient's anxiety and aggression toward "femaleness." On Card VI the patient responded to the TLS procedure by avoiding the obvious phallic symbol and giving as his response "testicles," located in the tiny bumps in the lower invaginated section. Adding the Rorschach data to that previously obtained, the examiner was now firmly convinced of the hysterical nature of the patient's disorder and prepared to render a case formulation that would lead to a diagnosis and prognosis for specific treatment.

The patient whose case is under discussion lost his father early in life; thus the dominant figure in his life was his mother. The satisfaction of safety needs, survival itself in fact, demanded that he learn to do things the way she wanted them done and therefore adopt many of her habit patterns—in other words, partially identify with her, a woman and, from what we know, a punitive, hypochondriacal one. The patient resented his mother's domination. He thought of her as brutal and had a considerable amount of aggression directed toward her. She did not, obviously, contribute to his feelings of confidence in himself. With this substratum—habit patterns learned from a woman, fear and resentment against his mother, insecurity because of his inability to get along well with his mother, plus his small size—the boy was thrust into a competitive masculine society and expected to behave like a little man. He learned to adapt by compliance. Fortunately, he was bright; hence he learned to win respect from his peers by being a good scholar. He made an adjustment; that is, he learned some socially acceptable ways of satisfying basic psychological needs. He married. From what we know of learning principles, we can predict his fear and resentment of his wife, manifested in this case by the need to dominate her, to demand unflagging attention from her, and to leave her at will by his frequent business trips. A son arrived. Now his wife could no longer fuss over him as much as she used to when he came home from his trips. The patient punished his wife. He became sexually impotent and exhibited ejaculatio praecox. He made no attempt to correct this situation. He displayed aggression toward his son. (It should be noted that during these years there was a gradual development of a heart condition.)

These attempts to satisfy security needs were inadequate. Fortunately, the patient did well in his work for he rose to a position of some power and influence. Previous to his stroke, however, he had a cardiac disease, was sexually impotent, had a fairly unhappy home condition; nevertheless he was successful in his work and had no apparent mental illness. These were important factors in a precarious psychological balance, but it was a balance. The problem, therefore, is one of understanding the onset of his psychological illness.

That the patient had psychological deficit will be conceded. That this deficit is one of psychogenic origin we have demonstrated to our own satisfaction. According to our theoretical formulation, deficit is a function of stress arising from the deprivation of needs. After his stroke, the patient suffered a loss of intellectual capacity, thereby being deprived of his ability to satisfy security needs by status and performance on his job and, in addition, became wholly dependent on his wife. (Note that immediately after his incident the patient was forced into stimulus situation similar to that of early childhood and that, by the principle of generalization, there would be a tendency to respond similarly.) We can formulate it in an oversimplified manner somewhat as follows:

$$P.D. = \frac{Stress \text{ (deprivation of security, prestige, and cognitive needs)}}{X \text{ (intellectual defenses, defenses against excessive dependency, fear and aggression toward women, tendency toward hysterical symptoms, submissiveness toward masculine figures of authority, etc.)}}$$

After his stroke the patient suffered an increase in stress and a decrease in X, with consequent increase in deficit. He was driven by security needs to utilize other learned patterns—his defenses against women, his tendency toward hysterical symptoms. These patterns proved unsatisfactory thereby increasing deficit, which precluded the reinstatement of intellectual capacity—a vicious cycle. The prognosis for this patient was good. He could be treated as an outpatient, being not dangerous to himself or to others. He had the capacity to establish a good working relationship with a male therapist. The patient's se-

curity needs were met in therapy, thus decreasing stress and deficit, and
the patient's intellectual defenses were restored. After relatively few
interviews, the patient reached his previous level of efficiency and went
back to work. In treatment no attempt was made to effect any profound
change in the patient; rather, the goal was to achieve the same, admittedly precarious, psychological balance that had obtained prior to
the patient's cerebral hemorrhage.[5]

ANXIETY REACTION IN A VETERAN

The patient was referred to the clinical psychologist for diagnosis
by his neuropsychiatrist. The psychiatrist had diagnosed the patient as
suffering from anxiety hysteria, had treated him over several interviews,
and had not obtained the response to psychotherapy he expected.
The questions, now, were why had the patient not responded to therapy
and what to do about it.

The patient was a 33-year-old army veteran, married, with two children, a college graduate, and a business man. He was a tall mesomorph,
neatly dressed, soft-spoken, and somewhat reserved in manner. His
complaints concerned a nervous stomach, nausea, occasional headaches,
and a sense of panic when too many people got too close to him. He
was working every day, but had to avoid all social engagements. His
general nervousness and anxiety caused him considerable distress on
unpredictable occasions, even on the job.

The symptoms first appeared a short time after he had been wounded
and captured by the enemy. He, along with other prisoners, was
loaded into a boxcar for transportation to a prison camp. The prisoners were packed so tightly into the locked car that they could only
stand. For three days and nights they traveled thus, not being allowed
to leave the car for any purpose whatsoever, so that the car became
a filthy mess. Added to that, several of the prisoners died and had to
be kept in the car until the end of the journey. It was during this
trip that the patient first experienced his present symptoms. Other
than on this trip, the patient was symptom free during his military service and after discharge. The symptoms recurred one month after the
birth of his first child, a girl. Since then, the symptoms have persisted
without any periods of relief. The patient recounted a long history of
medical consultations and treatment before he was finally referred to
a psychiatrist for therapy.

[5] The student will note that, in spite of the ahistorical protestation of the theoretical
approach presented, case history material was used in the case formulation. We do
not, as yet, have the diagnostic devices that will enable us to dispense with historical
material. Even if we had these devices, we would, of course, still be interested in the
etiology of the patient's illness for research and teaching purposes.

The patient had only one sibling, a sister three years younger. Of her, he said they had fought continually. "She was father's favorite," he emphasized. He described his father as a good businessman, one who had built up a successful business of his own. The father was a quiet, rather reserved man, even inclined to be taciturn. He was strict, but fair. He insisted on such qualities as courtesy, promptness, neatness, and the like in his son. "I cannot now and never could think it so important to be precisely punctual," the patient commented after talking about his father. The mother was described by the patient as being warm and loving. As a child, the patient made friends easily, and, he said, looks back to it with happy memories. Once he had a narrow escape from drowning and has not liked water since. In high school and college he had many friends, dated frequently, and participated in sports. One summer during his college days, the patient had a job as an inspector in a canning factory. He said he had to quit the job because he could not bring himself to report the results of his inspection for fear of involving the workers.

With the onset of war, the patient enlisted in the army and became a paratrooper. He got along well in the army and was promoted regularly. He was wounded and captured on his first encounter with the enemy and, except for the incident previously reported, he endured fairly well the vicissitudes of being a prisoner of war. After discharge he entered his father's business and soon thereafter his father retired, leaving him in charge. The patient married. He describes his wife as being very efficient, almost meticulous. "She took very good care of me," he said, using the past tense. His wife's mother died when she was a baby, and she had been reared by her father, of whom she was very fond. The patient and his wife got along very well together and were reasonably happy. This state of affairs continued until about one month after the birth of their first child when, as has been mentioned previously, the patient's symptoms began to trouble him again.

The Wechsler-Bellevue indicated the patient to be of superior intellectual capacity with significant impairment, psychogenic in nature. On the verbal subtests he showed his most profound drop in weighted scores in the Arithmetic-Digit Span subtests. Such a finding is often associated with anxiety. On the performance subtests his most pronounced drops were noted in the Picture Arrrangement and Digit Symbol subtests. The first is sometimes found in patients who have difficulty in their relations with people and the second in patients who are depressed. In addition, there was a fair amount of intratest variability. Although the scatter is marked, the general performance is in keeping with that found in outpatients; for example, a weighted score of 16 was obtained for the Comprehension subtest and 13 for Similarities.

The Wechsler-Bellevue, here, served the purpose of providing the initial check on organicity versus psychogenesis. It served as an estimate of deficit and rendered information leading to preliminary hypotheses concerning the nature of the patient's disorder.

As an additional check on deficit the Bender-Gestalt was given and scored (Pascal and Suttell, 1951). The patient obtained a standard score of 67 where the mean for the standardizing population is 50 and the standard deviation is 10. Again, the patient showed some deficit, but it was well within the limits of an outpatient population. The Bender gave no indications of organicity, the Gestalten were fairly well executed.[6] There was gross tremor in most of the line drawings. The over-all order of the designs on the paper were logical, but the initial careful sequence gave way to crowding to make room for the last two designs. On Design 2 he began by carefully making the little circles and aligning them correctly, but initial spacing and alignment were lost in the crowding toward the right-hand edge of the paper in order to complete the design. The drawings were larger than those of most normal subjects. Such performance suggests (among other things) anxiety and a childish impulsiveness.

The Draw-A-Man test was administered. Both man and woman were drawn with many fine little lines. Noteworthy was the remarkable lack of differentiation between the sexes, with the female being a little larger. Again, the performance suggested anxiety and in addition, an inference could be made about the patient's conception of himself in the masculine role, his feelings of inadequacy, and his lack of sexual maturity. More hypotheses about the patient could be drawn from these two time-saving tests, but enough have been given to indicate the nature of the interpretations and the usefulness of the tests.

The Rorschach and the Thematic Apperception Test corroborated the impressions formed from the tests previously discussed. The patient was found to be suffering from a neurosis of psychogenic origin, with anxiety evidently his chief reaction to stresses. The patient's feelings of inadequacy in the masculine role, passivity, anxiety, and inability to express aggression against figures of authority; his need for a succorant mother figure; his sense of helplessness; and his tendency to withdraw were clearly depicted in these projective techniques. His response to TAT Card 1, which shows a boy with a violin, was particularly revealing: "This apparently is a little blind boy who's studying or going to study the violin. His instructor wants him to feel the violin and commit to memory all its parts so he'll be familiar with it when he starts his lesson." Assuming positive identification with the main character of

---

[6] For a review of Bender-Gestalt test performance and organicity the student is referred to Billingslea (1963) and Garron and Cheiftez (1965).

the story, it was not difficult to hypothesize the patient's blind groping, his acceptance of instruction, and his sense of helplessness. The process in interpretating projective tests is that of setting up a series of hypotheses, which are either rejected or confirmed to the point of subjective certainty as interpretation proceeds.

With the data at hand, we are now ready to conceptualize this case. The patient's psychological deficit can be classified as moderate. He is in good contact with reality. His practical judgment is relatively unimpaired. He is efficient enough to keep his job. He is not dangerous to himself or others. He should respond to outpatient treatment. We see the patient as having had a fairly stable, succorant early environment. At the age of three, with the advent of his sister, the patient experienced some difficulty. He evidently was unable to establish a warm, secure relationship with his father. We surmise that his mother continued somewhat overprotecting. The boy seemed to have grown up rather fearful of his father, anxious for his approval, and unable to find any security in the relationship. His mother provided a warm, secure haven within which he could develop and, for the most part, successfully cope with his environment.

If we skip now to the situation existing immediately prior to the patient's illness, we see the patient laboring under the stress of filling his father's role as head of the business, but counterbalancing this stress by his new-found security with a wife who succored him. The patient managed fairly well until the birth of his daughter. His wife, kept busy by the infant, was unable to give him the attention he had obtained previously. In addition, there was a parallel to the stimulus situation that had obtained at the birth of his own sister and a generalization of response. Stress, then, comes from his sense of helplessness, his feelings of inability to win his father's approval. His defenses, the ingredients of the X factor, do not work. Partial withdrawal is not enough, dependency on a mother figure is partially taken away from him; compliance toward masculine figures of authority does not work since he is the "boss." Psychological deficit occurs, and the tendency toward anxiety reinstates itself.

In order to answer the original question, why the patient did not respond to the psychiatrist's treatment, we have to understand the patient's attitudes toward male figures of authority. He is fearful of them, anxious to please, but threatened. The patient's defense in such a situation is to withdraw, which he did. The patient's prognosis with a male therapist is good with one who is not paternalistic or otherwise authoritarian, but who can give security in a democratic, nonthreatening fashion. Such a treatment approach was undertaken and the patient responded rapidly, with the loss of deficit and symptoms, to the acceptance of a safe dependent relationship with the therapist. This dependency relationship was, then, used by the therapist to teach the patient new habits for satisfying his security needs.

OBSESSIVE-COMPULSIVE NEUROSIS

The patient was referred to a psychological clinic by his family physician because of extreme nervousness and a tendency toward high blood pressure. The patient was a 34-year-old accountant, married, with no children. He was medium-sized, walked with a limp, quite verbal, and extremely tense. He complained of "nervous tension," insomnia, inability to make up his mind about things, a constant concern for the future. He was always trying to "figure out" the future. He could never be satisfied in his work, about its correctness, and would spend hours checking and rechecking. He was always returning to the house to find out whether or not he had turned off the gas or put out the lights. He had recurring fantasies of getting away from it all, to be a vagabond, a beachcomber. Eight years ago he had a "nervous breakdown." It happened while he was attending school in the morning and working in the afternoon. He drove his car back and forth from work to school all day, not being able to make up his mind to go to either. Finally, he collapsed and was picked up and taken to a hospital where he was completely inactive for weeks. He has had symptoms similar to those he now described for many years before his nervous breakdown and since.

The patient is the youngest of three siblings, having two sisters older than himself. His father was a salesman for a manufacturing concern. He was a gifted musician. The patient described his father as a man with a good deal of charm, but also as an alcoholic. The patient said he remembered many occasions when he tried to persuade his father to come away from a saloon, many occasions when promised trips were not taken because his father could not be coerced to leave off drinking. In his teens, the patient once, in a rage, beat up his father in defense of his mother. He urged his mother to divorce his father, which she did when the patient was 15. Of his mother the patient said they got along fairly well but as he got older she used to come to him with all her troubles and became "too dependent" upon him. The patient said he got along well with his sisters but had little to do with them.

It appears the patient had a satisfactory life until the age of six, according to what he could remember. At six he was afflicted with poliomyelitis and left with an incapacitating crippling of his right leg. Thereafter followed years of consultations with physicians, several operations and much time spent in hospitals. The patient said he was unable to play with the other children very actively. He fell behind in his school work and seemed always to be striving to catch up with his age group. It was after this illness that the father began to drink heavily. At the age of nine the patient contracted a close relationship with a neighborhood boy a year older than himself. This boy was his best friend—in fact, his only close friend. They indulged in homosexual practices that continued sporadically for 13 years. There were other homosexual partners during adolescence. In spite of his difficulties, the patient did well in high school. He entered college and with much hardship, due to his having to work his way through, did well. During his senior year in college he met his future wife.

After college the patient was employed by an accounting firm. He then began attending school part time to obtain an advanced degree. It was during this period that he had his "nervous breakdown," mentioned previously. Meanwhile he had been seeing his wife-to-be at rather frequent intervals, particularly at drinking parties. Finally, she asked him to marry her, and with some reluctance, he did. His wife is the sort of person who seems calm and unruffled under even very trying circumstances. She drinks heavily but not to the extent of becoming intoxicated. She has worked steadily at her profession, a designer, since their marriage. The patient says his nervousness, his constant questioning of the future, and his doubts leave her unperturbed. She humors him, soothes him, but refuses to become disturbed by him. Since their marriage his symptoms have remained at a steady state, never quite reaching the extremity experienced just previous to his hospitalization.

The patient was administered the Rorschach and Bender-Gestalt tests. On the Bender he obtained a standard score of 95. His performance was characterized by guidelines, many erasures, and attempts at meticulousness that failed to achieve the performance necessary for an average score. He was scored for such things as converting dots to circles, touch-ups, work-over, and double lines. Thus, although the Gestalten were faithfully preserved, the details of his performance counted heavily against him. He returned the next day after having taken the test and asked to recheck the count on Designs 1 and 2. Such performance on the Bender suggests the self-doubts of the patient, the tremendous energy expended in an effort to control his anxiety, and the failure of such behavior in achieving satisfactory results, as reflected in the high score.

The Rorschach showed an emphasis on the whole and tiny detail locations, with a consequent neglect of the more usually perceived larger parts of the ink blots. Such emphasis is not uncommon in compulsive individuals. In fact, many of the characteristics of the Rorschach records of obsessive-compulsive individuals noted by Schafer (1950) were seen in this record. Perhaps his first reaction to the ink blots might be illuminating. On Card I he gave but one response. After six seconds, holding the card upright, he noted that it was symmetrical and then said it looked like the pelvis. Such a response enables us to set up several hypotheses. We note, first of all, that the response is deviant; that is, it is uncommon. Few subjects note the symmetry of the cards and then give the response "pelvis." The first reaction to the card tends to be coldly intellectual, as opposed to the subject who responds with a "female figure," "Santa Claus," etc. Our patient notes the card is symmetrical. Such a response shows the epitome of the rigidity and constriction implied in Rorschach's form response. It divides the world in half so to speak; it is distant; it shies away from the warmth of any content of the blot. His attempt at content is barren, an anxiety-laden response, a bone. We note that the bone mentioned is often substituted for a sexual response and that this response is given to a "female" card (Pascal et al., 1950). We hypothesize that the patient's reaction to this particular stress is to attempt to control by intellectualization; that this reaction fails; it results in anxiety; and that anxiety may be connected with the sexuality of a female figure. Further, such a response tells us something of the extent of the patient's psychological deficit. So much for the kind of clinical reasoning that lies behind the interpretation of a single Rorschach response.

Space does not permit us to go through the whole protocol and illustrate the process of rejecting and/or confirming initial and later hypotheses based on successive responses. We shall, instead, proceed with the case conceptualization in which test results and case history material are interwoven.

The physician, having checked the patient neurologically, ruled out cortical damage; the patient is suffering from a psychogenic disorder. Although the patient displays psychological deficit, it is not severe enough to cause loss of judgment to the extent that the patient is unable to maintain himself in his environment. The habit patterns that we are able to identify through tests and case history material are not such as would result in harm to himself or others. The patient, therefore, seems treatable as an outpatient. We can, if we like, call his disorder a "neurosis." He has many of the characteristics of the obsessive-compulsive. He is also depressed, which is not surprising. His history also indicates sexual perversion. What we call him makes little difference. We know the patient is disturbed; he knows it and wants treatment. Our problem is to formulate a diagnosis that will indicate his treatability under a particular set of conditions.

Let us see if we can identify the patient's stresses, his deprivations. Perhaps we can do this best if we look into his history. He was a child with much love for his father, but this father, in essence, rejected him. Much of the history that the patient recounted had to do with attempts to get back his charming father. His mother he seems to have accepted, but she had relatively little value to him. Even at an early age she looked to him for strength, instead of being a source of strength and security for him. The patient experienced a physical illness that made it difficult for him to compete with his fellows both in and out of school. His need for the security of a relationship with an older masculine figure led to the establishment of a homosexual relationship. He sought this security on other occasions. This behavior increased his already existing doubts about his own masculinity. He loved his father, yet he did not want to be a man like him; he was ambivalent, in the Freudian sense (Fenichel, 1945). He could not rest in the security of becoming a man "just like Daddy" and being rewarded for such behavior; on the contrary, becoming a man like his father meant becoming a drunkard. Yet, he loved his father. The patient's inability to cope physically with his fellows, his homosexual behavior, all add to his doubts about himself, which extend to his environment. He doubts whether he has ever done anything right. He has to check and recheck. Perhaps if he could have things just so, as in accounting—have the world static so it will not change . . . ?

The obsessions and compulsions become part of the patient's defenses against his self-doubts, but they are not satisfying. He learned that he can successfully compete with his fellows on an intellectual level. He has also in him a tendency to withdraw, to escape from it all. Perhaps the student can identify the patient's stresses: the threat to security inherent in the deprivation of the need to belong, as a man, the need to be satisfied with himself in this role, the need to be a man to his wife, etc. He should also be able to identify the X factors, the tendency to control by intellectualization, the obsessive-compulsive characteristics, the withdrawal tendencies, the hostility toward figures of authority, the easy acceptance of a dependent relationship with a mother figure (the wife). It was predicted that this patient could establish a secure relationship with a very consistent, very reliable male therapist. It was predicted that the patient would doubt the therapist, attempt to control by intellectualization, and attempt to withdraw. These predictions were found to be correct as psychotherapy slowly, but successfully, progressed.

SUMMARY

The neurotic reaction is differentiated from psychotic behavior in that there is no gross distortion of reality or pervasively extreme personality disorganization. In making an appraisal of any neurotic condition, the clinical psychologist uses a variety of psychological tests and case history material to arrive at a diagnosis. Three broad classes of variables are considered by the clinician: (1) psychological deficit, which has to do with the severity of the disorder; (2) stress arising from need deprivation; and (3) the defenses and habits used to satisfy deeply rooted needs. In this approach to diagnosis, little emphasis is placed on taxonomy; but, rather, the purpose of diagnosis is to make the best prediction possible with respect to the practical problems of patient management and to arrive at a prognosis for specific psychological treatment.

REFERENCES

ALBEE, G. W. 1950. Patterns of aggression in psychopathology. *J. consult. Psychol.*, 4, 465–68.

ASH, P. 1949. The reliability of psychiatric diagnoses. *J. abnorm. soc. Psychol.*, 44, 272–77.

BAUER, J. 1945. *Constitution and disease.* (2d ed.) New York: Grune & Stratton.

BILLINGSLEA, F. Y. 1963. The Bender-Gestalt: A review and a perspective. *Psychol. Bull.*, 60, 233–51.

BORING, E. G. 1913. Learning in dementia praecox. *Psychol. Rev.*, 15, 1–101.

CATTELL, R. B., and SCHEIER, I. H. 1961. *The meaning and measurement of neuroticism and anxiety.* New York: Ronald.

COMMITTEE ON NOMENCLATURE AND STATISTICS OF THE AMERICAN PSYCHIATRIC ASSOCIATION. 1952. *Mental disorders.* Washington, D.C.: The Association, Mental Hospital Service.

EYSENCK, H. J. 1952. Schizothymia-cyclothymia as a dimension of personality. II. Experimental. *J. Psychol.*, 20, 345–84.

EYSENCK, H. J. 1957. *The dynamics of anxiety and hysteria.* London: Routledge.

EYSENCK, H. J. (ed.). 1961. *Handbook of abnormal psychology.* New York: Basic Books.

EYSENCK, H. J. 1963. Psychoticism or 10 psychotic syndromes. *J. consult. Psychol.*, 27, 179–80.

FELDMAN, DOROTHY, PASCAL, G. R., and SWENSEN, C. H. 1954. Direction of aggression as a prognostic variable in mental illness. *J. consult. Psychol.*, 18, 167–70.

FENICHEL, O. 1945. *The psychoanalytic theory of neurosis.* New York: Norton.

GARRON, D. C., and CHEIFTEZ, D. I. 1965. Comment on "Bender-Gestalt discernment of organic pathology." *Psychol. Bull.*, 63, 197–200.

HODGES, A. 1953. Double alternation behavior as a function of chronological and mental age. Doctor's dissertation, Univer. of Tennessee.

HULL, C. L. 1917. The formation and retention of association among the insane. *Amer. J. Psychol.*, 28, 419–35.

Hunt, J. McV., and Cofer, C. N.   1944.   Psychological deficit.   In J. McV. Hunt (ed.), *Personality and the behavior disorders*.   New York: Ronald. Pp. 97–1032.

Hunter, W. S.   1920.   The temporal maze and kinesthetic sensory processes in the white rat.   *Psychobiol.*, 2, 1–18.

Hunter, W .S., and Bartlett, S. C.   1948.   Double alternation behavior in young children.   *J. exp. Psychol.*, 38, 558–67.

Huston, P. E., and Shakow, D.   1948.   Learning in schizophrenia.   I.   Pursuit learning.   *J. Pers.*, 17, 52–74.

Kallman, F. J.   1946.   The genetic theory of personality.   *Amer. J. Psychiat.*, 103, 309–22.

Lewin, K.   1936.   *Principles of topological psychology*.   New York: McGraw-Hill.

Lorr, M., and Rubenstein, E. A.   1955.   Factors descriptive of psychiatric out-patients.   *J. abnorm. soc. Psychol.*, 51, 514–22.

McGeoch, J. A., and Irion, A. L.   1951.   *The psychology of human learning*.   New York: Longmans.

Maslow, A. H.   1943a.   A theory of human motivation.   *Psychol. Rev.*, 50, 370–96.

Maslow, A. H.   1943b.   Dynamics of personality organization.   I.   *Psychol. Rev.*, 50, 514–39.

Maslow, A. H.   1943c.   Dynamics of personality organization.   II.   *Psychol. Rev.*, 50, 540–58.

Mehlman, B.   1952.   The reliability of psychiatric diagnoses.   *J. abnorm. soc. Psychol.*, 47, 577–78.

Murray, H. A., et al.   1938.   *Explorations in personality*.   Fair Lawn, N.J.: Oxford Univer. Press.

Overall, J. E., and Gorham, D. R.   1962.   The brief psychiatric rating scale.   *Psychol. Rep.*, 10, 799–812.

Pascal, G. R.   1951.   Psychological deficit as a function of stress and constitution.   *J. Pers.*, 20, 175–87.

Pascal, G. R.   1959.   *Behavioral change in the clinic: A systematic approach*.   New York: Grune & Stratton.

Pascal, G. R., Bayard, J., Cole, M. E., Feldman, D. A., and Swenson, C. H.   1953.   Studies of prognostic criteria in the case histories of hospitalized mental patients: Introduction, methodology, and significant variables.   *J. consult. Psychol.*, 17, 163–71.

Pascal, G. R., and Jenkins, W. O.   1959.   The Hunter-Pascal concept formation test: An experimental approach to the measurement of cortical capacity.   *J. consult. Psychol.*, 15, 159–63.

Pascal, G. R., Ruesch, H. A., Devine, C. A., and Suttell, B. J.   1950.   A study of genital symbols on the Rorschach test: Presentation of a method and results.   *J. abnorm. soc. Psychol.*, 45, 286–95.

Pascal, G. R., and Suttell, B. J.   1951.   *The Bender-Gestalt Test*.   New York: Grune & Stratton.

Pascal, G. R., and Swenson, C. H.   1952.   Learning in mentally ill patients under conditions of unusual motivation.   *J. Pers.*, 21, 240–49.

PASCAL, G. R., and ZEAMAN, J. B. 1949. A note on the validity of Wechsler-Bellevue scatter. *Amer. J. Psychiat.*, 105, 840–42.

RAPAPORT, D., GILL, M. and SCHAFER, R. 1945. *Diagnostic psychological testing.* Vol. 1. Chicago: Year Book Publications.

REISER, M. F., and BAKST, H. 1959. Psychology of cardiovascular disorders. In S. ARIETI (ed.), *American handbook of psychiatry.* New York: Basic Books.

SCHAFER, R. 1950. *The clinical application of psychological tests.* New York: International Universities Press.

SELYE, H., and FORTIER, C. 1950. Adaptive reaction to stress. *Psychosom. Med.*, 12, 149–57.

SIPPRELLE, C. 1954. An empirical test of Pascal's formula. *J. Pers.*, 23, 197–206.

SMITH, D. M. 1951. An analysis of aggression among patients in a mental hospital. Doctor's dissertation, Univer. of Pittsburgh.

WARDEN, C. J., et al. 1951. *Animal motivation: Experimental studies on the albino rat.* New York: Columbia Univer. Press.

WEISENBERG, T., and McBRIDE, K. E. 1935. *Aphasia.* Fair Lawn, N.J.: Oxford Univer. Press.

WELLS, F. L., and RUESCH, J. 1945. *Mental examiner's handbook.* New York: Psychological Corp.

WITTENBORN, J. R., and HOLZBERG, J. D. 1951. The generality of psychiatric syndromes. *J. consult. Psychol.*, 15, 372–80.

13

The Psychoses

HERBERT C. QUAY *

The psychoses represent the most serious of the behavior abnormalities in that they are the most debilitating, generally have the most adverse personal and social consequences, and, in many cases, are refractory to present treatment procedures.

The primary feature of the psychotic disorders is the disintegration of effective personal and social behavior. Psychotic individuals are impaired in their ability to test and adequately evaluate reality. In many cases emotional responsivity is underactive, overactive, or inappropriate to the situation.

Psychotic disorders generally account for about 65 to 70 per cent of first admissions to mental hospitals. Further broken down, the functional disorders account for about 33 to 40 per cent, with schizophrenia at about 25 per cent. The organic psychoses account for the remaining 30 to 40 per cent; the largest single subcategory being that of chronic brain syndrome with cerebral arteriosclerosis. This latter finding goes hand in hand with the fact that patients in mental hospitals are increasing in average age. However, psychoses generally represent only about 10 to 20 per cent of the caseload of outpatient psychiatric clinics. Thus, it can be seen that treatment of these conditions much more frequently involves removal to a controlled environment with the subsequent loss of the services of the patient as provider or homemaker.

CLASSIFICATION

Classically, the psychotic disorders have been divided into the organic and the functional and such separation is maintained to some extent in

* Herbert C. Quay, Ph.D. (University of Illinois), Director of Research, Children's Research Center, University of Illinois.

the current nomenclature (American Psychiatric Association, 1952). Table 13-1 presents a condensed form of the classification system as it involves psychotic disorders. It should be noted that the diagnostic scheme recognizes that either an acute or chronic brain syndrome may be present without psychotic manifestations. Thus, it is not correct to infer that a chronic brain syndrome associated with cerebral arteriosclerosis is necessarily a psychotic condition. Rather, the qualifying phrase "with psychosis" must be added to the diagnosis (American Psychiatric Association, 1952, p. 12). However, when psychotic manifestations are present in the clinical picture and other evidence indicates organic involvement, the primary diagnosis is one of either chronic or acute brain syndrome associated with whatever etiology is operative.

However, the functional-organic dichotomy, even to the extent it is currently in vogue, implies a separation of the psychological from the physiological that is misleading. As an obvious example, it is well known that the type of symptomatology developed by an individual after the onset of an organically demonstrable brain dysfunction is frequently seen to be related to his premorbid personality characteristics. The rather rigid and suspicious senior citizen often becomes obstreperous and openly paranoid when suffering from a chronic brain syndrome associated with cerebral arteriosclerosis. At the same time, the symptomatology of the functional disorders can be altered by drugs that obviously intervene at a physiological level. The wildly overactive manic depressive may become calm and rational; improvement in level of activity and emotional balance may be dramatic following the administration of tranquilizing medication.

In clinical practice, the task is more realistically one of assigning some relative weight to the organic or the more purely environmental or psychological factors, for it is such relative weights and their interactions that generally influence what treatment procedures may be attempted and the degree to which restoration to the premorbid level of functioning is likely.

Subtypes. Despite the apparent neatness of the subcategories of the functional disorders implied in the classificatory system, they differ in significant ways from the subcategories of the organic psychoses. First of all, they are based on symptomology rather than on etiology. Rarely will a diagnosis of acute brain syndrome associated with trauma be made without the physical signs of cerebral insult being demonstrated along with the behavioral symptomatology generally associated with the organic dysfunction. However, a diagnosis of schizophrenic reaction, catatonic type, is not dependent upon demonstrating any etiological agent. The etiology for this subtype of schizophrenia cannot be shown

Table 13–1. Psychotic Disorders in Current Nomenclature (American Psychiatric Association, 1952), in Abbreviated Form

---

Disorders of psychogenic origin or without clearly defined physical cause or structural change in the brain

   I. Involutional psychotic reaction

  II. Affective reactions
    A. Manic depressive reaction, manic type
    B. Manic depressive reaction, depressive type
    C. Manic depressive reaction, other
    D. Psychotic depressive reaction

 III. Schizophrenic reactions
    A. Schizophrenic reaction, simple type
    B. Schizophrenic reaction, hebephrenic type
    C. Schizophrenic reaction, catatonic type
    D. Schizophrenic reaction, paranoid type
    E. Schizophrenic reaction, acute undifferentiated type
    F. Schizophrenic reaction, chronic undifferentiated type
    G. Schizophrenic reaction, schizo-affective type
    H. Schizophrenic reaction, childhood type
    I. Schizophrenic reaction, residual type

 IV. Paranoid reactions
    A. Paranoia
    B. Paranoid state

  V. Psychotic reaction without clearly defined structural change, other than above

Disorders caused by or associated with impairment of brain-tissue function

   I. Acute brain disorders
    A. Disorders due to, or associated with, infection
      1. Acute brain syndrome associated with intracranial infection
      2. Acute brain syndrome associated with systemic infection
    B. Disorders due to, or associated with, intoxication
      1. Acute brain syndrome, drug or poison intoxication
      2. Acute brain syndrome, alcohol intoxication
        a. Acute hallucinosis
        b. Delirium tremens
    C. Disorders due to, or associated with, trauma
      1. Acute brain syndrome associated with trauma
    D. Disorders due to, or associated with, circulatory disturbance
      1. Acute brain syndrome associated with circulatory disturbance
    E. Disorders due to, or associated with, disturbance of innervation or of psychic control
      1. Acute brain syndrome associated with convulsive disorder
    F. Disorders due to, or associated with, disturbance of metabolism, growth, or nutrition
      1. Acute brain syndrome with metabolic disturbance
    G. Disorders due to, or associated with, new growth
      1. Acute brain syndrome associated with intracranial neoplasm
    H. Disorders due to unknown or uncertain cause
      1. Acute brain syndrome with disease of unknown or uncertain cause
    I. Disorders due to unknown or uncertain cause with the functional reaction alone manifest
      1. Acute brain syndrome of unknown cause

Table 13–1. (Continued)

II. Chronic brain disorders
  A. Disorders due to prenatal (constitutional) influence
    1. Chronic brain syndrome associated with congenital cranial anomaly
    2. Chronic brain syndrome associated with congenital spastic paraplegia
    3. Chronic brain syndrome associated with mongolism
    4. Chronic brain syndrome due to prenatal maternal infectious diseases
  B. Disorders due to, or associated with, infection
    1. Chronic brain syndrome associated with central nervous system syphilis
      a. Meningoencephalitic
      b. Meningovascular
      c. Other central nervous system syphilis
    2. Chronic brain syndrome associated with intracranial infection other than syphilis
  C. Disorders associated with intoxication
    1. Chronic brain syndrome associated with intoxication
      a. Chronic brain syndrome, drug or poison intoxication
      b. Chronic brain syndrome, alcohol intoxication
  D. Disorders associated with trauma
    1. Chronic brain syndrome associated with birth trauma
    2. Chronic brain syndrome associated with brain trauma
      a. Chronic brain syndrome, brain trauma, gross force
      b. Chronic brain syndrome following brain operation
      c. Chronic brain syndrome following electrical brain trauma
      d. Chronic brain syndrome following irradiational brain trauma
  E. Disorders associated with circulatory disturbances
    1. Chronic brain syndrome associated with cerebral arteriosclerosis
    2. Chronic brain syndrome associated with circulatory disturbance other than cerebral arteriosclerosis
  F. Disorders associated with disturbances of innervation or of psychic control
    1. Chronic brain syndrome associated with convulsive disorder
  G. Disorders associated with disturbance of metabolism, growth, or nutrition
    1. Chronic brain syndrome associated with senile brain disease
    2. Chronic brain syndrome associated with other disturbance of metabolism, growth, or nutrition (includes presenile, glandular, pellagra, familial amaurosis)
  H. Disorders associated with new growth
    1. Chronic brain syndrome associated with intracranial neoplasm
  I. Disorders associated with unknown or uncertain cause
    1. Chronic brain syndrome associated with disease of unknown or uncertain cause (includes multiple sclerosis, Huntington's chorea, Pick's disease, and other diseases of a familial or hereditary nature)
  J. Disorders due to unknown or uncertain cause with the functional reaction alone manifest
    1. Chronic brain syndrome of unknown cause

to be different than that for other subtypes of schizophrenia; it remains, in fact, basically unknown.

Then, too, prognosis is involved. The prognosis for a chronic brain syndrome is generally clear cut. The damage is done, and while symptoms may fluctuate, anything like full recovery to the premorbid functioning is unlikely. For the subtypes of schizophrenia, no such prognostic statements can be made with any degree of certainty.

A further complication is that there is also less certainty about the coherence and homogeniety of the symptom clusters themselves. Studies in which the degree of agreement between psychiatrists in the assignment of subtype diagnoses has been demonstrated to be quite poor (Ash, 1949; Schmidt and Fonda, 1956) have suggested that the current symptom clusters arrived at out of clinical observation are inadequate. Correctives have been suggested through the use of multivariate statistical procedures in developing the symptom-based syndromes (Lorr, Klett, and McNair, 1963; Wittenborn, 1951), and through the use of an item-validity approach seeking symptomatic and other behavioral and background factors that can be statistically related to prognosis (Phillips, 1953; Wittman, 1941).

The latter approach has had considerable success in delineating two forms of schizophrenia: the "process" and the "reactive." In the process type, there is an insidious and gradual development of the psychosis, a lack of clear-cut precipitating factors, a poor level of premorbid personality and social adjustment characterized by withdrawn or "schizoid" behavior, and a presenting symptomatology consisting generally of a lack of affective behavior but with good orientation, an absence of confusion, and a clear sensorium. Conversely, reactive schizophrenia is generally typified by a rapid onset of the psychosis, some demonstrable precipitating factors, a generally adequate premorbid personality and social adjustment, and presenting symptomatology consisting of fluctuating affective behavior, frequently at a high level of intensity, disorientation, and confusion. (Langfeldt, 1956.)

Considerable recent research has concentrated on studying this dichotomous classification and differences have been demonstrated in thought processes (Becker, 1956), autonomic responsiveness (King, 1958), sensitiveness to censure (Rodnick and Garmezy, 1957), and prognosis (Kantor, Wallner and Winder, 1953). It has also been suggested that the psychological functioning of the process group is much more like that of patients suffering organic brain dysfunctions than is the functioning of the reactive group (Brackbill, 1956; Tutko and Spence, 1962).

THE CLINICIAN'S TASK

The task of the clinician is that of making a differential diagnosis not only between the psychotic disorders and other abnormal conditions and between one form of psychotic disorder and another. There are other even more important considerations. The clinician needs to concern himself with such questions as: To what degree has this patient's social and intellectual competence been impaired? Can he make a living for himself and his family even under the most nurturant of environmental circumstances? Must he be hospitalized or can he be treated on an out-patient basis? Is recovery likely? To what extent can he be expected to regain personal and social adequacy? Is he dangerous to himself or others? All of these practical questions are of utmost concern to the patient, to his family, to cooperating social agencies, and to society as a whole. To the extent that the clinical psychologist can help in answering them, to that extent will his value to the diagnostic and treatment team be enhanced.

In accomplishing his task, the clinician must be knowledgeable about, and sensitive to, many different things. He must be able to recognize the behavioral symptomatology associated with psychotic disorders. In some cases he must be skillful in actually eliciting such behavior from the patient; the schizophrenic does not always freely admit to his hallucinations nor is the paranoid always open about his feelings of persecution. In assessing the meaning of what appears to be a gross behavioral abnormality, the clinician must be sensitive to cultural differences. For example, auditory hallucinations of the voice of God are not highly unusual among followers of certain more primitive religious sects. To conclude that hallucinations in a person of such belief were indicative of psychosis would be erroneous. Alertness and sensitivity to less obvious forms of behavioral abnormality is also a requisite for the good clinician. A tremor or language handicap that would go unnoticed by the untrained observer might suggest the presence of an organic brain dysfunction to the clinical psychologist.

The clinician must also be highly knowledgeable about his diagnostic instruments. In a general sense, psychological tests are ways of collecting samples of behavior under controlled conditions with the further condition that the samples of behavior collected can be interpreted by reference to norms for the general (or some specific) population. Since diagnostic testing is discussed in detail elsewhere in this volume (see Chapters 3, 4, and 5), suffice to say here that the clinician should know both the strengths and weaknesses of his tests. He should be particularly aware of factors other than psychopathology that can influence patient performance, for example, verbal intelligence and facility, reading skills, cultural background, and many others.

The clinical psychologist's contribution to the clinical process can best be seen in the context of a number of complete case histories. In these histories, contributions of the various professional disciplines can be seen to operate together to provide a total integrated picture out of the history, and the current status of the patient's functioning. Clinical teamwork has arisen because no one discipline can provide all of the information needed to make the most rational decisions affecting the future of a behaviorally disordered person.

The following cases have been selected to illustrate three different types of psychotic disorders and the psychologist's contribution to the process of clinical diagnosis. They represent composites of actual cases, such composites serving to illustrate better important features of both the psychoses and the clinical process. As near as possible the original language and syntax have been preserved to give as much of the actual flavor of clinical records as possible.

CASE A: MALE, AGE 32
Events Leading to Hospitalization

For six months prior to his admission the patient had been living in a low-cost rooming house just on the fringe of the central business area of a middle-sized city. He had been employed, or so his landlady thought, as a dishwasher in a cafeteria where his meals were provided as part of his wages. While the land-lady generally did not take more than a passing interest in her roomers as long as they paid their rent, she realized one morning that she had not seen Mr. A in over a week. Fearing that he had left owing her a week's rent, she entered his room with the key to find him in bed fully dressed and staring at the ceiling. He refused to get up and would respond only in monosyllables, mumbling vaguely that he wanted to be left alone. The police were called and he was removed, only mildly protesting, to the local precinct. He could give no coherent reason for his behavior and, according to the police, said a number of things that "didn't make sense." His behavior resulted in a physician being called in to examine him. Hospitalization was recommended. The patient's father was located, and he consented to sign the commitment papers and institutional placement was shortly effected.

Mental Status of Examination

The patient was oriented for time, place, and person. He could see no reason why he had been brought to the hospital and did not consider himself to be ill in any way. Some mild feelings of persecution were elicited in that he complained that some of the other people in a rooming house where he had last lived talked about him as being an "oddball." Hallucinations were denied and no systematized delusional material could be elicited. Affect was flat and expressed emotion was almost nonexistent. The events leading to his being hospitalized were not regarded by the patient as being unusual—"All I wanted was to be left alone."

Social History

Parents. The social history was provided by the father; the mother had died of cancer at the age of 56, three years before the patient's hospitalization. The father is currently retired and is living in a retirement home operated for members of a union in which he has been a life-long member. Now aged 66, he completed grammar school and then became a carpenter's apprentice. He has been steadily employed until his retirement except for a brief period in the early

1930's. He married the patient's mother when he was 31 and she was 24; despite the age difference in his favor, it was clear that the mother was the more dominant of the two. She was a high school graduate who had been employed as a stenographer at the time of her marriage. The father indicated that he thought his marriage had been a happy one but that his wife had devoted herself almost completely to her son after his birth.

Patient's Early Life. The patient was born during the third year of his parents' marriage; there were no other children. As an infant and young child the patient was small, frail, and frequently ill, although never seriously. While his mother was devoted to him, at the same time she was restrictive of his contacts outside the home.

Education. During his school years Mr. A was a competent, if not an outstanding, student, graduating in the upper quarter of his class. On his mother's urging he had taken a commercial course despite the fact that he would have likely succeeded in college had he been able to go. He was not active in extracurricular groups and had few friends; he dated only rarely. The majority of his free time was spent in reading or in home activities with his mother.

Marital History. The patient has never married and since his discharge from the service has shown absolutely no interest in women.

Military and Occupational History. After graduation from high school the patient was drafted into the Army. During basic training he was hospitalized briefly after having been frequently on sick call for a series of very vague somatic complaints. No organic factors were found and the patient was returned to duty without a diagnosis. After completing basic training he was assigned for training as a finance clerk. He served in this capacity for the remainder of his three years in the service in grades up to the equivalent of corporal. His off-duty hours were generally spent in the post library. He had no close friends and virtually no contact with women. His leaves were spent with his parents.

Following his discharge he obtained a clerical position in a large bank. For the first few years he performed creditably but his work became less and less accurate and he became even more withdrawn and preoccupied. He finally became unable to perform the duties of his job and was discharged. There then followed a series of clerical jobs, each terminated because his preoccupation and asociality precluded his adequate performance of the work involved. The termination of his last job coincided with the onset of his mother's illness. For two years he did nothing beyond caring for her. On her death he abruptly moved out of the family home. For the three years prior to his hospitalization he had one menial job after another, being barely able to support himself. He had essentially no contact with the father during these years.

A consideration of the social history, carefully taken in the social service department, in terms of factors relating to prognosis as outlined in such approaches as the Phillips' Scale (Phillips, 1953) and the Elgin Prognostic Scale (Wittman, 1941) led to the almost inescapable conclusion that the prognosis was very poor. Social relationships and sexual adjustment had never been even near normal and the long and insidious onset of the psychotic process was clearly manifest in the occupational history.

Psychological Evaluation

Mr. A entered readily into the testing situation but did not appear to be particularly emotionally involved. His reaction to the test materials and to both success and failure with them were generally flat. There was little in the way of spontaneous comment and elaboration of test responses was at a minimum. The examining clinical psychologist noted that the picture was one of flattened affect, and loss of spontaneity.

On the Wechsler Adult Intelligence Scale the patient obtained a verbal IQ of 93, a performance IQ of 91, and a full-scale IQ of 93. There was little scatter among the subtest except for the similarity subtest, which was considerably lower. Analysis of the nature of the responses to items of this subtest revealed a tendency for individualistic, although not really concrete, types of responses. To the item "In what way are an orange and a banana alike," the patient replied, "I have both of them on my sink at home." The use of such "private" concepts and categorization behavior has been demonstrated by McGaughran and Moran (1956) to be characteristic of schizophrenia. In view of the patient's intelligence test performance and the school achievement in earlier years the current IQ suggests an over-all impairment in intellectual functioning.

Rorschach responses were analyzed in terms of levels of perceptual development (Friedman, 1953). This approach to the test responses revealed the presence of many of the more poorly differentiated responses with a paucity of highly differentiated and integrated responses. A clear-cut example of confused and regressive thinking was provided by a response in which Mr. A related one part of the blot to another by saying, "This must be New York because that down there is Philadelphia and New York is north of Philadelphia." The over-all picture of performance on the Rorschach Test suggested, according to the findings of Becker (1956), the likelihood of a process schizophrenia.

On the Minnesota Multiphasic Personality Inventory the presence of a psychotic disorder was strongly suggested by the profile when analyzed in terms of the signs for psychosis suggested by Meehl (1946) and given further validation by Peterson (1954). Despite the fact that no single clinical scale was at a T score of greater than 70, four ($F > 65$; $Sc > Pt$; Pa or Sc or $Ma > Hs$ and D; $D > Hs$ and Hy) of Meehl's six signs were present. The failure of any scale to reach a T score of 70 was at least suggestive of the presence of a chronic rather than an acute condition. The patient's profile is presented in Fig. 13–1.

Taken together, the results of the separate psychological tests present a picture highly suggestive of a schizophrenic disorder of an insidious and debilitating type. In this respect the psychological findings were highly consonant with the evidence for a process schizophrenic reaction suggested by the social history and mental status examination. The psychological tests were particularly valuable in assessing the degree to which regression in thought processes were then manifest.

Diagnosis and Prognostic Considerations

The official diagnosis was schizophrenic reaction, chronic undifferentiated type. However, the fact that the patient presented the features of process schizophrenia in dramatic form provided more useful information. Obviously Mr. A has gradually come to the point where he is personally and socially ineffective and can no longer maintain himself in society. Were a sheltered

The Minnesota Multiphasic Personality Inventory

Starke R. Hathaway and J. Charnley McKinley

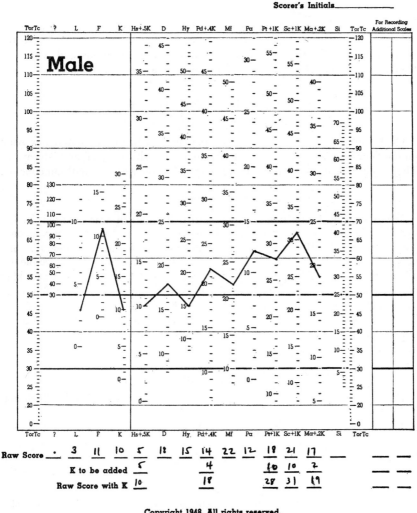

Scorer's Initials_____

Raw Score . 3 || lo ζ 18 15 14 22 12 18 21 17 ___ __ __

K to be added ___ ζ ___ 4 ___ lo lo 7 ___ __ __

Raw Score with K lo ___ 18 ___ 28 31 19 ___ __ __

Fig. 13–1. MMPI Profile of Case A.

atmosphere available outside the hospital, he might be able to adjust to a highly protected, nondemanding life. In his case however, no such possibilities existed and continued hospitalization was warranted. The prognosis was considered extremely poor and it was thought likely that the patient would be a long-term hospital resident.

DISCUSSION

In this case, the unique contribution of the clinical psychologist was to discover and to point up the deep degree to which the patient's thought processes had regressed even though the clinical picture of superficial functioning seemed not severely impaired. This feature of Mr. A's functioning, coupled with the systematic indications from the social history of an insidious and long-term breakdown of competence, was crucial in arriving at a correct diagnosis.

CASE B: FEMALE, AGE 24
EVENTS LEADING TO HOSPITALIZATION

On his arrival home from work the patient's husband had found her lying on the floor weeping copiously and screaming that she was evil and "decayed." The family physician was called and hospitalization was effected immediately.

MENTAL STATUS

When seen by the examining psychiatrist, the patient was oriented for the fact that she was in a hospital but did not seem to be aware that she was on a psychiatric ward. Her memory for the preceding few days was cloudy. She exhibited alternate periods of crying and motor overactivity. She frequently alluded to herself as "rotting away inside"; her ideas as to how this was taking place were specific enough at times to suggest that they were frankly delusional in character. At one time she said that "bugs are eating away at my insides." Hallucinations were denied by the patient although the examiner noted his impression that she had likely been subject to auditory hallucinations of voices accusing her of evil behavior.

SOCIAL HISTORY

Early History. The social history was provided by the husband. Birth and early development were normal, and while the patient was considered to be rather "high strung" throughout her childhood, she was not considered to be a behavior problem. The patient's parents, both in their late 50's, are reported to be living and well. Patient's husband reported that her mother was considered to be "nervous" and did require psychiatric care at the time of the menopause.

Educational-occupational History. The patient was an above-average student in high school where she was also moderately active socially. Her dating tended to be restricted to one boy at a time on whom she tended to become rather dependent. After graduation from high school the patient entered a small state university where she met her husband who was then in his junior year. The patient left college at the end of her sophomore year to get married. She has never been employed.

Marital History. As noted above, the patient married after the completion of her sophomore year in college at which time her husband received a degree in business administration. They then moved to an urban area when her husband joined the sales department of a moderately large corporation. Since their marriage her husband has had to spend a considerable amount of time away from home because of the demands of his job. Their income has been limited but is gradually increasing and the prospects are now excellent for the coming years. While both husband and wife have expressed a desire to have children, they have not as yet been able to do so although each has been assured that there are no physical factors interfering. They currently reside in a rather small apartment, which is, however, adequate for their needs. While the patient has attempted to fill her time with social affairs outside the home, over the past year she has become increasingly concerned over the amount of time her husband must spend in travel. On returning from a week-long trip about two weeks prior to her admission, her husband found her in an agitated state and obviously very upset. The patient finally confessed that she had had an affair with a man whom she had met during the course of one of her women's group activities. The husband was deeply hurt, and sought counsel from his minister, who advised him to do his best to forgive his wife while taking a serious look at the factors that may have led to her transgression. The patient also received some counseling from a physician whom they had been consulting in their attempt to have children. She continued to remain rather upset however and this period terminated in the events leading to her hospitalization.

Psychological Evaluation

When Mrs. B was seen by the psychologist, tranquilizing medication had already acted to attenuate her emotional lability. She was also in better contact with reality and realized that she had suffered some sort of emotional upset.

Intelligence testing revealed a full-scale IQ of 102 with a verbal IQ of 103 and a performance IQ of 99. Her over-all functioning seemed somewhat below expectations based on her educational achievement. The lowering of her score appeared to be primarily the function of depressed performance on the arithmetic, digit span, and digit symbol subtests. This was interpreted as being due to the interfering effects of a high level of anxiety.

Anxiety was also reflected in her MMPI profile (Fig. 13–2). The presence of three of Meehl's signs (T scores on four or more scales > 70, $F > 65$, $D > Hs$ and Hy) suggested a psychosis.

The Rorschach was not revealing in serious regression in perceptual processes. However, there was a tendency for color to predominate over form in determining perceptions; a feature generally thought to be indicative of emotional lability.

The over-all picture of Mrs. B's psychological functionings suggested a person of above-average intelligence whose ability to deal constructively with the environment was currently being impaired by a high level of anxiety and extremely poor emotional control. While her perceptual processes were not

The Minnesota Multiphasic Personality Inventory
Starke R. Hathaway and J. Charnley McKinley

Scorer's Initials_____

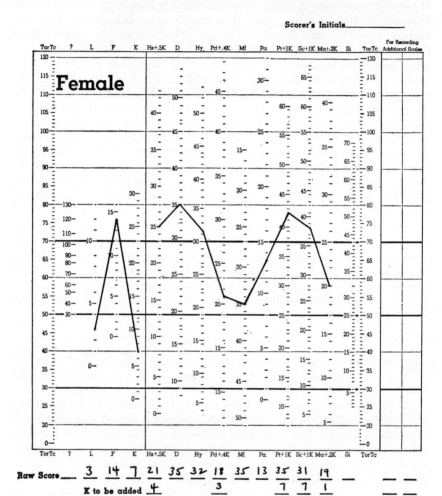

Fig. 13–2. MMPI Profile of Case B.

thought to be seriously regressed at the time of testing, there was evidence of some impairment in reality testing.

DIAGNOSIS AND PROGNOSTIC CONSIDERATIONS

Mrs. B received a diagnosis of schizophrenic reaction, schizoaffective type. Her history and functioning strongly suggested her schizophrenic breakdown to be of the reactive type. Her premorbid adjustment and presenting symptomatology were not indicative of the presence of the more debilitating process psychosis. The prognosis for her recovery from her present attack is considered quite good. Clearly she needs support and likely much more than the ordinary individual. She will always need to avoid stressful situations, and it is likely that she will not be able to handle tension-producing factors that would not seriously upset a better integrated personality. However, with understanding from her husband and the development of constructive interests outside the home, perhaps including employment or continuation of her education, she should be able to function on an adequate social level.

DISCUSSION

For this patient a crucial function of the clinical psychologist was to ascertain that (in marked contrast to the first case) thought processes were not seriously regressed. The fact that the psychological tests indicated a high level of anxiety and an extreme emotional lability, thus suggesting a more acute psychotic condition, rather than a reorganization of the personality along a lower developmental level, was very helpful in arriving at a correct formulation of the case.

Help for Mrs. B required the collaboration of the clinical team. During the ensuing months Mr. B was able to gain a considerable understanding of his wife's needs, as well as his own, through continued contacts with the social worker. Mrs. B was maintained on tranquilizing medication by the psychiatrist while she underwent supportive psychotherapy with a clinical psychologist.

She enrolled in a local college, taking a limited load, and was making satisfactory progress after a year. It is likely that without the continued cooperation of the three disciplines the outcome might have been much different.

CASE C: MALE, AGE 29
EVENTS LEADING TO HOSPITALIZATION

The patient had been brought to the hospital by his employer who had gone to his apartment to check on his absence from work for two days. This in itself was not highly unusual, but the patient had a sizable sum coming to him for saleswork made the previous week. The patient was confused and disoriented and had dried blood in his right ear. He was belligerent but agreed to accompany his employer to the hospital.

MENTAL STATUS EXAMINATION

Patient was confused and restless and had little memory of the previous several days. He vaguely recalled an altercation in a tavern that subsequent investigation found to have been a major brawl leading to the arrest of the participants—not including the patient. He was grandiose at times and delusions were suspected. Although no aphasic symptoms were noted, organic involvement was suspected and neurological workup was ordered.

SOCIAL HISTORY

Parents. The social history was provided by both parents. The father is age 53, in good health, and employed in a machine shop. He claims to be a steady worker but admits that at times alcohol is a problem. The mother is now 49 years old, is a housewife, and suffers from mild hypertension. The parents have been married 31 years, never divorced or separated. The union has produced four children, all male. The patient was the second child. The oldest sibling is employed as a factory worker in another city. The third is currently serving in the United States Army while the youngest attends high school. None of the siblings have ever been hospitalized with the exception of the patient. To date, only the patient has graduated from high school.

Patient's Early Life. Birth and early development were uneventful. The patient was always large for his age and inclined to be somewhat aggressive. He was considered to be a behavior problem in grammar school but was never expelled. He was generally punished physically by his father for misdeeds. His academic performance in high school was spotty and he was considered by his teachers to be overly aggressive. Although known to juvenile authorities for truancy and for fighting in public places, he was never considered a serious delinquent. He was always interested in automobiles and had some mechanical aptitude.

Marital History. The patient was married at age 25, is the father of two children, now ages 2 and 3, and has been divorced for the past year. He sporadically contributes to the support of his children but shows little interest in them. The wife is employed as a salesclerk in a distant city where her parents reside. From the beginning the marriage was stormy. The wife obtained a divorce after she was severely bruised during an incident provoked by her having censured her husband for excessive drinking.

Military and Occupational History. The patient is currently an Army reservist, having served a brief period of active duty after enlistment. His initial adjustment to active duty was marked by one episode of absence without leave and fighting for which he was courtmartialed and fined. He has held a number of jobs all related to the automotive field. He is currently a used-car salesman, his income as such being highly variable. He has been fired from at least two jobs for aggressiveness. He is frequently suspicious and distrustful of his coworkers, especially other salesmen. He drinks heavily on occasion and sometimes has suffered blackouts during binges.

Summary of Social History. The patient has always been rather aggressive and difficult. His history suggests an antisocial, or at least an aggressive, personality structure. The degree to which alcohol is involved in his difficulties was not readily ascertained.

PSYCHOLOGICAL EVALUATION

Although confused and restless Mr. C cooperated adequately for testing. On the Wechsler Adult Intelligence Scale he obtained a verbal IQ of 98, a performance IQ of 89, and a full-scale IQ of 94. On the Halstead battery of tests for the detection of organic brain damage, the patient's impairment index was .8 indicating considerable likelihood of organic dysfunction (Halstead, 1947; Reitan, 1955). Tests of finger tapping revealed that the left hand was not functioning as well as it should with relation to the right.

The MMPI suggested the presence of multiple somatic complaints and subjective feelings of anxiety and depression. The presence of a functional psychosis was contra-indicated by the MMPI profile (Fig. 13–3).

The Minnesota Multiphasic Personality Inventory
Starke R. Hathaway and J. Charnley McKinley

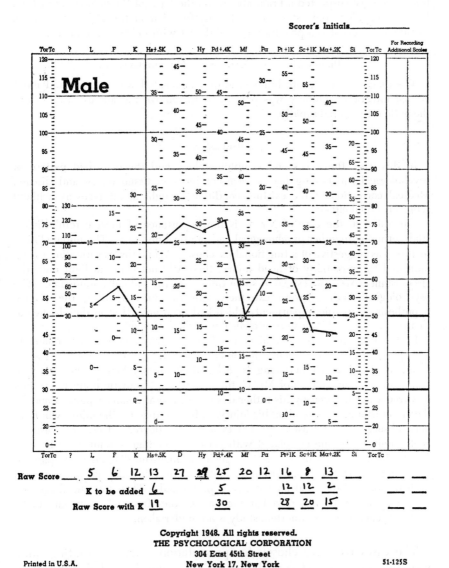

Fig. 13–3. MMPI Profile of Case C.

The over-all impression given by the results of the psychological test was one of organic involvement rather than functional psychosis. Neurological study was recommended.

NEUROLOGICAL EVALUATION

While no abnormal signs were found in the clinical neurological examination, the neurologist suspected a brain abscess on the basis of the behavioral picture. Electroencephlographic study indicated dysfunction in the right hemisphere. Skull X-rays revealed a penetrating skull defect with indriven fragments.

PROGNOSIS AND DIAGNOSTIC CONSIDERATIONS

The diagnosis was acute brain syndrome associated with trauma and intra-cranial infection. Surgery was performed to remove the abscess after which the patient recovered rapidly.

DISCUSSION

In this case, the behavioral symptomatology and the disturbed pattern of psychological functioning had a clear-cut basis in tissue injury and disease. Medical correction of the existing condition brought about recovery without serious residual effects.

Illustrated in the case of Mr. C is the importance of most careful clinical study bringing together psychological and physical findings. The initial clinical picture was suggestive of a functional psychosis. While the precipitating events indicated the possibility of head injury, these did not come to light until the circumstances were investigated some time after the patient's admission. The psychological findings were extremely valuable in supporting the clinical hypothesis of organic impairment, which had been arrived at in the absence of clear-cut behavioral indicators or clinical neurological signs.

It should be pointed out that cases of acute brain syndrome are relatively infrequent in clinics and mental hospitals. More frequently such cases will be seen by psychologists functioning as part of the neuropsychiatric team in a general hospital. In the case of Mr. C, the fact that a traumatic brain injury had occurred was obscured by his rather dyssocial general behavior pattern and by the circumstances surrounding his injury. More frequently the injury will have been observed or at least suspected to a greater degree. However, cases of acute brain syndrome associated with causes other than trauma may be confused with functional psychoses. In such instances misdiagnoses are particularly tragic as the true nature of the patient's disorder may go unrecognized until the patient dies and an autopsy is performed. Then too, the diagnostic error may never be recognized if the patient dies from what appears to be "natural" causes and postmortem study is not undertaken.

The cases we have chosen for presentation, while illustrating quite well the function and contribution of the clinical psychologist, are in some ways misleading. Not all cases seen in the clinical setting can be so neatly diagnosed. In many instances the picture will remain clouded despite the best efforts of the clinical team. Psychological tests can yield results that are at variance with both the clinical impressions of the patient's behavior and the outcome of the case. No clinician is without his collection of test negatives who turned out to be clever and even dangerous paranoids and test positives who were later seen not to be nearly as psychologically disordered as the tests indicated.

In the case of the psychotic disorders we have tried to make it obvious that the team approach is a necessity in both diagnosis and treatment. No amount of individual psychotherapy would have been able to maintain Mr. A in society. The positive outcome in the case of Mrs. B could not likely have been brought about without the help received by her husband and the anxiety-ameliorating effects of continued medication even though she was receiving personal counseling. The case of Mr. C could have ended in tragedy had not the clinical team gotten the patient into the hands of the neurological surgeon. The clinical psychologist never forgets that there is nothing more complex than human behavior and that all disciplines concerned with it, particularly with its disordered forms, need all the help they can get.

SUMMARY

The psychoses are the most serious of the personality disorders. They are associated with a loss of contact with reality and a disintegration of personal and social competence. Psychotic disorders are generally divided into two major groups: the organic and the functional. While various subtypes of both groups are recognized, the clinically derived categories for the functional disorders have not proved to be especially useful in that they are not related to either etiology or prognosis. More recent attempts to develop subcategories by statistical means appear more promising.

In working with the psychoses, the clinical psychologist must not only attempt to differentiate between psychoses but must also direct his efforts toward answering questions relative to degree of disability and to prognosis. The crucial task is the assessment of the degree to which perceptual and conceptual regression or deterioration has occurred. These factors appear to be the most important determinants in the eventual outcome of functional psychotic disorders.

Clinical teamwork is particularly important in the diagnosis and management of the psychoses. Psychological, social, and medical intervention may all be necessary to bring about the highest degree of rehabilitation of the individual suffering from psychotic disorder.

REFERENCES

AMERICAN PSYCHIATRIC ASSOCIATION. 1952. *Diagnostic and statistical manual: Mental disorders*. Washington, D.C.: The Association.

ASH, P. 1949. The reliability of psychiatric diagnosis. *J. abnorm. soc. Psychol.*, 44, 272–77.

BECKER, W. C. 1956. A genetic approach to the interpretation of the process-reactive distinction in schizophrenia. *J. abnorm. soc. Psychol.*, 53, 229–36.

BRACKBILL, G. A. 1956. Studies on brain dysfunction in schizophrenia. *Psychol. Bull.*, 53, 210–26.

FRIEDMAN, H. 1953. Perceptual regression in schizophrenia: An hypothesis suggested by the use of the Rorschach test. *J. proj. Tech.*, 17, 162–70.

HALSTEAD, W. C. 1947. *Brain and intelligence: A quantitative study of the frontal lobes*. Chicago: Univer. of Chicago Press.

KANTOR, R. E., WALLNER, J. M., and WINDER, C. C. 1953. Process and reactive schizophrenia. *J. consult. Psychol.*, 17, 157–62.

KING, G. F. 1958. Differential autonomic responsiveness in the process-reactive classification of schizophrenia. *J. abnorm. soc. Psychol.*, 56, 160–64.

LANGFELDT, G. 1956. The prognosis in schizophrenia. *ACTA Psychiat. Neurol. Scand.*, Suppl. 110, pp. 1–66.

LORR, M., KLETT, C. J., and McNAIR, D. 1963. *Syndrome of psychosis*. Oxford, England: Pergamon.

McGAUGHRAN, L. S., and MORAN, L. J. 1956. "Conceptual level" vs. "conceptual area" analysis of object sorting behavior of schizophrenic and nonpsychiatric groups. *J. abnorm. soc. Psychol.*, 52, 43–50.

MEEHL, P. E. 1946. Profile analysis of the MMPI in differential diagnosis. *J. appl. Psychol.*, 30, 517–24.

PETERSON, D. R. 1954. The diagnosis of subclinical schizophrenia. *J. consult. Psychol.*, 18, 198–200.

PHILLIPS, L. 1953. Case history data and prognosis in schizophrenia. *J. nerv. ment. Dis.*, 117, 515–25.

REITAN, R. M. 1955. An investigation of the validity of Halstead's measures of biological intelligences. *Amer. Med. Assn. Arch. Neurol. Psychiat.*, 73, 28–35.

RODNICK, E. H., and GARMEZY, N. 1957. An experimental approach to the study of motivation in schizophrenia. In M. R. JONES (ed.), *Nebraska symposium on motivation*. Lincoln: Univer. of Nebraska Press.

SCHMIDT, H. O., and FONDA, C. P. 1956. The reliability of psychiatric diagnosis: A new look. *J. abnorm. soc. Psychol.*, 52, 262–67.

TUTKO, T. A., and SPENCE, JANET A. 1962. The performance of process and reactive schizophrenics and brain injured subjects on a conceptual task. *J. abnorm. soc. Psychol.*, 65, 387–94.

WITTENBORN, J. R. 1951. Symptom patterns in a group of mental hospital patients. *J. consult. Psychol.*, 15, 290–302.

WITTMAN, PHYLLIS. 1941. A scale for measuring prognosis in schizophrenic patients. *Elgin State Hospital Papers*, 4, 20–33.

14

Psychopathic and Criminal Behavior

L. A. PENNINGTON *

The origins of delinquency and crime, the management and rehabilitation of the delinquent and the criminal, and the prevention of antisocial behavior are major social and research problems confronting the public in general and the behavioral scientists in particular. The unassailable fact that crimes are committed by people leads directly to the frontiers of knowledge about human action where theories of personality, of cultural and social organizations, and of research methods do not always join. By and large, two groups of investigators show major concern with the problem: the penologists and the clinicians. The former, ordinarily criminologists and sociologists by training and experience, are now less prone to accept the constitutional and hereditarian biases of the early twentieth century. Rather, they tend to approach the issues by applying methods of research from the social sciences where stress is placed largely upon the facts and principles of group behavior. In their studies one meets the hypothesis that criminal behavior is the result of competing value systems arising from the disorganization present in social institutions and neighborhood areas (Barnes and Teeters, 1959). Cultural conflict is thus a focal point. A second hypothesis comes from the clinicians —prison psychiatrists, psychologists, and social workers,[1] among others.

* L. A. Pennington, Ph.D. (Brown University), Consulting Clinical Psychologist, Danville, Illinois.
[1] The term "orthopsychiatrist" is often applied here, for it combines the three professions just named. Major goals of the American Orthopsychiatric Association, founded in 1930, are the identification, treatment, and prevention of behavioral difficulties in children and the improvement of the mental and physical health of parents.

This view posits that in each and every criminal act, psychogenic factors specific to the individual are either involved or responsible. These students have therefore ordinarily studied those prison inmates judged guilty by the courts of crimes [2] against persons. Their approach is largely descriptive, clinical, and idiographic. The sociologists, on the other hand, have studied the many inmates judged guilty of crimes against property. Their approach has largely been culturally oriented and nomothetic.

Each group of specialists has upon occasion gone from its research data and has formulated hypotheses in efforts to account for antisocial behavior. Differences in professional backgrounds, research interests and methods, and theoretical positions have provided areas for controversy. For example, the prison psychiatrist is critical of the overemphasis placed at times by the penologist upon norms of conduct within the inmate's home community and of the latter's lack of interest in conflicts present early in the family setting. The penologist is likewise critical of the psychiatrist's seeming ambiguity when he endeavors to differentiate the habitual criminal from the situational one on grounds of "emotional instability," "feelings of insecurity," "psychopathic tendencies," and other terms. He points out that prison psychiatrists and psychologists have not been able predictively to select for segregation purposes the "good" risks from the "bad" ones on the basis of interview and psychodiagnostic tests alone (McCord and McCord, 1959). The penologist accordingly may take a dim view of the clinician's assumption of relationships between concrete criminal behavior and abstract personality-test variables. He continues to stress the *act*, to study it in relation to the forces of cultural conflict. The clinician, on the other hand, focuses upon the doer, upon his deeds in relation to his conflicts, and his strivings. These two approaches are only now slowly merging (Glueck and Glueck, 1962).

In retrospect it is not surprising then to find a twofold taxonomic system operative within the prison walls. The administrative penologist has ample need for a workable one the better to segregate and hence to maintain discipline, as well as to reduce the number of untoward events. The psychiatrist needs a handy system by virtue of tradition, a job that yearly requires a statistical tally of the numbers of variously diagnosed inmates, and because of his need to choose those capable of profiting from a widening variety of rehabilitative measures and procedures. So it has come about that the criminologist speaks of the habitual, accidental, and professional classes of criminals. The habitual are the recidivists, the

---

[2] "Crime" is defined as an intentional act in violation of the law. It is said to be committed without defense or excuse, and is punished by the state through the courts as a felony or as a misdemeanor. The terms "crime," "criminal," "delinquency," and "delinquent" are therefore strictly social and legal concepts. They denote—they do not explain.

repeaters. The accidental are viewed as "normal" or situational in that they once reacted too soon and unwisely in what was for them a stressful situation. The professional criminals—those few who are apprehended— are by choice, experience, and skill engaging in crime just as another might study to become an accountant. Some place these three classes on a continuum that reflects the interplay of cultural forces in the arousal of the antisocial act. At one extreme is the social criminal who performs misdeeds for clearly discernible (e.g., economic) goals. The professional criminal, who by virtue of his strong emotional ties with antisocial elements in his culture embarks upon a career in crime, is of this order. His behavior is approved by his group. At the other extreme is the individualized criminal whose conduct stems from undecipherable forces that no social group can tolerate. The so-called insane criminal is a case in point. Between these extremes are found the accidental criminals whose felonies are considered as atypical responses to unusual stress. Society can "understand" their crimes and, in so doing, may at times take a strong stand in their behalf. The habitual criminal, on the other hand, by virtue of his own weaknesses coupled with relatively minor environmental stress, repeatedly misbehaves. Society can tolerate him for a time only to react strongly later. It is in this category that the law, criminology, and penology ordinarily place the sociopath and the psychopath. This classification, or one of its substitutes, tends to highlight the fact that criminal intent and capability of accepting responsibility for one's acts—"competence" before the law—are important variables that the lawyer, judge, and administrative penologist must consider in their respective positions. The psychologist assigned to a prison's diagnostic center can thus expect to meet in each new group of inmates a number who are considered "normal" when culturally viewed. Each, from the psychologist's view (Grigsby, 1963) will, however, have his own set of personality characteristics and conflicts. And some will react strongly to confinement by such patterns as anxiety and somatization states, strong guilt with ideas of reference, excitements, escape mechanisms as illustrated by malingering and the Ganser Syndrome, reactive depressions, and brief psychotic episodes. In this connection it is estimated that the percentage of prison inmates suffering from clear-cut emotional disturbances of whatever kind centers around 25 per cent (Macdonald, 1958).

The second categorization is, of course, psychiatric and in general follows the nomenclature devised by leaders in that professional group. The psychiatric and neurological examinations, usually accompanied by psychodiagnostic evaluations (Burgemeister, 1962), are often done initially by order of the court to aid in the early decision upon such matters as intent and competence. Once judged guilty, the prisoners are then sent to prisons which vary in degree of security (minimal to maximal), reformatories, prison farms, or more specialized penal institutions. Later on these inmates are again clinically studied, "screened," segregated, and transferred if necessary to institutions best suited to the prisoner's needs and rehabilitation.

The sociological and the psychiatric classification systems are now often used interchangeably by members of those professions working in the broad field of delinquent and criminal behavior (Huffman, 1962). Sociological and psychological data are therefore necessary in prison case worker evaluations, because, among other reasons, the former system now includes a class of inmates known for their deviant behavior patterns. And the clinician, too, makes frequent reference to individual prisoners who exhibit "neurotic character patterns" and "dyssocial reactions," for example. And it should be mentioned that prisons and related institutions are increasingly in need of the services the psychologist can provide. Such settings, multiplying in number with the increases in population and the incidence of antisocial behavior, provide practicum (in-service to the inmate and the staff) and investigative functions. In the first, the duties of the psychologist are similar to those in any institutional setting. In the second, the psychologist can structure and carry out research projects for the study of relatively extreme deviations in behavior. From these efforts much needed information is collected (Wilkins, 1963). Earlier studies, for example, allow the psychologist to state that the sociolegal concepts of delinquency and crime merely denote the narrow band of character defects within that broad spectrum known as abnormal behavior.

THE CHARACTER DISORDERS: AN OVERVIEW

Objective measurements of personality variables coupled with modern factor-analytic approaches and clinical observations all pinpoint the fact that one aspect of a person's life style is his character, that is, those fairly permanent traits that carry an evaluative connotation (Cattell, 1964). And research workers and clinicians concur that deviant behavior patterns among children can be divided into one of two major categories: the *personality problems* in which feelings of inferiority, insecurity, and inadequacy, coupled with social withdrawal, predominate; and the *conduct problems* in which the hallmark is the expression of impulses against society in an overt way. The former are often considered "neurotic" manifestations. Conduct problems, on the other hand, are observed in their clearest forms in what the psychiatrists have long called the *character disorders* where defects in superego functions are reflected. Many of today's delinquents and criminals are found in this group. Thus, while studies (Peterson, 1961) clearly portray these two groups of problems among children, one can find clinical observations that extend this grouping into the teens and the adult years where a relatively high incidence is noted especially in the vital statistics compiled at community mental health centers (Pennington, 1959). For it is there that numerous individuals are first professionally seen and where clinical workers must differentiate those in this group from those who are psychotic or are neurotic. Adequate identification is of major importance inasmuch as treatment methods differ. Too, the task is complicated by the fact that it is fairly commonplace for a borderline psychotic patient to "act out" his impulses and hence superficially seem an arresting example of the character disorders. Such masking, so to speak, is one of the many reasons why the expressions "acting out" and "acter-outer" have little diagnostic precision (Bellak, 1963).

If we explore current usage by attention to the character disorders, we note, first, those whose traits are faulty in a comparatively mild degree. It is here that one finds the personalities described as either passive-dependent, passive-aggressive, or as overly aggressive. Usually such adults, occasionally in trouble with the law and often known to numerous social agencies in a community, have had a long history of overprotection and permissive rearing to which they react unwittingly by demanding the same from society or by displaced frustration and open aggression. Marked dependency needs and related habit patterns are usually basic. Second, we find other disturbances involving trait complexes (Eysenck, 1959) where severe deviations are encountered by society and the clinical worker. The personality is by development distorted to such a degree that only minimal stress is tolerated. Here one finds the schizoid, the cycloid, the inadequate, and the paranoidal personalities. Many of these come to the attention of the courts by virtue of their limited tolerance to stress. Characteristically most show interaction between the id, ego, and superego with the latter less effective as a brake to impulse release. They are differentiated from the milder character disorders by reference to the variables of complexity and severity. The third group of character disorders is usually designated as the sociopathic and refers to those who appear almost, if not entirely, lacking in superego functions. They impress the observer as completely selfish, affectionless, guiltless, and aggressive. They lack the brakes upon behavior that most citizens demonstrate. They differ from the "dyssocial" person in that the latter has adequate ego strength and has an internalized and active superego albeit from an environment where impulse release is condoned and hence in direct conflict with the social group in which the person now finds himself. The dyssocial individual "adjusts" well only in a setting similar to that of his rearing. The sociopath does not get along in any setting.

THE PSYCHOPATH AND THE SOCIOPATH

Toward the close of the nineteenth century the German school of psychiatry under the leadership of Emil Kraepelin, the great classifier, proposed a seven-fold typology of the expression "psychopathic personalities" defined at the time by the exclusion of the psychotic, the neurotic, and other fairly well established classes of disordered behavior (Koch, 1888). This typology has since been dropped, but the generic term remains. G. E. Partridge in 1930, stressing exclusively social maladjustments, suggested "sociopath" as more descriptive. In 1952 the American Psychiatric Association officially dropped the older term and began the official use of the newer one. At present, despite this official action, both concepts are in use. Clinicians agree that there are in society those who are devoid of guilt and affection. They do not agree at the grass roots level on which word to use in routine designation. So some use one and some use the other. This confusion is clouded still more at the level of research by the fact that investigators have isolated two groups within the heretofore loosely defined category of psychopathy and have appropriated both terms. So, under the circumstances of history and by virtue of current research trends, both concepts must undergo aeration. We shall start with the psychopath.[3] And by so doing we shall clarify both terms.

The Psychopath Viewed Behaviorally. The psychopath cannot be described as neurotic or psychotic in the usual sense. Nor does he suffer from obvious brain damage. He is not mentally deficient. Psychopaths are not physically inferior. Many are predominantly mesomorphic in somatotype (Glueck and Glueck, 1962). Indeed, they give upon superficial appraisal the suggestion of unusual physical, mental, and neurological health. They talk well and usually earn from average to high-average ratings on tests of general intelligence (Frost and Frost, 1962). Rarely do they seek the clinic for help. And when they do, the law is not

---

[3] For centuries professional workers and laymen alike have realized the presence of "characters" in their midst. No one has quite known how to describe, label, treat, control, or prevent their deviant behavioral patterns. Numerous efforts in the past hundred years have been made at the local, state, and federal levels by recourse to all sorts of professional and other methods in vogue at the time. The terms "psychopathy" and "sociopathy," the former devised by psychiatrists and the latter by a psychologist counsellor working in a reformatory, remain with us. For those who insist upon the use of the single term "sociopath" to designate these "characters," one can recall Slater's comment in 1948 to the effect that if we were to drop the expression "psychopath," we would have to replace it with another equally ill defined. In this chapter the stand is taken, in agreement with objective test data, that these terms are not synonymous and that indeed each does designate a different group within the category of the character disorders. It is thus not necessary to drop either of these purely descriptive terms already part of our classification systems.

far behind. With their superficially engaging conversations and wiles, they live well for the moment, with intermittent stops at Skid Row. The immediate gratification of the sudden impulse, without concern for the consequences, describes the life style. A fair number appear to come from average to better socioeconomic backgrounds. Others, by their histories, have been reared in "tainted" families of such natures as to lead a few earlier writers to conclude that the condition is genogenic (Slater, 1948). But all, regardless of their backgrounds, make failures of living and show degrees of antisocial behavior, poor judgment, and no insight. Defective in self-control, they are preyed upon by impulse and, when challenged for the ill-fated consequences of their acts, they are facile in the projection of blame upon members of their long-suffering families or upon society. Lies are preferred to the truth. In feelings the psychopath has been described (McCord and McCord, 1956) as guiltless, affectionless, callous, and aggressive. His shallow thoughts, when verbalized as they usually are, are replete with rationalizations and projective content. Cleckley (1964) has described him as inconsistently unreliable, shameless, and incapable of object-love, therewith exhibiting an affective poverty accompanied by a casual experimental sexuality. Aggressive, when frustrated, to the extent of injuring others, he is not suicidal. Devoid of vocational goals and heavily alcoholic of the "binge" type, the psychopath contributes his share to the nomadic and prison populations. Numerous psychopaths are therefore in and out of penitentiaries but one cannot, even so, equate psychopathy with criminality. Many prison inmates are not psychopaths and, incidentally, do not accept well the inmate who is.

Data from social histories show that as children the adult psychopaths were well known in their neighborhoods as "problem children." Early in their teens they were usually declared "delinquents" and not long after became in the eyes of the law "criminals." It has been estimated that from 5 to 10 per cent of problem children are of this type (Bender 1947). Others estimate that perhaps 15 per cent of delinquents are psychopathic. From 3 to 10 per cent of prison populations appear to fall into this category. Two per cent of admissions to state psychiatric hospitals are so viewed. These estimates point up an important datum: the incidence of psychopathy is far lower than some assume. This small group, even so, contributes heavily to the drain on the public purse and to the misery heaped upon families and the community. It should be mentioned in this connection that few psychopaths, by virtue of their extreme life styles, remain long undetected.[4] The following case report of John is

---

[4] Interestingly enough, observation indicates that toward middle age the psychopath "settles down." At any rate, there are fewer of them. Several hypotheses have been suggested. Many will have been arrested and will be serving "time." Others will

illustrative, while the sketch on Clyde pictures a group often confused with psychopathy.

THE CASE OF JOHN

Born to an unmarried circus acrobat while she was "on the road," he was at the age of ten days placed by her in a "private" orphanage where he remained for four or five months.   There followed a series of placements in marginal foster homes for the next two years, with frequent returns to the orphanage.   When "about three," the child was taken by the maternal grandmother, who worked seven days each week as a waitress in a restaurant of questionable repute, it was reported.   The mother continued her circus life, with only rare visits to her family.   The child, unattended during the day, was under the supervision of "whatever neighbor happened to see what was going on."   The mother took the child, aged five, with her into her third marriage.   Informants agreed that constant bickering between mother and husband accompanied by "kicks and kisses doled out to John" characterized the situation.   The mother, shortly separated from her husband, moved from city to city.   The child completed the eighth grade meanwhile after attending nine different school systems.   Indifferent to all people, incorrigible from the earliest years, known to many social agencies and juvenile court officials in a dozen or more cities, John did as he pleased, still does, even though in the past six years he has been jailed at least ten times on charges of vagrancy, attempted assault, and thievery.   Upon release from prison farms and jails he is at once committed by his mother, now married to her seventh husband, to state psychiatric hospitals, from which John promptly escapes, only to be imprisoned for another series of antisocial acts.   In appearance John is alert, prepossessing, likened by one observer to a "bank teller," seemingly compliant until frustrated. He then responds with immediate aggression and empty threats.   Demanding in manner and word he appears an emotionally labile, healthy infant.   Records from six different psychiatric hospitals report six diagnoses all reading "psychopathic personality."   Selected psychological test findings indicated one of superior verbal intelligence with spotty performances on subtests requiring the manipulation of concepts and other symbols.   Reactions to the word association test items were rapid, and, upon retesting, largely identical in content.   Stories on the TAT were superficial descriptions of the cards.   The Rorschach protocol, limited to eight responses, consisted entirely of inanimate objects ("sticks and

---

have met fatal accidents and illness-caused deaths contingent upon their adventuresome styles of life.   Others, perhaps shaken by the pace of the early years, settle down in degree and become known to the shifting scene as alcoholics and migrant workers. Some consider decline in libidinal urge a factor.   Then, too, others admitted to psychiatric hospitals may now be given the diagnosis of "chronic alcoholism," for example. Indeed, some may do what the youthful psychopath glibly mentions as his "goal" for the later years—"I want to settle down on a chicken ranch."   The criminologist, however, tells us that even within the prison community the psycopath "burns out" and ceases to be a trouble-maker.   It is entirely possible that the psychopath in prison settles down because he must.   As one, aged 36, recently said: "I got tired of banging my head against the walls.   They always won."   Evidence is needed to clarify these piecemeal observations.

stones"). Psychological examining was continued three weeks later, during which interval the patient was initiated into psychotherapy. Results from certain of these tests are reported in a later section of this chapter.

THE CASE OF CLYDE

Equivalent in age, education, and IQ to John, Clyde was reared in one house by both parents until he "left home" at 16. The father, an electrician, was a "hard worker—to keep his wife in clothes so she could advance socially and join the Country Club," it was reported by a tart informant. Clyde was ever his mother's favorite, while Susan, two years older, was the father's child. The mother, embittered by her husband's inability to earn more and more money and by his "uncouth manners," turned more and more to her handsome son as the one who would some day rescue her from her "humdrum" life. The father, reacting in his own way, became alcoholic until he, when Clyde was 16, lost his job. An aunt reported that Clyde "got anything he wanted by yelling for his mother, and Susan had her own way by asking her dad." Clyde, "well-behaved and with the nicest manners," athletic, and sought after by his peers during grade and high school, was no longer able to connive to gain spending money from his mother when his father "retired," in their manner of speaking. All had to go to work to make both ends meet. Clyde then ran away. He held a long series of "temporary" jobs in various cities between his home in the east and the west coast, returning periodically to "disgrace us all." This included going drunk to church and disrupting the services as well as undressing at the Country Club's Christmas formal dance. Numerous small checks written on the feared father's now nonexistent bank account led repeatedly to a series of imprisonments, where the diagnostic evaluations were always that of "psychopathic personality." After serving 30 months of a three-year sentence and after three divorces, Clyde was placed on parole, then committed by his mother, after having made certain by a personal visit that he "won't be locked up or hurt in any way," to a psychiatric hospital where detailed social history, psychiatric examinations, psychological, and therapeutic interviews indicated the existence of strong guilt reactions, the presence of recurrent and mounting tensions culminating in antisocial, impulsive acts for which he in the past had been imprisoned only to be "appointed a trusty," thereby (proudly stated) "always making a fine record." Parole was threatened by Clyde's theft of "my best friend's" electric guitar, which a day later was returned in person to the police station by a penitent Clyde. Revenge motivations directed toward the father and a competitively possessive attachment for the mother combined to produce a personality laden with guilt, masochistic trends, Oedipal conflicts, and free-floating anxiety.

This overview of those customarily designated as psychopathic personalities suggests a uniformity that is only superficial. It is true that both John and Clyde were repeatedly so diagnosed. But it is noteworthy that their histories are highly dissimilar. So, too, were their performances on selected psychological tests. Clyde, unlike John, shortly also was able to participate a bit in treatment sessions. These indicators, among others, document the current trend toward the recognition of two distinct groups one of which can be termed *psychopathic* and the second as *sociopathic*.

Current Views. Dogma abounds in the absence of facts. Numerous viewpoints have been posited as to the causes of this group of character disorder. There are those, chiefly influenced by the early German school of psychiatry, who continue to stress the role of constitution and heredity. No conclusive evidence has been provided in support of such a contention. In fact, data from other areas tend to refute heredity as a casual agent. A second approach toward understanding this group of antisocial personalities is the neurological. Specialists have tried to investigate the role played by developmental anomalies, early diseases, and injuries to the central nervous system. Evidence in support of this hypothesis rests primarily upon the incidence of abnormal tracings in the electroencephalograms. The psychopath is said by some to show abnormalities, either unusually slow or with rapid resting waves, sometimes with spikes consequent to hyperventilation tests, in from 50 to 85 per cent of the cases studied (Kennard, 1953; Silverman, 1947). Simon *el al.*, however, in a study of 96 male psychopaths, carefully screened for the exclusion of those with neurological and physical anomalies and well selected on the basis of social histories and clinical evaluations, report that only 28 per cent of their group showed the deviant tracings. Of the "worst" psychopaths in the group, 25 in number, only 5 showed abnormal waves. In noting that their findings are in disagreement with other studies, they state that clinical criteria are now available (and used by them) by which to screen out those antisocial personalities whose histories are complicated by organic anomalies. Levy and Kennard (1953) in their study of 100 prison inmates, chosen on the basis of three patterns on the MMPI (*Pd* deviation, normal, and abnormalities other than *Pd*), report that 50 per cent of those with high alpha indices also showed high scores on the *Pd* scale. They judge that it may some day be possible to distinguish two classes of criminals. The first group would be comprised of those with high *Pd* peaks and normal EEG records. These to their view would be classed as psychopaths and would require maximal custodial care. The second group would be composed of those with normal or neurotic MMPI profiles, along with a high incidence of abnormal waves. These could be considered as suitable for psychotherapy directed toward uncovering specific psychopathology. It is interesting to note that John's wave tracings were normal whereas the tracings for Clyde were not. One can conclude, then, that the presence of defective cortical rhythms is not the sine qua non of psychopathy. Diagnosis by the EEG approach is not now possible.

It is conceivable, of course, that neurological and psychogenic variables could either interact or function in isolation to produce the character disorders. Extreme affective deprivation during the early years could alone result in the psychopathic (and sociopathic) ways of living. Perhaps less extreme deprivation, coupled with undetected brain dysfunction, could produce much the same patterns in maladjustment. Thus, EEG tracings, the social history, and detailed professional clinical evaluations remain essential before a diagnostic statement can be offered (McCord and McCord, 1959).[5]

A third interpretative approach is that developed by American psychiatrists. Karpman, on the staff at St. Elizabeth's Hospital in Washington, D.C., until his death in 1962, contended with vigor that the rubric of "psychopathy" was greatly overused. In his view 85 per cent of those so termed were "secondary" in type, that is, not really psychopaths at all. He firmly excluded the schizoid, the cycloid, the antisocial neurotic, the psychotic who "acts out," and the obviously brain damaged, stating "they only act like psychopaths." The remaining 15 per cent were considered *true, pure, idiopathic,* or *primary* psychopaths in whom no available tool or professional skill could detect the presence of personality dynamics. These individuals revealed no evidence of conflict or of psychogenic reasons for their behavior. Karpman designated these by coining the term *anethopathy.* In short retrospect his view has merit in that it does remove from consideration many who do not belong. It also has merit in that it calls specific attention to the motivational forces resulting in alloplastic behavior. But it does not account for the anethopath and for John whose case report illustrates the concept. Cleckley, in proposing another view, assumes the basic difficulty is a disorder in meaningfulness. He stresses the operation of unspecified psychogenic factors resulting in a semantic defect that, in turn, he labels as a regressive adjustment mechanism. This seems to imply that the psychopath has at one time not been psychopathic, that an unspecified series of events

[5] Cohn reports for every psychopath with defective rhythms he can find another with normal tracings. He considers it feasible that the former may have suffered head injuries consequent to their psychopathic styles of life, hence the abnormal recordings. This observation by Cohn is consistent with the view that two sets of factors in isolation or by interaction could be responsible etiologically for psychopathic and sociopathic behavior patterns. Arthurs and Cahoon (1964) document this judgment in their clinical and electroencephalographic studies of two groups of "psychopaths," the "true" ones and those with "neurotic" traits. They emphasize an unspecified involvement of the hypothalamus in those cases with defective cortical rhythms. In this connection Dr. Narabayashi (1963) and his students report reduced aggressiveness in one "psychopath," along with 59 other non-psychopaths, following stereotaxic amygdalotomy. Their single case is described as "non-epileptic and a drug addict." Lovett Doust *et al.* (1954) report in London similar effects of photic R.S.B.T. (Rhythmic Sensory Bombardment Therapy) on three cases of "paranoidal, inadequate psychopaths." Thus far, these approaches have not been evaluated; the findings are nonetheless noteworthy. (See Author Index for references.)

has occurred, with the result that the thoughts, feelings, and actions—although maintaining a masklike resemblance to normality—are disjoined, thereby requiring the patient to come to terms societally by the development of a regressive adjustment process called *semantic deficit*. Cleckley considers these personalities as psychotic and recommends the development of research centers devoted to their study. In evaluation he has called attention to another of the outstanding attributes of the group, that is, their affective poverty. But one cannot find in their histories clear evidence for normative behavior prior to the so-called regression. Indeed, the psychopath has from the earliest years been atypical in behavior. *Fixation,* not regression, might be a better term.

A fourth interpretative view is that provided by psychoanalytically oriented workers (Alexander, 1930; Freud, 1924; Reich, 1925). Freud, interested in the autoplastic disorders more recently designated as the psychoneuroses, noted that in certain seemingly neurotic patients the symptoms were less perceptible. They appeared to act out their conflicts (the alloplastic or modern character disorders) in one or more of the following avenues: by demanding that they be treated as exceptions; by breaking down consequent to success even to the point of creating situations conducive to failure; and by antisocial acts committed out of unconscious guilt. Reich preferred to call such a patient an "impulse-ridden character," a term still in use today. Alexander first used in 1923 the designation "neurotic character" to denote them. According to him the "acting-out" individual suggests in action and shows by psychoanalytic study the presence, as in the true neurotic, of regression and repression. Distorted psychological development during the early years with subsequent defective development of, and unhealthy relationships between, the ego and the superego are held responsible for the release of primitive impulses, themselves signposts indicative of the nature of repressed conflicts. The neurotic character has an avenue through activity for getting temporary gratification, just as the autoplastic neurotic gratifies by the development of symptoms. It is held that the self-defeating component is indispensable for the gratification of the neurotic character's impulses, as is suffering to the neurotic. The former succeeds in "actualizing his world of fantasy despite the fact that by so doing he brings disaster upon himself." Here, then, is a group of people who by virtue of their unconscious motivations act out their conflicts, thereby ensuring punishment by imprisonment and other means. Alexander emphasizes that these are not habitual (dyssocial) criminals who by introjection have identified with the undesirable aspects of parental figures or ego-ideals. The neurotic character, by virtue of his early rearing, is defective in his capacities to relate to parent figures with the result that he never learns normally to identify himself with others. Parenthetically, the case of

Clyde is illustrative. And it is also here that the term "sociopathic personality" can be used by those who prefer to avoid the psychoanalytic concept of the neurotic character. If one retains, as the culture is doing, the concept of the psychopath for purposes of designating the few extreme deviates (from Karpman), and if one uses the term "sociopath" for pointing out the relatively many neurotic characters (from Alexander), the problem of terminology disappears.

Clinicians and criminologists, often assuming that the psychopath and the sociopath are one and the same, have tried to diagnose, manage, control, and treat those so designated by identical approaches. This error can be corrected, if the psychopath is placed relatively low on a personality dimension briefly designated as ego development. The sociopath then occupies a range farther along the continuum in the direction of the psychoneurotic. The two groups are thus placed in a perspective that permits quantification and discussion of their differences in relation to principles of ego and superego development. Indeed, placement can be achieved by the measurement of ego and superego strengths, anxiety, and tension, for example. One is reminded in this connection of Eysenck's (1959) dimensional studies in which he indicates that the psychopath is more similar to the psychotic than to the autoplastic neurotic. Reference to Fig. 14–1 indicates that the psychoneurotic is high on ten-

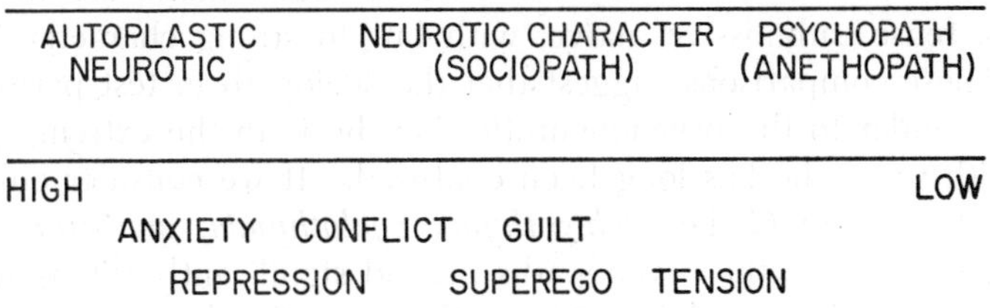

AUTOPLASTIC NEUROTIC	NEUROTIC CHARACTER (SOCIOPATH)	PSYCHOPATH (ANETHOPATH)
HIGH		LOW

ANXIETY   CONFLICT   GUILT

REPRESSION   SUPEREGO   TENSION

Fig. 14–1. Hypothesized covariation of nosological groups and symptom formation.

sion, anxiety, guilt, conflict, and repression. The true psychopath, on the contrary, is low or, according to some, completely lacking in these characteristics. The so-called neurotic character, or sociopath, falls between the two. Thus, when Alexander describes his alloplastic neurotic as manifesting unconscious guilt, conflict, and repression, he is not at odds with Cleckley and Karpman who deny the presence of these attributes to those they consider psychopathic. Surely one reason for the vast array of disagreement in the literature on the topics of the psychopath and the sociopath comes from the fact that different observers have described "psychopaths" who belong at different points on the continuum and who represent different stages in personality growth.

The measurement of pertinent variables subsumed in the above interpretation has been achieved in part by the administration of the Cattell Sixteen Personality Questionnaire. A prison population consisting of 30 extreme psychopaths, 30 sociopaths, and 30 "normal" criminals, coupled with data already available from autoplastic neurotics and several hundred normal adults, have been studied by Pennington and Fairweather.[6] The data indicate that one can describe the criminal psychopath (Karpman's anethopath) as aloof, cold, solitary, extremely weak in character integration, weak in ego and superego functions, crude, and relatively free from anxiety and tension. He is strongly attention-seeking, demanding, and overly aggressive. The correspondence between the test profiles and clinical judgment is fairly close. John's profile (A), reproduced in Fig. 14–2, is illustrative. Surprising to some is the fact that the psychopath scores low on the "sophistication scale" (Factor N). The explanation rests upon the strong tendency to confuse the psychopath with the antisocial neurotic (sociopath) who does indeed score high on "N," as shown by Clyde's profile (B) in Fig. 14–2.

The standard scores earned on the Cattell questionnaire by the sociopath differ from the normal, the psychoneurotic, and the psychopath in several ways. These individuals are high on the scale denoting "general neuroticism," average in superego functions, and high in anxiety, tension, and sophistication. Psychoneurotics, on the other hand, are desurgent, anxious, tense, submissive, naïve, with fair to strong character integration. These comparisons suggest that the sociopath in test performance is more similar to the psychoneurotic than he is to the extreme psychopath with whom he has long been confused. If we consider only three scales (A, C, and G, i.e., *schizothymia-cyclothymia, ego-strength,* and *superego function*), the psychopaths proved significantly different at the 1 per cent level of confidence from the neurotic character (sociopath) and the normal prisoners on Scales A and G. The two character-disordered groups, however, did not differ significantly on Scale C, although both differed at the 1 per cent level from Cattell's normal population. On the Taylor Anxiety Scale (1953), the lie scores did not differentiate the criminal groups. The difference between the means on the anxiety test items per se were significant at the 2 per cent level for all three samples. The psychopaths earned extremely low scores on this scale. They appeared, as a group, aloof, relaxed, demanding, crude, and deficient in

---

[6] The psychopaths in this sample were rigidly selected and correspond to the group described by Karpman. They come from the 5 per cent of the penitentiary's population carrying this diagnosis. Each had been so diagnosed from three to eight times in their careers at different prisons. The sample included those who did not "volunteer"—a requisite according to Karpman and others. Cooperation, once the "gimmick" had been explained away, was adequate by virtue of a reward that had value in a prison barter system.

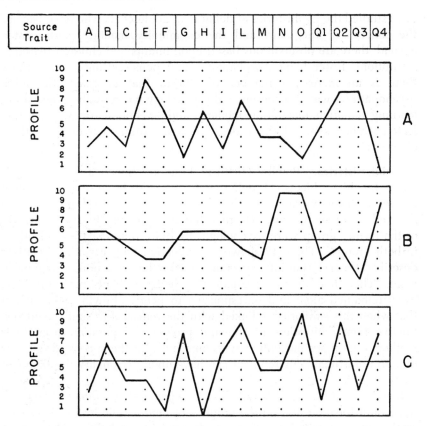

Fig. 14–2. Profiles of three patients on the Cattell Sixteen Personality Factor Questionnaire. Profile A is of John, the criminal psychopath. Profile B is of Clyde, the neurotic character (sociopath). Profile C is that of an extremely anxious psychoneurotic male of comparable age, education, and intelligence. (Profile charts reprinted with permission granted by author and publisher, Champaign, Illinois: Institute of Personality and Ability Testing.) Continued administrations of this scale (1965) to selected nosological groupings have, in general, supported scalar distinctions between the psychopath and the sociopath as well as between them and the psychoneurotic and normal populations.

character development. The sociopaths were, on the other hand, tense, anxious, and symptom laden.

SELECTED STUDIES

Numerous investigations over the years have accumulated that relate to this discussion; these fall into three classes. First, certain workers have studied the life histories of delinquent adolescents who have become the concern of the court and the community mental health center. Second, there are observations based upon infants and children reared in institutions, foster homes, orphanages, and penal settings. And, third, there is an increasing number of studies that approach the adult psychopath by way of experimental psychology whereby the processes of learning , emotion, motivation, memory, and perception are explored. Selected studies, some of them already classic, from each of these three classes are considered below.

Social Histories. Bowlby (1946) at London's famed Tavistock Clinic chose for his subjects 44 delinquents referred because of persistent thievery. They were matched with those in a second group of 44 referred for other reasons. He reported that possibly 14 and clearly 12 of the former group were psychologically quite different from all others in both groups. These 12 showed no affection and warmth. Relatives described them during infancy as unmoved either by kindness or punishment. They stole; they were truant; they lied in glib and brazen fashion. They remained aloof and unresponsive to peers. Bowlby pointed out that when this similarity is linked with the remarkably similar and distinctive family histories—all showing prolonged separation from their mothers—one notes not only a syndrome but also the specific distortions that an unfortunate environment can have upon personality development (Bowlby, 1956).

Bowlby, designating these children as *affectionless characters,* refused to account for their acts on the grounds of neuropathic history inasmuch as the rate of mental disorder was lower in their families than in all others combined. He concluded that a broken home, especially if accompanied by early separation from the mother, is highly significant when it occurs while the infant is forming ties with objects. Bender, in another classical study (1947), analyzed the emotional difficulties of over 5,000 pre-adolescent children admitted for observation to the children's wards at Bellevue Hospital, New York City. She reported that from 5 to 10 per cent comprised what she called the "psychopathic behavior disorders." Careful study of this group led her to conclude that the major difficulty stemmed from their inabilities to form relationships and to identify with others, with subsequent defects in concept formation, and hence in social and emotional development. She held that the developmental processes became fixated at the earliest stage because there were few if any satisfactions derived from experiences. Because there were no conflicts, there was no anxiety. The ego remained defective and the superego did not appear. She judged that the first year of life was the most vulnerable, although prolonged breaks in affective and object relations between the ages of two and four did, if severe, result in a social agnosia rather than in autoplastic neurotic symptoms. It was observed, too, that these children learned slowly to talk and were defective in telling time. Such children, when beset by frustration triggered by their rigid adherence to momentary perceptual patterns, could do little more than imitate the actions and verbal expressions of those about them. These defects were once thought to be fixed and irreversible. Alpert (1964), however, has been able to demonstrate that such irreversibility is fortunately not true. Bender's and Bowlby's characterizations foreshadow the pseudoaffectivity of the adult psychopath, his rigid efforts to play an everchanging series of roles, his obvious difficulties with abstractions and with the concept of time. These workers suggest that the defects stem from a cluster of factors designated here as the lack of opportunity to introject and to relate through identification with others. Too, their observations, reanalyzed and restated by Bender in 1962, are supported by those who have studied the background factors in 100 cases of unwed mothers where it was found that more than half, coming from homes early broken by death or desertion of the fathers, were suffering from relatively severe character disorders (Donnell and Glick, 1952). The results from these early studies have been, in general, substantiated over the years. One can now say that, as a rule, the greater the affective deprivation [7] during the very early years of life the more asocial the child. Findings by Szurek (1942), Heaver (1943), and by Greenacre (1948) have sometimes been mentioned as contradictions to this conclusion inasmuch as they reported that extreme permissiveness and overindulgence by mothers were accompanied by "psychopathic" behavior patterns in their children. Indeed, these investigators of the 1940's suggested that the mothers unconsciously encouraged their offspring to adopt antisocial reactions. More recent evaluations indicate that these workers were dealing with one set of personality dynamics within the neurotic character disorders rather than with the dynamics-free true psychopath (Pennington, 1959).

Studies of Infants. Several students in this country and in Europe have reported observations relative to the behavior of infants reared under the very conditions deduced by those who have worked "backwards" via the social history (see above). One series of such studies has been chosen for discussion here. These investigators were concerned with the effects of hospitalism upon physical and psychological developmental variables of infants under one year of age. These studies included prolonged

---

[7] One must here think in terms of degrees of severe deprivation and not in terms of total physical isolation where in the latter instance the result is complete retardation in all spheres. Detailed summaries on these points can be found in reports by Yarrow (1961), Kozol, (1961), and Maughs (1961).

periods of observation, the administration of psychological tests, and a careful study of environmental factors. The infants were studied in a series of different situations including (1) intact professional homes; (2) a penal institution where the mothers reared their children under supervision for the first year; (3) a European foundling home where the infants from birth were reared under the control of a changing shift of nurses, one each assigned to 10 or more infants; and (4) families residing in an isolated fishing village. Observations were made on three auto-erotic acts: genital play, rocking, and fecal play as exhibited by a total of 170 infants in the first three of these environmental settings. The investigators concluded that autoerotic activity was covariant with the pattern of emotional relationships between the mother and child, inasmuch as in their absence these activities were almost nil (i.e., the foundling home). Rocking behavior was most prevalent among those children where the tie with the mothers was neither completely absent nor well balanced. Of 20 such instances, 17 of the mothers were studied in detail by tests, interviews, and social histories. All were found to be emotionally immature and labile with resulting high incidences of violent, unpredictable emotional outbursts vented upon the children. The infants responded somewhat in kind, showed excessive rocking, and a characteristic profile on the Hertzer-Wolf Babytests where social adaptation (S) and manipulative performance (M) were both notably retarded. These workers judged that these two scales measured relatively well the infant's ways of dealing with his environment. The M-sector indicated how the child handled and mastered toys, for example. On the S-sector a measure was obtained that quantified the infant's relationships with libidinal objects. Infants, unable to form stable object relationships, rocked by the hour. The mother, so labile that relationships could not be formed with any degree of stability in time and space, aroused in a sense this rocking behavior—a symptom of arrest in object relationships whereupon the whole body, as opposed to its parts, were erotically stimulated. When the mother-child relationship changed after long intervals of consistent handling, fecal play with part-objects emerged. When the ties were normal, genital play appeared. These workers (Spitz and Wolf, 1949) therefore extended and amplified the meaning of Bowlby's deduction of maternal separation. Roudinesco and her students (1952), working with foundlings in French orphanages, showed that age at separation, the length of the interval, the number of changes in foster homes, and the quality of the substitute mothering were also important variables. Apparently physical *and* psychological factors must be considered when one defines maternal separation as influential in the development of deviant behavior patterns. A mother can be physically present and psychologically absent. It is pertinent to mention that infants reared in the

manners described above have been found as adolescents to show the
"psychopathic" and neurotic character patterns under discussion in this
chapter.

Experimental Studies. These aim to test the accuracies of selected
clinical observations reported in textbooks and hence to extend knowledge about those who compromise the character-disordered group. Fairweather (1953), working with the criminal population described earlier,
required each subject to learn in 25 trials under one of three conditions
a list of 10 nonsense syllables. In the first situation, all subjects were
unrewarded. In the second, each was told at the outset that he would
(and did) receive two packages of cigarettes at the end of the session.
The third was told at the start that they would receive the cigarettes
"if they did as well as the others did yesterday." Figure 14–3 portrays

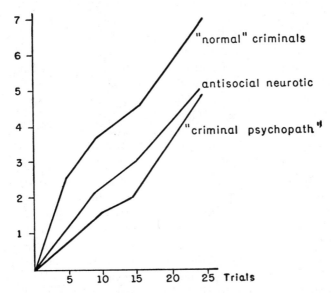

Fig. 14–3. The mean number of correct anticipations of nonsense syllables on every fifth trial by "normal criminals," antisocial neurotics, and
psychopathic subjects. (Courtesy of G. W. Fairweather.)

one finding. Data in Table 14–1 show that the extreme psychopath
learned best when reward was *uncertain*. Here, he reached the performance level achieved by the "normal" prisoner without incentive.
The dictum that the psychopath does not learn from experience therefore
requires qualification couched in terms of motivating conditions, one of
which apparently is novelty. In another study (Johns and Quay, 1962)
the investigators required experimental and control neurotic and psycho-

Table 14–1. Mean Number of Correct Anticipations of Nonsense Syllables on the 5th, 10th, 15th, 20th, and 25th Trials by Criminal Psychopaths Under Conditions of *No Incentive, Incentive,* and *Uncertainty*

Superiority of the third condition is indicated after the use of Fisher's *t* test, which showed the difference between the means of the last two groups significant at the 5 per cent level of confidence.

Group	Trials				
	5	10	15	20	25
No incentive	.6	1.4	1.9	2.7	4.2
Incentive	.7	1.8	2.6	3.9	4.2
Uncertainty	1.8	2.7	3.3	4.3	6.4

pathic subjects to compose a sentence using a verb and the choice of six personal pronouns all presented on cards. For the first 20 trials all 64 subjects made up their sentences with the choices of pronouns recorded. From trials 21 through 80 the experimenter said the word "Good" to the 34 experimental subjects at the end of a sentence that started with the pronouns "I" and "We." Control subjects of course heard no such remark. The results showed that the psychopaths were less sensitive to this secondary reinforcement. The neurotic offenders responded more often to the social reward of "Good" than did the psychopaths. Indeed the latter group did not exhibit any increase in frequency of pronoun usage significantly different from that shown by the unreinforced control group. From one viewpoint the novelty and the uncertainty elements were absent in this setting just as they were in a study devised by Lykken (1957) who found his 19 psychopathic subjects to demonstrate defective avoidance learning in a mental maze where all alternatives had three of four shockfree exits. Too, he reported that the experimental psychopaths showed the least galvanic skin reactivity to the electric shock stimulus as well as the least manifest anxiety on selected psychological scales. It seems likely that the true psychopath does indeed, as Eysenck (1957) has intimated, condition poorly.[8] This great need for novelty and uncertainty coupled with the psychopath's slowed response by conditioning to verbal rewards has considerable significance for educators and therapists responsible for teaching and training children with conduct problems of the psychopathic type (Quay, 1963). Educational methods must in some way make heavy use of repetition as well as apply liberal

[8] The psychopath's personality is such that one might expect him to condition poorly in the absence of anxiety and in the presence of his extraverted quest for novelty (Fairweather, 1953; Kadlub, 1956). One wonders how Lykken's subjects would have reacted in the mental maze, if the one shock-exit had been changed from trial to trial. Psychopaths, for example, in a highly familiar corridor will routinely turn the opposite of the only correct direction that leads out of the building.

dosages of novelty, that is, unexpected, even startling, rewards. Experimental studies, too few in number to generalize from, seem to point toward the hypothesis that the psychopath does indeed learn from experience, but under circumstances different from those effective with nonpsychopaths.

To continue, Sherman (1953), studying the recall of previously learned meaningful and nonsense materials, has reported the superiority (following interpolated learning) in retention of both types of material by the psychopath as contrasted with normal prisoners and with hospitalized neurotic patients. These findings support the clinical observation that the psychopath's rote memory is indeed good; recent events interfere little with his recall of the past. Glaudin (1953) presented by tachistoscopic means a series of neutral, id, and superego five-letter nonvulgar words all of equal frequency in current usage. He reported that these 18 words, 6 in each class, were recognized significantly more rapidly by the normal criminals than by the psychopaths who, in turn, perceived them significantly more rapidly than hospitalized neurotic patients. As a group, the psychopaths alone required more exposures to perceive the id words than the neutral ones at the 1 per cent level of confidence. These findings, along with those reported by Fairweather on serial rote learning, those by Johns and Quay, by Lykken, and by Sherman (whose results showed the psychopath's forgetting to be relatively less under conditions of retroaction), suggest the presence of psychodynamic mechanisms operative in the extreme psychopath that some have denied him. It is hazarded that with continued clinical and experimental studies the psychopath and his cousin, the antisocial neurotic character (see Table 14-2), will provide the behavior sciences with basic insights into the psychogenesis of, and the interactions among, temperament, personality, and character. These insights are certain to have important theoretical and practical values.

TREATMENT AND THE PSYCHOPATH

For many years the psychopath and the neurotic character have been confused in the diagnostic process. This has sometimes led to the denial of treatment to both. The reason for this seems to lie in the early failures reported largely by the psychoanalysts in their "analyzing" psychopaths. This is to say that if the psychopath cannot be analyzed and if the neurotic character and the psychopath are one and the same, then there is little that can be done for either. This viewpoint has therefore resulted in the denial of therapeutic assistance for many who likely could have been guided toward a marginal adjustment within the law. This attitude is now changed especially with reference to the neurotic

Table 14–2. Selected Characteristics in Which the Pure Psychopath and the Antisocial Neurotic Character Perceptibly Differ in Clinical Experience *

The Psychopath	The Antisocial Character Neurotic
1. Severe affective deprivation in the very early years	1. Overindulgence more common; deprivation factor less severe
2. Social histories show grandmothers often serving as mother surrogates	2. Far less often noted
3. "Bad" from earliest years	3. Onset of antisocial conduct usually in 'teens
4. Trouble-maker in prison	4. "Trusty"; "good records"
5. Social isolate	5. Less noted in degree
6. Crime often minor	6. Crime more serious
7. Weak sex drive	7. Average to strong sex drive
8. Appear calm, relaxed, unconcerned	8. Tense, anxious, remorseful upon occasion
9. No insight verbalized	9. Insight superficial, but verbalized in degree
10. Tenuous emotional ties with people and objects	10. Occasional strong ties, often with "wrong" objects and persons
11. Psychological deficit on tests involving symbol manipulation	11. None
12. Below-average score in mechanical aptitudes	12. Often earn high scores
13. Rarely athletic	13. Usually athletic
14. "Time" has little meaning	14. Time meaningful, but flaunted
15. Behavior *appears* unmotivated, bizarre	15. Dynamics *suggested* by superficial view of acts
16. Remote memory excellent	16. Memory blanks apparent

* This table focuses on one thesis of this chapter, the nonidentity of the two groups. In the antisocial neurotic character, one usually finds overindulgence by a parent, a later onset of antisocial activity (sometimes in the neighborhood's "good boy"), strong ties with people, hypersexuality, often superior mechanical aptitude, guilt, evidences of tension, anxiety, conflict, and limited insight. The two groups above can be clinically and psychometrically differentiated. A carefully documented social history is essential. The items in this table must be interpreted in line with the continuum described earlier (see Fig. 14–1). The attributes of the psychopath portray him as a nomadic lone wolf who seeks novelty and hence makes few if any ties with people. A law unto himself, so to speak, he quickly becomes known to local police and as quickly ends within prison walls. His recidivism rate is high, and he is ever a poor risk for parole and for probation.

character disorders. The true psychopath, however, remains to some a therapeutic enigma. To others—and their number is increasing—the adult and the child psychopaths are at least given the benefits of professional doubts. Their efforts, upon occasion, have tended to disprove the once-accepted notion that nothing constructive could be done with such disordered behavior. Table 14–3 lists a wide range of methods that have been used within this century with the psychopath either in or out of an institutional setting. Several of these reports are lacking in details. Some lack adequate control groups. Others provide incomplete statistical treatment of the data collected. Many suffer from the absence of the highly necessary followup studies.   And, too, as one might expect, several suffer from loose definitions of terms.   Nonetheless, there are indeed those today who firmly maintain that these extreme behavior problems upon occasion can be successfully treated by the use, modification, and extension of existing psychotherapeutic and rehabilitative (see Chapter 22) approaches.   The time has not yet come when it can be said that all are treatable, but certainly some are.   There is evidence to suggest that the psychopath may well respond better when treated in an inpatient setting than when the same effort is made outside the prison, school, or hospital walls (Pennington, 1959).   At any rate, it is professionally sensible to recommend that a trial at treatment should be offered those who seek it, even if the client is pursued by the law to ensure compliance. And this pursuit does at times provide an element of uncertainty that the therapist can effectively use in therapeutic management of the adult psychopath.   For it is fairly commonplace for the adolescent and the adult psychopaths, under seemingly the most adverse circumstances for effective psychotherapy, to participate in their own devious ways and to achieve an interval of adjustment just within the law.   This interval is often at first short lived.   But some psychopaths, perhaps remembering their marginal adjustments of months or years ago, do return for additional help.   Therapeutic approaches must work in the present (uncovering with the primary psychopath is futile for there is little or nothing to uncover) and must make heavy use of novelty and uncertainty.   The adult psychopath's primitive affect hunger (powerfully concealed and behaviorally denied by the "I couldn't care less" antisocial attitudes), his anticipation of continued, repetitive rejection, and his quest for the novel and the different as a strong defense mechanism perhaps of the reaction formation type, permit the therapist now and then to reach him by verbal or nonverbal means.   For example, the therapist's ignoring the adult psychopath when the latter is certain the therapist wants to see him is at times accompanied by the psychopath's hunting for the therapist and wanting to talk with him.   It is helpful at the level of hypothesis to view this seeking out of the therapist not only as a quest for the increasingly uncertain but also, more dynamically, as a quest for reassurance from the significant parent who never gave it when the child did catch up with him (Donnelly, 1964).   In this abbreviated example, the psychopath is expecting (with some uncertainty) rejection when seeking out the elusive therapist.   Once the client finds him, reassurance is given, contrary to the expectations.   A foothold can thus sometimes be gained by such a maneuver that hits home to the psychopath.   Such devices can be used for brief verbal exchanges all of them reality oriented. Individual psychotherapy is thus one of the methods frequently used by those professional workers who do accept primary psychopaths as clients.

This choice of approach implies the presence of personality dynamics as well as the need to modify treatment methods to fit these dynamics. Of course, hypnosis (Linder, 1944), sedation, tranquilizers (Eysenck, 1963), and other medical adjuncts have been combined with it (see Table 14–3).

Table 14–3. Treatment Methods Applied to the Adult Psychopath *

	References
A. Inpatient Settings	
1. Isolation and punishment	Stafford-Clarke, 1951
2. Group therapy	Abrahams, 1947
3. Forced conformity	Glaser, 1948
4. Psychodrama	Lassner, 1950; Corsini, 1951
5. Individual psychotherapy	Weber, 1952
6. Hypnoanalysis	Lindner, 1944
7. Psychoanalysis	Bromberg, 1954; Beacher, 1962
8. Drug therapies	McCord, 1956
9. Electroshock	Green, Silverman, Geil, 1944
10. Milieu therapies	Craft, 1964; Papanek, 1958
11. Lobotomy	Darling, 1945
12. Rehabilitation methods	See Chapter 22.
B. Outpatient settings	
1. Individual psychotherapy	Schmideberg, Lindner, Greenacre, and Thorne.
2. Milieu therapy	Cambridge-Somerville Project (McCords, 1959).

* This overview conceals the complexities of the problems in this simplified listing of methods some of which have been used in combination. Those interested in additional reading will find the references a start toward more detailed study.

The psychotherapeutic avenue has also been used by Tietelbaum and others (1965) with the secondary psychopath where sociopathic behavior patterns (e.g., sophisticated wheeling and dealing, gambling, stealing) predominate. These workers stress the presence of a weak ego (marked inadequacy feelings, loneliness, and helplessness) and a superego that is either highly restraining in certain behavioral areas and quite lax in others or one that builds up guilt following impulsive acting out. Such persons thus act more aggressively because they lack ego controls. Individual psychotherapy with this sociopathic group aims toward building up the low frustration tolerance along with improved perception of reality. The primary psychopath, therefore, differs from the secondary in terms of superego and ego strengths in defense mechanisms. The latter makes use of dissociation, externalization, projection, and hence masks more complexly his anxiety-inducing conflicts. The primary psychopath is on the other hand a primitive seeker of acceptance and reassurance in the guise of anticipated rejection. His defense, if he has one, is one of resignation and an exaggerated "I don't care" attitude.

A second method is milieu therapy and usually, although not necessarily, involves the psychopath's residence within an institutional setting where the concept of the therapeutic community (Jones, 1956) is demonstrated in daily life. Perhaps the best illustration of this in its historical antecedents was Aichhorn's school founded in 1918 at Oberhollabrunn, Austria (Aichhorn, 1935, 1965). More recently, Stürùp in Herstedvester, Denmark, and Craft (1964) at Balderton Hospital in Notts, England, have reported their efforts with milieu therapy. The latter, along with his psychologist and statistician colleagues, placed 50 psychopaths for one year under either a self-governing environment coupled with group psychotherapy, or under a paternalistic, disciplined setting without therapy. Both groups had routine work assignments. A followup study 14 months later indicated the statistical superiority of the latter setting as measured in terms of recidivism rate and readmissions. In view of what is known about the lack of limits in the psychopath's childhood, these findings are not surprising inasmuch as the subjects remained for a relatively short time in either setting. Nor is it surprising that others (McCord and McCord, 1959) in the detailed re-evaluation of the Cambridge-Somerville (Massachusetts) Project (1935–45) and the 325 delinquent boys who remained at home while receiving counseling and guidance (as opposed to the control group of 325 boys who did not receive "help") arrived at the same conclusion. Both studies, however, suggest the possible success of a total push by way of milieu therapy in the treatment of the psychopath and his cousins in antisocial behavior.

The milieu method, applied to child psychopaths, is well illustrated by Papanek and his co-workers at New York City's Wiltwyck School for Boys where individual and group therapeutic approaches are combined as well as demonstrated in the residential school community. The behavior patterns of a hundred or so boys, taught much in the Aichhorn manner through permissiveness and affection, showed significant changes during their stay at the school. The psychopaths are reported (McCord and McCord, 1956) to have changed more than did the neurotic and psychotic children placed in the school for appropriate treatment. The aggressive fantasies were significantly reduced and the superego functions were strengthened. Authority figures were viewed less often as punitive and more often as supportive. Thus, milieu therapy with boys aged 8 to 14 years has been found effective in changing the behavior patterns of antisocial children. Studies of these children have clearly proved that the psychopath's need for love is still present. It has not been extinguished. The need is merely fended off by the aggressive behavior. These investigators were also able to demonstrate that the psychopathic child's drive to aggression is no stronger than that of his cousins in antisocial behavior. It is merely that the psychopath lacks the internal brakes for its control, much as Tietelbaum has said for the adult psychopath (1965). The conclusion seems warranted that milieu therapy in a residential school setting, such as at Wiltwyck, is effective in reversing, at least in degree, the psychopathic child's antisocial behavior.

Summarily, then, the primary psychopath and the sociopath do reflect the presence of personality dynamics that can be therapeutically managed by the use and modification of available methods. The child psychopath profits from milieu therapy in a residential setting. The adult psychopath can profit from modified psychotherapeutic methods that involve the use of uncertainty. The neurotic character or the sociopath can also be worked with constructively. It is no longer necessary to claim, without prior therapeutic effort, that nothing can be done. The problems in the applications of these approaches are, of course, numerous. But to venture is to learn about these unique personalities that manage to disrupt a family, a community, and, upon occasion, a state and the world. And while no one expects the psychotherapist to "cure" all clients suffering from a neurotic difficulty, there are laymen and professional workers in other fields who seem to expect 100 per cent success in the behavior scientist's efforts with the conduct disorders. Such wishful thinking is likely a measure of the magnitude of the problems created by such antisocial characters. At any rate, treatment effort is greatly needed. One can hazard, even so, that if all therapists bent all their workday energies toward correcting the problems of the conduct disorders, the psychopath, the sociopath, and the neurotic character would still be present in our midst. The answer seems to lie in a twofold approach. First, the problem is one of treating those children and adults already so behaving. Psychotherapy and milieu therapy are ways that appear to work in such instances. Second, the problem is one of *prevention* and of the two is much more difficult and time consuming. Here, the approach must be with the parents of budding psychopaths and sociopaths. Vital statistics of various kinds have repeatedly indicated that delinquent children are so reared by delinquent parents (Glueck and Glueck, 1965).[9] Evidence suggests that much the same is true for conduct-disordered children. So adult educational avenues for young parents coupled with counseling approaches in mental health centers will have to be tried with the very people the least likely to seek and accept either. Until this twofold approach can be made, then our society can continue to expect increments in the numbers of conduct disorders as well as increases, too, in the rates of delinquency and crime.

[9] Professor and Mrs. Sheldon Glueck, ever trying to do something constructive about these and related problems, provide a concise summary of their research and its meanings in *U.S. News and World Report* LVIII, No. 17 (1965), 56–62. They plead that parents learn to show affection and apply discipline.

SUMMARY

A major purpose of this chapter has been to set forth the similarities and differences between the primary psychopath and the antisocial neurotic character, psychoanalytically viewed. Data from experimental studies on learning, conditioning, memory, retroactive inhibition, the psychogalvanic reaction, and perception, coupled with differences in profiles on objective personality scales, factor analytically derived, document this clinically apparent distinction. Just which terms are to be used to designate these two groups within the spectrum of the conduct (or personality) disorders remains a moot question. The American Psychiatric Association in 1952 resolved this issue by discarding the term "psychopathic personalities" and substituting for it "sociopathic personalities." The subtypes were then officially designated as "antisocial" and "dyssocial." This action does not erase the fact that antisocial personalities are of two types and that each sometimes needs to be designated. In this chapter the position is taken that the more primitive of the two can be termed the primary psychopath and that the second, where personality psychodynamics are clear enough for the untrained to suspect and decipher, can be called the "neurotic character" or "the sociopath." Numerous students agree on the presence of the two groups regardless of terminology. Evidence thus far available makes it clear that the expression of "psychopath" is no longer a wastebasket category. It can and does have relatively precise meaning. The same can be said for the secondary psychopath (sociopath).

Second, differential diagnosis in the area of the conduct disorders can best be done by the team approach. The social worker's detailed workup is essential, just as is the psychodiagnostic appraisal and the psychiatric evaluation. Accuracy in diagnosis saves time in therapeutic planning and its application.

Third, an admittedly psychogenic interpretation has been developed to account for those in our society who fall within the rubric of the conduct disorders, antisocial type. The origins of the seemingly many variations in antisocial behavior patterns stem from extremely faulty rearing practices present during the early critical years of life. Major defects in the identification process delimit the growth and differentiation of ego and superego functions. Affective deprivation, maternal separation, absence of limits, and perhaps inconsistent overindulgence, accompanied by the defective identification aforementioned, are the clinical aspects of the child's learning to behave in the antisocial, psychopathic manner. Clinical conceptualizations and learning theory therefore have here a fertile field for continued investigation. The primary psychopath, learning differently from the nonpsychopath, becomes a worthwhile subject for experimentation. He can contribute both to clinical and experimental areas of scientific endeavor.

Fourth, the primary psychopath and the antisocial neurotic character can upon occasion undergo treatment. Psychopathic children have been found to profit from milieu therapy in a residential school setting. Adult psychopaths have profited from modified psychotherapeutic efforts. The less extreme ones can now and then be managed on an outpatient basis. Forced conformity to treatment by way of the police and courts is not a deterrent and can be used constructively by the therapist. Heavy use of uncertainty in any setting is a method that helps the therapist reach the adult psychopath. Denial of treatment effort to those correctly diagnosed as primary psychopaths is no longer sensible.

Thus, the psychopath, most often found in the prison community where he comprises a small percentage of the population, is often studied by the clinician and the penologist from different frames of reference. The latter sometimes considers him unimprovable and a candidate for maximal security regimens. The former views him as a unique personality whose psychodynamics require investigation and understanding before their existences are denied. Psychological and other studies indicate the presence of dynamic forces that upon occasion can be changed in direction and in degree by therapeutic effort. Prevention is a far more vast and complex problem than is the problem of treatment. Parental education regarding rearing methods coupled with counseling of parents already faced with antisocial behavior in their young children can resolve the difficulty in some degree in time. As it now stands, increases in the number of conduct-disordered persons and in delinquency and crime can be expected.

REFERENCES

ABRAHAMS, J., and McCORKLE, L. 1947. Group psychotherapy at an army rehabilitation center. *Dis. Nerv. System*, 8, 50–62.

AICHHORN, A. 1935. *Wayward youth.* New York: Viking.

AICHHORN, A. 1965. Delinquency and child guidance: Selected papers. Fleischmann, O. Kramer, and Ross (eds.), New York: International Universities Press.

ALEXANDER, F. 1930. The neurotic character. *Int. J. Psychoanal.*, 11, 292–311.

ALPERT, A. 1959. Reversibility of pathological fixations associated with maternal deprivation in infancy. *Psychoanalytic Stud. Child*, 14, 169–85.

ARTHURS, R. G. S., and CAHOON, E. B. 1964. A clinical and electroencephalographic survey of psychopathic personality. *Amer. J. Psychiat.*, 120, 875–77.

BARNES, H. E., and TEETERS, N. K. 1959. *New horizons in criminology.* (3d ed.) Englewood Cliffs, N.J.: Prentice-Hall.

BEACHER, A. I. 1962. Psychoanalytic treatment of a sociopath in a group situation. *Amer. J. Psychother.*, 16, 278–88.

BELLAK, L. 1963. Acting out: Some conceptual and therapeutic considerations. *Amer. J. Psychother.*, **17**, 375–89.

BENDER, L. 1947. Psychopathic behavior disorders in children. In R. M. LINDNER and R. V. SELIGER (eds.), *Handbook of correctional psychology.* New York: Philosophical Library. Pp. 360–77.

BENDER, L. 1961. Psychopathic personality disorders in childhood and adolescence. *Arch. Crim. Psychodynamics*, **4**, 412–15.

BOWLBY, J. 1946. *Forty-four juvenile thieves: Their character and home-life.* London: Bailliere, Tindall & Cox.

BOWLBY, J., AINSWORTH, M., BOSTON, M., and ROSENBLUTH, D. 1956. The effects of mother-child separation: A follow-up study. *Brit. J. Med. Psychol.*, **29**, 211–47.

BURGEMEISTER, B. B. 1962. *Psychological techniques in neurological diagnosis.* New York: Hoeber.

CATTELL, R. B. 1964. *Personality and social psychology.* San Diego: R. R. Knapp.

CLECKLEY, H. 1964. *The mask of sanity.* (4th ed.) St. Louis: Mosby.

COHN, R. 1964. DC recordings of paroxysmal disorders in man. *Electroencephalography clin. Neurophysiol.*, **17**, 17–24.

CORSINI, R. 1951. The method of psychodrama in prison. *Group Psychother.*, **3**, 321–26.

CRAFT, M., STEPHENSON, G., and GRANGER, C. 1964. A controlled trial of authoritarian and self-governing regimes with adolescent psychopaths. *Amer. J. Orthopsychiat.*, **34**, 543–54.

DARLING, H. F. 1945. Shock treatment in psychopathic personality. *J. nerv. ment. Dis.*, **101**, 247–50.

DONNELL, C., and GLICK, S. J. 1952. Background factors in 100 cases of Jewish unmarried mothers. *Jewish soc. Serv. Quart.*, **29**, 152–60.

DONNELLY, J. 1964. Aspects of the psychodynamics of the psychopath. *Amer. J. Psychiat.*, **120**, 1149–54.

EYSENCK, H. J. 1957. *The dynamics of anxiety and hysteria.* London: Routledge.

EYSENCK, H. J. 1959. *The structure of human personality.* (2d ed.) London: Methuen.

EYSENCK, H. J. (ed.). 1963. *Experiments with drugs: Studies in the relation between personality, learning theory and drug action.* New York: Macmillan.

FAIRWEATHER, G. W. 1953. *Serial rote learning by psychopathic, neurotic, and normal criminals under three incentive conditions.* Doctor's dissertation, Univer. of Illinois.

FREUD, S. 1924. Some character-types met with in psychoanalytic work. In *Collected papers*, Vol. 4. London: Hogarth. Pp. 318–44.

FROST, B. P., and FROST, R. 1962. The pattern of WISC scores in a group of juvenile sociopaths. *J. clin. Psychol.*, **18**, 354–55.

GLASER, E., and CHILES, D. 1948. An experiment in the treatment of youthful habitual offenders at The Federal Reformatory, Chillicothe. *J. crim. Psychopath.*, **9**, 376–425.

GLAUDIN, V. 1954. *Speed of visual recognition of operationally defined prim-*

itive, social, and neutral printed words in so-called criminal psychopathic, neurotic, and normal subjects. Doctor's dissertation, Univer. of Illinois.

GLUECK, S., and GLUECK, E. 1962. *Family environment and delinquency.* Boston: Houghton Mifflin.

GREEN, E., SILVERMAN, D., and GEIL, G. 1944. Petit mal electro-shock therapy of criminal psychopaths. *J. crim. Psychopath.,* 5, 667–95.

GREENACRE, P. 1947. Problems of patient-therapist relationship in the treatment of psychopaths. In R. M. LINDNER and R. V. SELIGER (eds.), *Handbook of correctional psychology.* New York: Philosophical Library. Pp. 378–83.

GRIGSBY, S. E. 1963. The Raiford Study: Alcohol and crime. *J. crim. Law, Criminol., Police Sci.,* 54, 296–300.

HEAVER, W. L. 1943. A study of forty male psychopathic personalities. *Amer. J. Psychiat.,* 100, 342–46.

HUFFMAN, A. V. 1962. The behavior patterns of criminals. *J. soc. Ther.,* 8, 15–33.

JOHNS, J. H., and QUAY, H. C. 1962. The effect of social reward on verbal conditioning in psychopathic and neurotic military offenders. *J. consult. Psychol.,* 26, 217–20.

JONES, M. 1956. The concept of a therapeutic community. *Amer. J. Psychiat.,* 112, 647–50

KADLUB, K. J. 1956. *The effects of two types of reinforcement on the performance of psychopathic and normal criminals.* Doctor's dissertation, Univer. of Illinois.

KARPMAN, B. 1951. Psychopathic behavior in infants and children: A critical survey of existing concepts. *Amer. J. Orthopsychiat.,* 21, 223–72.

KOZOL, H. L. 1961. The dynamics of psychopathy. *Arch. crim. Psychodynamics,* 4, 526–41.

LASSNER, R. 1950. Psycho-drama in prison. *Group Psychother.,* 3, 77–91.

LEVY, S., and KENNARD, M. 1953. A study of the electroencephalogram as related to personality structure in a group of inmates of a state penitentiary. *Amer. J. Psychiat.,* 109, 832–39.

LINDNER, R. M. 1944. *Rebel without a cause.* New York: Grune & Stratton.

LYKKEN, D. T. 1957. A study of anxiety in the sociopathic personality. *J. abnorm. soc. Psychol.,* 55, 6–10.

McCORD, W., and McCORD, J. 1956. *Psychopathy and delinquency.* New York: Grune & Stratton.

McCORD, W., and McCORD, J. 1959. *Origins of crime: A new evaluation of the Cambridge-Somerville youth study.* New York: Columbia Univer. Press.

MACDONALD, J. M. 1958. *Psychiatry and the criminal: A guide to psychiatric examinations for the criminal courts.* Springfield, Ill.: Charles C Thomas.

MAUGHS, S. B. 1961. Current concepts of psychopathy. *Arch. crim. Psychodynamics,* 4, 55–57.

PAPANEK, E. 1958. Re-education and treatment of juvenile delinquents. *Amer. J. Psychother.,* 12, 269–96.

PARTRIDGE, G. E. 1928. A study of 50 cases of psychopathic personality. *Amer. J. Psychiat.,* 7, 953–73.

PENNINGTON, L. A. 1959. The treatment of the adolescent male acter-outer. In *Proceedings*, 3d Annual Meeting of Clinic Administrators, Illinois Department of Public Welfare, Allerton Park, Monticello, Ill., March 5–6, 1959.

PETERSON, D. R. 1961. Behavior problems of middle childhood. *J. consult. Psychol.*, **25**, 205–9.

QUAY, H. C. 1963. Some basic considerations in the education of emotionally disturbed children. *Except. Child.*, **30**, 27–31.

QUAY, H. C., and HUNT, W. A. 1965. Psychopathy, neuroticism and verbal conditioning: A replication and extension. *J. consult. Psychol.*

REICH, W. 1925. *Der triebhafte Charakter.* Leipzig: Internationaler Psychoanalytischer Verlag.

ROUDINESCO, J. 1952. Severe maternal deprivation and personality development in early childhood. *Understanding Child*, **21**, 104–8.

SCHMIDEBERG, M. 1947. The treatment of psychopaths and borderline patients. *Amer. J. Psychother.*, **1**, 45–70.

SHERMAN, L. J. 1954. *A study of retroactive inhibition in normal, autoplastic neurotic and criminal psychopathic subjects as a function of meaningful and nonsense material.* Doctor's dissertation, Univer. of Illinois.

SILVERMAN, D. 1947. Electroencephalography: Use in penologic practice. In R. M. LINDNER and R. V. SELIGER (eds.), *Handbook of correctional psychology.* New York: Philosophical Library. Pp. 72–97.

SIMON, B., O'LEARY, L., and RYAN, S. S. 1946. Cerebral dysrhythmia and psychopathic personality. *Arch. Neurol. Psychiat.*, **56**, 677–85.

SLATER, T. O. 1948. Psychopathic personality as a genetic concept. *J. ment. Sci.*, **94**, 277–82.

SPITZ, R. A., and WOLF, K. M. 1949. Autoerotism: Some empirical findings and hypotheses on three of its manifestations in the first year of life. In *Psychoanalytic study of the child.* Vols. 3–4. New York: International Universities Press. Pp. 85–120.

STAFFORD-CLARK, D., POND, D., and DOUST, L. 1951. The psychopath in prison: A preliminary report of a cooperative research. *Brit. J. Delinqu.*, **2**, 117–29.

STÜRÜP, G. K. 1952. The treatment of criminal psychopaths in Herstedvester. *Brit. J. med. Psychol.*, **25**, 31–38.

TAYLOR, J. 1953. A personality scale of manifest anxiety. *J. abnorm. soc. Psychol.*, **48**, 285–90.

TEITELBAUM, S. H. 1965. The psychopathic style of life and its defensive function. *Amer. J. Psychother.*, **19**, 126–36.

THORNE, F. C. 1959. The etiology of sociopathic reactions. *Amer. J. Psychother.*, **13**, 319–30.

WEBER, L. 1952. Working with a psychopath. *J. abnorm. soc. Psychol.*, **47**, 713–21.

WILKINS, L. T. 1963. Juvenile delinquency: A critical review of research and theory. *Educ. Res.*, **5**, 104–19.

YARROW, L. J. 1961. Maternal deprivation: Toward an empirical and conceptual re-evaluation. *Psychol. Bull.*, **58**, 459–90.

15

Adult Development and Aging

JAMES E. BIRREN *

By age twenty-one, when the average person legally comes of age, he has lived only about 29 per cent of his life-span. The more than fifty years to follow coming-of-age constitute the adult phase, the longest and most important part of the life-span: the "pay off years" for the individual and society. New and interesting careers are developing around the research and service required in a technological society to meet the needs of the mature population. There are now almost as many people over the age of sixty-five in the United States as the total population of all ages in Canada, approximately 19 million. The fastest rate of growth of the United States population is at the ends of the age spectrum, the under eighteen and the over sixty-five. This increase in the young and old defines the pressure points for psychological services, although we are better prepared to cope with the problems of the young.

This chapter will describe some of the developmental principles and issues of the adult phase of the human life cycle. In past decades, developmental psychology gave its attention primarily to the early years or, at most, to the school years. More recently, perspectives have broadened with the realization that the adult is continually undergoing transformations of a biological, psychological, and social nature. Such a dynamic viewpoint is necessary to deal rationally with the personal and social problems associated with advancing age.

* James E. Birren, Ph.D. (Northwestern University), Professor of Psychology, and Director, Institute for the Study of Retirement and Aging, University of Southern California.

THEORIES OF AGING

It is important for the student of the psychology of adult development and aging to recognize that his frame of reference for aging is different from that of the biologist and sociologist. Theoretical explanations of aging vary with the discipline. Biologists tend to be concerned with length of life so that length of life becomes a variable dependent on other variables frequently molecular or genetic in nature. The psychologist interested in aging tends to be concerned with the changes in the capacities and skills of an individual in adapting to environmental stimulation. Such changes tend to be explained in terms of biological alterations in the individual differential experience over the life-span and changes in motivation. The sociologist, in turn, is interested in such qualities of external behavior as the individual's acquired social roles in relation to the age grading of expected behavior by society. As in the maturation of a child, it is difficult to speak about aging of the individual as a unitary process. One way to conceive of the collective changes of aging is to view the individual as a "host" that is altered with age so that vulnerability to many specific environmental stimuli is altered. Thus, age changes are noted in resistance to infection, emotional trauma, or susceptibility to accidents. Viewed in this way, the scientific problem is one of finding out if there are common processes that underlie altered vulnerability of the host.

Although the individual is a high-turnover system with new molecules and cells replacing old ones, stability, as well as change, characterizes our biological organization and individuality. At the psychological level, each of us has an awareness of continuity from childhood and of a unique existence. Experience, being cumulative, helps to impart to us a conviction of a direction to events. Biologically as well as psychologically, there is time direction to the organism; that is, we move toward continual differentiation. Theories of aging represent one of the frontiers of science, and the student will find that the variables employed shift with the level of biological organization being considered in relation to age, that is, molecules, cells, tissues, organs, organisms, or populations (Brues and Sacher, 1965). Such explorations can lead the psychologist to considerations of the nature of time and the mechanisms of imparting time direction in the organism (Reichenbach and Mathers, 1959) and concepts of development that embrace the facts of all phases of the life-span.

As early as 1835, a book appeared by Quetelet, *On Man and the Development of His Facilities*. Quetelet recognized that the influence of both biological and social factors determines how man develops and how long and how well he lives. What is important is that Quetelet was trained as a mathematician and developed the concept of the average man around which measurements are distributed according to the laws of chance. This concept, now commonplace, was revolutionary in the early part of the nineteenth century. We now use such terms to discuss issues of age and individual differences, using distributions, averages, and correlations among traits. Another intellectual giant of the nineteenth century was Francis Galton. By the year 1879, he had already described the reduction in high-tone sensitivity with age in human subjects. He had also gathered data on auditory and visual reaction time, antedating many subsequent experiments on sensorimotor slowing with advancing age. (Welford and Birren, 1965.)

PERSONALITY IN AGING

There are characteristic issues that face adults during phases of the life-span and evoke different responses, for example, career and job choice, adaptation to choice of mate, childbearing and child rearing, children's maturing and leaving home, menopause, career plateau, style of life in retirement, death of peers and spouse. Most problems or developmental tasks are readily met, although some may be particularly taxing to a vulnerable individual and evoke emotional crises (Kuhlen, 1959).

One way of describing aging has been in terms of personality in which the term *personality* stands for the organization of behavior tendencies in the individual. Within this framework, many of the important questions are at best only partially answered, for example, "Which personality characteristics are stable with advancing age, and which show change?" and "Are there personality types such that some individuals remain active with advancing age and some deteriorate?" A follow-up study was made of the personality characteristics of 300 couples engaged to be married (Kelly, 1955). Data were obtained on 215 of the original 600 engaged individuals in a 16- to 18-year follow-up. Vocational interest and personal values seemed most stable among the characteristics measured, whereas attitudes were found to be unstable (only 8 per cent consistency). One point of interest that bears upon the adaptation in marriage was the fact that there was no observable change in the degree of correlation of personality variables between husband and wife. Viewed as a whole, the study suggests that the normal adult does show significant change representing the adaptations to adult life. These changes can be viewed as changes in personality. At the same time, the changes are not so great that the individual loses his uniqueness in the population of adults. The study does prepare us for the view that there are continuing adaptations of the personality over the adult life-span.

One of the characteristics imputed to older adults is a tendency to rigidity, an unchangingness of attitudes, beliefs, and habits of behavior. An important study by Chown (1961) did find some evidence of rigidity in older adults. Her study of 200 individuals from the age of twenty to eighty-two years indicated that, on 16 different tests of rigidity, scores were more related to intelligence than to chronological age. This leaves us with the possibility that what is called "rigid behavior" in older adults could be the result of a changing capacity to make rapid discriminations and reason, as much as it could be a result of a "rigid frame of mind" leading to an inability to reason quickly and well.

A group of investigators at the University of California viewed retirement as a stimulus to which the individual had to react (Reichard *et al.*, 1962). Classifying individuals according to their personality, they made comparisons among the individuals in terms of their adjustment to aging. Three clusters of individuals appeared to adapt well to aging and retirement. These were (1) the mature group having a constructive approach to life, (2) the "rocking chair type" of somewhat passive individuals who depended heavily on others, and (3) the "armored type," who were maintaining high well-developed defenses against anxiety. The two clusters of individuals who adjusted poorly to aging were (1) the "angry," who were hostile and characteristically blamed others, and (2) the "self-haters." While these personality types probably do not have universal properties, they do suggest ways of characterizing individuals as to their likelihood of handling late-life problems.

One of the most important aspects of the ability to adjust to the changes of late life is the extent to which individuals interact with others. That is, the disposition to move toward high interaction with others can be regarded as a characteristic of personality. Studies carried out at the University of Chicago indicate that in some individuals there is a reduction of participation in many activities with advancing age. This has been termed a "disengagement" from social roles. One view about aging has been that the changes in the environment of the older person make it harder for him to participate in his characteristic activities, and he thus becomes disengaged from social roles. The contrasting point of view is that, as individuals age, they are often willing to be disengaged from their social interactions (Cumming and Henry, 1961). It is likely that both processes occur. The aged widow of limited income has very little social mobility and opportunity to maintain her previous social roles. Another person may move to a lower level of activity to conserve energy. The importance of such contrasting examples lies in their relevance to attempts to improve the life satisfaction of aging individuals; that is, "Will this be brought about by constriction of psychological involvement and activities or by the increased involvement in activities?" Social-role participation to an appropriate degree probably protects the aging from overreactions to commonplace changes in daily life. The level at which pressure for social participation can be unproductive is uncertain.

CHANGES IN MOTIVATION

Studies of interests and activities of adults over the life-span indicate that there are changes in motivation. Indeed, as we grow older, we seem to disengage from some activities and engage more in others. Interest in participation in sports and playing bridge, for example, declines over the adult years, while visiting museums, gardening, and bird watching increase (Strong, 1931). After age twenty-five, men tend to become less interested in exciting hobbies that involve danger, rapid adjustment, and strenuous activity. Both men and women appear to maintain an intellectual curiosity about the world throughout the life-span. Generally, the values that individuals place upon leisure activity are less related to age than they are to social class and personal adjustment (Havighurst, 1961).

Sexual Activity. Sexual behavior, particularly in the male, has been taken as an index of motivational change with age. The interview data obtained by Kinsey *et al.* (1948) showed an almost linear decline in sexual activity in males from ages sixteen to twenty to ages fifty-five to sixty. Availability of suitable sexual partners is probably more of a problem for the aging male adult than any diminished sex drive. Commonly overlooked is the fact that lower mobility and lower availability of a partner can be greater contributors to undesirable sexual adjustment in an older adult than previously existing personality traits or attitudes.

Crime. Changes in the frequency of certain crimes with age is an indication of underlying changes in motivation (Fig. 15–1). Thus rape tends to be a relatively young man's crime, with 34 per cent of arrests for rape occurring in the under-twenty-year group; only 8 per cent of men arrested for forcible rape are over the age of forty. Similarly, auto theft is a young man's crime. Seventy-four per cent of automobile thefts are committed by people under the age of twenty. Crimes that increase with age include vagrancy and drunkenness. The young offender attempts to steal the immediate object he wants, whereas the older adult tends to manipulate stolen property obtained by others or plan embezzlement or forgery. The crimes of youth tend to be impulsive in character, whereas those of later life tend to be crimes resulting from long-established habit patterns. Sex differences in crime are large, with men outnumbering women 36 to 1 in burglary and 30 to 1 in automobile stealing.

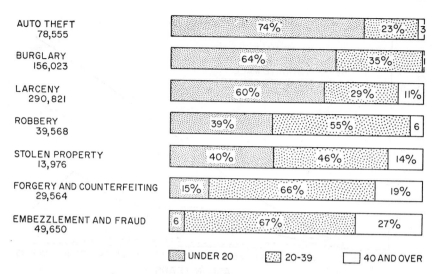

Fig. 15–1. Type of crime and age. Per cent of crimes by age group for 1962. From U.S. Department of Justice, Crime in the United States, Uniform Crime Reports, 1962 (Washington, D.C.: Federal Bureau of Investigation, 1963).

Suicide. One of the most dramatic changes in later life is the increased suicide rate among white males. It goes up almost as a straight line from late adolescence through the remaining life-span. Although suicide among men shows a constant rise over the adult life-span, females show a much slower increase, and, toward the end of the life-span, the rate declines. Complicating the picture are the facts that the nonwhite population has a much lower rate of suicide and the rate for the nonwhite male does not increase after age fifty-five. Thus, the explanation of the suicide rates is a complex function of sex differences, social class, and age (Fig. 15–2). Provocations to suicide attempts in older people are factors of physical infirmity, chronic illness, and frequently the diagnosis of an incurable disease. Why the white male reacts more often by suicide to changes involving illness compared with the nonwhite male requires further research to answer. There may be factors in the culture surrounding the nonwhite that do not lead to the development of the self-directed hostility or, alternatively, guilt that suicide frequently implies.

AGE AND MENTAL ILLNESS

It is important not to identify the 19 million people "over sixty-five" with victims of mental problems. Most adults live through their life-spans

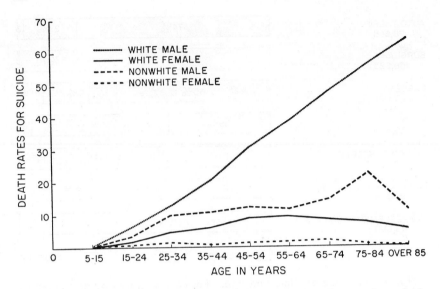

Fig. 15–2. Effects of age, sex, and race on the death rates for suicide. From U.S. Department of Health, Education, and Welfare, Special Reports (Washington, D.C.: Bureau of Vital Statistics, 1956).

without serious limitation of function. The statistic "5 per cent" is often cited as an index of severe disability in the aged, based on the proportion in institutions of all types. Yet there is no valid figure, since measures of physical and mental health among the aged await development, as does their application to representative samples of the population. It can be assumed, however, that, as more knowledge is acquired about the years after middle life (somewhere between ages thirty-five and forty, depending on sex and other factors), more conditions requiring professional attention will be identified. This will not be a change in the well-being of the population so much as an improvement in epidemiological fact-finding and the delineation of new syndromes in the population. Perhaps more disability will be uncovered in the aged, since science has penetrated less deeply into the phenomena of late life than elsewhere.

It is important to distinguish between aging and pathology in considering the facts about adult life. Aging is defined as the characteristic changes individual members of a species show as they advance in chronological age in some constant environment. Aging is a process, and, while closely related to chronological age, it is not identical with it. Chronological age is an index to the position of an individual in the life-span dynamics of biological, psychological, and social transformation. However, while chronological age is a powerful descriptive index, it is not an adequate explanation of the transformations that occur in adults.

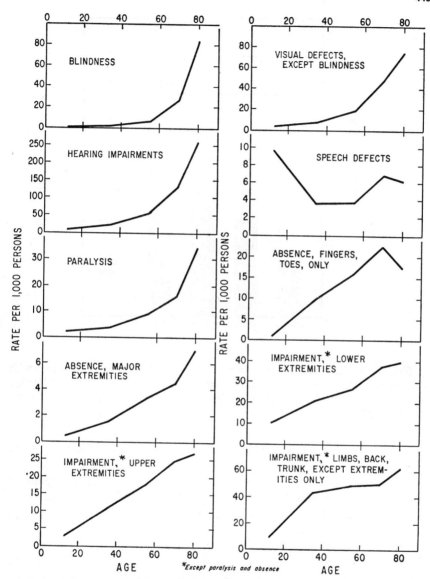

Fig. 15–3. Age and impairments. Number of impairments per 1,000 persons according to type of impairment and age. From U.S. Department of Health, Education, and Welfare, Health Statistics (Washington, D.C.: Public Health Service, 1959. Series B-9).

Many sources of influence alter the individual's capacity to adapt to environmental stimulation; for example, a host alters with age so that his vulnerability to an infection or emotional trauma can increase. Changing

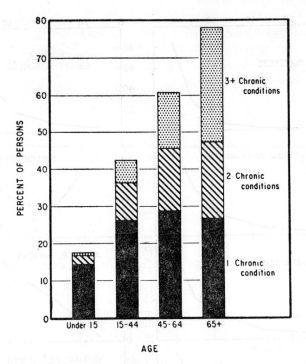

Fig. 15–4. Chronic Illness in relation to age. Percentage of persons with chronic conditions according to age group. From U.S. Department of Health, Education, and Welfare, Health Statistics (Washington, D.C.: Public Health Service, 1959, Series B-18).

vulnerability with age is seen in accident rates, curves of mortality from specific diseases, or duration of hospitalization for disease. The concept of aging relates to the changing vulnerability of a host to the agent or agents whose presence is the necessary condition for the appearance of a syndrome whether it be mental or physical. (See Figs. 15–3 through 15–5.)

The late-life mental diseases actually occur more frequently than does schizophrenia or psychoneuroses. What masks the picture is the fact that schizophrenia patients tend to remain in hospital for long periods. Although the mental diseases of the senium are the most frequent of all classes of mental illness, they by no means form the typical picture of growing old. Because of dramatic instances of aged relatives who undergo severe intellectual deterioration, there is a tendency among even sophisticated observers to identify advancing age with mental incompetence. Relatively few persons of any age group will ever be institutionalized; about 1 to 2 per cent of the older population may be expected to be hospitalized for senile mental illness. This leads to the distinction

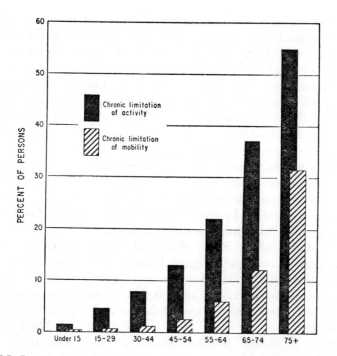

Fig. 15–5. Percentage of persons with any degree of chronic limitations of activity and mobility according to age. From U.S. Department of Health, Education, and Welfare, Health Statistics (Washington, D.C.: Public Health Service, 1959, Series B-11).

between normal, or "healthy," aging and psychiatric illnesses. In writing about the clinical psychiatry of late life, Post (1965) quotes sources that indicate that between the ages of twenty-five and seventy-five years there is a sixfold increase in the likelihood of being admitted to a mental hospital. Post reports that, viewed in absolute terms, of every 1,000 boys in the city of London, at some time in their life 8 will be admitted for schizophrenia, 8 for manic-depressive psychoses, and 21 for psychoses of old age. Slightly higher rates were observed for girls, although, for both sexes, the range was somewhere between 3 and 6 per cent for individuals who will be in a mental hospital at some time in their life. The likelihood is greater than half that the institutionalization will be for a psychosis late in life.

BRAIN SYNDROMES

A considerable number of organic brain diseases have been differentiated in the older patient (Allison, 1962), since the brain is highly sensitive to the lack of oxygen and its cells cannot survive for more than a very few minutes if circulation or diffusion of oxygen is interfered with. Arteriosclerosis leading to diminished blood flow to the brain is a serious condition in older individuals. However, by no means does limitation of cerebral circulation account for all or even a majority of organic brain deteriorations in late life. A study by Simon and Neal (1963) of 505 patients admitted to a mental hospital indicated that about a fourth of the cases showed cerebral arteriosclerosis and presumed interference with blood flow as the main finding. A higher proportion, 61 per cent, were found to display significant brain disease without arteriosclerosis being the primary factor. Other research, on healthy elderly men, indicates that a reduction of blood flow to the brain and a decline in brain metabolism are by no means the expected pattern in older individuals. Age itself is by no means presumptive of a decline in cerebral blood flow and metabolism (Dastur et al., 1963).

Earlier studies of the brains of individuals in relation to clinical pictures suggested neuropathological findings and behavioral symptoms. More detailed observations of the neuropathological changes, as well as the behavioral characteristics, suggest that, as might be expected, there is a close interrelationship between behavior and organic integrity of the brain in late life. A study by Corsellis (1962), of 300 brains from patients in a mental hospital, shows a good correlation between clinical diagnosis and subsequent neuropathological findings. While organic brain change and general physical disability are important contributors to the behavioral changes of elderly patients, it can by no means be assumed that all behavioral symptoms are irreversible. Numerous studies have shown that a substantial proportion of late-life organic mental states are reversible even at the present relatively undeveloped stage of our knowledge of the etiology of such states.

AGE AND SLOWNESS OF BEHAVIOR

The slowing of behavior with age in man and other animals was for a long time not considered an important or systematic problem in psychology or physiology. This may have resulted from the fact that the slowness of the older organism was overly obvious.

Slowness of behavior with age has been reliably observed in man and other mammals in a wide variety of contexts. It can be taken as fact that most of the slowness of behavior associated with advancing age can be attributed to the time taken or required by the central nervous system in mediating the input and output relations in behavior. Generally, not much of the slowness with age can properly be attributed to poor motility of joints or muscular contraction. Also, limitations of sensory input or the primary sensations are not usually the major contributors.

Observation suggests that the older person can do most if not all of the things he did at a younger age but not do them quickly. Early research indicated that the diminution of sensorimotor speed with age is not limited to one sense modality or to a particular motor response. While the evidence was circumstantial that the slowing was general or diffuse, proof was needed that aging individuals were or were not independently quick or slow, depending on the particular task. With this issue in mind, Birren, Riegel, and Morrison (1962) carried out an experiment in which the form of the response (quickness of button pressing) was held constant while the complexity of stimuli was systematically varied. Under all stimulus conditions used, elderly subjects were found to be slower than young adult subjects. This could have been predicted from previous work; however, the additional point was established that the speed of response to the various types of stimuli was more highly intercorrelated among older subjects. Thus, in a group of young subjects (eighteen to thirty years), the "speed factor" accounted for 29 per cent of the variance compared with 43 per cent of the variance in older subjects (sixty to eighty years). Since the experimental stimuli were varied, including verbal associations as well as numbers and colors, there is reason to believe that a rather broad or general factor emerges with age and imposes a common limitation on the speed of all behavior mediated by the central nervous system. Young adult subjects appear to be task-specific in their response speed; that is, they are quick or slow depending on the nature of the task. With increasing age, people tend to show a characteristic slowness of response regardless of the nature of the task.

That this general quality of slowness is not limited to effector or motor response processes is also shown in the work of Chown (1961). She gave a wide range of intelligence, speed, and "rigidity" tests to 200 men who ranged in age from twenty to eighty-two years. Of considerable present importance is her conclusion:

The most marked change in the interrelationships between factors with age was in the role of speed. The speed tests formed their own unique factor in the young group, maintained this to a lesser extent in the middle group, and were loaded most highly on the nonverbal intelligence factor in the old group. Thus among old people, but not among the young, these speed tests became a measure of intellectual capability and of the extent of the preservation of this function. [Chown, 1961, p. 361.]

Such evidence suggests that the limitation of speed with age does not to a major degree involve the most remote elements of the input-output processes but, more importantly, involves association time and the time to select appropriate response elements. The slowness of behavior with advancing age is less suggestive of punctate neurological damage, which might be associated with disease, than of a primary change in the

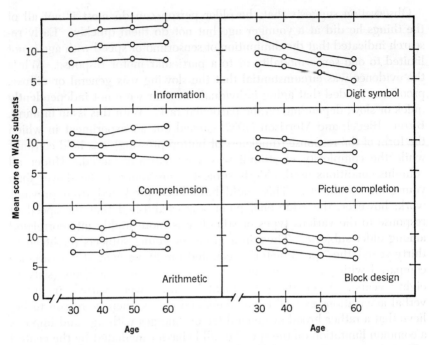

Fig. 15–6. Age and education level in relation to mean scores on the subtests of the Wechsler Adult Intelligence Scale. On each subtest, the upper curves are based on individuals with an educational level of thirteen years or more; middle curves, from eight to twelve years; and lower curves, less than

nervous system. The implications of the expression "primary age change in the nervous system" are not always clear. Here it is taken to mean a progressive change that will eventually appear in every individual who lives long enough. To be regarded as a primary manifestation of aging, the constellation of functional and structural changes should appear independently of any particular disease or environmental condition. A primary age change would eventually be shown by all individuals despite optimum health, education, good personal habits, and advantageous social and physical environments. This does not imply that environmental differences and disease could not interact with a primary process and modify the appearance and the rate of change. Conceptually, one is distinguishing the contribution of environmental differences and disease from an invariant transformation of members of a species, recognizing that in real life these factors are interacting. A highly relevant question is whether older persons judged to be healthy, in the sense of freedom from disease, show a slowness of behavior characteristic of their age group.

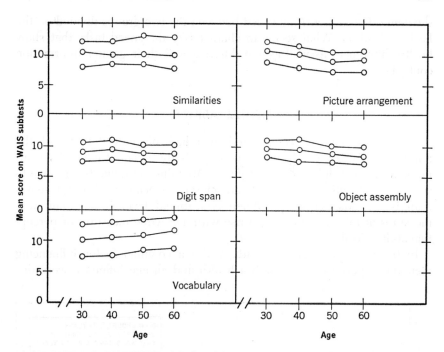

eight years. Age intervals: 25–34, 35–44, 45–54, and 55–64. From J. E. Birren and D. F. Morrison, Analysis of the WAIS subtests in relation to age and education, *J. Geront.*, 1961, **16**, 366.

A group of forty-seven men above the age of sixty-five were studied at the National Institute of Mental Health with regard to a broad range of physiological, medical, psychological, and social characteristics. Among the measurements was that of simple reaction times, which in these subjects were not significantly different from those of previous subjects less well selected for good health. In addition, when the group of forty-seven men was divided into two groups, one of optimum health and the other with subclinical or symptomatic disease, no difference in reaction time was found. This would suggest that slowness of response occurs with advancing age even in individuals relatively free from disease.

The above facts would initially seem to contradict some previous data, which indicated that senile dementia patients were particularly slow in doing a rather simple task involving speed of writing. Both sets of data appear to be valid representations of the changes that occur with age and, in the one instance, are exacerbated by disease. In the healthy group of forty-seven elderly men previously cited, writing speed was faster than among a previous sample less well selected for health. Also, the men differed in writing speed between the two groups divided on the basis of health. What seems to characterize the speed tasks that show health differences as well as age differences is their greater information content.

MENTAL ABILITY

One factor that has contributed to a lack of understanding of the normal trends in mental ability with age is the unequal educational attainment among different age groups. Over the age range twenty-five to sixty-five, educational level is more closely associated with test scores than is chronological age. When educational level is held constant, measures of information tend to rise with age while measures of perceptual ability decline. (See Fig. 15-6.)

In the older population, health is also a common factor influencing mental-test performance. Both a health and an age influence were dis-

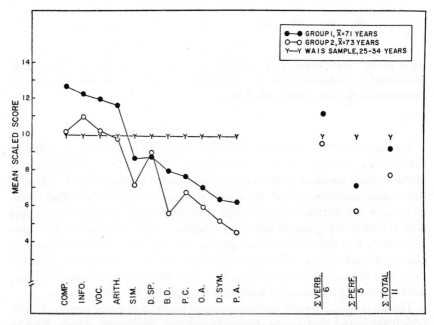

Fig. 15–7. Age and health differences in mean curves on the subtests of the Wechsler Adult Intelligence Scale. Healthy elderly are in group 1; elderly men with mild asymptomatic diseases are in group 2; mean values for young adults are given as Y. From J. E. Birren, R. N. Butler, S. W. Greenhouse, L. Soholoff, and M. R. Yarrow (eds.), *Human Aging* (Washington, D.C.: Public Health Service Publication No. 986, 1963, p. 151).

tinguished in one study that assessed the physical well-being of subjects who were also studied with regard to their abilities and personalities. (See Fig. 15–7.)

TERMINAL DECLINE AND TERMINATION

Facing terminal changes in health and death itself is the final task of life. Terminal deterioration in an individual may extend from a few days to a few years. This part of the life-span should be distinguished from the previous epochs, since characteristics of the individual during this phase may show abrupt changes not obviously consistent with the previous behavior of the individual. Abruptness of measured cognitive changes are coming to be regarded as prodromal of death (Kleemeier, 1961). The normal psychology of the end of the life-span needs the illumination of considerable research. The last days of life can be provocative, result in a surprising recall of early-life events, and prompt an individual to become involved with a review of his life. Psychological reactions to the stimulus of awareness that the end of life may be close vary: Some deny it; some accept it passively; and some even welcome it. Butler has discussed the function of the life review (1963) in terms of four tasks facing the dying individual: management of his reactions to the symptoms of his terminal state, adaptation to the impending separation from loved ones and friends, adjustment of his life perception, and reaction to a transition to an unknown state. This phase of the life-span is but little understood, and, as more information becomes available, professional services will be more constructive for the normally aged.

SUMMARY

Over two-thirds of the life-span of the average person is spent as an adult, yet psychology has only recently begun to be seriously concerned with the problems of the adult phase of the human life cycle. The adult is continually undergoing transformations of a biological, psychological, and social nature. Acceptance of this dynamic viewpoint is necessary if one is going to deal rationally with the personal and social problems associated with advancing age. As there are in childhood, there are characteristic problems to face at phases throughout adult portion of the lifespan, that is, the developmental tasks of adult life. Developmental problems and tasks are successfully met by most people, although some problems can be taxing to vulnerable individuals and evoke psychological crises.

Advancing age brings with it an increase in many well-recognized forms of disease and disability that require professional care. Distinguishable from such frequent pathology is a pattern of normal aging, which most persons experience. Facing terminal changes in health and then death itself is the final task of life. Far from being without content, the terminal stages of life can be provocative to the individual and result in a surprising recall of early-life events, prompting some people to experience a "life review." Professional psychological services at this stage, as at all earlier adult ages, will improve and become more insightful as needed further research and study are carried out on the developmental psychology of the adult years.

REFERENCES

ALLISON, R. S. 1962. *The senile brain.* Baltimore: Williams & Wilkins.

BIRREN, J. E. 1964. *The psychology of aging.* Englewood Cliffs, N.J.: Prentice-Hall.

BIRREN, J. E., BUTLER, R. N., GREENHOUSE, S. W., SOKOLOFF, L., and YARROW, M. R. 1963. *Human Aging.* Washington, D.C.: Public Health Services Publication No. 986.

BIRREN, J. E., RIEGEL, K. F., and MORRISON, D. M. 1962. Age differences in response speed as a function of controlled variations of stimulus conditions: Evidence of a general speed factor. *Gerontologia,* **6,** 1–8.

BRUES, A. M., and SACHER, G. A. (eds.). 1965. *Aging and levels of biological organization.* Chicago: Univer. of Chicago Press.

BUTLER, R. N. 1963. The life review: An interpretation of reminiscence in the aged. *Psychiatry,* **26,** 65–76.

CHOWN, SHEILA. 1961. Age and the rigidities. *J. Geront.* **16,** 353–62.

CORSELLIS, J. A. N. 1962. *Mental illness and the aging brain.* Fair Lawn, N.J.: Oxford Univer. Press.

CUMMING, ELAINE, and HENRY, W. E. 1961. *Growing old.* New York: Basic Books.

DASTUR, D. K., LANE, M. H., HANSEN, D. B., KETY, S. S., BUTLER, R. N., PERLIN, S., and SOKOLOFF, L. 1963. Effects of aging on cerebral circulation and metabolism in man. In J. E. BIRREN, R. N. BUTLER, S. W. GREENHOUSE, L. SOKOLOFF, and M. R. YARROW (eds.), *Human Aging.* Washington, D.C.: Public Health Service Publication No. 986. Pp. 59–76.

HAVINGHURST, R. J. 1961. The nature and values of meaningful free-time activity. In R. W. KLEEMIER (ed.), *Aging and Leisure.* Fair Lawn, N.J.: Oxford Univer. Press. Pp. 309–44.

KELLY, E. L. 1955. Consistency of the adult personality. *Amer. Psychologist.,* **10,** 659–81.

KINSEY, A. C., POMEROY, W. B., and MARTIN, C. E. 1948. *Sexual behavior in the human male.* Philadelphia: Saunders.

KLEEMEIER, R. W., JUSTISS, W. A., JONES, A., and RICH, T. A. Intellectual changes in the senium. Unpublished manuscript.

KUHLEN, R. G. 1959. Aging and life-adjustment. In J. E. BIRREN (ed.),

Handbook of aging and the individual. Chicago: Univer. of Chicago Press. Pp. 852–97.

POST, F. 1965. *The clinical psychiatry of late life.* Oxford, England: Pergamon.

REICHARD, SUZANNE, LIVSON, FLORINE, and PETERSEN, P. G. 1962. *Aging and personality.* New York: Wiley.

REICHENBACH, MARIA, and MATHERS, RUTH A. 1959. The place of time and aging in the natural sciences and scientific philosophy. In J. E. BIRREN (ed.), *Handbook of aging and the individual.* Chicago: Univer. of Chicago Press.

SIMON, A., and NEAL, M. W. 1963. Patterns of geriatric illness. In R. H. WILLIAMS (ed.), *Processes of Aging.* New York: Atherton Press. Pp. 449–71.

STRONG, E. K. 1931. *Change of interest with age.* Stanford, Calif.: Stanford Univer. Press.

TOBIN, S. S., and NEUGARTEN, BERNICE. 1961. Life satisfaction and social interaction in the aging. *J. Geront.,* 16, 344–46.

WELFORD, A. T., and BIRREN, J. E. (eds.). 1965. *Behavior, aging and the nervous system.* Springfield, Ill.: Charles C Thomas.

III

TREATMENT APPROACHES

III

16

Psychotherapy: An Overview

John G. Watkins *

The approach to the treatment of human ills by relationship and social interaction is as old as the history of mankind itself. Our study of ancient cultures discloses that early man (as well as primitive tribes of today) used charms, incantations, amulets, dances, rituals, and magic words as therapeutic agents. In fact, it is estimated that one form of psychotherapy, suggestion, has probably been used to treat more cases of illness than all other therapeutic agents put together, throughout the entire history of man.

THE MEANING OF PSYCHOTHERAPY

Strictly speaking, *psychotherapy* refers to the "treatment of the mind." However, since physical methods such as use of drugs and surgery are not usually so classified, the restricted meaning, treatment *by* the mind— hence, treatment by relationship, or by human behavioral techniques— would seem more precise. Accordingly, we would regard the use of a placebo as a psychotherapeutic technique, but not the use of a psychotropic drug, where the behavioral change is induced chemically.

Since psychotherapy is practiced by many different practitioners—psychiatrists, social workers, speech therapists, and others, as well as psychologists—definitions often reflect not only different theoretical orientations but also the languages of different professional disciplines. Thus,

* John G. Watkins, Ph.D. (Columbia University), Professor of Psychology, and Director of Clinical Training, University of Montana.

psychotherapy defined as "The art of treating mental diseases or disorders" (Hinsie and Shatzky, 1945) makes good sense to the medical psychiatrist. The psychologist, as a behavioral scientist, might prefer a definition such as "Psychotherapy is a certain kind of social relationship between two persons who hold periodic conversations in pursuit of certain goals: namely, the lessening of emotional discomfort and the alteration of various other aspects of client behavior" (Shoben, 1953). Most definitions of the term can be classed under the following four categories, depending on the emphasis placed on different goals:

1. Relief of symptoms
2. Development of a feeling of personal adequacy, maturity, and integration
3. Improvement of the ability to give and receive love, to react in empathic and socially constructive ways toward others
4. Adjustment to the demands, work opportunities, and laws of society

Psychotherapists of every persuasion would usually maintain that they seek all of the above objectives. Yet, it is apparent, as one considers the various techniques and theoretical assumptions, that each approach places greater weight on certain of the above goals than on others.

Because of these widely differing views of just what constitutes the process, what are its goals, what are its theoretical bases, and what are its techniques, courts and legislatures have found it an almost impossible job to define and hence regulate its practice. In psychotherapy, some person, called a "patient" or "client," who is suffering from some pain, impairment of function, anxiety, fear, depression, personality disturbance, or ineffectiveness of ability to achieve his goals, for reasons that are not considered to be physically or organically based, seeks the services of another person, called a "psychotherapist." This therapist will attempt to intervene through social-relationship techniques, primarily verbal, in the behavioral patterns of such a person for the purpose of changing them in a direction considered to be more desirable by the person, his therapist, his family, his employer, the law, or society in general. What a confusing situation is this, with which the young clinician must cope in trying to understand just what psychotherapy is all about. To compound the difficulties, the various disciplines concerned—medicine, psychology, psychiatry, social work, the clergy, the courts, and others—have often quarreled over property rights. To whom does the right to administer such treatment belong? What should his training be? What does he do? How does he do it? And how does he know that he has done it?

The next few chapters in this book will be devoted to a consideration of the major approaches to psychotherapy as understood and practiced by clinicians each of whom is especially skilled and knowledgeable in one of these areas. I will try in this chapter to lay a broad basis for the more detailed consideration of specific approaches later, and to present in outline form a listing of the various theories and techniques that might be contained within the word "psychotherapy."

HISTORY AND BACKGROUND

Evidences of the practice of psychotherapy during historical times can be traced back as far as 2000 to 3000 B.C. Early writings of Egyptian and Babylonian physicians, as well as reliefs found in the Egyptian tombs, have clearly established that psychological approaches to treatment were used in those periods. The priest-physicians of ancient Greek culture placed their patients on stone couches within the temples and spoke to them soothingly, reducing anxieties through what Plato called "beautiful" logic, hence interpretation. One is reminded here of the technique called "psychoanalysis" to be devised many centuries later.

During the medieval period, psychotherapy stemmed primarily from church dogma and consisted primarily of the use of punishment and reward for the reinforcement of Christian beliefs and the elimination of heresy. There was a decline of humanitarianism, and rigid methods of control were the order of the day.

During the later Middle Ages, the fear of witchcraft became so strong that the insane were often tortured and put to death if scourging and other torture failed to drive the witches from their bodies and behavior. Gone was the humane treatment of disturbed individuals who in earlier times had often been regarded as inspired, holy men.

In the eighteenth century, a revival of liberalism, and concern for humanitarian concepts, such as culminated in the French Revolution brought new attitudes toward the treatment of the mentally ill (Bromberg, 1954). Pinel in 1780 struck the chains from the insane who were imprisoned in asylums, and, for the first time in many centuries, the emotionally maladjusted individual was regarded as a human being, possessing worth and integrity, and deserving kindness and constructive treatment designed to restore him to society. Not that such a transition in attitude came easily or rapidly. Even Benjamin Rush, a great humanitarian psychiatrist of the early 1800's, employed the tranquilizing chair, a device in which the disturbed patient was so completely strapped that he was incapable of any movement whatsoever—thus tranquilizing his behavior.

This same period featured the earliest explosions of interest in the psychotherapeutic technique of hypnotic suggestion, the history of which was to be marked by such names as Mesmer, Braid, Liebeault, and Bernheim (1964). In fact, it was through early work in this modality that

Freud came by his concepts of unconscious motivation and initiated the studies that culminated in the theories and techniques of psychoanalysis, a major treatment approach about which much more will be said in a later chapter.

Perhaps we can say that the modern practice of psychotherapy began at this point, around 1890, and at this point we will leave its historical consideration to discuss in greater detail the nature of the process, the relationship, and the therapist.

PSYCHOTHERAPY: THE PROCESS

We are confronted here with two different terms that appear to describe the same similar processes, namely, *counseling* and *psychotherapy*. In both, a therapist talks with a troubled person for the purpose of assisting him with his personal difficulties. Some psychologists even consider the terms synonymous. However, the two do differ in respect to the nature of the problems they generally undertake to solve and the objectives, even though there is much overlap.

The "counselor" most often attends primarily to matters of vocational and educational adjustment or to marital problems. He tends to call his subjects "clients," rather than "patients," they being considered as normal people with problems and not as mentally ill. Furthermore, the disturbance is generally more mild or limited. In "psychotherapy," we are often concerned with more highly disturbed people, those whose behavior has deviated so far from the average that they can no longer be regarded as "normal," and whose problems often have roots that reach deeply into subliminal or unconscious processes within the individual. They are not susceptible of manipulation except by rather intricate and "deep" approaches. The goal, also, usually entails a more drastic personality reorganization.

The modern tendency is to regard the disturbances of the psychotherapeutic patient as due to faulty learning; psychotherapy then is a kind of corrective relearning (Szasz, 1960). Viewed in this way, both the counselor and the psychotherapist become teachers. It should be noted that such views tend to define the process as more psychological than medical in nature. They have, accordingly, often evoked considerable opposition by certain members of the medical profession who feel that the process should be defined as a part of medicine and its practice limited to medically trained therapists.

Psychotherapy, as a psychological approach to treatment, has been divided into many different schools. Each of these is supported by a varying body of psychological theory. Each has its own rationale, its own goals, and its unique methodology. However, we have not yet reached that point in psychological science where we can clearly evaluate the respective claims of these varied approaches. The young clinician is, accordingly, advised to become acquainted with as many as possible, weighing, evaluating, and borrowing, toward the time when he can develop his own rationale and technical skills in the field. We are like the blind men and the elephant. No one has the truth and all the truth yet. Progress will be made only if we can avoid the rigidity of premature identification with a single approach, to the exclusion of the stimulation from fruitful hypotheses stemming from different theories. A rather open-minded eclecticism seems wisest at this stage of development, albeit there is greater personal security and freedom from anxiety with adherence to a single, consistent doctrine.

It is interesting to note that every system and technique of therapy has its reported successes. It seems as if a disturbed individual can be treated with benefit by a tremendous number of different tactics. One therapist, for example, thinks of psychotherapy in terms of learning theory. He regards himself as a teacher, or conditioner, and treatment as a process of emotional relearning or behavioral correction through reinforcement. Another clinician sees in psychotherapy a problem of perceptual reorganization, a forming of new Gestalten and new figure-ground ties. His task is to direct the patient's attention toward the inadequacies and inefficiencies in his perception of objects, events, and people, both past and present. Other therapists assume that the job is to free the patient to mobilize his resources and redirect his own energies toward goals of greater self-integration and improved social adjustment. To still others, treatment means probing and exploring unconscious processes, the better to expose hidden conflicts. Some therapists see the restorative forces as arising largely in the patient, with their own roles as catalytic. Others conceive of themselves as "giving" or "loaning" support, energy, and understanding. Still others seek to initiate the constructive changes through stimulating or controlling the patient's behavior. Indeed, the way one views the process relates clearly and directly to his own theoretical frame of reference.

Even so, in all these different views, we see a distressed patient communicating with an attentive therapist in a close and confidential relationship. We see the therapist as a sincere person who is trying to understand his patient in the light of a chosen reference frame. At times during this verbal interaction (called variously the "therapeutic interview," "session," or "hour"), the therapist imparts a bit of his understanding to his patient in the form of suggestions, advice, hints, interpretations, or reflections of feeling; he reinforces "good" behavior through confirmation, praise, or rewards; or he offers some other reaction that he considers appropriate in the light of his grasp of the patient's problem, his theoretical view, and his technical skill. If the therapy is successful, the patient uses the therapist's reactions to modify his behavior in some way. He alters his attitudes toward himself and others; he mobilizes resources; he lives more happily.

At some time in this process, there comes a moment when the patient, the therapist, or both arrive at the decision that it is time to terminate their relationship, that the goals have been achieved, or are unachievable, have been replaced, or have been achieved as much as seems feasible without undue further effort, time and cost. Sometimes the treatment is terminated when the patient feels misunderstood and, in a fit of anger, refuses to come for further interviews. The many complications of quitting are as complex as the beginning and intermediate aspects of the process.

At this point, the therapist may undertake some evaluations of the success of the procedure. However, most workers in the field will hold that the results may require months or years to become fully manifest. Constructive trends may be set in motion that overcome previous destructive processes within the patient and take time for their full evolvement and realization. The criteria for evaluation will be discussed more later, but they are not as yet very objective and reliable.

To the critics of psychotherapy, it can be pointed out that patients seek the process, are willing to invest considerable sums of money and time, and report that they have benefited, and that such reports are often concurred in by their therapist, family, and friends. There is, however, no universality for such beneficial results, and there are many unsuccessful treatment cases who continue to suffer and misbehave while they seek one therapist after another in the vain hope of finding a "doctor" or technique that will work for them.

THE PSYCHOTHERAPIST

Since the second edition of this text, there has been a tremendous growth in the number and training of psychotherapists. At that time (1954), an estimate was presented to the effect that there were only about 1,000 competent psychotherapists in the United States. Today, the number must surely approach 5,000 highly competent practitioners. If we include all the members of the American Psychiatric Association, the psychoanalysts, both medical and non-medical, the therapeutically trained psychiatric social workers, the psychological counselors, the clinical psychologists, and the pastoral counselors, there may be as many as 20,000 practitioners of the art of psychotherapy actively treating cases in 1966. It is surprising, in spite of this great expansion within a decade, that the demand continues to exceed the supply. Perhaps as the general standard of living and personal incomes have increased, disturbed people have acquired more resources to obtain psychotherapeutic help. At any rate, we still have not met the demand.

What are the personal qualifications for the psychotherapist? Someone facetiously defined "psychotherapy" as the interaction of two people, one of whom thinks he is less sick than the other. It is scarcely necessary to defend the thesis that he who treats should be a better-adjusted person than his patient. This, however, has not always been the case. A few individuals with strong, unresolved emotional problems continually seek to enter this field as a means of trying to solve their own difficulties. These disturbed people, if admitted as practitioners, might then project their own problems onto their patients. It is not always easy to know what is "I" and what is "thou," and the therapist who has serious blind spots in regard to his own shortcomings makes a poor guide along the road toward psychological health. It has, therefore, been considered axiomatic that the therapist must be reasonably free from severe emotional problems, either by "nature" or through successful, intensive personal therapy. In fact, advocates of certain approaches (such as psychoanalysis) maintain that the latter is preferable.[1]

In descriptions of the successful therapist, we find such adjectives as "human," "warm," "understanding," "accepting," "tolerant," and "kind." Inasmuch as therapy is often viewed as a form of parental "rerearing," it appears that the therapist can be likened to the good parent. In fact, the patient often views the therapist as a parent figure and treats him accordingly.

The modern psychotherapist has arrived in this profession by one of several educational routes. He may be identified with one of several professional disciplines. Until recently, psychiatry has been the most closely associated with psychotherapy. The *psychiatrist*, as a doctor of medicine, has extended his study of organic pathology into the field of psychological pathology, which he terms "mental illness." Not all psychiatrists, however, practice psychotherapy, some preferring, because of either inclination or lack of training, to approach the problem of behavior disturbance by way of physical techniques. The young psychiatrist of today has had training as a *resident* in a psychiatric clinic or hospital. This period of some three or more years follows his medical internship and includes training in psychotherapeutic methods.

The psychoanalyst is more commonly a physician who has completed a course of training involving a personal analysis followed by a combination

[1] It should be noted that some attempts have been made in mental hospitals to establish therapeutic groups in which patients treat patients, although with supervision by a trained psychotherapist. Perhaps, in certain kinds of conditions, it is possible for an individual to be helped by one whose adjustment is poorer than his own. Such special situations do not warrant generalization to the professional, trained therapist.

of courses, seminars, and the conducting of several analyses under the close supervision of an experienced (training) analyst. There are now several centers in this country that provide analytic training to psychologists and other non-physicians. Accordingly, the number of non-medical analysts in this country is on the increase, approaching in this respect the situation previously found in Europe, where a number of so-called lay analysts were trained and practicing.

Clinical psychologists ordinarily possess the Ph.D. degree with one or more years of internship experience in clinical settings. Almost all of the doctoral training programs for clinical psychologists in approved universities today provide some form of training in psychotherapy, either through university courses and practicums or through supervision in internship settings. In fact, emphasis on training in psychotherapy is growing and coming to occupy an increasingly prominent position in the training of psychological clinicians. A number of psychotherapeutic societies such as the American Academy of Psychotherapists, The Council of Psychoanalytic Psychotherapists, and the Psychologists Interested in the Advancement of Psychotherapy have been organized that are composed in large measure of non-medical members. A few such as the American Psychoanalytic Association still require the M.D. degree for membership. These reflect the medical orientation that psychoanalysis adopted in this country in 1937 and that has prevailed ever since.

Closely allied with the clinical psychologists are the *counseling psychologists,* who have their own division in the American Psychological Association, and their own specialty-board diploma issued by the American Board of Examiners in Professional Psychology, which is the full equivalent in quantitative requirements to the diploma in clinical psychology that is issued by the same board.

With somewhat less stringent requirements, *counselors* often operate in a high school or college guidance center. They have generally limited themselves to types of non-crippling personal problems or to vocational and educational guidance; they may or may not possess the doctoral degree. The doctorate is now a standard minimal requirement for employment as a clinical or counseling psychologist in any of the branches of federal service.

The psychiatric social worker has come from the profession of social work. In various clinics, these practitioners often undertake therapy with patients as well as adjunctive therapy with members of the patients' families. The *psychiatric nurse,* by virtue of her strategic position in the hospital ward, has almost unlimited opportunity to practice various forms of psychotherapy, usually supportive in nature. In some hospitals, experiments have shown that the nurse and the psychiatric aide (ward attendant) can both function as auxiliary psychotherapists under the supervision of a fully trained psychiatrist or clinical psychologist, especially in administering continuous reinforcement to desirable behaviors as exemplified in the therapeutic approach called "operant conditioning." The *speech therapist* trained in speech pathology often practices various forms of psychotherapy, since speech disturbances have come increasingly to be identified as problems of the entire person and his living conditions. Psychotherapy is also inevitably performed by the *general medical practitioner* in the course of his regular office and hospital practice. In fact, if he is not aware of psychotherapeutic techniques and does not employ them to some extent continuously, he may well develop the antagonism of his patients to his ministrations. Medical schools today, while not training the general physician intensively in complex psychotherapeutic techniques, try to offer him some acquaintance with these procedures.

Finally, we should note the current tendency for members of the clergy to seek and secure training in counseling and limited techniques of psychotherapy. The *pastoral counselor* is appearing in increasingly frequent numbers. Special schools, seminars, and institutes are continually giving training to men of the cloth in the recognition and amelioration of emotional disorders. People in this profession are often the first to whom the disturbed person turns for assistance, counsel, and support.

The practice of psychotherapy by psychologists may be in psychiatric hospitals, mental hygiene clinics, child guidance clinics, general medical and surgical hospitals, counseling centers, university clinics, institutions for the mentally defective, schools for child and adult rehabilitation, prisons, or private practice. The tendency has been toward an increased broadening in the utilization of the services of the clinical psychologist. His role has often become that of a psychological consultant in all types of behavior problems where he brings to the situation specialized training and skills, involving diagnostic, therapeutic, and research methodology. His earlier primary role as a giver of tests seems to be declining.

The independent private practice of psychotherapy by psychologists has been opposed by substantial elements in the psychiatric and medical professions. The American Psychiatric Association has exerted great efforts to define the role of the clinical psychologist as ancillary to that of the medical psychiatrist and to limit his activity in psychotherapy to the treatment of cases assigned him by psychiatrists, his treatment to be under their supervision.

The unwillingness of the psychological profession to accept this role has culminated in much conflict between the two APA's and struggles over the certification laws within the respective states. However, in general, the trend has been toward increasing independence and responsibilities for the psychologist. The American Psychological Association, through its ethical-practices code, insists that the psychologist is bound to see that the medical needs of his patients are provided for. Most psychologists prefer to establish good working relationships with the medical profession and to collaborate with physicians in order that medical conditions will not go undiagnosed or untreated when disguised as behavioral problems.

At the present time, half of the states have some form of legal certification or licensure of psychologists. Perhaps another dozen or so states have some regulation of the practice of psychologists through the self-certification provided by examining boards established by the state psychological associations. Almost all of these require the doctorate as a prerequisite for certification. Many of the certification laws have the right of privileged communication written into them, thus affording to the psychological practitioner the protection usually granted to the physician, the attorney, and members of the clergy.

The American Board of Examiners in Professional Psychology provides a high-level certification involving some five years of advanced experience and examinations in addition to the doctoral requirement. Its diplomates thus can be compared in the quantity of their training to the specialists certified by such medical boards as the American Board of Surgery, the American Board of Physical Medicine, and the American Board of Psychiatry and Neurology. In a highly specialized area, another board, also recognized by the American Psychological Association, the American Board of Examiners in Psychological Hypnosis, issues diplomas certifying high-level competence in clinical or experimental hypnosis.

Perhaps the majority of clinicians still function in a hospital or clinic setting that involves a team approach to the problems of diagnosis and treatment. This has the advantages of providing built-in protection for the practitioners and of pooling the therapeutic thinking of individuals from several complementary disciplines. Traditionally, the psychiatrist made the initial medical evaluation, the social worker prepared a social case history, and the psychologist administered a battery of psychological tests. After staffing, the cases were usually "assigned" by the psychiatrist as "captain" of the team to the respective team members for therapy.

In some settings, this pattern of practice continues today. In others, the psychologist has become more nearly equal in rank and responsibility to the psychiatrist. In still others, there seems to be a paralleling of services between the Psychology Service and the Psychiatric Service, while occasionally institutions concerned with therapy and rehabilitation have no psychiatrist, but instead have staff psychologists who collaborate directly with non-psychiatric physicians. The team approach still has much to recommend it. There are many who believe it superior to the individual practice of psychotherapy by either the psychiatrist or the psychologist.

Although often at loggerheads over matters of status, independence, and legislation through their professional associations, individual practitioners in general throughout the country report the most amiable of personal relationships between psychologists and psychiatrists, with the tendency to value each other on the basis of individual competence rather than professional affiliation. This has coincided with the increased recognition by medical practitioners of the rigorous and competent training of the psychologist, and by the psychologist of his own limitations in dealing with conditions that are both psychological and physiological.

THE TREATMENT SETTING

For what kinds of behavior deviations is psychotherapy recommended? In the past, the psychoneuroses were the primary syndromes treated by these approaches. The trend continues, however, toward application to an ever widening variety of disturbances. For example, the psychotic disorders have been found responsive to a number of types of psychotherapy, especially when these have been integrated with the various psychotropic drugs that have in recent years been developed to alleviate anxiety and reduce depression. Criminal behavior including the problem of the so-called psychopathic personality has received increased attention by both individual and group psychotherapeutic approaches. The entire range of psychophysiological disorders such as emotionally caused disturbances of the gastrointestinal tract, the cardiovascular system, the skin, and the allergies are now often approached psychotherapeutically as well as through the more widely used somatic therapies. Even such conditions as the disorders of old people, epilepsy, tuberculosis, and other illnesses commonly regarded as physical in origin have been found to respond favorably to psychotherapy. It is known that pain can be displaced from one part of the body to another; anxiety and tension can increase the suffering of a physical involvement, and disturbed behavior can render difficult or impossible the patient's cooperation with the physician. Through the work of psychological therapists, these physical illnesses may be modified, or at least the treatment of them by physiological techniques may be rendered increasingly feasible or effective. For example, hypnotic suggestion practiced by psychologists has induced a state of relaxation making possible the insertion of a gastroscope for the diagnosis of a peptic ulcer. It has made bearable to some patients the changing of dressings on painful burns or the treating of dental caries. Thus, we see that psychologists are becoming increasingly ingenious in the ways in which they employ psychological procedures to help and influence the entire practice of medicine.

The supervision of the psychotherapist raises many questions. In the past, this was carried out in the medical setting by the psychiatrist. However, the sheer physical limitations of time, coupled with the fact that increasing numbers of clinical psychologists have received psychotherapeutic training at least equal if not superior to that of their psychiatric colleagues, have tended to bring the therapeutic role of the psychologist in the medical setting into greater independence. No one would quarrel with the contention that junior clinicians, psychological or psychiatric, require extensive periods of supervision during their training and in the early years of their practice. There seems to be no substitute for directed experience in which the young psychologist can share in the insights of the more experienced practitioner. It is generally recognized that it is the skill and experience of the supervisor, combined with the relationship established between therapist and supervisor, that matters, rather than the latter's professional-group identification.

The attitudes of supervisors vary. Some conceive of supervision as the close observation of the young therapist, imparting to him a greater understanding of his patient and the therapeutic relationship, seeing to it that he does not make mistakes, and teaching him on the spot particular techniques useful in a given case at a specific time. Other supervisors view the supervisory relationship as a growth situation similar to psychotherapy itself, in which both members, through interaction, improve their capacities to interrelate. From this viewpoint, the patient at times seems somewhat secondary to the interaction beween supervisor and supervisee. Perhaps the majority of supervisors function somewhere between these two attitudes.

Interest in group therapy has grown considerably in the past decade, partly because it reduces the per-patient cost of treatment but also because it adds certain elements that are not to be found in the one-to-one treatment situation. Furthermore, through participation in therapeutic groups, either as patients themselves or as auxiliary therapists, young psychologists get firsthand acquaintance with the group process. Many training situations employ one-way-vision screens, hidden microphones, tape recordings, and "sitting-in" tactics to permit the younger therapist-in-training to get the "feel" of a therapeutic hour. It is in this process of supervision (or "controls" as it is termed in psychoanalytic training centers) that most of the learning of therapeutic technique occurs. Here, the inexperienced therapist can share the experiences of the senior clinician and develop best his own skills and sensitiveness. Psychotherapy cannot be learned merely from reading. The opportunity to work with the experienced psychotherapist is a privilege to be sought by the clinician-in-training.

APPROACHES TO PSYCHOTHERAPY: THEORY AND TECHNIQUE

The various therapeutic approaches are divided for convenience into those that are largely *supportive* and those whose aim is a more significant and permanent reorganization of personality structure. The latter are often termed *reconstructive*. It is recognized that in any supportive approach one can find reconstructive elements, just as one can find supportive elements in the reconstructive or intensive approach. It is, accordingly, not possible to categorize exactly any one procedure. We might, however, conveniently define as supportive those methods that aim at relieving symptoms by the use of motivation, suppression, ego strengthening, and re-education without altering the basic personality structure. Reconstructive therapies include those procedures that attempt the indirect relief of symptoms through a significant reorganization of the patient's customary modes of personality interaction with others. This occurs in a close interpersonal relationship with the therapist. Self-understanding, or insight into one's inner motivations, generally accompanies this process. Certain therapists consider this insight the agent causing the emotional growth; others consider it a by-product of progress in personal development. By virtue of these definitive statements, Table 16–1 has been arranged to designate various approaches considered primarily supportive or reconstructive. Certain ones, of course, clearly fall within one category or the other, while others are sufficiently borderline to leave room for controversy.

To differentiate these two classes at the level of a personality theory, one can refer to the reference frame developed by Federn (1952) and Weiss (1960), who describe personality in terms of postulated economic, dynamic, and topographical aspects. By the *economic* aspect is meant the quantity of energy invested in any drive or psychological state. By *dynamic* aspects they mean the direction and pattern of energy interactions and, hence, the structure of the drives and defensive maneuvers. *Topography* refers to the basic attitudinal positions of the individual, the sets that were acquired earliest and that underlie and modify later acquisitions of behavior. In psychoanalytic theory, these represent fundamental investments of love and hate (libido positions). These latter characteristics are considered to be structured at primitive levels within the person and are not within his realm of consciousness.

From this viewpoint, supportive procedures are those that change the economic pattern by displacing energy from one aspect to another of the functioning personality. They may involve the substituting of one defense for another. Such procedures would not change the basic topography. On the other hand, it is apparent that the reconstructive therapies aim at a more permanent and comprehensive revision involving not only economic and dynamic but also topographical changes. In psychoanalytic circles, this is referred to as altering the "basic character structure." From the standpoint of behavioral and learning theory psychologies, these three terms tend to lose meaning. The operant conditioner, for example, would not concede that his manipulations that modify external and apparent behavior are "superficial," that they do not change the fundamental bases of behavior that the psychoanalyst describes as unconscious and relatively inflexible under the term *basic character structure.* Without attempting at this time to resolve the differences in viewpoint, we can but note that the *supportive* therapies are concerned primarily with the more immediate and apparent manipulations of observable behavior. The reconstructive therapies aim at intervening in the process within the patient between the input of stimuli and the output of response. They tend to be more closely related to the psychoanalytic view of human personality.

Attention is now turned to a brief characterization of those supportive and reconstructive approaches listed in Table 16–1. Because the following chapters consider in detail the most often used techniques, few details will here be offered relative to the client-centered, psychoanalytic child therapies and operant conditioning approaches. Table 16–1, nonetheless, provides, summarily, an inventory of the techniques one is most likely to encounter either in one's reading or in clinical practice.

SUPPORTIVE PSYCHOTHERAPEUTIC TECHNIQUES

Reassurance, suggestion, advice, reasoning, persuasion, and motivational procedures such as rewards and punishments, as Thorne (1950) has indicated, can be effective when properly and appropriately used. These methods are time-honored and are a common stock in trade of the general medical practitioner as well as many vocational and personal counselors. However, they have their limitations, inasmuch as their use by the inexperienced can preclude an awareness of deeper problems presented by the unsophisticated and inarticulate client.

When a patient talks about his difficulties, he becomes less afraid of them. He becomes less sensitive, or *desensitized.* This enables him to cope with concepts he had previously regarded with such fear, anxiety, and guilt as to place them outside the realm of effective control. The supportive therapist well knows the value of mere self-expression. This may be continued to the point of a true *verbal catharsis*, or outpouring of strong feelings and violent tensions. Sometimes the patient becomes so involved in his released emotions that he weeps or shouts. This experience, known as *abreaction*, is deliberately provoked by the therapist and

Table 16–1. A List of Supportive and Reconstructive Techniques *

Supportive Methods	Reconstructive Methods
Reassurance	Psychoanalysis and modifications
Suggestion and advice	The Washington "cultural" school
Reasoning and persuasion	Sullivan-Fromm
Motivational procedures: rewards and punishments	Horney's approach
Desensitization	Stekel's active approach
Ventilation and verbal catharsis	Ferenczi's active approach
Poison-pen therapy	The Chicago school
Abreaction	Herzberg's "active psychotherapy"
Counseling, directive and non-directive	Karpman's "objective psychotherapy"
Educational, vocational and personal	Deutsch's "sector analysis"
Rest	Mowrer's two-factor learning theory
Progressive relaxation	Reich's character analysis
Autogenic training	Character-analytic vegototherapy
Hypnotherapy	Federn's "ego psychology"
Re-education: conditioned reflex therapy	Berne's "transactional analysis"
Aversion or conditioned avoidance	Dollard and Miller's integration of psychoanalysis and learning theory
Operant-conditioning approach	Jung's "analytical psychology"
Wolpe's therapy by reciprocal inhibition	Rank's "will therapy"
Environmental manipulation	Relationship therapy (Taft-Allen)
Social service	Roger's "client-centered therapy"
Chemotherapies (as psychotherapies)	Experiential therapy (Whitaker-Malone)
Remedying physical defects	Adler's "individual psychology"
Plastic surgery	Meyer's "psychobiology"
Physiotherapy	Kelly's "constructive alternativism"
Occupational therapy	Hypnoanalysis
Manual arts therapy	Therapy under drug-induced narcosis
Food therapy	Grinker and Spiegel's "narcosynthesis"
Recreational activities	Horsley's "narco-analysis"
Dance therapy	Play therapies
Music therapy	Levy's "release therapy"
Art therapy	Moreno's "psychodrama"
Bibliotherapy (prescribed reading)	Group therapies (reconstructive)
Group therapy (Supportive)	Gestalt therapy
Religious therapies	Korzybski's "general semantics"
Confession	Existential analysis
Pastoral counseling	Szondi's "fate analysis"
Participation in church activities	Religious experience
Christian Science	Zen psychology

can have a tremendously relieving effect, especially when the previously repressed emotions have stemmed from some traumatic experience the patient could not master.

At times, the patient needs temporary relief from his tensions, such as can be found in enforced *rest* or through the systematic training of muscle behaviors found in *progressive relaxation* (Jacobson, 1938) or *autogenic training* (Schultz and Luthe, 1959). Hypnosis is sometimes

* See Chapters 16–22 in this volume.

used to induce a state of relaxation, during which it has been found that therapeutic suggestions appear to have increased effectiveness. The methods of inducing the trance state and of implanting effective suggestions (*hypnotherapy*) have been described by Bernheim (1964) Meares (1961), Watkins (1949) and Weitzenhoffer (1957), among others.

Since psychotherapy is a kind of unlearning or relearning procedure, current learning theories have been utilized to devise treatment techniques. *Conditioned-reflex theory*, for example, has been employed to recondition alcoholics so that they become nauseated rather than pleasantly stimulated by the smell of whiskey. By association of the ingestion of liquor with an emetic, an *aversion*, or *conditioned avoidance*, is established. The *operant conditioning* theories of B. F. Skinner (1953, 1957), which are described in greater detail in other chapters—9, 17, and 21— have been found effective in the modification of neurotic and psychotic behavior through the positive reinforcement of more constructive responses.

The strong feeling of inferiority related to physical disfigurement can occasionally be relieved by corrective *plastic surgery*. In fact, any type of medical attention may have a suggestive, therapeutic effect. Certain patients are so accustomed to receiving drugs from their physicians that the mere administration of "something" by him is sufficient to relieve their symptoms, even though this *placebo* is quite inert psychologically.

By means of movies, television, radio, and reading, we observe the lives of others, participate vicariously in their experiences, and become modified in the process. Therapists at times, therefore, prescribe *bibliotherapy*, or the reading of material they believe will constructively help their patients. The inspirational value of great works of literature as well as the intellectual stimulation provided in well-written books on human adjustment can often be salutary.

Manipulation of the environment, whereby the patient's residence or his job is changed, may supportively relieve him of pressures with which he can no longer cope. The removal of an embittered mother-in-law from the home of a quarreling couple may permit them to improve their marital relationship. The social caseworker is trained in methods of environmental manipulation and may well be consulted when such procedures are indicated.

Additional supportive measures are the exercise of muscle groups through electrical stimulation, rubbing, massage, and heat (*physiotherapy*). This includes the manipulation of tools to make toys, designs, art work, and other creative products as in *occupational therapy* and *manual arts therapy*. *Recreational activities* involving attending or participating in games, sports, plays, and shows often have a beneficial effect on a disturbed patient. Participation in other activities such as *dance, music,* and *art* may frequently benefit him by mobilizing his more creative and constructive motives.

Group therapies can be organized along either supportive or reconstructive lines (Bach, 1954; Corsini, 1957). And finally, it should be noted that *religious* organizations provide supportive therapy through confession and participation in church activities as well as pastoral counseling.

RECONSTRUCTIVE PSYCHOTHERAPEUTIC TECHNIQUES

These methods, as indicated in Table 16–1 are relatively numerous. Historically, the first of these to gain wide use was the psychoanalysis, which was developed by Sigmund Freud (1935, 1953) and his students. Because Chapter 19 is devoted in its entirety to this approach, only selected modifications will be discussed here.

Among the most significant of these variants of orthodox psychoanalytic therapy is that of the Washington "cultural" school, involving the contributions of Sullivan (1953) and Fromm (1955). Sullivan and his co-workers placed great emphasis on the significance of interpersonal relationships in the development and distortion of personality functioning. They perceived the therapist as a "participant" observer. The role of transference (termed by Sullivan "parataxic reactions") toward both the therapist and other significant figures was an important facet of their therapeutic approach. Fromm described various types of individuals, such as the receptive personality, the exploitative personality, the hoarding personality, and the marketing personality, and emphasized the therapeutic goal of maturity, which he defined as the capacity for love and productive work.

Karen Horney (1950), to turn to a second modification, broke with the Freudian analysts to form the American Institute for Psychoanalysis, centered at Philadelphia. Her therapeutic objective was self-realization, a reaching toward mature growth. The neurotic was viewed as having created culturewise an unrealistic "idealized self." To actualize this, the neurotic developed false pride, many "neurotic claims," and compulsive behavior patterns that Horney designated as "shoulds." These became organized into characteristic personality-type solutions such as the expansive, the self-effacing, the morbidly dependent, and the resigned. Therapy was viewed as the process of assisting the patient to realize the nature of his true self through an understanding of the neurotic structure. Sullivan, Fromm, and Horney did not differ too significantly from the Freudian analysts in the actual procedures they used within the therapeutic interviews.

A number of attempts have been made to shorten analytic therapy. These involve efforts to use more active procedures. The Chicago psychoanalytic group under the leadership of Alexander and French (1946) experimented with increased control of transference reactions, flexibility in the frequency of sessions, increased interpretative activity by the analyst, and more limited goals, with the result that, on occasion, patients improved with only twenty to sixty sessions as compared with the several hundred common in classical psychoanalysis. Others who developed active approaches to analytic treatment were Stekel (1943), who emphasized dream interpretation; Ferenczi (1953); and Herzberg (1946), who combined psychoanalysis with selected supportive techniques that aimed at strengthening the ego through the assignment of tasks progressively graded in difficulty. Karpman (1949) used the patient's autobiography as a source for written queries returned to the patient for answering. Interpretations were typewritten, and bibliotherapeutic reading was assigned. Deutsch (1949) had his patients associate to key words obtained from their autobiographical social histories.

Mowrer (1950) stressed the view that psychoneurosis is an immaturity, an underlearning of social adjustment techniques. He felt that it was a weak, immature, "id dominated" ego that attempted to repress the societal controls represented by the superego. Neurotic anxiety was then caused by the return of the repressed superego. He perceived the therapist as the ally of social maturity, the superego. Through a relational struggle reprojected upon the therapist (transference), the immaturity of the ego is corrected.

Wilhelm Reich (1949) noted the presence in some of his patients of characteristic resistances in great strength, which he designated as "character armor." Penetration of this armor by consistent analysis of the negative and resistant manners of the patient toward the analyst was necessary in order to release unconscious material. Later, he developed the concept that these resistances became "frozen" into typical postures, poses, muscular spasms, tics, and other physical reactions, which he termed the "muscular armor." In his "Character-Analytic Vegetotherapy," he described procedures for analyzing this "muscular armor." He considered orgastic potency as the therapeutic goal.

Federn (1952) and his disciple, Weiss (1960), described analytic techniques for the resolution of problems of the ego. They hypothesized a special energy, termed "ego cathexis," the deficiency of which resulted in the appearance of such psychotic symptoms as estrangement and the depersonalization, depending on whether the weakness appeared in the heart of the ego or at its boundaries. A method of treating psychoses called "psychoanalysis in reverse" was developed that involved returning overvalent primitive material to a state of repression and re-establishing ego defenses. Federn's views appear to have considerable significance, but, unfortunately, his style of writing was so difficult that his concepts have not had wide circulation. Berne (1961) used Federn's theories to develop an interesting approach, termed "transactional analysis," in which the roles of the internalized parent and child are analyzed. Berne stressed the unconscious "games" played by people in their relationships with each other.

Jung (1953–64) and Adler (Ansbacher, 1956) were early disciples who broke with Freud to found their own schools of analysis. Jung conceived of the human psyche as being divided into a conscious area, a personal unconscious, and a region he called the "collective unconscious," which included the heritage of the human race as passed down through the generations.

Jung held that this collective unconscious contained "archetypes," which represented basic concepts and images derived from constitutional factors. The goal of treatment was "individualization," the integration and experience of the complete self. His therapeutic techniques did not differ too greatly from Freud's, except that the patients were usually seen in a sitting-up posture, not lying on a couch. Much emphasis was given to the analysis of dreams.

Another rebel from the Freudian view was Adler, who emphasized the role of feelings of inferiority as opposed to sexual problems. He taught that each person developed a "style of life," which was related to his order of birth in the family constellation and was characterized by a seeking for superiority. Adler put less emphasis on unconscious motivations.

Still another of Freud's protégés who broke with him was Otto Rank (1950), who believed that neuroses stemmed primarily from the "trauma of birth." Rank believed in developing an intensive relationship during therapy and taught that the patient possessed a "will," which, if stimulated, might resist the treatment so strongly as to defeat it. He placed great emphasis on the therapist being permissive and letting the patient "will" for himself.

Influenced by the relationship therapies of Taft (1936) and Allen (1942), the client-centered approach was developed by Rogers (1942, 1951) and his associates. In chapter 18, the principal concepts and techniques of this therapeutic method will be discussed.

Adolf Meyer (1957) tried to weld all the therapeutic techniques into a global method, both analytic and supportive, which included also the biological and medical approaches to treatment. He termed this comprehensive system "psychobiology." He stressed the securing of complete histories and developed a diagnostic classification system based on his approach to "reaction types." Therapists who follow Meyer, while not discarding psychoanalytic procedures, tend to emphasize environmental, manipulative, and other supportive procedures. They accent the "commonsense" view of the patient in his environment.

Kelly (1955) developed an approach that he termed "constructive alternativism." In this, he postulated that a person's processes are psychologically channelized by the ways in which he anticipates events. From this fundamental postulate, he drew a number of "corollaries," which represented an explanation of the process by which personality and its disturbances developed and on the basis of which he suggested a more or less experimental approach to therapeutic technique.

The use of hypnosis as adjunctive to selected supportive procedures has already received mention. Wolberg (1947), Gill and Brenman (1959), Schneck (1963), and Watkins (1963), among others, have integrated hypnosis with psychoanalytic techniques into an approach called "hypnoanalysis." Transference reactions, dream material, projective techniques, automatic writing, regression, and other reactions have been used to study selected elements of mental life in intensive analytic-type treatments. Kline (1963) has described some interesting studies and presented a theory that shows the relationship of this approach to the more traditional psychoanalytic methods.

Abreaction under narcosis induced by barbituate drugs was used by Grinker and Spiegel (1945) during World War II in conjunction with psychoanalytic procedures by means of which traumatic incidents were dramatically relived and integrated within the patient. They referred to this procedure as "narcosynthesis." In England, Horsley (1943) treated patients with psychoanalytic methods combined with a drug-induced narcosis wherein the major purpose was the determination of the content of repressions and their "working through" to ego integration. He called his approach "narco-analysis."

Brief mention might be made of various acting approaches to treatment, such as Levy's *release therapy* (1939), used primarily with children, and Moreno's *psychodrama* (1947). Therapeutic groups are often treated reconstructively as well as supportively through the application of many analytic procedures. There are innumerable variations.

Efforts have been made to utilize the *Gestalt* principles of perception as the basis of therapy (Perls, Goodman, and Hefferline, 1951). Szondi (1952) has described a system based on the concept that individuals are determined by their "destinies."

An approach to treatment that has received relatively less attention than it deserves is "general semantics." Its founder, Korzybski (1948), pointed out that neurotic behavior may stem from a lack of clear understanding in the use of words and their meanings. His therapy consisted of teaching the patient-student correct word habits to replace the faulty orientations in language previously acquired.

A recent significant movement in psychotherapy has derived from the work of certain phenomenological philosophers who were searching for the meaning of existence. This is *existential therapy*, as developed through the writings of Kierkegaard (1954), Heidegger (1949), Binswanger (1963), and May (1958). Although the actual techniques of treatment are not carefully specified or distinguished from the more common analytic methods, the patient's manner of "being-in-the-world" is the focus of treatment. The existentialists have opened up a new way of viewing the goal of treatment, especially in a world in which so many disorders stem from a lack of meaning to life. An oriental search for the purpose of life that is in some ways similar is exemplified by the *Zen psychologists* (Watts, 1957). Through a rigorous training, which teaches that one thing is as good as another and that striving is worthless, they aim at achieving the state of complete role identification known as "*satori.*" This is somewhat similar to Horney's "realization of the true self" and Jung's "individuation."

Finally, it should be noted that many people have been helped in significant ways through intensive *religious experiences* such as are found in conversions. These may occur spontaneously and without specific therapeutic intervention by trained therapists.

It is obvious that the number of theories offered to account for emotional maladjustment and its treatment is legion. No person can master them all. The student is invited to investigate further the major systems currently in use, which are described in greater detail in succeeding chapters.

THE EVALUATION OF THERAPEUTIC IMPROVEMENT

The measurement of progress in therapy is a most difficult and challenging problem. Neither the criteria for recovery nor the procedures for their appraisal are presently adequate. Rating scales and observations by family members, friends, associates, the referring physician, the therapist, and the patient himself can be employed to ascertain the degree to which the various objectives of treatment have been attained. Batteries of psychological tests have been used to record any real or potential changes. Experienced clinicians study evidences of change in manner, attitude, behavior, and social adjustment, as well as in reported dreams. A criterion employed by certain client-centered therapists is based on the difference between the patient's idealized self and the way he views his self as measured by a "Q sort" of cards containing descriptive words that the patient considers and rates in terms of how strongly they apply to him. It is assumed that, as therapy is successful, the difference will decline. Hesterly and Berg (1958) were able to show that immaturity as demonstrated in the responses of adult schizophrenics to the Perceptual Reaction Test was similar to that exhibited by normal children, suggesting that this measure might be effective in estimating extent of recovery from psychotic breakdown. Grayson and Olinger (1957) have noted that the ability of the psychotic to simulate normalcy on the MMPI is suggestive of his potential treatability.

Attempts have been made to study physiological changes, for example, in pulse rate, blood pressure, and psychogalvanic responses as related to improvement. It has been shown that such changes do occur. In some cases, they are highly related to anxieties initiated within the therapeutic interview. It has yet to be shown that these indicators can be effectively used as measures of progress or therapeutic success.

Not only the outcomes of treatment have been subjected to investigation, but also the processes that occur within psychotherapy. A symposium sponsored by the National Institute of Mental Health and the American Psychological Association (Rubenstein and Parloff, 1959) brought forth a series of papers on the evaluation of psychotherapeutic process and outcome. In Chapter 23, some of these studies will be described in more detail.

It is obvious that the research worker in psychotherapy must be well trained in experimental techniques. He must also be a seasoned clinician who has a firsthand acquaintance with the treatment of many patients. There are few psychologists at the present time who can meet both criteria. The need to develop experimentally oriented and clinically experienced psychotherapists is great if the field is to advance from art to science.

SUMMARY

Psychotherapy is perhaps the oldest form of treatment known to man. Today, there are so many different approaches, theories, and schools that it is impossible to master them all and very difficult for the young clinical psychologist to become familiar even with all the major ones (Watkins, 1960). Most definitions of "psychotherapy" include one or more of the following objectives: the relief of symptoms, the development of a feeling of adequacy, the ability to give and receive love, the adjustment to society. The tendency now is to emphasize the process as a kind of relearning and, hence, subject to the principles of learning.

Psychotherapists come from a number of different professional disciplines, with medicine, psychiatry, psychology, social work, and the clergy as the most prominent. Because of the difficulty of defining the process, there have been jurisdictional quarrels among these disciplines, notably between psychiatry and psychology. However, during the last decade, the independence of psychologists in the practice of psychotherapy has made rapid strides.

Current discussion in the field is centered on the problems of training and supervision. Supervision of experience is admittedly the crucial factor in the training of psychotherapists. There are too few training centers, and training is inadequate in most of those that are now operating, for either psychologists, psychiatrists, or others.

Therapeutic approaches can be divided primarily into those that are supportive, and rely on educative and suggestive techniques that aim at the modification of observable behavior, and those that are reconstructive. These latter seek for an indirect change in behavior and symptoms through "deep" and systematic reconstruction of what is called "basic character structure."

Psychoanalysis is the prototype of the reconstructive methods, and most of them stem from modifications of this system. The two approaches that have attracted the greatest amount of attention in recent years are the operant conditioning methods, based on the investigations and theories of B. F. Skinner, and the existential therapies, which stem from the philosophic teachings of S. Kierkegaard. These two represent the ultimate in opposite poles of thought: The first stems from objective, behavioral science; the second is subjective, with its roots in psychoanalysis, philosophy, and religion. A comprehensive, validated, and generally agreed-upon theory of human personality on which integrated psychotherapies can be built is still lacking.

There has been a substantial increase of interest in objective research studies aimed at measuring the outcomes of therapy and determining the variables relevant for success and failure. Investigations have focused on the relative efficacy of different techniques, the nature of the process, and the characteristics of the successful therapist. Research advance is hampered by the lack of investigators who are well trained both as therapists and as scientific experimentalists. The student in clinical psychology is enjoined to refrain from identifying strongly with one school or theory during his formative years. A broad knowledge of different ones will enable him to grow into a more mature, sensitive, and sophisticated therapist through the integration of the best thinking from many viewpoints.

REFERENCES

ALEXANDER, F., and FRENCH, T. M. 1946. *Psychoanalytic therapy.* New York: Ronald.

ALLEN, F. H. 1942. *Psychotherapy with children.* New York: Norton.

ANSBACHER, H. L., and ANSBACHER, R. R. (eds.). 1956. *The individual psychology of Alfred Adler.* New York: Basic Books.

BACH, G. R. 1954. *Intensive group psychotherapy.* New York: Ronald.

BERNE, E. 1960. *Transactional analysis in psychotherapy.* New York: Grove.

BERNHEIM, H. 1964. *Hypnosis and suggestion in psychotherapy.* New Hyde Park, N.Y.: University Books.

BROMBERG, W. 1954. *Man above humanity.* Philadelphia: Lippincott.

CORSINI, R. J. 1957. *Methods of group psychotherapy.* New York: McGraw-Hill.

DEUTSCH, F. 1949. *Applied psychoanalysis.* New York: Grune & Stratton.

FEDERN, P. 1952. *Ego psychology and the psychoses.* New York: Basic Books.

FERENCZI, S. 1916. *Contributions to psychoanalysis.* (Published also under the title *Sex and psychoanalysis.*) Boston: Badger.

FREUD, S. 1935. *A general introduction to psychoanalysis.* New York: Liveright.

FREUD, S. 1953. *Collected papers.* Vols. 1–5. London: Hogarth and Institute of Psycho-analysis.

FROMM, E. 1951. *The sane society.* New York: Holt, Rinehart & Winston.

GILL, M. M., and BRENMAN, M. 1959. *Hypnosis and related states.* New York: International Universities Press.

GRAYSON, H. M., and OLINGER, L. B. 1957. Simulation of "normalcy" by psychiatric patients on the MMPI. *J. consult. Psychol.,* **21,** 73–77.

GRINKER, R. R., and SPIEGEL, J. P. 1945. *War neuroses.* Philadelphia: Blakiston.

HEIDEGGER, M. 1949. *Existence and being.* Chicago: Regnery.

HERZBERG, A. 1946. *Active psychotherapy.* New York: Grune & Stratton.

HESTERLY, S. O., and BERG, I. A. 1958. Deviant responses as indicators of immaturity and schizophrenia. *J. consult. Psychol.,* **22,** 389–90.

HINSIE, L. E., and SHATZKY, J. 1945. *Psychiatric dictionary.* Fair Lawn, N.J.: Oxford Univer. Press.

HORNEY, K. 1950. *Neurosis and human growth.* New York: Norton.

HORSLEY, J. S. 1943. *Narco-analysis.* Fair Lawn, N.J.: Oxford Univer. Press.

JACOBSON, E. 1938. *Progressive relaxation.* Chicago: Univer. of Chicago Press.

JUNG, C. G. 1953–64. *The collected works of C. G. Jung.* New York: Pantheon Books (published as No. 20 in the Bollinger Foundation Series).

KARPMAN, B. 1949. Objective psychotherapy. *J. clin. Psychol.,* **5,** 193–236.

KELLY, G. A. 1955. *The psychology of personal constructs.* 2 vols. New York: Norton.

KIERKEGAARD, S. 1954. *Fear and trembling and the sickness unto death.* New York: Doubleday.

KLINE, M. V. 1963. *Clinical correlations of experimental hypnosis.* Springfield, Ill.: Charles C Thomas.

KORZYBINSKI, A. 1948. *Science and sanity.* (3d ed.) Lakeville, Conn.: International Non-Aristotelian Library Publishing Co.

LEVY, D. M. 1938. Release therapy in young children. *Psychiatry,* **1,** 337–90.

MAY, R., *et al.* (eds). 1958. *Existence: A new dimension in psychiatry and psychology.* New York: Basic Books.

MEARES, A. 1961. *A system of medical hypnosis.* Philadelphia: Saunders.

MEYER, A. 1957. *Psychobiology.* Springfield, Ill.: Charles C Thomas.

MORENO, J. L. 1947. *The theatre of spontaneity.* New York: Beacon House.

MOWRER, O. H. 1950. *Learning theory and personality dynamics.* New York: Ronald.

NEEDLEMAN, J. (ed.). 1963. *Being-in-the-world: Selected papers of Ludwig Binswanger.* New York: Basic Books.

PERLS, F. S., GOODMAN, P., and HEFFERLINE, R. 1951. *Gestalt therapy: Excitement and growth in the human personality.* New York: Julian Press.

RANK, O. 1950. *Will therapy and truth and reality.* New York: Knopf.

REICH, W. 1949. *Character analysis.* New York: Orgone Institute Press.

ROGERS, C. R. 1942. *Counseling and psychotherapy.* Boston: Houghton Mifflin.

ROGERS, C. R. 1951. *Client-centered therapy.* Boston: Houghton Mifflin.

RUBENSTEIN, E. A., and PARLOFF, M. B. (eds.). 1959. *Research in psychotherapy.* Washington, D.C.: American Psychological Association.

SCHNECK, J. M. 1963. *Hypnosis in modern medicine.* (3d ed.) Springfield, Ill.: Charles C Thomas.

SCHULTZ, J. H., and LUTHE, W. 1959. *Autogenic training.* New York: Grune & Stratton.

SKINNER, B. F. 1953. *Science and human behavior.* New York: Macmillan.

SKINNER, B. F. 1957. *Verbal behavior.* New York: Appleton-Century-Crofts.

STEKEL, W. 1943. *The interpretation of dreams.* New York: Liveright.

SULLIVAN, H. S. 1953. *The interpersonal theory of psychiatry.* New York: Norton.

SZASZ, T. S. 1960. The myth of mental illness. *Amer. Psychologist,* **15,** 113–18.

TAFT, J. 1936. *Dynamics of therapy in a controlled relationship.* New York: Macmillan.

WATKINS, J. G. 1949a. *Hypnotherapy of war neuroses.* New York: Ronald.

WATKINS, J. G. 1949b. Poison-pen therapy. *Amer. J. Psychother.,* 3, 410–18.

WATKINS, J. G. 1960. *General psychotherapy: An outline and study guide.* Springfield, Ill.: Charles C Thomas.

WATTS, A. W. 1957. *The way of Zen.* New York: Pantheon.

WEISS, E. 1960. *The structure and dynamics of the human mind.* New York: Grune & Stratton.

WEITZENHOFFER, A. M. 1948. *General techniques of hypnotism.* New York: Grune & Stratton.

WOLBERG, L. R. 1964. *Hypnoanalysis.* (2d ed.) New York: Grune & Stratton.

WOLPE, J. 1958. *Psychotherapy by reciprocal inhibition.* Stanford, Calif.: Stanford Univer. Press.

17

Direct Methods of Treatment

ARTHUR J. BACHRACH AND WILLIAM A. QUIGLEY *

INTRODUCTION

For the purposes of this chapter, we will limit the coverage of direct methods of treatment to two areas—*behavior modification* and *physiological methods*. The former term *behavior modification*,[1] is used in the sense expressed by Watson (1962): "Studies of behavior modification are studies of learning with a particular intent—the clinical goal of treatment" (p. 19). Thus, the emphasis will be on learning techniques and their application to the treatment of clinical disorder. The second section, dealing with physiological methods, will cover techniques ranging from drugs to surgery developed toward the goal of treating emotional disorders. What makes these diverse methods of behavioral modification and physiological techniques somewhat similar is the emphasis on the *direct* method of treatment. In both general approaches, there is an assumption that behavior can be altered clinically by direct modification. The behavior therapist, for example, usually does not concern himself with postulated inner mediating processes (such as the "unconscious") in a clinical disorder—he tries to define a behavioral process to be modified in terms of a specific response class; so, for example, in a neurotic disorder, the behavior therapist does not approach the problem as one

* Arthur J. Bachrach, Ph.D. (University of Virginia), Professor and Chairman, Department of Psychology, and William A. Quigley, M.A., Graduate Research Assistant, Department of Psychology, both of the Arizona State University.
[1] Israel Goldiamond, in a recent personal communication, expressed the thought that *behavior modification* is a term covering many types of behavior change, including reading, language acquisition, and similar teaching programs. He would prefer to reserve the term *behavior therapy* for the specific kind of behavior modification involving treatment in interpersonal contact.

of uncovering unconscious wishes, let us say, but rather as one of a specific response to be modified. As an illustration, a phobic reaction, a fear of some object such as an automobile, is described in the American Psychiatric Association nomenclature: "The anxiety of these patients becomes detached from a specific idea, object, or situation in the daily life and is displaced to some symbolic idea or situation in the form of a specific neurotic fear." The behavior therapist [2] such as Wolpe, whose work we will cover in fuller detail, chooses to see a phobic reaction as a learned (or conditioned) response that can be altered or modified as can any other learned response. The symbolic or unconscious factors are not considered. Eysenck (1959) equated the symptom with the disorder when he observed: "Learning theory does not postulate any such 'unconscious causes,' but regards neurotic symptoms as simple learned habits; there is no neurosis underlying the symptom, but merely the symptom itself. *Get rid of the symptom and you have eliminated the neurosis.*" This is essentially the position adopted by behavior therapists, that behavior is itself a response class that can be controlled and modified without their concerning themselves with modifying underlying root causes such as "conflict." Many such therapists would not deny the possibility that symbolic factors exist but would merely indicate that they do not find them useful in the modification of behavior. We will return to this problem later.

Physiological techniques such as psychosurgery (lobotomy and amygdalotomy, for example) or drug therapy do not assume the need for inferring underlying root causes for emotional disorder. While such practitioners may accept the possibility that depression is a result of intensive guilt in the individual, the drug therapy is based on the assumption that pharmacological agents will have a direct effect on specific neural structures and result in biochemical alterations that are presumed to mediate behavior. If a monoamine oxidase (MAO) inhibitor effects a biochemical change in an individual, the therapist may find the patient "energized" and less "depressed," and he may infer that, somehow, the guilt of the patient has been eased, but this is an inference superimposed on the pharmacological action. In a similar fashion, lobotomies, in which neural tracts in the forebrain were severed by surgical intervention in a patient, were considered by some investigators to be a cut in the connection between id and ego, assuming that the id, as a reservoir of primal urges, was located functionally in the thalamus, while the ego, as a region of contact with the outer world, was functionally set in the frontal lobes. Thus, severing a bunch of fibers between the thalmus and

---

[2] We will follow Ullman and Krasner (1965) and Reyna (1965) in essentially using *behavior therapy, behavior modification* and *conditioning (learning) therapy* as interchangeable terms.

the frontal lobes (actually an oversimplification of the procedure) was equated with detaching id from ego.[3] Such inferences, whose validity is questionable, are not necessary to the formulations of the therapist initiating a surgical procedure, who may view a patient as being dangerously violent and in need of some drastic treatment that will quiet him. The rationale for this kind of intervention is also questionable and will be considered in detail later on.

The direct methods of treatment represented by behavior modification and the physiological techniques have other aspects in common—in both, there has been a rush to application with an empirical derring-do often lacking solid theoretical or research foundation. The excited promises attendant upon lobotomies (and before that, electric shock and insulin coma therapy, and, after that, drugs) did not really meet hopeful expectations. The big boom in drug therapy, during the psychopharmacology heyday in the late 1950's has settled down a decade later to a reasonable level of research and clinical application, a sensible fraction of the earlier activity. The faddist tendencies so often encountered in clinicians—uncritical excited acceptance, followed by uncritical rejection—are reminiscent of the situation in programed learning, a very important area of educational research, which was characterized in its early days by a rush to the building of teaching machines (without the programs to put in them) and a promise that this was the dawn of a new era in education. The hangover after this intoxication came soon, and it is now possible to approach these potentially valuable teaching methods with an appreciative but sober eye. The danger that the very real and powerful techniques available in behavior therapy may be obscured by the same uncritical use and rejection will be considered in greater detail when we turn to a critique of the methods. For the moment, after this aside regarding booms and busts, let us return to another look at the relationships between learning theory and psychoanalysis.

LEARNING THEORY AND PSYCHOANALYSIS: SOME OBSERVATIONS

The methods of behavior modification, as we have noted, are clearly learning (or teaching) methods and are clearly accepted as such by be-

---

[3] This reification of an abstraction such as the ego by giving it neuroanatomical locus is not surprising in view of the strong neurological background Freud had. Throughout his writings, neurological analogies abound. In discussing the functions of the ego, for example, Freud (1949) observed that speech "brings the material in the ego into a firm connection with the memory-traces of visual and more particularly of auditory perceptions. Thenceforward the perceptual periphery of the cortex of the ego can be stimulated to a much greater extent from inside as well." The terms used in this quotation, particularly the word *cortex*, have a neural flavor. Also, see Pribram (1962).

havior therapists. The centrality of learning in psychology as a whole was described by Hilgard (1956), when he observed that

Psychologists with a penchant for systems find a theory of learning essential because so much of man's diverse behavior is the result of learning. If the rich diversity of behavior is to be understood in accordance with a few principles, it is evident that these principles will have to do with the way in which learning comes about.

(It should be noted here that Hilgard, in talking about behavior as a "result of learning," is close to following a traditional differentiation of learning as a process sometimes associated with observed behavior, usually referred to as "performance.")

The importance of learning theory was also noted by Hefferline (1962), who observed that "The statement that learning is a support of clinical psychology will receive general, albeit bored, assent," indicating that it is rather a platitude to assume the central place of learning in psychology. Hefferline went on, however, to discuss some comments by David Rapaport, a spokesman for psychoanalytic thinking with regard to learning, particularly the position that current learning theory has doubtful relevance to clinical practice:

Learning theory seems to be the academic theoretical backbone of the majority of recent, mass-produced clinical psychologists. But since this theory cannot guide their clinical work, they rely there increasingly upon psychoanalytical propositions, whose theory they have not studied. [1962, p. 97.]

Hefferline further commented on Rapaport's observations by noting that Rapaport sought to solve his learning theory problem by substituting another, psychoanalytically based, theory of learning for the academic, theoretical model:

These . . . experimental analogues of "freudian mechanisms" would neither be embarrassing to nor incompatible with psychoanalytic theory if no claim were made that in man, too, the mechanisms of the primary processes and of the defenses are products of conditioning. . . . Psychoanalytic theory at present cannot escape this embarrassment, since it has no learning theory of its own to pit against conditioning. . . . Psychoanalysis will be completely free of embarrassment from this quarter only when it has a learning theory which not only fulfills its own empirical and theoretical requirements, but is also broad enough to account for conditioned phenomena—including the conditioned analogues of "unconscious mechanisms"—as special cases. [1962, pp. 97–98.]

Rapaport's statements reaffirmed the importance accorded learning theory in psychology and accepted the relevance of a theory of learning (though not necessarily the current ones) for clinical thought and practice. The latter criticism, questioning the meaningfulness of current theories of learning as used by behavior therapists, is echoed in a recent paper by

Breger and McGaugh (1965). In general, it is possible to say that therapists whose methods are based on learning theory have either attempted
a *rapprochement* between psychoanalysis and learning theory as developed in the experimental laboratory (Dollard and Miller, 1950) or have
openly rejected the methods and theories of psychoanalysis (Wolpe, 1958,
1962, 1965). Others such as Mowrer (1950), Masserman (1946, 1954) and
Ferster (1963) have suggested that some of the behaviors explained
psychoanalytically, such as repression, might be studied in an experimental analysis of conditioned aversive control, one of the experimental
analogues Rapaport has found aversive.

If a *rapprochement* exists, it must be based on the assumption that,
different though the interpretations of behavior may be among learning
theorists and psychodynamically oriented practitioners, they are dealing
with the same behaviors. In the case involving anorexia nervosa to be
discussed in a later section, it will be noted that the cause of the drastic
reduction in the frequency of eating in this and similar patients is inferred
by psychodynamically oriented therapists to be a fear of oral impregnation, that is, a fear of becoming pregnant by eating. The *behavior* is the
same as viewed by either practitioner: It is primarily in the interpretation
of etiological factors that the rift appears.

Earlier, we observed that the behavior therapists do not concern themselves with postulated inner mediating processes such as the "unconscious mind," which may be a useful concept in a psychodynamic
framework. This does not mean, we believe, that both schools cannot
effectively use a concept such as *symptom* if the term is used in its proper
sense. Goldiamond, Dyrud, and Miller (1965) consider *symptom* to be a
valid behavioral term, noting that symptomatic behavior reflects behavioral deficits. They present a case of a student with a behavioral
deficit, by which they mean that "consequences which maintain certain
critical behaviors are not available to the patient" and are replaced by
other behaviors. This student

was assigned a difficult project upon which his grade and continuation in the
program were contingent. He explained how his inability to do the work
stemmed from early childhood experiences and relations with authority figures,
all of which was quite interesting to his listeners, who maintained such autobiography by their attention. To one friend, he berated the system and claimed
the instructor had it in for him. Disagreement maintained this behavior. With
another friend, he discussed his sorry plight and the probability that all his
efforts would have been wasted, and received sympathetic comments. These
various behaviors were maintained by their audiences. They continued for
an extended period of time and were his continual topic of conversation. As
long as they continued, the project was not tackled.

With regard to this student in particular, the completion of the difficult project was accompanied by a cessation of the other behaviors, no longer needed, no longer "symptomatic."

For the theorist and practitioner attempting some *rapprochement* via the study of symptom behavior, another case, presented by Lief, a practicing psychoanalyst, has much of value (Lief, 1955). Lief reported the case of a thirty-eight-year-old woman whose presenting symptoms included an inability to drive her car and difficulty in sleeping. In the discussions during the therapeutic sessions, it seemed as though these symptoms related to an earlier incident involving her husband when he was hospitalized:

One particular Sunday she decided to visit her husband earlier than usual —he was in the hospital recuperating from an illness—and so she attended an early church service that morning. When she walked into the hospital room, about two hours sooner than she was expected, she saw a young woman—a pretty redhead—holding her husband's hand. The girl got up and left hurriedly with a murmured apology. Upon the wife's insistent demands, the husband confessed a two-year's intimate relationship with the girl, a waitress in a drugstore. The wife fainted and had to be carried to another room and put to bed.

Following this episode, the wife developed a profound depression, and she also developed a phobic avoidance of many things adventitiously associated with the traumatic experience. The time of the original experience was involved in that she woke up with panicky feelings on Sunday mornings for months after what she termed the "shock." The places were also involved: Going to church upset her so that for a while she actually remained away, although she was ordinarily a conscientious, almost compulsive, church-goer. The hospital where the trauma had occurred was avoided like the plague, and she would suffer unbearable anxiety if she came within blocks of it. Various accessory cues also became significant: Although the dress she was wearing that day was an expensive one, she threw it out. She likewise threw out all drugs bearing the label of the drugstore where the redhead worked, and she ordered her husband never to buy anything from, much less frequent, that drugstore. If she came anywhere near the store she would become panicky, and so she made wide detours to avoid it. The delivery wagons of the drugstore gave her the same frightened feeling. She also began to develop a phobic avoidance of all places where she learned her husband had taken the girl— motor courts, restaurants, even particular streets and highways. For a time it was almost impossible for her to drive her car.

The behaviors reported in this case may be discussed as symbolic behaviors by a psychodynamically oriented therapist, but they may also effectively be considered by a behavior therapist in terms of learning theory with respect to three major events: a *noxious event* (the scene in the hospital), a lowered responsivity ("profound depression"), and *generalized avoidance*. The spread of effect, in learning terms, from the original noxious stimulus, took three chains, one generalizing from the church and two generalizing from the hospital:

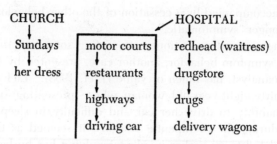

The avoidance responses (staying away from the drugstore, etc.) fit into the avoidance paradigm stated by Schoenfeld (1950):

$$S_1 \;\text{------}\; / \;\text{------}\; S_2$$
$$R_{T(av)}$$

where S_1 is a "warning" stimulus associated with the subsequent occurrence of S_2, the "painful" stimulus, and $R_{T(av)}$ is the response by which the person "terminates" the warning stimulus (escapes it) and avoids the painful stimulus. There are also evident, in this case, certain "superstitious" aspects of behavior that are of interest. The originally neutral (or even positive) stimuli of the drugstore, church, temporal events such as Sundays, and her prized dress took on negative stimulus characteristics somewhat adventitiously. Superstitious behavior, so-called, occurs adventitiously in association with certain events (Lief's paper is called "sensory association of phobic objects") and is maintained presumably by intermittent reinforcement as an avoidance response. Superstitious behavior is stable and resistant to extinction (Skinner, 1948; Skinner and Morse, 1957; Bachrach, 1962a; and Herrnstein, 1966). Much of what is called "neurotic behavior" appears to be clearly related. Such a recasting of this case, as presented by Lief, in learning theory terms may not contribute more to an understanding of the "dynamics" of the behavior, but it does, we hope, indicate that psychodynamicists and behaviorists may meet in a consideration of the symptoms.

All of what has gone before in this discussion has been an introduction leading to the specific consideration of the behavior therapies. Our plan is now to present an account of the dominant schools of behavior therapy, the classical conditioning school and the operant conditioning school, followed by a critique, *en famille*, of the methods and theoretical positions.

BEHAVIOR MODIFICATION

Classical Conditioning. Among the current practitioners of behavior therapy, two separate, though congenial, schools of thought predominate:

the group that derives its methods primarily from Pavlov and Hull, as represented by Wolpe and Eysenck, and those whose techniques and orientation come, in the main, from Skinner. The latter group finds exponents such as Bijou (see Chapter 21) and Krasner. The Wolpe-Eysenck group has taken much from Dollard and Miller (1950), whose endeavors link Freudian and Hullian theory [4] have been briefly noted above, and has avowedly concerned itself with neurotic behavior, which it regards as learned behavior: "Neurotic behavior consists of *persistent habits of learned (conditioned) unadaptive behavior acquired in anxiety-generating situations* . . . therapy depends upon the unlearning of this behavior" (Wolpe, 1962, p. 555). Anxiety, central to the theory, "refers specifically to those responses predominantly of the autonomic nervous system, with which the individual characteristically reacts to noxious (painful) stimuli" (Wolpe, 1962, p. 555), responses that include rapid pulse, increased generalized muscle tension, and rise in blood pressure. Reyna (1965, p. 171) elaborates on the unadaptive characteristics of this neurotic behavior when he observes: "In describing the neurotic behavior as learned, the emphasis is on indicating that this behavior is initially the result of various external operations such as reinforcement, generalization, and contiguity rather than on postulated unobservable inner forces." Conditioning of neurotic behavior is assumed. In the present discussion, we will concentrate on Wolpe as representative of the classical conditioning school.

To understand better the systems expounded by Wolpe, it is necessary to have some comprehension of the learning theory advanced by Hull. Hull, in his *Principles of Behavior* (1943), defined learning:

The essential nature of the learning process may . . . be stated quite simply. Just as the inherited equipment of reaction tendencies consists of receptor-effector connections, so the process of learning consists in the strengthening of certain of these connections as contrasted with others, or in the setting up of quite new connections.

---

[4] Ullmann and Krasner (1965, pp. 18–19) consider why Hullian conceptualization should be more compatible with psychoanalytic concepts: "Hull distinguished between performance, the overt behavior, and habit, the modification of the central nervous system, which mediates learning and which is not directly measurable. A performance is the product of habit strength and drives such as hunger and thirst. Important concepts for behavior therapy, particularly those of tics, are those of reactive inhibition and conditioned inhibition. All activity produces some fatigue and this fatigue produces a drive (reactive inhibition which decreases with rest) and a negative habit (conditioned inhibition). The Hullian system with its concept of drive and mediation through habit is perhaps a stronger explanatory tool than Skinner's system and certainly lends itself more readily (compare Dollard and Miller, 1950) to the translation of psychoanalytic concepts." While Wolpe might not find it reinforcing to effect a liaison with psychoanalytic concepts, the Hullian element of drive, particularly anxiety as a conditioned drive that may be inhibited by counterconditioning, is quite compatible with a Freudian as well as a Pavlovian model.

For Hull, these "connections" occurred internally, mediated by nervous-system stimulation. So, an external stimulus, S, has as its function the stimulation of an afferent system, *s*, which, in turn, effects a motor impulse, *r*, within the nervous system. The final response, external R, does not have to occur for learning to take place—the critical connection is the *s-r* connection, leading to a "habit." Wolpe (1950) reflected this neurophysiological view of learning within a Hullian model when he observed that "learning is subserved by the development of conductivity between neurones in anatomical apposition" (p. 613). He also used the Hullian concept of *drive* neurophysiologically to account for anxiety production: "When stimuli . . . become able to produce anxiety responses, they necessarily produce anxiety drive (with concomitant central neural excitation) as an antecedent" (p. 614).

Anxiety as a drive and the reduction of this anxiety drive were also central to Wolpe's point of view and his methodology. The reduction of anxiety as drive becomes reinforcing, according to Mowrer (1950): "Not getting 'punished,' or 'injured,' is rewarding *only if punishment is expected,* i.e., only if the subject is anxious or fearful, and if this expectation in some way gets *reduced*" (p. 93). The reduction of anxiety, for Wolpe, was explained by the use of the concept of *inhibition,* particularly *reciprocal inhibition,* which Wolpe (1962) described as follows: "*If a response inhibitory to anxiety can be made to occur in the presence of anxiety-evoking stimuli, it will weaken the connection between these stimuli and the anxiety responses*" (p. 562). By *counterconditioning* the responses, Wolpe attempts to alter the neurotic, maladaptive anxiety responses. To condition a response incompatible with anxiety is a key technique. Thus, the relaxation techniques used by Jacobson (1938) are used by Wolpe in the belief that relaxation is incompatible with anxiety and that the conditioning of relaxation as an alternative response serves anxiety reduction.

It would appear that an alternative response incompatible with the anxiety responses inhibits these responses by inhibiting and thus reducing anxiety drive. The drive reduction makes possible the establishment of neural connections subserving a learned inhibition of the anxiety as a response to the particular stimuli that were antecedent to it at the time. [Wolpe, 1950, p. 616.] [5]

Wolpe has also worked as part of the counterconditioning of neurotic responses, on *desensitization,* a systematic technique he described in detail (Wolpe, 1958, 1959, 1962) in which relaxation therapy is followed by a catalog of anxiety-producing situations ranked as an "anxiety hierarchy," followed, in turn, by a relaxed period in which the patient (usually under hypnosis) is asked "to imagine the least disturbing item in the list"

[5] Much of the thinking regarding counterconditioning and similar techniques derives from work of an earlier period, such as the studies of Dunlap (1932). See also Guthrie (1938).

(Wolpe, 1962, p. 564). The imagining of the anxiety-producing stimuli, beginning with that reported as of least intensity, is counterconditioned, proceeding up the list until the most anxiety-producing item is invoked.

Proceeding in this manner, the therapist is eventually able to present the "strongest" item in the hierarchy without arousing any anxiety. At every stage it has been found that freedom from anxiety to an imagined stimulus confers freedom from anxiety upon confrontation with the real equivalent (though sometimes the latter lags behind). [Wolpe, 1962, p. 564.]

Wolpe expects that the responses to the imagined stimulus, under conditions of relaxation (incompatible with anxiety), will reciprocally inhibit the fear response. An example of such an "anxiety hierarchy" might be found in a patient with a "fear of death" in whom Wolpe might find the rating of lowest intensity in thinking about death, with the highest intensity found in the sight of a coffin with a corpse in it, and, perhaps, with the sight of a tombstone at a median level of intensity. Such successive ordering of anxiety-provoking stimuli, especially in the imagined situation, produces obvious problems of measurement (see page 497), but the technique of systematic desensitization as a counterconditioning or reciprocal inhibition method is in use (Lang and Lazovik, 1963). As a method, it is clearly related to such techniques as Eysenck's graded stimulus situations.

One final technique used in the methods of inhibiting anxiety responses by Wolpe is that of the *assertive* response. Wolpe (1958) stated that the response of anxiety and that of expressing resentment are incompatible. Therefore, if a person is able to assert himself in an anxiety-producing situation, let us say, with his boss or his wife, where previously he "bottled up" his resentment, the expression of resentment will inhibit the anxiety. Here again, a hierarchy of difficult situations may be established in which the individual is assertive in increasingly more anxiety-provoking situations until the most intense is handled. Wolpe also considers that feeding responses are incompatible with anxiety, explaining that "eating voraciously because of heightened hunger drive, the patient obtains a reciprocal inhibition of any anxiety responses that happen to be occurring within him at that time" (Wolpe, 1954).

In short, Wolpe's basic principle of reciprocal inhibition is predicated on the assumption that anxiety drive can be reduced by the evocation of responses incompatible (reciprocally inhibitory) with the anxiety response. His greatest reported successes in this regard have been with such specific response classes as phobic behavior.

Operant Conditioning. Earlier, we saw that the Wolpe-Eysenck group views neurosis as learned behavior (as conditioned anxiety and maladaptive habits). Operant conditioners, by and large, do not concern them-

selves too much with even this much theoretical analysis of neurotic behavior, contenting themselves with attempts to specify the behavior so
that it may be brought under control.

Skinner, in comparing Freudian and behavioral approaches, observed,
"Where, in the Freudian scheme, behavior is merely the symptom of a
neurosis, in the present formulation it is the direct object of inquiry"
(1953, p. 376). Skinner considers neurosis itself to be an "explanatory
fiction" (1953, p. 373) and noted that it has had the unfortunate result of
encouraging therapists "to avoid specifying the behavior to be corrected
or showing why it is disadvantageous or dangerous. By suggesting a
single cause for multiple disorders it has implied a uniformity which is not
to be found in the data" (1953, p. 373). Skinner's strongest objection to
this explanatory fiction of neurosis is that it focuses on inner, inferred, unobservable causes rather than on observed, manipulable variables involved in the establishment and maintenance of such behavior: "it has
encouraged the belief that psychotherapy consists of removing certain
inner causes of mental illness, as the surgeon removes an inflamed ap-
pendix" (1953, p. 373). Dealing with "repression" of unacceptable
thoughts, as in the Freudian system, Skinner suggested it is more important to avoid the inner causes and to concentrate on asking "why the
response was emitted in the first place, why it was punished, and what
current variables are active" (1953, p. 376). Admittedly, these questions
are difficult, if not impossible, to answer, but the statement illuminates
critical variables used by operant conditioners in their behavior analysis:
the specification of the response, the conditions under which it was first
established, and the currently active variables that maintain it. Given
these data (or even lacking the conditions under which the response was
established), the behavior therapist using operant methods tries to bring
the behavior under control.

It is apparent, as we have noted also with regard to the Wolpe-
Eysenck group, that most of the discussions so far with regard to operant
methods in behavior therapy have dealt with mildly disturbed behaviors,
usually called "neurotic." Severely disturbed behaviors, the psychoses,
have been considered by a number of therapists to be essentially no
different in the matters of specifying the responses and bringing certain of
them under control (Ayllon and Michael, 1959; Isaacs, Thomas, and
Goldiamond, 1960; Ferster and DeMyer, 1962, as examples), but, while it
is true, as Grossberg (1964) has observed, that behavior therapy applied
to psychotics has resulted (in some instances) in beneficial behavioral
change such as increased sociability, decreased verbalization of delusional material, and a diminution of phobic overreactions, "very few
investigators have reported hospital discharges attributable to treatment"
by behavior therapy. (Success has been greatest with neurotic reactions,

a fact true of the Wolpe-Eysenck group as well.) We may conjecture many reasons for this. Wolpe, for example, believes that, whereas neurotic behavior is learned, psychotic behavior is largely physiologically based in biochemical and neurophysiological disorder.

Skinner (1953), in discussing control, noted that a person may have been under inadequate control because he

may not have been in contact with controlling agents, he may have moved to a different culture where his early training is inadequate, or he may not be readily accessible to control. Therapy will then consist of supplying additional controlling variables. When the individual is wholly out of control, it is difficult to find effective therapeutic techniques. Such an individual is called psychotic. [1953, pp. 379–80.]

Implicit in this view is the thought that there is in such patients a behavioral deficit (see page 370) in which the lack of controls established is of such a magnitude as to make therapy extremely difficult. When Skinner uses the phrase "wholly out of control," he is not depicting a wild-eyed madman; he is clearly describing a behavioral deficit.

Lindsley (1960) has made the point that the disturbed psychotic behavior such as rocking behavior or smearing feces on the wall replaces normal behavior (i.e., behavior considered "appropriate") under the control of environmental contingencies. Lindsley feels that the emphasis on the study of psychotic behavior might well be directed toward analysis of the deficit, considering that the disturbed behavior is replacing normal behavior and that the *lack* of the latter, rather than the *presence* of the former, is the key problem. This point was also well made by Ferster (1963): "there is no question, . . . that the depressed patient who stays in bed all day knows how to dress or drive his car or carry out the activities associated with his work. The significant fact is that the performances do not occur. . . . The question is what variables are responsible for the low frequency" (1963, p. 254).

Success with psychotic patients, as noted above, has been limited to specific changes such as increasing the social contacts in the ward and improving self-care. A study reported by Ayllon (1963), for example, showed how stealing food, hoarding towels, and wearing an excessive amount of clothing were brought under control in a hospitalized chronic schizophrenic patient weighing 250 pounds. The consequences contingent upon her behavior were clearly established: Stealing food resulted in her being taken from the dining room and missing a meal; wearing too much clothing was reduced by weighing her on a scale and setting certain limits of weight that would allow her to go to the dining room—too much weight resulted in denial of access to the meal. The technique of satiation was used in controlling the towel hoarding in her room. Towels were brought into the room in large numbers, the maximum being 625. The patient had indulged in rather compulsive behaviors of stacking and folding the towels in the early stages; when the number reached a magnitude of around 600, the situation apparently became aversive so that, by the third week of the treatment, she was saying, "Take them towels away. . . . I can't sit here all night and fold towels." This is an illustration of the typical kinds of control established in dealing with certain behaviors among psychotic patients. While such changes, as Grossberg noted, have not often resulted in discharge from the hospital, their importance should not be underestimated. Discharge might indeed be dependent on the building of many individual minor behaviors. Self-control is a therapeutic goal. Moreover, the control of even minor bits of psychotic behavior gainsays the notion that such patients are "out of touch with reality."

Let us turn now to a specific consideration of the techniques used by operant conditioners in behavior therapy. More detailed discussions of operant conditioning may be found in several good references (Keller and Schoenfeld, 1950; Skinner, 1953; Sidman, 1960, 1962; Verhave, 1966). We will content ourselves with a discussion of the basic principles and illustrative material. The *experimental analysis* of behavior, a term preferred by most practitioners of operant conditioning for the methodologies involved, stems from early work by Skinner (1938) and is largely concerned with the control of behavior by its consequences: "behavior can produce changes in the environment, and where such changes come to alter the probabilities of the behavior involved, the behavior is considered *operant* behavior, namely, it operates on the environment and in so doing is altered thereby" (Goldiamond and Bachrach, 1963, p. 2). We may then consider a consequence of behavior to be an environmental change that does not occur unless the behavior occurs.

The behavior is, accordingly, necessary and sufficient for such a change, and a change of this type shall be referred to as "response-contingent" consequences. Response-contingent consequences, where they exert an influence over future behaviors of that class, may have two effects upon such behavior: they may maintain it, or they may attenuate it. We shall refer to a response-contingent consequence which maintains behavior as a "reinforcement," and a response-contingent consequence which attenuates behavior as a "punishment." [Goldiamond and Bachrach, 1963, p. 2.]

Further to illustrate reinforcement, Sidman's definition (1960) reads: "any event, contingent upon the response of the organism that alters the future likelihood of that response." By definition, positive reinforcement tends to increase the likelihood of a response recurring; punishment tends to decrease its probability.

Frequently, students are confused by the terms *punishment* and *nega-*

tive reinforcement because they are, seemingly, used interchangeably.[6]
Skinner observed,

We first define a positive reinforcer as any stimulus the *presentation* of which
strengthens the behavior upon which it is made contingent. We define a negative reinforcer (an aversive stimulus) as any stimulus the *withdrawal* of which
strengthens behavior. Both are reinforcers in the literal sense of reinforcing or
strengthening a response. Insofar as scientific definition corresponds to lay
usage, they are both "rewards." In solving the problem of punishment we
simply ask: What is the effect of *withdrawing* a *positive* reinforcer or *presenting*
a *negative?* An example of the former would be taking candy from a baby; an
example of the latter, spanking a baby. [1953, p. 185.]

Keller noted (1954) that a "negatively reinforcing stimulus is one that
strengthens the response that takes it away . . . [and] also a stimulus
that weakens the response that produces it."

There are situations in which reinforcement and punishment do not
work exactly as predicted. Continued punishment (and continued reinforcement) may lose effectiveness in controlling responding. This does
not greatly alter the general set of principles of reinforcement but, rather,
focuses on the serious need for careful specification of conditions under
which responses and consequences are developed and maintained.
Again, quoting Goldiamond and Bachrach,

. . . very often reinforcement or punishment can yield results which are contrary to what is expected, and then it may be assumed fallaciously that they
do not work. In actuality, what is involved is that the conditions under which
they are used govern their effectiveness and direction, and it is to the specification of these conditions that attention has been directed. [p. 3.]

This point, of specifying the conditions under which reinforcement (and
punishment) has been effective, was elaborated on by Verhave and
Bachrach (1964) in discussing the findings of Bijou and Baer (1963) that
a smiling puppet is not always a social reinforcer for children, a result
that prompted the latter investigators to propose a systematic investigation
of the conditions under which the effectiveness of such reinforcement is
present and lacking. Verhave and Bachrach suggested that the effectiveness of a reinforcer is conditional on certain circumstances (such as the
physiological condition, the deprivation level, and the reinforcement history of the organism) and, following up on Pavlov's term "condition*al*
reflex" (poorly translated as "condition*ed* reflex"), further suggest a term
"conditional conditioned reinforcement." Pavlov's "condition*al* reflex"
meant that the reflex would occur, given certain conditions. "Conditional
discrimination" (Lashley, 1938) meant the same. "Conditional conditioned reinforcement" is too cumbersome, and, in its stead, Verhave and
Bachrach suggest the term *"provisional reinforcement,* by which [is

6 See Sidman (1966).

meant] reinforcement whose effectiveness is constrained by other organismic and/or environmental conditions—it is effective *provided that
certain conditions are met*" (p. 8). This question will be further explored
in a critique of behavior therapy beginning on page 503.

THE OPERANT PARADIGM. Goldiamond (1962, pp. 294–95) contributed
a clear and precise paradigm for discussing operant behavior. He noted
that Dollard and Miller (1950) listed the four variables of learned behavior as "drive, response, cue, and reinforcement," and he indicated that
these are identical to the variables considered in the following paradigm:

$$. . . . \text{SV (state variables)}$$

Controlling stimuli:
  S^D-S^Δ (discriminative)—R (Response)—S^r-S^o (differential reinforcement)
  SS^C (Constant)

To modify Goldiamond's explanation of this paradigm somewhat, presenting
a discriminative stimulus (S^D) in the presence of other constant stimuli (SS^C)
will occasion a Response (R); whether this response recurs is contingent upon
the consequences (S^r) of that response (under these specific conditions) and the
state variables (SV) usually referred to as "needs," "motivation," "deprivation,"
and the like which make the consequences of the response effective in controlling it. Assuming that behavior is governed by its consequences under
specified conditions, discriminative behavior can be produced, maintained and
altered if the constant stimuli, the discriminative stimuli, the response contingencies and the state variables are specified and controlled. [Bachrach, Erwin,
and Mohr, 1965, p. 160.]

Ullmann and Krasner (1965, p. 29) suggest that "all behavior modification
boils down to procedures utilizing *systematic environmental contingencies
to alter the subject's response to stimuli.*" This programing of therapy,
as it were, in a systematic fashion is crucial to behavior therapy. Whether
the principles used in classical or operant conditioning methods of behavior modification are sufficient (or even correct) may be debated (see
page 506), but the advantages of systematically programing a course to
follow fit in with a scientifically laboratory-based set of procedures, allowing optimally for testing the principles. As Goldiamond, Dyrud, and
Miller noted, "A *program* merely consists of a systematically arranged
sequence of procedures and behavioral requirements" (1965, p. 118). We
would not use the modest, qualifying "merely" in such a description; it is
critical in using behavior therapy to specify the behaviors of both
therapist and patient.

In any laboratory procedure, a critical variable is the base-line behavior
—the behavior (operant level, for example) recorded before any experimental treatment is begun. This permits a comparison with posttreatment
states and also allows the experimenter to check out changes as they occur. A beginning of a systematic program to accomplish this in psychotherapy was suggested by Phillips (1960). Three bits of information in

such a program are crucial: what the individual was like beforehand, what procedures are followed (behaviors of therapist and patient), and what criteria for change are used for detection of any alterations that occurred? Phillips, in his work with parents and children, specifically asks these questions in defining his criteria for change ("success"):

Are the symptoms less frequent than before? This is a tally of specific responses on the part of the child; it requires that the parent-observer, as well as the therapist-observer, describe the behaviors in response terms—not "He is aggressive" but, rather "He destroyed his younger brother's toy on two occasions during a period of a week." If the occasions for such destructive acts occur with less frequency (a measurable datum), it is a specific fact. Pinpointing of the behaviors that have apparently resulted in the child's being referred for therapy provides specific criteria for change and, obviously, also permits determination of modification procedures.

Are the symptoms less intense or of less duration than before? While such a question is patently of greater subjectivity than a question regarding frequency of occurrence, some sort of criterion for intensity as a dimension is possible and is clearly related to frequency.

Does the child or parent recover faster after any occurrence of disruption? Here the question centers around *latency,* another specifiable behavioral dimension; it allows a specific statement of the amount of time elapsed before a child or parent returns to a steady state after a behavioral disruption, also permitting comparison with pretherapy latencies.

Phillips' criteria for success are obviously not ideal from an experimental standpoint, but, dealing with experimental variables of *frequency* (*rate*), *intensity,* and *latency* as they do, they can become a basis for behavioral criteria much more meaningful than some vaguely conceived "increase in ego strength."

Goldiamond, in the above-discussed operant paradigm, and Phillips both set up a type of programed systematic means of analyzing the procedures and effects of behavior modification. Goldiamond's thinking was most influential in the planning of a course of treatment for a patient, a thirty-seven-year-old woman diagnosed as suffering from anorexia nervosa on the basis of a drastic reduction in eating, with attendant weight loss. This case, reported by Bachrach, Erwin, and Mohr (1965), as noted, used the Goldiamond paradigm specifically in mapping out the program for the behavior modification and will be dealt with in some detail. This woman at the age of eighteen (Fig. 17–1), weighed approximately 120 pounds, her customary weight for a number of years. Over a period of several years, her weight dropped from this level to 47 pounds on admission to the hospital for treatment (Fig. 17–2 and 17–3). Two basic ques-

Fig. 17–1. Patient at age eighteen, weight approximately 120 pounds, before the onset of *anorexia nervosa.*

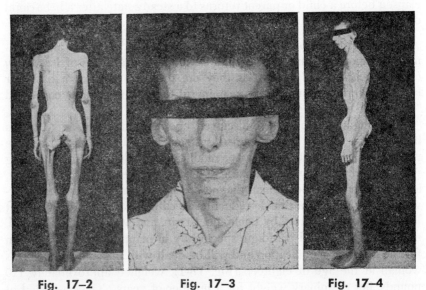

Fig. 17–2   Fig. 17–3   Fig. 17–4

Patient in December, 1960, at age thirty-seven, after onset of *anorexia nervosa,* weight 47 pounds.

tions were posed: "One, how do we get this patient to eat? And, to effect this, under what conditions will eating occur?"

The patient, divorced and childless, was admitted to the University of Virginia Hospital Medical Service on December 14, 1960, with a presenting complaint of "Why do I have this block about food?" Her weight loss started around 1943, when she went to 110 pounds. Her weight gradually dropped to around 65 pounds in 1949. Between 1949 and 1960, when she was admitted to the hospital at the University of Virginia, she lost an additional 18 pounds. Physical examination on admission showed edematous ankles and feet, ulcers in several protuberances such as the back of the skull, knees, elbows, and ankles, and cavernous ulcers over the right buttock and pubis. Extensive endocrinological tests were run, including ACTH stimulation of the adrenals with concomitant plasma corticoid measurements, radioactive iodine uptake, and urinary 17 ketosteroids. All the test results were within normal limits; the only abnormalities detected on laboratory examination were considered to be secondary to the decreased food intake. A complete medical history appears in the original paper cited above and will not be covered, except for particular highlights. No attempt was made to get a psychiatric history from this patient, nor was psychotherapy per se attempted by anyone. The experimental questions noted above—"how do we get this patient to eat?" "Under what conditions will eating occur?"—formed the design basis. She was not given any drugs such as tranquilizers. An occasional hypnotic for sleep and vitamins were the only drugs she received. The patient was transferred to the Psychiatric Service and assigned to a psychiatric resident (Erwin), who called in a staff psychologist (Bachrach); both of these arranged for a medical student (Mohr) to be assigned to this case so that all three could work out a behavioral program of therapy. Interpretations of why the patient stopped or decreased eating were eschewed as inferential. Psychodynamic explanations such as those advanced by Nemiah (1958, 1963) and Wall (1959) usually involved conflict over aggression, sexual conflict, and a fear of oral impregnation. While such interpretations may have some validity, they are essentially unproved. It was considered by the three authors to be more effective to treat the non-eating as a specific response to be brought under control—eating behavior to be restored.

The patient was originally placed in an attractive hospital room with pictures on the wall, flowers on the table, and a lovely view of the university grounds from the window. She had free access to visitors, books, records and a record player, television, and magazines. Because these activities were apparently reinforcing to her, they were taken away to be used as response-contingent reinforcers, that is, as reinforcers contingent upon eating behavior and nothing else. She was transferred to a

barren room, denied visitors, and allowed to have books and other reinforcers only on a reinforcement schedule. It might be said at this point
that the full cooperation of the family and the hospital administration
was sought and received. The nurses, graduate and student staff, were
specifically told in detail what the plan was, to illustrate the behavior-
modification techniques to be used and to enlist their support, to remove
the natural feeling that this was "inhuman treatment." The last was not
hard to do, because of the lack of success achieved by other therapies
including drugs, and the very real danger that this patient (the most
serious anorexia case recorded in the medical literature, according to the
intern who examined her) would die. The feeling that it would be more
inhuman to let her return home with a grave prognosis was conveyed to
the staff. The psychiatric staff was equally cooperative.

The three authors of the case study took turns eating meals with her
at first. They set up a reinforcement schedule

somewhat gross in its characteristics and difficult to achieve, but nevertheless
attempted; this involved verbal reinforcement of movements associated with
eating. When the patient lifted her fork to move toward spearing a piece of
food the experimenter would talk to her about something in which she had an
interest. The required response was then successively raised to lifting the food
toward her mouth, chewing, and so forth. [p. 157.]

The same scheduled increase in required response was applied to the
amount of food consumed.

At first, any portion of the meal that was consumed would be a basis for post-
prandial reinforcement (a radio, TV set, or phonograph would be brought in by
the nurse at a signal from the experimenter); if she did not touch any of the
food before her, nothing would be done by way of reinforcement and she would
be left until the next meal. [p. 157.]

The requirement for consumption, upon which reinforcement was based,
was raised until she had to clear the plate to earn the reinforcer. The
meals were also closely increased in caloric value. Other reinforcers
were gradually added, such as eating with other patients in the ward
solarium and taking walks around the university grounds.

When the patient hit a plateau of weight gain at one point (not unexpected for a short period, inasmuch as her lying down rebuilt body constituents), the question arose as to whether she might be vomiting her
food after the experimenters or nurses left. The plateau continued for a
longer period than might have been expected on the basis of the rebuild-
ing process, so the contingent behavior (actually not behavior in itself
but, rather, dependent on eating behavior) was made weight gain instead
of food consumed. Thus, when any evidence of weight gain was reinforced, the plateau ceased and weight gain continued.

Returning to Goldiamond's operant paradigm (see page 496), the authors of the case report on this anoretic patient visualized the variables to be as follows (Bachrach, Erwin, and Mohr, 1965, pp. 160–161):

State Variables: (SV): Essentially unknown: we could not evaluate with any degree of assurance those needs, motives or other inferred conditions that might have occasioned her drop in eating rate. The reinforcement history of any organism first studied is always an unknown; experimentally, the task is to manipulate deprivation states so that the past reinforcement history is less relevant and thereby bring the deprivation variables under experimental control. In the present case, the patient's past reinforcement history was inferred to have occasioned positively reinforcing values for such events as music, reading, social contact and the like and these could then be put on a deprivation schedule.

Controlling Stimuli: The discriminative stimuli to which we wished the patient to respond (S^Ds) were those which eventually were to exercise some measure of control over her behavior, particularly eating behavior. Therefore, two S^D classes were considered, one for the inpatient controlled environment, the other for outpatient control. The Inpatient S^Ds included the Experimenters as mealmates, the various utensils (plates, forks, knives, *et cetera*) and temporal S^Ds such as specific times for eating meals with no in-between eating. The Outpatient S^Ds included the alarm clock for mealtime, the purple tablecloth as an S^D for eating (particularly important if the table is used for other purposes such as sewing) and, again, temporal S^Ds in the form of specific mealtimes.

Constant Stimuli: (SS^C): In the hospital it would include the major stimulus class of the room itself and the various objects contained therein; the stimulus change from an attractive hospital room to a barren one is a shift in SS^C classes, limiting the number of S^Ds in the room by removing flowers, pictures, and similar stimuli. The SS^C as an outpatient would be more varied and less controlled but would include major stimulus situations such as the home and church.

Response: (R): Clearly, the response to be manipulated was eating. Weight gain, which supplanted eating *per se* as a reinforced event, is obviously contingent upon eating, the major response.

Differential reinforcement: ($S^r = S^o$): In the hospital room, the reinforcements included social contact, television, radio, records, reading; the response of eating was reinforced by these events. Not eating (and no weight gain) occasioned lack of reinforcement (S^o) and, later, verbal disapproval, presumed aversive (S^a). As an inpatient, the S^rs were expanded to include walks around the grounds of the university, eating in restaurants, choosing her own menu and eating with other persons of her choice, as well as verbal approval as social reinforcement.

The patient was in the hospital from December 14, 1960, and was transferred to the Psychiatric Service on January 3, 1961, and the experiment was begun on February 1, 1961. She was discharged as an outpatient on March 25, 1961, weighing 64 pounds, 14 pounds more than she had when she had been transferred. Her weight gradually rose to a level of 85 pounds by June 20, 1962, when her last hospital recorded weight was taken (Fig. 17–5 and 17–6). During that summer, all three of the authors

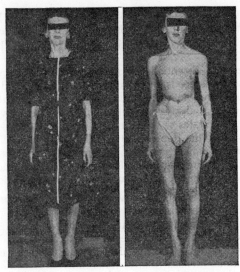

Fig. 17–5   Fig. 17–6

Patient in June, 1962, at age thirty-nine, after operant conditioning therapy, weight 85 pounds.

who had conducted the experiment left the University of Virginia, and contact was maintained through correspondence. Her self-reported weight on January 15, 1963, was 76 pounds, and she wrote that she was trying with some success to maintain work and social life. This case has been presented in some detail, but a fuller account of all the medical and behavioral aspects may be obtained by reference to the original paper.

The use of operant methods in such a case is illustrated by a quotation from Barrett (1962), who noted, "The basic datum of the free-operant method is the frequency of a specific and reliably defined response within a controlled experimental environment. The method is most readily applied, therefore, in cases where changes in the rate of a repeated movement are of primary concern." This, indeed, appears to be the real strength of operant methods. For this reason, as we shall discuss further in a critique of behavior therapy, it is apparent that many problems exist when one considers the possibility, suggested by Ullmann and Krasner (1965, p. 61), that "one likely future development of behavior therapy will be work with *larger units of behavior with increasingly general social application,*" "larger units" such as "interest, enthusiasm and attention." It may be true, as these authors suggest, that reliable observers can define these broad response classes sufficiently well to apply reinforcement techniques to their control, but it should be kept in mind that the most success with the very valuable operant methods has been, as Barrett said, with "specific and reliably defined responses within a controlled experimental environment." The farther one gets from specificity and controlled environment, the less effectiveness one may expect from the methods, and the more dubious are the interpretations of the results.

Conclusions and a Brief Critique of Behavior Therapy. The therapies based on conditioning methods, classical and operant, discussed in the previous sections fall heir to all the strengths and weaknesses of the laboratory-developed concepts on which they are generally based. The strength of these methods is that they are, at their best, based on specific and reliably defined response frequency measures. As we mentioned in discussing Phillips' work (see page 497), "lessened destructiveness" in a child may be measured by the number of times he engages in a specific destructive act (or, for example, the number of siblings' toys he wrecks within a period of a week compared with the week before). While some critics may say that such individual behavioral acts are minor, it is nonetheless true that the inference that a child is "destructive" is drawn from such behavioral manifestations. While they may be a minor part of an entire behavior pattern, they are objective indications. Skinner (1953b)[7] has pointed out that a personality description is, in effect, a description of a response class emitted with frequency. To say that a person is "hostile" is to suggest that he emits behavior interpreted by others as hostile with a higher frequency than most other behaviors. The conditioning methods are at their best when the responses are clearly defined and when the environment is carefully controlled. This is obviously true in the laboratory; it is equally true in the therapeutic situation. The reason, we feel certain, is that, as Grossberg (1964), reviewing the results of behavior therapies observed, "Behavior therapies have been most successful when applied to neurotic disorders with specific behavioral manifestations" (p. 81). Thus, the laboratory specification of behaviors appears a critical necessity also in clinical applications of behavior therapy, a point we have made several times because of its fundamental nature.

The laboratory problems inherited by behavior therapies are among the general theoretical problems faced by psychology as a field studying learning and behavior. Specifically, we are referring to the problem of defining the crucial concepts basic to the experimental analysis of behavior: *stimulus, response,* and *reinforcement.* As noted, these are theoretical problems faced by experimental psychologists, whatever their persuasion happens to be.

[7] Also see Allport's work on personality (1937).

DEFINING STIMULUS AND RESPONSE. The first theoretical problem is the separation, if possible and if, indeed, appropriate, of *stimulus* and *response*. In their introductory text, Keller and Schoenfeld (1950) defined *stimulus* and *response* in the following fashion:

A stimulus may be provisionally defined as a "part, or change in a part, of the environment," and a response may be defined as "a part, or change in a part, of behavior." We shall recognize, however, that a *stimulus* cannot be defined independently of a response. An environmental event becomes a stimulus by virtue of the fact that it is followed by a response. [p. 3.]

Bugelski (1956) wrote, "It is unfortunately true that there is no agreement yet on the meaning of the term 'stimulus'. It is usually defined in terms of a response, as: a stimulus is that which causes (or is followed by) a response, but there we are, perhaps, even worse off" (p. 82).

There is little need to go on to a point of tedium reiterating this fact: stimulus-response psychologies basic to experimental methodologies have yet to arrive at a definition of *stimulus* [8] independent of the response with which it is associated. To be sure, we may set up experiments in which the stimulus is defined as the key at which the pigeon pecks, with its discriminative qualities (red changed to green, etc.), but a clear topography of stimulus definition is needed.

The definition of *response* is inherently related. Keller and Schoenfeld (1950) defined a *response*, following the above-mentioned statement that a response is "a part, or change in a part, of behavior" by the observation that "Activities of our muscles and glands (the so-called bodily effectors) make up our responses" (p. 3). Perhaps the topography of the response is more easily described. We may define a response within an experimental context as the pecks of a pigeon at a key, the bar pressing of a rat, or the number of times an individual emits a noun within a ten-minute verbal output. Such response classes are reasonably discrete.

The definition of a response is equally theoretically important.[9] Again to quote Barrett (1962) with regard to response measure in operant conditioning (but equally applicable to other conditioning techniques), "The basic datum of the free operant is the frequency of a specific and reliably defined response within a controlled experimental environment." Within such a framework, we must agree, in large measure, with the comments of Breger and McGaugh (1965) that, when Wolpe asks a patient to imagine an anxiety-producing scene (such as a corpse in a coffin, perhaps) and then asks him to relax, while visualizing this scene as a reciprocally inhibitory response, "The 'imagination of a scene' is hardly an objectively defined stimulus, nor is something as general as 'relaxation' a specifiable

[8] See also Cumming and Schoenfeld (1963).
[9] See Mueller and Schoenfeld (1954).

and clearly observable response" (p. 340). Nor can we see the "larger units of behavior" such as "interest, enthusiasm and attention" previously mentioned from Ullmann and Krasner (see page 502) as "specific and reliably defined responses" as Barrett would define them. There are undoubtedly specific responses emitted by individuals that may be interpreted by the observer as "interest" or "attention," but the risk of observer bias and the growing distance from a laboratory response definition are very real. The advantage of a good laboratory method is clarification of the data and response measures, and this should always be kept in mind in theory as well as in application.

THE PROBLEM OF REINFORCEMENT. Basic to the behavior therapies represented by conditioning is the concept of reinforcement. Earlier we referred to Sidman's definition of *reinforcement* as "any event, contingent upon the response of the organism that alters the future likelihood of that response" (1960). The problem of defining reinforcement or isolating the "reinforcing stimulus" becomes somewhat knotty when one turns to the generalized conditioned reinforcers such as "approval," "attention," and money, which are related to the "socially acquired motives" so important to formulations in social psychology. Social theorists consider primary reinforcers (such as food) to be insufficient in controlling events, and they appeal, in their stead, to such socially derived reinforcers or social motives. Skinner (1953a) discussed conditioned reinforcers:

A conditioned reinforcer is generalized when it is paired with more than one primary reinforcer. The generalized reinforcer is useful because the momentary condition of the organism is not likely to be important. The operant strength generated by a single reinforcement is observed only under an appropriate condition of deprivation . . . but if a conditioned reinforcer has been paired with reinforcers appropriate to many conditions, at least one appropriate state of deprivation is likely to prevail upon a later occasion. [p. 77.]

And again: "Eventually generalized reinforcers are effective even though the primary reinforcers on which they are based no longer accompany them . . . we get attention or approval for its own sake" (p. 81) and "we play games of skill for their own sake" (p. 81). This apparent functional autonomy of conditioned reinforcement ("for its own sake") has disturbed some critics of behavior therapy. Chomsky (1959), in a review of Skinner's book on verbal behavior, observed that when we say that a person "reads what books he likes . . . *because* he finds it reinforcing to do so . . . we can only conclude that the term 'reinforcement' has a purely ritual function" (p. 38).

Newman (1951) stated that "one has the suspicion that if we completely understood secondary reinforcement we should understand the whole mechanism [of reinforcement]" (p. 419). Verhave and Bachrach (1964), who reviewed the literature on generalized secondary or conditioned reinforcement, observed that, "Although the concept of a generalized conditioned reinforcer has had wide appeal and appears a valid explanatory concept for many types of complex social behavior, the experimental analysis of the concept and the behaviors assumed to be involved has hardly begun" (p. 6). These authors refer to Kelleher and Gollub (1962), who stated, in a review of experimental research on conditioned positive reinforcement, that, "despite the systematic importance of generalized conditioned reinforcers, very little research has explicitly evaluated their effects" (p. 587). Much of the relevant literature on conditioned discrimination and conditioned reinforcement reviewed by Verhave and Bachrach led them to the conclusion that

The circumstances under which conditioned reinforcers function are far from understood. The specific nature of the constraints have not been dealt with experimentally since most of the reinforcers in social and psychotherapeutic situations are conditioned reinforcers and experimental clarification of their status and the conditions under which they are effective and ineffective has great theoretical and practical importance. [1964, p. 10.]

This very brief commentary on the most significant theoretical problems of definitions of *stimulus, response,* and *reinforcement* has only touched the surface of the issues. It is true that successes have been achieved through the use of conditioning techniques in certain therapeutic situations. It is also true that these situations are invariably ones in which the response classes have been specific, clearly and reliably defined, and the environmental conditions have been well controlled. To move from such circumscribed situations to more complex ones requires a step-by-step experimental analysis of the concepts basic to the methods.

SOME OBJECTIONS TO BEHAVIORISTIC MODELS IN THERAPY. Objections to a behavioristic methodology in psychotherapy are essentially of two types—the one that objects to the mechanistic, "dehumanized" view of the individual and the other that holds that "the laws or principles of conditioning and reinforcement which form the basis of [the behavior therapists] . . . learning theory are insufficient explanations for the findings from laboratory experiments, let alone the complex learning phenomena that are encountered in psychotherapy" (Breger and McGaugh, 1965, p. 339). The former position, that of the "dehumanization" or oversimplification of human behavior was reflected by Shlien (1962) in his comments on a paper presented by Krasner entitled "The Therapist as a Social Reinforcement Machine" (1962). Shlien observed, in a discussion of the problem of using behavioristic techniques to control human behavior, "I'm afraid . . . there is an attractive simplicity in such work that will lure people into mechanical techniques prematurely" (p. 109). This position has merit if it refers to a concern about the technician's uncritically applying principles as yet not entirely clarified. But Shlien offered little more than an alternative that is characterized by over-simplicity in itself when he suggested that changing the behavior of other humans is a "political problem" and not a scientific one, that the "scientific problem is to find and understand the internal mechanisms of behavior change," adding, "Once we find the basic mechanism, there may be many applications" (p. 109). The same mote appears to lie in the eye of the other critics of behavioristic approaches to therapy quoted above, Breger and McGaugh. Many of their arguments are cogent,[10] but they offer, as an alternative to the methods of the behavior therapists, a system based on "central mediators," "strategies," and "plans" (p. 339). In their view, learning is "the process by which information about the environment is acquired, stored and categorized. This cognitive view is, of course, contrary to the view that learning consists of the acquisition of specific responses; responses, according to our view are mediated by the nature of stored information" (p. 355). This cognitive view (rather a computer-oriented view of information gathering-analysis-storage and action) is a reasonable theoretical system from many standpoints.

Unfortunately, to paraphrase the quotation from Breger and McGaugh presented earlier, such a learning theory is insufficient to account for findings in the laboratory and much less sufficient for the explanation of complex learning phenomena encountered in psychotherapy. Potentially productive theories such as those espoused by Staats and Staats (1963) use central mediating processes and reinforcement alike as constructs whose validity must be continually examined experimentally. With the present state of knowledge, it is probably as presumptuous for Wolpe to say "Neurotic behavior is unadaptive learned behaviour that despite repeated evocations fails to become extinguished" (1950, p. 613) as it is for Breger and McGaugh to say "Neuroses are not symptoms (responses) but are strategies of a particular kind which lead to certain observable (tics, compulsive acts, etc.) and certain other less observable, phenomena (fears, feelings of depression, etc.)" (1965, p. 355). The former definition is couched in terms more familiar to the laboratory, but it is, perhaps, true that it is not a great deal clearer than the latter.

Objections such as those raised by Shlien and by Breger and McGaugh are basically theoretical problems similar to those we have discussed as problems of definitions of *stimulus, response,* and *reinforcement.* Shlien's hope for a "basic" mechanism of behavior change and Breger and Mc-Gaugh's concern with the cognitive analysis of behavior have identical foci of problems in theory, variant though they may appear with each other and with the behavioristic models.

[10] Much of their thinking follows up work of Krech (1951).

POSSIBLE FUTURE DEVELOPMENTS IN BEHAVIOR THERAPY: THE "LIFE CYCLE" OF A METHOD. Often, throughout this chapter, we have expressed concern about the future of behavior therapies, concern that the potentially valuable methods may suffer the same fate as so many other clinical techniques—uncritical and enthusiastic acceptance, followed by uncritical and disappointed rejection. Clinicians have a rather happy-go-lucky cynicism about therapeutic methods—witness, for example, the amused comment made by Thompson (1952, p. 590) at a conference on biological methods in the treatment of mental illness: In commenting on the use of niacin therapy in emotional disorders, he wryly remarked, "When I return home I shall treat as many patients as possible while the cure lasts." There is ample reason for such an attitude—the history of therapies is such as to support a "here today, gone tomorrow" outlook. In fact, it is possible to describe a fairly typical "life cycle" of a therapeutic method.

The application of a particular technique may begin with an accidental discovery or a relationship between events. Cerletti, for example (see page 514), found in his clinical practice that epilepsy and schizophrenia rarely if ever occurred in the same person (this has not since been confirmed). He considered the possibility that the convulsive seizures were, in some way, antagonistic to the disorder of schizophrenia. Hence, he induced shock in patients with schizophrenia. Marsilid (see page 543) was originally used as a drug for the therapy of tuberculosis. A finding unrelated to the antituberculosis aspects of the drug was the apparent effect it had on some depressed tuberculosis patients of making them more active and apparently less depressed. Hence, on the basis of the unanticipated side effect, the drug was tried on psychiatric patients as a "psychic energizer." The use of monoamine oxidase (MAO) inhibitors emerged therefrom as an area of clinical research.

Not all applications have such serendipitous beginnings, of course. Programed learning had its general basis in intensive research such as Skinner's (1958) on shaping behavior. There is, however, a similar life cycle in all such applications, which runs as follows: First, after the initial proposal of the usefulness of a particular method—let's stick to therapeutic techniques for this—there is a high frequency of published papers and verbal reports (at professional meetings, for example, on clinical applications of the therapy. These papers and reports are almost inevitably of the case-study type—an empirical report on method X used on n number of patients with certain results. Following the case-study phase of the life cycle are a drop in the frequency of the case reports and an increase in the studies in which method X is compared with other methods (drugs versus electric shock therapy, for example) in terms of clinical effectiveness. This *comparison* phase leads into the next, or *follow-up,* stage, in which other reports (presented with much less frequency than the other types) appear, bringing the long-range results of therapy to the light: "Lobotomies 10 years later . . ." The final phase of the life cycle of the technique is the re-evaluative phase, in which the *mode of action* of the method is explored. Here, the physiological effects of certain drugs are examined. Biochemical changes attendant upon shock therapy are investigated, etc. In sum, the sequential phases *case study, comparison, follow-up,* and *mode of action* may portray the life cycle of a method. Applying this to the behavior therapies, we find that these techniques are for the most part in the first phase, that of case reports. For example, Ullman and Krasner's book called *Case Studies in Behavior Modification* (1965) consists solely of case studies. Their other work (Krasner and Ullman, 1965) called *Research in Behavior Modification* offers some intensive papers on research, in which much of the material is entirely based on case reports. This is perfectly sound practice; what is now probable is an increase in the frequency of such case studies for a period, followed (if our life cycle holds true) by a drop in case reports and an increase in comparative studies (not necessarily done by the practitioners themselves —behavior modification versus psychoanalytic therapy or nondirective therapy). The follow-ups and, ultimately, the mode of action in which such concepts as response and reinforcement will have to be considered carefully from a theoretical standpoint will be discussed in greater detail later. Application in the field always is ahead of the research that tests it —clinical exigencies may demand this—but application divorced from research and theory has limited utility.

Goldiamond, Dyrud, and Miller (1965, p. 111) make a good case for the orchestration of practice, science, and technology. "First," they say, "we have practice."

By practice, we mean the attempt to solve by our behavior certain problems of an empirical nature. In their solution, whatever skills, artistry, and knowledge we have are put to use. The critical thing is to get the job done. Another stage, which may develop out of such problems, is science. In science, we may attempt to systematize our procedures and knowledge. Such systematization may suggest an application to other problems, and we shall limit the term, technology, to such application of science. The technician, having demonstrated some successes in the areas of his application, may be asked to solve problems for which his technology is only partly sufficient. He may then in addition call upon unformulated skills, procedures from other disciplines, intuition, and artistry; and we have practice again. This practice may lead to further science, to further technology, to further practice, to further science, and so on. In each case, the practice incorporates more and more scientific elements and the sciences incorporate more and more from the problem areas and technologies, so that the relationship between the three is an ascending spiral rather than a circle or an unidirectional arrow.

Ullmann and Krasner, in predicting the future of behavior modification, foresee a growing cadre of "psychotechnicians trained in the application of behavior modification techniques. With an effective body of information and technique, the pressure for applied rather than research personnel will increase" (p. 60). Thus, the technologists of Goldiamond, Dyrud, and Miller will come upon the scene. The crucial problem, however, is limned in two phrases in this statement: "with an effective body of information and technique" and "applied rather than research personnel." First, we must be supremely confident that an effective body of data exists upon which to base this technology (the *science* of Goldiamond *et al.*), and, second, we must be sure that there are scientists (research personnel) to provide the necessary thinking through and analysis of the techniques used by applied personnel. It is undoubtedly true that the field of behavior therapy, with its worthy social goals, its theoretical simplicity (deceptive though it may be), and its empirical success (under certain circumstances), will attract many psychotechnicians. It is, therefore, a field in danger of being ruined by amateurs.

PHYSIOLOGICAL METHODS OF TREATMENT: SOMATOTHERAPIES

Introduction. In this section we will deal with the physiological treatment methods that derive, in general, from biologically oriented formulations of the etiology of emotional disorders. The basic theoretical frame of reference is provided by the belief that behavioral, emotional, or "mental" disorders are manifestations of underlying physiological-biochemical aberrations. The "direct" methods of treatment to be considered in this section are, in a stricter sense, not direct, inasmuch as their use is predicated on the assumption that the physiological changes that may be crucially responsible for the disorder can be altered by surgical or pharmacological action upon the neural substrates of the body. The treatment of the disorder is, then, in effect, secondary to the intervention with physicochemical events.

The approach in physiological treatment methods, therefore, is an attempt to control or modify the biological substrates assumed to be responsible for aberrant behavior patterns. It is important to note, in this respect, that an ideal scientific and rational plan of treatment for such disorders would require an understanding of the underlying biogenic factors specific to the disorder. Unfortunately, the acquisition of detailed knowledge of such factors has lagged considerably behind the development of increasing numbers of physiologically based treatment methods. At several points throughout this chapter, we have indicated recognition of and concern about, the problem of practical and empirical approaches' preceding scientific and experimental examinations of therapies. It is, as we have noted, inevitable that clinical applications of treatment methods will outdistance the experimental laboratory investigations of these methods, but there is also an inevitable cost in fads of application that might actually delay the development of effective techniques. It would be desirable to have physiological treatments, for example, developed in accordance with an understanding of biological factors. This has been rarely true; much of the application of physiological treatment techniques has been based on accidental empirical assumptions such as the one, described on page 514, in which Cerletti and Bini, following a suggestion by Von Meduna, developed shock therapy as a treatment method for schizophrenia purely on the basis of clinical observation that since epilepsy and schizophrenia did not occur in the same patient, seizures "must" be in some fashion antagonistic to schizophrenia. Inducing seizures by electric current applied to the patient's head was the next empirical, and perhaps logical, step.

We would not attempt to minimize the role of accident in scientific discovery. On the contrary, we have much respect and, indeed, awe of it (Bachrach, 1965), and frequently it leads to exciting research. Recent investigations, for example, of possible effects of aspirin on coronary disease stemmed from an observation that there was a lower incidence of coronaries in arthritic patients than might be expected. Aspirin, frequently used in large doses with such patients, is known under certain conditions to have anticoagulatory blood effects and, therefore, might have some reasonable basis for beneficial effects in coronary thrombosis. But this is obviously and most importantly a "hunch," an empirical lead to follow in careful clinical and experimental investigation before any widespread use of this as a treatment procedure is adopted. Often, in medicine, the development of an effective treatment has preceded any understanding of the disease process. To date, biochemists have not been able definitively to demonstrate how insulin lowers the blood sugar level, yet insulin has been effectively employed in controlling diabetes. It should be remembered, however, that the use of insulin emerged from years of careful, dedicated laboratory work on animals by Banting and his associates.

The cautious minuet between experimental research and clinical application is important. The clinician, with his immediate need for treatment procedures, can be alert to possible leads for research in methods and their application. The use of such methods simply because they are "plausible" should be approached with *much* caution. Dews (1962), in an incisive essay on drugs, discussed the gap between plausible and established accounts of drug action, taking as an example the work on reserpine and 5-HT (5-hydroxytryptamine):

The limitation in specificity of drug actions weakens the inferences that can be made from observed behavioral effects of a drug—even a drug with a well-established type of action. It has been shown that morphine can liberate histamine. . . . No one appears to have suggested that the analgesic effects of morphine are dependent upon its histamine-liberating properties. Yet, when reserpine was shown to liberate 5-HT a few years ago, the suggestion was quickly made that the behavioral effects of reserpine were dependent on its ability to liberate 5-HT. [p. 429.]

This "plausible" hypothesis was based on incomplete evidence, but at least it was a hypothesis that could bear some testing and, if demonstrated, might lead to effective treatment of psychotic states. But the multiplicity of drug action (for example, resperine also liberates catecholamines and other amines), among other critical factors, dictates caution in hypothesis formulation and, above all, in the clinical use of untested techniques.

With this brief background and cautionary tale, we may now turn to a consideration of current physiological methods which may be classified into four broadly defined treatment categories: shock and convulsive therapy, psychosurgery, miscellaneous physiological methods, and psychopharmacological therapies. The material for this discussion has been drawn, in the main, from American and English literature during the period 1945 to June, 1965. The methods to be covered have been extensively discussed by Alexander (1953), Sargent and Salter (1954), Hoch and Pennes (1958), and Freeman (1958). More recently, in a comprehensive text on somatic treatment methods, Kalinowsky and Hock (1961) discussed modern drug therapies and the numerous modifications of shock therapy, insulin treatment, and psychosurgery.

The primary objective of the present discussion will be to examine the available data on therapeutic results of the various physiological treatment methods in order to obtain, insofar as is possible, an estimate of their effectiveness. For more specific and detailed information about the techniques *per se,* the above-noted group of publications should prove quite useful.

Shock and Convulsive Therapy

INSULIN SHOCK THERAPY (IST). Also called "insulin coma therapy" (ICT), insulin shock therapy was introduced by Sakel in 1933. His initial observation was that insulin therapy could be used to reduce the distressing symptoms of the newly abstinent morphine addict. On the basis of these results, Sakel decided to try insulin in treating other forms of excitation. Quite by accident, when he attempted to determine optimal dosage, some of the schizophrenic patients being treated fell into coma. Sakel observed that, when these patients emerged from coma, not only had the excitement abated, but the psychotic symptoms as well had lessened and in some cases even disappeared. Within a few years of the initial impact, the technique had received widespread acclaim as the most successful form of therapy for mental illness that had yet been found. In the first flush of enthusiasm, a number of reports were published indicating that insulin shock therapy was extremely successful in treating a variety of psychotic disorders. The majority of reports that have accumulated in the literature since 1933 have agreed on the therapeutic superiority of ICT over routine hospital care (Leiberman *et al.*, 1957; West *et al.*, 1955; Palmer *et al.*, 1950; Brannon and Graham, 1955).

Apart from its empirical value, ICT has remained a theoretical stumbling block. The mechanism of the mode of action of ICT is still unknown, and no explanation has gained general acceptance. Various theories have proposed a multitude of physiological, biochemical, and psychological explanations, but experimental evidence has generally been lacking.

The rationale for its use, other than that based on its empirical value, is still to a large extent obscure. In general, extensive use of ICT in the past 25 years suggests that the treatment can help reduce the symptoms of schizophrenia, especially during the early stages of the disorder. However, later reports have not been as favorable, particularly regarding the permanence of the beneficial changes, which usually appear soon after a series of treatments. Even today, opinions still vary considerably as to the efficacy of ICT. Several large-scale statistical surveys of the literature on ICT have indicated that there may be very little, if any, significant improvement-rate difference between treated and control populations. Staudt and Zubin (1957) found 58 per cent improvement immediately after treatment and 46 per cent at one year, tapering off to about the nonspecific treatment control rate of 30–40 per cent for the two- to five-year follow-up period. Another finding was that the most successful results with both ICT and ECT (electroconvulsive therapy) occur in the same type of patients, who tend toward a good prognosis even without such treatment. The statistical data they report indicate that the relapse rate in the insulin-treated group is higher than in the control spontaneous remission groups. The initially higher ICT improvement rate drops progressively closer to the control improvement rate and is approximately equal to the latter after five years' follow-up.

One of the difficulties encountered in reviewing the enormous literature on treatment results is that only a few studies attempt to follow the necessary control techniques and principles. By far the majority of studies report results with only a small number of patients, in whom the improvement is largely a matter of the clinician's personal judgment. Valid comparison of different reports is impossible, owing to the lack of control of such factors as diagnostic standards and methods of evaluation of response.

These difficulties, coupled with the more critical evaluation of long-range effects after first enthusiasm, have certainly increased the reluctance of many clinicians to emply ICT. The current literature also suggests a marked decline in interest in the treatment, which may well reflect a decline in its use in hospitals. Another important reason for this stems from the impact of tranquilizers and the use of electro convulsive therapy. Furthermore, from a purely practical point of view, ICT is much more time-consuming and expensive to administer.

ELECTROCONVULSIVE THERAPY (ECT).[11] In 1938, Cerletti and Bini described a method of producing convulsions by electricity and began its use in the treatment of schizophrenia. The theoretical basis of this procedure is the apparent antagonism between epilepsy and schizophrenia also suggested by Von Meduna. Underlying this theoretical basis were the observations that the two disorders rarely occurred together and that spontaneous generalized seizures sometimes had a therapeutic effect in schizophrenia.

Cerletti and Bini believed that the convulsion itself was the therapeutic agent, rather than the electric current *per se*. The method gained wide practical acceptance despite later revision of the theoretical rationale. More recently, the use of ECT has declined, again owing to the impact of the tranquilizers. This decline is best illustrated by an almost total disappearance from publications during the past few years in the American and English literature.

Later reports on the results of ECT indicate apparently more divergence of opinions concerning the therapeutic value of ECT than exists for ICT. In some respects, ECT has been considered more efficacious in the affective disorders than in schizophrenia, and of little or no value in the psychoneuroses except where there are depression features. The sources of the difficulties in the evaluation of ECT are essentially the same as for the other somatotherapies, namely, the inability to relate or match treated populations in different studies and the tremendous differences in methods of evaluation of response. Such factors as the number of patients studied, the diagnostic standards, and the duration of illness and hospitalization prior to treatment are seldom if ever comparable in any two studies.

The most recent large-scale statistical survey indicates that ECT provides higher immediate remission and improvement rates than does routine hospital care. Staudt and Zubin (1957) reported an initial 52 per cent improvement rate with ECT as compared with the corresponding nonspecific rates and control rates of 25 per cent and 30–40 per cent. Another large-scale survey, reported by Alexander (1953), indicates an initial improvement rate of about 50 per cent for 7,357 cases with con-

[11] Sometimes referred to as "electroshock therapy" (EST).

vulsive therapy, as compared with a 30 per cent spontaneous remission rate among 11,081 schizophrenics. One survey did not find a significant statistical difference between ECT and routine hospital care. Appel *et al.* (1953) reported an immediate improvement rate of 32 ±10 per cent with ECT and a routine-hospital-care rate improvement of 29 ±10 per cent. A meaningful comparison of these statistical data is difficult to construct. For one thing, the methodological approaches in these three surveys differ considerably. As a general overview and summary of an enormous clinical literature, they indicate what might be taken as a consensus of opinion, namely, that ECT may produce immediate improvement rates that are by and large superior to those of routine hospital care. Furthermore, there seems to be some indication that the use of ECT results in an average decrease in hospitalization time.

The studies on long-range follow-up after ECT indicate that there is very little, if any, significant improvement-rate difference between treated and control groups. In fact, Staudt and Zubin (1957) found a negative sort of relation between length of follow-up period after ECT and percentage of patients recovered, much improved, or improved. They reported an immediate effect of about 52 per cent; after one year, 48 per cent; and after two years, 46 per cent. The five-year follow-up group showed only a 39 per cent effect. After five years, nonspecific treatment in the preshock period produced 42 per cent improvement, while parallel control groups in the shock period yielded a 25 per cent improvement rate. (The lower improvement for the shock-period control group may have been due to selection of patients with poorer prognoses as controls.)

By and large, the most successful results with both ECT and ICT occur in the same type of patients, who tend toward a good prognosis even without such treatment. One important factor that seems to be inversely related to favorable outcome is the duration of illness prior to treatment, while the symptom picture related to favorable outcome seems to be that of the acutely agitated or depressed paranoids.

Much effort has been expended in the attempt to reduce or eliminate the undesirable side effects and complications of standard ECT without reducing the therapeutic effect. One of the most frequent complications of the modified ECT is vertebral fractures produced by violent muscular contractions. For this reason, one of the very popular modifications of ECT has involved the use of pharmacological agents for the control of the convulsion. Commonly, neuromuscular blocking agents are used to lower the incidence of fractures and dislocations and reduce general systemic stress by controlling the intensity of the peripheral convulsion.

Another modification, on which there is a large literature, is of the parameters of electrical stimulation. Some of these variables are wave form, pulse duration, intensity and frequency, mode of current onset, number of electrodes, and placement. The principal objective here, as with the chemical modifications, has been that of reducing the dangerous complications of the standard ECT while either maintaining or improving the therapeutic effect. In the past 20 years, there has accumulated a very large applied clinical literature on the efficiency of these and other modifications. An earlier exposition by Liberson (1953) reviewed many of these modifications and attempted to correlate the various alterations with the therapeutic effect.

A general survey of the American-English literature on ECT over the past 20 years reveals some interesting trends in the development of this treatment.[12] The first 10-year period, from 1945 to 1955, was dominated almost exclusively by the clinical applications—"case-study" types of reports for which either the standard ECT method or some chemical or electrical modification was employed. In the second 10-year period, from 1955 to the present, there has been a rather interesting trend away from the straight clinical case study. There has been a good deal of interest, for example, in the mode of action of ECT, the main questions being concerned with how the convulsion is produced and whether, in fact, the convulsion is the therapeutic factor (Fleming, 1958). These studies have generally been physiological or biochemical (Gour and Bijargava, 1957; Brill et al., 1957). Others have investigated such factors as the role of fear in ECT (Crumpton et al., 1963) and the relation of changes in memory to improvement in ECT (Korin et al., 1956; Cameron, 1960). A number of studies have involved comparisons of clinical effects of ECT with those of other newer methods of treatment (i.e., drugs).

An important point is that recently there has been an almost total disappearance of the clinical-application type of report.[13] This decline in the straight clinical application of ECT may be due to several factors. Certainly prominent among these has been the tremendous impact of the modern drugs for the treatment of mental illness. Another factor in the decline of ECT has been the growing recent conviction that longer-range follow-up reveals very little improvement over either the nonspecific treatments or the drug therapies. Furthermore, there has perhaps been a certain amount of pressure to keep "up-to-date" with newer treatment methods, and ECT apparently has become old-fashioned.

COMBINED INSULIN COMA–CONVULSIVE TREATMENT. The possibility of combining ICT and ECT has received some attention in the past. The

---

[12] See page 507 for the "life cycle" of a treatment method.

[13] A careful survey of *Psychological Abstracts* provides evidence for the decline of reports on ECT; it also documents the case study to mode of action shift. This is also true of other techniques such as ICT.

aim has been to secure a summation of the presumed therapeutic benefits of each procedure. The rationale for such combined treatment has been generally based on the observation of sudden improvement after "spontaneous" convulsions in insulin hypoglycemia. The specific indications for the use of combined therapies have not been precisely defined. A common indication for combined treatment has been when the patient fails to improve on either ICT or ECT. Although there are a number of reports on clinical applications in the literature, there have been no controlled studies designed to evaluate the relative effectiveness of either ICT or ECT as compared with the combined treatment. The most common observation in the clinical literature has been that the combined treatment does not differ significantly as to improvement percentages. Recent reports on the use of combined treatment have, in fact, not appeared in the literature, which, in all likelihood, indicates a very minor role in current direct therapy.

PHARMACOLOGICAL CONVULSIVE THERAPY (INHALANT CONVULSIVE TREATMENT). This has been used as an alternative procedure to ECT. There are some general opinions that this procedure may be used as effectively as ECT for the same therapeutic purposes and is accepted more readily by some patients. A variety of agents have been employed, one of the more common being hexafluorodiethel ether (Indoklon). As yet there have been no controlled studies to evaluate the relative effectiveness of this treatment. The general indication, however, is that it does not differ significantly from ECT in terms of therapeutic success.

CONVULSANT PHOTOSHOCK TREATMENT (PHOTOPHARMACOLOGICAL TREATMENT). The pharmacological production of generalized therapeutic convulsions by means of intravenous Metrazol was early abandoned for a number of reasons. In particular, these were the undependability of seizure production, the severity of seizures, and the production of marked apprehension in the patient during the period of induction.[14] As an alternative to this procedure and to ECT, a technique was developed in which a seizure is produced by using intermittent photic stimulation in conjunction with intravenous hexazole. Apparently, many of the difficulties encountered with Metrazol are for the most part avoided by using this technique. Ulett, Smith, and Gleser (1956) evaluated convulsant photoshock therapy and reported the technique to be of value in the treatment of the affective psychoses; although, the therapeutic results were not shown to be superior to those of ECT.

Psychosurgery. The initial developments in the area of psychosurgery

[14] It was frequently called the "blue flame" because of the reported visual (and apparently frightening) stimulation of a flamelike perception.

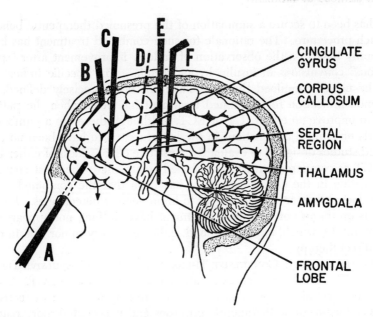

Fig. 17–7. Schematic representation of psychosurgical techniques (after Scoville, in L. Bellak [ed.], *Schizophrenia* [New York: Logos Press, 1958]) (see text): *A*—transorbital lobotomy; *B*—topectomy, cortical undercutting; *C*— Grantham operation (stereotaxic electrocoagulation); *D*—septal stimulation; *E*—stereotaxic amygdalotomy; *F*—stereotaxic thalamotomy.

can be credited to Moniz and Lima, of Portugal, who were the first to recommend and perform a surgical interruption of the frontal association pathways as a treatment for psychotics. Subsequent to the publication of Moniz' monograph in 1936, the operation was introduced into the United States by Freeman and Watts (1941). Within the period of a few years, the operation had been widely adopted and was the subject of an ever increasing body of literature.

Many neurosurgeons developed modifications of the original operation, which were advanced as being markedly superior in one respect or another. All this activity gave rise to a great variety of psychosurgical techniques. Unfortunately, adequate evaluation of the relative efficacy of different techniques on comparable series of patients has been grossly lacking.

Even after almost thirty years, and certainly as many thousand operations, psychosurgery remains very much a controversial issue. The source of much of this controversy can be reduced to two basic questions. One concerns evaluation: *"is psychosurgery effective?"* The other question is

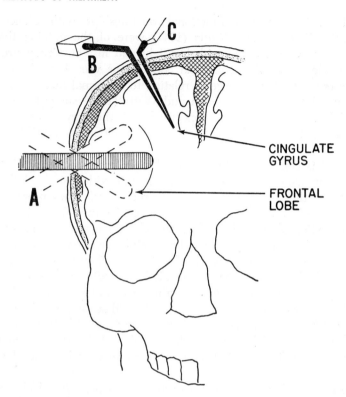

CINGULATE
GYRUS

FRONTAL
LOBE

Fig. 17–8. Schematic representation of psychosurgical techniques (after Scoville, in L. Bellak [ed.], *Schizophrenia* [New York: Logos Press, 1958]) (see text): A—Freeman and Watts' "closed" standard lobotomy; B—Scoville's cingulate gyrus undercutting; C—Livingston's cingulate gyrus subcortical sectioning.

"what is the mechanism of action?" If we find that psychosurgery is sometimes effective, we should be able to formulate an explanation of its effectiveness, and such an explanation, gaining support from available empirical evidence and reduced to verifiable propositions, could constitute a theoretical rationale for psychosurgery.

In the absence of adequate explanation, the only rationale for psychosurgery will be expressed in terms of its empirical value. By and large, this situation describes the current condition of psychosurgery. Although a great many theories have been advanced, to date no one has proposed a completely adequate explanation of the assumed therapeutic effects of psychosurgery. Moniz' original conception was that, in mental illness, there is an alteration of frontal lobe function to the extent that cells become fixed in abnormal functional relationships with diencephalic structures. Freeman and Watts (1941) were of the opinion that the frontal lobes are concerned with foresight and insight. They proposed that the role of the thalamofrontal connections was that of mediating affective (emotional) discharge in relation to abnormal ideas of self-concern. In a later paper, Freeman and Watts (1948) suggested that the frontal lobes might indeed be concerned with the very structure of the ego itself or at least with the elaboration of consciousness of self in various relationships.

Paul and Greenblatt (1958) proposed an interesting theory of frontal lobe function, which they attempted to integrate with observed behavioral changes after the various psychosurgery procedures. They proposed that the frontal and prefrontal lobes are involved in foresight and planning, whereas the thalamus and hypothalamus mediate affective behavior. The projections of thalamic nuclei to the frontal lobes, on the other hand, mediate the conscious experience of emotion. They suggested that the cutting of these fiber connections so alters the subjective component of the affective response that tensions do not accumulate in the elaboration of past experience. They proposed, therefore, that the individual is more completely bound to immediate stimuli, being less able to elaborate affective experience. The patient, they suggested, being free from past emotional entanglements, is thus able to make new behavioral adjustments.

Some support for this theory is derived from the clinical observation that pathological emotional states may be controlled by sectioning the thalamofrontal radiations. Still, there are a number of problems that make the task of inferring brain functions from postoperative data a complex and risky business. In the first place, tissue damage is never limited to the specific site of the lesion. Even with very discrete cortical lesions, there is usually widespread degeneration of thalamic cells and fibers. Another factor that makes interpretation a difficult matter is the complexity of thalamic connections with other brain structures. Thus, it would seem that the effects of frontal lesions could be the manifestation of altered function in widespread areas of the brain. The notion of the localized action of psychosurgery in this case would seem to be a gross oversimplification. It is possible that adequate explanation of psychosurgical effects will require an understanding of the functional integration of neural systems. At present, our knowledge of complex neural interaction is quite insufficient for the task of explaining (or understanding) the mechanism of psychosurgical effects.

As it stands, the only substantial support for psychosurgery is derived from the evaluation of its empirical value. To a large extent, developments in psychosurgery have been guided by the principle "better a doubtful remedy than none."

Psychosurgery is used today only when all other methods have failed, and even then with reluctance. Its use since the introduction of the modern drug therapies has greatly decreased. Patients are selected for operation on the basis of symptoms rather than diagnosis. The best results are said to be obtained in those patients who manifest severe tension, agitation and distress, emotional aggressiveness, hostility, and excited impulsive behavior. The operation is definitely contraindicated in patients showing cruelty and avoidance of responsibility.

It is claimed that the best results in lobotomy are secured in agitated depressions and in severe obsessive-compulsive reactions (Noyes and Kolb, 1963). Most commonly, psychosurgery has been used in the particularly severe and stubborn schizophrenic reactions. It has also proved useful for the relief of intractable pain, as in the case of terminal malignancy (i.e., inoperable cancer).

The various operations for prefrontal lobotomy have been designed to sever the connections to, or remove tissue primarily from, the prefrontal cortex and anterior cingulate gyrus. The principal objective of many of these operative techniques is that of cutting the projection pathways from the anterior and dorsomedial thalmic nuclei.

From a historical point of view, the most important procedures have been the full *bilateral lobotomy*, the *orbital lobotomy*, and the *transorbital lobotomy*. Procedures involving cortical ablations or undercutting have also been widely employed and will be considered here briefly. Finally, we will outline certain recent developments such as the *Grantham operation*, *thalamotomy*, and the most recent, *amygdalotomy*.

The full *lobotomy*, also known as the "standard operation," was developed by Freeman and Watts as a modification of Moniz' original procedure. The operation, performed "blind" through small burr holes in the skull, consists of cutting the white matter in both frontal lobes. The interruption of these fiber connections with the thalamus is, as in other forms of lobotomy, supposed to disassociate by surgical means the pathological thinking from its emotional reverberations.

The *bilateral orbital lobotomy* was developed in an attempt to avoid unnecessary sacrifice of brain tissue. Dax and Radley Smith (1946) carried out extensive studies of the comparative effects of fiber sections in various areas of the frontal lobes on an equivalent series of cases. They reported their findings in patients who had received an "upper section," a "middle section," and a "lower section." Apparently, their results indicated a certain specificity of the lesion in terms of therapeutic effect. These investigators reported that depressions were more readily relieved by a lower section; aggressiveness of catatonic schizophrenics, by an upper section; and paranoid schizophrenics, by a middle section.

Transorbital lobotomy is an example of this general approach. In this operation, a pointed instrument (leukotome) is passed through the conjunctival sac and orbital plate into the orbital surface of the frontal lobe, where an arc swing of the instrument cuts the inferior quadrant of the frontal lobe.

Advocates of transorbital lobotomy stress that complications and mortality are less frequent than in other forms of psychosurgery. The underlying theory, as in other forms of lobotomy, suggests that the surgical interruption of fiber tracts disassociates pathological thinking from its emotional reverberations. Among the advantages of this technique are the apparent facts that undesirable personality traits after this operation are much less frequent and seizures are also greatly reduced.

Bimedial lobotomy consists of cutting only the medial half of the white matter of both frontal lobes. This technique, which is simply a modification of the standard lobotomy, was developed to avoid the undesirable personality features observed after the standard operation. Some reports, to be considered in more detail below, suggest that this operation is followed by generally better therapeutic results than is the full bilateral or unilateral operation.

A variation of the "closed" lobotomy technique has been described by Grantham (1951). This procedure, the *Grantham operation*, consists of electrocoagulation of the lower and upper medial quadrants of the frontal lobe, using a stereotaxic apparatus. Some preliminary reports on the clinical effects of this procedure will be discussed later.

The *gyrectomy* procedure consists of the operative removal of cortical tissue. The Columbia-Greystone Project group used this method, termed *topectomy*, in an extensive study. Although initially this operation was hailed as an excellent treatment, later carefully controlled evaluation of the original series suggested that this technique was not as successful as conventional lobotomy. Cortical undercutting consists of undercutting specified areas of the frontal lobe. The procedure is much like the topectomy, except that the isolated tissue is left in place.

The *cingulectomy* operation was developed on the basis of evidence that suggests that the cingulate gyrus is an important autonomic effector area, as well as a suppressor center for both cortical activity and peripheral motor function. Pool (1951) reported the effects of isolating or removing the anterior cingulate gyrus bilaterally. The results obtained were not at all encouraging.

The *thalamotomy* procedure was conceived as a method of interrupting the frontothalamic connections without sectioning fiber tracts. This procedure consists of placing small circumscribed lesions by stereotaxic methods in the dorsomedial nuclei of the thalamus either by electrolysis or by electrocoagulation. A similar procedure, called *hypothalamotomy*, has also been employed as a follow-up when lesions in the thalamus have been found to be clinically inadequate.

The advantage of thalamotomy and hypothalamotomy over surgery of the frontal lobes is said to be mainly that of avoiding complications with postoperative convulsions and severe personality defects, both of which frequently follow the standard prefrontal lobotomy procedures. A serious limitation of these procedures, however, is the relatively high mortality rate they produce.

Quite recently, Narabayashi and his associates (1963) reported some initial observations on the clinical effects of *stereotaxic amygdalotomy* in treating behavior disorders. Earlier reports of the destruction of the human amygdaloid and periamygdaloid areas, by Freeman and Williams (1953) and Terzian (1950), were far from conclusive in their findings. Among the various behavioral changes reported were decrease in aggressiveness, initial increase in aggressiveness, emotional lability, motor restlessness, abnormal interest in food, and hypersexuality.

Narabayashi and his associates (1963) reported that stereotaxic amygdalotomy was performed bilaterally on 21 patients exhibiting severe behavior disturbances. For 17 of the 21 patients, "the operation resulted in marked reduction in the emotional excitability and a normalization of the patient's social behavior and adaptation." The clinical improvement of most patients was evaluated over a six-month period, and it was observed that such dramatic results were indeed quite permanent and stable over the postoperative follow-up period.

A puzzling aspect of this work is the apparent discrepancy between the types of behavioral changes noted by Freeman and Williams (1953) and those reported by Narabayashi and his associates (1963). The problem here is that in several instances the behavioral effects of amygdalotomy reported by Freeman and Williams (1953), such as hyperactivity, aggressiveness, and emotional lability, were exactly the types of behavior disorders Narabayashi and his associates (1963) claimed to have successfully treated with amygdalotomy. Narabayashi and his associates (1963), for example, reporting on one case (Case 21), stated that the patient exhibited a disturbance of behavior consisting of a labile mood, poor concentration, and aggressiveness. After the operation, they reported, "There was . . . a very complete and dramatic change in the patient's mood and behavior. She was able to read and pay attention very quietly and no longer had a tendency to violence and irritability" (Narabayashi et al., 1963, p. 9). Another case in point is that of a five-year-old boy with a diagnosis of hyperactive feeblemindedness, who was reported to have shown marked improvement following bilateral amygdalotomy. The authors commented, "The hyperactivity had been completely abolished and his entire attitude and behavior had become completely normal. His speech had improved and his concentration span had greatly increased in length" (Narabayashi *et al.*, 1963, p. 9).

Although these initial reports are indeed very encouraging, it is necessary to remember that as yet they have not been subject to controlled analysis or follow-up evaluation. It is possible that the conflicting reports that have appeared in the literature on the effects of amygdalotomy have resulted from variations in the size and location of the lesions produced. In order to compare the various behavioral effects, it will be necessary to obtain detailed histological information on the nature and extent of these lesions.

In any case, it is certainly not possible at present to make any conclusive statements concerning the therapeutic effect of the amygdalotomy procedure. We must await the findings of further carefully controlled evaluative studies, and certainly the histological verification of the lesions employed. Some research in amygdalotomy is in its preliminary stages at New Castle State Hospital, in Indiana, and we will be looking with great interest for reports of this work.

One of the more interesting developments in recent years has come as a rather marked departure from traditional psychosurgical procedures. Heath and his associates, at Tulane University, have been conducting extensive investigations on the efficacy of "rewarding brain stimulation" as a means of treating or controlling a variety of behavioral disorders. Of particular interest are the preliminary reports on *septal stimulation* (Heath, 1954) and *intracranial self-stimulation* (ICSS) (Heath, 1963).

In 1954, Heath and his associates reported on the effects of septal stimulation in schizophrenic patients. Their report, which presented detailed accounts of studies of patients before and after septal stimulation, indicated that about one-third of the patients so stimulated improved clinically.

Quite recently, the Tulane group reported on a series of studies in which it incorporated and modified certain of the animal ICSS methods for human investigation. A study was described (Heath, 1963) in which a patient was equipped with a small portable self-stimulator with three buttons, permitting delivery of electric stimuli of fixed parameters to any one of three brain sites. One patient, age twenty-eight, failed to respond to conventional treatments. He had electrodes implanted in fourteen predetermined brain regions and fixed to remain in exact position for prolonged study. The ICSS study was begun by randomly exploring the effects of stimulation at the various electrode placements. They found that stimulation of the septal region produced the most positive results.

The patient would press the septal button on his stimulator at relatively high rates and over extended periods of time.

In explaining why he pressed the septal button with such frequency, the patient stated that the feeling was "good." The authors of the study reported that the patient further explained that the feeling was as if he were building up to a sexual orgasm. He reported that he was unable to achieve the orgastic end point, however, explaining that his frequent, sometimes frantic, pushing of the button was an attempt to reach the end point (Heath, 1963, p. 573, patient No. B–7).

An additional effect of the septal stimulation was that it alerted the patient, thereby combating his narcolepsy. As an interesting sidelight, Heath reported that, by virtue of the patient's ability to control symptoms with the stimulator, he was employed part-time, while wearing the unit, as an entertainer in a night club. It was reported that a second patient (No. B–10) responded most frequently by pressing the button that provided a stimulus to the centromedian thalamus. A most interesting observation was that this stimulus did not induce the most pleasurable response; in fact, they reported, it induced irritability. The subject reported that he was almost able to recall a memory during this stimulation, but could not quite grasp it. "The frequent self-stimulations were an endeavor to bring this elusive memory into clear focus." At times, the patient noted, this was an intolerably frustrating effort. He reported, however, that the frustration and anger resulting from stimulation of the centromedian thalamus were alleviated with stimulation to the septal region.

The finding that a "self-provided" brain stimulation can immediately eliminate painfully frustrating emergency states would appear to have widespread implications for the development of therapeutic methods to favorably alter disordered behavior.[*]

The evaluation of clinical results in psychosurgery has, in large measure, derived from the long-range follow-up or longitudinal type of study. These studies have usually observed the patients at various intervals after surgery. The patient's progress is often measured in terms of a number of different criteria. A rating is thus assigned signifying a specific level of improvement.

A significant drawback in this method of evaluation is that it tends to generate an isolated statistic such as an improvement rate, which is very difficult to interpret outside the context of the diagnostic standards, the clinical criteria of change, and the measurement techniques employed in the particular study. All too often, these critical factors are not clearly specified in the report. Without this information, the isolated improve-

[*] See R. G. Heath, Electrical self-stimulation of the brain in man, *Amer. J. Psychiat.,* 1963, 120 (6), 571–577.

ment statistic can have no particular significance or relevance and, in fact, would seem quite meaningless.

The constituents of an adequate study would necessarily include a careful description of the types of cases selected, the criteria of clinical change, and the measurement techniques employed. In addition to these, a most valuable datum is the improvement rate in a carefully matched control series given an equal amount of hospital attention.

It is somewhat discouraging that only a handful of studies in the enormous literature on treatment results ever attempt to follow these essential control techniques and principles. Much of the controversy in the literature over the relative merits of the various operative techniques stems from the fact that valid comparison of different reports is impossible owing to variations in essential elements of experimental design. By and large, evaluation in psychosurgery has amounted to the accumulation of isolated statistics that, on closer examination, are not too meaningful.

A study reported by Freeman (1953) is a good example of the isolated-statistic approach. In a study of some 1,000 patients of all types one to sixteen years after lobotomy, Freeman (1953) reported satisfactory adjustment out of the hospital in over two-thirds of the cases. The improvement of the transorbital patients was found to be generally superior to that of the patients who had received other types of surgery. Six years after transorbital lobotomy, 80 per cent of the patients were out of the hospital and showing satisfactory adjustment. In the five- to ten-year period following prefrontal lobotomy, about 70 per cent of the surviving schizophrenic patients were out of the hospital. Freeman suggested that the observed superiority of transorbital lobotomy is, in all probability, related not only to the limited nature of the operation itself but also to the application at an earlier period in the disorder.

One finding was that results became progressively worse with increasing chronicity. Freeman reported that delay of surgery into the second year after hospitalization cut the results to 52 per cent, whereas postponement of five to ten years brought the release rate down to 30 per cent. Freeman used these data to make a case for the advisability of the earlier application of surgery. A fallacy in this argument is that the statistical trend Freeman found in lobotomized patients exactly parallels the trend in nonlobotomized patients. For this reason, there are many who consider lobotomy for a patient with an acute illness of recent onset indefensible. Certainly, with the introduction of the major tranquilizers, there has been a growing reluctance to apply psychosurgery, and this perhaps has been the major factor contributing to the marked decrease in usage of psychosurgery in recent years.

Considering the number of different psychosurgical techniques that have been advanced, it is somewhat surprising that so few comparative studies have been conducted. As a result, it is most difficult, if not impossible, to say which operations are most effective. Frequently, one technique has been advanced as being superior to all others without comparative observation or controls. Adequate evaluation of the relative efficacy of different operations or comparable series of cases has been done in only a few hospitals.

One study, conducted under Greenblatt and Solomon (1953), carefully investigated the therapeutic effectiveness of three different operative procedures. In this study, full bilateral, unilateral, and bimedial operations were compared in essentially equivalent chronic schizophrenic patient groups.

The levels of clinical improvement for each of the surgical groups at the five-year follow-up were reported by Paul, Fitzgerald, and Greenblatt (1957). They assigned a "marked" improvement rating to those patients who showed complete relief of all disturbed (or psychotic) symptoms such as inappropriate speech and behavior, severe anxiety and tension, delusions, and hallucinations. "Moderately" improved patients were those who showed substantial reduction of most symptoms. A "slightly" improved rating was assigned to patients who showed improvement in only certain areas, other symptoms remaining relatively unchanged. "Unimproved" patients showed no changes, and "worse" ratings applied to patients whose postoperative psychotic behavior was more severe than that observed preoperatively.

One finding was that the bimedial operative group showed greater improvement than the other two operative groups. The authors stated that "In both a one-year and five-year follow-up, bimedial lobotomy cases were found to be adjusting on a level superior to patients who received either full or unilateral operations" (Paul, Fitzgerald, and Greenblatt, 1957). The significant improvement rate for the combined operative groups, 114 patients in all, was reported to be 46 per cent at the end of five years.

The authors of the study further noted that, at five years, the bimedial patient was more likely to be tractable and often showed "greater ease in developing object relationships than either the bilateral or unilateral patient." These investigators summarized their findings with the comment that bimedial lobotomy appeared to be the procedure of choice in the chronic, hopeless schizophrenic patient. They also suggested that some patients unresponsive to psychosurgery might still do well on chlorpromazine or other ataractics (see discussion of drug therapy). The only major drawback with the bimedial operation appears to be the relatively high rate of convulsive complications it incurs.

By comparison, Freeman (1956) reported that the incidence of postoperative seizures in a group of transorbital patients was only .25 per cent. In contrast to this, the follow-up studies by Paul *et al.* (1956, 1957) revealed an incidence of 24 per cent convulsive seizures in the bimedial group. This rate was found at the five-year follow-up, which indicates the persistence of the complication. (The rate at the end of the first postoperative year was 21 per cent.)

Some preliminary reports on the clinical effects of the operative procedure described by Grantham and Spurling (1953) have generated interest in recent years. The technique is said to elicit improvement in a very significant proportion of cases and to reduce postoperative convulsive seizures dramatically.

Grantham and Spurling (1953) reported that lesions produced by electrocoagulation in the medial ventral quadrant of the frontal lobe were effective in producing clinical improvement in psychotic patients without postoperative convulsive seizures and with only minimal undesirable personality changes. A further study by McIntyre *et al.* (1954) utilized the Grantham technique on a small group of psychotic and neurotic patients. Their general findings were in agreement with those reported earlier by Grantham (1953). They noted that the schizophrenic patients "made good social recoveries with relative freedom from intense anxiety, tension and guilt." In most cases, there was also a marked reduction of aggressive, hostile, and explosive behavior patterns. The authors of the study suggested that the favorable therapeutic effects noted in their patients were most likely related to the disappearance of high levels of anxiety and tension that existed prior to the operations.

Although these results appear quite promising, it must be remembered that they are as yet only preliminary, corresponding in the main to the first, case-study stage in the life cycle of the treatment. It will of course be necessary to subject this treatment method to further controlled observation and follow-up evaluation. To our knowledge, there has been no report of a follow-up study on the initial observations in the use of electrocoagulation.

In contrast to the studies cited above, which generally report favorable therapeutic results, a few carefully controlled studies have uncovered certain significant limitations in the effectiveness of the various psychosurgical procedures. Robbin (1959) conducted a study in which the therapeutic results in cases treated by standard lobotomy were compared with those with patients of the same diagnosis and matched for age, sex, and chronicity of distribution, but not treated by lobotomy. Robbin found that the proportion of schizophrenic patients discharged after the operation was greater than in the control group, but the number of subsequent re-admissions was also greater for the postoperant group. In fact, the long-term results were found to be quite comparable in the two groups. In general, the most successful results with lobotomy tend to occur in the same type patients as show a good prognosis even without surgery, lending serious question to the rationale for surgical intervention.

In an earlier study, Robbin (1958) compared the results in 198 cases treated with lobotomy with those in 198 controls, again matched for chronicity, age on admission, sex, etc. Summarizing his findings, he indicated that the lobotomy did *not* appear to (1) improve the chances of discharge from the hospital, (2) accelerate discharge, (3) reduce the chances of re-admission, (4) delay re-admission, (5) reduce the number of re-admissions, or (6) significantly improve hospital behavior as judged by ward personnel.

The relevant point concerning these findings is that they certainly do not lend support to the notion of an empirical rationale for the lobotomy operation. By and large, the greatest measure of support for the therapeutic efficacy of these procedures can be traced to the "first-enthusiasm" type of case study and its none too critical follow-up.

Despite the promising results of innumerable initial reports on various psychosurgical procedures and even several impressive follow-ups, there seems to be an increasing recent conviction that the carefully controlled study reveals little, if any, significant improvement-rate difference between postoperant and control groups.

Some optimistic studies have boosted the clinical improvement rate to well over 50 per cent (Freeman, 1953). Unfortunately, such figures are not too meaningful without careful description of the types of patients selected, the criteria of improvement, and the measurement and evaluation techniques employed. Furthermore, without a control series matched for diagnosis, chronicity, age on admission, sex, etc. (see Robbin, 1958), the isolated improvement statistic provides very little information. Indeed, when such controlled observations are employed, one is often unable to demonstrate substantial benefits in clinical improvement rates.

Practitioners faced with the difficulties of constructing and consistently applying a theoretical rationale have had no choice but to rely mainly on the empirical value of the treatment as a rationale for its use. But the evidence gathered in support of such a rationale is all too often derived from the enthusiasm of preliminary reports. We have seen that original claims made for a particular treatment method prove quite often to be overly optimistic. The final statement on the therapeutic efficacy of a technique usually comes into view only gradually in the light of carefully controlled evaluation, which is unfortunately so often lacking.

The topectomy operation, developed by the Columbia-Greystone group, is a relevant example. It has been noted that initially this operation was hailed as an excellent treatment; follow-up evaluation based on carefully controlled studies, however, suggested that this technique was not as successful as conventional lobotomy (Pool, 1951).

Development and application of psychosurgical techniques, as well as other direct treatment methods, have been guided in large measure by the essentially pragmatic principle "If it works, use it." Unfortunately, the uncritical acceptance of preliminary evidence has frequently led to erroneous conclusions about the therapeutic value of a particular treatment.

It would seem, therefore, only reasonable to add certain qualifying statements to our pragmatic principle. We would tend to agree with the principle of an empirical rationale, but, before a treatment is recommended for general application, we would want to be quite certain that carefully controlled evaluation demonstrates its efficacy. Equally important is an explanation of *how* the treatment "works." By and large, there has been very little progress along these lines in psychosurgery.

Miscellaneous Physiological Techniques. *Rhythmic sensory bombardment therapy*, as first reported by Doust and Schneider (1954), consisted of the rhythmic application of intermittent photic, sonic, or tactile stimulation to the patient. These investigators treated 51 patients in various diagnostic categories for five to six days per week, one hour per treatment, in courses of 20 treatments. After a two-year follow-up, more than 50 per cent were judged to have demonstrated adequate remission, 25 per cent were considered improved, and 20 per cent showed no lasting effects. The criteria of improvement in this study were mainly concerned with relief of symptoms such as disorganization of thought, severe anxiety and tension, delusions, and inappropriate speech and behavior. Best results occurred with affective disorders, neurosis, and sociopathic personalities, and some improvement was considered to have occurred in persons diagnosed as paranoid.

Nonconvulsive electrical stimulation has been applied peripherally (Jones *et al.*, 1955) as a therapeutic procedure in instances of mental disorder. The impetus for this technique came from the previously observed efficacy of electric shock to the legs in producing arousal from barbiturate coma; the results appeared to be as effective as the more usual procedure of transcerebral stimulation. Such arousal was considered to result from excitation of the reticular activating system, which presumably would occur regardless of electrode site. To gather preliminary data on the role of the reticular activating system in electroconvulsive therapy as distinct from the convulsion per se, Jones and his co-workers subjected 15 patients, 7 of whom were labeled "schizophrenic," to nonconvulsive, peripheral electrical stimulation at the legs and lumbosacral region. Results were equivocal, and no follow-up data were reported.

Subcoma ambulatory insulin treatment was introduced by Polatin and Wiesel (1940) and appears under a variety of labels such as "subcoma," "half-coma," or "superficial coma." The designation is largely dependent on the particular techniques employed, that is, insulin dosage, duration of hypoglycemia, stage of hypoglycemia achieved, total length of treatment course, and other factors. In less intensive methods, only mild hypoglycemia is produced; in more intensive procedures, the degree of hypoglycemia may correspond to the light-coma phase of insulin coma therapy.

Greaves, Regan, and West (1955) report 79.2 per cent improvement in 133 schizophrenics during the period 1942–52. Improvement was based on the criterion of symptomatic relief and subsequent ability to profit from psychotherapy, the principal consideration in their work. For this reason, percentage improvement figures must be regarded as inconclusive as regards subcoma insulin treatment alone.

Euseef (1952) reported on the use of *intravenous insulin* for subcoma treatment. The results among 12 schizophrenics compared favorably with those in the control group subjected to insulin coma therapy by intramuscular insulin. As with coma insulin, best effects with subcoma insulin occurred in the schizoaffective states, in excited catatonia, and with certain patients with acute onset and short duration of illness.

In general, results with subcoma insulin treatment appear to range from those obtained with full insulin coma to relatively little effect. The most consistent effect is sedative in nature with a reduction in anxiety and tension in various mental disorders.

The first report on the use of CO_2 (*carbon dioxide*) came from Loevenhart et al. (1929). By means of an inhalation apparatus, they introduced a progressively increasing CO_2-oxygen gas mixture usually up to a ratio of about 35 per cent CO_2 and 65 per cent oxygen. They found that, in some psychotic cases, immediately following such an administration there would occur a two- to three-minute period of complete symptomatic remission or, in some cases of mute or noncommunicative patients, a vigorous expression of psychotic thinking. Owing to the brevity of these effects and complete absence of any long-lasting benefit, this procedure was abandoned in the case of the psychotic patient.

Meduna (1950) employed CO_2 with a group of 100 psychoneurotic patients composed mostly of persons diagnosed as having anxiety neurosis, spastic colitis, cardiac neurosis, female frigidity, male impotence, stuttering, character neurosis, and other ailments. Of this group, 68 showed a degree of improvement he considered to be "cured," using treatment sessions varying from 20 to 150. No follow-up data were made available.

Psychopharmacological Therapies. The use of drugs in the treatment of emotional disorders has a long history from the time of the ancients, when Celsus (*ca.* A.D. 14), for example, used an opiate for patients who were unable to sleep, administering draughts of "decoction of poppy." In the seventeenth century, drugs such as Usnea were used to treat nervous disorders. Usnea, a particularly prized entry in the pharmacopeia, was derived from moss of a special sort—that found on the skulls of criminals whose punishment had been hanging in chains. This drug was used until the nineteenth century, and, indeed, the first edition of the *Encyclopaedia Britannica,* in 1771, had a section on the uses of Usnea in therapy. In recent years, the use of such sedative agents as belladonna and phenobarbital was common in treating emotional disorders such as psychosomatic and anxiety conditions. Agents such as Metrazol (see page 517) were used in treatment to induce shock in the early twentieth century. It was not, however, until the years around 1950 that the beginning of widespread and investigated uses of psychopharmacological agents was well under way. The reasons for this are many and varied. Any science is dependent on other sciences for advances; neurology's strides forward were aided immeasurably by the development of the electron microscope; drug therapy was advanced in large measure by improvements in physiological, biochemical, and pharmacological methods not developed until recent years.

In this section, we will concentrate on psychopharmacological agents of five major types: the ataractic drugs, emotional tranquilizers, antidepressants, central nervous system stimulants, and psychotomimetic drugs. The first two groups, the ataractics (sometimes called the "major tranquilizers") and the emotional tranquilizers, have been so divided in practice because of their clinical use. For more exact reference, however, we have placed them in the same group of tranquilizers in the chart on page 534, and their placement therein is based on chemical classification.

ATARACTIC DRUGS. One of the most dramatic advancements in direct treatment methods has come about through the development of the ataractic drugs. Although these drugs have also been referred to as the "major tranquilizers," they actually are said to exert a much broader effect than that implied by the term *tranquilizer.* Tranquilizers are usually described as agents that reduce excitement and agitation while inducing sleep or "clouding consciousness." The drugs properly classified as ataractics are said to do much more than eliminate agitation. They may facilitate social adjustment, eliminate delusions and hallucinations, or make mute patients communicative. An important characteristic of the ataractic drugs that is often overlooked is their ability to affect behaviorally disturbed persons suffering from "mental illness." The ataractics, as a rule, do not bring "freedom from confusion" or "peace of mind" to normal persons. In fact, such drugs may not affect the normal person at all or may even supplement his ongoing level of confusion.

In the course of the past ten years, the ataractic drugs have become the primary means of treatment in the mental hospital. Since their introduction, there has been a marked decline in the use of other somatic treatment methods, particularly ECT, ICT, and psychosurgery. These drugs have dramatically altered the atmosphere of wards for disturbed patients. It is rarely necessary to tie violent patients down in their beds or to force them into isolation rooms. Ward personnel have been reduced because patients no longer require close supervision and can, in fact, do many things for themselves that were previously beyond their capacities.

Perhaps the most impressive and encouraging fact of all is that many state institutions for the first time in their histories report more discharges than admissions. The average length of hospitalization has, indeed, been reduced so markedly that, despite an over-all increase in the general population, the predrug increase in patient population has been halted and even reversed.

The final report of the Joint Commission on Mental Illness (1961) stated that the major tranquilizers "have delivered the greatest blow for patient freedom in terms of nonrestraint since Pinel struck off the chains in the Paris asylum 168 years ago."

Along with this newly achieved success, a number of disappointments and drawbacks have been uncovered. As a rule, we find that initial observations and preliminary reports have tended to be somewhat optimistic and are often subject to considerable qualifications in the light of further investigations.

A most significant drawback is the fact that many of the ataractic drugs have been found to produce dangerous side effects such as liver damage (jaundice) and hemolitic changes (eosinophilia, leucopoenia). Adverse effects in the cardiovascular system include tachycardia, hypotension, and cardiovascular accidents. Most pronounced of the central nervous system side effects are the extrapyramidal symptoms and motor restlessness.

Cole (1960) suggested that, in some cases, the "side effects" may be directly related to the observed therapeutic effect. He stated that the ataractic drugs "can produce a pharmacological straight jacket in which the patient is so stiff and sedated as to make any type of behavior, disturbed or otherwise, impossible" (Cole, 1960, p. 171).

The ataractic chlorpromazine was first suggested for its antihistaminic and sedative actions. Later, the discovery of its effects on the regulation of body temperature and blood pressure led to its use in surgical procedures. Incidental observations of its effects on behavior finally resulted in its present use as one of the major tranquilizing drugs (Russell, 1960).

Chlorpromazine (Thorazine) is said to possess three major pharmacological properties. In clinical terms, the first and foremost is said to be a capacity to alleviate anxiety, tension, apprehension, and agitation without inducing sleep, clouding "consciousness," or depressing "mental" acuity. A second property is an ability to potentiate central nervous sys-

REFERENCE CHART
Principal Psychopharmological Agents Used in Therapy
(See text.)

Classification	Generic or Chemical Name	Proprietary (Trade) Name (All Registered ®) and Manufacturer
I. *Tranquilizers*		
A. Rauwolfia derivatives	Alseroxylon	Rauwiloid (Riker)
1. Mixed alkaloids	Reserpine	Serpasil (Ciba)
2. Single alkaloids	Rescinnamine	Moderil (Pfizer)
	Deserpidine	Harmonyl (Abbott)
B. Phenothiazine derivatives	Chlorpromazine hydrochloride	Thorazine (Smith, Kline & French)
	Promazine hydrochloride	Sparine (Wyeth)
	Mepazine	Pacatal (Warner-Chilcott)
	Prochlorperazine	Compazine (Smith, Kline & French)
	Perphenazine	Trilafon (Schering)
	Triflupromazine	Vesprin (Squibb)
	Trifluoperazine	Stelazine (Smith, Kline & French)
	Thioridazine	Mellaril (Sandoz)
	Thiopropazate	Dartal (Searle)
	Fluphenazine hydrochloride	Prolixin (Squibb)
C. Diphenylmethane derivatives	Benactyzine	Suavitil (Merck, Sharp & Dohme)
	Hydroxyzine hydrochloride	Atarax (Roerig)
	Azacyclonol hydrochloride	Vistaril (Pfizer)
		Frenquel (Merrell)
D. Propanediol derivatives	Meprobamate	Miltown (Wallace); Equanil (Wyeth)
	Mephenesin	Tolserol (Squibb)
	Mephensin carbamate	Tolseram (Squibb)
	Phenaglycodol	Ultran (Lilly)
E. Gamma amino-butyric acid (GABA) derivatives	Haloperidol	Seranace (Searle)

Classification	Generic or Chemical Name	Proprietary (Trade) Name (All Registered ®) and Manufacturer
II. *Antidepressants*		
A. Dibenzazepine derivatives	Imipramine	Tofranil (Geigy)
B. Monoamine oxidase (MAO) inhibitors	Nialamide	Niamid (Pfizer)
	Iproniazid	Marsilid (Roche)
	Phenelizine	Nardil (Warner)
	Phenoxypropazine	Drazine (Smith, Kline & French)
	Tranylcypromine	Parnate (Smith, Kline & French)
	Isocarboxazid	Marplan (Roche)
C. Amitriptyline hydrochloride derivatives		Tryptizol (Merck, Sharp & Dohme)
		Saroten (Warner)
		Laroxyl (Roche)
III. *Central Nervous System (CNS) Stimulants*		
	Amphetamine sulfate	Edrisal (Smith, Kline & French)
	Dextro-amphetamine sulfate	Dexedrine (Smith, Kline & French)
	Methylamphetamine hydrochloride	Desoxyn (Abbott)
	Methylphenidate hydrochloride	Ritalin Hydrochloride (Ciba)
	Pipradol	Meratran (Merrell)
	Deanol	Deaner (Riker)
IV. *Psychotomimetic (Psychedelic) Drugs* * (see Metzner, 1963)		
A. Phenylethylamine derivatives	Mescaline	
B. Lysergic acid derivatives	Lysergic acid (LSD)	
C. Tryptamine derivatives		
1. Alkyl derivatives	Dimethyltryptamine (DMT)	
	Diethyltryptamine (DET)	
2. Hydroxy derivatives	Bufotenine	
	Psilocybin	
D. Piperidyl benzilate esters	Ditran	
E. Phencyclidine	Sernyl	

* Psychotomimetic drugs are, in the main, limited by federal law to investigational use only and are distributed by the pharmaceutical industry as experimental drugs to qualified researchers.

tem depressants such as anesthetics, narcotics, and sedatives. The third important property is the potent antiemetic effect the drug is said to exert. Descriptions are given in the literature of the use of chlorpromazine in treating anxiety and tension states, senile agitation, somatic conditions complicated by emotional stress, alcoholism, nausea and vomiting, disorders in children, hiccups, psychiatric disorders, and drug addiction (Mendelsohn, 1959; Heilizer, 1959). Descriptions are also given of the use of chlorpromazine in relieving pain in cancer, surgery, and obstetrics. It is said to reduce psychomotor activity and has been used in combating hyperactivity (Heilizer, 1959). The most important use of the drug, of course, has been in controlling psychotic symptoms. Basically, the ataractic drugs are antipsychotic, whereas the so-called emotional tranquilizers are more commonly used in controlling neurotic tension and anxiety.

By and large, professional hospital personnel have great confidence in the therapeutic value of the ataractic drugs. The major difficulty, however, has been that of demonstrating their efficacy in objective research. If either the patient or the investigator believes strongly enough that a drug is beneficial, he is more likely to report the occurrence of desirable effects. To control for the effects of suggestion or bias, one technique has been to administer a placebo [15] to a control group while the test drug is administered to an experimental group. The effects of the test drug may then be compared with the effects of the placebo. In carefully controlled studies, a double- or single-blind design is often used—in which case, neither the patients nor the evaluators are supposed to know who is receiving the test drug and who is receiving a placebo.

A number of studies employing double-blind designs have demonstrated the effectiveness of the major tranquilizers (Feldman, 1956; Hollister, 1956; Shepherd, 1956; Tenenblatt, 1956; Kilgore, 1959; Casey, 1960). Olson and Peterson (1962) administered chlorpromazine in a double-blind study to three groups of chronic schizophrenic patients for one month. The following month, one group received an inert placebo, a second group received no treatment at all, and a third was treated with thioridazine (Mellaril) (see p. 534), an ataractic similar to chlorpromazine. The proportion of patients who showed no behavior change as a result of the change of regimen in the second month was 15 per cent in the no-treatment group, 71 per cent in the inert-placebo group, and 92 per cent in the substitute-tranquilizer group. Thus, it appears that the ataractic

[15] Shapiro (1964), in an extensive review of the literature on the placebo, presents an interesting discussion of factors influencing the placebo effect and their implications for psychotherapy. He defines *placebo* as any therapeutic procedure that is given deliberately to have, or, unknown to the giver, has, an effect on a patient, symptom, syndrome, or disease, but that is objectively without specific activity for the condition being treated.

was somewhat superior to the placebo, but, interestingly enough, the placebo was far superior to no treatment at all.

A number of other studies have employed the discontinuance technique in the evaluation of chlorpromazine and related ataractic agents. In a double-blind study, Good, Sterline, and Holtzman (1958) discontinued chlorpromazine therapy for 112 schizophrenic patients for three months or longer and substituted a placebo. Ratings of behavior in the hospital ward, personality tests, and intellectual tests showed a definite regression in a number of patients when the drug was withdrawn. Diamond and Marks (1960), in a similar study, reported that at three months there was a tendency for the placebo group to show deterioration relative to the medication subjects, but at six months the superiority of the medication group was definite both in terms of psychiatrists' ratings and in terms of ward behavior ratings.

By far the vast majority of reports in the literature on chlorpromazine have not followed control design principles. Bennett (1957) reviewed 962 articles on chlorpromazine that were published between 1952 and 1956. He found that only ten reports described controlled studies. Typically, a single investigator administered a drug to a small group of patients and reported his observations in terms of clinical course, side effects, and percentages of patients who, in his judgment, had improved. It was not at all clear whether the clinical changes reported were attributable to the drug under study, to chance fluctuations, or to some other source such as staff enthusiasm. Control groups, objective measures, statistical tests of probability, and methods for evaluating bias, error, and other sources of variation were used only occasionally.

Rauwolfia Derivatives. The root of the Indian plant *Rauwolfia serpentina* was used for many centuries in that country as a treatment of a wide variety of diseases including such disorders as anxiety states, manic psychosis, and epilepsy. It was not until the last decade, however, that the active agent, a colorless crystalline alkaloid, was chemically isolated from the root in pure form and identified as reserpine. At present, the following alkaloids have been isolated in the pure state and found effective as tranquilizers: deserpidine (Harmonyl), rescinnamine (Moderil), and reserpine (Serpasil).

Pharmacologically, these agents produce symptoms of sympathetic suppression and parasympathetic mobilization and predominance. The major symptoms are miosis (pupillary contraction), bradycardia (slowed heart action), increased secretory and motor activity of the gastrointestinal tract, ptosis, and hypotension. The mechanism of sympathetic suppression is thought to be due to inhibition of certain hypothalamic regions associated with sympathetic functions. Pharmacologically, the rauwolfia derivatives have an effect on the metabolism of serotonin (5-hydroxytryptamine). Initially, it was thought that the behavioral effects of reserpine were dependent on its ability to liberate serotonin. Later, however, it was demonstrated that reserpine also exerts a pronounced effect on the metabolism of other catecholamines (epinephrine and norepinephrine), which, of course, suggests the possibility of additional modes of action [16] (Dews, 1962). At present, there seems to be no generally accepted explanation of the tranquilizing effects of these drugs.

Generally speaking, the clinical effects of the rauwolfia derivatives resemble those of chlorpromazine. Typically, the patient receiving these drugs is lethargic and somnolent. Recent evaluation of the therapeutic effects, in fact, suggests that the mode of action of these drugs may in large measure be that of a "psychopharmacological straitjacket." The apparent results are quite possibly due to the increased somnolence during the hours of the day when the patient would normally be awake.

The most important clinical use of reserpine has been in acute schizophrenia with tension and anxiety or in milder chronic reactions of the restless, combative, hostile, overactive, and threatening patient. It has generally been observed that the improvement in behavior of the overactive and aggressive patient is less marked than that observed after the use of chlorpromazine. Experience has shown that reserpine may have a sedative effect on the irritable, quarrelsome, demanding, or hostile senile patient, and it is generally believed that the use of reserpine will enable many ambulant senile patients who would otherwise require institutional supervision to remain in the care of their families.

Among the common contraindications are symptoms of hypotension or heart disease. These drugs are not usually recommended for patients in poor general health, and they are definitely contraindicated in patients suffering from depression.

The most dangerous complication in the use of reserpine is said to be in the sudden advent of severe depression after several weeks of treatment. Furthermore, the drug has been reputed to produce serious adverse effects on the gastrointestinal tract, such as small gastric erosions or ulcers, sometimes leading to perforation. In higher doses, reserpine has quite often been found to produce epileptic convulsions or a midbrain syndrome manifested as decerebrate rigidity (Cattell and Malitz, 1960).

In the light of present knowledge of the variety of adverse reactions to reserpine, there seems to be a growing reluctance among clinicians to recommend this drug, especially in view of the demonstrated effectiveness of the various phenothiazine derivatives (p. 534). Occasionally, a reserpine preparation is used in combination with chlorpromazine in the treatment of schizophrenia. Many believe at present that there is very

[16] See page 544 for discussion of difficulties encountered in the "plausible explanation" of the mode of action of a drug.

little evidence to commend such a procedure. In general, it appears that the major clinical applications are shifting more and more to the ataractic phenothiazines, with a concomitant decrease in the use of the rauwolfia drugs.

The pharmacological properties and, indeed, the clinical uses of the other phenothiazines (such as those listed under "phenothiazine derivatives" in the reference chart on page 534) are essentially similar to those of chlorpromazine. The general indications for the prescription of these drugs are the same as those for chlorpromazine. They do, however, commonly differ from chlorpromazine and each other in the variety and severity of their toxic properties. In the discussion to follow on these phenothiazine compounds, we will consider only the more widely used drugs, noting where possible the important similarities to, and differences from, chlorpromazine, with respect to clinical application and toxic side effects.

Promazine, sold commercially as Sparine, has been recommended particularly for use in cases of delirium tremens and in the treatment of the senile and arteriosclerotic brain syndromes, since it is claimed to have a less hypotensive effect than chlorpromazine. There is evidence that toxic manifestations such as jaundice and hypoplastic anemia are less likely to occur, but cases of agranulocytosis and convulsive seizures have been reported to have occurred with its use.

Prochlorperazine, known under the trade name "Compazine," is recommended for use in the treatment of various neurotic conditions, for the relief of anxiety. It has a powerful antiemetic action and thus is useful in the control of nausea and vomiting. It also has been administered in the treatment of numerous psychosomatic conditions and is reported to be of quite some value. It is effective at a lower dosage than chlorpromazine and is said to have less sedative effect in therapeutic doses. In larger doses, however, it has been found to give rise to extrapyramidal symptoms more frequently and of greater intensity.

It has been claimed that this drug has led to improvement in schizophrenic patients who have not responded to chlorpromazine. These claims, however, are controversial and the most general application is apparently as yet reserved for the nonpsychotic conditions.

Perphenazine, sold under the trade name "Trilafon," is considered to be more potent weight for weight than Compazine. Its action is claimed to be more rapid than that of chlorpromazine, and therapeutic doses are smaller. The clinical condition for which it is said to be particularly effective is that of emotional tension and agitation. It does not produce as much drowsiness as chlorpromazine, and its general toxic effects are said to be rare in therapeutic doses.

Trifluoperazine, known commercially as "Stelazine," is said to be particularly useful in activation of the chronically apathetic, withdrawn, or depressed schizophrenic, in contrast to chlorpromazine, which often aggravates these types of behaviors. The drug is said to act rapidly in effecting therapeutic results. It does not produce drowsiness, and, in fact, is claimed to exert an "awakening effect." There have been a number of claims that this drug is the most effective of all the ataractic tranquilizers in the treatment of schizophrenia. This contention has not been substantiated, however, and many clinicians still consider chlorpromazine to be the most effective drug for this illness. The major side effect seems to be extrapyramidal symptoms, which are said to be more frequent and pronounced than those produced by the other phenothiazines.

Is is certainly justifiable to say that as yet no final conclusions have been reached regarding the comparative therapeutic values of the various phenothiazine preparations now available. There is a good deal of information relating to their individual specific properties, but studies of their comparative therapeutic values, employing objective measures of clinical change, and methods for evaluating bias, error, and other sources of variation, have been far too few.

Gamma Aminobutyric Acid (GABA) Derivatives. Haloperidol (Serenace) and trifluperidol are two of the more recent additions to the group of ataractic tranquilizer drugs. Their therapeutic properties are broadly similar to those of the ataractic strenothiazine. Their chemical structure, however, is fundamentally different from that of the others of that group and, in fact, is quite similar to that of gamma aminobutyric acid. The therapeutic effects of these compounds are reportedly broadly similar to those of chlorpromazine and other ataractic phenothiazines, and they have been recommended for use in similar conditions.

A study comparing haloperidol and trifluperidol with chlorpromazine, involving a group of hospitalized acute schizophrenic patients, has been reported by Pratt, Bishop, and Gullart (1964). The therapeutic response was evaluated by means of 16 quantitative measures including the Beckomberger Rating Scale, the MACC Behavioral Adjustment Scale, and the Tulane Test Battery. Clinical laboratory data including blood pressure and pulse rate were also recorded for each patient. The investigators reported the mean percentage change in scores from pretreatment to final evaluation on each of the 16 measures for each of the three groups. The main finding was that there were only slight differences between groups for most of the measures. The mean percentage change for the trifluperidol group, however, was greater than for the chlorpromazine group on 13 of 16 measures. Gains for the haloperidol group were greater than for the chlorpromazine group on 11 of 15 measures.

The true value of these drugs as therapeutic agents as yet remains to be determined. The Pratt *et al.* (1964) report suggests that they might at least be as effective as chlorpromazine. Brandrop and Kristjansen (1961) also reported favorable results with haloperidol in a controlled clinical test. The only disadvantage appears to be a relatively higher incidence of extrapyramidal side effects with the GABA derivative than with chlorpromazine. Although these drugs have been subjected to rather extensive clinical trials in this country, the manner in which they act is still unknown. As yet it is not possible to make any reasonable prediction of their therapeutic potentialities.

THE EMOTIONAL TRANQUILIZERS. The term *emotional tranquilizer* refers to any of a group of drugs that, though quite different in chemical structure, are alleged to have in common the ability to diminish emotional tension without concomitant interference with normal conscious processes or motor activity. These drugs are different from sedatives and hypnotics: Sedatives achieve a calming effect but with some clouding or diminution of awareness, whereas hypnotics are used to induce sleep.

Perhaps the most promising emotional tranquilizer is chlordiazepoxide (Librium), the major effects of which are considered to be relief of emotional and muscular tension, anxiety, apprehension, and fear (Jenner *et al.*, 1960). In certain cases, the drug appears to exert anticonvulsant effects. As with all the emotional tranquilizers, the degree of response to chlordiazepoxide varies greatly among users.

Meprobamate (Equanil, Miltown) generally produces effects similar to, but less powerful than, those attributed to chlordiazepoxide. An important factor in choosing between these two drugs is that continued use of meprobamate can lead to addiction, whereas no such addiction has been reported in the use of chlordiazepoxide. Clinical evaluation of meprobamate in a paper by Kleh *et al.* (1959) led to the conclusion that this tranquilizer was effective in anxiety states and musculoskeletal disorders in which spasticity was a predominant feature. In a controlled study by Loranger and Prout (1962), the effects of meprobamate combined with benactyzine (Deprol) on hospitalized patients were judged to be no different than the effects of the central nervous system stimulant Deanol or a placebo. In passing, it seems important to note that the administration of two drugs together, as occurred in this research, makes it impossible to attribute specific effects to either compound, thus frustrating the goal of the drug-evaluation study. Tucker and Wilensky (1957), using a placebo control group, reported significant anxiety and tension reduction in chronic schizophrenics using meprobamate therapy.

Hydroxyzine (Atarax, Vistaril) is another fairly popular tranquilizer, with much the same effects as meprobamate. Methylpentynol (Oblivon) has properties similar to those of Hydroxyzine and meprobamate and, in sufficiently large doses, can be used as a hypnotic. Methylpentynol corbamate (Oblivon C) has the same properties as methylpentynol, but its action lasts longer.

The place of the emotional tranquilizers in the treatment of psychiatric disorders appears secure despite the fact that the therapeutic value of these drugs remains to be convincingly demonstrated in controlled evaluation. It appears that the main indication of therapeutic value of these drugs has been derived from numerous, small, simple case-study reports. The general consensus has been that there is value in the judicious use of emotional tranquilizers, probably for at least three major reasons: (1) Generally, they appear helpful in bringing relief to persons suffering from anxiety and emotional tension. (2) They do not produce as much general sedation as barbiturates and are relatively free of adverse side effects. (3) Addiction is less likely with these drugs than with sedatives or hypnotics. It must be realized that the final general assessment and recognition of the therapeutic value of any drug rest not only on its widespread use but most critically on the basis of carefully controlled evaluation. General experience has shown that original claims nearly always prove to be overly optimistic, and only gradually, as the evidence of controlled studies accumulates, will the therapeutic value of the drug be assessed.

ANTIDEPRESSANT DRUGS. The first drugs discovered to be of some use in the treatment of depression were selective stimulants of the central nervous system (CNS), such as the amphetamine group (represented by Dexedrine). One of the drawbacks with these drugs, however, is their propensity to produce habituation and addiction.

In the past ten years, three different types of drugs that counteract depression have been discovered. These are (1) imipramine, (2) the monoamine oxidase (MAO) inhibitors, and (3) amitripyline. The mechanism of action of these drugs in modifying the depressive state is essentially unknown. One explanation proposed for the pharmacological action of the antidepressants is the elevation of CNS amines resulting from suppression of the action of the enzyme monoamine oxidase (Goldman, 1960). Although the monoamine oxidase inhibiting drugs have been found to exert antidepressant effects in clinical studies, other antidepressant agents such as imipramine (Tofranil) do not inhibit this enzyme. It is possible that these drugs also exert their antidepressant effect through neuramine potentiation at the cerebral level, but through some mechanism other than blocking the metabolic breakdown pathway. Sainz and Bigelow (1962) have studied the relative antidepressant activity of these three chemical groups and have presented some evidence in support of the neuramine-potentiation hypothesis.

The antidepressant agents are generally considered to constitute the method of choice in treatment of depressive reactions. They are prescribed now as the initial form of therapy and are considered preferable to ECT (Goodman, 1960).

One of the most powerful antidepressant agents is imipramine (Tofranil). Blair (1957) first reported its clinical effects. Since then, it has been investigated in a number of closely controlled studies and has gained widespread application in psychiatry (Cole, 1959; Saavedra, 1960; Bertagna, 1959). Moreover, a general consensus seems to be emerging to the effect that imipramine is the most effective drug in the treatment of endogenous depressions. The MAO inhibiting agents, on the other hand, are said to be most effective in the treatment of reactive depressions.

The antidepressant activity of the monoamine oxidase inhibitor iproniazid (Marsilid) was discovered almost by accident (Floody, 1958). The application to psychiatry originated in the clinical observation that iproniazid, then used as an antitubercular agent, seemed to produce in some patients a marked alleviation of depression. When the drug was tried on cases of psychiatric depression, it was found to possess a strong antidepressant action (Goldman, 1960). Its therapeutic potentialities were cut short, however, by the discovery of dangerous side effects. One of the more serious of these, toxic hepatitis, apparently results from the inhibiting action of iproniazid on liver MAO.

In view of these findings, iproniazid was eventually withdrawn from the market. However, the positive findings of antidepressant action stimulated research for a drug with equal or greater antidepressant effect but with fewer and less serious side effects.

Within a few years, a number of MAO inhibitors were developed. Each was claimed originally to have high antidepressant and low toxic effects. The most commonly used drugs in this group have included isocarboxazid (Marplan), nialamide (Niamid), phenelzine (Nardil), and tranylcypromine (Parnate).

In view of an impressive number of clinical reports, it appears that the recently developed MAO inhibitors are generally effective in combating depressions of most categories. There is much controversy, however, over the relative values of different agents, and even over whether these agents are more useful than placebos. A particular area of controversy concerns whether clinical response is related to diagnostic categories. Overall and his associates (1964) have been concerned with the question of the specificity of action of different antidepressant drugs. In comparing the clinical effects of thioridazine, an antipsychotic drug, and imipramine, an antidepressant, they reported essentially no significant differences between the drugs. The study did not confirm the specificity of action normally attributed to antipsychotic and antidepressant drugs. Lauer

(1958) seems to have made the point that the MAO inhibitors are most effective in treating the reactive depressions. Imipramine, as was noted above, is said to be most effective in treating the endogenous depressions (Goldman, 1960). The difficulty here, in large measure, is that of verbally characterizing any emotional state. The absence of unambiguous definitions allows for great variability and ambiguity in classification, which, in turn, are reflected in disagreements in the literature as to the efficacy of various drugs in treating one form of depression as against another. As Dunlop (1964) observed, there are at present 58 classifications of depression, based on a mixture of etiology and symptomatology. We conclude that a refinement in the global concept of depression is clearly indicated, particularly if clinicians are determined to claim specific antidepressant actions for the various drugs.

The widespread acceptance of these drugs is clearly seen by their increased use in psychiatry and the continuing search for still more active compounds. Yet, the final statement on their efficacy is still to be made. It is important to keep in mind the general rule that original claims, based on the clinical trial, are nearly always optimistic. Moreover, side effects not originally obvious may gradually manifest themselves until, with the accumulation of evidence, it becomes clear that they are of critical importance. It is certainly justifiable to say that as yet no final conclusions have been reached regarding the therapeutic value of these drugs. All too often, the final evaluation of a drug involves the discovery of serious side effects.

Amitriptyline is one of the newer drugs to appear on the antidepressant market. Marketed as Elavil, this drug is said to have actions, indications, and side effects similar to those of imipramine (Burt, 1962). It is not a monoamine oxidase inhibitor and is, therefore, thought to act like imipramine, but knowledge of its actions and toxicity is less extensive than with imipramine.

The interesting thing about this drug is that it is said to have the specific potentiality to combat both depression and anxiety and agitation simultaneously (Burt, 1962; Skarbek and Smedberg, 1962). This contention is still open to doubt, however, as far as the majority of cases are concerned. If these initial findings are confirmed in further investigation, there can be no doubt that this drug will come to play an increasingly important role in pharmacotherapy.

The effective chemical treatment of the various depressions has been perhaps one of the major therapeutic developments in psychiatry. Here again, however, as with other direct treatment methods, there seems to be much controversy and confusion over the possible mechanism of action. It seems that this will not be clarified until the etiology of the biochemical and neurobiological reactions underlying these conditions is understood.

CNS STIMULANTS. Central nervous system stimulants are often described as agents that act in a way opposite to that of the tranquilizers. Where the tranquilizers are said to calm and quiet emotional reactions, the stimulants supposedly exert an excitatory effect on the central nervous system including those levels associated with the highest and most complex levels of behavior. Such drugs have also been called "psychic energizers," owing to their reported potentiality to counteract "mental and physical exhaustion." For many years, these drugs were recommended for the treatment of depression. Current clinical usage has tended to restrict the application of these drugs to cases of "simple depression," "mental exhaustion," and "neurasthenia," particularly since the advent of the so-called antidepressant agents.

Two drugs that have been extensively used for their "central stimulant" properties are amphetamine and methamphetamine. World War II stimulated a great deal of interest in the effects of these drugs as agents potentially able either to improve performance on a complex motor task or to prevent the decrement in performance that usually results from fatigue or sleep deprivation. In general, the reports indicate that both drugs are effective in delaying or mitigating fatigue-induced performance decrements, without causing adverse behavioral effects in most subjects (Cuthbertson and Knox, 1947).

The drugs will fortify a subject for a long period of psychomotor effort, but will not improve relative performance levels. Furthermore, it has been reported that a subject under the influence of these stimulants can perform a greater amount of psychomotor work, but the proportionate number of errors does not decrease (Newman, 1947).

Under certain conditions such as prolonged use with sleep deprivation, the amphetamine drugs have been shown to produce rather marked performance decrements in what has been called "behavioral toxicity" (Cole, 1960). The most common side effects are due to the drug's stimulation of the central nervous system. Such symptoms are irritability, tenseness, excitability with tremor, and increased reflexes are frequent examples. In the worst cases, mental confusion, hallucinations, and delirium may occur. If the dose is a large one, the original stimulant effects are usually followed by depressive symptoms and rather pronounced exhaustion. Along with these "central" effects, a number of "peripheral" side effects have been reported, including cardiovascular symptoms, hyperventilation, dryness in mouth, nausea, vomiting, and diarrhea. Another effect of the amphetamine drugs is an anoretic action, because of which the drugs are often specifically used to reduce appetite and control weight.

The drug phenmetrazine (Preludin) resembles amphetamine in its actions but differs from it in being a particularly potent anoretic agent that has less stimulant action on the central nervous system and little effect on the cardiovascular system. The drug is commonly used in weight control, and often misused for its central stimulant properties. Patients taking this drug for weight control have been known to become quite dependent on it as a "morning eye opener."

Phenidylate (Ritalin) is another member of the CNS stimulant group that is said to have behavioral effects resembling those of the amphetamine compounds. The advantage claimed for this compound is the absence of side effects characteristic of the amphetamine derivatives. It is said to exert little action on the appetite, blood pressure, heart rate, or respiration. Clinically, Ritalin is used in treatment of chronic "mental exhaustion," neurasthenia, and simple depression. It is generally believed to be less potent in action than the amphetamine compounds and less liable to cause irritability, restlessness, insomnia, or euphoria. Nevertheless, its effects are thought to be such that prolonged use may produce habituation or even addiction.

The drug deanol (Deaner) is properly placed in a group with amphetamine and phenidylate only in terms of the similarity of the clinical conditions for which it is recommended. Chemically and pharmacologically, it is very different.

Deanol [17] is thought to be a possible precursor of acetylcholine. The role of acetylcholine in the functioning of the central nervous system has not yet been definitely established, but there is a good deal of evidence that, in the periphery (motor end plates and autonomic ganglia), it acts as a chemical mediator in the transmission of the nerve impulse. Pfeiffer (1957) presented evidence to show that cholinergic agents, when given in sufficiently large doses, can produce remissions in schizophrenic patients. Hypotheses were advanced to the effects that a possible reduction of the level of acetylcholine in the brain could be a cause of certain psychotic reactions and that the administration of an agent that the body can readily utilize to make acetylcholine could counteract it.[18]

Deanol is claimed to stimulate the central nervous system including the reticular activating system and, in consequence, to cause improvement in "mood" and remission of depressive behavior patterns. It is said to produce an increase in psychomotor energy and a feeling of well-being and

---

[17] The chemical name of this agent is "diethylaminogthanol"; its generic or approved name is "deanol"; and the proprietary name is "Deaner."

[18] Acetylcholine and choline are both thought to be unable to pass the blood brain barrier. Deanol, however, as a precursor of choline, will pass into the brain. After its administration, the level of acetylcholine in the brain is said to rise.

affability. The amount of sleep required may be reduced, with increased alertness on waking (Pfeiffer, 1957). In addition, it is said to provide an increase in muscular tone. A remarkable feature of its use is that its action is slow in onset and may take as long as three or four weeks to become manifest. Correspondingly, its effects are reported to wear off slowly after the drug is withdrawn. It is claimed to produce neither habituation nor addiction.

Its clinical uses apart from that reported by Pfeiffer (1957) have been mainly in the treatment of chronic fatigue states, mild depression, and migrainous headaches. By and large, its therapeutic potentialities have not as yet been subjected to careful evaluation, and, to be cautious, one must suspect an element of optimism in original claims and preliminary reports. Further experience and clinical trials are necessary before a more complete statement of its therapeutic value can be made.

As a general overview, it can be said that many of the "central" stimulant properties of this group of drugs have been well established. There is no doubt that these drugs, especially the amphetamine derivatives, produce in many people a pronounced feeling of well-being (often amounting to euphoria), alertness, and industry, sometimes involving a capacity for longer hours of work than would otherwise be possible. It has also been established that, after such periods of artificial activation, there occurs a period of inactivation, characterized by lethargy, depression, and general unproductivity. In terms of action and reaction, it might be that every step forward under stimulation requires one marktime step in recovery. The danger of habituation or addiction probably stems in large measure from the fact that withdrawal of the drug after prolonged use commonly leads to depression and exhaustion. By and large, the drugs in this group are considered to have a limited but definite place in the temporary treatment of chronic fatigue states and mild depression.

PSYCHOTOMIMETIC DRUGS. The term *psychotomimetic* refers to the capacity of certain drugs to produce behavioral effects that are alleged to resemble the clinical psychoses. Largely because of this assumption, research interest in such drugs became intense, for it appeared that the experimental creation of a controllable and temporary "model psychosis" would be of great value in yielding information concerning the etiology and treatment of "real" psychotic conditions. More recently, enthusiasm in this respect has cooled, chiefly as a result of the lack of operational, measurable criteria that would delimit the psychotic behavior the effects of these drugs are presumed to imitate (see, for example, Bakker and Amini, 1961).

The list of so-called psychotomimetic drugs is long; perhaps the most widely investigated include mescaline, lysergic acid (LSD), psilocybin, dimethyltryptamine (DMT) and sernyl. Confusion concerning the mechanisms of actions of these drugs, and, indeed, with respect to any sort of adequate demonstration of their effects, is reflected in the wide and varied nomenclature currently in use with respect to these drugs, which includes such terms as *hallucinogen, psychotogen,* and *psychedelic.* The specific effects produced by such compounds are extremely labile, and wide variations are reported both within and between subjects. Effects reported range from feelings of euphoria and religious ecstasy, to varied visual, auditory, and tactile hallucinations, to extreme anxiety, paranoia, and catatonia-like states. It is hypothesized that effects are to a large extent influenced by the subject's expectations, the experimental environment, instructions, "personality structures," and other aspects of "set" and "setting" (Leary *et al.,* 1963).

While, on the surface, it would seem that the use of these psychotomimetic agents as therapeutic tools would be in opposition to their use as producers of disturbed behavior, a rationale suggested for their use in therapy has been that the drugs release deep-lying "unconscious" fantasies and repressed material. Hence, the marked behavioral changes are considered to be, in a sense, cathartic. The brief compass of this chapter does not permit a detailed study of the reported research in the psychotomimetic drugs within a nontherapeutic framework. Review of this may be found in such volumes as Cholden (1956) and Garattini and Ghetti (1957). For our immediate purposes, the applications of these psychotropic agents will be discussed as they have appeared in therapeutic settings.

Almost all the research in this area is similar to four questionnaire studies (Ditman *et al.,* 1962; Sherwood *et al.,* 1962; McGlothlin *et al.,* 1962; and Leary *et al.,* 1963) that present rather comparable results on the use of psilocybin with normal and patient populations. Percentages of subjects reporting lasting benefits or changes were 50 per cent, 85 per cent, 58 per cent, and 62 per cent, respectively, for the four studies. Percentages of subjects reporting a "pleasant" experience were 72 per cent, 85 per cent, 66 per cent, and 70 per cent. Evaluations of the longevity of these and other claims have produced conflicting results. These authors pointed out that their respective studies were reports of *subjective* claims, and they emphasized the need to supplement such data with studies of behavioral indexes.

Lysergic acid has been used in the treatment of alcoholics (Smith, 1958; Chwelos *et al.,* 1959; MacLean, *et al.,* 1961; Jensen, 1962). Patient populations in these four studies varied somewhat, but, typically, only the most difficult cases of chronic alcoholism were selected for study and treatment. Patients were followed up over an average of one year, showing an average of about 50 per cent complete abstinence. Only one study (Jensen) provided a control group of alcoholics not given LSD; his results showed 58 per cent abstinence after one year for the LSD-treated group as compared to 13 per cent for the control group.

Ling and Buckman (1954) reported successful treatment in sixteen selected cases of female frigidity, using LSD and the CNS stimulant Ritalin in combination with psychotherapy. Cohen and Elsner (1959) reported after a follow-up of 6–19 months, on success with 15 of 22 neurotics through the use of LSD as an adjunct to psychotherapy. They tentatively concluded that LSD intensifies the patient-therapist relationship, permits a more direct approach to basic problems, and facilitates the vivid and affect-laden recovery of repressed experiences.

Reported therapeutic effects of LSD–25 were recently summarized by Schmneige (1963) as follows:

Those using LSD in multiple doses as an adjunct to psychotherapy feel that it is so useful because of its ability to do the following: (1) It helps the patient to remember and abreact both recent and childhood traumatic experience. (2) It increases the transference reaction while enabling the patient to discuss it more easily. (3) It activates the patient's unconscious so as to bring forth fantastic and emotional phenomena which may be handled by the therapist as dreams. (4) It intensifies the patient's affectivity so that excessive intellectualization is less likely to occur. (5) It allows that patient to better see his customary defenses and sometimes allows him to alter them. Because of these effects, therapists feel that psychotherapy progresses at a faster rate. . . . Those who administer lysergic acid in a single dose have as their goal, in the words of Sherwood *et al.* (1962) an overwhelming reaction in which an individual comes to experience "himself in a totally new way. . . . Frequently, this is accompanied by a transcendental feeling of being united with the world. . . . Some spectacular, and almost unbelievable, results have been achieved by using one dose of the drug."

In keeping with the last two sentences above, Leary (1964) presented an interesting contribution covering the achievement of revelatory, transcendental, or religious sorts of experiences through the use of LSD, psilocybin, and other psychedelic (consciousness-expanding) substances.

Although the therapeutic possibilities of these compounds are, on the whole, interesting, the compelling fact concerning this whole area of research, as pointed out by Unger (1964), is that not a single methodologically acceptable controlled study of the efficacy of psychedelic agents as adjuncts to psychotherapy has yet been performed. The many claims of dramatic therapeutic changes in such highly treatment-resistant conditions as chronic alcoholism, severe chronic neurosis, and severe personality disorder must thus be regarded as unproved.

The many unknowns regarding such powerful psychotropic drugs as lysergic acid make it extremely critical that considerable caution be used in their research and therapeutic use.

SUMMARY

This consideration of the direct methods of treatment, including the behavior therapies and various physiological methods, has touched on several of the techniques available.

In the section on behavior modification and behavior therapies, the discussions of the relationship of learning theory to psychoanalysis and of the techniques based on classical conditioning and operant conditioning approaches were designed to present a summary of current thinking about behavior modification, including theoretical and practical objections to such techniques.

In the second section, dealing with physiological treatment, four major areas were covered, including shock and convulsive therapies, psychosurgery, miscellaneous physiological methods (such as rhythmic sensory bombardment therapy, anoxic treatment, and ambulatory insulin treatment), and psychopharmacological therapies, the use of drugs in treatment.

Throughout the chapter, the authors have attempted to present a concise description of the background and uses of the various therapeutic methods, along with an evaluation of their effectiveness where possible. There has been a central theme: There is a marked need for carefully controlled evaluation of clinical methods. Almost universally, in evaluating the techniques, it has appeared quite clear that a need exists for a careful description and measurement of the behaviors involved before and after the use of various therapies. It is basic to these methods that there is a need for careful description of base-line behavior, an exact statement of the therapeutic procedure itself, and, finally, a detailed description of the changes presumably brought about by the therapy. It is a failing of almost all the techniques presented that such careful descriptions of pretreatment and posttreatment behavior (as well as an exact analysis of the technique itself) have been weak or, indeed, often lacking.

Another theme that appears throughout the discussion is that of the history of many of the methodologies. We have attempted to describe a "life cycle of a method," which seems to characterize clinical techniques in general. The record usually begins with an enthusiastic array of case studies. These and reports gradually decline, to be replaced by a comparison of the particular method with other methods used. There is later, perhaps, a follow-up of the effectiveness as seen in patients who have been previously treated with the technique. Finally, the literature consists of some consideration of a mode of action, for example, the bio-chemical changes that may be attendant on electroconvulsive therapy. This life cycle of a method points up the perhaps uncritical acceptance of therapeutic technique, based on initial presumed success, which is followed by more sober and conservative analysis. It again illuminates the extremely important need for measurement, description, and careful analysis of therapeutic techniques involved.

The direct methods of treatment involving behavior therapies and the various physiological methods are widely used and continue to be im-portant aspects of the general therapeutic approach to emotional dis-order. Because of their importance, they should be known and studied with the goal of improving their effectiveness.

REFERENCES

ALEXANDER, L. 1953. *Treatment of mental disorder.* Philadelphia: Saunders.

ALLPORT, G. 1937. *Personality: A psychological interpretation.* New York: Holt, Rinehart & Winston.

APPEL, K. E., MYERS, J. M., and SCHEFLEN, D. E. 1953. Prognosis in psy-chiatry: Results of psychiatric treatment. *Amer. med. Assn. Arch. Neurol. Psychiat.,* **70,** 459–68.

AYLLON, T. 1963. Intensive treatment of psychotic behaviour by stimulus satiation and food reinforcement. *Behav. Res. Ther.,* **1,** 53–61.

AYLLON, T., and MICHAEL, J. L. 1959. The psychiatric nurse as a behavioral engineer. *J. exp. Analysis Behav.,* **2,** 323–34.

BACHRACH, A. J. 1962a. An experimental approach to superstitious behavior. *J. Amer. Folklore,* **75,** January–March, 1–9.

BACHRACH, A. J. (ed.). 1962b. *Experimental foundations of clinical psy-chology.* New York: Basic Books.

BACHRACH, A. J. 1963. Operant conditioning and behavior: Some clinical applications. In H. LIEF, V. F. LIEF, and N. R. LIEF (eds.), *The psycho-logical basis of medical practice.* New York: Hoeber.

BACHRACH, A. J. 1965. Some applications of operant conditioning to be-havior therapy. In J. WOLPE, A. SALTER, and L. J. REYNA (eds.), *The con-ditioning therapies.* New York: Holt, Rinehart & Winston. Pp. 62–75.

BACHRACH, A. J., ERWIN, W. J., and MOHR, J. P. 1965. The control of eating behavior in an anorexic by operant conditioning techniques. In L. ULL-MANN and L. KRASNER (eds.), *Case studies in behavior modification.* New York: Holt, Rinehart & Winston. Pp. 153–63.

BAKKER, C. B., and AMINI, F. B. 1961. Observations of the psychotomimetic effects of Sernyl. *Comprehensive Psychiat.,* **2,** 269–80.

BARRETT, B. H. 1962. Reduction of rate in multiple tics by free operant con-ditioning methods. *J. nerv. ment. Dis.,* **135,** 187–95.

BENNETT, I. F. 1957. Chemotherapy in psychiatric hospitals: Critical review of the literature and research trends. In VA DEPARTMENT OF MEDICINE AND SURGERY, *Transactions of 1st Research Conference on Chemotherapy in Psychiatry.* Washington, D.C., 15–20.

BERTAGNA, L. 1959. Chimiothérapie des états dépressifs (Chemotherapy of depressive states). *Cah. Laennec, 19*(2), 27–36.

BIJOU, S., and BAER, D. 1963. Some methodological contributions from a functional analysis of child development. In L. LIPSITT and C. SPIKER (eds.), *Advances in child development and behavior.* New York: Academic Press. Pp. 197–231.

BLAIR, D. 1957. Treatment of severe depression by Imipramine: An investigation of 100 cases. *J. ment. Sci., 106,* 891.

BLAIR, D. 1963. *Modern drugs for the treatment of mental illness.* Springfield, Ill.: Charles C Thomas.

BRANDROP, E., and KRISTJANSEN, P. 1961. A controlled clinical test of Haliperidol. *J. ment. Sci., 107,* 778–82.

BRANNON, E. P., and GRAHAM, W. L. 1955. Intensive insulin shock therapy: A five year survey. *Amer. J. Psychiat., 11,* 659–63.

BREGER, L., and McGAUGH, J. L. 1965. Critique and reformulation of "learning theory" approaches to psychotherapy and neurosis. *Psychological Bull., 63,* 338–58.

BRILL, N. Q., CRUMPTON, E., EIDUSON, S., GRAYSON, H. M., HELLMAN, L. I., RICHARDS, R. A., STRASSMAN, H. D., and UNGER, A. A. 1957. Investigation of the therapeutic components and various factors associated with improvement with electroconvulsive treatment: A preliminary report. *Amer. J. Psychiat., 113,* 997–1008.

BUGELSKI, B. R. 1956. *The psychology of learning.* New York: Holt, Rinehart & Winston.

BURT, C. G., *et al.* 1962. Amitriptyline in depressive states. *J. ment. Sci., 108,* 711.

CAMERON, D. E. 1960. Production of differential amnesia as a factor in the treatment of schizophrenia. *Comprehensive Psychiat., 1,* 26–34.

CASEY, J. F., BENNETT, I. F., LINDLEY, C. J., HOLLISTER, L. E., GORDON, M. H., and SPRINGER, N. N. 1960. Drug therapy in schizophrenia. *Amer. med. Assn Arch. gen. Psychiat.* 2, 210–20.

CATTELL, J. P., and MALITZ, S. 1960. Revised survey of selected psychopharmacological agents. *Amer. J. Psychiat., 117,* 449–55.

CHOLDEN, L. (ed.) 1956. *Lysergic acid diethylamide and mescaline in experimental psychiatry.* New York: Grune & Stratton.

CHOMSKY, N. 1959. Review of B. F. SKINNER, *Verbal behavior. Language, 35,* 36–58.

CHWELOS, N., BLEWETT, D. B., SMITH, C. M., and HOFFER, A. 1959. Use of LSD-25 in the treatment of chronic alcoholism. *Quart. J. Stud. Alcohol, 20,* 577–90.

COHEN, S., and EISNER, B. G. 1959. Use of lysergic acid diethylamide in a psychotherapeutic setting. *Amer. med. Assn Arch. Neurol. Psychiat., 81,* 615–19.

COLE, C. E., PATTERSON, R. M., CRAIG, J. B., THOMAS, W. E., RISTINE, L. P.,

STAHLY, M., and PASSAMANICK, B. 1959. A controlled study of efficacy of oproniazid in treatment of depression. *Amer. med. Assn Arch. gen. Psychiat.*, 1, (November), 513–18.

COLE, J. O. 1960. Behavioral toxicity. In L. UHR and J. G. MILLER (eds.). *Drugs and behavior.* New York: Wiley. Pp. 100–183.

CRUMPTON, E., BRILL, N. Q., EIDUSON, S., and GELLER, E. 1963. The role of fear in electroconvulsive treatment. *J. nerv. ment. Dis.*, 136(1), 29–33.

CUMMING, W. W., and SCHOENFELD, W. N. 1962. Behavior and perception. In S. KOCH, (ed.), *Psychology: A study of a science.* Vol. 5. New York: McGraw-Hill.

CUTHBERTSON, D. P., and KNOX, J. A. 1947. The effects of analeptics on the fatigued subject. *J. Physiol.*, 106, 42–58.

DAX, E. C., and RADLEY SMITH, E. J. 1946. Discussion of prefrontal lobotomy. *Proc. Royal Soc. Med.*, 39, 448.

DEWS, P. B. 1962. Psychopharmacology. In A. J. BACHRACH (ed.), *Experimental foundations of clinical psychology.* New York: Basic Books. Pp. 423–43.

DIAMOND, L. S., and MARKS, J. B. 1960. Discontinuance of tranquilizers among chronic schizophrenic patients receiving maintenance dosage. *J. nerv. ment. Dis.*, 131, 247–51.

DITMAN, K. S., HAYMAN, M., and WHITTLESEY, J. R. B. 1962. Nature and frequency of claims following LSD. *J. nerv. ment. Dis.*, 134, 346–52.

DOLLARD, J., and MILLER, N. E. 1950. *Personality and psychotherapy.* New York: McGraw-Hill.

DOUST, J. W. L., and SCHNEIDER, R. A. 1954. Rhythmic sensory bombardment therapy (R.S.B.T.): A new treatment for patients with psychiatric disorders. *Amer. J. Psychiat.*, 110, 854–55.

DUNLAP, K. 1932. *Habits: Their making and unmaking.* New York: Liveright.

DUNLOP, E. 1964. The choice of antidepressants in various types of depression. *Psychosom. Med.*, 5, 107–10.

EUSEEF, G. S. 1952. Indication for the intravenous injection of insulin in hypoglycemic shock therapy. *Dis. nerv. System*, 16, 10–15.

EYSENCK, H. J. 1959. Learning theory and behaviour therapy. *J. ment. Sci.*, 105–75.

FAZEKAS, J. F., LACY, B. S., WALKER, A. E., and GARVES, N. J. 1956. A controlled blind study of effects of thorazine in psychotic behavior. *Bull. Menninger Clinic*, 20, 25–47.

FERSTER, C. B., and DeMYER, M. K. 1961. The development of performances in autistic children in an automatically controlled environment. *J. chronic Dis.*, 13, 312–45.

FLEMING, T. C. 1956. An inquiry into the mechanism of action of electric shock treatments. *J. nerv. ment. Dis.*, 124, 440–50.

FLOODY, R. J., *et al.* 1958. Marsilid toxicity. *Dig. nerv. ment. Dis.*, 13, 541.

FRANK, J. 1950. Some aspects of lobotomy (prefrontal leucotomy) under psychoanalytic scrutiny. *Psychiatry*, 13, 35.

FREEMAN, W. 1953. Level of achievement after lobotomy. *Amer. J. Psychiat.*, 110, 269–76.

FREEMAN, W. 1958. Prefrontal lobotomy: Final report of 500 Freeman and Watts' patients followed for 10 to 20 years. *Sth. Med. J.*, 51, 739–45.

FREEMAN, W., and WATTS, J. W. 1948. Frontal lobe and consciousness of self. *Psychosom. Med.*, 3, 111–19.

FREEMAN, W., and WATTS, J. W. 1948. Frontal lobe functions as revealed by psychosurgery. *Dig. Neurol. Psychiat.*, 16, 62.

FREEMAN, W., and WILLIAMS, J. M. 1953. Effect of amygdaloidectomy. *Amer. med. Assn Arch. Neurol. Psychiat.*, 70, 630.

GARATTINI, S., and GHETTI, V. (eds.). 1957. *Psychotropic drugs.* Amsterdam: Elsevier.

GEIS, L., STEBBINS, W. C., and LUNDIN, R. W. 1965. *Reflex and operant conditioning, the study of behavior.* Vol. 1, Parts 1 and 2. New York: Appleton-Century-Crofts.

GOLDIAMOND, I. 1962. Perception. In A. J. BACHRACH (ed.), *Experimental foundations of clinical psychology.* New York: Basic Books. Pp. 280–432.

GOLDIAMOND, I., and BACHRACH, A. J. 1963. *Applications of an experimental analysis of behavior to the problem of traffic safety.* Preliminary report to Governor's Committee on Traffic Safety, State of Arizona.

GOLDIAMOND, I., DYRUD, J., and MILLER, M. D. 1965. Practice as research in professional psychology. *Canad. Psychologist*, 110–128.

GOLDMAN, D. 1960. Pharmacological treatment of depression. *Dis. nerv. System Suppl.*, 21, 74.

GORDON, H. L. 1958. *The new chemotherapy of mental illness.* New York: Philosophical Library.

GOUR, K. N., and BHARGAVE, S. P. 1957. Biochemical studies in electric convulsive therapy. *J. ment. Sci.*, 103, 257–69.

GRANTHAM, E. C. 1951. Prefrontal lobotomy for the relief of pain with a report of a new operative technique. *J. Neurosurg.*, 8, 405.

GRANTHAM, E. C., and SPURLING, R. G. 1953. Selective lobotomy in the treatment of intractable pain. *Ann. Surg.*, 137, 602–8.

GREAVES, D. C., REGAN, P. F., and WEST, L. J. 1955. An evaluation of subcoma insulin therapy. *Amer. J. Psychiat.*, 112, 135–39.

GREENBLATT, M., and SOLEMAN, H. C. (eds.). 1953. *Frontal lobes and schizophrenia.* New York: Springer.

GROSSBERG, J. M. 1964. Behavior therapy: A review. *Psychological Bull.*, 62, 73–88.

GUTHRIE, E. R. 1938. *The psychology of human conflict.* New York: Harper & Row.

HEATH, R. G. 1954. *Studies in schizophrenia.* Cambridge, Mass.: Harvard Univer. Press.

HEFFERLINE, R. F. 1962. Learning theory and clinical psychology—an eventual symbiosis? In A. J. BACHRACH (ed.), *Experimental foundations of clinical psychology.* New York: Basic Books. Pp. 97–138.

HEILIZER, F. 1959. The effects of chlorpromazine upon psychomotor and psychiatric behavior of chronic schizophrenic patients. *J. nerv. ment. Dis.*, 128, 358–64.

HEILIZER, F. 1960. A critical review of some published experiments with chlorpromazine in schizophrenic, neurotic, and normal humans. *J. chronic Dis.*, 11, 102–48.

HERRNSTEIN, R. J. 1966. Superstitious behavior: A corollary of operant conditioning principles. In W. K. HONIG (ed.), *Operant behavior.* New York: Appleton-Century-Crofts.

HILGARD, E. R. 1956. *Theories of learning.* (2d ed.) New York: Appleton-Century-Crofts.

HOCH, P. H. 1959. Drug therapy. In S. ARIETI (ed.), *American Handbook of Psychiatry.* New York: Basic Books.

HOFFMAN, H. 1966. The experimental analysis of discriminated avoidance. In W. K. HONIG (ed.), *Operant behavior.* New York: Appleton-Century-Crofts.

HOLLISTER, L. E., TRAUB, L., and BECKMAN, W. G. 1956. Psychiatric use of reserpine and chlorpromazine: Results of double-blind studies. *Psychopharmacology*, 42, 65–74.

HULL, C. L. 1943. *Principles of behavior: An introduction to behavior theory.* New York: Appleton-Century-Crofts.

ISAACS, W., THOMAS, J., and GOLDIAMOND, I. 1960. Application of operant conditioning to reinstate verbal behavior in psychotics. *J. Speech Hearing Disorders*, 25, 8–12.

JACOBSON, E. 1938. *Progressive relaxation.* Chicago: Univer. of Chicago Press.

JENNER, F. A., et al. 1960. Controlled trials on chlordiazepoxide (Librium). *J. ment. Sci.*, 107, 575.

JENSEN, S. E. 1962. A treatment program for alcoholics in a mental hospital. *Quart. J. Stud. Alcohol*, 23, 243–51.

JONES, C. H., SHANKLIN, J. G., DIXON, H. H., BROOKHART, J. M., and BLACHLY, P. H. 1955. Peripheral electrical stimulation, a new form of psychiatric treatment. *Dis. nerv. System*, 16, 323–32.

KELLEHER, R., and GOLLUB, L. 1962. A review of positive conditioned reinforcement. *J. exp. Analysis Behav.*, 5, 543–97.

KELLER, F. S. 1954. *Learning: Reinforcement theory.* New York: Random House.

KELLER, F. S., and SCHOENFELD, W. N. 1950. *Principles of psychology.* New York: Appleton-Century-Crofts.

KILGORE, J. M. 1959. Follow-up evaluation on a controlled, blind study of effects of chlorpromazine on psychotic behavior. *J. clin. exp. Psychopathol.*, 20, 147–61.

KLEH, J., EHRMANTROUT, W., and FAZEKAS, J. F. 1957. The choice of psychotropic drugs in the treatment of neuropsychiatric disorders. In S. GARATTINI and V. GHETTI (eds.), *Psychotropic drugs.* Amsterdam: Elsevier.

KORIN, H., FINK, M., and KWALWASSER, S. 1956. Relation of changes in memory to improvement in electroshock. *Confinia Neurologica*, 16, 88–96.

KRASNER, L. 1962. The therapist as a social reinforcement machine. In H. H. STRUPP and L. LUBORSKY (eds.), *Research in psychotherapy.* Vol. 2. Washington, D.C.: American Psychological Association. Pp. 61–94.

KRASNER, L., and ULLMANN, L. P. (eds.). 1965. *Research in Behavior modification.* New York: Holt, Rinehart & Winston.

KRECH, D. 1951. Cognition and motivation in psychological theory. In W. DENNIS (ed.), *Current trends in psychological theory.* Pittsburgh: Univer. of Pittsburgh Press.

LANG, P. J., and LAZOVIK, A. D. 1963. Experimental desensitization of a phobia. *J. abnorm. soc. Psychol.,* 66, 519–25.

LAUER, J. W., INSKIP, W. M., BERNSOHN, J., and ZELLER, E. A. 1958. Observations on schizophrenic patients after iproniazid and tryptophan. *Amer. med. Assn Arch. Neurol. Psychiat.,* 80, 122–30.

LEARY, T. 1964. The religious experience: Its production and interpretation. *Psychedelic Rev.,* 1, 324.

LEARY, T., LITWIN, G. H., and METZNER, R. 1963. Reactions to psilocybin administered in a supportive environment. *J. nerv. ment. Dis.,* 137, 561–73.

LEIBERMAN, D. M., HOENIG, J., and AUERBACH, I. 1957. The effect of insulin coma and E.C.T. on the three-year prognosis of schizophrenia. *J. Neurol., Neurosurg. Psychiat.,* 20, 108–13.

LIBERSON, W. T. 1953. Current evaluation of electric convulsive therapies. *Res. nerv. ment. Dis.,* 31, 199–231.

LIEF, H. I. 1955. Sensory association in the selection of phobic objects. *Psychiatry,* 18, 331–38.

LINDSLEY, O. R. 1960. Characteristics of the behavior of chronic psychotics as revealed by free-operant conditioning methods. *Dis. nerv. System, Monogr. Suppl.,* 21, 66–78.

LING, T. M., and BUCKMAN, J. 1964. The treatment of frigidity with LSD and ritalin. *Psychedelic Rev.,* 1, 450–58.

LOEVENHART, D. S., LORENZ, W. F., and WATERS, R. M. 1929. Effect of carbon dioxide on psychotic patients. *J. Amer. med. Assn,* 92, 880–83.

LORANGER, A. W., and PROUT, C. T. 1962. A controlled evaluation of deanol and benactyzine-meprobamate. *New England J. Med.,* 266, 1073–78.

McGLOTHLIN, W. M. 1962. *Long lasting effects of LSD on certain attitudes in normals: An experimental proposal.* Rand Corp.

McINTYRE, H. D., MAYFIELD, F. H., and McINTYRE, A. P. 1954. Ventromedial quadrant coagulation in the treatment of psychoses and neuroses. *Amer. J. Psychiat.,* 11, 112–20.

MACLEAN, J. R., MACDONALD, D. C., BYRNE, U. P., and HUBBARD, A. M. 1961. The use of LSD–25 in the treatment of alcoholism and other psychiatric problems. *Quart. J. Stud. Alcohol,* 22, 34–45.

MASSERMAN, J. H. 1954. Experimental approaches to psychodynamic problems. In G. MURPHY and A. J. BACHRACH (eds.), *An outline of abnormal psychology.* New York: Random House. Pp. 435–62.

MASSERMAN, J. H. 1946. *Principles of dynamic psychiatry.* Philadelphia: Saunders.

MEDUNA, L. J. 1950. *Carbon dioxide therapy.* Springfield, Ill.: Charles C Thomas.

MENDELSOHN, R. M., PENMAN, A. S., and SCHIELE, B. C. 1959. Massive chlorpromazine therapy: The nature of behavioral changes. *Psychiatric Quart.*, 33, 55–76.

METZNER, R. 1963. The pharmacology of psychedelic drugs. I. Chemical and biochemical aspects. *Psychedelic Rev.*, 1, 69–115.

MOWRER, O. H. 1950. *Learning theory and personality dynamics.* New York: Ronald.

MUELLER, C. G., JR., and SCHOENFELD, W. N. 1954. Edwin R. Guthrie. In W. K. ESTES *et al., Modern learning theory.* New York: Appleton-Century-Crofts.

NARABAYASHI, H., NAGO, T., SAITO, Y., YOSHIDA, M., and NAGAHATA, M. 1963. Stereotaxic amygdalotomy for behavior disorders. *Arch. Neurol.*, 11–26.

NEMIAH, J. C. 1958. Anorexia nervosa: Fact and theory. *Amer. J. digestive Dis.*, 3, 249–71.

NEMIAH, J. C. 1963. Emotions and gastrointestinal disease. In H. LIEF, V. F. LIEF, and N. R. LIEF (eds.), The psychological basis of medical practice. New York: Hoeber. Pp. 233–44.

NEWMAN, E. 1951. Learning. In H. HELSON (ed.), *Theoretical foundations of psychology.* New York: Van Nostrand. Pp. 390–451.

NEWMAN, H. W. 1947. The effect of amphetamine on performance of normal and fatigued subjects. *J. Pharmacol. exp. Therapeutics*, 89, 106–8.

NOYES, A. P., and KOLB, L. C. 1963. *Modern clinical psychiatry.* Philadelphia: Saunders.

OLSON, G. and PETERSON, D. 1962. Intermittent chemotherapy for chronic psychiatric inpatients. *J. nerv. ment. Dis.*, 134, 145–49.

OVERALL, J. E., HOLLISTER, L. E., MEYER, F., KIMBELL, I., and SHELTON, J. 1964. Imipramine and thioridozine in depressed and schizophrenic patients: Are there specific antidepressant drugs? *J. Amer. med. Assn*, 189, 605–8.

PALMER, D. M., RIEPENHOFF, J. P., and HANAHAN, P. W. 1950. Insulin shock therapy: A statistical survey of 393 cases. *Amer. J. Psychiat.*, 106, 918.

PAUL, N. L., FITZGERALD, E., and GREENBLATT, M. 1956. Five-year follow-up of patients subjected to three different lobotomy procedures. *J. Amer. med. Assn*, 161, 815–19.

PAUL, N. L., FITZGERALD, E., and GREENBLATT, M. 1957. The long term comparative clinical results of three different lobotomy procedures. *Amer. J. Psychiat.*, 113(9), 808–14.

PAUL, N. L., and GREENBLATT, M. 1958. Psychosurgery and schizophrenia. In L. BELLAK (ed.), *Schizophrenia: A review of the syndrome.* New York: Logos Press.

PFEIFFER, C. C. 1957. Stimulant effect of 2-dimethylaminoethanol—possible precursor of brain acetylcholine. *Science*, 126, 610–11.

PHILLIPS, E. L. 1960. Toward an "automatic" child psychologist. *Psychological Rep.*, 6, 384.

POLATIN, P., and WIESEL, B. 1940. Ambulatory insulin treatment of mental disorders. *N.Y. State J. Med.*, **40**, 843.

POOL, J. L. 1951. Psychosurgical procedures. *Dig. Neurol. Psychiat.*, **19**, 3.

PRATT, J. P., BISHOP, M. P., and GALLANT, D. M. 1964. Comparison of haloperidol, trifluperidol, and chlorpromazine in acute schizophrenic patients. *Current Therapeutic Res.*, **6**(9), 526–71.

PRIBRAM, K. H. 1962. The neuropsychology of Sigmund Freud. In A. J. BACHRACH (ed.), *Experimental foundations of clinical psychology.* New York: Basic Books. Pp. 442–70.

REYNA, L. J. 1965. Conditioning therapies, learning theory, and research. In J. WOLPE, A. SALTER, and L. J. REYNA (eds.), *The conditioning therapies.* New York: Holt, Rinehart & Winston. Pp. 169–80.

ROBBIN, A. A. 1958. A controlled study of the effects of leucotomy. *J. Neurol., Neurosurg. Psychiat.*, **21**, 262–69.

ROBBIN, A. A. 1959. The value of leucotomy in relation to diagnosis. *J. Neurol., Neurosurg. Psychiat.*, **22**, 132–36.

RUSSELL, R. W. 1960. Drugs as tools in behavioral research. In L. UHR and J. G. MILLER (eds.), *Drugs and behavior.* New York: Wiley.

SAAVEDRA, A, MARIÁTEGUI, J., and BOGGIANO, L. 1960. La imipramina en los estados depresivos (The use of imipramine in depressive conditions). *Rev. Neuro-Psiquiat., Lima*, **23**, 195–228.

SAIGER, G. L. 1964. The Food and Drug Administration Information Center on Adverse Reactions and Hazards. Paper presented at a Special Conference on Drug Information Services, American Society of Hospital Pharmacists, Lexington, Ky., Feb. 24, 1964.

SAINZ, A., and BIGELOW, N. 1962. Relative antidepressant activity of various chemical groups. *Psychiatric Quart.*, **36**(4), 633–54.

SCHMNEIGE, G. R. 1963. The current status of LSD as a therapeutic tool: A summary of the clinical literature. *J. med. Soc. N.J.*, **60**, 203–7.

SCHOENFELD, W. N. 1950. An experimental approach to anxiety, escape, and avoidance. In P. J. HOCH and J. ZUBIN (eds.), *Anxiety.* New York: Grune & Stratton. Pp. 70–99.

SCOVILLE, W. B., WILK, E., and POPE, A. 1951. Selective cortical undercutting. *Amer. J. Psychiat.*, **107**, 730–38.

SHAPIRO, A. K. 1964. Factors contributing to the placebo effect. *Amer. J. Psychother.*, **18**, 73–88.

SHEPHERD, M., and WATT, D. C. 1956. A controlled clinical study of chlorpromazine and reserpine in chronic schizophrenics. *J. Neurol., Neurosurg., Psychiat.*, 19, 232–35.

SHERWOOD, J. N., STOLAROFF, M. J., and HARMAN, W. W. 1962. The psychedelic experience: A new concept in psychotherapy. *J. Neuropsychiat.*, **3**, 370–75.

SHLIEN, J. 1962. Group discussion: Therapist's contribution. In H. H. STRUPP and L. LUBORSKY (eds.), *Research in psychotherapy.* Vol. 2. Washington, D.C.: American Psychological Association. P. 108.

SIDMAN, M. 1960. *Tactics of scientific research.* New York: Basic Books.

Sidman, M. 1962. Operant techniques. In A. J. Bachrach (ed.), New York: Basic Books. Pp. 170–210.

Sidman, M. 1966. Avoidance behavior. In W. K. Honig (ed.), *Operant behavior*. New York: Appleton-Century-Crofts.

Skarbek, D., and Smedberg, D. 1962. Amitriptyline: A controlled trial in chronic depressive states. *J. ment. Sci.*, 108, 859.

Skinner, B. F. 1953a. *Science and human behavior*. New York: Macmillan.

Skinner, B. F. 1953b. Some contributions of an experimental analysis of behavior to psychology as a whole. *Amer. Psychologist*, 8, 69–78.

Skinner, B. F. 1958. Teaching machines. *Science*, 128, 969–77.

Smith, C. M. 1958. A new adjunct to the treatment of alcoholism: The hallucinogenic drugs. *Quart. J. Stud. Alcohol*, 19, 406–17.

Staats, A. W., and Staats, C. K. 1963. *Complex human behavior*. New York: Holt, Rinehart & Winston.

Tenenblatt, S. S., and Spagno, A. 1956. A controlled study of chlorpromazine therapy in chronic psychotic patients. *J. clin. exp. Psychopath.*, 17, 81–92.

Terzian, H. 1958. Observations on the clinical symptomatology of bilateral, partial or total removal of the temporal lobe in man. In M. Baldwin and P. Bailey (eds.), *Temporal lobe epilepsy*. Springfield, Ill.: Charles C Thomas. Pp. 510–29.

Tucker, K., and Wilensky, H. 1957. A clinical evaluation of meprobamate therapy in a chronic schizophrenic population. *Amer. J. Psychiat.*, 113, 698–703.

Ulett, G. A., Smith, K., and Gleser, G. 1956. Evaluation of convulsive and subconvulsive shock therapies utilizing a control group. *Amer. J. Psychiat.*, 112, 795–802.

Ullmann, L., and Krasner, L. (eds.). 1965. *Case studies in behavior modification*, New York: Holt, Rinehart & Winston.

Unger, S. M. 1964. LSD and psychotherapy: A bibliography of the English-language literature. *Psychedelic Rev.*, 1(4), 442–49.

Verhave, T. (ed.). 1965. *The experimental analysis of behavior: Selected readings*. New York: Appleton-Century-Crofts.

Verhave, T., and Bachrach, A. J. 1964. *Social stimuli and provisional reinforcement*. Technical Report, Contract Nonr 2794(03), Group Psychology Branch, Office of Naval Research, June, 1964.

Wall, J. H. 1959. Diagnosis, treatment and results in anorexia nervosa. *Amer. J. Psychiat.*, 115, 997.

Watson, R. I. 1962. The experimental tradition and clinical psychology. In A. J. Bachrach (ed.), *Experimental foundations of clinical psychology*. New York: Basic Books. Pp. 3–25.

West, F. H., Bond, E. D., Shurley, J. T., and Meyers, C. D. 1955. Insulin coma therapy in schizophrenia. A fourteen-year follow-up study. *Amer. J. Psychiat.*, 11, 583–89.

Wolpe, J. 1950. The genesis of neurosis. *S. African med. J.*, 24, 613–16.

Wolpe, J. 1958. *Psychotherapy by reciprocal inhibition.* Stanford, Calif.: Stanford Univer. Press.

Wolpe, J., Salter, A., and Reyna, L. J. (ed.). 1965. *The conditioning therapies.* New York: Holt, Rinehart & Winston.

Wycis, H. T. 1950. Thalamotomy. *Amer. med. Assn Arch. Neurol. Psychiat.*, 64, 299.

18

Relationship and Client-

centered Therapies

WILLIAM U. SNYDER *

Approaches to psychotherapy that have been the source of widespread interest are the client-centered and relationship therapies. This is a development for which psychologists are largely responsible, and it possesses certain distinct characteristics because of that fact. The focal interest is the feelings of the client himself, rather than the symptoms he relates. One of the outstanding characteristics is an attitude of permissiveness on the part of the therapist.

HISTORY

The historical origins of relationship and client-centered therapy are found in the will therapy of Otto Rank and the relationship therapy of Jessie Taft. Originally a student of Freud, Rank (1945) later differed with him concerning the nature of the therapeutic relationship. He believed that in psychotherapy, as in every other life experience, a conflict exists between the "wills" of the two persons involved. Therefore, it was his opinion that the client should be allowed free opportunity to exert his will in dominating the counselor. Rank was much impressed with the notion of birth trauma, a concept that refers to the emotional pain that separation from the mother is believed to cause the newborn child. He assumed that every life experience duplicates this situation, and that the patient who has not found a successful means of adjusting to this separa-

* William U. Snyder, Ph.D. (The Ohio State University), Professor and Chairman, Director of Clinical Training, Department of Psychology, Ohio University.

tion suffers a neurosis. For Rank, therefore, each therapy situation was an experience in readjusting to the separation from a person who represented the loved parent. Eventually, the ending of treatment was itself thought to have symbolic value for the client as a part of this relationship.

This conception of will therapy was brought to this country by Jessie Taft, a social worker and psychologist, who translated Rank's writings into English. Taft (1933) placed great emphasis on the relationship that exists between the two persons in a therapeutic interview. She believed that this relationship was more important than the decisions or the intellectual explanations of behavior that might be made during therapy. The situation was, therefore, made very permissive, and the client was allowed to express any attitude that he felt.

This point of view spread in this country between 1930 and 1940 so that eventually a number of people were utilizing similar concepts. John Levy's relationship therapy, David Levy's attitude therapy, and Frederick Allen's approach to psychotherapy with children are among the more important examples. Carl Rogers also was influenced by this approach. In 1940, he began to modify this point of view in the direction of an even more permissive relationship. By 1942, his ideas had been sufficiently crystallized to be published in the book entitled *Counseling and Psychotherapy* (1942). These views were developed and elaborated and have been described most adequately in Rogers' book *Client-centered Therapy* (1951).

DESCRIPTION OF THE METHOD

The relationship and client-centered methods developed along an empirical line so that the techniques used appeared before the theoretical explanation of the method. In order to produce a permissive relationship and to avoid directing the interview, the therapist uses both positive and negative principles. Not only does he perform certain functions, he also carefully avoids certain others common to traditional counseling (see Chapter 2). Among the techniques the therapist uses less often are the giving of information, the giving of advice, the use of reassurance and persuasion, the asking of questions, the offering of interpretations, and the giving of criticism. The major activity performed consists of the attempt to help the client recognize or clarify the feelings associated with what he is saying. The following is an example of clarification of feeling:

Client. Everything gets to going so badly that finally you end up by not going to class. You get sort of nonchalant. But you know damn well that you wanta get the work. You're lying to yourself.

Therapist. You want to use some kind of defense when things are going so badly.

Client. Yes. It didn't happen so much this summer.

Therapist. That kind of defeating situation makes you feel that the best thing to do is just to give up and admit defeat.

Client. I want to give up, but there are too many other factors—too many people depending on me. It makes the idea of being alone in the world attractive.

Therapist. You feel you have other people expecting a good bit of you, and it's a disturbing sensation.

Client. Right.

Reassurance and interpretation are used more sparingly in the client-centered techniques, although some variation exists among therapists in this respect. Most of them are inclined to rely on the recognition of feeling as being in itself reassuring. Other reassuring elements of the interview are the therapist's tone of voice, his choice of words, facial expressions of interest, and his general poise and bearing. Occasionally, some therapists may commend the client. Interpretations are somewhat more directive as techniques, since the therapist proposes his ideas of the nature of the client's problem, and so they are used sparingly. An interpretation is best described as any statement that attempts to suggest a motivation of the client. The therapist using relationship methods seeks to avoid saying why the client may have acted as he did, but rather waits until the client himself can give the explanation.

The giving of information is a technique that is traditionally associated with counseling. In the relationship therapies, however, this is less frequently used, because it is considered a counselor's attempt to make the decision as to what behavior is appropriate for the client. When a client seems actually to lack information and expresses a need for it, a therapist may refer him to a convenient source. He usually avoids giving it himself, because to do so has been found to alter the relationship, placing the responsibility for the progress of therapy on the therapist, rather than maintaining it as a joint responsibility. In certain infrequent cases, when the client exhibits strong needs that the therapist give him information, the latter may comply in order to avoid breaking rapport by assuming a negativistic, and thus directive, role.

In addition to the specific techniques indicated, there is another aspect of the treatment, which is not so much a technique as a generalized attitude of therapist acceptance of the client himself. The therapist consistently makes an effort to accept the client, and this is done largely by the process of responding to his feelings. Feelings are responded to and accepted whether they are positive or negative, and whether they involve the client or his associates, particularly when they involve the therapist himself. This attitude of warmth and permissiveness on the part of the therapist gives the client the feeling that he is understood and that he is free to work out his problems in his own way.

As a result of the procedures employed by the therapist, certain client reactions follow. Typically, the first interview is one of catharsis—with the client "pouring out" his problem. Late in the interview, there is almost always a pause when the client either asks or implies the question "What are you going to do about this?" At that point, the therapist structures the situation and gives the client the opportunity of deciding whether he wishes to continue. The client, because the situation tends to place responsibility upon him, makes progress in working out an under- standing of his difficulties and reaches a solution that, for him, is accept- able and effective.

In client-centered therapy, the client's progress usually follows a regular series of steps. At the beginning of the treatment, the client states his problem, generally expressing many negative feelings toward himself or others. He may even express doubt as to his ability to work through the problem. After a considerable amount of negative expression—and this varies among clients—tentative statements of positive attitudes toward the situations that have previously been described in negative terms are hazarded. Meanwhile, there is a growing amount of insight. At first this is not significant, but, as the treatment continues, it deepens and frequently reveals a growth in understanding the dynamics that have influenced the client. At times, this includes insights relating to the client's childhood and reveals a tendency toward a more complete under- standing of his personality. Next, a recognition of the steps that seem necessary to bring about changes in the situation usually develops. Often a retreat or relapse in progress characterizes the client's effort to decide whether or not he wishes to take these steps.

Eventually, in the case making satisfactory progress, the client makes a choice in the direction of acts that will help him to eliminate his problem. These plans he at first tries tentatively, or in a testing mood, but, as he becomes aware of the fact that they are proving satisfactory, he makes rapid and more sweeping revision of his former modes of behavior. The client is then likely to recognize that he is no longer in need of treatment, although it is not unusual for him to wonder whether the improvement will be lasting and want to continue the treatment interviews through an experimental period. Usually, however, the client reaches the conclusion that a real change has taken place and that, although he has not reached the solution to every problem in life, he now feels prepared to approach problems in a different manner and to handle on his own initiative most of them as they arise. Thus, the question as to how long treatment is to last is no problem. It generally lasts until the *client* reaches the stage of feel- ing prepared to proceed without treatment.

There is some variation regarding the frequency of interviews, but in general they tend to take place once or twice a week. This is usually decided at the first interview. It may be modified as treatment proceeds, but always by agreement. The interviews are usually held regularly and follow a systematic schedule. The client's just "dropping in" is not an accepted procedure in this method. Also, clients are discouraged from seeking extra interviews and from telephoning the counselor at his home. These are discouraged because the importance of limiting any human relationship is recognized, and *over*dependence on the part of the client is avoided. There is often an attempt to encourage an affectional relationship with the counselor. The relationship is kept warm and understanding, but it is always a professional relationship. The personality and past activities of the therapist are not usually discussed with the client.

The most frequent length of the interview is 50 minutes. With young clients, the periods are usually shorter. The therapist never permits telephone calls to interrupt the counseling. He carefully keeps the appointment, but, if the client is late, no effort is made to make up the time missed. Lateness on the part of the client is considered to be an indication of resistance to the therapy, unless clear evidence indicates otherwise. In effect, the therapist lets the client know that there are limitations on the demands he is permitted to make, but that, except for certain limitations, the entire period is to be used as he wishes. The therapist also avoids certain techniques used in a more traditional approach, such as using his influence with officials on behalf of the client. It is implicit in the technique that the client receive from the therapist a relationship, but he does not receive assistance in living.

THEORETICAL FOUNDATIONS

Several basic assumptions that underlie the use of this technique were discussed by Rogers and his followers. Rogers stressed the following four: (1) The individual possesses a drive toward growth, health, and adjustment; (2) client-centered therapy stresses the emotional aspects of adjustment rather than the intellectual ones; (3) the method is more concerned with the immediate situation than the emotional situations of childhood; and (4) the treatment relationship is itself a growth experience. The last three are rather descriptions of the technique and would not likely be disputed. The first concept, however, that of the drive toward growth and adjustment, meets with some opposition. Most specialists in psychotherapy agree that a motivation on the part of the client toward cure facilitates treatment. Rogers (1946) stated that the individual has the "capacity and strength to devise *unguided* the steps which will lead him to a more mature and more comfortable relationship to his reality."

Anderson (1946) defended this technique on the theoretical grounds that it "cuts the vicious circle of aggression breeding aggression." He demonstrated experimentally that the responses of many persons in social situations are aggressive ways of meeting aggression, and only when these responses are characterized by understanding, and hence by the integrative function, do they tend to bring about a different attitude in the person.

Another interesting theoretical contribution to the relationship and client-centered approaches is Shaw's (1946) description of the way insight is achieved in a therapy relationship. He defined "insight" as the ability to use symbols formerly unavailable by virtue of repression. When a person disapproves of an idea, this disapproval is a conditioned stimulus to the arousal of anxiety. The person reduces anxiety by repression. If the person is able to symbolize the idea and bring it into consciousness, this process is described as insight. Client-centered therapy brings about insight because it gives considerable opportunity for the client to verbalize and thus to symbolize more adequately the repressed incidents. In many situations, this verbalization is not sufficiently complete to allow the reconditioning to take place. Shaw also pointed out that the verbalization in an acceptance-oriented situation considerably facilitates the reconditioning.

A further development of this idea was proposed by Shoben (1948, 1949), who, in two articles, attempted to explain client-centered therapy in terms of familiar concepts from what is usually called "learning theory." He proposed that psychotherapy occurs through three interrelated processes: (1) reduction of repression and instigation of insight through *symbolic reinstating* of the stimuli for anxiety, (2) reduction of anxiety by *association* of the anxiety-producing stimuli with the comfortable therapeutic *relationship,* and (3) re-education through the therapist's reinforcement of the patient's tentatively formulated new goals and means to goals. Shoben related his theory to Mowrer's two-factor learning theory, in which the learning of "voluntary" responses is affected through the principle of reinforcement, and the learning of involuntary responses is effected through the principle of contiguity.

As thinking about client-centered therapy develops, it becomes apparent that there is a new recognition of the significance of the client's subjective experiences that are inherent in the situation. Rogers' emphasis has shifted toward the more personalistic frame of reference, and especially toward emphasis on the self concept. In his book *Client-centered Therapy,* he advances a theory of personality based on 19 phenomenological propositions, and a theoretical justification of his methods. Several of these propositions, shown below, help to explain quite well the dynamics of a therapeutic relationship.

The organism has one basic tendency and striving—to actualize, maintain, and enhance the experiencing organism.

The best vantage point for understanding behavior is from the internal frame of reference of the individual himself.

Most of the ways of behaving which are adopted by the organism are those which are consistent with the concept of self.

Any experience which is inconsistent with the organization or structure of self may be perceived as a threat, and the more of these perceptions there are, the more rigidly the self-structure is organized to maintain itself.

Under certain conditions, involving primarily complete absence of any threat to the self-structure, experiences which are inconsistent with it may be perceived, and examined, and the structure of self revised to assimilate and include such experiences.

When the individual perceives and accepts into one consistent and integrated system all his sensory and visceral experiences, then he is necessarily more understanding of others and is more accepting of others as separate individuals. [1]

Another theoretical development has been the recognition of the qualities of the relationship itself, and its importance as one of the major factors in effecting the therapeutic change. The present writer has suggested that every therapy situation possesses a number of distinctive qualities or variables,[2] of which seven are at present evident. Each of these variables exists on a quantitative continuum. The following table gives the seven variables, together with their extremes of quantity.

Table 18–1. Variables of the Therapy Interview, and Their Quantitative Extremes

Variable	Range of Extremes
Relationship	Emphatic to distant
Control	Permissive to authoritarian
Behavioral level	Emotional to intellectual
Time orientation	Past to future
Etiological orientation	Dynamic to nosological
Level of expression	Verbal to activity
Dependence *	Supportive to nonsupportive

* This variable almost certainly is not "pure," but rather is dependent on several of the others, particularly on relationship and control.

Snyder proposed that the first two of these variables, or possibly the first three, are especially important. Together with Dr. George T. Lodge, he worked out a diagrammatic method of presenting the probable coac-

[1] Quoted from Carl R. Rogers' *Client-centered Therapy* by permission of the publishers, the Houghton Mifflin Co., Boston.

[2] Simultaneously, but quite independently, Bordin (1948) and Collier (1950) each developed a similar idea.

tion between any two of these variables.[3] Using the first two as an example, a chart can be constructed, as in Fig. 18–1, to show all possible relationships of the two variables, relationship and control, which are represented in the figure by the vertical and horizontal axes, respectively.[4] The extremes of each axis are indicated in the diagram. Considering,

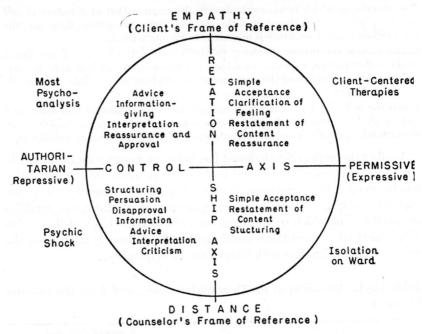

Fig. 18–1. Coaction of relationship and control phenomena in psychotherapy.

then, the midpoint in one of the quadrants, for example, the upper right quadrant, one finds represented a therapy situation that constitutes a maximum amount of empathic relationship with a maximum amount of permissiveness. It becomes apparent that this sounds like a description of good client-centered therapy. Conversely, in the lower left (or "southwest") quadrant, one perceives a situation comprising a maximum of both repressive control and nonempathic relationship. Such a situation might exist, therapeutically, in some of the examples of psychic shock therapy, as described by Fisher (1944) or Rosen (1962). It is also apparent that

[3] Since the development of this scheme, Lodge and Snyder learned of the somewhat similar conception described as "Interpersonal Dimensions of Personality," developed by Freedman, Leary, Ossorio, and Coffey (1951).

[4] It should be pointed out that the two factors are seen from the perspective of the therapist in this coaction compass. A different compass could be constructed showing the factors of relationship and control as perceived from the client's frame of reference.

different techniques, no matter what their therapeutic system, can be classified on the same variables. For example, the giving of advice or the clarification of feeling might vary considerably with regard to the aspects of both control and empathy.

By means of such a diagram, it is possible to approach differences between different therapies from a more adequately descriptive point of view. For example, all of the relationship therapies including psychoanalysis and client-centered therapy cluster at the top of the "Coaction Compass": The similarities among these therapies are greater than their differences.

Perhaps, during the past decade, one of the most important developments has been a return to recognition of the significance of the relationship qualities in the psychotherapy situation. Snyder (1961) devoted a book to a study of this aspect of therapy and, in a recent casebook (1963), further illustrated the importance of the part that the therapist-client relationship plays in therapy. He recognizes as well the part dependence plays in the building of many therapeutic relationships. Snyder also called attention to the important contributions made to the current thinking about therapy by the learning-theory-oriented therapy of Dollard and Miller (1950). In the attempt these two authors made to relate psychoanalysis to the laboratory of experimental psychology, perhaps the most important developments in the theory of psychotherapy have occurred; probably half of the therapists in this country now practice an electic type of therapy, drawing elements from the relationship and client-centered therapies, from the learning-theory approach to the conditioning of behavior, and from the theory and methods of psychoanalysis.

EXPERIMENTAL INVESTIGATION

Many interesting researches have been conducted on the nature and use of relationship techniques in therapy. Rogers (1942) was the first to publish a phonographic transcription of this counseling process. This technique of phonographic recording is now widely used as a scientific tool by psychologists. Covner (1944) investigated the interview process and the methods by which counselors record their interviews as compared to the phonographic transcription just mentioned. A comparison of nondirective and directive counselors' techniques was made by Porter (1943), who found marked differences in the amount of counselor participation in the interviews.

Snyder (1945) extended the program of studying the nondirective process itself by making an analysis of 48 counseling interviews, 30 of which were phonographically recorded. He showed that *clarification* of the client's *feeling* comprised about half of the counselor's activity.

Simply accepting what the client said comprised 30 per cent. *Structuring*, or telling the client what to expect from the treatment process, and the use of *approval* and *encouragement* comprised most of the remaining 12 per cent. Little use was made of persuasion, disapproval or criticism, interpretation, or the giving of information. With regard to this analysis in relation to the client, one-third of his statements were descriptions of his problem; understanding or insight was low at the beginning of treatment, but, in the last phases, 30 per cent of the statements were insightful. Discussion of plans for the future, initially nonexistent, increased to 12 per cent during the latter part of treatment. Several years later, Seeman (1946) replicated this study on subjects who had been counseled at Chicago at a more recent time, and found an even stronger client-centered tendency existing then.

A group of studies by the Psychotherapy Research Group at the Pennsylvania State University (1953) included some contributions to the "process" type of studies. The group added refinements to the coding categories. To Snyder's original "Clarification of Feeling," they added the variant "Clarification of Unverbalized Feeling." The Group also added five subdivisions to the classification "Client's Statement of Problem." These were "Symptomatic Statements," "Explanatory Statements," "Historical Statements," "Anticipatory Statements," and "Statements of Relief from the Problem."

Another contribution of the Penn State Group to the process type of study was Gillespie's (1951) system of classifying resistance. He identified and validated 13 different classifications of resistance, grouped under three headings: (1) "Resistance to the Therapist," (2) "Resistance to the Therapeutic Process," and (3) "Resistance Within the Client."

A significant development in the classifying of content of the therapeutic interview was the contribution by students of Bordin (Rausch *et al.*, 1956) of differentiating nine different levels, or "depths," of interpretation, of which the deeper six were new concepts, ranging from simply connecting two aspects of the contents of previous client statements, to dealing with inferences about material completely removed from the client's awareness. This method of classifying interpretations has enjoyed rather widespread use. Perhaps the most distinctive innovation in the analysis of *client* content in the therapy interaction was the classification scheme constructed by Dollard and Auld (1959), who, following a lead of E. J. Murray (1956), developed H. A. Murray's system of needs and "presses" into a very effective scoring system for the material the client brings to the interview. Earlier schemata for similar sorts of classifications were the Distress Relief Quotient (DRQ), of Dollard and Mowrer (1947), and the self reference analysis (PNAvQ), of Raimy (1948). A modification of several of these systems, with distinct innovations, was developed by Strupp (1957), who made classifications of the type of therapeutic activity, depth-direct-edness, dynamic focus, initiative, and therapeutic climate. Strupp's scheme sharpened most of the earlier systems a bit, placing their cate-gories in somewhat more logical order and giving clearer definitions of focal points on different continua of measurements, although most of the concepts employed had already been developed by the earlier investi-gators.

COMPARISON OF RELATIONSHIP AND CLIENT-CENTERED METHODS WITH OTHER THERAPIES

One of the early comparisons of client-centered and other therapies occurs in studies by Fiedler (1950). He employed the "Q" technique to compare counselors' opinions regarding the characteristics of good and poor therapy, and found that there was more agreement among experi-enced counselors of several different systematic orientations than there was between experienced and inexperienced counselors of the same sys-tem. In fact, he found that even laymen can describe the ideal thera-peutic relationship in terms similar to those of the experts. He also demonstrated that some of the Adlerians and analysts place themselves in a more tutorial, authoritarian role, as contrasted with the opposite reac-tion of the client-centered therapists. These analyses of Fiedler, were, of course, based on *attitudes about* good therapy rather than on the actual therapeutic practice itself.

Perhaps the person who has done the most work on comparing dif-ferent methods of therapy is Strupp (1960), who summarized a decade of work in his book *Psychotherapists in Action*. In several different projects, Strupp compared the responses given by differing "schools" of therapists to filmed presentations of therapeutic interviews. He was par-ticularly interested in comparing the client-centered with the psycho-analytic therapies. He also compared the behavior of more experienced with that of less experienced therapists. There were very marked dif-ferences between analysts and Rogerian therapists, and between psy-chiatrists and psychologists. (These two dichotomies tended to parallel each other.) Strupp felt that more experienced, more directive, more diagnostically oriented, and "warmer" therapists, who preferred working with neurotic, rather than with more deeply disturbed, clients, also tended to produce more therapeutic results with their clients. Here, the relationship aspects of therapy would seem to be favored, whereas the client-directing sorts of activities seemed less effective, in Strupp's opinion. Unfortunately, the study did not analyze actual responses in therapy, but only reported probable responses in a therapy-like situation.

Experimental Evaluation of Client-centered Therapy. An outstanding evaluation of the nondirective technique is a study by Muench (1947). Twelve clients were treated nondirectly after having been given three personality tests—the *Rorschach,* the *Kent-Rosanoff Free Association Test,* and the *Bell Adjustment Inventory.* After treatment, the clients were re-tested. The results showed statistically significant improvement in the Rorschach scores for 11 of the 12 cases, in the Kent-Rosanoff scores for 9 of them, and in the Bell Adjustment scores for 7 clients. The cases showing the greatest improvement on the basis of psychological test indexes were those the therapists also considered successful. Although Muench did not have a control group for his study, a very satisfactory control study was made by Hamlin and Albee (1948).

Haimowitz (1948) conducted a much more elaborate study along lines similar to Muench's, but with 56 clients and a control group. Also, elaborate procedures of retesting were utilized. Her results strongly confirm Muench's. Mozak (1950) attempted a similar study but used two different tests in addition to the *Rorschach, Bell,* and *Kent-Rosanoff.* These were the *Minnesota Multiphasic Personality Inventory* and the *Hildreth Feeling-Attitude Scale.* Cowan (1950) used the *Bernreuter Personality Inventory.* All three of these measures showed positive changes in personality variables in the experimental, or counseled, group. It seems, therefore, that client-centered therapy is generally being shown to effect personality changes.

An attempt to develop a multiple criterion of a successful outcome of therapy was a significant contribution from the Penn State studies in client-centered therapy. The criterion was made up of a client's rating scale filled out at the conclusion of therapy, a counselor's rating scale filled out by both the counselor and an independent judge who had read the entire case, and a ratio between the positive and negative feelings found in the first and last interviews. Tucker (1952) describes these criteria more fully.

A different sort of evaluation study is that of Thetford (1949), who analyzed changes in physiological functioning after therapy. Subjects who underwent therapeutic sessions showed more rapid recovery than control subjects on several measures of physiological changes after an experimentally induced frustration. These changes were based on galvanic skin response and variations in heart rate.

A very elaborate series of evaluative studies was carried out at the University of Chicago under the direction of Rogers (Rogers and Dymond, 1954). In this situation, a block of integrated studies was developed on the tape-recorded therapy interviews of 29 clients, conducted by 16 staff members. Many pre- and post-therapy measurements and tests were employed, and an effort was made to control numerous variables by the use of control waiting periods and special control groups. In a lengthy discussion of results, Rogers and Dymond reported significant changes in self concept, in ability of clients to relate to others in their environment, in personality and integration, in attitudes toward others, and in general behavioral approaches to life situations. Youthfulness, sex (female), duration of therapy, immediacy of beginning therapy when requested, and high motivation for therapy all seemed to be factors relating to more successful outcome of the therapy. This block of studies is one of the most definitive ever produced by *any* school of therapy; it is impossible to summarize here all of its significant findings relating to the nature of client-centered therapy and the factors which bring about successful therapeutic change. It should be studied by all serious practitioners of psychotherapy.

Another rather elaborate study of outcome was reported by Snyder (1961), who analyzed the tape-recorded interviews of 20 of his own clients. All of these clients had been given several personality tests, and also had taken a specially developed measure of client affect toward the therapist after each of their interviews; the therapist had similarly taken the same affect test, as he felt the client might have filled it out on the same day, and had also, after each interview, taken another test measuring the therapist's affect toward the client. Several other ratings and rankings were also employed to measure the relationship between therapist and client in more than 500 interviews. The most striking findings of this study were the marked reciprocity between client's and therapist's affects, and the fact that clients with attitudes and values similar to those of the therapist tended to develop a better mutual relationship with the therapist, and their therapy also seemed to be considerably more successful, as measured against seven different criteria of goodness of therapy outcome.

RANGE OF APPLICATION

Evidence is now being accumulated as to the appropriate use of the relationship and client-centered methods. Their most obvious area of applicability has been with college students. These clients usually meet the prerequisites for effective therapy, that is, adequate intelligence, emotional freedom from family, sufficient maturity without too much rigidity of personality, freedom from excessive environmental limitations, and, in most cases, a desire for help. Because the problems of college students usually lie within their own personalities, the technique is especially effective with them. Relationship therapies seem also to have a useful role in the counseling of marital adjustment problems, because most of these are the product of emotional immaturity. The method has frequent applicability to the area of vocational counseling. When the vocational problem consists largely of emotional difficulties associated with making a job choice, this method is quite successful. Another area in which it has been used successfully is in counseling on parent-child problems. Here, therapy with the parent is frequently combined with the use of play therapy with the child.

The relationship method has wide application to the treatment of the emotional problems of normal persons and of the mildly psychoneurotic. Anxiety states and hysterical symptoms have responded quite satisfactorily. It has been used less frequently with psychotics. The method has not been as successful with persons of low intelligence; actually, most of the more successful published cases have been those of persons of better than average intelligence. Advanced age also seems to be a contraindication for the usefulness of this technique. It is seldom used with clients over fifty, although certainly variations in personal flexibility exist. A certain degree of ability to verbalize is desirable, and people so emotionally disturbed that they find this difficult do not respond well to the technique. Finally, the *excessively* dependent person makes poor use of the method. While this is not invariably true, and while a skilled therapist can do much to reduce dependence, it is still apparent that the client who is willing to take on the management of his own life makes a better subject than the one who wishes to maintain an immaturity based on dependence.

Thus far, the discussion in this chapter has been descriptive, theoretical, and investigatory in nature. Believing that most readers will find an illustration of the method interesting, the author will devote the next section of this chapter to a recorded excerpt from a case of relationship therapy. Because the limitation of space prevents recounting the entire treatment process, only a small part of the treatment has been included here. If the reader is interested in further study of client-centered or relationship therapies, he should consult Rogers' *Client-centered Therapy* (1951), or he may be interested in the book *Dependency in Psychotherapy* by the writer (1963).

A CASE ILLUSTRATING RELATIONSHIP THERAPY

The Case of Calvin Kennedy [5]

Calvin Kennedy was a thirty-seven-year-old assistant professor of art in a large university. He was married, with four children, a son and daughter in junior high school and two much younger sons. He held a Ph.D. degree and was considered to be a good teacher and a rather talented artist. He got along well with his colleagues, except for his dean, who disapproved of his work and considered him lacking in creativity and rebellious toward authority. Dr. Kennedy usually took the leadership in opposing the dean, who was considered

[5] Written permission to quote from, and to report on, this case has been obtained from the client and from the therapist, William U. Snyder. Names and places have been altered for obvious reasons.

ultraconservative by the members of the art department. Dr. Kennedy resented the fact that the department chairman allowed him to assume leadership in this regard and thus incur the brunt of the dean's wrath.

The principal reasons Dr. Kennedy gave for requesting therapy were a number of psychosomatic complaints, of which claustrophobia, diarrhea, and heart palpitations were the most frequent. He often found himself having to leave large groups of people because he felt panic in their presence; however, he had taken many physical examinations including several in metropolitan medical centers and had always been told that he was in excellent physical condition. Dr. Kennedy also felt dissatisfied with his professional progress and feared that he would never receive a promotion, because of his friction with the dean. After several interviews, he also mentioned another "problem"; he engaged regularly in extramarital sexual relations, although he insisted that he was deeply fond of his wife. These relationships were fairly easily effected, owing to the fact that Dr. Kennedy spent most of his afternoons and evenings at the studio, which was located on the campus, and not at home. He also taught several out-of-town extension courses, which provided him with additional opportunities for clandestine assignations.

The client was given the Minnesota Multiphasic Personality Inventory (MMPI) and the Edwards Personal Preference Schedule (EPPS) at the beginning of therapy, and the latter test was repeated after every fifth interview. He also took Snyder's *Client Affect Scale* after every interview, and the therapist likewise took Snyder's *Therapist Affect Scale* after every interview. Scores obtained on these tests were as follows (high scores are starred):

MMPI T-scores		EPPS Need (T-score)	First Test	Last Test		Client Affect	Dependency	Therapist Affect
L-score (lie)	30	Achievement	56	56	(1)	48	17	23
F (validity)	55	Deference	38	52	(2)	30	20	44
K (plus-getting)	60	Orderliness	38	63*	(3)	69	12	63
Hypochondriasis	72*	Exhibition	66*	57	(4)	59	15	56
Depression	60	Autonomy	60*	58*	(5)	54	10	54
Hysteria	72*	Affiliation	48	48	(6)	55	19	47
Sociopathic	73*	Introception	44	57	(7)	86	13	61
Sex inversion	73*	Succorance	51	53	(8)	64	20	55
Paranoia	56	Dominance	55	59*	(9)	39	10	49
Psychasthenia	64	Abasement	33	25	(10)	73	13	74
Schizophrenia	60	Nurturance	56	48	(11)	60	12	71
Hypomania	78*	Change	55	49	(12)	47	11	59
		Endurance	51	36	(13)	77	17	47
		Heterosex.	58*	58*	(14)	35	6	44
		Aggression	42	35	(15)	omitted	–	56
		Consistency	47	42	(16)	omitted	–	31
					(17)	49	17	−15
					(18)	73	9	28
					(19)	75	12	−15
					(20)	74	14	51
					(21)	71	11	43
					(22)	73	14	40
					(23)	omitted	–	15

* High score.

The MMPI scores reveal a tendency toward hysteria or hypochondriasis, and a marked drive, or "push," such as might be found in a professionally or socially ambitious person. The elevated sociopathic and sexual inversion scores could be explained as being typical of persons with an advanced educational status, but they might also reveal some independence from social norms, and some problems with sexual identity. Thus, sexual problems and those in the area of aggression and passivity seem to be in evidence.

The EPPS scores suggest some preoccupation with needs in the areas of narcissism, sexuality, and self-directedness. After therapy, there were signs of problems in the area of needs to be dominant and orderly.

In terms of his test scores, there appeared to be a fairly high amount of mutual positive affect between Dr. Kennedy and the therapist. The client did not reveal an excessive amount of dependence in the test scores.

Progress in the therapeutic interviews is reported in the therapist's case notes, which are summarized below. Verbatim excerpts from the tenth interview are also given.

First and Second Interviews, September 25 and October 2

A general review of the problems, indicating symptoms of a typical anxiety neurosis with pronounced hypochondriacal reactions, marked achievement drive, and much evidence of social mobility striving. Although bored with teaching, the client revealed a compulsion to work hard, but wonders, "How much is *enough* work?" He particularly likes the creative and original aspects of his profession.

Third Interview, October 9

The client asked for reassurance that the therapy would do him some good. He discussed his intolerance of sickness, and his irritation with himself for having physical problems (not yet admitted as psychosomatic). After some interpretations of this matter by the therapist, he indicated his concern about being sufficiently masculine, and his attempts to appear strong and rugged. He then mentioned, for the first time, his extramarital behavior and his rather constant search for a more active sexual partner than he has previously encountered. The discussion then shifted to his need to attack father figures, particularly his dean. He described his own father as being rather brutal in his treatment toward the client; he, in turn, pushes his oldest son, a rather passive boy, to become more aggressive in his relationships with others.

Fourth Interview, October 16

The client reported a marked amount of euphoria after the last interview. Some of the sexual material was reviewed, and the therapist made a highly generalized reference to the possible relationship between promiscuity, excessively masculine behavior, and the fear of castration. This led the client to a discussion of the play "Tea and Sympathy," which he had recently seen and which caused him a great deal of anxiety. He mentioned his belief that his genitals were unusually small, but the therapist challenged this and said such beliefs were very common and frequently were a sign of fears of sexual inadequacy. The client readily accepted this interpretation as being very applicable to himself. At the end of the interview, the therapist cautioned the client that he would probably experience some anxiety after this interview.

FIFTH AND SIX INTERVIEWS, NOVEMBER 2 AND NOVEMBER 6

The client had requested his MMPI and EPPS scores, and these were sent to him the day before the next regular interview. However, that same day he called to cancel his appointment because of a special out-of-town trip and to schedule two subsequent appointments before another trip. In the fifth interview, he mentioned some anxiety he had experienced because of the evidence of psychosomatic problems revealed on the MMPI. The rest of the two interviews was spent in reporting sexual difficulties with his wife, who he said was too passive in the sexual relationship, although otherwise a very fine wife. Although he felt he could never divorce his wife, he did enjoy his extramarital affairs, and, perhaps even more, he enjoyed a continuous fantasy he had about a brief affair he had experienced with a girl in Italy almost twenty years ago. She still represented his sexual ideal; she was very aggressive about sex and did most of the seducing, which he enjoyed. There was also some discussion of his general feelings of inadequacy and insecurity.

SEVENTH INTERVIEW, NOVEMBER 20

Dr. Kennedy had arrived at a new understanding of his wife's inability to praise him very much. The therapist connected this with her inability to take an active part in the sexual relationship, and perhaps to their early marriage relationship, and to her middle-class background. The client discussed his lower-class background and rather marked early poverty and mentioned that, because of the crowded living conditions, he had shared a bedroom with his grandmother until he was seventeen years old. She had been excessively fond of him and oversolicitous, in contrast to his parents, who had been preoccupied with their work and homemaking and had ignored him. He reported no sense of discomfort when he was around women, but said all of his anxieties occurred in the presence of men, and these were particularly acute in situations where there was any degree of physical intimacy, as in sports or at stag parties.

EIGHTH INTERVIEW, NOVEMBER 27

Most of the discussion centered around whether or not to give up promiscuous sex; the client thinks he should but doesn't want to, and believes he can continue it without spoiling his marriage. He asked the therapist to decide whether he should give up this behavior, but the therapist refused. Dr. Kennedy requested an opinion as to the maturity of this behavior, but the therapist would not give one and asked for his, in turn. The client stated his belief that conformity is not necessarily a sign of maturity. The therapist asked him about the interrelationship between personal integration and social integration. The client grew quite resistant to discussion of this topic, and the resistance was interpreted. He then indicated that he was planning to start a new affair but did not like the fact that he would have to deceive his wife again. He switched the discussion to the topics of his annoyance with his sister's constant complaints of sickness and with his mother's lameness and of his consequent rejection of his mother. His need for perfection in his own body image was interpreted to him. This led to a discussion of his dislike of his own dependence feelings, and those of other persons directed toward himself.

Ninth Interview, December 4

Repression of anger was discussed, and Dr. Kennedy indicated that he had recently allowed himself to express anger toward a student, and had felt very good about his freedom to do so. The therapist mentioned the psychological concept of displacement, and the client recounted numerous instances of his displacing hostility and aggression onto his children, particularly his oldest son, who irritates him because he seems to be lacking in masculinity. The interview was slow, and the therapist described the phenomenon of resistance.

Tenth Interview, December 11
(Quoted in slightly condensed verbatim form;
last fourth is fully condensed.)

C. As I remember, we were talking about my relationships with my family — my immediate family — and my feelings about this. (Pause) It's quite hard for me to get into this, in a sense. (Resistance) I don't know quite where to start. I think I have pretty deep feelings of loyalty to the family, and this feeling of loyalty is linked with feelings of dissatisfaction over being married. (Conflict) Maybe it would help if I went back and tried to tell you a little about how I happened to meet my wife and how I got into the arrangement. I had not gone steady with very many girls. In high school, I met a girl and went with her for a long period of time. I went steady for about three years. It was a very stormy adolescent type of thing where we were constantly arguing about things like religion and—I was [working evenings] and couldn't take her dancing—and we were storming all the time. And, while I was going with her, I started going with another girl for a very short period of time — going with the two at once (slightly deprecating laugh), and this girl had a very tragic time after I left her, and while I was going with her I liked her very much but I always felt kind of odd because she was not at all warm or emotional in any sense, so I stopped going with her. And about this time I went to college, and I dated quite a bit the first year. And I was working the physical side of the street pretty hard in the first year, and kids got kind of sore at me. I was a little bit older because I had worked before I went to college, and the girls, particularly, started to gang up when they found out what was happening. A lot of the kids wouldn't even talk to me. It was a very difficult sort of thing. So I went to one of the psychology professors. He gave me some pretty good advice, I thought. He, his first reaction was, "Oh, let this thing blow over. It's not going to be something that will keep up." So we waited awhile, and it didn't blow over. It got worse. Then I went back and talked again, and he suggested that maybe if I would find some girl who was above reproach in the minds of all these other folks, that if I went with her and dated her for a long enough period of time that this would blow over, and this would be a good way to do it. So, I, I — this was rather difficult because I could hardly get a girl to talk to me, let alone date me, and so my wife came into the picture. She was in a math class with me, and so I called her up one night and made a contact this way, and we started working together, and I started dating her fairly frequently on weekends and Friday nights whenever I could and — well — we just kind of stayed together. We were in college together, dating and engaged over about a three-year period. And I went into service — and we were married before I went into service. And she still finished at school. And this was the kind of a basis on which we met, actually. And I always worried — I think always in the back of my mind is the basis on which we met. It's always been a kind of a sore spot. Really, the period of my needing to go with her was quite short-lived. I could have stopped going with her — had just a temporary thing — but I chose to keep on with her because I liked to be with her, but this was always in the back of my mind as an element in our meeting — that I didn't care for her. We were married, as I said, and I went into service, and she finished out her year. We had about a month together before I went overseas. Then I had a little over a year overseas. And then we came back, and we were together for the remainder of the war. We were all through the Midwest and the Southwest.

In the interim, when I came back from overseas, I've told you about the adjustment — it was difficult to make. The fact that we had a youngster — we had a very stormy time. I was in the Army, when the baby was small, and we were living in two rooms, which I had built myself out of an old filthy hut. There just wasn't room enough to move around, and I was feeling a lot of pressure from what had happened overseas. We lived in this thing, and her reaction was to turn to the boy, very strongly. She would, at his slightest whim, respond. This, coupled with my own feelings of being trapped in the marriage, just kind of made it rough for me. This kind of antagonistic feeling carried on for a long time until we had a blowup and the whole thing kind of smoothed out. And from that time on it's been rather positive. In that period, from the time that I came back from overseas until the time that we had the so-called blowup, there was a lot of friction, a lot of bickering, but it never really came out in quarrels and that sort of thing. It came out mostly in me, rather than in her. In me it was a matter of being irritated, that is, speaking harshly at everything and nothing, taking off and not coming back at night, going up to the studio and working long hours and finding excuses for not going home, eating alone a lot. In her, the reaction was one of drawing closer to the kids and being very hurt but not showing it. Then, since that point — well, then, right after coming out of the war, we went to live with her parents while I was finishing school, and her mother is very moralistic about things, and her mother and father always have been very close, living on a farm, and I used to take off nights. I'd just take off nights and go off by myself and listen to band music and come home late at night. And she was under a lot of pressure from her mother about why did I do this, and she was pretty hurt until the point when we had this clearing of the air, and, since that time, I think, things have been considerably better. There is a great deal better understanding, although I still have feelings of being trapped and wishing I weren't married at times. But I can't say really that they are deep-seated feelings, the kind that would get me into trouble. I don't know. They would have, had they continued to be the same kind of feelings I had had up to the time that our girl was born. Since then, they haven't been as strong, but there is still that little gnawing feeling every once in a while.

T. Why do you think that made a difference? Her birth?

C. I don't think it was her birth, as such, that made a difference, though it may well have been. I reached the point where I probably made a decision that something had to be done. And, when my wife went home to her mother for a period of time, a couple of weeks while she was carrying the baby, I had a girl come in and do the housework. We had people living upstairs, and we were living downstairs. And I took this girl everywhere with me, and we went swimming in the nude at a public beach at night, and I knew what would happen, and I wasn't even interested in this girl particularly. ("Acting out") It was a kind of final resentment against the whole thing, as I picture it now. And, when my wife came back, rather than trying to carry on this farce of what I was doing with this girl, I just told her all of the problems that I felt—the physical and emotional side of things—and we had a rather stormy period, and then the baby was born, and things have been better ever since then, I think, and I attribute it to getting it out in the open. It may also be that, now that she had a second child, that there was not so much attention on her part toward the boy, though she's the kind of mother that would be like this. The youngsters wouldn't have to be in difficulty at all, but just turn over in bed, and she would be up and out of her own bed and over straightening the covers. In other words, she'd carry this love and affection thing to the extreme. The point is, even now, and this irritates me a little bit, the youngsters can want anything – in other words, they can get away with murder. I think I'm disturbed at this because I see it's not good for them. But I think I could also recognize that there's a little bit of jealousy on my part. (Insight)

T. It bothers you that she's that overprotecting of them, but it also bothers you a little bit that she's not that protective to you. (Clarification)

C. Um hmm. Yeah. I think this enters into the picture. She doesn't see me as having that kind of need. In fact, she expects male *children* to supply that kind of affection for her (said with a certain hard quality in the voice), and it's not really a good reciprocal kind of thing. It isn't that we share each other in that sense.

T. Um hm.

C. She's tremendous in emergencies. She's a very level kind of a person, very even, doesn't easily get upset. She's a perfect nurse; you would get a lot of attention by being ill. There could be a relationship here, couldn't there, between —

T. Your somatic problems, and that fact?

C. Yeah. I don't know, but it's really not out of the realm of possibility though. (Insight)

T. She doesn't meet any need of yours for dependency, or protection, and she doesn't act like a mother toward you in any sense. She expects you, as a matter of fact, to be protective toward her. (Interpretation)

C. Yeah. This — when we were first married, not when we were first married, but when we started housekeeping and were living together, she would expect me to make every decision, no matter what, as to what I wanted for supper type of thing. It wasn't just normal politeness like "What would you like tonight?" It was almost to the point of being a "Should we have rye or raisin bread?" kind of thing. And it's only within the last couple of years that I've been able to get her to handle financial matters at all. Now I just completely turn the whole thing over to her—lock, stock, and barrel. And she does it now because I thought this was something that she ought to be less dependent on me about. You know, in talking about this dependency, the thought flashed through my mind that I remember one time that I told you about this ideal dream girl, and it was that I wanted someone who would dominate me—a very strong person. Well, I don't suppose I could really live with someone who was like that; nevertheless, it may be an element that is missing within my own marriage. (Insight)

T. Um hmm.

C. She's not a Casper Milquetoast type person. She's not a person who lets people walk on her. I mean, she doesn't put up with that kind of thing. She can be angry and be upset, but it takes an awful lot. In other words, she's almost *too* good, in a sense. Her breaking point is so far removed from most people's breaking point, she'll put up with so much guff that it is sometimes hard to live with.

T. Um hmm. It sounds as though she has a rather rigidly stereotyped notion of the ideal mother-wife role, possibly associated with certain socioeconomic strata, and that she follows this rather strictly. The good wife-mother does not do certain things and does do other things, and this is a fairly rigidly conceived pattern of behavior, which happens not to meet your needs—or perhaps your conception of the ideal wife-mother role, or at least the ideal mate role. (Interpretation)

C. Yeah. There's a kind of a conflict there. I like certain elements of what she does real fine. (He goes on to discuss how she "waits on" him without questioning whether she should, but, if a lock is broken on the door, she wouldn't try to fix it, because she would feel that was his job. He attributes this to her mother's complaining about men taking advantage of women. Describes his wife's mother as a "real martinet type of woman." Discusses how this affects the sexual relationship.) Yet, you know, this is something I'm just coming to see, that I never have before, one would think such a person would tend to be prudish, but she's not a prude by a long shot. I mean she can tell and listen to a shady story. She can hear one without discomfort, and she can laugh at it in mixed company without being upset. It's just, she's not prudish, and yet — she's not exactly what I would want her to be in this area.

T. Let's see, you started going with her. You chose her deliberately—or the psychologist chose her—as someone whose impeccable reputation could by association clean up your somewhat dubious one in that particular cultural setting. And then you went with her, and this rather rapidly effected this change in their perception of you, or did what you wanted it to do, I guess, and then, you said, you didn't break off. You kept going together. And you liked certain things that she brought you. (Summarizing) I wonder why, at this point, I mean this was the time when you had a chance to choose, really, why did you go on with this girl who was very nice and could help your reputation but had certain deficiencies, or did you want to find someone else? (Challenging)

C. Well, first of all I don't think I could have identified her deficiencies, at that time. We had a normal type of courtship, and I had no indication that she was not interested in sex at all. We didn't have intercourse until months after we were married, actually, but we would have strenuous necking to the point where I would be certain that she would be interested in that kind of activity. I think there was something deeper than this. I think actually I was attracted by her family. Her family had some things that my family did not. I think there was a kind of security arrangement there. Her mother, for example, is a lot like myself, in many ways. Her mother is very competent in being able to get things done. (Insight) When I think of what I was attracted by, I used to go there on Sundays right after working all week, and working nights — be completely bushed — and I'd sleep all day Sunday at their house, and this I was allowed to do. This was considered perfectly normal. We were going together during the Depression years, and pickings were pretty slim at my house, and, that being a farmhouse, the Sunday dinners were just absolutely fabulous as far as I was concerned. My mother's idea of a Sunday meal would be French fried potatoes, period. Her mother, on the other hand, likes to entertain, and this impressed me. And her dad was a very interesting fellow. Had a tremendous life—worked in the copper mines in the West, ran away from home when he was a kid, etc. There was a feeling of adventure in the family, and, I think, some kind of status. (Insight)

T. What socioeconomic level would you say, do you know what level they were? (Questioning interpretively)

C. Um hm. They would be middle, or lower middle.

T. Middle, or even rural upper middle do you think? (Information)

C. I don't think upper middle.

T. What socioeconomic status do you think *your* family had? (Teaching discrimination)

C. Lower middle.

T. Um hm. Some of the things you have described about their situation would make me wonder just a little bit whether it was lower middle or upper lower. (Challenging)

C. Mmm.

T. Their standards, for example, their permitting you the sexual freedom that they did, your discussion of the role of the grandmother in your family, your discussion of the eating habits — (Persuasion)

C. Um hum. If you would use some of the Warner criteria about type of house, etc., I think it would be middle; I'm not sure. It may very well — there was a difference, let's say. My father, my mother, and my uncles were all skilled printers.

T. Well, what I am trying to get at is only an objectification of the social difference there. (Explanation) And your perception is that, I wonder whether you're saying that she represented a way of life that was nicer or a social improvement. Social mobility maybe. (Interpretation)

C. Definitely. I think this is definitely in the picture. *Her* mother's people are early American stock. They laugh about the "Mayflower" days and that sort of thing, and they have silver in their family that was brought over in the 1600's. And her father's family were people who were direct-line descendants of nobility. So, I mean, that was definitely in the picture, and it did appeal to me. More than that, though, I think was their immediate way of life in their family. There was none of the bickering and carrying on that was in my own family. In other words, just by going there and resting on a Sunday afternoon gave me a great feeling of security. (Insight)

T. So that not just status but a style of living was also more acceptable and, in fact, was desirable.

C. Um hmm.

T. And the part that comes along with it, that you didn't know about, would be the frigidity. You didn't know, for example, that in this group the girl distinguishes between petting and intercourse. (Information)

C. Well, you know, I think I'm changing my feelings. I think there's not so much frigidity on *her* part as there is a lack of understanding and appreciation on my own. (Pause) I'm seeing it differently. I think the symptoms are exactly the same, but I think the relationships are different. (Insight)

T. That's pretty important, isn't it? (Approval)

C. Yeah. I think this is related more to me than it is to her. Part of it, part of this lack, part of this inability on her part to come to me I can understand when I look back on it.

T. In other words, you're saying you're not always approachable. (Clarification)

C. Um hm. And even though this business cleared the air, an awful lot of the experiences we've had together as husband and wife would be the kind that would lead to pretty deep scars, I would think. For instance, this time when I told her about all these experiences — that would be one. The fact that we had a rather abnormal marriage to begin with. We were married in secrecy, which would be in violent opposition to her mother. In fact, this was a very difficult thing for her mother to forget. And then not being able to be together, and not being able to consummate the marriage over such a long period of time, and then my going overseas — a month of almost frantic living before I went overseas, and then the coming back after being away for a year, and my expecting a level of operation which would be — in other words which I probably should have approached as a newlywed, almost, I was approaching it as an experienced partner, which she couldn't take. I can see these things a lot clearer now. (Insight)

T. Um hm. This is what I was trying to get at when I said that possibly those first months had been so difficult, plus any revelation she might have had of what had happened overseas, that she found it hard to accept you. (Explanation)

C. Yeah. But if you couple that to the fact that she has this perfect wife-mother picture in her mind, she could never let me know that this was what was bothering her. And the only way it would show up would be in this not being able to come to me in sex. (Insight)

T. Then you're saying you don't really think she is frigid. You're saying that in the difficulty in the personal interaction between the two of you, that you feel somewhat responsible. (Clarification of feeling)

C. Um hm. There's another little thing in here that's eluded me that's related to myself, too. I can feel it more than I can say it. I think it has to do with my expectation level, too; it's probably pretty warped. I've been living with this perfect dream, that's probably not nearly as perfect as I dreamed it would be over the last 13 or 14 years, plus this rather Hollywood ideal of what one expects from a sexual relationship, plus the inadequacy — the feelings of inadequacy that I've identified within myself in relation to this penis sort of thing — in other words, sex is a kind of a — maybe I've been using it as a way of building my own ego, superego, everything — (Insight)

T. Um hmm. A symbol for you of adequacy. (Clarification)

C. Yeah. That's it. And I would be approaching this thing, and it really not being what it *could* be, I would have to find a scapegoat for what I'm not finding in it.   (Insight) Maybe I'm not — I'm sure I'm not building some feeling here —

T. Are you saying you wonder if it's as important as you've made it seem?

C. (Pause) I hate to think of — I have the feeling that if this therapy is going to make me want to give up sex, I don't want therapy.   (said with a laugh) (Resistance)

T. I don't see why the therapy would need to — (Challenging) You're saying that sex is still pretty nice to you.   You don't want to give the impression that you're ready to become a hermit!   (Clarification)

C. Yeah.   But, realistically, I think what you are saying is right.   I'm trying to make it into something it isn't.   I'm trying to use it to another end, and it isn't meeting that need.   I'm hanging onto it too hard.   (Pause) (Insight)

   This dissatisfaction over these feelings, unhappiness, have created a problem between my son and me.   At times, there have been pretty strong feelings of resentment on my part, and I've tried very hard to not show these. They're certainly not at the surface level, except as they come out, sometime; again, my characteristic reaction when I'm bothered is this irritation thing that we talked about, where I would flash out at something.   And I'm not really angry at the person when I do this.   I'm really being angry at myself.   I think I've come to see that now.

Summary of Remainder of Interview.   The client thinks he has felt too much irritation with his son.   In the past he has felt jealous and angry because of his wife's attention to the boy.   Nevertheless, he also has some positive feelings toward him.   He has tremendous pride in the boy's intellectual, musical, and athletic abilities.   However, he also is irritated because musical and athletic activities come to his son so easily that he doesn't have to work at them in order to be good.   The client wishes his son would exert enough effort in these two areas to be really competent.   He realizes that the reasons for his feelings are that he identifies with his son and doesn't want him to make the same mistake that he himself did.   He (the client) could have been quite outstanding in these areas, but never made the effort.

   The client recognizes that his level of aspiration for his son has always been unrealistically high.   He always chose toys a year or more too old for the boy. Intellectually, he knew what one should expect of a child of a certain age, but emotionally, because he identified his son with himself, he always expected too much.   He can forgive his daughter any weaknesses, but not his son.   For his wife, the reverse is true.   The client has always wanted to be "tops" himself, but didn't exert the effort to be.   He thinks he sees himself as a potential "A" performer who operates at the "B" level.   He believes his feelings toward his son are changing, though.   His wife also thinks that the relationship between the two is improving because of therapy.   She has commented on his spending more time with the boy.   This hasn't been accomplished consciously; it has occurred without his being especially aware of it.

ELEVENTH INTERVIEW, DECEMBER 18

A very significant interview.   Dr. Kennedy reported much improvement in his social relationships, and then described his dependence needs toward his wife in the matter of sex.   He wants her to seduce him, rather than the reverse, and this rarely happens. He considers her sexual responses normal, but her demands for love excessive. When these demands become too strong for him, he withdraws from her sexually and goes on long sprees of indulging in masturbation, about which he feels a great amount of guilt. He indicated his feeling that the therapy was helping him greatly, and his desire to continue it.

Twelfth Interview, January 8

Again quite significant. The client discussed his anger because sometimes his wife will abandon sexual intercourse when only partially completed, if she hears some noise suggesting that one of the children is restless or uncomfortable. He would like to leave his wife and join the girl he knew in Italy; they still carry on a rather sporadic correspondence. The therapist interpreted the client's concern about lack of aggressiveness in a sexual partner, and his desire to be seduced, and the client began to see some implications of homosexuality in this behavior. This made him extremely uncomfortable. He works harder to give his partner an orgasm than to achieve one for himself, and he considers this to be abnormal.

Thirteenth Through Sixteenth Interview, January 15 Through February 18

In the next several interviews, Dr. Kennedy discussed some exacerbations of his symptom picture. First, he mentioned a recent event where he had brought a current mistress to live at his house for several days during which his wife and children were visiting the grandparents. ("Acting out.") He realized that this event was a possible source of neighborhood gossip, and might even cause him very serious trouble if the information got back to his wife, but he said that, if she was unwilling to take such news in a mature manner, she would just have to get a divorce. He discussed how these affairs give him a sense of recaptured youth, and also some sense of attainment or adequacy. They counteract his omnipresent feelings of inadequacy and general as well as sexual incompetence.

In the next interview, he indicated that he had taken another physical examination and that the physician had noticed some possible elevation of blood pressure but did not think it was at all serious—probably only the result of tension. The therapist discussed the nature of psychosomatic reactions and indicated how anxiety could quite possibly bring about changes in the cardiovascular behavior. He suggested a possible relationship between the physical symptoms and sexual or professional tension and anxiety. The client accepted these interpretations easily.

In another interview, he discussed his mixed feelings toward the dean; he dislikes him and disapproves of his philosophy and his way of dealing with people, but also he is uncomfortable when he fights with the dean. He envies the dean's apparent signs of rugged masculinity, but also suspects that this behavior is a façade for deeply felt feelings of inadequacy. He feels that he and the dean have much in common, because both of them fear that they might really be incompetent people, but the client feels that the dean is better able to compensate for these feelings than he is.

In the sixteenth interview, he discussed intense feelings of depression he was currently experiencing. He is thinking about changing jobs, since he sees little future in his present one. Also, his wife rejected his sexual advances during the past week, and this both angers and depresses him.

Seventeenth Interview, March 4

During the last two weeks, the client had been out of town frequently, and he had also failed to fill out his regular postinterview questionnaires after the last two interviews. The therapist raised this issue and challenged the client's negligence as a sign of therapeutic resistance. Dr. Kennedy admitted that, although he had been busy with trips, he had also felt that the last two interviews had been rather unproductive. The therapist interpreted this to mean that, while the interviews had actually been quite significant, they had also probably been personally quite *threatening* because of the problems that had been discussed. The client accepted this interpretation. He then discussed the new position he is considering as a full professor and chairman of an art department at a small but highly reputed liberal arts college. He would like this position but feels it would demand more circumspect behavior on his part (discontinuing the extramarital activities); he showed some reluctance to "compromise [his] principles and be dominated by the middle class mores," which this would entail. He discussed some of the reasons why social mobility is so important to him (he has been reading Havighurst on this topic); his father has always pushed him, and still does, to get ahead in the academic hierarchy. In fact, his father considers anyone below the level of dean as being a subordinate; he thinks professors are just "hired hands," which he felt was his own status in life (skilled labor, really). Finally, Dr. Kennedy showed some regret about not having filled out the posttherapy scales, recognizing that the therapist would naturally consider this as resistance. He filled out his scales, this time, within an hour after therapy.

Eighteenth Interview, March 15

First, the client discussed his rather profound hostility toward authority figures. He then asked the therapist to suggest a topic for further discussion. The latter complied, suggesting, (1) authority figures, (2) the client's sense of inadequacy, and (3) his relationship with his wife. Dr. Kennedy traced his hostility back to many incidents with his father, and with other persons. At present, he said, he no longer perceives his father as an authority figure, since he pays little attention to what his father says. He digressed into a discussion of his childhood sleepwalking and how his parents would "catch him at it." Later, he brought up his adolescent fears of blindness and of fainting, and the therapist interpreted all of these as signs of sexual problems. The client rejected these interpretations rather categorically.

Nineteenth and Twentieth Interviews, March 18 and March 26
(Uneven scheduling was caused by client's trips.)

Dr. Kennedy started the discussion by recounting how he tends to look upon, and use, his wife as a personal servant. He then talked about his social-mobility drive, indicating that he feels it to be very intense. He would like to be a dean, but only because of the social status, not because he would like the work. He recently visited the school he is considering joining, and, before going, he bought his boys new shoes so that they would make a good impression. The therapist raised the issue of a possible conflict between his social-mobility drive and a sense of contentment with his creativeness and artistic productivity. It was decided that this was a common conflict in upper-middle-class circles, and the client professed to see no way of resolving it.

In the next interview, Dr. Kennedy arrived at the insight that his wife was "too good" for him. She always does things in the most socially approved way, and she is rather puritanical. He also perceived her "controllingness," which, though subtle, is profound. She will never "surrender," nor will she ever show that she is interested in sex. She is the perfect mother, but in this she tends to be a "Madonna type," and this doesn't make for a compatible sexual relationship. ("Spouse phobia" or the Freudian "split-imago" problem is very evident here.)

Twenty-first Interview, April 1

Dr. Kennedy reported that he had accepted the new position at the other college; he felt that this would solve most of his problems. He made many profuse expressions of gratitude to the therapist for helping him to arrive at the point of being able to take this "constructive step." He then discussed his sense of identity with the success of the members of his family, which he believes to be unusually strong. His wife has spoiled his daughter and is now unable to manage her very well. This causes him embarrassment when she misbehaves in public. He has a feeling of personal failure whenever a member of his family is unsuccessful or misbehaves. He discussed his own deep-seated feelings of personal inferiority. Then he indicated some regret at the prospective ending of the therapy relationship.

Twenty-second and Twenty-third Interviews, April 8 and April 15

The client seemed to have little to talk about at the beginning. He mentioned a minor anxiety attack he had experienced the previous day. He has decided to give up all extension teaching, and also to stop his extramarital affairs; he feels that his new responsibilities will demand more circumspect behavior on his part, and, while he mildly resents being dominated by social pressures toward conservativism and dignity, he enjoys the prospects of the enhanced status his new position will supply. Again he expressed much gratitude for the therapy sessions, and he asked for an evaluation of his most recent Edwards personality tests; this interpretation was given him in the final interview.

In the last interview, he talked briefly about the possibility of shifting to the field of psychology if he was not happy in his new position (positive transference?); this impulse seemed transitory, and he recognized its unrealistic character. He talked about his feeling of never having been accepted by other children when he was little, and how this had become less of a problem in college, and perhaps even less so in his professional life, although he still recognizes that he has some residual social problems to cope with in his life experiences. The interviews ended on a very friendly note.

SUMMARY

Relationship and client-centered therapies comprise relatively new techniques that have for historical antecedents the methods of will therapy by Otto Rank and relationship therapy by Jessie Taft. They consist primarily of therapist techniques of clarifying the feelings the client expresses. The therapist continually tries to keep the orientation centered on the client's feelings, rather than on his symptoms. He also tries constantly to keep the responsibility for the direction of the interview in the hands of the client himself. In addition, he generally avoids giving much advice, criticism, persuasion, or interpretation, and he seldom gives information; occasionally, he may ask some direct questions. His use of reassurance and approval is limited and carefully controlled.

The techniques are based on the belief that the client will make the most satisfactory progress if the therapy situation is one in which he is freed from the usual inhibiting factors and from emotional blocks that prevent him from working out the most effective means for meeting his life problems. They are also based on the tenets that the client is capable of such growth and that this growth is likely to be prevented if techniques of direction are used. A warm, positive, permissive relationship is established with the client, who can feel totally accepted by the therapist.

There are certain criteria for the selection of cases for which these techniques are more effective. In general, situations that (1) favor independence from external controls on the part of the client, (2) indicate at least average intellectual ability, and (3) reveal the desire for change make this method most appropriate.

A significant development in this field of therapy was the introduction of the technique of electrical recording of the interview, which made numerous research investigations possible. Adequate systems for the analysis of the material presented during the interviews have been devised, so it has been possible to study the activities occurring during the therapy sessions. A start has been made in the direction of associating the client-therapist relationship in the therapy interview with existing knowledge in the field of learning theory.

REFERENCES

ANDERSON, H. H. 1946. Directive and nondirective psychotherapy: The role of the therapist. *Amer. J. Orthopsychiat.*, **16**, 608–14.

BORDIN, E. S. 1948. Dimensions of the counseling process. *J. clin. Psychol.*, 4, 240–44.

COLLIER, R. M. 1950. A basis for integration rather than fragmentation in psychotherapy. *J. consult. Psychol.*, 14, 199–205.

COVNER, B. J. 1944. Studies in phonographic recordings of verbal material. III. The completeness and accuracy of counseling interview reports. *J. gen. Psychol.*, 30, 181–203.

COWAN, E. L., and COMBS, A. W. 1950. Follow-up study of 32 cases treated by nondirective psychotherapy. *J. abnorm. soc. Psychol.*, 39, 281–97.

DOLLARD, J., and AULD, F., JR. 1959. *Scoring human motives: A manual.* New Haven: Yale Univer. Press.

DOLLARD, J., and MILLER, N. E. 1950. *Personality and psychotherapy.* New York: McGraw-Hill.

DOLLARD, J., and MOWRER, O. H. 1947. A method of measuring tension in written documents. *J. abnorm. soc. Psychol.*, 42, 3–32.

FIEDLER, F. E. 1950. A comparison of therapeutic relationships in psychoanalytic, nondirective and Adlerian therapy. *J. consult. Psychol.*, 14, 436–45.

FISHER, V. E. 1944. Psychic shock treatment for early schizophrenia. *Amer. J. Orthopsychiat.*, 14, 358–68.

FREEDMAN, M. B., LEARY, T. F., OSSORIO, A. G., and COFFEY, H. S. 1951. The interpersonal dimension of personality. *J. Pers.*, 20, 143–61.

GILLESPIE, J. F., JR. 1951. Verbal signs of resistance in client-centered therapy. Doctor's dissertation, Pennsylvania State College.

HAIMOWITZ, NATALIE R. 1948. An investigation into some personality changes occurring in individuals undergoing client-centered therapy. Doctor's dissertation, Univer. of Chicago.

HAMLIN, R. M., and ALBEE, G. W. 1948. Muench's tests: A control group. *J. consult. Psychol.*, 12, 412–16.

MOZAK, H. 1950. Evaluation in psychotherapy: A study of some current measures. Doctor's dissertation, Univer. of Chicago.

MUENCH, G. A. 1947. An evaluation of nondirective psychotherapy by means of the Rorschach and other tests. *Appl. Psychol. Monogr.* No. 13.

MURRAY, E. J. 1955. A method for studying psychotherapy. Doctor's dissertation, Yale Univer.

PORTER, E. H., JR. 1943. The development and evaluation of a measure of counseling interview procedures. II. The evaluation. *Educ. psychol. Measmt*, 3, 215–38.

PSYCHOTHERAPY RESEARCH GROUP. 1953. *Group report of a program of research in psychotherapy.* University Park: Pennsylvania State Univer.

RAIMY, V. C. 1948. Self reference in counseling interviews. *J. consult. Psychol.*, 12, 153–63.

RANK, O. 1945. *Will therapy; and truth and reality.* New York: Knopf.

RAUSCH, H. L., et al. 1956. A dimensional analysis of depth of interpretation. *J. consult. Psychol.*, 20, 43–48.

ROGERS, C. R. 1942. *Counseling and psychotherapy.* Boston: Houghton Mifflin.

ROGERS, C. R. 1946. Significant aspects of client-centered therapy. *Amer. Psychologist*, 1, 415–22.

ROGERS, C. R. 1951. *Client-centered therapy.* Boston: Houghton Mifflin.

ROGERS, C. R., and DYMOND, ROSALIND F. 1954. *Psychotherapy and personality change.* Chicago: Univer. of Chicago Press.

ROSEN, J. N. 1962. *Direct psychoanalytic psychiatry.* New York: Grune & Stratton.

SEEMAN, J. 1949. A study of the process of nondirective therapy. *J. consult. Psychol.*, 13, 157–68.

SHAW, F. J. 1946. A stimulus-response analysis of repression and insight in psychotherapy. *Psychol. Rev.*, 53, 36–42.

SHOBEN, E. J., JR. 1948. A learning theory interpretation of psychotherapy. *Harvard educ. Rev.*, 18, 129–45.

SHOBEN, E. J., JR. 1949. Psychotherapy as a problem in learning theory. *Psychol. Bull.*, 46, 366–92.

SNYDER, W. U. 1945. An investigation of the nature of nondirective psychotherapy. *J. gen. Psychol.*, 33, 193–224.

SNYDER, W. U. 1963. *Dependency in psychotherapy.* New York: Macmillan.

SNYDER, W. U., and SNYDER, B. JUNE. 1961. *The psychotherapy relationship.* New York: Macmillan.

STRUPP, H. H. 1957. A multidimensional system for analyzing psychotherapeutic techniques. *Psychiatry*, 20, 293–306.

STRUPP, H. H. 1960. *Psychotherapists in action.* New York: Grune & Stratton.

TAFT, JESSIE. 1933. *The dynamics of therapy in a controlled relationship.* New York: Macmillan.

THETFORD, W. N. 1949. The measurement of physiological responses to frustration before and after nondirective psychotherapy. Doctor's dissertation, Univer. of Chicago.

TUCKER, J. E. 1952. Investigation of criteria for evaluating nondirective psychotherapy with college students. Doctor's dissertation, Pennsylvania State College.

19

Psychoanalytically Oriented Therapy

JOEL R. BUTLER, FELICIA A. PRYOR, AND
HENRY E. ADAMS *

Psychoanalytic treatment is uniquely important because it is the foundation from which all later psychotherapeutic treatment methods received support in varying degrees. *Psychotherapy*, of course, is the generic term for the psychological treatment of human problems, and psychoanalysis is just one of many forms of psychotherapy. Nevertheless, the broad impact of psychoanalysis has been overwhelming in drawing attention to the remediation of emotional problems. Thus, any real understanding and appreciation of the psychoanalytically oriented psychotherapies presuppose a knowledge of psychoanalytic theory (see Chapter 2, page 47). Analytic therapies are based on certain assumptions developed by Sigmund Freud. The most important of these assumptions are psychological determinism, motivation, psychological economics, the genetic approach, and the unconscious.

Psychological determinism refers to the principle that all behavior has determinants and is not the result of chance. Thus, the simplest facts of normal behavior, such as forgotten names or dreams, as well as the peculiar behavior of the disordered personality, are purposeful and meaningful. Such behavior can be traced, if we know enough, to a highly complicated set of antecedents.

* Joel R. Butler, Ph.D. (Louisiana State University), Associate Professor of Psychology, Felicia A. Pryor, Ph.D. (Purdue University), Assistant Professor of Psychology, both of the Louisiana State University, and Henry E. Adams, Ph.D. (Louisiana University), Assistant Professor of Psychology, University of Georgia.

Motivation in psychoanalytic thinking represents an assumption that the purposes of human behavior are to seek pleasure and avoid pain. It is on this assumption that much therapeutic activity is based. Conscious motivation provides the therapist with a tool with which he can search for the underlying cause of human behavior. Any idea, object, or activity that may be observed in one's self is considered to be conscious.

The *unconscious,* which is the underlying source and impetus of behavior according to psychoanalytic thought, consists of all those impulses that are outside of awareness. The assumption of motivation implies that unconscious, as well as conscious, motivation is goal-directed and purposeful. Thus, through those activities to which the individual is able to attend and respond, the therapist is able to assess the content of the unconscious, and in that way he can begin to make sense out of behavior.

All energy for human activity is derived from the metabolic processes of human physiology, and energy used for psychological pursuits is called *libido,* or life energy. Freud originally believed the libido was sexual in character, but later psychoanalytic therapists expanded the concept of libido to include all energy-utilizing activity needed to preserve life, including such psychological activity as the search for affection and security. A normal, healthy person's body produces sufficient energy for normal personality functioning, but a psychologically unhealthy person requires an inordinate amount of energy to deal with his problems.

Psychoanalysis maintains that libido is distributed with order and in a way that seeks to maintain *psychologically economical* homeostasis within the organism. This balance is continuously being disturbed, not only by changing external, or environmental, influences but also by the very process of life itself. Unexpended libido can be stored up for later utilization on new experiences, but there is a tendency for the individual to use his libido in old, habitual ways of responding, which sometimes are no longer adequate. Accordingly, life appears to be something of a struggle between these opposing tendencies. On the one hand, the individual seeks to use old patterns of behavior, and, on the other hand, he finds he must respond flexibly to changes that have taken place within and around him in order to maintain equilibrium.

The *genetic approach* emphasizes the past personal history of an individual as being able to account for his present behavior. Present behavior is seen merely as the result of an individual's adaptations to experience during earlier developmental periods, particularly those of childhood. However, since no one is aware of all the past events in his life, psychoanalytic therapists have postulated that most of a person's early formative experiences are kept outside his awareness, in the unconscious.

THE UNCONSCIOUS

Freud believed that unconscious forces were the main motivators of man's behavior, but later psychoanalytically oriented theorists tended to de-emphasize the motivating influence of the unconscious. These later theorists believed the psychological struggles that shaped the personality were more interpersonal than intrapsychic. For example, Horney believed conflicts that produced psychological disorders were caused by disruptions in early interpersonal relationships; Adler believed they were due to infantile inferiority feelings; Jung believed they were due to a disregard of one's spiritual nature; and Sullivan believed unresolved conflicts were due to lack of ego integration. Nevertheless, in spite of such differences, the unconscious processes remain of singular importance for all psychoanalysts in their actual psychotherapeutic practice.

Assumption of the existence of an unconscious allowed psychoanalytic theorists to account for the influence of past conflicts on present personality. Unresolved conflicts are not allowed into functional awareness, because any expression of them brings punishment to the individual through his superego or his society. Thus, the only evidence we have of unconscious processes comes through such behavior as memory lapses, dreams, neurotic symptoms, and psychosis. Before identification of the unconscious, this behavior was believed to be of little value in the understanding and treatment of mental disorder. However, knowledge gained by the psychoanalytic theorists through an understanding of dynamic mechanisms of the unconscious has provided psychotherapists with a base and structure for psychotherapeutic treatment procedures.

The theory of analytic treatment states that, once unconscious forces become conscious, the psychic energy previously used to defend the personality against them is freed, and the former strong effect they had on the personality is diminished. The work of psychoanalytic therapy is to effect this transformation from the unconscious to the conscious. As indicated, content of the therapy hour and the thematic events brought into consciousness, as well as interpretations given to this material, will differ according to the orientation of the therapist. For example, a Freudian analyst will emphasize repressed sexual frustrations, whereas a neo-Freudian will emphasize the breakdown of early interpersonal relationships. Yet, in spite of differences in emphasis and terminology, all psychoanalytic therapists use similar techniques to get at unconscious content. Most important of these techniques are free association, dream analysis, hypnosis, psychological slips, projective techniques, and the life pattern.

VIEWS ON FREE ASSOCIATION

Free association refers to psychological associations that come into consciousness when conscious control is relaxed. This technique, which developed from the "talking cure" and Freud's interpretation of dreams, is actually the principal therapeutic method for bringing repressed material into consciousness.

The patient is asked to relax, not to try to be conversational or directional, but to say everything that comes into his mind regardless of whether it might be considered objectionable, shocking, or insignificant. He is asked, in short, to give himself up to the unconscious processes. It is not a request or an invitation for the patient to confide in the therapist all of his secrets or innermost thoughts, for such would require conscious control. Instead, the patient is asked to talk with no idea of either revealing or concealing. Generally, information given in free association will be fragments of thoughts, hopes, feelings, and judgments, and occasionally complete memory events. As idiosyncratic as the process must be to each individual, allusions of the association will demonstrate a consistency of theme. Thus, the analytic process of free association provides for acquisition of information by both patient and therapist about the unconscious problems of the patient. However, free association is very difficult, and the patient will unconsciously try all kinds of methods to resist it. Resistance to free association is so powerful that psychoanalysts see it as a central problem in therapeutic treatment (see page 607). As the patient, with the therapist's help, comes to recognize the information for what it is, that is, the revelation of unresolved needs, order will occur from the seemingly unrelated associations, and resistance will be broken down.

Jung on Free Association. Jung used dream analysis more frequently than free association as a therapeutic technique. Jungian analysts find that their patients can more easily give themselves up to their unconscious processes in recall of dreams than in the process of free association. Jungian analysts will, however, use free association when it seems necessary.

Adler and Horney. Later psychotherapeutic analysts felt that free association was secondary to the analyst's responsibility to direct and interpret the therapeutic session, whereas, in the orthodox psychoanalytic session, the patient is allowed more complete freedom in directing the analytic session. Though neoanalysts use free association, they think that too much information thus revealed is irrelevant and unnecessary for treatment. Therefore, they are less likely to allow the patient to associate as freely than are the more orthodox psychoanalysts. Adler did not believe that genuinely uninhibited free association was even possible.

Sullivan. Sullivan brought together the orthodox view of free associa-tion with the later psychoanalytic view. A Sullivan analyst will use this technique only when the patient's avoidance behavior indicates he has repressed important material. Then the analyst will say something like "Well, I wonder what is really the nature of this problem! Please tell me, now, whatever comes into your mind." It is believed that, by means of an objective attack on blind spots in his memory, the patient utilizes the process of free association. As he talks freely, he works toward answering the question at hand and gains insight into his problem. Thus, the Sullivan analyst directs the interview up to a point and then helps the patient to a limited, but effective, use of free association.

THE ROLE OF DREAM ANALYSIS

Freud noted the importance of dream analysis quite early in his work. Dream analysis has been found to be of such value in psychoanalysis that, next to free association, it is the most frequently employed technique for assessment of the unconscious. Dreams allow impulses to express them-selves with a minimum of ego interference. Thus, it is found that dreams of normal people do not differ in any essential form from those of neurotics. The fact that almost everyone forgets his previous night's dreams indicates it is only with wakefulness that the ego can re-establish control over unconscious processes and repress those impulses that have gained expression in one's dreams. Often, the only neurotic symptoms shown by a normal person may be expressed in his dreams.

Psychoanalytic dream theory contends that, like all behavior, dreams have definite meaning. Since they may express id impulses and wishes, they must be censored to render them acceptable. For this reason, people usually dream in symbols that serve to hide or distort their true meanings. These dream symbols become part of the resistance built up against a person's understanding his dreams. Understanding is further hindered because the dream symbols themselves are also censored by the ego. However, since there is a relationship between the symbol and the re-pressed impulse, it is possible for the analyst to interpret a dream. For example, a father may appear in dreams symbolically as a king or some other person in authority. Siblings may be symbolized as little animals or peculiar kinds of creatures. Birth is often represented by some refer-ence to water. Dying is represented by a long journey or traveling. However, symbols cannot always be interpreted universally, of course; sometimes a symbol has special meaning for an individual. Also, each analyst will interpret the dream symbol as it best fits his theoretical frame-work. Thus, though a long journey may be interpreted by an orthodox Freudian as symbolic of dying, Horney would have been likely to interpret a long journey as the patient's unending search for security, Jung might have interpreted it as a breakdown in the patient's resistance to his unconscious processes, Adler would have been likely to have interpreted it as the patient's forlorn search for his idealized goal, and Sullivan, in contrast to the others, would probably have seen such a dream symbol as representing a great gulf in the patient's interpersonal relationships.

Dream symbols actually highlight the distinction between manifest dream content, that is, actual dream material reported by the patient, and latent dream content, or the dream's unconscious meaning. Tracing what is manifest in the dream to its underlying meaning is one of the important techniques used by psychoanalysts to bring repressed material into consciousness. In the psychoanalytic framework, the dream is not a mysteriously inspired psychic event, but only the disguised expression of a wish.

Three important rules should always be observed by the analyst when he seeks to interpret dreams: (1) He must consider the surface meaning of the dream, whether reasonable or absurd, as relatively unimportant and superficial, since it is the unconscious impulse that must be understood. (2) The analyst must attempt to find substitute ideas for every element in the dream, no matter how far removed they may be from the manifest content of the dream. Remember, the dream is merely a distorted substitute, too. (3) The analyst should allow for the spontaneous appearance of the unconscious thought through its own processes. The therapist, whatever his theoretical orientation, will not try to interpret a dream as an isolated event in a person's life. Instead, he will interpret it with full knowledge of a person's life and, on the basis of such knowledge, will try to relate the dream fragments to the total experience of the individual.

Jung on Dreams. Of all the psychoanalysts considered, Jung was most concerned with understanding the process involved in psychoanalytic analysis of dreams. Jung found that conscious control is commonly most relaxed during the process of dreaming. Jung's interpretations differed from the Freudian dream interpretations because Jung was much more likely to encourage his patients to interpret their dreams as prophecies, that is, as a means of understanding present difficulties and future strivings rather than as explanations for the genesis of one's mental disorder. This, of course, was in line with Jung's idea that therapy should be concerned with the individual's present and future problems rather than his past conflicts.

Jung also had much to say about the importance of dream symbols. Briefly, he believed they had both an objective and a subjective component. Through dream analysis, Jung would seek to separate the symbols into their components. For example, the objective element of the dream symbol would be concerned with the individual's objective problems. The subjective element would involve an interpretation of the dream's personal meaning, as understood through myths and one's collective unconscious. After the dream symbols had been thus interpreted, a Jungian analyst would help his patient integrate them into his psychic life as guideposts for future behavior.

HYPNOSIS, FREUDIAN SLIPS, PROJECTION, AND LIFE PATTERN

Hypnosis. While early psychiatric practitioners used hypnosis almost exclusively in such neurotic disorders as hysteria, Freud was one of the first psychoanalysts to point out its ineffectiveness as well as its dangers. Under hypnosis, many patients have unusual recall ability so that events that have been repressed or long forgotten can be brought into consciousness. However, the reliving of such experiences under hypnosis does not have the same effect on the patient as do emotional abreaction and insight gained through psychoanalysis. Under hypnosis, the patient rarely is able to accept the knowledge revealed by him, and the process itself may serve only to frighten him. Also, he is quite likely later to forget the hypnotically revealed episode. Even if he is not amnesic for the material revealed in hypnosis, the anxiety produced by his recall may interfere with the normal therapeutic process. Thus, though hypnosis is a valuable tool for providing the therapist with information about the patient's conflict areas, it is used with great caution by the psychoanalyst and only adjunctively to other psychoanalytic techniques.

Psychological Slips. Based on the psychoanalytic assumption of determinism, it is assumed that everything a person does, even his mistakes, has a meaning and a purpose. Human mistakes include common events of everyday life such as forgetting a friend's name, calling a person by another person's name, forgetting or being late for an appointment; and remembering an experience incorrectly. Such errors may be insignificant or important to the person concerned, but they are usually not accidental. The *sense* behind the slip may appear quite obvious, as in the case of the new and energetic school principal who was appealing to his school board for a new *scoreboard* for his athletic field and said, "Gentlemen, I want you to know that on these grounds we have the worst, the most dilapidated and malfunctioning, *school board* in the state!" At other times, it is more difficult to find the relationship between the slip and the unconscious choice.

Such slips of the tongue are probably the most common examples of psychological slips, but there are also slips of the pen and misreadings, that is, when someone writes something other than what he meant to write or reads something other than what was actually written. All the sense organs are vulnerable to such slips: One may mis-hear, mis-smell, mis-taste, mis-feel, or mis-see any particular phenomenon. Interestingly, Freud also considered jokes to be a form of psychological slip. As Goethe said of Fichtenberg, "Where he makes a joke, a problem lies concealed."

A person will often make a slip when he is tired, unwell, excited, or concentrating on some other activity. Forgetting of people's names, for example, often seems to occur when the ego is less actively in control than usual. Such errors can occur also when one is apparently quite normal and healthy, and they usually stubbornly persist so that when we make one slip we may well make another in attempting to correct the first. This brings to mind the example of the girl who spent an evening with Charley and said, "Goodnight, Harry — oh, I'm sorry, John. Oh, what is your name?" Psychoanalysis does not insist that every single mistake that may occur has a meaning, although it is believed that such is probable. Errors result from the mutual interference of two different intentions. One is the intention that is interfered with, the other is the interfering tendency. The intention that is interfered with is not of great concern to the psychoanalyst. However, production of the interfering tendency, the slip, shows its relationship to the unconscious processes as do dreams and free association. Since psychological slips are produced by a lessening of ego control, the psychotherapist uses them in much the same way dreams and free association are used. Since slips often have readily identifiable unconscious meanings, they provide the patient and the therapist with additional source material for a more accurate identification of the patient's unconscious desires.

Projective Techniques. Techniques of presenting ambiguous stimuli, upon which a person may project certain aspects of his dynamic characteristics, are actually not part of the psychoanalytic technique proper. Projective techniques are used primarily as assessment techniques, as opposed to the types of therapeutic techniques we have been considering so far. Freud, without identifying it as such, did utilize a kind of projective device in his early work. He would ask a person to give his free association to a particular word. Later psychotherapists, instead of using a word as a stimulus, substituted many different kinds of stimuli. Thus, a projective technique may be any unstructured and ambiguous stimulus to which a response can be elicited. Since the stimulus itself has little structure, the individual must rely wholly on his own background and experiences. In this way, he will, of necessity, relinquish conscious control and "project" his own personality, his desires and impulses, into the stimulus.

Two major projective tests in use today, the Rorschach and the Thematic Apperception Test, were developed by psychoanalytically oriented psychiatrists. Today, such tests are used by clinical psychologists to probe into the dynamics and content of the unconscious. To make appropriate use of such tests, however, the examiner must be well trained in psychoanalytic principles. No single response is considered adequate for personality differentiation or evaluation, because it is the whole pattern of responses that points to important features of a person's unconscious activity. Thus, the test subject may react to the test stimuli as a series of dirty pictures, as episodes of violence, or as a pretty landscape with flowers. Whatever he sees as the theme of the test is used by the psychoanalyst as a key to an understanding of his more general personality functioning. (See Chapter 4, by Jules D. Holzberg, pages 106–153, for a discussion of projective methods.)

Life Pattern. As the genetic approach would suggest, information that may be obtained about an individual's past behavior provides material that is useful in understanding his present behavior and in predicting his future behavior. The notion of a life style is most properly credited to Adler, though Freud had similarly noted the existence of the "repetitive compulsion," in the neurotic character. Such a compulsive pattern would constitute the neurotic's life style and would result in the continual reappearance of unsolved life problems. If a problem has never been solved, the individual goes about not solving it in his same inadequate and unsuccessful fashion. This sets up a cycle of failure and frustration characteristic of the neurotic process. For example, men and women who have been divorced because of unsuccessful relations with their first mates will often marry a person with the same or similar disliked traits. There is even one recorded case of a man who married three different one-legged women! In psychoanalytic techniques, study of the life pattern appears as incidental to psychoanalysis. It, like hypnosis and psychological slips, is used in conjunction with free association and dream analysis as a psychotherapeutic technique.

STAGES OF PERSONALITY DEVELOPMENT AND CHARACTER FORMATION

All schools of psychoanalytic thought attach great importance to the genetic approach as a means of understanding human behavior. Psychoanalysts believe there are certain developmental factors that determine adult behavior. However, psychoanalysts differ among themselves as to which factors are of major importance. Orthodox analysts emphasize the importance of biological development, specifically sexual development, and the proper investment of libido. Later psychoanalytic theorists placed their emphasis on such factors as the person's social climate and his early relationships with other people. In spite of these differences, few of the later psychoanalysts examined the developmental stages of personality. Sullivan was the only neo-Freudian who actually tried systematically to define and analyze the developmental stages of personality in terms of interpersonal conflicts. Thus, since orthodox stages remain the main source of information about the way in which adult character is formed, they will be examined first. Then, developmental stages identified by the later psychoanalysts will be examined briefly.

According to the orthodox Freudian view, development of the personality takes place in progressively differentiating stages. Each stage is based on a part of the body from which the developing person derives pleasure (*erogenous zones*). For normal development to take place, the individual must successfully complete each of the stages. An overinvestment of libido in any particular stage will lead to a certain amount of abnormal development at that phase (*fixation*), and later growth will be incomplete owing to an insufficient amount of libido remaining for investment in the later stages.

According to the neo-Freudian viewpoint, development follows much the same progression, but what lead to later immature behavior are disruptions in the child's early interpersonal relationships, and not fixations on a child's erogenous zones. These later theorists felt that normal development was dependent on the warm and affectionate acceptance and guidance of an individual as a child. If the individual is given such a background, it is believed he will develop a satisfactory life style (Adler) and his defensive strategies will work in harmony with those of society (Horney). However, should the person's early life be fraught with hostility, anger, rejection, and fear, his life style will reflect anxiety and ambivalence, his reality testing will be inadequate (Sullivan), and his defensive strategies will interfere with later social participation.

Oral Stage. The center of infantile activity during the early stages of development is the mouth. Not only does it provide the child with nutritional ingestion necessary for his survival, it also provides the infant with his main source of pleasure. The oral stage is divided into two main parts—*oral erotic* and *oral sadistic*. The oral erotic stage is associated with the pleasure of taking in objects, especially incorporation of food, and is related later in life to acquisitions that give pleasure. Since this stage is concerned with satisfactions of instinctual needs, it is said to be dominated by the id. Residuals of this stage would include such activities as smoking, thumb-sucking, and the gourmet-type pleasures. If the personality is moderately fixated at this stage, it will produce personality characteristics of a glutton, a gourmet, or a fellator. Should the fixation be particularly severe, it is hypothesized that the individual will develop schizophrenia of the catatonic type. In catatonic schizophrenia, the regressive phenomenon is so pronounced that the individual may assume fetal positions and display an infantile rage reaction.

The object upon which the libido is fixated in the oral erotic stage is autoerotic. The object of the oral sadistic stage is narcissistic. The oral sadistic stage is associated with the pleasure of being able to control other objects through oral aggression, or biting. Later residuals of this stage would be such activities as gum-chewing, nail-biting, nagging, gossiping, cynicism, and argumentativeness. If there is moderate fixation at the oral sadistic stage, it would result in such personality characteristics as are evidenced by a cynic or an agitator. If there is severe fixation at the oral sadistic stage, it will result in various addictions—drug, alcoholic, etc., or manic-depressive disorders of affect.

In addition to the residuals noted above, another aspect of development in the oral stage is concerned with the growth of an individual's dependence feelings. Since the infant is most helpless during the oral stage, it is at this stage that he develops either basic trust in the world or basic anxiety (Horney). Whichever has been his experience will influence the way he participates in his later life experiences (Adler). Sullivan referred to the oral stage as the *infancy stage.* He believed that the child's concept of himself is formed in this stage through his relations with a "significant other," usually the mother. If the mother is warm and accepting, the child views himself and his world as good. If the mother is cold and rejecting, the child views himself as bad and begins to develop anxiety due to fear of disapproval accompanied by a loss of euphoria and empathy. According to Sullivan, the infancy stage lasts from birth to about the age of two, when the child begins the development of language.

Anal Stage. This is the stage when the child first meets injunctions and impositions of the external world and begins to think of himself as a separate entity. A primary learning task in the anal stage is that of toilet training. The child must learn to control the physiological impulse to empty his bowels and to postpone the pleasure that comes from such a release. The mother's attitude and method in toilet training will have far-reaching effects in determining the child's later character. The anal stage, like the oral stage, is divided into two parts: the *anal erotic* and the *anal sadistic.* The anal erotic stage is associated with the pleasure that comes from pleasing others and by the giving of oneself. In this case, the mother rewards the child for giving up his bowel contents in the expected fashion. Residuals of this stage in later life would be such activities as generosity, philanthropic extravagance, masochism, and sometimes creativity and productivity. Severe fixation at this stage would result in grandiosity and paranoid schizophrenia. The object choice would be narcissism and partial love.

The anal sadistic stage would be associated with the pleasure of retaining. It differs from the oral sadistic stage in that it is not merely the "taking in" that is pleasurable, but it is also the keeping that gives one pleasure. It does not matter whether or not one enjoys getting the things, it is having them (not even necessarily using them) that is all the fun. In this case, one keeps one's "valuable" bowel contents in order to punish mother for her strictness and angry impositions. Residuals of the anal sadistic stage are such traits as compulsiveness, pedantry, miserliness, stinginess, obstreperousness, ambivalence, and the general withholding of pleasure. Another reaction to a strict toilet-training regime may be quite different. In this instance, the child may try to control the mother by expulsion instead of retention of his feces. This kind of reaction results in such character traits as destructiveness, disorderliness, cruelty, uncontrolled temper tantrums, and sadism. Severe fixation at the anal stage is believed to result in obsessive compulsive neurosis or paranoia.

In addition to receiving toilet training, the child learns something about independence and social interaction. He also learns something of the value of possession and the reality principle. The reality principle states that one will delay present gratification in order to gain later, greater gratification. Since this stage is concerned with the child's relationship to reality, the anal stage is said to be dominated by the ego.

Sullivan identified the most important learning task of the anal stage (childhood) as the development of language and not toilet training. He believed that manipulation of symbols gives the child control over other people. Also, since this is the stage in which the ego is being developed, the child begins to see relationships among events. However, Sullivan believes that, since the ego is just in the beginning stages of development, distortions (particularly interpersonal relationships) in the perceived relationships will result and will lay the foundation for later autistic thought processes.

Additionally, the child begins to develop ambivalent feelings toward himself and others. Such feelings are produced by inconsistent relations the child has with adults. He finds he is accepted at some times and rejected at others. Thus, he begins to develop feelings of both affection and hostility for the same persons.

Phallic Stage. This is the stage of development in which children first discover sexual differences. At the time they learn about these differences, they are also beginning to engage in genital autoerotic activity. Accompanying this masturbatory activity is the child's sexual wish. Since the genital area is the erogenous zone of this stage, sexual stimulation, pleasures, and desires are derived from that area. The very closest members of the opposite sex toward which the child can direct his sexual impulses are his parents. Of course, the child has not yet learned that having sexual desires for his parents is believed to be immoral; that is, he has not yet learned how to be innocent. Thus, the parent is the child's first love choice. Love choice refers to both physical and psychological components of the sexual impulse. Choice of the parent as the love object brings about the *Oedipus complex* when the boy child desires the mother and the *Electra complex* when the girl child desires the father.

OEDIPUS COMPLEX. When the little boy desires his mother, he begins to compete with his father for her affection. As time goes on, the child becomes less tolerant of his father and comes to believe that the father is growing intolerant of him. Thus, the son is both hostile toward and afraid of the father. If the father becomes jealous, he will threaten the child, particularly when the child is engaged in masturbation or some other sexual display. The child begins to fear castration, and this fear makes him extremely anxious (Freud called this anxiety *castration anxiety*). In order to relieve this extreme anxiety, he must repress his sexual desire for the mother and his hostility toward the father. As he represses these things, he is able to identify with the father, and, in that way, he will have successfully resolved the Oedipal conflict. By identifying with the father, the boy can exert his masculinity without fear and can vicariously enjoy his mother. If the boy is unable to resolve the Oedipal conflict, he may show such behavior as that of a "mama's boy." Other examples of an inadequate Oedipal resolution would be the young man who continually prefers the company of older women to that of those of his own age, the individual whose sexual needs are satisfied by sexual foreplay rather than sexual intercourse, or the man who is unable to even contemplate sexual intercourse with a woman, because, in his mind, women should be above such a "base" activity.

ELECTRA COMPLEX. Somewhat the same process occurs in the phallic stage for girls. The girl desires the father and sees the mother as the threatening person. This results in the Electra complex and growth of the girl's *castration complex*. However, Freud felt that the girl is not as threatened by the mother as the boy is by the father. Having less anxiety, she does not need to so thoroughly repress her desires for her father or her hostility toward her mother. Since her mother has been seen as a loving person in the earlier stages, and since care by the mother is still very much needed for the girl's survival, she finds it relatively easy to identify with the mother. By this identification, the girl exerts her femininity and vicariously shares the father's affection with the mother. Since so little anxiety is aroused in girls, they feel free to show affection for their fathers much more openly. Also, Freud found that it is not unusual for women to have fantasies about incestuous relations and sexual ravishment. The fact that more girls than boys actually have had incestuous relations seems to confirm the difficulty women have in effecting an adequate resolution of the Electra conflict.

Another problem that occurs in the Electra situation stems from the girl's castration complex. Since the girl finds herself without a penis, she may develop feelings of inferiority (this is called *penis envy*). She may see herself and her entire sex as worthless and unimportant. Such a feeling may result in the kinds of personality traits displayed by the woman who is masculine and aggressive, is promiscuous, or has an abnormal desire to bear a male child. Another way a girl fixated at the phallic stage may react is to attempt to, psychologically, take the male's organ away from him. Thus, she may ridicule the male, dominate the male, or use other tactics to "cut him down to size."

Primarily, the learning task of the phallic stage is development of satisfactory attitudes toward one's own sex and toward the opposite sex. With proper resolution of the child's conflicts at this stage, sexual impulses are expanded to include feelings of tenderness, love, and compassion. Another learning task in this stage is concerned with establishing a relationship to authority and to the rules of society. For the first time, the child has felt guilt. Thus, it is thought that the phallic stage is the stage in which the superego begins its development. Fixations at the phallic stage would include ambivalence toward parents and incestuous fantasies. A moderate fixation at this stage could result in an improper sex role identification or in such sexual perversions as exhibitionism, voyeurism, or fetishism. A severe fixation at this stage would result in hysteria or psychopathic behavior. Since the phallic stage is concerned with appropriate choice of love object, it has been referred to as a "little puberty." Orthodox Freudians believe that, by the end of this stage, the basic personality of the individual is established.

Jung views the Oedipal situation as a *possession complex* in which children of both sex want to possess the mother. As pleasure in the genital zones increases, the possession complex is coupled with jealousy toward the parent of the same sex. Jung viewed the first five years of life as presexual, but he acknowledged that, with the emergence of the Oedipal situation, behavior was motivated by a drive toward pleasure. Incestuous desires, however, were viewed by Jung merely as a symbolic wish to return to the womb.

Adler viewed the Oedipal situation as a "vicious, unnatural result of maternal overindulgence." He also advanced the idea that the individual's concept of masculinity and femininity resulted from cultural stereotyping, and not just from libido investment.

Horney believed the Oedipal conflict resulted from an unhealthy family situation. She felt that the problems produced in this stage were due to anxiety aroused in the child by two conditions: (1) the child's ambivalence toward his parents and (2) an unusual amount of familial sexual stimulation.

Sullivan explained the Oedipus complex in terms of familiarity and strangeness between parent and child. When the child is like-sexed, the parent feels a sense of familiarity toward him. Thus, the parent establishes an authoritarian relationship with the child, which, in turn, results in hostility from the child. When a sense of strangeness occurs, the parent tends to respond in a gentler fashion, and this consideration is returned by the child. Sullivan believed that, if no such pressures existed, no Oedipal complex would exist.

Latency Stage. This stage of development is a plateau at which sexual impulses are repressed and the child is concerned with the firm establishment of his proper sex role. In this phase, the child integrates all his past learning and coordinates activities of his continuously developing id, ego, and superego. He spends much of his time role playing in the relatively nonthreatening atmosphere of his same-sex peers. Also, the child develops skills in social interaction with people outside the immediate family. Typically, he leaves home for the first time to go to school. If he has not been prepared for this independence, he will suffer separation fears and anxiety about a loss of love. Fixations during this period will result in a preference for same-sex companions, and it has been hypothesized that a severe fixation at this stage will result in homosexuality.

Sullivan was the only neo-Freudian who described the latency stage. He defined the phase as the *juvenile era* but added little new knowledge to the orthodox psychoanalytic view. He, like the other psychoanalysts, felt that this period was concerned with the child's establishment of his culturally defined sex role, with the child also learning about competition, relations to people outside the home, and social interaction with other authority figures.

Preadolescent Stage. Many neo-Freudians believe that, between the latency and genital stages, there is another stage of development, known as the *preadolescent stage* (Sullivan). This stage is concerned with the mature emergence of the sexual impulse and the societal restrictions of that impulse. When the conflict between these two factors is too great, the sexual impulse is unable to be sublimated, and it breaks through, producing anxiety, aggression, and a recurrence of the Oedipal or Electra fantasies.

Genital Phase. This is the last stage of psychosexual development. The child who has progressed normally to this stage will enjoy a healthy, well-adjusted adulthood. The genital stage begins at puberty and lasts for the remainder of the individual's life. Heterosexual relations and adjustment are the main activities in this phase. Owing to physiological changes of puberty, the child can no longer repress his or her sexual impulses and finds himself or herself in another Oedipal or Electra conflict. The conflict is not so grave this time, since the child has already met and resolved it in the phallic stage, and the child is now able to direct his or her sexual impulses toward a more appropriate love object—a peer of the opposite sex.

Sullivan called the final phase of development the *adolescent stage,* but he, like the other neo-Freudians, added few new insights to the orthodox view of this phase. He saw adolescence as the time at which a person reaches his adult level of sexual expression as well as his maturity and competence in dealing with, and relating to, other people.

PSYCHOANALYTIC TREATMENT TECHNIQUES

Psychoanalytically oriented psychotherapy has been given many different names, and theorists have claimed that these newly named therapies were, actually, different treatment methods. However, none of the therapies of the neo-Freudians are sharply differentiated from the others or from their basis in psychoanalysis. The differences lie mainly in the theoretical and semantic foundation on which each is based.

Since analytic theory is the basis of etiological psychotherapy, most forms of psychological treatment are similar in practice. The etiological approach is concerned with exposing the patient to past emotions and emotional situations. It is believed that, owing to the patient's former position of weakness (childhood), he was unable to deal effectively with his emotions. In the supportive and favorable atmosphere of therapy, however, traumatic experiences can be re-examined and dealt with by him in what is now a position of strength. Thus, the patient may correct the effect of these past experiences with current but similar emotions and, by so doing, may diminish the harmful influences of these previous emotional experiences.

According to psychoanalytic theory, personality disorders, particularly neuroses, occur when an idea or impulse conflicts with an individual's value system and with the reality orientation of his ego. In order to protect the person from anxiety aroused by this conflict, the ego exerts a counterforce. However, the counterforce does not resolve the conflict; it merely pushes the idea or impulse out of awareness. Because the impulse is repressed, it becomes pathogenic. The individual is unable to achieve satisfaction, pleasure, or achievement when he is wasting so much of his psychic energy in a continuous repression of his unresolved conflicts. Since all people have repressions, the difference between psychological health and illness is one of quantity and not quality.

Highly charged impulses will often seek substituted satisfaction or expression through the formation of symptoms. The task of analytic treatment is to make the repressed, unconscious material conscious in order to free the patient's valuable but limited libido for more effective use. Thus, the patient will be able to use his libido for achievement of realistic, mature satisfactions instead of substitute satisfactions in the form of symptoms, inappropriate object choices, and defense mechanisms.

As mentioned earlier, psychoanalysts differ among themselves as to the cause of conflicting circumstances that give rise to mental disorders. Jung believed there was a "neurosis of the times" brought about by lack of emphasis on the spiritual side of life. According to Jung, mental disorders developed because of a conflict between the opposite poles of personality (physical and spiritual; introvert and extrovert; *anima* and *animus*). Adler, on the other hand, thought that mental disorders resulted from a lack of understanding of idealized goals of superiority. In Horney's system, mental illness results from disturbances in interpersonal relationships during childhood, which, in turn, lead to a feeling of basic anxiety. Sullivan, in contrast to this, contended that neurosis resulted from a lack of ego integration. Whatever the theoretical school, substitute reactions are indicative of psychological pain and personality imbalance. When such symptoms appear, certain treatment procedures should be undertaken to remove the pain and restore the balance. Most important of these procedures are regression, resistance, transference, interpretation, and termination.

REGRESSION, RESISTANCE, AND TRANSFERENCE

Regression. The psychoanalytic therapy session provides an atmosphere in which the patient can regress to his fixated stage of development. Having regressed to the stage at which his problem began, the patient can, with therapeutic help, resolve his conflicts and proceed to higher levels of psychological growth. "Ye shall be born anew" is the poetic statement of what happens in the therapeutic process. Treatment regression differs from regression expressed through formation of neurotic or psychotic symptoms, because treatment regression allows the patient to uncover and resolve his conflicts, whereas regression outside of treatment is used to push unresolved and frustrating conflicts into the unconscious.

Frustration is what brought the individual to the therapist. This frustration may be the cyclic frustration of neurotic symptoms, or it may be basic goal frustration. Whatever its character, it is a powerful motivator and is used as such by the therapist in treatment.[1] Since all patients are not at the same level of frustration, however, a major problem in psychoanalysis is maintaining an optimal level of frustration. If frustration is too great, the patient will leave, and, obviously, treatment cannot be accomplished without the patient. If the frustration is too little, the patient will merely incorporate it into his already functioning neurotic defenses. However, under optimal levels of frustration, the patient will resort to methods used when he was frustrated as a child. Thus, he abandons current defenses and "proceeds backward" to his fixated stage of personality development. Through the regressive phenomenon, the patient begins to feel as if he were a child and to feel as dependent on the therapist as he had felt on stronger adults as a child. Other techniques such as transference, free association, and therapeutic interpretation can now be used most effectively.

Jung felt that treatment regression was more of a symptom than a cure and that it was a "very suspicious circumstance" if a patient tried to explain his illness in terms of a long-past event. He felt that such action merely pointed up the patient's infantile inability to live up to his present circumstances. Thus, regression as a therapeutic process is less important to a Jungian analyst than to an orthodox analyst. However, a Jungian analyst will bring regressive material into consciousness in order to free libido, but this is considered to be of only secondary importance. The main activity of a Jungian analyst is to provide appropriate channels through which the patient may express his newly liberated libido.

Since Adler did not accept the Freudian view of regression, he did not routinely use it as part of his treatment technique. He ascribed great importance to the understanding of early childhood memories because they contributed significantly to revelation of the formation of the patient's life style. Adler's psychology assumed that people tended to repeat infantile performances because they found that such behavior was successful. As a treatment technique in an Adlerian analysis, regression would be used only to uncover past experiences so that the therapist could make predictions about the patient's future behavior. In addition, Adler noted that, when infantile behavior was symptomatic, it would disappear through therapy when the patient found that such behavior was no longer successful. Adler contended this was due to the patient's intellectual understanding of the problem.

Horney believed that, because neurosis was due to a disturbance of human relationships, it was not vitally necessary to take a person back to

---

[1] It should be noted that not all psychoanalytic therapists use frustration as a therapeutic technique. Adler, for example, took great pains to keep the level of tension as low as possible. He would tell the patient a joke about a person with a similar disorder and point out that such a condition can be taken more lightly, or he would quote stories, poems, or fables in order to reduce the frustration in therapy.

his former level of development. She felt that regression could be viewed as just a special form of the repetitive compulsion of the neurotic and should be discouraged in the treatment session.

Sullivan was not at great variance with orthodox Freudians on the concept of regression. He believed that regression was brought about through the self dynamism as a protection against anxiety, and that symptoms could be explained by repression. However, he thought that the more highly organized aspects of personality could not be helped by the regressive phenomenon. The reason for this lay in Sullivan's contention that, even though the mentally ill person may have regressed to a state very much like early infancy, he would not be able to learn as does the infant, because every step forward for him would bring about anxiety and subsequent repression. For Sullivan, therapy was not simply starting over again from a previous fixated state; it was an attempt to make the patient understand his self dynamism and be less afraid of it.

Resistance. Resistance is the patient's unconscious defense against therapeutic destruction of his old, unsatisfactory behavior patterns. The patient will show resistance throughout the therapeutic procedure because he will always want to protect some part of his mind from analytic intrusion. Resistance is concerned with keeping the repressed conflicts in the unconscious. Any ego defense mechanisms may be used to maintain resistance, but repression is the defense most frequently used. Repression and resistance represent the ego's censorship of unacceptable thoughts that are being brought into consciousness through therapy. Since resistance must be removed in order to dissipate the strength of repression, it is the duty of the analyst to seek out resistance and make the patient aware of it. Thus, the analyst will identify and interpret, and, at the right time, inform the patient of, resistive and repressive phenomena.

The most important techniques available to the therapist for the control of resistance are free association, interpretation, and transference. Free association, as earlier noted, helps to bring to light much repressed, unconscious material. However, there are many methods of resisting free association. The patient may remain silent or maintain either that he simply cannot think of anything or that he thinks only of trivial, unimportant things. He may refuse to freely associate by saying that he has found a thought too bizarre, too objectionable, or too unreasonable to mention to the analyst. The obsessive patient may clutter up his associations with overconscientious detail, or the anxious patient may become so frightened by his revelations that he cannot tolerate any further expression at the moment.

Another way of attacking resistance is through the ego, since resistance is largely a function of the ego. It is well to remember that the patient is not passive in psychoanalysis. He is motivated toward good health or he would not be in analysis. Because of these motives, he is compelled to be cooperative, so he uses his intelligence and rationality when they are reinforced by the interpretative process. Thus, therapeutic interpretations may be used effectively to overcome resistance. However, the therapist must be aware of the many kinds of resistance the patient may use against interpretations. The patient may, for example, fail to understand or hear the ideas the analyst presents to him. He may engage in long, global discussions, using his newly acquired psychological terminology. This kind of resistance is called intellectualism and is often found in the intelligent college student who says, "This is an interesting concept, but I don't believe it, and besides, it just doesn't apply in my case." Other difficult resistances to deal with are hidden manifestations of resistance, such as a flattening of affect and depersonalization. The analyst should not be caught attempting to dichotomize resistances, however, for all of them must be overcome in order to expedite the treatment process.

Probably the most difficult form of resistance to deal with is transference. Though it is a particularly tenacious resistance, it is one of the most important and productive of the treatment procedures. As a form of resistance, transference displaces the new frustrating object—the therapist —with the old frustrating object. Instead of merely recalling old feelings and emotional states, the patient reproduces them in the new frustrating situation of therapy. In this way, he tries to guard against bringing old conflicts into the conscious and reinforces his old behavior pattern. Examples of resistance in the form of transference occur when the patient bitterly attacks or criticizes the analyst, his theory, or his techniques. He may fall in love with the analyst and use his charms to make the therapist let up on his treatment attack. He may make unreasonable demands on the therapist. He may become dissatisfied with the results of therapy and stop treatment. He may reduce his productivity or remain silent. He may fail to keep an appointment, always with a superficially "good" reason. He may continually be late for appointments. He may forget to pay his bills. Use of transference as resistance should not be condemned, however, because transference is of great use in the treatment procedure. It brings the old conflict situations back to the patient in a most convincing fashion, and, in spite of the patient's efforts, it makes conscious much important repressed material.

Adler believed that resistance was a "depreciation tendency" directed toward disparagement of other people. In psychotherapy, such disparagement is often directed against the psychotherapist in the form of doubt, criticism, tardiness, special requests, acting out, or relapses. Since the therapist is seen as obstructing neurotic strivings of the patient, he is regarded as the obstacle that prevents the patient from reaching his superiority ideal.

As the patient improves, he will become even more energetic in his attempts to thwart the success of treatment. Resistance, according to the Adlerian view, can be neutralized only by continually directing the patient's attention through therapeutic interpretations to the repetitiveness of his behavior. Another device used by the Adlerian analyst is never to let himself be placed in a position of authority or superiority. Thus, the therapist is a co-worker, not a teacher, father, or savior, and psychotherapy in the Adlerian manner is an exercise in cooperation.

Horney saw resistance as protection of repressed feelings, and she believed that such protection was necessary to maintain the homeostasis of the neurotic. In the treatment process, of course, resistances would be broken down in the orthodox psychoanalytic manner.

Sullivan regarded resistance as a problem in communication. Sullivan found that, whenever a threatening subject was introduced in therapy, it produced anxiety in the patient. Consequently, the therapeutic session would not proceed as well as it had before threatening material had been introduced, and the patient would begin to use devices to avoid a straightforward confrontation with the threatening stimulus. Sullivan believed it was the therapist's duty, as the expert in interpersonal relations, to break down resistances by objectively and rationally considering them. Thus, the patient is not allowed the delusion of resistance. He must examine and dispose of the disturbing topic before therapy is allowed to proceed.

Transference. Transference deals with the displacement of the patient's old feelings and attitudes from the previous conflict situation into the new therapeutic situation. The actions of a patient in transference provide an excellent example of the repetitive compulsion that is so often a part of the disordered personality. Thus, transference is not unique to therapy but is probably the patient's habitual way of responding to frustrating interpersonal experiences. The transference phenomenon is important to the therapeutic process because it allows the patient to experience an emotional catharsis or abreaction, which is necessary for the complete working through of repressed conflicts. Accompanying the abreaction are therapeutic interpretations that provide the patient with intellectual insight into his disorder. This combination of emotional and intellectual catharsis brings about the corrective, reconstructive, and re-educational aspects of therapy.

What is occurring in transference is that the patient is simulating or reproducing conflict situations that confronted him long ago. Once transference is evidenced, it is the therapist's duty to point out to the patient that what he is experiencing now did not originate in the therapeutic situation but instead is related to his past. The therapist further makes it known to the patient that circumstances in which the original conflicts occurred have all changed. Today, the patient is in a position of strength; he no longer needs to use repression to deal with his conflicts, and, with therapy, he can understand and deal with his impulses in more effective ways.

By shifting the patient's disorder from the original conflicts into the therapeutic situation, transference creates a new neurosis, the transference neurosis, to replace the original one.[2] The patient's symptoms begin to abandon their original purpose and take on new meaning in the transference relationship. The new neurosis is artificial but allows the conflicts to be transformed in their original form into a more easily managed, externalized form. Once externalized, the problems cannot be taken back, and, in this manner, the patient's repetitive compulsion is broken, old conflicts are made conscious, and his libido is freed.

Such a healthful resolution is possible because the intensity of feelings in transference is much less than it was during the original conflicts. Also, the therapist's responses are different from the responses elicited in the original situation. This is true because the therapist accepts the "unacceptable" impulses of the patient and, in that way, helps the patient to accept them in himself. The therapist's responses will differ also because he is, actually, a different person. Under such conditions and in a position of strength, the patient's ego is forced to readjust its basic pattern and become more reality-oriented.

There are three problems a beginning therapist must be aware of in the process of transference. These problems are concerned with (1) premature results, (2) regression, and (3) countertransference. The first of these involves the superficial improvement shown by the patient as a result of regression to the oral, dependent stage of development. In this situation, the individual will try hard to do those things he thinks the therapist wants him to do. The inexperienced therapist may see this behavior as a cure. The patient is no longer showing his symptoms and is behaving in an appropriate manner. However, the patient's neurosis in this instance has not been remedied; it has been displaced.

The second problem the therapist must guard against is related to the first. The analyst must decide whether the regressive transference is a resistance against the conflict or an attempt at a mastery of it. Orthodox psychoanalysts believe that an evaluation of the amount of original cathexis at the point of fixation would determine which of these two regressive components is at work. However, sometimes it is difficult for the therapist to correctly determine the extent of cathexis at each stage. Thus, the therapist should try to guard against showing undue interest

---

[2] For this reason, Freud originally classed anxiety hysteria, conversion hysteria, and the obsessional neuroses as a group of transference neuroses.

in any particular stage, in order to force the patient to dwell on the stage of his own interest. If the analyst responds to regressive material other than that which attempts to resolve the old conflicts, he will have unwittingly allowed the patient to use therapeutic interpretations as an effective resistance.

The third condition a psychotherapist must guard against is countertransference. The analytic situation is a highly unique and objective approach for the understanding and treatment of human behavior. It depends largely on the objective and impersonal attitude of the therapist. The therapist neither yields to nor rejects the patient's demands. However, it is a mistake for the therapist to dehumanize himself and make himself into an unemotional robot or a blank screen. It is important that he is a person, for transference can take place only in an interpersonal relationship. Since the therapist is human, however, he must recognize the problems involved in countertransference.

The origin of countertransference is in the unresolved personal problems of the therapist. His feelings are invested in much the same manner as are the patient's, but, hopefully, the therapist's problems are much less intense. Signs of countertransference are many, and it is important for the therapist to be able to recognize them. Countertransference may be marked by anxious or defensive behavior on the part of the therapist. He may not pay attention to what the patient is saying; he may even fall asleep. He may deny provoked anxiety. He may find it difficult to shift attacks. He may become oversympathetic or overinvolved. If he becomes too closely identified with the patient, he may find himself making mistakes in interpretations, or he may lose his patience and get angry. There have been cases when, owing to countertransference, a therapist has become so emotionally involved with his patient that he has fallen in love with her, and even married her. Other evidences of countertransference are continual lateness for appointments, missing appointments, or giving one patient more time than that allowed to other patients. It can be seen that such behavior does not lead to objectivity, so the therapist experiencing countertransference would tend to be a less effective participant in therapy.

When countertransference is evidenced, the therapist should get a colleague to supervise these therapeutic sessions, or he should get therapeutic help in order to locate and resolve the source of his countertransference feelings. Because of the countertransference phenomenon, many schools of psychoanalysis feel that an analysis of the therapist in training is an indispensable part of his professional education. These psychologists believe that such an experience is the only effective guard against countertransference.

Jung had surprisingly little to add to the orthodox psychoanalytic view of transference. However, Jung was the psychoanalyst who made thera-pists aware of the importance of countertransference. He saw therapy as a learning situation for the therapist as well as for the patient. According to the Jungian view, much of the influence of therapy is related to the personality of the analyst. Not only is the therapist a confessor who grants society's forgiveness to the patient, but he also is a fellow partic-ipant in the therapy session. The confessional act leads to transference, which, with the help of therapeutic interpretations, will provide the in-dividual with insight. However, this is still not enough to effect a change in the patient's behavior. The therapist, working with the patient, must find new goals for the patient's freed libido. Thus, Jung felt that a truly successful analysis would not only affect the behavioral goals of the patient, but would affect the goals of the therapist as well.

Since Adler considered that the goal of therapy was the socialization of the individual, Adlerian therapists believe the artificial situation of trans-ference should be avoided. Members of this group of therapists think transference is created only with a view toward pointing out the sexual components of an individual's relationship with others. Also, they believe that transference tends to further the patient's inferiority feelings. Thus, Adlerian therapists contend that the creation of transference adds to the patient's problem. They find it is an easy way to gain affection, but it is, in their view, a false goal in therapy. To avoid such a trap, an Adlerian therapist must help the patient take full responsibility for his own con-duct, and learn to profit from his own mistakes. Though this is a laborious process, Adlerian therapists believe it is actually a simpler and far healthier process than transference.

The goal of analysis, according to Horney, was to break the neurotic's "vicious circle," or repetitive compulsion. She placed particular em-phasis on the directive role of the therapist. A Hornerian therapist, thus, would be a leader in the therapeutic relationship and, as such, would not foster transference. Horney also believed a therapist must be aware of the dangers of countertransference and guard against becoming emo-tionally involved with the patient, in order to maintain his objective direc-tion of the therapy.

Sullivan's view of transference was similar to that of orthodox psycho-analysts. He believed that transference is part of the self dynamism used to protect the personality from anxiety aroused by therapeutically re-awakened childhood threats. Sullivan saw transference in terms of a repetitive phenomenon, and he believed the therapist should interpret the patient's attitudes and early experiences as such. He did not believe that all interpersonal events that transpired between the patient and his therapist were repetitive. However, since transference did occur and caused the therapist to be re-created to fit in with the needs of the patient, it was the duty of the therapist to clarify his distortion through the process of interpretations.

INTERPRETATIONS AND TREATMENT TERMINATION

Interpretations. Interpretations are statements used by the therapist to help the patient gain insight into his own behavior. These statements are based on the therapist's understanding of the individual in treatment and on his knowledge of the general principles of psychoanalytic theory. Interpretations may deal with any aspect of the therapeutic situation; what is interpreted will depend to a large extent on the progress of therapy.

In the early part of analysis, interpretations will take the form of questions that act like probes into the patient's feelings and responses. They may often have to be rephrased or repeated before they will be accepted and understood by the patient. Thus, when using interpretations, the therapist must guard against just saying, "How did you feel?" or merely repeating, "Why?" after every statement. The patient would recognize the superficiality and laziness of such an approach and resent it. Questioning techniques the therapist uses should be relevant and parsimonious and should act as a wedge into the slightly opening door of self-knowledge. Effective questioning would include such statements as "What occurs to you after telling me that?"; "I wonder what made you think of that"; or sometimes, more simply, the therapist may "raise an eyebrow" or say, "Oh, really—hmm." Later therapy interpretations may become more informative or explanatory, for instance, in describing to the patient the nature of transference.

Even though in interpretations the therapist is actively making important contributions to treatment, he must always remember that interpretations should be, primarily, incentives for the patient's self-examination. The therapist must maintain the position that he is helping the patient make interpretations. The goal of the interpretive process is for the patient to be able to make interpretations for himself. For this reason, the therapist should not jump into a silence to provide an interpretation. He must remember that the patient is always working in therapy, even during periods of strong resistance, such as silences or angry demonstrations. Interpretations must be used sparingly and only when the patient is at a point where he can almost formulate them for himself.

It is difficult for an individual to accept any kind of statements about himself, especially statements of a very personal nature. Thus, not only should the patient be brought to a point where he can formulate interpretive statements for himself, but, also, the therapeutic atmosphere must be one of calm support and acceptance. Further, the patient needs to have respect and affection for the therapist in order not to be threatened by an interpretation. The therapist must remember that pronouncements do not cure. It is only as the patient is able to understand and act on his own formulated responses that a cure is effected. Thus, the therapist must never condescend, be paternal, or make adviser-type statements. For example, the therapist should not say, "Now, here is what you should do," or "This is the way it is," "You really should try this," or "I know," or "The only thing to do is . . . ." More acceptable phrasing would be "What do you think?" "Why do you suppose this situation keeps recurring for you?" Since interpretations are used to penetrate the defensive armor of the patient, the interpretive process shows a great similarity to the analytic process in general. When the patient reaches the point where he is able to give more interpretations than he is getting, his re-education is nearing completion.

Jung, as did all good psychoanalysts, varied the quantity and quality of his interpretations according to the personality type of the patient. He believed an introvert should be given very extensive and detailed interpretations, whereas an extrovert would be satisfied with straightforward prescriptions for behavioral change. Of course, many of Jung's interpretations dealt with the objective and subjective nature of the patient's symbols. Also, in a Jungian analysis, the therapist can be questioned, and he, like the patient, must try to provide an adequate and appropriate answer.

Adler believed that interpretations should be made on the basis of the therapist's understanding of the specific life style of the patient, his specific problem situation, and the specific significance of his symptoms. He believed that such an understanding could come about only through empathy, intuition, and guessing. He thought interpretations should take place in a free and friendly conversation in which the patient would always take the initiative.

Adler found that the patient, particularly in neurosis, strenuously resists disruption of his life style. However, these resistances can be broken down by therapeutic interpretations, and by the correct predictions the therapist makes regarding the patient's behavior. Once the patient sees how accurate the behavioral predictions are, he is able to accept the therapeutic interpretations, and, in this way, he begins to gain some insight into his life style.

Though the patient is allowed to indicate the direction of the therapeutic session, an analyst following Horney's method would deliberately conduct the course of the analysis. An analyst with Horney's orientation would use interpretations more liberally than orthodox psychoanalysts to clarify a patient's statements, to point out contradictions in a patient's behavior, and to make suggestions for the patient to pursue.

Sullivan's view of interpretations differed only slightly from that of orthodox Freudians. Sullivan's major difference was concerned with the content that was clarified in interpretations. For example, though he believed that interpretation of early life experiences was important, he would not interpret them as sexual fixations at a developmental stage; instead, he would interpret them as problems in social relationships, brought about by the patient's pursuit of satisfaction and security. As previously indicated, all psychoanalysts tend to base interpretations on their own particular theoretical and semantic base.

Termination of Treatment. A particularly important element of analytic treatment is the proper time for treatment to terminate. The therapist has the major responsibility for the evaluation of the patient for termination of treatment. Therefore, he must guard against certain common pitfalls. For example, transference is often seen as the turning point in treatment, but it must not be seen as the end. Also, symptom removal may occur quite rapidly, and the patient may feel that he no longer has need for additional treatment. However, such progress is only limited success and must not be taken as a basic cure.

There are, of course, no commonly accepted criteria for termination. However, in the therapist's evaluation of the patient, there must be at least indications of many more successes than failures in two major areas: the patient's acceptance of himself and the patient's effective participation in his relationship with others. In the first area, the therapist's evaluation should be concerned with such things as the patient's self-esteem, his self-confidence, and his ability to deal healthily and adequately with his conflicts and with himself. In the second area, that of interpersonal relations, it is necessary for the therapist to evaluate such things as the patient's affectional relationships, his ability to deal appropriately with others, and his ability to feel comfortable in social groups. Social interactions should be marked by pleasure, by sensitivity to the needs of others, by patience, and by an interest in the activities of others. The ability to work, to function on a job, and to enjoy recreational or play activity would also be considered.

As in the general therapeutic process, the patient must come to acceptance of the end of treatment at about the same time as the analyst. When the patient begins to enjoy his effective participation in society, and when he no longer needs the therapist to interpret for him, he is quite likely to suggest termination. If, after an evaluation of the patient's behavior, the analyst feels that therapy can be discontinued, he should direct the sessions toward that end. A word of caution must be given at this point; it is not unusual for symptoms to reappear on a temporary basis when the patient feels the responsibility of his coming independence. These symptoms are to be expected and can be dealt with through interpretation.

Jung viewed psychotherapy as a process intended to heal the division between the opposite elements of one's personality. Thus, Jung would terminate treatment when there was evidence of symptom removal, when the patient achieved an acceptance of his total self, and when the patient had found new meaning and purpose in life.

Increased social cooperation and a better understanding of one's life style were the two most important elements of a successful Adlerian analysis. Every gesture, every word, and every movement of the patient must have evidenced these goals before termination was considered. However, in general, Adler found that increases in social awareness and correction of one's life style could be achieved within two to three weeks by the mildly disturbed patient, and the more severely disturbed individual could be helped within a period of from two to three years.

The main purpose of an analysis by an adherent of Horney is to help the patient regain his spontaneity, find his measure of value, and gain the courage to be himself. Thus, an analysis should be terminated when the patient's neurotic strategies are no longer needed and the patient's idealized self image is replaced by a realistic acceptance of his true self.

Sullivan contended that an individual entered into psychoanalysis because he was unable to solve his own problems and could not use all of his given abilities effectively. Thus, the therapist's major job in analysis was to rid the patient of behavior that interfered with an efficient use of his abilities and to help the individual solve his problems. A Sullivan analysis would be terminated when the patient's interfering obstacles were overcome and the patient was able to use most of his abilities in an adequate adaptive process.

PRACTICAL CONSIDERATIONS

Freud compared psychoanalysis to a surgical operation and contended that, in order for analysis to be successful, it must be carried out under the most favorable conditions. One of these conditions is the ruling out of medical problems. The best way this condition can be met is to require the patient to undergo complete physical examination by a competent physician before therapy is initiated. Also, before therapy is to begin, it is important to evaluate the patient's attitude toward treatment. Since therapy rests largely in the hands of the patient, he must be motivated toward health. For this reason, treatment should never be entered into when the patient has been forced, tricked, or otherwise falsely coerced into entering therapy.

Since analysis is a radical and disturbing series of events, the patient should be advised that important decisions such as those involved in changing jobs, getting married or divorced, etc., should be deferred until analysis is completed. Further, the patient should be advised that therapy is a tentative and nonmagical procedure that guarantees no cure. He should be made aware of the fact that the major burden of treatment rests with him, the patient. He should be informed that treatment is a long process and that any real results will not be evident for some time. However, the patient has every right to expect that beneficial changes will occur if he is taken and kept in treatment. The patient also has a right to expect that he will not be abandoned by the therapist before treatment is completed. If an emergency arises and the analyst is not able to treat the patient, then he should refer him to another therapist and help the patient to accept such a compromise.

Often a preliminary discussion is held with the patient in which these and similar questions are discussed. Other matters that are often discussed are such things as the hour and length of time allotted for the patient's appointments, frequency of treatment, estimated length of treatment, and payment arrangements. There should be an agreed-upon hour and session duration that are rather rigidly adhered to. Often the patient will miss appointments, be late, or wish to run over the allotted time, but the therapist must recognize these as signs of resistance, interpret them to the patient as such, and refuse to be manipulated by them.

Appointments must be frequent enough to ensure treatment continuity. Analysts differ among themselves, however, as to just how frequent these appointments should be for maximum effectiveness. Thus, a patient may be seen every day or once every fortnight, depending on his condition and the point of view of the analyst. Horney, for example, saw her patients two or three times a week, whereas Freud usually saw his patients an hour every day.

Length of treatment, like appointments, is dependent on the severity of the patient's problem and the orientation and goal of therapy. It may vary from a few months to many years. A Jungian analyst, for example, may discontinue treatment after only a few weeks. Jung used termination as a treatment device in order to throw the patient back on his own resources and discourage overdependence on the therapist. However, the patient is expected to re-enter treatment with the Jungian analyst within a short time, and such a process of treatment-termination-treatment may continue for several years, even for a lifetime. As can be seen from this example, treatment may last from a minimum of two weeks (Adler) to a lifetime (Jung), though a complete analysis generally can be expected to take from two to seven years.

Concerning the question of charges, payment should be frankly discussed and not hidden by a false cloak of professional dignity. Within generally accepted professional limits, fees should be commensurate with the patient's ability to pay. Rarely should treatment be given without charge. The patient's motivation to get better is increased if each therapy session is costing him energy expenditure in terms of money, as well as time and effort. Occasionally, the payment of fees may be part of the patient's pathology. For example, an anal sadistic character may hold back fees as part of his retentive character, or an oral erotic character may shower his therapist with gifts. These are both resistances and should be handled through interpretations. At no time should a large debt accumulate, because then the value of payment would be lost, and only rarely should a gift be accepted. As indicated, some therapists cover all these topics in a preliminary discussion. Others, however, believe that these matters are handled most effectively as they are raised by the patient in the natural course of therapy.

Other areas for the therapist's consideration are concerned with such matters as the therapist-patient interaction in treatment, that is, the importance of the formalities of social courtesy and politeness, the use of a chair or a couch, sitting face to face with, behind, or beside the patient, etc. The answers to such questions are dependent on two considerations. First, how these practices will affect treatment of the patient and, second, what is most natural and comfortable for the therapist.

All actions in therapy are oriented toward beneficial treatment of the patient. Thus, whether or not a couch is used is largely dependent on the therapeutic results sought. If the patient can freely associate more productively on a couch than on a chair, a couch should be used. If he is more comfortable in a face-to-face relationship, a chair should be used. Freud, of course, used a couch because he felt it was easier for a patient to give himself up to his unconscious processes when lying down and not faced by the therapist. Sullivan favored the use of a chair, because he felt it emphasized the equalitarian relationship between the therapist and the patient. However, in terms of success, either arrangement is so idiosyncratic that it should be varied in order to meet the needs of both patient and therapist.

In regard to interaction between the patient and the therapist, it should be remembered that, in order for therapy to be successful, the therapist must remain rational and objective. Since close friendships do not lend themselves to rational, objective behavior, any action that would tend to foster such a relationship should be discouraged. Thus, a therapist would rarely discuss his hobbies or personal life with the patient. However, whether or not the therapist opens the door for the patient, helps the patient into a chair, or lights the patient's cigarette is a matter of individual preference. Freud, as would be expected, did none of these things. Following the strict Victorian tradition, he maintained the role of the respected, rather distant, *Herr Doktor* who felt that matters of politeness were of little importance to the major job of treatment. Adler, in a more equalitarian fashion, sought to reduce tension in the treatment session. Not only did he observe the normal rules of courtesy, but he also tried to begin each treatment session with an appropriate joke or fable. As can be seen from these examples, interactions between the therapist and the patient should be based on the natural personalities of both.

SUMMARY

Psychoanalysis is concerned with the psychological treatment of mental disorders. Since psychoanalytic therapeutic procedures are based on an etiological approach, it is similar to many other forms of psychotherapy. Underlying the etiological approach are certain assumptions of psychoanalytic theory that provide the structure and base for treatment methods used in psychoanalysis. These assumptions include psychological determinism, motivation, psychological economics, the genetic method, and the unconscious.

Since it is of singular importance in therapeutic practice, psychoanalytic therapists have devised various methods to get at the contents of a patient's unconscious. The most important of these methods involve free association, dream analysis, hypnosis, psychological slips, projective techniques, and the life pattern.

The genetic approach offers another important area for understanding of human behavior and character formation. The major psychoanalytic stages of development concerned with the growth of personality are the oral, anal, phallic, latency, and genital stages. Neo-Freudians have varied in assessing the time limits and importance of these stages. They have also included other stages such as infancy, pre-adolescence, and maturity.

Analytic treatment can best be understood in terms of regression, resistance, transference, interpretation, and termination. Treatment is concerned with bringing repressed material into consciousness. There is a resistance to this procedure, but two of the major resistances, regression and transference, may be used in treatment. Regression helps the patient to obtain an emotional resolution of his conflict. Transference substitutes a more easily handled neurosis for the original neurosis. Interpretations provide the patient with the intellectual insight needed for the synthesis and understanding of repressed material. Finally, termination is important insofar as it relates to the total treatment process, and certain guidelines should be considered for the evaluation of a successfully completed analysis.

REFERENCES

ADLER, A. 1927. *Understanding human nature.* (Translated by W. B. WOLFE.) New York: Garden City Books.

ADLER, A. 1959. *The practice and theory of individual psychology.* (Translated by P. RADIN.) Ames, Iowa: Littlefield.

ALEXANDER, F. 1961. *The scope of psychoanalysis 1921–1961* (selected papers). New York: Basic Books.

ANSBACHER, H. L., and ANSBACHER, ROWENA R. (eds.). 1956. *The individual psychology of Alfred Adler.* New York: Basic Books.

BLUM, G. S. 1953. *Psychoanalytic theories of personality.* New York: McGraw-Hill.

BOTTOME, PHYLLIS. 1957. *Alfred Adler, apostle of freedom.* London: Faber & Faber.

BREUER, J., and FREUD, S. 1957. *Studies on hysteria.* (Translated and edited by J. STRACHEY in collaboration with ANNA FREUD.) New York: Basic Books.

DRY, A. M. 1961. *The psychology of Jung: A critical interpretation.* London: Methuen.

FENICHEL, O. 1941. *Problems of psychoanalytic technique.* New York: Psychoanalytic Quarterly.

FENICHEL, O. 1945. *The psychoanalytic theory of neurosis.* New York: Norton.

FORDHAM, FRIEDA. 1956. *An introduction to Jung's psychology.* Harmondsworth England: Penguin.

FREUD, S. 1938. *The basic writings of Sigmund Freud.* (Edited by A. A. BRILL.) New York: Random House.

FREUD, S. 1953. *A general introduction to psychoanalysis.* (Translated by JOAN RIVIERE.) New York: Doubleday.

FROMM-REICHMANN, FRIEDA. 1950. *Principles of intensive psychotherapy.* Chicago: Univer. of Chicago Press.

HALL, C. S., and LINDZEY, G. 1957. *Theories of personality.* New York: Wiley.

HARPER, R. A. 1959. *Psychoanalysis and psychotherapy: 36 systems.* Englewood Cliffs, N.J.: Prentice-Hall.

HORNEY, KAREN. 1939. *New ways in psychoanalysis.* New York: Norton.

JACOBI, JOLANDE. 1943. *The psychology of Jung.* New Haven: Yale Univer. Press.

JUNG, C. G. 1939. *The integration of personality.* New York: Farrar & Rinehart.

MENNINGER, K. 1958. *Theory of psychoanalytic technique.* New York: Basic Books.

MULLAHY, P. 1948. *Oedipus: Myth and complex.* New York: Hermitage House.

MUNROE, RUTH L. 1955. *Schools of psychoanalytic thought.* New York: Holt, Rinehart & Winston.

SULLIVAN, H. S. 1954. *The psychiatric interview.* New York: Norton.

SULLIVAN, H. S. 1956. *Clinical studies in psychiatry.* New York: Norton.

WALKER, N. 1957. *A short history of psychotherapy in theory and practice.* London: Routledge.

WAY, L. 1950. *Adler's place in psychology.* New York: Macmillan.

WOLFF, W. 1956. *Contemporary psychotherapists examine themselves.* Springfield, Ill.: Charles C Thomas.

20

Group Psychotherapy

HUBERT S. COFFEY *

Among the many developments that have been directed toward the alleviation of psychological discomfort, none will stand out more strikingly than the phenomenal interest in group psychotherapy that has characterized the field of psychotherapy during the past quarter of a century. Perhaps the greatest impetus to its expansion as a therapeutic technique has been World War II. The need to treat large numbers of patients suffering from the pangs of emotional discomfort engendered through the necessity of adjusting to the various conditions of military life directed the attention of many therapists toward group treatment. For many therapists, this seemed at first a necessary expedient but not the preferred method of treatment. But, also, many have found in employing group treatment that it has certain virtues that recommend it as a method of treatment quite without any consideration of expediency.

The earliest attempts to use a group approach to psychotherapy were reviewed by Klapman (1946). As will be seen from his review, much of the early effort was of a didactic type where the patient functioned in a classroom-like situation and where the role of the leader-therapist was not unlike that of a lecturer. In this pedagogical approach, it was common for the therapist to introduce a predetermined topic for consideration, to outline the major points, and to stimulate the group to participate in the discussion. In this approach, there was little attention given to what is now commonly referred to as *group processes,* and the main emphasis was on producing better motivation and understanding. Often such group meetings were held with the topic oriented to a somatic illness such

* Hubert S. Coffey, Ph.D. (University of Iowa), Associate Professor of Psychology, University of California at Berkeley.

as tuberculosis, and often the groups consisted of patients whose attitudinal difficulties might be focused toward specific somatic or physiological conditions. Much of it was what Klapman saw as inspirational-repressive.

It was, indeed, inevitable that dynamic theory would influence group therapy, just as its impact on psychological theory and individual therapy was being felt. The therapeutic problems of persons in a group seem so closely parallel to those of persons in individual therapy that it was natural that group therapists who are psychoanalytically oriented would begin to be concerned with problems of transference, resistance, interpretation, and working through. As psychotherapy in America took on a more dynamic coloration, the perception of groups as involving relationships not only to a leader but among patients as well began to arouse speculation. It was also natural that those who were interested in the client-centered frame of reference would also bring to group therapy this point of view. Gradually, the view of group therapy as an expedient method of mass treatment or as an analogue of classroom procedure began to give way to more dynamic formulations. Today, the field of group therapy involves workers of many different points of view, functioning in a great variety of settings, working with many different kinds of patients, and concerned with a great range of therapeutic problems. Therefore, it is difficult in this brief chapter to give anything like a complete survey of what is going on in the field of group psychotherapy at present. Rather, we shall be concerned primarily with the common problems group psychotherapists have encountered and some of the techniques that have been used.

A survey of the literature makes it perfectly clear that it is more fruitful to speak of group psychotherapies than of group psychotherapy. For, although group psychotherapies hold in common the single element of involving a number of patients in the therapy situation, the methods employed depend to a high degree on the kind of patient and setting with which therapy is performed. For this reason, I have chosen to discuss group psychotherapy under four distinct headings: therapy with neurotic patients, therapy with hospitalized patients, T group training, and conjoint family therapy. Group therapy with children will be discussed in the next chapter.

THERAPY WITH NEUROTIC PATIENTS

Most of the reports of group psychotherapy are concerned with the adult neurotic patient, seen most typically in some kind of outpatient clinic setting. Therapeutic treatment depends in no small measure on assumptions that are implicit in the patient's coming to the clinic voluntarily for treatment. Although every patient manifests some ambivalences and resistances in seeking treatment, except under unusual circumstances, it is the discomfort that accompanies his neurotic symptoms that motivates him to seek help. Also, it is his anxiety about himself that serves him in the utilization of the group for treatment. However one may conceptualize the group process, the anxieties of patients serve as a kind of cohesive substratum through which group therapeutic processes develop and work. Where these anxieties are accessible, there is ready potential for group formation. It should be pointed out here that this point would be of less significance were it not for the fact that, in some kinds of groups where such anxieties are not accessible, the method of group treatment will of necessity be different. Failure to see these differences leads to inappropriate procedures. (See the section on group therapy with hospitalized patients.

In dealing with neurotic patients, theorists in group psychotherapy have much in common, while at the same time they tend to emphasize rather different points of view. All would agree very likely with Frank and Ascher (1951) that group psychotherapy provides a situation of support, stimulation, and reality testing for the patient. Here, the group is seen as a situation where patients agree that whatever is said has significance and that there is freedom to say it. A social climate is built up wherein the patient's inalienable rights are those of expressing his feelings and of sharing with the group whatever occurs to him. The support element is expressed in the willingness of other patients to reassure him, so, though there may not be other places where he can talk in this way, the group social climate is one in which he can feel perfectly safe in saying what he wants to say. This attitude makes it relatively comfortable for the patient to ventilate his anxieties and hostilities in the presence of others without fear of resentment or punishment. Likewise, the confidence of each patient in participating in this manner tends to bring into consciousness many aspects of his life that he might have repressed or denied unconsciously. For example, the patient who relates an incident of childhood when he felt himself to be punished unjustly may have found the voice to speak of such an event after having listened to another patient recount a similar event. We feel here not only the element of support but also a real element of stimulation during which those aspects of life heretofore inaccessible to verbalization becomes verbalized because of the participation of another group member.

The role of the group leader, or therapist, in developing this social climate is one of great importance. It is clear that his attitude of permissiveness and lack of judgmental function promotes openness in the group. Support and stimulation as a function of group participation is in a large measure related to how the leader is seen, and what it is felt he will permit. Often the initial orientation of the group may be facilitated by the leader's interpretation of "This is a group where we can indicate how we feel about things—where we can say anything we like." It goes without saying that, for this norm to be ultimately accepted, the leader must act in accordance with the precept as well as verbalize it.

Such groups do not fulfil their function solely in terms of ventilation and catharsis. Rather, the next step, that of *reality testing*, lies at the very heart of group psychotherapy. If we can assume that each neurotic patient brings to the group situation an inadequate self image, a distorted view of other persons, or both, the process of group discussion is one in which he continually tests the adequacy of these perceptions and corrects them in view of the evidence he is able to obtain in the course of group relationships. In large measure, the group exists to develop the type of personal reality-testing situations, nonthreatening in character, without external consequences, that provide him with materials by which his own perceptions may be corrected. In a real sense, this situation, so different from others he has known, so artificial in its lack of organic relation to other aspects of his life, is a highly compacted version of what normally happens in the psyche-group relations (Bion, 1961) of the child as he develops in his peer relationships. It may not be an overgeneralization to hypothesize that it is persons who have been deprived of such psyche-group relationships who feel the need for the therapy, and that this, indeed, is one reason why group therapy itself may be the effective medium for them.

Reality testing cannot be thought of solely or even primarily in the sense of shared verbalizations. From the moment of its inception, the group situation involves a network of human relationships, both verbal and nonverbal, and, because of the anxieties with their strong interpersonal components, these human relationships will be emotionally charged. It is no wonder then that, after an initial phase of getting acquainted has been welcomed and lived through, the group is likely to become concerned with the attitudes toward each other that are acted out in terms of pairing, rivalry, hostility, and mutual support. One of the advantages of group therapy as seen by its advocates is that the group provides multiple stimuli for each member, and each member works through a variety of relationships on the dimensions of love-hate and domination-submission, all at the same time, in a situation that approximates real-life more closely than the typical individual therapy relationship does.

The role of the leader in this conception of the function of reality testing seems to most writers to be crucial. If we recognize no major points of controversy in his functions as one who promotes a social climate wherein support and stimulation can be developed, we do see a diversity of viewpoints in the extent to which he functions as a representative of social reality through his presence—through his role as clarifier and interpreter. Perhaps, before we discuss theoretical differences in such a role, it should be pointed out that the group situation does provide the therapist with an abundance of data about all of the patients and their interrelationships in the group, concerning which he can make his interpretation. However, what the therapist does with respect to reality testing is closely connected with his conception of the dynamics of group formation. Here we see the source of rather widely distinct techniques.

Interpretation of the Group Process. The search for a theoretical foundation that explains group formation led many group therapists to Freud's insightful and provocative work on group psychology (Fairweather, 1964). Acceptance of his theory of the primal horde and the relation of the siblings to the father has induced many therapists to construct the therapy situation as one that bears symbolic resemblance to its mythical prototype; the therapist sees himself as the father figure and often has associated with him as a coleader, although of lesser authority, a female therapist. The assumptions here are that the therapy situation should reincarnate the family and that the therapists should re-enact symbolically the parental roles, while sibling rivalries for the parental figures are the very core of group relationships. Although this analogue may be recognized metaphorically, its consequences in leader reactivity and role are seldom made explicit. Of more significance is the fact that it is a setting where interpretation is oriented to the total group. Shaskan (1952) has formulated the theory in his statement that "because individuals have the same relation to the leader, they can relate to (identify with) one another and thus form the group. Interpretation made to the group presupposes that individuals are considering similar material."

Shaskan's technique, which derives from that of Schilder (1938), is to provide for a situation of group interaction whereby such an interpretation is facilitated. He has his patients form a circle and then begins the session of therapy by asking a patient for comment. The patient is free to say whatever he thinks, ask any question that comes to his mind, or address any comment or question to the leader or to another patient. On the other hand, he may not choose to respond in any verbal way, and the patient sitting next to him is then asked for comment. Any patient in the group is free to respond spontaneously to any other patient, and sometimes the comment of one patient may provoke a lively discussion. At other times, the consecutive comments of patients may be quite isolated, apparently unrelated associations. In any case, whenever a comment or question is addressed to the leaders, they do not respond in this portion of the session. About three-quarters of the way through the session, the leaders, a male therapist and a female therapist, devote five or ten minutes to an interpretive summary. This summary is devoted exclusively to the question of what the group was doing and never singles out particular patients; it is totally group-oriented. After the summary, five or ten minutes are devoted to a discussion of the interpretation. A dramatic example of this method is given in some detail by Shaskan in his discussion of what happens when the group shares a common fantasy. The interpretation of the material is not only in line with the disposition to give group interpretations, but it also fits neatly—perhaps too neatly—the psychoanalytic formulation of group formulation. A series of papers by Shaskan and his colleagues is based on this approach to group therapy and sets forth in lucid exposition many derivatives from the basic psychoanalytic point of view.

Perhaps the most extreme position with respect to interpretation and the relation of the therapist to the group is that characteristic of group therapy at the Tavistock Clinic, in London. Although it is extreme as compared to most practices in America, in some ways one can agree with its advocates that it is a logical next step. This logic is related to the fact that the Tavistock practice has been influenced by a thoroughly psychoanalytic position, the implications of which are rigorously adhered to, and by a clinical application of Lewinian field theory, particularly as its implications have been developed by Bion (1961). It is of interest here to note that, until recently, little or no effective communication between group therapists and those interested in group dynamics has been possible; but, with Bion's work and some recent attempts (Thelen and Whitaker, 1958; Watson, 1952) to apply his more clinically oriented concepts to group process as seen in small-group discussion situations, a bridge seems to have been made.

Ezriel and Sutherland have formulated the Tavistock position with great clarity. The position of Ezriel (1950) might be summarized as follows:

1. Treat *all* material as transference material to be used for "here and now" interpretations; 2. Everything a patient says or does during a session is considered as expressing his need for a relationship with the therapist; 3. Distinction between types of object relationships before therapist can interpret: (1) object relationship with group and the therapist, the required one; (2) a relationship which the patient feels would be calamitous if he gave in to his desire of entering the avoided object relationship.

Of greater significance, but in no way independent of the above summary, is the reliance of the Tavistock therapists on what they conceive to be "common group tension." This common group tension occurs when several people meet in a group

. . . and each member projects his unconscious phantasy objects upon various other group members and then tries to manipulate them accordingly. Each member will stay in a role assigned to him by another only if it happens to coincide with his own unconscious phantasy and it allows him to manipulate others in appropriate roles. Otherwise, he will try to twist the discussion until the real group does correspond to his phantasy group. The result of each member['s] doing this is that there will soon be established a common denominator, a common group tension, out of each member's individual dominant unconscious tension. [Ezriel, 1950.]

The role of the therapist is to analyze the role assumed by each group member in dealing with the common group tension. It is in this way that the defense mechanism of the patient in dealing with *his own* dominant unconscious tension is demonstrated. Reality testing, according to Ezriel, begins when it is demonstrated to the patient that he adopts one course of behavior and avoids another because he fears the supposedly disastrous consequences of the latter.

The function of the therapist in this view is one of locating the common group tension and of relating individual defensive behavior to it. Thus, the Tavistock therapist does not eschew individual interpretation as long as it is group-relevant and as long as the criterion of group relevance is formulated as common group tension. Within this frame of reference, what has sometimes been called "individual interpretation" may well be called by Tavistock therapists "group interpretations."

Individual Therapy in Groups. Another conception of group therapy that many see as considerably different from those whose exclusive aim is group interpretation is a form of group therapy that might well be called "therapy in groups." In this form of group therapy, there is no attempt to posit any basic group process or to relate group therapy to any particular historical theory of group formation. Rather, the attempt is to utilize the conditions that obtain in a group under certain types of leadership, namely, support and stimulation, and focus upon the individual problem as it is expressed in the group situation. Many of the therapists who function in this manner refer loosely to something called "the group process," but what they usually mean is the permissive attitude of the therapist that begets an attitude of mutual confidence in which patients are free to discuss their own and each other's problems.

Coffey and his colleagues have studied a number of therapy groups, using as their point of departure an interest in the theoretical formulations of Harry Stack Sullivan. Specifically, they have attempted to view the therapy situation as an interpersonal situation wherein the conscious and unconscious social roles of patients are given optimal opportunity to be seen in relation to each other. Their assumption has been that neurotic problems often lie in the disparity between what the patient sees himself as doing and what is communicated to others, which too often has the patients' unconscious social roles as the source. Most of their groups followed the same pattern of development, and this was significantly influenced by the facts that they uniformly were conducted for the same number of sessions and that the termination point was known to all at the beginning of the sessions. These authors could distinguish between three phases of group development in which the roles of the patients and the functions of leadership can be distinguished.

First, there is the period of *defensiveness and resistance*. In this phase, the patient brings out his neurotic social role; he tends to repeat in his approach to therapy the same social role that had proved so ineffective in real-life situations. The tasks of the therapist during the first phase are to allow defensive roles to develop, to encourage patients to describe their views of themselves and their problems, and to avoid the development of a leader-centered group.

The second phase was termed the period of *confiding*. In this phase, emphasis is placed on data such as dreams, fantasies, early memories, and parental relations, which patients relate. This phase is one in which anxiety about maintenance of conscious social roles is less evident, and patients are freer to deal with unconscious material. The leader's function is that of supporting excursions into unconscious roles and using data from the first phase to support or clarify the leader or group interpretations. The confiding period is one of great group cohesion, and, although neurotic disparities between conscious and unconscious roles may be expressed in many different ways, the recognition of problems of each other by group members and their acceptance of idiosyncrasies develop a close interpersonal bond. At this time, members contribute associations and interpretations with reference to the content of the active members, and these interpretations often set the pace for the therapist as they indicate the readiness for interpretation in relation to the evident feeling and the available evidence as seen in interpersonal relations.

The third stage was called the *integrative-prospective* stage. The group continues to produce genetic and symbolic material, and the interpretations of the therapist and members take into account more evidence produced by the patients in the group, and are therefore likely to be more integrative and extensive. Much of the time during the last 7 sessions of the 24 is devoted to comprehensive summaries for each person. Particular emphasis is given to the honest and positive relations that have evolved in the group. The amount of change achieved in the therapy seems to be directly related to the integration of the social role.

The question "Who are you?" a modal self-inquiry of phase one, becomes related to the modal question of phase two, "Why are you this way?" The therapeutic failures are those who cannot accept the definition of their roles in phase one, and who continue the defensiveness through the later sessions—usually increasing their isolation from other members. Answers to the theme question of phase three, "Where do you go from here?" depend on the progress in the preceding stages. The individual, now aware of his rigid social techniques and inner conceptions of "self" and "other" on which they are based, has new views of himself and the world, which move him toward change. He understands the interpersonal techniques by which he handles anxiety. He understands the effect his social role has on others. He understands better the dilemmas and defenses of others. He has some insight into the unconscious self conceptions that motivate his defensive behavior. He glimpses the root of his derogatory self conception in the traumata of the past. He becomes aware of the irrational expectations he projects onto "significant others," and the genetic causes for his current misperceptions of others. He realizes that he has changed his role and dropped his social defenses in the group, and he is encouraged to do so in his life outside the group.

I shall illustrate these three stages by reference to the behavior of a group member, Jones. In the first stage, Jones described himself as nurturant, nonaggressive, genial, and friendly and said he saw the world as friendly. But, even though he was describing "who" he was according to an optimistic self conception, he was seen by others in the group as dominating, directive, defensive, and hostile. The perception of him by others was based primarily on what he did in the group, how he challenged other members, and how he sought to take the reins of the group in his own hands. In this phase, the great discrepancy between his self conception and the way others saw him was laid out on the table, probably where Jones could see it for the first time. It was clear that Jones was bringing into the group the same social mechanisms he used in his relations outside the group, even though in the outside world they had proved ineffective and led to acute anxiety. The culture of the external world was not organized to permit him to be aware of his social mechanisms, but, rather, placed him constantly on the defensive.

In the second phase of the group development, Jones uneasily entered the area of confiding. He was stimulated to do so by the beginning of an awareness that what group members were responding to in him was something he had never seen in himself. For the first time, he began to see that his behavior of coercion and dominance in the group did not coincide with his self image of virtuous deference and humility. When this disparity began to become more apparent to him, he began to be willing to surrender himself to the group in a spirit of self-examination. The group was supportive and sympathetic as he told his life story—an orphaned refugee child raised by cold and unfriendly aunts who punished and exploited him; his encounter with unsympathetic adults, including a rejecting schoolmaster; his need to develop a martyr's role, using virtuous superiority and psuedohumility to coerce others. His dreams were of misunderstood figures valiantly facing a hostile world. The genetic and projective content indicate clues as to why the person functions with his particular unconscious social role, and Jones, in relating this material, began to see that his domineering direction of group members and resistance to the leader and to the group were to provoke the rejecting hostility that stemmed from his deepest expectations from the past. The very process of sharing with the group his own parataxic distortions when this very process involved a process of acceptance by the group through its support and cautious interpretations was one that encouraged insight and change.

In the third phase, Jones began to make significant changes in his social reactions in the group. Emphasis was placed on expanding these changes with people in his daily life. In many of the sessions, Jones, along with others, reported on his success and failures in dealing with persons more realistically. Jones discovered to his surprise that the professor he feared and distrusted was actually in sympathy with his progress. He learned that his dormitory enemy suffered from shyness similar to his own. He found that his past social techniques had been self-defeating and isolating, and he grew in confidence and self-acceptance within the group, which served as a training laboratory for his life outside the group. The therapeutic failures, unlike Jones, are those who cannot accept the definition of their role as perceived by others from the very beginning. Since they cannot afford at this time to accept the relevant data the group has concerning them and is willing to share with them, they remain defensive and isolated. Sometimes, the group serves as a type of "socializing" experience that continues to motivate them to attend, and that may actually provide a softening up of defenses that need to be managed with slower timing and greater continuous repair than can be accomplished in brief group therapy.

In many essential ways, this approach has much more in common with the Tavistock approach than it would seem at first glance. (1) There is an emphasis on emotional relationships operating at the moment in the group, rather than on the content of discussions *per se*, (2) Interpretations to patients in the group are based on material produced in the group, and no use is made of information about the patient that is not derived from his behavior or verbalizations in the group, (3) The group forms a "culture" different from that of the outside world, and, whether it is thought of as a re-enactment of basic familial group processes or as a kind of "laboratory" in social relations, it is a milieu where the patient can think, feel, and act in a way that is not possible in any other group relationship, (4) The function of the group is to internalize within the patient a new methodology for understanding himself and understanding others. The insight that comes from interpretation of transferences and countertransference is designed to help him assess the present methodology he has for coping with the world. In the group situation, insight is not always gained from a preoccupation with the particular patient's problem, but he may gain understanding where the focus of attention is on another, providing there is an emotional connection between the other person and his own problem.

Bion (1961) has contributed significantly to the understanding of group process by differentiating between "emotionality" and "work" in the group. He has defined "emotionality" in terms of such modal processes as fight-flight, dependence, and pairing. Although he is less definitive about what "work" is, it can be seen as those aspects of group process wherein the energies of the group are organized to resolve problems of group tension and transference. Bion also refers to emotionality as "basic assumptions." He is inclined to see groups as working through stages from dependence through the fight-flight and pairing dimensions.

The usefulness of his concepts with respect to the therapists' analysis of the group process and its implication for interpretation is shown in the following illustration. A therapy group of eight patients had been holding weekly meetings for about three months. The patients were all men ranging in age from twenty-two to forty-five, and all were veterans with service-connected disabilities. The first five or six sessions were devoted to safe, peripheral, and irrelevant content. As this was an "open" group, some members dropped out and others were added during the course of treatment. Each time a change in personnel occurred, there tended to be some movement away from more personal and emotionally significant discussion. The therapist made some interpretations about the "flight" from important considerations and, by his permissive attitude but unwillingness to supply direct support, consistently worked toward liberation of the inevitable dependence on the leader. The group began to have a sense of "working" when the problem of one of the members was discussed in great detail.

At the very next meeting, a new member came into the group. He was a man of about fifty—an alcoholic, whose recent career had been one of sliding down the social scale. He talked rather more than is usual for a new member in his first meeting, and showed obvious signs of having been drinking.

At the next meeting of the group, he was even more garrulous, but, after he had talked for about 20 minutes—recalling incidents from what he reconstructed as a glorious past—the hostility of the group was turned on him. One member was extremely vociferous, saying that the newcomer was wasting the time of the group, that the group did not care about the new patient's past exploits, and indicating a great deal of resentment at his

monopolizing the time of the group when the group had many "more important" things to do. This vehement spokesman was joined by others,
and all expressed impatience with the new member, who retreated hastily,
indicating his submission to the will of the group.

Naturally, the therapist had several concerns here. He was concerned
lest the new member be driven from the group by the tide of hostility.
He was concerned about the possible success of the "pathology" of group
insensitivity and hostility. He saw that he should not go to the rescue of
an individual member, because such succor would mean that the other
group members must again work through their dependence problems with
the therapist. He could not side with the group, because this would only
fortify the group in "fight emotionality," which it would need to work
through all over again. What he did do, however, was to see the group
as having a "common group tension," which was communicated at the end
of the meeting in an interpretation. For 20 minutes before the close of
the session, the group "worked" hard on the problems they had been dealing with in the previous sessions before the new member came into the
group, but, during this time, the new member was excluded, and the group
showed signs of uneasiness about his treatment. What the therapist said
in providing an interpretive summary was about as follows:

We were concerned this evening about Mr. Smith. When he talked about
himself, we developed real hostility toward him. We were worried that he
might upset our way of working. We have taken a long time to get down to
"brass tacks," and now that we feel we are really working we want nothing to
disturb it. We realize that Mr. Smith was doing what we have been doing for
a long time, but have recently given up. The reason we felt so vehement in our
hostility is that we feel we are on shaky ground. We are tempted all the time
to go back to our ways of "flighting" from the problems we are now working on.
And, because we feel insecure about this, we are more likely to have strong
feelings about any behavior that would tempt us. But Mr. Smith has shown
us how far we have moved toward work and away from peripheral issues. Our
feelings of hostility had as much to do with ourselves as they did Mr. Smith.

This interpretation seemed correct to the group, and they joined in
recognizing its pertinence to their feelings and behavior. Further, it set
the boundaries sufficiently wide to include the new member, for, since
all could now see that he served as a focus for anxieties that actually were
more about themselves than about him, and now they could recognize
and deal with these displaced feelings, Mr. Smith could enter the group as
a full-fledged member. He did just that.

Bion's contributions to an understanding of the group-dynamic process
in therapy groups have a further point of interest for the theorist. It
seems to me that research in the dynamics of discussion groups that has
utilized his concepts of work and emotionality has made possible the
greatest progress in understanding of both the movement of groups toward

goals and the functions of leadership. Thelen (1958), at the Human Dynamics Laboratory, at the University of Chicago, is at present analyzing task-oriented and training groups, using Bion's categories.

The underlying process of emotionality and the balance between emotionality and work seem to be as significant in understanding the dynamics of nontherapy groups as in understanding therapy groups. Further, the function of leadership in both types of groups seems to involve a balance of the forces Bion describes, although it seems useful to distinguish the therapy groups we have been discussing from the discussion and action groups studied by students of group dynamics. It seems to be essential to understand any group formation partly in terms of the irrational and noncognitive elements that are joined with the rational and cognitive.

Eric Berne (1961) drew on rather different metaphors in order to formulate a therapeutic approach to group therapy. In his volume *Transactional Analysis in Psychotherapy,* the key concepts are the hypotheses that (1) all interactions can be viewed in terms of child, parent, and peer components and (2) relationships can be understood in terms of child-parent, parent-child, and peer-peer models. "Transactions" in the group can be made in terms of these internalized object relationships, which become manifest in the patient interactions and are the focuses of analysis by the therapist and the group members. Another concept that is utilized is that patients in the group as well as outside it develop "games" in which they carry on defensive relations with each other, and these "games" are actually communication structures that hide real feelings. The assumptions are that the "games" have a universal quality and that, if they can be seen for what they actually are, they expose much of the motivational and manipulative aspects of interactions that produce distortions in relationships that otherwise might be more authentic. The group is treated as a microcosm of society, and the transactions are seen as reflecting the ways in which individuals perpetuate unrealistic, asocial, and unproductive methods of interpersonal relations.

The present author has tried to draw a distinction between therapy and nontherapy groups that parallels the dichotomy Bion developed independently (1961). But the present author (1950) used the distinction Jennings made between "psyche groups" and "socio groups." Here, the difference was described in the focus and in the emphasis given to one or the other of the group processes. It was maintained that, while the effective action group must have visualized goals, and the cognitive and rational elements must predominate, there must be strong "psyche group forces" operating to ensure that involvement and ego satisfaction are obtained and work is carried through. In contrast, in therapy groups, the emphasis is on "psyche group process," wherein the group exists not to achieve a group action goal but to provide the kind of relationships whereby individual needs and goals can be realized.

Some Specific Issues in Group Therapy with Neurotics. Some persistent questions are frequently considered when one discusses the area of group psychotherapy. They have to do with practical considerations in the formation of the group and in its conduct. Unfortunately, there are few definitive answers available, although many opinions are expressed. In this section, I shall consider some of these questions and discuss some of the issues the group therapist must consider in formulating his own approach.

SELECTION OF PATIENTS. Perhaps the first questions that occur to the group therapist is "Who should be in the group? How shall the group be composed?" For years, the questions were considered almost solely in terms of clinical or diagnostic criteria. Either careful efforts were made to compose groups on the basis of diagnostic homogeneity (i.e., all patients were anxiety hysterics) or equally careful consideration was given to create diagnostic heterogeneity. Powdermaker and Frank (1953) concluded,

. . . on the basis of our own experience we concluded that, except for alcoholism, none of the attributes usually considered in grouping—age, intelligence, education, marital status, clinical diagnosis—are significant in themselves, either in determining which patients are suitable for group therapy or in selecting those to be treated in the same group.

It is the opinion of the author that perhaps the most important consideration for the usual group therapy situation is that the differences in educational and intellectual level be not too extreme. Above all, when there is a wide range of educational difference, the extreme should not be represented by only one patient in the group. It is very easy to isolate such a member. Since communication is the life blood of the group, obvious barriers to communication in terms of language differences and cultural differences should be avoided. On the other hand, it is my experience that, except for extremes, clinical criteria within the neurotic classification have little significance in group composition. Powdermaker and Frank also found that, in composing groups of psychotic patients, the social role, that is, ascendant versus submissive, talkative versus silent, hostile versus congenial, was a more important basis for selection. Groups seem to do best where there is a variety of roles played by the patients. It has been my experience that this is true with neurotics as well. I have often relied on the impression of the intake worker rather than any clinical diagnostic material. Further, I have found that ambulatory psychotics often function well in a group of neurotic patients. There seems to be something to the folklore that a psychotic patient who is able to communicate well is able to cut through the defensive group façade. In other words, in terms of the concepts of Bion, he is able to deal directly with the problems of emotionality in the group. This freedom on the part of a patient can add immeasurably to the therapeutic force of the group.

SIZE OF GROUP. There seems to be uniform agreement that, in the group therapy we have been considering, the maximum number of patients in the group should be 8. This agreement is indicated, not by any explicit principles, but by the fact that relatively isolated therapists, sometimes quite variant in point of view, seem to indicate 5 to 8 patients in the group as optimal. The more didactic groups, of course, often had the appearance of assemblages, as 20 to 30 patients were present. There is a real question whether, other than for historical significance, these groups should be thought of as examples of group psychotherapy.

SEX OF PATIENTS. Perhaps the most common situation is to find groups composed only of men or only of women. This is in part dictated by the fact that many of the groups that are reported are in Veterans Administration mental hygiene clinics, where there is a preponderance of male patients, or in hospitals where there is a sex-segregation policy. This is not to gainsay the fact that there are many groups composed of both men and women. There seems to be more general preference for the all-male or all-female groups on the basis of therapeutic principle. If one assumes that the group therapy situation must be viewed as part of the transference phenomenon, then, as Slavson pointed out (1951), a mixed group may favor the tendency to act out. He wrote,

During certain stages, the patients develop libidinal desires for the therapist as a parent substitute which for obvious reasons they cannot satisfy. They displace (or retransfer) them upon a fellow patient who may resemble either the natural parent or the newly-evolved parental image with which the patient invests the therapist. The activation of the libidinal drives and the proximity of an object for its [sic] gratification in the group favor the tendency to act out.

There are other considerations that favor single-sex groupings. Since much of the material brought out deals with sexuality, mixed groups feel greater inhibition in the discussion. This seems to be true where there are both male and female patients, even though the presence of a male therapist in a female group or a female therapist in a male group seems not to have this effect. As a matter of fact, as we have seen, some group therapists prefer the presence of both mother and father substitutes or symbols as therapists.

Powdermaker (1951) seems also to have implied that the cohesive forces needed for therapy groups are themselves derivatives of the natural group forces of late childhood and early adolescence. In group therapy, she felt, there are certain dynamic forces that do not appear in individual therapy. Further, she saw that therapy groups can function "at various levels comparable to the different levels of maturity and development in the latency period and adolescence." Coffey (1952) pointed out how the gang of early adolescence is the example par excellence of "psyche group process." Since the ties in the latency period are principally homosexual in character, there would seem to be a compelling logic in favor of single-sex groups. It goes without saying that exploitation of the homosexual character of group formation for therapy has nothing to do with the problem of homosexuality as a clinical entity.

Yet, there have been very productive groups composed of both men and women. These groups almost invariably bring up the question of sexual feelings toward one another. The problem then is for the therapist to have the courage and sensitivity to interpret the feelings—to distinguish between feelings of closeness and those of situational acting out. Perhaps above all, it is important for him to perceive the symbolic dimensions of the sexual attitudes rather than cathect sexuality as a kind of personal emancipation on the part of the patient.

THE ROLE OF COTHERAPIST. It is not uncommon for groups, as we have seen, to employ two therapists. The practice is frequently based on the assumption that patients react more realistically and Oedipal conflicts are activated more easily by a family constellation that includes both a male and a female therapist. Just as frequently, the second therapist acts as an observer and may remain quite passive in the therapeutic role. If the therapist is quite active, it has been found by many to be valuable to have a second person, who is able to pay close attention to the dynamics of the group, and with whom an analysis of group process can be shared. Frequently, the method involving a cotherapist is used as a training device for the second therapist. For some therapists, there seems to be a concern about what the presence of two therapists does with respect to transference problems. It is my belief that this becomes a problem only when the group has to deal with rivalries and antagonisms between therapists. Likewise, it is probably well for one therapist to take a visibly dominant role in leadership, while the other remains primarily an observer.

ANONYMITY. There seem to be clear advantages in having patients in the group see as little of each other outside the group as is possible. This is always a problem over which there is little control when group therapy is practiced in a residential setting. But, with patients who meet once or twice a week in an outpatient-clinic setting, there is some tendency to form extrasessional social groups, and I feel that it should be discouraged. Defensiveness and resistance often develop through sociability that tends to break down the work orientation of the therapy sessions.

The problem arises usually through some encouragement of extrasessional sociability by the therapist. Sometimes, it is founded on a misguided conception of "democratic practice." On their own, few patients are likely to continue relationships from the group on the outside. It has also been my experience that neighborhood therapy groups involve almost insuperable difficulties. If the group is sufficiently "dynamic" to deal with transference material, it provokes problems in external relationships. If there is a norm involving unhampered continuation of the neighborhood relationships, the group rarely gets past those of an ordinary social group, which may be frustrating if the level of aspiration is toward a "dynamic" objective.

OPEN AND CLOSED GROUPS. The issue of whether members should be added to the group during the process of treatment or whether, once the group has been started, no new members should be allowed to join the group is usually decided on the basis of practical considerations. It is my guess that few therapists would advocate the use of open groups because of a supposed therapeutic superiority of these groups over closed groups. Rather, the open groups exist because, in many clinic and hospital settings, this is the only way in which treatment can be extended to a number of patients.

There may be some advantages in the open groups, and, if the policy is dictated by practical considerations, the therapist need not regard such necessities as wholly without virtues. The entrance of a new member into the group calls for his orientation, which often in mature groups is performed spontaneously by another group member. Further, the withdrawal of a member, while it may precipitate a brief reaction in the group, confronts the group with a situation that can be interpreted and worked through. A new member often occasions a reworking of rivalries and competition in the group, and sometimes helps the movement by a consolidation of forces. It is not my experience that the new member is universally the focus of aggression and hostility, as Slavson seems to have thought (1951), but there is danger of the therapist's being oversolicitous and the group's attempting to draw the member too quickly into itself. Emotional problems are just as likely to center around those of inclusion and separation as anything else, and, when these are seen in their meaningfulness to group process, there should be little concern about their disruptive effects.

A closed group has some obvious advantages to the therapist, for there is a greater sense of knowing and of control. The importance of this is not to be overlooked.

GROUP PSYCHOTHERAPY WITH HOSPITALIZED PATIENTS

It was inevitable that a great deal of group psychotherapy would be performed in hospitals. Not only were its beginnings in the hospital setting, but, in many ways, it seems an admirable answer to the need for treatment for patients who, because of shortage of personnel, would not otherwise be able to obtain it. Many of the accounts in the literature of group psychotherapy describe experiences with psychotic patients in hospitals.

There is no need to remind the reader that the psychological situation of the psychotic patient is vastly different from that of the neurotic patient, and that living within a hospital setting produces a constellation of forces different from those that characterize the patient who comes to the clinic once or twice a week for a group therapy session. But, all too often, although the distinctions between the life situations of the patients are fully recognized, no distinctions are made with respect to therapeutic goals and techniques. It has been my observation that therapists often use the same type of leadership technique with all psychotic patients that they use with nonpsychotic patients, even though they recognize different dynamics functioning in the lives of the patients.

One of the most interesting questions is that of why the techniques used with nonpsychotic patients usually are ineffective with psychotics. It is closely related to the fundamental difference between the two types of disorder: In the case of the nonpsychotic, for a variety of reasons, the anxieties of the patients are accessible. It is these anxieties that form the group cohesion in which emotionality occurs and can be fruitfully explored.

The hospitalized patient seldom has this accessible anxiety, for it is in the nature of psychotic disorder that it is a kind of "solution" to anxiety. This does not mean that the psychotic does not sometimes feel agitated and unhappy, but, for the most part, this agitation and unhappiness get systematized on a level of unreality that is not accessible to the level of reality and, hence, is not productive of interpersonal relations that are meaningful on the level of reality, as in the formation of a group.

Efforts of therapists to get psychotics to form groups in which the therapist sees himself as a permissive but quite inactive agent are usually doomed to failure, for there is no central core of interpretable relationships. What seems necessary is greater directiveness on the part of the therapist in supplying a core of activity to which the psychotic patient can relate. For this reason, I emphasize the greater activity on the part of therapist than would occur in a nonpsychotic group.

"Activity" of the therapist means a great many things. In some groups, it means increasing the degree of socialization among patients who are typically incapable of responding to each other except in the most peripheral way. The therapist may spend his time with the group in exploring relationships with many different patients, but his aim may be to produce more social interaction. The objective of producing more social ties between patients is related primarily to developing a level of social reality in which the patient can feel sufficiently comfortable to talk about himself and his anxieties. It is a paradoxical but evident truth that anxieties cannot be dealt with unless the social reality makes it possible for the patient not to escape to an autistic irreal comfort. The manifest objective of the therapist here is to help the psychotic patient exchange the autistic comfort of irreality for the emotional comfort of social reality. This requires an imaginative, sensitive therapist who will explore many possibilities of developing a social reality that communicates to the uncommunicative patient and, in turn, helps him to become communicative.

Therapists have used certain devices by means of which to develop this social reality in addition to making every effort to increase socialization in the patient. Some therapists have used recordings to play back to the group, which has served to focus discussion. In one group, the recording machine itself produced paranoid reactions on the part of the patients, confirming their hallucinatory dispositions. But these threats were assuaged when the imaginative therapist allowed each of the patients to examine the recording apparatus and taught them to use it.

In another therapy project, all the patients were shown movies that depicted various interpersonal relationships designed to be used with mental hygiene groups. These were presented on a Monday, and the patients in this ward were divided into small discussion groups on subsequent days. Sometimes, the substance of the movie was reflected in the group discussions; other times, it was not. Usually, it served as a springboard for discussions. Often, the discussion had little relevance to the theme of the movie or little import for the emotional problems of the patients. But almost always it served as a point of common stimulation around which social relationships could develop. There was noticeable improvement in the course of this treatment, in the direction of less conflict and less extreme agitation.

The problem of personnel in such a program dealing with several hundred patients is one to be considered. The medical director of the hospital reasoned that persons interested in performing this type of group psychotherapy could do so, and this included nurses, attendants, psychiatric social workers, clinical psychologists, and psychiatrists. Each group had two therapists, and the groups themselves numbered from 12 to 15 patients, considerably more than is common in nonpsychotic groups. After the group sessions, the staff got together in groups and talked through the various problems that had been encountered. Also, patients could go to whichever group they chose, and, while most of them felt more comfortable in a particular group, some shifted from one group to another before they would settle down to a "home room." In addition to the therapy groups, there was a "day room group," which consisted of those, often temporarily upset, patients who wanted to go to no group. It is my opinion that the next step in this project should be one of bringing together patients who have become both comfortable and active in such groups and helping them form a group that would go beyond the socialization objective to more "dynamic" considerations.

Group psychotherapy with psychotics, even in its infancy, suffers from the heavy hands of tradition and doctrine. There are many opportunities to be creative and experimental, which, indeed, are what the field most needs. At the same hospital as that discussed above, an interesting liaison between group psychotherapy and occupational therapy has been under way. In this project, patients work at their occupational activities in the "O.T. shop" for a given length of time. Often, the patients are "hopelessly regressed," and their activities consist of the simplest type of elementary manual arts: painting a board, hammering a nail, etc. After the given activity period, the patients are brought together for a short "sharing period" in which they are encouraged to communicate to each other and to the therapists what they have been doing during the activity session. Although this occupies a small percentage of the total time, it is very significant in utilizing their recent experience as the basis for communication. The technique is very much like that of a kindergarten teacher. Actually, many of the therapists visited kindergarten rooms in order to observe procedure they thought might be relevant to therapy with these patients.

Therapy with psychotic patients involves relating therapy techniques to the realistic therapeutic aspiration of the therapist as indicated by the age of the patient and the progress of mental illness. A young therapist became interested in a group of old men who had been in a hospital since World War I. Many of them were stabilized psychotics, harmless schizophrenics, but leading very unproductive, extremely isolated lives. A plan for foster-home care had been in course in the hospital for some time, but few seemed eligible, and fewer were successful in placements. The young therapist organized these prospective guardian-care patients into a therapy group. Their routine consisted of having coffee together, each member of the group taking turns in preparing and cleaning up afterward. Much of this time was spent in singing old songs. Some of the time was spent in discussing ambivalences about leaving the hospital, in rivalries with each other, in relating experiences. A close bond was formed of an almost purely social character. But the change from almost complete lack of communication to real conversational comfort, from petulant antagonisms to real ability to assume simple responsibility in cooperative effort, was phenomenal. It is not surprising that a significant percentage of these men went on to become successful guardianship placements and fit into families emotionally prepared to receive them. Perhaps the most amazing thing was that the young therapist once said in timid apologetics that she didn't think this was really therapy!

Some of the same questions that were raised about nonpsychotic groups have been raised with respect to psychotic groups. Powdermaker and Frank (1951) showed quite clearly that, in selection of hospitalized

patients for therapy groups, characteristic patterns of patient behavior
that they call "group roles" are the most important. They pointed out
that their most successful group was one in which the group roles of
patients were complementary. Two types of roles seemed to provide impetus to the groups' therapeutic movement, either directly or as a catalyst:

One is the type of patient who expresses his feelings freely, intensively, and
directly, especially in regard to his sexual phantasies and aggressive impulses.
Such a patient tends to provide a focus for the conflicts common to all members.
In this capacity he assumes the function of a leader in the group and maintains the interests and tensions of all the members at a level about the minimum
required for effective therapeutic interventions by the doctor. Another is the
type of patient who is freely verbal and responds compliantly when the doctor
talks to him. Through such a patient, the doctor may frequently liquidate the
group silences and raise issues involving withdrawn patients. Needless to say,
the doctor must not become dependent upon him but must use him with dis-
cretion.

Powdermaker and Frank (1953) described in great detail, both by using
summaries of their experience and by presenting situational analyses, the
activity of the therapist in working with groups of hospitalized patients.
A number of their points may be summarized here to indicate the general
ways in which they are in agreement with the author that the role of the
therapist with psychotic patients must be most active. Their com-
pendium of illustrations of these points is recommended to the reader.
They seem to agree that

1. Sitting or standing next to a patient, some physical contact, helped
induce the patient to speak.
2. Outside relationship with the patient might serve as the induction
into group relationships. Quoting opinions expressed by the patient in a
conversation outside the group often gave the patient a feeling of reassurance, or, in many cases, gave the patient the opportunity to expand
his views. If they were contrary to those of the group, he might have the
confidence to defend them.
3. The therapist must be consistent in his behavior and in his statements
to the group. He is often called upon to demonstrate this consistency by
accepting trying consequences. He must be able to accept both intense
hostility toward him and intense and primitive sexual feelings directed
toward him.
4. The therapist must not be loath to reward by offering praise and approval to patients who speak, present personal problems, make relevant
comments on the statements of others, act as group leaders, or show some
insight into their own problems or the problems of others.
5. The therapist should feel free to vary his position with respect to the

group. Sometimes, the practice of walking around the room from patient to patient permits the therapist to encourage relationship with patients who might otherwise remain on the periphery of the group. Certainly, the therapist must carefully encourage patient participation through active facilitation without at the same time exerting pressure that will make the patient become apprehensive and withdraw. His ability to recognize and appropriately reward the patient who moves a few inches nearer the center of the circle without overwhelming him involves great sensitivity and clinical skill.

6. Often, the therapist may use the words and phraseology of one patient when responding to another. Respect for each patient is demonstrated simultaneously. Further, making generalizations from one patient's remark to another patient in emphasizing the relevance of problems, or emphasizing similarity of problems, experiences, and emotions of two or more patients, by the therapist is a way of establishing a matrix of relationships, and it must be done quite actively by the therapist.

7. Continuity of relationship can be promoted by the therapist's referring questions to another patient or to the group as a whole, by reviewing the events of a meeting at the beginning of the next, and by applying general statements to the immediate group situation.

The nature of psychosis and the relatively new use of group psychotherapeutic techniques make the field one that is comparatively unexplored. We have few studies that indicate any very promising results, although Powdermaker and Frank (1953) indicated clear differences in the direction of improved mental health between patients who received group psychotherapy and ones who did not. Future research and exploration in the field should help, not only in developing more effective methods but also in developing criteria by which we can predict which patients are most likely to respond to group psychotherapy, and what type of group psychotherapy is needed.

Since the significant contribution by Powdermaker and Frank to the understanding of group psychotherapy with psychotics, Fairweather (1964) published an intriguing account of his work with psychotics in a VA hospital at Menlo Park, California, and his contribution can be predicted to be an enduring one to the field of social psychiatry as well as group therapy. His approach was that of developing problem-oriented groups in the wards of psychotic patients and establishing the locus of responsibility for the treatment of patients in the group itself. With the right of veto maintained by the staff psychiatrists, it has been possible for patients to develop group cohesion supporting realistic group standards and to make workable decisions concerning individual and group behavior. This has extended beyond the confines of the hospital to the community where patient living groups have been established, with employment and recreation arranged by group effort. Further studies on the project in community living will be published soon.

Although somewhat beyond the scope of this chapter, the pioneering work of Maxwell Jones (1953) should be mentioned, primarily because of the great influence it has had on the concept of the total hospital as a "therapeutic community." In Jones's concept, all the various activities of the hospital were joined to have a direct bearing on the treatment of the patient, and, since his demonstration that this had a beneficial effect in releasing patients, there has been a widespread practice of using hospitals as day-care or night-care centers, or in the establishment of "halfway houses," where the patient could test under rather protected conditions his ability to be out of the hospital and still not be subjected to the stresses and strains of complete absence from supervision and care. One effect Jones's work has had has been to develop the concept of "community groups" within the hospital where a large number of patients, sometimes as many as 150, meet together to ventilate their feelings and give criticisms. Many of these groups have been seen to have been largely ineffective, for, unlike those involved in Fairweather's method (1964), they are seldom given responsibility, nor are they involved in learning how to make decisions that affect their own destinies.

The concept of the therapeutic community has made some important changes not only in group therapy but in hospital administration as well. A frequent method of utilizing this concept in hospital administration is to "regionalize" the placement of patients so that those who belong to a particular geographical locality will be housed in the same or adjacent hospital wards. This has facilitated the development of groups whose members can move easily into their particular community along with others with whom they have formed associations in the hospital. Again, group therapy here has centered around visits to the home community in preparation for trial visits and has dealt with anxieties that occur in preparation for life outside the hospital.

Individual and Group Therapy. It is a common practice to have patients in both individual and group therapy at the same time. No careful studies have been made of the relationship and interaction between the two forms of treatment. It is usually thought that group therapy stimulates the patient to work out in individual therapy some of the problems of which he becomes more aware in the group. The group, in this case, acts as a catalyst for individual therapy.

Some patients can accept individual treatment only after they have functioned in the supportive atmosphere of the group. Their fears of self-exposure are overcome in a situation where others are revealing themselves. Other patients, who have gone a long way in individual treatment toward working through their problems, can use the group as a tapering-off, a controlled reality-testing, experience.

Certainly, no hard and fast rules govern policy in this area. Perhaps the most important essential is for the individual therapist and the group therapist to be in agreement about each other's function and to be in full communication where there are significant policy issues to be decided. Rivalries between therapists can be very disruptive to the patients' progress and welfare.

Usually it is thought that a patient should not have the same therapist for both individual and group sessions. There is a tendency to drain off in the one session material that might be dealt with in the other if the patient is reacting to the same individual in both situations. Individual therapy for one patient in the group by the group therapist may engender insuperable rivalries among members of the group, as well as lead to inhibition of the particular patient in the group setting.

An exception to the above consideration was a patient who was seen by the author in both individual and group therapy. He was an ambulatory schizophrenic who at first found it difficult, if not impossible, to participate in any way with the group. He was helped to participate by feeling the support of individual therapy carried into the group by the person of his therapist. However, nothing from individual therapy was ever brought up in the group without the prior consent of the patient.

Group Therapy with Special Objectives. Sometimes, within the organization of a hospital, it is thought advisable to organize therapy groups with specific objectives in mind. They tend to be groups that have as their objective the orientation of the entering patient to the hospital, or they have as their purpose the orientation of the patient to life outside as he is preparing to leave the hospital. In both instances, the medium of the group seems most useful for attaining the objective.

Orientation groups frequently combine material about the hospital's regimen with feelings patients have about entering the hospital. From what is known about studies of morale, there should be a real function for such a group. It has the advantage of getting the patient into treatment immediately, while his own motivation for improvement, associated with the crisis that brought him to the hospital, is high. Even though a patient may be in a state of shock or initially depressed, it is my experience that such groups help give the patient an opportunity to ventilate his immediate feelings toward hospitalization, and, by working through this problem, they help him to develop a treatment attitude and perspective that may be important for his improvement. The social structure of most hospitals is one in which the patient and his individuality get lost. The "orientation group" helps him see the hospital for what it is and also helps the hospital see him.

The "exit group," or the group designed to orient patients to life outside the hospital, is concerned with the opposite objectives. Here, the common group tension is about ambivalence in leaving the hospital, because of fear of failure on the outside. These groups are often concerned with attitude toward employers, families, and neighborhoods. Often, the problems patients feel they have difficulty in facing are reality problems that require social skills they need to develop. Often, hospitalization itself contributes to the deterioration of such skills if they were once possessed. Some interesting work has been done by workers at St. Elizabeth Hospital at Washington, D.C., in using psychodrama to help patients to develop skills or meeting situations outside the hospital. Frequently, the spontaneous dramas are concerned with interviews with employers about jobs, during which questions concerning mental illness come up. Behavior in the group may actually contribute diagnostically to the decision as to whether the patient is ready to leave. Often, it contributes to the resolution of ambivalence for the patient. Certainly, it establishes a symbolic bridge between the "inside" and the "outside."

T GROUP TRAINING

Although not designed to serve patients in hospitals or clinics and not originally developed for therapeutic purposes, in the last two decades there have developed quasi-therapeutic groups known as "T" groups or "sensitivity training" groups. These groups originated in connection with the training programs of the National Training Laboratory, at Bethel, Maine. The groups are formed to increase the self-awareness and improve the communication modes of the participants. The emphasis is exclusively on what occurs in the group, the "here and now." This unusual group approach has had an important place in the conduct of managerial training and in educational groups consisting of physicians, nurses, psychologists, social workers, and teachers.

The relevance of T group training for a student of group therapy is twofold: (1) What started out as an exercise primarily directed toward the preparation of persons for social action roles has now become a method of increasing the awareness of the person's own effect on others in a group where interpersonal relations are a major focus. As someone has said, it is "therapy for normals." (2) T group training is increasingly being used as a method of preparing students in psychiatry, psychology, and psychiatric social work for work in therapy groups. It offers an opportunity to be in a group that is oriented to processes similar to those confronted in therapy but organized in such a way that the participant feels comfortable in not being formally classified as a patient.

CONJOINT FAMILY THERAPY

Among the developments related to group therapy that have appeared in recent years is the growth of interest in *conjoint family therapy*. The term was coined by D. D. Jackson, of the Mental Research Institute, in Palo Alto, California, and the concept was made operational by Virginia Satir (1964), of the Institute, and by John Bell, of the U.S. Public Health Service. In this form of group therapy, the parents and the child or children are seen together by the therapist. The major emphasis is on the dysfunctions of communication in interpersonal relationships, and the role of the therapist is centered on clarifying the meanings communicated at verbal and nonverbal levels and the discrepancies between these levels. Charles Fulwiler developed a therapist's observation technique, for use in conjoint family therapy, that permits the therapist to move in and out of the group, with the family members sometimes interacting among themselves and sometimes interacting with him after he has shared an observation with them. These specific methods are described in writings by the authors mentioned. All of them focus on the interpersonal communications of family members meeting together as a group.

SUMMARY

As a method of treatment, group psychotherapy has developed from a stage where it was considered primarily an expedient in treating large numbers of patients to stage where many group psychotherapists see the method as having therapeutic advantages in its own right. As methods of treatment have developed, increased interest and speculation have focused on the *group process*. Group therapists agree that the permissive social climate of the group in providing support and stimulation for the patient is a necessary characteristic of group formation, although it may be achieved in a variety of ways. Real differences in techniques tend to center around the problems of reality testing and interpretation.

It is increasingly being recognized that the function of the group psychotherapist in working with groups of psychotic patients involves a more active and directive role on his part. The collaboration of the group therapist with other therapeutic activities seems also to indicate promising leads. Perhaps, what is most needed in the use of group psychotherapy with the hospitalized patient is greater freedom on the part of the therapist to try out unconventional techniques rather than follow set patterns, many of which have been inappropriately adapted from methods of working with groups of nonpsychotic patients.

The increased interest and research in the field of group dynamics should pave the way for future clinical study with groups and help emancipate the field of group psychotherapy from some of the doctrinaire assumptions about the nature of group formation that have tended to make therapeutic techniques too rigid. Important empirical studies are being conducted with the use of careful observational methods, and these have already contributed to the solution of some practical issues. Group psychotherapists, in this connection, have been more willing than individual therapists to record their sessions by mechanical and observational methods. This attitude toward the collection of data concerning the therapeutic process and the willingness to explore methodology augur well for future development in the field.

REFERENCES

BELL, J. E. Family group therapy. *U.S. publ. Hlth Monogr. No. 64.* Washington, D.C.: Government Printing Office.

BERNE, E. 1961. *Transactional analysis in psychotherapy: A systematic individual and social psychiatry.* New York: Grove.

BION, W. R. 1961. *Experiences in groups.* New York: Basic Books.

BRADFORD, L. P., GIBB, J. R., and BENNE, K. D. 1964. *T group theory and laboratory method.* New York: Wiley.

COFFEY, H. S. 1952. Socio and psyche group process: Integrative concepts. *J. soc. Issues,* 8, 65–74.

COFFEY, H. S., FREEDMAN, M. B., LEARY, T. F., and OSSORIO, A. 1950. Community service and social research: Group psychotherapy in a church program. *J. soc. Issues,* 6, 3–63.

EZRIEL, H. 1950. A psychoanalytic approach to group treatment. *Brit. J. med. Psychol.,* 23, 59–74.

FAIRWEATHER, G. 1964. *Social psychology in the treatment of mental illness: An experimental approach.* New York: Wiley.

FRANK, J. D., and ASCHER, E. 1951. Corrective emotional experiences in group therapy. *Amer. J. Psychiat.,* 108, 126–31.

FREEDMAN, M. B., LEARY, T. F., OSSORIO, A., and COFFEY, H. S. 1951. Interpersonal dimensions of personality. *J. Pers.,* 20, 143–61.

FREUD, S. 1948. *Group psychology and analysis of the ego.* London: Hogarth.

JENNINGS, H. H. 1950. *Leadership and isolation.* New York: Longmans.

JOHNSON, J. A. 1963. *Group therapy: A practical approach.* New York: McGraw-Hill.

JONES, M. 1953. *The therapeutic community.* New York: Basic Books.

KADIS, A., et al. 1963. *A practicum of group psychotherapy.* New York: Harper & Row.

KLAPMAN, J. W. 1946. *Group psychotherapy: Theory and practice.* New York: Grune & Stratton.

MULLAN, H., and ROSENBAUM, M. 1962. *Group psychotherapy: Theory and practice.* New York: Free Press.

POWDERMAKER, FLORENCE B. 1951. Psychoanalytic concepts in group psychotherapy. *Int. J. group Psychother.*, 1, 16–22.

POWDERMAKER, FLORENCE B., and FRANK, J. D. 1953. *Group psychotherapy.* Cambridge, Mass.: Harvard Univer. Press.

ROSENBAUM, M., and BERGER, M. 1963. *Group psychotherapy and group function: Selected readings.* New York: Basic Books.

SATIR, VIRGINIA. 1964. *Conjoint family therapy.* Palo Alto, Calif.: Science and Behavior Books.

SCHILDER, P. 1938. *Group therapy.* New York: Norton.

SHASKAN, D. A. 1952. Demonstration of a common phantasy in a group. *Int. J. group Psychother.*, 2, 250–54.

SLAVSON, S. R. 1951a. *Introduction to group therapy.* New York: International Universities Press.

SLAVSON, S. R. 1951b. The dynamics of analytic group psychotherapy. *Int. J. group Psychother.*, 1, 208–17.

THELEN, H., and WHITAKER, DOROTHY. 1958. *Emotional dynamics and group culture.* New York: New York Univer. Press.

WATSON, JEANNE. 1952. Some social psychological correlates of behavior. Doctor's dissertation, Univer. of Michigan.

WHITAKER, DOROTHY, and LIEBERMAN, M. A. 1964. *Psychotherapy through the group process.* New York: Atherton Press.

21

Therapeutic Techniques
with Children

SIDNEY W. BIJOU AND HOWARD N. SLOANE *

The psychological treatment of children, broadly conceived, consists of a variety of procedures. Some of these have been patterned after techniques developed for treating adults; others have evolved directly from treatment experience with deviate children. A brief initial review of the major types of programs currently in use may provide perspective. Methods are grouped according to the stimulating conditions that are modified to alleviate the problem, rather than on the basis of common historical origin of groups of methods. In other words, we shall ask what alterations can be made in the child's environment to effect changes in his behavior.

One possible class of alterations involves moving the child to a totally new environment, that is, foster-home or institutional placement. A second type of modification in stimulating conditions involves attempts to alter the current environment of the child. This may include (1) modification of the parents' behavior by advising, persuading, counseling, or admitting to psychotherapy; (2) making changes in the physical environment of the child; (3) changing the behavior of siblings through the various procedures outlined in this chapter. A third class of procedures involves setting up an adjunct environment in which to initiate changes in the child. Programs of this type often include some type of concurrent treat-

* Sidney W. Bijou, Ph.D. (University of Iowa), Professor of Psychology, and Howard N. Sloane, Ph.D. (The Pennsylvania State University), Research Assistant Professor of Psychology, both of the University of Illinois.

The nature and scope of the problems that children bring into the clinic were described in Chapter 6. This chapter extends the application of the clinical approach into the diagnostic and therapeutic functions. Because these are viewed as two continuous aspects of clinical practice, they are both discussed here.

ment of one or both parents, and can entail treating the child by one or both of the following procedures: (1) handling specific problems by what are often considered educational techniques, by providing information or such training in new skills as, for example, sex education or remedial reading and (2) dealing with the problems of the child by some sort of psychotherapy.

This chapter is concerned with the clinical techniques used in the last two programs above, which involve modifying the child's current environment or exposing the child to some adjunct environment. Many of the child therapies in the latter group are designated "play techniques." A label of this sort can give the erroneous impression that play per se is a therapeutic agent, or that play is a technique in some sense such that it can be contrasted with other psychotherapeutic methods for children. "Play" is a descriptive word that refers to the most common mode of behavior of the child; hence, a great deal of the activity found in all treatment approaches may be so described. Stimulating play in therapy provides occasions for the therapist to bring about changes. The extent to which play is used in the different therapies varies, depending on how it is introduced and controlled, as well as on the age of the child, the type of presenting problem, and the theoretical orientation of the therapist.

Clinical child methods will be considered in two parts. The first will be concerned with therapy; the second, with diagnosis. In exploring the various child therapies, we shall briefly trace the pioneer efforts, point out and discuss some of the differences in the therapeutic conditions for child and for adult treatment, describe the processes involved in some individual and group procedures, and, finally, evaluate research. In the second section, we shall point out the relationship between child therapy and child diagnosis, review some of the kinds of materials and activities employed in diagnostic procedures, and conclude with an appraisal of research on diagnostic play.

HISTORICAL BACKGROUND

The study and treatment of maladjusted children are relatively recent developments compared to the attention accorded maladjusted adults. Contributions to child treatment and diagnosis have come from psychiatry, education, psychometrics, experimental psychology, developmental psychology, and social work. Perhaps the greatest contribution to date, however, has come from those directly concerned with psychopathology. Outstanding was the work by Freud and his students.

It is well known that one of Freud's major concerns was the development of a psychotherapy for neurotic adults. Early in his work, he stated that the problems of the neurotic adult originated in the sexual conflicts of early childhood. From this he inferred that young children must have an active sexual life and vivid sexual fantasies. In 1906, he presented a case of phobia in a five-year-old child—the well-known case of Little Hans—in support of his contention (1925). Freud did not conduct the therapy. It was carried out by the boy's father, himself an analyst. Although the significance of some of the findings might be questioned, Freud's report did represent the first application of psychoanalysis to children and stimulated considerable interest. As Mahler (1945) pointed out, the group at that time best prepared to explore the application of psychoanalysis to children was not the regular practicing psychoanalysts but the psychoanalytically oriented educators. Thus, Hermine Hug-Hellmuth (1919) began to use psychoanalytic doctrine to guide her educational practices in the treatment of maladjusted children. In a case report presented in 1913, she described play as a basic part of her procedures with children under seven years of age and as an aid to the therapeutic process with children beyond that age.

About ten years later, Anna Freud and Melanie Klein reported clinical observations of therapy with children and offered their theoretical analyses. Although both claimed to adhere to psychoanalytic theory, each formulated different treatment procedures. Their divergence resulted from their differing conceptions of the psychosexual stages of early development, especially in relation to the theoretical nature of the transference neurosis and infantile ego. Anna Freud (1946) maintained that the classical techniques of adult analysis must be modified in application to child analysis because (1) the child is incapable of developing a transference neurosis, and (2) his infantile ego ideal is weak. In her treatment, she therefore devoted considerable time and effort to establishing a close relationship prior to analyzing the child's thought processes, and, during analysis proper, she applied a variety of techniques in an effort to reveal what she believed to be unconsciously based behavior. She was cautious about interpreting play activities. In addition, she introduced educational procedures to assist the child to develop new behavior. A more detailed account of her approach will later be described.

Melanie Klein (1949), on the other hand, theorized that a transference neurosis does develop in child analysis, provided a method equivalent to adult analysis is used. She contended, furthermore, that the child's superego is "overly severe" (rather than relatively weak) and that traditional analytic techniques strengthen rather than weaken the infantile ego. In her method, analytic interpretation begins at once, for she believed that the treatment relieved unconscious anxiety and brought the child rapidly into a therapeutic relationship. For her, free play by the child is equivalent to free association by the adult; hence, she believed that every playful action has a symbolic meaning within the framework of psychoanalytic theory. She did not use educational procedures, for she contended that the redirection of anxiety and guilt (the strong superego) through analysis would remove all symptoms.

The theoretical differences between these two European analysts touched off a controversy. Much has been written by the proponents of each "school" regarding the transference neurosis issue, the symbolic character of play activities, the role of educational procedures in treatment, and the ages and types of children who profit most by this kind of therapy.

These pioneer efforts greatly influenced the practices of psychiatrists, clinical psychologists, and social workers in the United States. They were also influenced by the procedures being developed by child guidance clinics in this country. Soon after the founding of the first psychological clinic for children, by Witmer, in 1896, others were established, all carrying on practices integrating the psychoanalytic and psychobiological principles of Freud and Adolph Meyer. By 1921, a relatively large number of clinics, most of them attached to mental hospitals, schools, courts, colleges, and social agencies, were adopting a comprehensive case approach involving a group of professional people. With the further development of these clinics, largely through the efforts of the National Committee for Mental Hygiene and the Commonwealth Fund, came further revisions in the techniques of child therapy. Characteristically, the trend has been toward developing methods that are not only less intense than those of Anna Freud and Melanie Klein but that also include supplementary programs for parents and provisions for modifying the child's living conditions. Among the outstanding contributors to this movement were Allen (1942), Kanner (1948), Levy (1939), Lowery (1939), Pearson (1949), Rogers (1939), Rogerson (1939), and Taft (1933).

Another group of therapies emerged from different historical antecedents. They are the behavior therapies founded on experimental studies rather than clinical analyses. The methods of treatment that have developed, though diverse, have several factors in common, primarily that they are all derived from "learning theory" of one sort or another, or from experimental data on stimulus-response relationships. Behavior therapy may be defined as the "attempt to alter human behavior in a beneficial manner according to the laws of modern learning theory (Eysenck, 1964, p. 1). Behavior itself is seen as the problem to which treatment is addressed; behavior is not considered a symptom of some underlying state or illness. This has led to a more circumscribed approach in treatment, which is designed to manipulate specific behaviors (e.g., specific unreasonable fears, enuresis, and socially isolate behavior) rather than general conditions. The goal of treatment is, therefore, to change behavior rather than to achieve insight, effect personality reorganization, or modify some other inferred condition or entity.

The research of Pavlov and Thorndike stimulated some early laboratory studies of behavior therapy. In the classical "little Albert" study, Watson and Rayner (1920) developed in the child a generalized fear response to small, furry animals by pairing the sight of a white rat with loud noise. The treatment of such fears was accomplished by feeding the child in the presence of the feared object (counterconditioning—first with the object at a distance and then with the object moved closer in gradual steps (Jones, 1924). In 1930, Dunlap used a form of behavior therapy in treating tics and other "habits" by means of "negative practice" (1930), and, in 1938, Mowrer published reports of a conditioning technique for the treatment of enuresis (1938). Also in 1938, Jacobson's book on treating neuroses, *Progressive Relaxation,* was published. Somewhat later, Dollard and Miller (1950) attempted to reinterpret psychoanalytic therapy in terms of Hullian learning concepts and principles.

COMPARISON OF ADULT AND CHILD THERAPIES

Before describing the current approaches, it might be instructive to point out the similarities and differences in the adult and child therapeutic situations. The following comparison along five dimensions will set forth, in a broad sense, some of the factors influencing the practices in each.

Motivation for Therapy. Through one set of conditions or another, the maladjusted adult comes to treatment seeking relief from a personal problem. The child, on the other hand, seldom comes for therapy because of the adverse conditions created by his problem. He comes because someone, usually a parent, has decided that professional help is needed. Not only does he lack motivation to change his behavior, but it is likely that the first indications that he is being brought for treatment arouse fear reactions. Some therapists (e.g., Anna Freud and Pearson) deal with this initial reaction by using the first few sessions as preparatory for treatment. They consider the child "ready for treatment" when he indicates that he has a problem and that the therapist can help him deal with it. Others (e.g., Allen and Axline) believe that therapy begins at the first contact, whether or not the child demonstrates an emotional reaction to the initial part of therapy. These differences in assumptions and procedures will be discussed in the next section, on the approaches to child therapy.

Ability To Verbalize. In psychoanalytic therapy with the adult neurotic, verbal behavior plays a central role. It is claimed that verbal associations with the therapist help the adult to identify, formulate, and communicate his reactions. The client must, therefore, be able to understand and discuss interpretations and to make new discriminations and generalizations (Dollard and Miller, 1950).

In contrast, the young child cannot engage in verbal associations effectively. He lacks the required linguistic skills and has not as yet developed serviceable skills in solving problems in symbolic form. Most of his reactions are expressed by gross motor activities. Furthermore, different activities—fantasy, dramatic play, and social behavior—are highly interrelated, making some discriminations difficult.

Family Relationships. Most adults in therapy on an outpatient basis do not live in a family situation in which they are highly dependent on their parents. Most children in therapy on the same basis live in the protective surroundings of their family. Furthermore, some or most of the relationships that generated the child's problem may still be in effect. Finally, continuation of therapy rests with his parents and not with the child. The significance of these intimate family relationships has led to the practice of carrying on collateral therapeutic work with parents to ensure continuation of treatment, to minimize parent-child interactions that may be contrary to the goals of treatment, and to maximize those thought to enhance treatment effects.

Strength of Therapeutic Relationship. Whether or not there is a difference between the adult and child therapies on the basis of the presence or absence of a transference neurosis depends on the meaning of the psychoanalytic concept of *transference.* Anna Freud defined the term thus: "By transference we mean all those impulses experienced by the patient in his relation with the analyst which are not newly created by the objective analytic situation but have their source in early—indeed, the very earliest—object-relations and are now merely revived under the influence of the repetition-compulsion" (1946, p. 18). Anna Freud claimed that a transference neurosis can be attained in both the adult and the child. Other analysts such as Fraiberg have claimed that "Although we utilize interpretation of transference in our therapeutic work and assist the child in understanding the unreal nature of his feelings toward the therapist, I cannot say from my own experience that I can credit the analysis of transference reactions with being the powerful agent of therapy in work with children that it is with adults" (1951, p. 305).

Physical Setting. Obviously, the physical settings of therapy for the adult and child differ. For the adult, the therapist provides an atmosphere conducive to quiet relaxation, with the furniture and furnishings appropriate for therapeutic interviews. For the child, he prepares a special playroom and play equipment that meet certain specifications.

APPROACHES TO CHILD THERAPY

Examination of specific therapeutic procedures is now in order. We shall see how therapists deal with the issues described and the justifications they offer for their practices. In general, the techniques and rationales are related to the therapist's conception of child development and behavior, personality development, psychopathology, and psychotherapy. Each approach is, therefore, presented within its own theoretical framework.

Child Analysis. The application of psychoanalysis to the problems of children merits first consideration simply because of the impact it has had on child-treatment methods. In terms of the number of children so treated, child analysis observes no such distinction. The great majority of children undergoing treatment are handled by the typical child guidance methods or the briefer psychotherapies to be considered in the next section.

The aim of child analysis is that of all therapies—to help the child achieve adequate functioning. To this end, child analysis is planned (1) to investigate the child's unconscious processes and fixed defense mechanisms, (2) to communicate to the child the interpretations derived from therapeutic analysis, and (3) to work on the follow-up consequences of the treatment (Pearson, 1949). In this program, the child is ordinarily seen five times a week, although, under special circumstances, he may be seen less often. The procedure involves two phases—rapport building and treatment proper. In the rapport-building phase, the child is gradually introduced to therapy and is helped to understand his problem. During this period, the child is given an opportunity to develop a fondness and respect for the therapist, who helps to advance the relationship by making himself useful to the child, helping him deal with outside opposing forces, playing the games he likes, protecting his health, and so on.

Treatment proper begins when transference is said to have been established. During this phase, the child plays with toys and engages in drawing, painting, and clay modeling. He is encouraged to describe his dreams and daydreams and his emotional reactions to situations in, and outside of, therapy. (Verbal association is used as part of therapy only with children at the prepuberty or puberty stages and older.) The responses observed are interpreted in terms of psychoanalytic theory. Reactions to the interpretations are reinterpreted. Educational procedures are inaugurated to strengthen the child's weak superego functioning, for it is believed that, at this stage, the superego is not as yet detached from external objects. It is contended that, if educational procedures do not accompany the analysis, the child may become difficult to manage, as a consequence of being freed from his repressions.

As to the desirability of working with parents, the view seems generally to be (1) treatment can be conducted with or without a working relationship with the parents, and (2) the more insight the child has into his problem, the less the need for cooperation of the parents. In practice, at one extreme, there are analysts who desire no contact with the parent, not even for information pertaining to the child's history or for accounts of outstanding changes in behavior during therapy. At the other extreme are those who believe that a successful analysis is possible only when the parents accept either analytic education or personal therapy. The middle-of-the-road group wants and seeks a cooperative working relationship with the parents. Their assistance is utilized to ensure continuation of the analysis, to assure the child of family support during therapy, and to provide information.

In terms of developmental stages, child analysis is regarded as appropriate for children having problems during the training period, the Oedipal conflict period, and the latency period. This would include children from about age three to eleven. Since child analysis is considered a "deep" therapeutic process, its practitioners generally agree that it should be reserved for those with severe forms of maladjustments or with neurotic traits of long standing. It, too, is stated that psychoanalytic therapy is fitting for youngsters who lack sufficient control (the extremely aggressive, for example) and for those whose problems, regardless of the specific form of the maladjustment, are due to disturbed family relations. Pearson (1949) believes that child analysis is most effective for children suffering from severe transference neurosis—anxiety states, conversion hysteria, and uncomplicated anxiety hysteria. He has also maintained that it is the only therapeutic method for dealing with the narcissistic neuroses and the childhood psychoses. In such cases, he has contended, it is necessary to modify the usual child-analytical procedures to reach and deal with the unconscious processes.

Briefer Analytic Child Therapies. The influence of Freud's work on the field of child therapy is seen when we consider the number of therapists and the variety of briefer child-treatment methods that have been based on analytic theory. We shall now note how these procedures are applied to an individual child and to groups of children.

Frequently, the individual approaches are subdivided into the free and the controlled methods. Newell (1941) maintained that the main difference between these lies in the activities of the therapist. In the free method, the child is given free reign in selecting what materials he wants to use and the form his play takes. The therapist's activities are kept at a minimum: He encourages activity, shows an interest in the child's play, and gives his undivided attention. In the controlled method, the therapist not only chooses the material that will be used but also describes a situation to the child, encouraging reactions to it.

INDIVIDUAL FREE THERAPY APPROACHES. The goal of the free therapies is to help the child gain or regain adequate functioning by strengthening, in theory, his ego defenses against "his instinctual impulses" (Pearson, 1949). Typically, therapy is conducted in a room equipped with running water, a sandbox, and toys (dolls, household equipment, soldiers, guns, and cars, for example).

During the first contact, the analyst structures the situation. Rogerson (1939) describes this procedure: The child is shown the toys, the sand, and other objects. He is told that this is the room to which he can come once a week or more. It is explained that he can make as much noise as he likes, say and do what he likes—in fact, do anything except break the windows or lights. It is also explained to him that other youngsters come to the room at other times and that, sometimes, when they are nervous, angry, or afraid, they tell the doctor about it and then feel better. During this first meeting, the analyst gives the child reassurance and his undivided attention. Genuine interest is shown in everything the child does and says. Ample time is allowed for the youngster to explore, examine, and test the situation. "When he feels and accepts the security offered, he is free and able to bid for understanding. In short, he shows that a positive relationship [1] has been established" (Rogerson, 1939, p. 22).

The therapist may now begin cautiously to make interpretations. This caution is indicated, Newell (1941) stated, because interpretations made too early either have no effect or arouse anxiety and resistance. With repeated therapy sessions, the child expresses more and more of his feelings and fantasies. At the same time, he gradually develops insight, and, little by little, he acquires an awareness of his real self and his life situation. As these changes occur, new anxieties are displayed, which are treated as part of the therapeutic process.

Virtually all analysts using the briefer approaches believe that parental cooperation is an essential part of the treatment program. In general, it is believed that, the more insight the child has regarding his problem, or the older the child, the less the need for parental assistance. The manner in which a parent cooperates depends on his or her adjustment status and the family situation. Some parents are believed to need analytic treatment; others, only educative and supportive therapy; still others, only discussions with reference to certain parent-child situations. In some treatment arrangements, the same analyst conducts therapy with both child and parent; in most, each family member sees a different analyst.

[1] The analyst-child relationship is referred to by some writers in this group variously as *relationship* (Rogerson, 1939), *transference*, (Tallman and Goldensohn, 1941), or *rapport* (Newell, 1941). Regardless of the designation for this characteristic, and without reference to nuances in meanings, the analytically oriented stress the importance of the therapist-child relationship in the treatment of children in the early and middle childhood stages of development.

GROUP FREE THERAPY APPROACHES. The group approach is widely used and is rapidly gaining more adherents. Most of the techniques have been patterned after the studies by Slavson (1943, 1947, 1950) and his colleague Ginott (1961). During the past 45 years, these therapists have conducted intensive programs for groups of children and adults. Four types of group psychotherapies are recommended for children: (1) play group psychotherapy with preschool children, (2) activity-interview psychotherapy with children in the latency period (situational therapy), (3) analytic group psychotherapy with girls in puberty, and (4) analytic group psychotherapy with adolescent girls. Each group is run according to the developmental status of its members. A comprehensive clinical study is made of each child to determine whether treatment should be individual, group, or a combination of both. The role of the group therapist is in many ways similar to that of the therapist in individual treatment, and group therapy procedures are, therefore, based on such concepts as transference, catharsis, and insight. Effective practice is said to depend on the perspicacity, skill, tact, and insights of the therapist (Slavson, 1950). Changes in group therapy are believed to be brought about by the same analytic processes that operate in individual therapy. Elements of reality testing and sublimation, however, are said to be added features that group therapy can provide.

Although many factors, clinical and nonclinical, are considered among the criteria for the selection of cases, generally children of "at least minimal intelligence" with problems centering around interpersonal relationships profit most. "In cases where the secondary outcomes such as feelings of inadequacy, sibling rivalry, and social maladjustments are the presenting problems, the earlier difficulties with parents can be allayed by exclusive group treatment" (Slavson, 1950, p. 233).

INDIVIDUAL EXPRESSIVE (CONTROLLED) THERAPIES. The expressive therapies, variously described as release therapy, active play therapy, or controlled play therapy, constitute the second category of the briefer analytic child therapies; with these the names of D. M. Levy (1939), Solomon (1951), and Conn (1939), as well as others, have been associated. From the child's viewpoint, these may be described as "expressive"; from the therapist's, as "controlled." All of these approaches attempt to provide a situation conducive to the expression of blocked emotional behavior. The cardinal principle, according to Levy, involves exploiting the child's own method of treating himself. Levy maintains that the child uses imaginative play as one method of releasing tensions created by anxiety. If his behavior produces adequate results in the anxiety-inducing situation, no tensions remain; if not, symptoms, in proportion to the severity of the disturbance, are formed.

According to the expressive therapists, the child obtains emotional release in three ways: (1) through nonthematic activities, that is, through acting aggressively toward the therapist; (2) through dramatic play in standardized situations, with dolls and toys depicting sibling rivalry, parent-child relationships, and the like; and (3) through specific play situations resembling experiences in his history. Sometimes a doll representing the therapist is added to these standard play situations (Solomon, 1951).

Expression is not believed to bring "cure" automatically. The crucial factor is the relationship. With positive transference (not technically considered a transference neurosis), the child's expressions can be treated by the therapist in such a manner as to reduce tensions. Interpretation is kept at a minimum or avoided. Levy claims that children between the ages of two and five can be relieved of their difficulties without knowing why they came to the therapist and without understanding the significance of the therapeutic relationship. In such instances, many children terminate treatment with a strong positive feeling for the therapist.

Criteria suggested (Levy, 1939) for the selection of cases for expressive therapy are (1) The child should be under ten years of age. (2) There should be a definite reaction pattern precipitated by a specific event such as a frightening experience, birth of a sibling, or death of a parent. (3) The problem should not be of long standing. (4) The traumatic experience should be in the past, that is, not continuing at the time of referral. (5) The child should be from a relatively normal family situation. Little collateral work with the parents is ordinarily required. The mother's role is mainly that of informant relative to the child's history, development, past and current family situation, and progress outside the therapeutic sessions.

Expressive therapy is often combined with other therapies. It may on occasion precede briefer analytic child therapy, or it may be integrated with child analysis, although this latter procedure is questioned by some (Pearson, 1949).

EXPRESSIVE THERAPY WITH GROUPS. Many child group therapies are based on the principles described for the individual expressive approach. Included are techniques based on puppetry, psychodrama, role playing, and music therapy. Puppetry will serve as an example. Bender and Woltmann (1936) explored this medium, using a variety of approaches and refining the therapeutic process by means of dramatic scripts. Before the puppet show starts, those in the audience are told they are expected to participate by telling the puppets what to do and how to do it whenever they can be of help. The puppets, especially the "hero," in turn, ask questions and call for advice from the audience, either in connection with the play or in asides. The puppets always portray types of people with whom the child has an affective bond. It is clear from clinical observation that shows of this sort can stimulate emotional behavior. Woltmann maintains that, in addition, "the real value lies in the follow-up discussions. The material elicited during group discussions also provides good starting points for follow-up individual therapy" (1951, p. 637).

Relationship Child Therapy. Rank's conception of dynamic psychotherapy supplies the theoretical basis for the relationship child-therapy approach. Rank contended that psychoanalysis, by interpretation and reinterpretation of conscious and unconscious reactions in terms of historical events, unnecessarily prolongs treatment. He argued that if these therapist-child interactions were interpreted as reactions to the therapist, one of several effects would be that treatment time could be reduced from years to a few months. Taft (1933) demonstrated the feasibility of this contention in her clinical work with both adults and children.

Allen (1942) modified some of Rank's principles and concentrated on refining and elaborating the techniques for children. He asserted that the term *relationship therapy* is misleading, inasmuch as all psychotherapies involve and depend on a therapeutic relationship. The point at issue for him was the significance of the relationship and the way it is used. In child analysis, the relationship is said to be used to obtain the historical background of the problem, to make unconscious processes conscious, and to re-create the past, thereby releasing anxiety associated with earlier experiences. In contrast, in child relationship therapy, the relationship is used to analyze immediate experience. At any rate, as Allen indicated, "children with personality and behavior difficulties can be helped to help themselves" (1942, p. 7). This was his guiding principle. Therefore, for him, the immediate goal of relationship therapy was to provide a situation that would allow the self-help process to run its course. Therapy begins immediately. The therapist, by words and actions, shows the child that he is aware of his feelings and that they are accepted as such. The child can engage in any and all kinds of conversation or activities whenever he pleases. He is, however, expected to adhere to limitations of time, and to the rules against destroying property or injuring the therapist. As the child expresses his feelings, the therapist provides interpretations in terms of the immediate treatment relationship. This is also what happens when the child makes references to past experiences and contemporary outside relationships. Such interactions, it is believed, give direction and meaning to the changes that transpire; they help the child re-evaluate himself. Changes occur when the child formulates a new definition of himself in the presence of an accepting person.

The basic assumption in this viewpoint is that all individuals have capacities to achieve a better adjustment. All can learn and grow. The therapeutic situation is created to stimulate the emotional growth that has been blocked in the life experiences of the child. The child places himself in a position to be changed; the therapist helps him make the change. The principles underlying change are the same as those that bring about changes from real-life participation. Growth takes place when the "child begins to discover the reality of his own strength. Now the child is able to make this experience his own, and to use it for his self-differentiation" (1942, p. 80). When these new forms of behavior are sufficiently strong, they transfer to "outside" behavior. The adherents of relationship child therapy believe that this approach is particularly effective in instances in which environmental manipulation has not been successful, with problems that seem to stem from inner tensions reflecting difficulties in interpersonal relationships, and with children with severe personality disturbances.

The principles of relationship therapy have been applied to group therapy. Groups formed on the basis of developmental status are used either as an independent treatment program or as an adjunct to individual therapy. For younger children, the group is conducted in a free play atmosphere; for older children, the procedures are similar to those described by Slavson as activity group therapy. While the children are attending group sessions, their mothers also are generally seen in an individual or group therapy relationship.

Play Therapy. Axline describes this as a "play experience that is therapeutic because it provides a secure relationship between the child and the adult so that the child has the freedom and room to state to himself in his own terms exactly how he is at that moment in his own way and in his own time" (1950, p. 62). This approach emanated from the work of Carl Rogers and his associates (1942, 1951). The more remote influences derive from Freud and Rank. From the former have come the concept of determinism, the therapeutic significance of permissiveness and catharsis, and the concept of play as a form of communication and expression. From the latter have come the notions that reactions observed in therapy are expressions of momentary feelings, that the feelings expressed are more important than the revealed content, that the usual authoritative role of the therapist can be successfully de-emphasized, and that free play activities have therapeutic value.

Treatment in play therapy, as in relationship child therapy, begins in the first session. The therapist at once attempts to establish a relationship in which the child feels accepted regardless of what he says or does. Although the child is made to feel that he can do as he wishes in the playroom, limits are set "to anchor the therapy to the world of reality and to make the child aware of his responsibility in the relationship" (Axline, 1947). No attempt is made to educate the child or to interpret the meaning of his reactions, historical or contemporary, in terms of an explicit theory of personality. The task of the therapist consists of recognizing and accepting the feelings expressed or reflecting them in such a way that the child can "use" them to his advantage. The basic assumption of play therapy is the same as that for client-centered psychotherapy, namely, "that the individual has within himself, not only ability to solve his problems satisfactorily but also that this growth impulse makes mature behavior more satisfying than immature behavior" (1947, p. 15). It is believed that, in an atmosphere of acceptance and permissiveness, fears are neutralized, defensive behavior is lessened, and relaxation ensues. The child is freed to learn new controls, abandon unwholesome modes of behavior, and explore new ways of feeling and behaving. Throughout, the therapeutic relationship has the crucial role.

It is not essential, according to Axline, to work with the parents while the child is in therapy. Such an arrangement may, however, help shorten the treatment period, particularly in the cases of handicapped children. Even if it is difficult or impossible to gain parental cooperation, the child's treatment program can proceed with the expectation of a favorable outcome. With or without their participation, it is not unreasonable to anticipate changes in the parents as a consequence of changes in the child.

Play therapy has been applied to groups (Axline, 1947; Cruickshank and Cowen, 1948; Fleming and Snyder, 1947; Mehlman, 1953). Group play therapy is considered suitable for children whose difficulties center around social maladjustment; individual treatment is considered more appropriate for those with severe emotional problems. Since it is not always possible to determine at the outset the basis and severity of the problem, the treatment program is often a combination of both approaches. In addition to being used with children having personal and emotional problems, these techniques have been used with maladjusted children whose problems are complicated with school problems (Axline, 1947; Bijou, 1965) and physical (Cruickshank and Cowen, 1948) and mental handicaps (Axline, 1949; Mehlman, 1953). Whether they are suitable for treating the childhood psychoses has not been determined (Axline, 1950).

Behavior Therapies. It will be recalled that these are the therapeutic approaches that have their antecedents in findings from experimental studies. In the sense that they are based on concepts and principles derived from animal and human investigations, they might be considered as instigating and developing a technology of psychotherapy. We discuss these treatment programs under two main headings—the classical conditioning approaches and the operant analysis approaches.

CLASSICAL CONDITIONING APPROACHES. The classical conditioning approaches are based on the research and writings of Pavlov and Hull. The outstanding proponents of this method of treatment are Wolpe (1958, 1964a, 1964b) and Eysenck (1960, 1964) and their colleagues. The most important concept on which they base treatment is that of "reciprocal inhibition" or "counterconditioning." Wolpe (1964b, p. 21) stated that "if a response inhibitory to anxiety can be made to occur in the presence of the anxiety-evoking stimuli so that it is accompanied by a complete or partial suppression of the anxiety response, the bond between these stimuli and the anxiety response will be weakened." *Anxiety* is defined as unadaptive conditioned autonomic responses, although the term is sometimes used in such a way as also to refer to the skeletal or muscular responses that mediate the autonomic responses, or that terminate or avoid the anxiety-evoking stimuli.

The emphasis given anxiety in both the etiology and the treatment of maladaptive behavior is a fundamental similarity among the classical conditioning approaches and the expressive therapies already discussed. As the burden of treatment is placed on reconditioning anxiety responses (conditioned autonomic responses) rather than on changing the mediating instrumental behavior or the escape and avoidance behavior generated, the approach stresses concepts that relate to classical conditioning rather than to instrumental conditioning. Reciprocal inhibition is derived from the Pavlovian concepts of excitation, inhibition, and disinhibition, and an early forerunner of the current classical conditioning therapies stressed these concepts quite directly (Salter, 1950).

Several therapeutic procedures are based on reciprocal inhibition, the commonest being the conditioning of relaxation responses, sexual responses, assertive responses, and respiratory responses to the anxiety-evoking stimuli. Of these, *systematic desensitization,* the technique of conditioning relaxation responses by using an adaptation of Jacobson's "progressive relaxation," is the most frequent (Wolpe, 1964b). Briefly, this consists of the graded exposure of the patient during "deep muscle" relaxation to the stimuli that elicit the anxiety responses, starting with the least upsetting stimulus and progressing carefully toward the more aversive. Wolpe refers to the procedure as "systematic deconditioning of anxiety responses along a stimulus dimension of generalization" (1962, p. 565). With adults, relaxation is sometimes taught using hypnosis, and the stimuli are presented by having the patient "imagine" situations described by the therapist, also often under hypnosis. However, hypnosis is not considered essential. With children various "positive emotions" rather than relaxation may be conditioned, and hypnosis is rarely used (Lazarus, 1962).

Treatment usually starts by the therapist's talking with the child and perhaps his parents to classify the types of situations that evoke anxiety and to rank the situations within each category from least to most upsetting. Each category of ranked stimuli is called a "hierarchy." A "snake hierarchy" for a specific child might contain items such as "hearing someone say 'snake' . . . seeing a snake . . . touching a snake," while a "parental-separation hierarchy" might include such items as "hearing parents talk of being some place without child . . . seeing parents dressing to go out . . . being alone in the house." Initial training in producing relaxation or positive emotions is then given, and perhaps practice in developing strong "images," and then desensitization proper, is instituted.

No explicit role is prescribed for parents. Information and history including data with which to construct the hierarchies may be obtained from the parents. Parents may be asked to make sure the child is not exposed to anxiety-evoking stimuli that are too intense or are further along a hierarchy than those stimuli to which the child has been desensitized, to avoid reconditioning, whereas, later in treatment, exposure in "real life" to these stimuli may be incorporated into the therapy.

Systematic desensitization has been used in treating children with various problems, particularly with phobic behaviors (Bandura, 1961; Bentler, 1962; Grossberg, 1964; Lang, 1964; Lazarus, 1959; Metzner, 1961; Meyer and Gelber, 1963; Rachman, 1962; Rachman and Costello, 1961; Schermann and Grover, 1962). Procedures that have rarely been used with children, or that have been widely used by various practitioners, are not reviewed (Gelber and Meyer, 1965; Jones, 1955; Neale, 1963; Reyna, 1964). No group work with children has been reported, although group procedures have been tried successfully with adults (Lazarus, 1961).

OPERANT ANALYSIS APPROACHES. The second major approach to behavior therapy with children involves the explicit use of operant conditioning procedures (see Chapter 6) and stems from the work of B. F. Skinner (1938, 1953, 1961). Emphasis is placed on discovering, and changing where indicated, important aspects of the child's current life situation, particularly the stimulus *consequences* that strengthen or weaken specific behaviors (Bijou and Baer, 1965). Focusing on the *relation* between the child's behavior and environmental events has obvious implications for a treatment program designed to change behavior. Helping the child to develop new and useful ways of acting by providing a suitable environment for the development of such behavior is stressed, rather than emphasizing, in planning treatment, the child's deficiencies.

In initiating treatment, a description of the problem and its history and other pertinent data are obtained from the parents or others familiar with the child. The child is observed, often while interacting with his family or other adults or with children. Next, the problem behavior and the situations in which it occurs are specified in precise descriptive terms and usually in terms of frequency of occurrences, as are the usual consequences of the behavior. The desired results of treatment are similarly described. A treatment program is then planned to progress in gradual steps from the current behavior to the desired behavior.

A decision is made as to the setting in which treatment will be carried out. If possible, this is done in the type of environment most relevant to the problem; if not, in the situation dictated by practical considerations. Thus, operant techniques that require special materials and recording have been applied to speech problems in a laboratory-clinic setting (Bricker, 1965; Salzinger *et al.*, 1965), and hospitalized autistic children have been treated and studied in the hospital (Demyer *et al.*, 1962; Ferster *et al.*, 1961, 1962; Hingten *et al.*, 1965; Risley and Wolf, 1966; Wolf *et al.*, 1964) and, after release, in the home (Risley and Wolf, 1966; Wolf *et al.*, 1964). A hyperactive child who created a schoolroom problem was treated in the classroom (Patterson, 1965; Patterson *et al.*, 1965), a setting that has been used for treating other behavior problems (Zimmerman and Zimmerman, 1962). Mothers and children with difficulties in interacting have been jointly treated in a playroom (Bijou and Baer, 1961; Russo, 1964; Straughan, 1964) and in the home itself (Hawkins *et al.*, 1965). Delinquent behaviors of retardates have been treated in a special institutional unit (Williams, 1965), and isolate social behavior, regressed crawling, "spoiled" crying with inadequate social skills, and fear of climbing play equipment have been treated in a nursery school (Allen *et al.*, 1964; Bijou, 1965; Harris *et al.*, 1964; Hart *et al.*, 1964; Johnston, 1966).

Objective daily records of the frequency with which the child performs the behaviors in question are obtained before treatment starts, to provide a base line against which to evaluate the effects of specific treatment procedures (Bijou, 1965). These records are continued throughout treatment and, when possible, for a period after its termination.

Before trying to change behavior, the therapist must have available for use effective reinforcers, that is, consequences that, when presented or withheld after specific acts of the child, will affect the future frequency of these behaviors. With many young children, social reinforcement in the form of attention, praise, smiles, etc., from adults is effective (Bijou, 1965; Harris *et al.*, 1964), while, with others, nonsocial reinforcers such as candy or some other food, toys, trinkets, money, or access to preferred activities are more effective or more practical (Bricker, 1965; Demyer and Ferster, 1962; Ferster and Demyer, 1961, 1962; Gelber and Meyer, 1965; Hingten *et al.*, 1965; Neale, 1963; Risley and Wolf, 1966; Salzinger *et al.*, 1965; Slack, 1960; Wolf *et al.*, 1964). If attention, praise, and social acts of others are found not to be effectual with a particular child, often a program is instituted aimed at making them reinforcing through special training (Lovaas *et al.*, 1964). Often, parental attentions are the most effective reinforcers, but parents may not give praise, attention, etc., frequently enough or at the appropriate times. Therefore, Wahler (Bijou, 1965) observed child-parent interactions in a play-therapy room and, by means of a signaling device, reinforced *parents* for attending to or praising certain behaviors and for ignoring or punishing others, thus changing the behavior of both parent and child. Social reinforcement from peers is often powerful with older children. Patterson (1965) made candy and other valuables for an entire school class contingent on successive reductions in the activity level of a single hyperactive student, and the other children then reacted to the hyperactive child's behavior in such a way that a more normal activity level developed. Neutral or punishing consequences have also been used. Extinction was found effective in reducing tantrums (Williams, 1959; Wolf *et al.*, 1964), stuttering (Jones, 1955), and "operant" vomiting (Wolf *et al.*, 1965), and punishment has been used when other procedures failed to remove "hyperactive mannerisms" that interfered with the treatment of psychotic children (Lovaas *et al.*, 1964). Avoidance of electric shock has been shown effective in developing social behavior in autistic children who completely lacked a social repertoire (Lovaas *et al.*, 1964).

Another factor considered important in treatment is the necessity for proceeding slowly and by "successive approximations" (White, 1959). When the presenting problem behavior has been described and the desired terminal behavior specified, the therapist does not passively await a full-blown instance of this final behavior to reinforce. A slow progression of changes from the current to the desired behavior is planned, and, at each point in treatment, variations in existing behavior that resemble the desired behavior even slightly are reinforced.[2] Other techniques may also be used to initiate or prime new behavior, such as imitation (Baer *et al.*, 1965; Bandura, 1961, 1965) or instructions, the new ways of responding then being reinforced.

Particular procedures are recommended to ensure that the behavior changes will continue when treatment ceases. Early in treatment, the child is reinforced very frequently after desirable new behavior. As treatment progresses, candy, praise, approval, etc., may be given less and less frequently after acceptable responses, with very intermittent reinforcement common in the terminal stages of treatment (Allen *et al.*, 1964), as behavior with a history of intermittent reinforcement is more resistant to extinction. Usually, the child's everyday environment (parents, peers, physical world) will reinforce and maintain in strength a well-developed and socially desirable behavior resulting from treatment, although it would not reinforce early pretreatment approximations of such behavior.

---

[2] This is similar to Herzberg's work (1941, 1945) in which he utilized successive approximations, providing a social reinforcement to the patient for a series of graduated tasks each of which approximated a more adequate set of behaviors.

The varying roles of parents in treatment have already been described, and these roles are usually considered to be more critical here than in the other approaches. As Krasner and Ullmann suggested (1965), these roles are frequently easier for parents to assume than the tasks assigned to them in other child therapies. It is suggested that this is due to the fact that the behavior required of the parents is specific and does not consist of generalized demands (e.g., "Be loving and warm"). As indicated, a major task of the therapist is often that of explicitly training parental behavior (Bijou, 1965; Hawkins et al., 1965). If the parents directly reinforce undesirable behavior, as when parents maintain "dependent" behaviors in an ill or otherwise impoverished child, it is difficult to develop and maintain any changes.

Treatment may take place on a one-to-one or group basis. For problems that involve social behaviors, group situations are believed to be the most suitable treatment settings. However, treatment is individual in the sense that therapeutic operations are individual and specific for each child; that is, each child receives individual treatment in a group setting utilizing the group situation (Baer, 1963). Unlike participants in some group therapies, many children in the group may not receive treatment.

The early exploratory nature of operant treatment approaches makes it impossible to state at present the range of problems to which it is applicable. No particular repertory such as speech is a prerequisite for treatment. Children with behavior disorders varying in severity from psychotic behavior (Wolf et al., 1964) to difficulties in the "normal" range (Hart et al., 1964) have been treated in experimental settings, and problems ranging from the interpersonal (Bijou, 1965) to the rehabilitation of simple motor skills (Johnston et al., 1966; Meyerson et al., 1966) have been handled.

Those using operant procedures stress the point that service demands and experimental-analysis requirements need not conflict. One illustration of this is the recording of base-line and later behavior. Although this experimental recording seems onerous and impeding in the clinical setting, it has, in fact, been found to be a reliable method for the clinician to determine whether or not his procedures are effective, and whether or not a change in procedure is indicated (Bijou, 1965). The psychotechnologically oriented clinician and the experimentalist are alike in that each is willing to be guided by observed results rather than by a priori considerations. The experimental psychologist learns about some aspect of child behavior by varying independent variables and observing the effect of this variation; the clinician develops his procedures by "trying things out" and seeing which have the desired effect. Thus, in operant behavior therapy, after the desired behavior is instituted, the pretreatment reinforcement conditions are often temporarily reinstated to try to recover the base-line behavior (Harris *et al.*, 1964). This experimental "reversal" procedure allows the experimentalist to learn more about the variables that influence behavior change, and it allows the clinician to pinpoint more precisely which techniques are effective.

Many aspects of operant therapy with children have been carried out by trained teachers (Harris *et al.*, 1964) and ward attendants (Wolf *et al.*, 1964).

RESEARCH ON CHILD THERAPY

Research efforts on child therapy have not approached in scope or number those devoted to adult therapy. However, some objective research on the outcome of treatment and on the treatment process does exist. The behaviors of the child and the therapist during play therapy have been studied (Landisberg and Snyder, 1946), as has the use of different play-therapy methods with different kinds of behavior problems (Axline, 1947; Bills, 1950; Cruickshank and Cowen, 1948; Mehlman, 1953). Operant behavior therapy studies, by "reversing" the experimental reinforcing conditions and reverting to the pretreatment situation, with consequent recovery of pretreatment behaviors, have demonstrated that the reinforcement operations planned as treatment do account for the changes observed (Bijou, 1965). Additional controls in some studies have interspersed between reinforcement period intervals in which praise, approval, or other possible reinforcers were given the child on a "free" or random basis which did not depend upon the child's behavior. During the "free" reinforcement periods new behavior was not learned or, if already learned, not well maintained (Hart *et al.*, 1965). These results suggest that what is important in treatment is not the *amount* of attention, approval, or "love" given the child but the functional relationship between behavior and these rewards. In general, however, few "process" studies with children are as yet available.

In contrast to this limited research on the child therapy process, much has been written about differing interpretations regarding adherence to doctrine, the reasonableness of procedures, misunderstandings over terms and principles, and "armchair" conclusions with respect to different approaches. Part of this difficulty arises because many therapeutic accounts are reported in a story-like manner, and the data and principles on which procedures and conclusions are based are discussed in terms that are meaningful to only a limited number of clinicians. Research data and principles said to underlie a particular therapy are often unrelated to what is suggested for the conduct of treatment. Nevertheless, progress continues insofar as there is a trend toward relating, in a closer and more concrete fashion, theory and data.

Reviews of the outcome of treatment with children are available. Levitt (1963, 1957) has covered most of the available research on the outcome of psychotherapy with children, and Eysenck (1961) has summarized and added to Levitt's 1957 data, combining them with similar data on the outcome of adult therapy. Combined, these reviews are based on approximately 10,000 child-therapy cases and conclude that about 60 to 65 per cent of both treated and untreated controls "improve," with no apparent differences between the groups. Unfortunately, many different kinds of child therapy are lumped together, although only a fraction of 1 per cent of these would fall in the class of behavior therapies. Serious objections can be raised about grouping all kinds of cases and combining the consequences of different techniques, and about the use of nontreated controls who "defected" before treatment and who may represent a select group. Levitt (1957) presented data that show that the treated and "defector" groups do not differ on 61 different measures (mostly estimates of severity), and the problems in both groups are rated equally serious by professionals. However, this does not rule out possible differences between the groups.

The limited number of children treated by operant techniques makes outcome data meaningless. Data available on classical conditioning treatments of children are only slightly better. In regard to these, Lazarus and Abramovitz (1962) reported 7 recoveries and 2 failures after a mean of 3.3 sessions in treating phobic children of ages seven to fourteen, and Lazarus (1959) reported no failures or relapses in treating 18 phobic children, the mean number of sessions being 9.5. The brevity of treatment is perhaps more significant than the outcomes in this sparse sample. Eysenck (1961) reports a high rate of success in treating problems such as enuresis by classical conditioning techniques. It will be interesting to see if this rate of favorable outcomes after only brief treatment is maintained as a larger number of children and a wider range of problems are treated.

CHILD CLINICAL DIAGNOSIS

Relationship Between Therapy and Diagnosis. It is generally agreed that therapy and diagnosis are closely interrelated procedures. Therapy takes place during the diagnostic process, and diagnostic findings are revealed during therapy. Depending on the problem, setting, and objective, the emphasis may be on one or the other. If the task is diagnosis, the clinical findings from psychometric tests, projective techniques, and analysis of play behavior (together with other information gathered by means of interviews and reports from schools, clinics, and other agencies) serve as a basis for making recommendations to treatment agencies. If the objective is treatment within the organization, the findings may serve to plan and guide at least the initial part of the treatment program.

Diagnostic Play Materials and Activities. What play materials and activities are selected for diagnostic work depend to a large extent on the clinician's theoretical orientation. Other important factors are the developmental level of the child, the nature of the problem presented, and the purpose of the evaluation. In light of the reason for referral and the available possibilities for treatment, the final consideration is practical. With severe time limitations and with facilities restricted to a desk or a table, limited materials known to minimize exploratory play are likely to be used. For example, a constellation of dolls representing the child's family and a schematic presentation of a house and a school might be the sole diagnostic equipment.

From the point of view of diagnosis, play materials and activities cannot be discriminated from projective techniques. It might be said, however, that findings from play procedures are interpreted on an even less formal basis than those from projective methods. Both projective techniques and play methods attempt to obtain diagnostic information by the behavior in response to vague, ambiguous, or suggestive stimuli.[3]

Diagnostic play procedures may be classified on the bases of the characteristics of the materials and the typical reactions to them. These classifications, in turn, may be subdivided in terms of (1) toys to stimulate dramatic play, (2) materials to encourage artistic production, and (3) situations to encourage role playing.

Toys To Stimulate Dramatic Play. Among the toys used to initiate fantasy, dramatic, or thematic play, one encounters a heavy emphasis on the use of dolls to represent parents, other authority figures, babies, and children of all ages. Also included are doll equipment, household furniture and furnishings, cars and trucks, blocks, guns, and the like (Jackson and Todd, 1950). As in the therapeutic approaches, presentation is either free or controlled. In the former case, the child is left to his own devices, whereas, in the latter, he is limited to materials taking one of several patterns (e.g., dolls representing a classical family situation—father, mother, sister, brother, and baby; dolls as a duplication of the child's family; or dolls and other materials symbolizing a general problem area). Lowenfeld (1935) prepared a standard set of materials (The World Test) consisting of 150 wooden toys representing not only people but also the physical and cultural things in the world. The child is shown the complete set and asked to create whatever he wishes. The clinician can discuss the

---

[3] The materials, methods of analysis, and types of interpretations used were considered in Chapter 4. In addition, Bell (1948) has reviewed the topics, and Stone (1950) has presented an evaluation of recent trends.

child's interactions with the materials, or he can allow the child to work independently.

MATERIALS TO ENCOURAGE ARTISTIC PRODUCTION. Most, if not all, of the devices used to encourage artistic production have been exploited for diagnostic purposes, including pencils, crayons, paints, finger paints, water and sand, modeling clay, charcoal, colored stones, story construction, incomplete sentences, and incomplete stories and pictures. We shall group those most frequently used under the following two headings: (1) drawing and painting constructions and (2) verbal constructions.

With the first group, the child is simply given paper, pencil, crayons, paints, and paint brushes and prompted to draw a specific individual group or situation, or anything he likes. Interest in this approach has led to the development of numerous ways of obtaining drawings and analyzing them. The child may be asked simply to draw a man, as in the Goodenough test of intelligence (1926), or he may be asked to draw his family (Hulse, 1951) or to draw or paint some interesting or emotional situation (Harms, 1941). Methods of evaluation range from a detailed record of movements and symbolic content (Woltmann, 1951) to a global qualitative judgment. When the child is allowed to draw or paint what he wishes (Naumberg, 1952), interpretations can be made of his reactions while working and of his final productions.

Finger painting, first introduced for educational and recreational purposes, has enjoyed a place among diagnostic materials because of its appeal and because colorful productions can be made readily. Napoli (1951) devised an elaborate scoring system for the use of this medium. He and others (Kadis, 1950) have suggested that the unique value of the method lies in the fact that it is free from motor limitations. Although it has been used for general diagnostic purposes, Kanner (1948) believes it is especially helpful when applied to children with obsessional reactions, those having bowel-training problems and anxieties with respect to cleanliness.

The second group of procedures in this category is used to initiate and encourage verbal constructions. Several of the techniques were described by Kanner (1948). After rapport has been established, the clinician asks the child to recount his dreams, his daydreams, or descriptions of his imaginary companions. Or he may be asked to pretend he is granted three wishes. More structured techniques require the completion of sentences or stories, as in the incomplete-sentence test for children that was developed by Rohde and Hildreth (1947). The favorable features of the incomplete-sentence approach include short administration time and flexibility, inasmuch as the stimulus phrases can be adapted to the immediate situation. Straightforward storytelling methods have also been used. Stories of a certain kind may be requested ("Tell me the best story you have ever heard."), or they may be stimulated by material such as a comic-strip character (Haggard, 1942).

SITUATIONS TO ENCOURAGE ROLE PLAYING. In this category, psychodrama and puppetry have been given considerable attention. Psychodrama, originally developed for adolescents and adults, has been used with young children as well. One of the techniques used by Moreno and Moreno (1945) involves selecting a number of the most characteristic roles representing individuals in any given community. Each child is then asked to take these roles. ("Show what he does.") Later, the roles are taken by a trained adult, and the child is asked to identify the characters portrayed. The child's level of development and "cultural age" are inferred from scores.

Diagnostic Integration. Diagnostic play provides a sample of behavior that can serve as a basis for inferences about the child's functioning. Combined with information from other sources, these findings are used for their implications for disposition (refer to another agency, institutionalize, offer therapy) and for planning of treatment. Although the first goal, disposition, is often reached by diagnostic evaluation, there is some question as to whether current assessment techniques offer much in guiding treatment (Bijou, 1965; Ferster, 1958, 1965). In fact, it often appears that unsureness as to the treatment implications of diagnosis, combined with relative security with respect to disposition, leads to a continual round of referrals reminiscent of "musical chairs." Everyone disposes of cases, but few treat them (Wolfensberger, 1965).

It is possible that this unfortunate situation is merely technological; that is, the current diagnostic rationale is sound, but current instruments are just not good enough. This leads to statistical considerations of reliability and validity. It is also possible that the usual rationale for diagnosis is inappropriate to its tasks. Treatment is a process of change in which, regardless of the theoretical partiality of the therapist, someone performs certain real-world operations that it is hoped will have a known effect on the child in treatment. Most current diagnosis techniques, however, usually provide normative-correlational information, and such information does not impart much about the functional relation of behavior to its surrounding environment, the "today" environment in which therapeutic manipulations occur (Bijou, 1965; Ferster, 1965). Finally, it is possible that serious deficiencies exist both in the usual rationale for diagnosis and in the current state of psychotechnology.

Research on Diagnostic Play. While the greatest interest in child psychology once centered mainly on descriptions of behavior and the attendant establishment of norms, play activities were given their full share of attention. Data were gathered describing the kinds of play and play materials that attracted children of different age levels, as well as the characteristics of each stage of play. In response to increasing demands from the applied fields, especially education and child rearing, and because of the shift in theoretical interest from a correlational to a functional approach, a new trend appeared. Studies of play delved into the analysis of development in normal children (Bijou and Baer, 1961, 1965; Hoffman and Hoffman, 1964; Lerner et al., 1941; Palermo and Lipsitt, 1963).

Experimental studies of play that can serve as a sound foundation for the development of diagnostic procedures are rare. Investigations by Sears and his co-workers were concerned with methodological problems of doll play (1947) and with measuring and relating, within a Hullian frame of reference, conditions antecedent and concomitant to this segment of child behavior (1951, 1951). Little consistent research followed these efforts. In a 1962 review of doll play, it was concluded that "an overall body of sensible, interrelated findings is not apparent" (Levin and Wardwell, 1962).

Recent research, reviewed by Lovaas et al. (1965), suggests some of the limitations of traditional doll-play procedures and describes alternatives that may overcome these limitations. As doll play is usually used, they point out, it is impossible to define either the specific stimulus characteristics of the situation or the functions of these stimuli with reference to the child's behavior or to obtain quantitative measures. To overcome these limitations, various apparatus were described that utilized automated dolls, puppets, or mother pictures and in which the "performance" characterized some social event such as "aggression" or "affection." Some convenient response of the child is necessary to produce these performances; thus, neither the characteristics of the stimuli nor their functional relations to the child's behavior are controlled by the child. Studies of aggressive responding and aggressive reinforcement, imitation, and effects of attention on children's behavior were reported, as well as plans to relate these procedures more directly to clinical evaluations.

All in all, however, the amount of published research on child diagnosis is regrettably small. The seven most recent volumes of the *Annual Review of Psychology* (1959–65) contain no index references to diagnostic procedures with children, other than scattered reports of a few tests, and no references at all to diagnostic play.

SUMMARY

Treatment techniques with children, frequently referred to as "play techniques" or "play therapy," stem for the most part from the theory and psychotherapeutics of Freud and his students. Contemporary practices have emerged from a combination of the theory and practice of psychotherapy with neurotic adults and functional conceptions of child behavior and development. There are six major approaches, not entirely discrete but sufficiently different in theoretical orientation or therapeutic goals to warrant individual consideration. Three of these are based directly on psychoanalysis: child analysis, briefer analytic child therapy, and expressive therapy. A fourth, relationship child therapy, is based on the Rankian variation of psychoanalysis; the fifth, referred to as "play therapy," is based on Rogers' viewpoint; and the sixth, called "behavior therapy," stems from the work of Pavlov, Hull, and Skinner. Thus far, research efforts have been devoted mainly to exploring treatment techniques. Little has been accomplished in the delineation of the functional relationships within the therapeutic process or in the evaluation of the results of treatment.

The diagnostic and therapeutic functions in clinical child psychology are intermeshed. Division between the two is made only for practical elucidative purposes. Many considerations are usually involved in the selection and use of diagnostic devices, the most important factor being the theoretical viewpoint of the clinician. Typical materials employed include toys to stimulate dramatic play and devices to encourage artistic production and role playing. Most of the investigations on diagnostic problems have been exploratory in nature. Studies planned to convert the more often used diagnostic methods into serviceable clinical instruments are still lacking.

REFERENCES

ALLEN, F. H. 1942. *Psychotherapy with children.* New York: Norton.

ALLEN, K. EILEEN, HART, BETTY M., BUELL, JOAN S., HARRIS, FLORENCE R., and WOLFF, M. M. 1964. Effects of social reinforcement on isolate behavior of a nursery school child. *Child Develpm.,* 35, 511–18.

AXLINE, VIRGINIA M. 1947a. *Play therapy.* Boston: Houghton Mifflin.

AXLINE, VIRGINIA M. 1947b. Nondirective therapy for poor readers. *J. consult. Psychol.,* 11, 61–69.

AXLINE, VIRGINIA M. 1949. Mental deficiency—symptom or disease? *J. consult. Psychol.,* 13, 313–27.

AXLINE, VIRGINIA M. 1950. Play therapy experiences as described by child participants. *J. consult. Psychol.,* 14, 53–63.

BACHRACH, A. J. (ed.). 1962. *The experimental foundations of clinical psychology.* New York: Basic Books.

BAER, D. M. 1963. Improving the behavior of nursery school children through social reinforcement. *Bull. ment. Hlth Res. Inst.,* 2(4).

BAER, D. M., PETERSON, R. F., and SHERMAN, J. A. 1965. Building an imitative repertoire by programming similarity between child and model as discriminative for reinforcement. Paper presented to SRCD, Minneapolis.

BANDURA, A. 1961. Psychotherapy as a learning process. *Psychol. Bull.*, **58**, 143–59.

BANDURA, A. 1965. Behavior modification through modeling procedures. In L. KRASNER and L. P. ULLMANN (eds.), *Research in behavior modification: New developments and implications.* New York: Holt, Rinehart & Winston.

BELL, J. E. 1948. *Projective techniques.* New York: Longmans.

BENDER, LORETTA, and WOLTMANN, A. G. 1936. The use of puppet shows as a psychotherapeutic method for behavior problems in children. *Amer. J. Orthopsychiat.*, **6**, 341–55.

BENTLER, P. M. 1962. An infant's phobia treated with reciprocal inhibition therapy. *J. child Psychol. Psychiat.*, **3**, 185–89.

BIJOU, S. W. 1965. Experimental studies of child behavior, normal and deviant. In L. KRASNER and L. P. ULLMANN (eds.), *Research in behavior modification: New developments and implications.* New York: Holt, Rinehart, & Winston.

BIJOU, S. W., and BAER, D. M. 1961. *Child development: A systematic and empirical theory.* New York: Appleton-Century-Crofts.

BIJOU, S. W., and BAER, D. M. 1965a. *Child development: The universal stage of infancy.* New York: Appleton-Century-Crofts.

BIJOU, S. W., and BAER, D. M. 1965b. Operant methods in child behavior and development. In W. K. HONIG (ed.), *Operant behavior and psychology.* New York: Appleton-Century-Crofts.

BILLS, R. E. 1950. Nondirective play therapy with retarded readers. *J. consult. Psychol.*, **14**, 140–49.

BRICKER, W. A. 1965. Speech work with autistic and mentally retarded children. Paper presented to SRCD, Minneapolis.

CAMERON, N., and MAGARET, ANN. 1951. *Behavior pathology.* Boston: Houghton Mifflin.

CONN, J. H. 1939. The play interview: A method of studying children's attitudes. *Amer. J. Dis. Child.*, **58**, 1199–1214.

CRUICKSHANK, W. M., and COWEN, E. L. 1948a. Group therapy with physically handicapped children. I. Report of study. *J. educ. Psychol.*, **39**, 193–215.

CRUICKSHANK, W. M., and COWEN, E. L. 1948b. Group therapy with physically handicapped children. II. Evaluation. *J. educ. Psychol.*, **39**, 281–97.

DEMYER, MARIAN K., and FERSTER, C. B. 1962. Teaching new social behavior to schizophrenic children. *J. child. Psychiat.*, **1**, 443–61.

DOLLARD, J., and MILLER, N. E. 1950. *Personality and psychotherapy: An analysis in terms of learning, thinking and culture.* New York: McGraw-Hill.

DUNLAP, K. 1930. Repetition in the breaking of habits. *Scientific mon.*, **30**, 66–70.

EYSENCK, H. J. (ed.). 1960. *Behavior therapy and the neuroses.* New York: Pergamon.

EYSENCK, H. J. (ed.). 1961. *Handbook of abnormal psychology: An experimental approach.* New York: Basic Books.

EYSENCK, H. J. (ed.). 1964. *Experiments in behavior therapy: Readings in modern methods of treatment derived from learning theory.* New York: Pergamon.

FERSTER, C. B. 1958. Reinforcement and punishment in the control of human behavior by social agencies. *Psychiat. Res. Rep.,* **10,** 101–18.

FERSTER, C. B. 1965. Classification of behavioral pathology. In L. KRASNER and L. P. ULLMANN (eds.), *Research in behavior modification: New developments and implications.* New York: Holt, Rinehart, & Winston.

FERSTER, C. B., and DeMYER, MARIAN K. 1961. The development of performances in autistic children in an automatically controlled environment. *J. chronic Dis.,* **13,** 312–45.

FERSTER, C. B., and DeMYER, MARIAN K. 1962. A method for the experimental analysis of the behavior of autistic children. *Amer. J. Orthopsychiat.,* **32,** 89–98.

FLEMING, L., and SNYDER, W. U. 1947. Social and personal changes following nondirective group play therapy. *Amer. J. Orthopsychiat.,* **17,** 101–16.

FRAIBERG, SELMA H. 1951. Clinical notes on the nature of transference in child analysis. In *The psychoanalytic study of the child.* Vol. 6. New York: International Universities Press.

FREUD, ANNA. 1946a. *Psychoanalytic treatment of children.* London: Imago.

FREUD, ANNA. 1946b. *The ego and the mechanisms of defense.* New York: International Universities Press.

FREUD, S. 1925. *Collected papers.* Vol. 3. London: Hogarth.

GELBER, H., and MEYER, V. 1965. Behavior therapy and encopresis: The complexities involved in treatment. *Behav. Res. Ther.,* **2,** 227–31.

GINOTT, H. G. 1961. *Group psychotherapy with children.* New York: McGraw-Hill.

GOODENOUGH, F. L. 1926. *The measurement of intelligence by drawings.* New York: Harcourt, Brace & World.

GROSSBERG, J. M. 1964. Behavior therapy: A review. *Psychol. Bull.,* **62,** 73–88.

HAGGARD, E. A. 1942. A projective technique using comic strip characters. *Charact. Pers.,* **10,** 289–95.

HARMS, E. 1941. Child art as aid in the diagnosis of juvenile neurosis. *Amer. J. Orthopsychiat.,* **11,** 191–210.

HARRIS, FLORENCE R., JOHNSTON, MARGARET K., KELLEY, C. SUSAN, and WOLF, M. M. 1964. Effects of positive social reinforcement on regressed crawling of a nursery school child. *J. Educ. Psychol.,* **55,** 35–41.

HARRIS, FLORENCE R., WOLF, M. M., and BAER, D. M. 1964. Effects of adult social reinforcement on child behavior. *Young Child.,* **20,** 8–17.

HART, BETTY M., ALLEN, K. EILEEN, BUELL, JOAN S., HARRIS, FLORENCE R., and WOLF, M. M. 1964. Effects of social reinforcement on operant crying. *J. exp. child Psychol.,* **1,** 145–53.

HART, BETTY M., REYNOLDS, NANCY J., HARRIS, FLORENCE R., and BAER, D. M. 1965. Application of reinforcement principles to cooperative play. University of Washington. Personal communication.

HAWKINS, R. P., PETERSON, R. F., and SCHWEID, EDDA. 1965. Treatment of mother and child in the home by operant conditioning techniques. University of Washington. Personal communication.

HERZBERG, A. 1941. Short treatment of neuroses by graduated tasks. *Brit. J. med. Psychol.,* 19, 36–51.

HERZBERG, A. 1945. *Active psychotherapy.* New York: Grune & Stratton.

HINGTEN, J. N., SANDERS, BEVERLY J., and DeMYER, MARIAN K. 1965. Shaping cooperative responses in early childhood schizophrenics. In L. P. ULLMANN and L. KRASNER (eds.), *Case studies in behavior modification.* New York: Holt, Rinehart, & Winston.

HOFFMAN, M. L., and HOFFMAN, LOIS W. (eds.). 1964. *Review of child development research.* New York: Russell Sage.

HUG-HELLMUTH, HERMINE V. 1919. *A study of the mental life of the child.* New York: Nervous and Mental Disease Publishing Co.

HULSE, W. C. 1951. The emotionally disturbed child draws his family. *Quart. J. child Behav.,* 3, 152–74.

JACKSON, LYDIA, and TODD, KATHLEEN M. 1950. *Child treatment and the therapy of play.* New York: Ronald.

JACOBSON, E. 1938. *Progressive relaxation.* Chicago: Univer. of Chicago Press.

JOHNSTON, MARGARET K., KELLEY, C. SUSAN, HARRIS, FLORENCE R., and WOLF, M. M. 1966. An application of reinforcement principles to the development of motor skills of a young child. *Child Develpm.*

JOHNSTON, MARGARET K., KELLEY, C. SUSAN, HARRIS, FLORENCE R., WOLF, M. M., and BAER, D. M. 1964. Effects of positive social reinforcement on isolate behavior of a nursery school child. Unpublished manuscript, Univer. of Washington.

JONES, E. L. 1955. Exploration of experimental extinction and spontaneous recovery in stuttering. In W. JOHNSON (ed.), *Stuttering in children and adults.* Minneapolis: Univer. of Minnesota Press.

JONES, H. G. 1960. The behavioral treatment of enuresis nocturna. In H. J. EYSENCK (ed.), *Behavior therapy and the neuroses.* New York: Pergamon.

JONES, MARY C. 1924a. The elimination of children's fears. *J. exp. Psychol.,* 7, 382–90.

JONES, MARY C. 1924b. A laboratory study of fear: The case of Peter. *J. gen. Psychol.,* 31, 308–15.

KADIS, ASYA L. 1950. Finger-painting as a projective technique. In L. E. ABT and L. BELLAK (eds.), *Projective psychology.* New York: Knopf.

KANNER, L. 1948. *Child psychiatry.* (2d ed.) Springfield, Ill.: Charles C Thomas.

KLEIN, MELANIE. 1949. *The psychoanalysis of children.* London: Hogarth.

KRASNER, L., and ULLMANN, L. P. (eds.). 1965. *Research in behavior modification: New developments and implications.* New York: Holt, Rinehart, & Winston.

LANDISBERG, SELMA, and SNYDER, W. U. 1946. Nondirective play therapy. *J. clin. Psychol.,* 2, 203–13.

LANG, P. J. 1964. Experimental studies of desensitization therapy. In J.

WOLPE, A. SALTER, and L. J. REYNA (eds.), The conditioning therapies. New York: Holt, Rinehart, & Winston.

LAZARUS, A. A. 1959. The elimination of children's phobias by deconditioning. Med. Proc., S. Africa, 5, 261–65.

LAZARUS, A. A. 1961. Group therapy of phobic disorders by systematic desensitization. J. abnorm. soc. Psychol., 63, 504–10.

LAZARUS, A. A., and ABRAMOVITZ, A. 1962. The use of "emotive-imagery" in the treatment of children's phobias. J. ment. Sci., 108, 191–95.

LAZARUS, A. A., and RACHMAN, S. 1957. The use of systematic desensitization in psychotherapy. South African med. J., 31, 934–37.

LERNER, E., MURPHY, L., STONE, L. J., BEYER, E., and BROWN, E. 1941. Methods for the study of personality in the young child. Monogr. Soc. Res. child Develpm., 6, (Whole No. 4).

LEVIN, H., and WARDWELL, E. 1962. The research uses of doll play. Psychol. Bull., 59, 27–56.

LEVITT, E. E. 1957. Results of psychotherapy with children: An evaluation. J. consult. Psychol., 21, 189–96.

LEVITT, E. E. 1963. Psychotherapy with children: A further evaluation. Behav. Res. Ther., 1, 45–51.

LEVY, D. M. 1939. Release therapy. Amer. J. Orthopsychiat., 9, 913–36.

LOVAAS, O. I., BAER, D. M., and BIJOU, S. W. 1965. Experimental procedures for analyzing the interaction of symbolic social stimuli and children's behavior. Child Develpm., 36, 237–48.

LOVAAS, O. I., FREITAG, G., KINDER, M. I., RUBENSTEIN, B. D., SCHAEFFER, B., and SIMMONS, J. Q. 1964a. Experimental studies in childhood schizophrenia. II. Establishment of social reinforcers. Paper presented to Western Psychological Association.

LOVAAS, O. I., FREITAG, G., KINDER, M. I., RUBENSTEIN, D. B., SCHAEFFER, B., and SIMMONS, J. Q. 1964b. Experimental studies in childhood schizophrenia. Development of social behavior using electric shock. Paper presented to American Psychological Association, Los Angeles, September, 1964.

LOWENFELD, M. 1935. Play in childhood. London: Gollancz.

LOWERY, L. G. 1939. Evolution and present status of treatment approaches to behavior and personality problems: Evolution, status and trends. Amer. J. Orthopsychiat., 9, 669–706.

MAHLER, MARGARET S. 1945. Child-analysis. In N. D. C. LEWIS and B. L. PACELLA (eds.), Modern trends in child psychiatry. New York: International Universities Press.

MEHLMAN, B. 1953. Group play therapy with mentally retarded children. J. abnorm. soc. Psychol., 48, 53–60.

METZNER, R. 1961. Learning theory and the therapy of neuroses. Brit. J. Psychol., Monogr. Suppl. 33.

MEYER, V., and GELDER, M. G. 1963. Behavior therapy and phobic disorders. Brit. J. Psychiat., 109, 19–28.

MEYERSON, L., KERR, N., and MICHAEL, J. 1966. Behavior modification in rehabilitation. In S. W. BIJOU and D. M. BAER (eds.), Readings in the *experimental analysis of child development and behavior.* New York: Appleton-Century-Crofts.

MORENO, F. B., and MORENO, J. L. 1945. Role tests and role diagrams of children. *Sociometry,* 8, 426–41.

MOWRER, O. H. 1938. Apparatus for the study and treatment of enuresis. *Amer. J. Psychol.,* 51, 163–65.

NAPOLI, P. J. 1951. Finger painting. In H. H. ANDERSON and GLADYS L. ANDERSON (eds.), *An introduction to projective techniques.* Englewood Cliffs, N.J.: Prentice-Hall.

NAUMBERG, MARGARET. 1952. Spontaneous art in therapy and diagnosis. In D. BOWER and L. E. ABT (eds.), *Progress in clinical psychology.* Vol. 1 (Sect. 1). New York: Grune & Stratton.

NEALE, D. H. 1963. Behavior therapy and encopresis in children. *Behav. Res. Ther.,* 1, 139–49.

NEWELL, H. W. 1941. Play therapy in child psychiatry. *Amer. J. Orthopsychiat.,* 11, 245–51.

PALERMO, D. S., and LIPSITT, L. P. 1963. *Research readings in child psychology.* New York: Holt, Rinehart, & Winston.

PATTERSON, G. R. 1965. The application of conditioning techniques to the control of a hyperactive child. In L. P. ULLMANN and L. KRASNER (eds.), *Case studies in behavior modification.* New York: Holt, Rinehart, & Winston.

PATTERSON, G. R., JONES, R., WHITTIER, J., and WRIGHT, MARY A. 1965. A behavior modification technique for the hyperactive child. *Behav. Res. Ther.,* 2, 217–26.

PEARSON, G. H. J. 1949. *Emotional disorders of children.* New York: Norton.

RACHMAN, S. 1962. Learning theory and child psychology: Therapeutic possibilities. *J. child Psychol. Psychiat.,* 3, 149–63.

RACHMAN, S., and COSTELLO, C. G. 1961. The etiology and treatment of children's phobias: A review. *Amer. J. Psychiat.,* 118, 87–105.

REYNA, L. J. 1964. Conditioning therapies, learning theory, and research. In J. WOLPE, A. SALTER, and L. J. REYNA (eds.), *The conditioning therapies.* New York: Holt, Rinehart, & Winston.

RISLEY, T., and WOLF, M. M. 1966. Experimental manipulation of autistic behavior and generalization in the home. In S. W. BIJOU and D. M. BAER (eds.), *Readings in the experimental analysis of child behavior and development.* New York: Appleton-Century-Crofts.

ROGERS, C. R. 1939. *The clinical treatment of the problem child.* Boston: Houghton Mifflin.

ROGERS, C. R. 1942. *Counseling and psychotherapy.* Boston: Houghton Mifflin.

ROGERS, C. R. 1951. *Client-centered therapy.* Boston: Houghton Mifflin.

ROGERSON, C. H. 1939. *Play therapy in childhood.* Fair Lawn, N.J.: Oxford Univer. Press.

ROHDE, A. R., and HILDRETH, G. 1947. *Sentence completion test.* New York: Psychological Corp.

Russo, S. 1964. Adaptations in behavioral therapy with children. *Behav. Res. Ther.*, 2, 43–47.

Salter, A. 1950. *Conditioned reflex therapy.* New York: Creative Age.

Salzinger, K., Feldman, R. S., Cowan, Judith, and Salzinger, Suzanne. 1965. Operant conditioning of verbal behavior of two young speech deficient boys. In L. Krasner and L. P. Ullmann (eds.), *Research in behavior modification: New developments and implications.* New York: Holt, Rinehart, & Winston.

Schermann, A., and Grover, V. M. 1962. Treatment of children's behavior disorders: A method of re-education. *Med. Proc., South Africa,* 8, 151–54.

Sears, Pauline S. 1951. Doll play aggression in normal young children: Influence of sex, age, sibling status, father's absence. *Psychol. Monogr.,* 65, No. 6 (Whole No. 323).

Sears, R. R. 1947. Influence of methodological factors on doll play performance. *Child Develpm.,* 18, 190–97.

Sears, R. R. 1951. Symposium on genetic psychology. III. Effects of frustration and anxiety on fantasy aggression. *Amer. J. Orthopsychiat.,* 21, 498–505.

Skinner, B. F. 1938. *The behavior of organisms.* New York: Appleton-Century-Crofts.

Skinner, B. F. 1953. *Science and human behavior.* New York: Macmillan.

Skinner, B. F. 1961. *Cumulative record.* (Enlarged ed.) New York: Appleton-Century-Crofts.

Slack, C. W. 1960. Experimenter-subject psychotherapy: A new method of introducing intensive office treatment for unreachable cases. *Ment. Hygiene N.Y.,* 44, 238–56.

Slavson, S. R. 1943. *An introduction to group therapy.* New York: Commonwealth Fund.

Slavson, S. R. (ed.). 1947. *The practice of group therapy.* New York: International Universities Press.

Slavson, S. R. 1950. *Analytic group psychotherapy with children, adolescents and adults.* New York: Columbia Univer. Press.

Solomon, J. C. 1951. Therapeutic use of play. In H. H. Anderson and Gladys L. Anderson (eds.), *An introduction to projective techniques.* Englewood Cliffs, N.J.: Prentice-Hall.

Stone, L. J. 1950. Recent developments in diagnostic testing of children. In Molly R. Harrower (ed.), *Recent advances in diagnostic psychological testing.* Springfield, Ill.: Charles C Thomas.

Straughan, J. H. 1964. Treatment with child and mother in the playroom. *Behav. Res. Ther.,* 2, 37–41.

Taft, Jessie. 1933. *The dynamics of therapy in a controlled relationship.* New York: Macmillan.

Tallman, F. F., and Goldensohn, L. N. 1941. Play techniques. *Amer. J. Orthopsychiat.,* 11, 551–61.

Ullmann, L. P., and Krasner, L. (eds.). 1965. *Case studies in behavior modification.* New York: Holt, Rinehart, & Winston.

WATSON, J. B., and RAYNER, ROSALIE. 1920. Conditioned emotional reactions. *J. exp. Psychol.*, 3, 1–4.

WHITE, J. G. 1959. The use of learning theory in the psychological treatment of children. *J. clin. Psychol.*, 15, 227–29.

WILLIAMS, C. D. 1959. The elimination of tantrum behavior by extinction procedures. *J. abnorm. soc. Psych.*, 59, 269.

WILLIAMS, T. 1965. An intensive training unit for delinquent retardates. The Rainier School, Wash. Personal communication.

WOLF, M. M., BIRNBRAUER, J. S., WILLIAMS, T., and LAWLER, JULIA. 1965. A note on apparent extinction of the vomiting behavior of a retarded child. In L. P. ULLMANN and L. KRASNER (eds.), *Case studies in behavior modification*. New York: Holt, Rinehart, & Winston.

WOLF, M. M., RISLEY, T. R., and MEES, H. L. 1964. Application of operant conditioning procedures to the behavior problems of an autistic child. *Behav. Res. Ther.*, 1, 305–12.

WOLFENSBERGER, W. 1965. Embarrassments in the diagnostic process. *Ment. Retardation*, 3(3).

WOLFF, W. 1948. *Expressive movement chart: Evaluation of emotional trends in pre-school children*. New York: Grune & Stratton.

WOLPE, J. 1958. *Psychotherapy by reciprocal inhibition*. Stanford, Calif.: Stanford Univer. Press.

WOLPE, J. 1962. The experimental foundations of some new psychotherapeutic methods. In A. J. BACHRACH (ed.), *The experimental foundations of clinical psychology*. New York: Basic Books.

WOLPE, J. 1964a. Behavior therapy in complex neurotic states. *Brit. J. Psychiat.*, 110, 28–34.

WOLPE, J. 1964b. The systematic desensitization treatment of neurosis. In H. J. EYSENCK (ed.), *Experiments in behavior therapy: Readings in modern methods of treatment derived from learning theory*. New York: Pergamon.

WOLPE, J., SALTER, A., and REYNA, L. J. (eds.). 1964. *The conditioning therapies*. New York: Holt, Rinehart, & Winston.

WOLTMANN, A. G. 1951. The use of puppetry as a projective method in therapy. In H. H. ANDERSON and GLADYS L. ANDERSON (eds.), *An introduction to projective techniques*. Englewood Cliffs, N.J.: Prentice-Hall.

ZIMMERMAN, E. H., and ZIMMERMAN, J. 1962. The alteration of behavior in a special classroom situation. *J. exp. Analysis Behav.*, 5, 59–60.

22

Rehabilitative Approaches

JOHN R. BARRY [*]

Rehabilitation has been referred to as a philosophy, an objective, and a method (Mayo, 1959). The focus in this chapter will be on the latter meaning, the methods or approaches in rehabilitation, and will refer primarily to activities in the United States, although in some respects, rehabilitation in the Scandinavian countries and in a few other countries is more advanced than in the United States.

The concept of rehabilitation has over the last several years been broadened to include almost every kind of service to those who are disadvantaged in any way in their attempts to achieve their individual potentials. A cogent discussion of several meanings of the term *rehabilitation* appears in an early section of the proceedings of an institute on the roles of psychology and psychologists in rehabilitation held at Princeton (Wright, 1959).

A recent committee of the National Rehabilitation Association has described rehabilitation as an individualized process in which the disabled patients, the rehabilitation professionals, and others, through comprehensive, coordinated, and integrated services, seek to minimize the disability and its handicapping and to facilitate the maximum rehabilitation of the handicapped individual. A key notion in this description is the active involvement of a team of professionals in the practical real-life problems of a disabled person (National Rehabilitation Association, 1965).

It is useful to distinguish between impairment, on the one hand, and the resulting disability, on the other. *Impairment* refers to an anatomical or functional change and is a medical or psychological term. However, the term *disability* refers to an administrative, judicial, or legislative judgment

---

[*] John R. Barry, Ph.D. (The Ohio State University), Professor of Psychology, and Director, Regional Rehabilitation Research Institute, University of Florida.

about the social and economic consequences of the impairment (Kessler, 1964; Nagi, 1964). There will be no distinction in the present chapter between the terms *patient* and *client*. The former is essentially a medical term and is most often applied to sick people. The term *client* usually refers to someone who needs, applies for, or gets services of some kind. In practice, once the patient leaves the strictly medical setting, he is more likely to be called a "client." The terms *handicapped* and *disabled* also tend to be used interchangeably, although the latter is becoming the more acceptable.

Sometimes a differentiation is made between *rehabilitation,* or restoring a person to the maximum possible extent, and *habilitation,* or helping a handicapped person to achieve productive and independent living for the first time. This latter term would apply to many rehabilitation services for the retarded and others impaired at birth. In practice, both objectives, habilitation and rehabilitation, are accomplished in similar ways, and often in the same setting and by the same professional staffs. In this chapter, no further distinction will be made between habilitation and rehabilitation. They will be discussed together.

While present-day rehabilitation has its roots in earlier health and psychological service programs, there were relatively few organized or formal rehabilitation activities prior to World War II (Pennington, 1954). Even the state-federal rehabilitation programs were relatively small. Services tended to be limited to vocational training related to the disability, rather than to involve its alleviation or its elimination (Garrett and Levine, 1962).

During World War II, the extreme shortages of all types of manpower, as well as the return from war of many disabled servicemen, provided the occasion, the need, and, indirectly, the means for rehabilitating large numbers of all types of disabled people. The manpower shortages during the war enabled disabled people to obtain work and prove their economic value to society. Exploration and research on new techniques of rehabilitation in the public and private sectors were strongly encouraged. Today rehabilitation has emerged as a primary focal point for many socially important efforts in the health, welfare, education, and economic fields.

At this point, it might be helpful to introduce the reader to one of the kinds of problems the rehabilitation worker may face. Many problem families need the combined help of several rehabilitation facilities and agencies. For example, the Jones family became visible to social agencies when Mrs. Jones applied for Aid to Dependent Children. Her husband had been in a tuberculosis hospital for six months. She had had a job as a waitress but had lost it because of extreme nervousness and poor vision. She also had had an operation for the removal of a rather large goiter.

Because of concern for the family, Mr. Jones was continually leaving the hospital without permission, which only aggravated his already severe condition. A family social worker attempted to explain to him the necessity of cooperating with the hospital, but his condition grew steadily worse. While the application for Aid to Dependent Children was under consideration, county welfare provided food orders and the Needlework Guild gave clothing and shoes. The health department treated the three children for worms and gave immunization shots. Glasses were given to one child by the Lions Club. Robert, the oldest son, aged eleven, ran away from home because the children at school laughed at his ragged clothes and made fun of him. He and his mother secured counseling at the local child guidance center to relieve some of the insecurity caused by his father's absence from home.

After Mr. Jones's death, his wife attempted to find work as a waitress but was rejected in several places because the goiter had given an unpleasant bulging appearance to her eyes. She was finally referred to the Vocational Rehabilitation Service for evaluation, rehabilitation, and eventual placement. She had done office work during the war, and psychological evaluation suggested certain clerical aptitudes.

She was fitted with glasses and enrolled full-time in a business college, with the vocational goal of becoming a secretary. A housekeeper was secured through Child Welfare, and in due time Mrs. Jones completed the course. The state employment service helped her to secure full-time employment, and this family is now self-sufficient. Without the help and cooperation of many different private and public service groups, this whole family might very well have become permanent public wards.

This brief case report illustrates several points that will be discussed below. First, most clients have multiple problems, some of which may be social in nature, and others, medical. Most clients have families who are deeply involved and affected by what happens to the client. Many agencies are needed to deal with the problems of the whole family in order to facilitate the rehabilitation of the breadwinner. The skills of many specialists are involved in rehabilitation, and different specialists play key roles at different points in the rehabilitation process.

Rehabilitation is a field of interest to psychologists outside the laboratory and in the community. It offers to the psychologist a broader frame of reference than ever before (Garrett, 1952). The psychologist in rehabilitation can see the effects of his ideas, skill, and work, and he can give service. In the subsequent parts of this chapter, the discussion will focus first on specific rehabilitation approaches and settings. Usually these are related; that is, vocational counseling may occur in placement-oriented rehabilitation settings, speech therapy in cleft-palate centers, etc. In most settings, several approaches are employed. There is, of course, a great deal of overlap. In a subsequent section of this chapter (pages 695–700), the activities of specific rehabilitation specialists will be described, including activities of clinical psychologists. Finally, some of the important psychological concepts in rehabilitation will be discussed briefly.

It should be noted that this chapter is intentionally *not* organized around specific disability groupings, but, rather, it is intended to cut across these diagnostic categories and to deal with rehabilitation practices and problems common to all kinds of patients, both the physically and the psychiatrically ill. It is sometimes convenient and very helpful to consider separately all the information available about the rehabilitation of a single group such as the mentally retarded, the deaf, the blind, or the mentally ill. An excellent book by Garrett and Levine (1962) is organized in this way around specific disability groupings. Of course, many of the practices and concepts appropriate for any one of these groups are also very useful with other groups. Some authors (Seidenfeld, 1956) combine both approaches in their writings. However, in the present chapter, rehabilitation approaches common to several disabled groups will be discussed.

Rehabilitation like most of the helping fields today is limited by great shortages of trained personnel and, in some areas of the country, by a shortage of facilities and other kinds of support. One way of meeting these shortages is to utilize available facilities and existing trained personnel for helping all kinds of disabled people rather than to limit them to working with a specific disability group. Workshops and day hospitals, for example, do not need to limit the types of patients served to a single disability group. Facilities may be shared by many kinds of disabled people and by many different specialists. Experience has repeatedly shown that multidisability rehabilitation settings were more helpful to patients, more stimulating to professional staff, and more economical than settings and facilities limited to a single group of disabled people.

One benefit of such settings is the increased communication among diverse professional specialists that can be fostered by rehabilitating many types of disabled persons together. A psychiatrist may be encouraged to talk to an orthopedist when both specialists work with patients who are receiving physical therapy side by side. The present lack of communication across the rehabilitation disciplines is emphasized by the relatively small number of professional journals written for such broad audiences. Most journals, even in the rehabilitation areas, are written for specific specialists, usually a very small number of them (e.g., *the Journal of Physical Medicine and Rehabilitation,* for psychiatrists; the *Rehabilitation Counseling Bulletin,* for rehabilitation-counseling psychologists). The importance of this point will become more obvious when the various specialists who typically participate in rehabilitation are described, later in the chapter.

SPECIFIC REHABILITATIVE APPROACHES

In a broad sense, all efforts to help a patient recover and return to his maximum level of functioning are, by definition, rehabilitation. All of the specialists to be described in the next section apply rehabilitation techniques broadly conceived. The physician, the counselor, and all of the other therapists use their particular specialized knowledge to enhance progress toward the goal of rehabilitating the patient. In this sense, rehabilitation approaches do not differ from those that have been described in the earlier chapters of this volume.

However, some specific rehabilitation approaches have developed out of the particular philosophy related to helping the disabled. These approaches all involve helping the patient to become more active, to work with increasing independence, and to regain or develop his self-confidence, self-direction, and functional skills to as great an extent as is possible. As early as possible in the course of the patient's illness or disability, attempts are made to interest him in providing for his own bodily needs, in feeding himself, in dressing, and in taking care of his personal appearance. Reading materials are provided. Other leisure-time activities are introduced. Every effort should be made at this time to interest the patient in becoming more self-sufficient.

Different techniques and procedures are, of course, related to, and appropriate for, the different phases of the patient's illness-treatment-recovery-rehabilitation cycle. Thus, immediately after a serious accident, physical therapy in a hospital setting is certainly more appropriate than and often must precede any prevocational evaluation or on-the-job training. The last-named kind of rehabilitation is more appropriate to a later phase of rehabilitation, after the patient has regained his physical functioning.

In this section, then, I will first refer briefly to certain rehabilitation settings in the hospital that are appropriate primarily for the recently or seriously handicapped patient. Then I will describe rehabilitation settings and approaches that are more appropriate for the patient after his rehabilitation has begun and he is moving out into the community. Finally, two national programs will be described, in which a number of these approaches and settings are combined. In practice, there are many such broad programs in the United States that might be mentioned, including The Goodwill Industries, the American Foundation for the Blind, The National Association for the Mentally Retarded, the National Association for Crippled Children and Adults, the Veterans Administration, and many others such as the numerous state-federal vocational rehabilitation programs carried on with the help of the Vocational Rehabilitation Administration, of the Department of Health, Education, and Welfare. However, because of space limitations, only two programs (the Veterans

Administration rehabilitation program and the state-federal vocational rehabilitation programs) will be described in any detail.

Hospitals. Within most community, regional, or specialized hospitals, there exist a number of rehabilitation services staffed by the various specialists listed in Table 22–1 (see page 695). Since the roles and functions of these specialists are to be described in the next section, this comment here is meant only to call attention to the fact that most rehabilitation can and should begin as soon as the patient starts to recover his functioning. One rationale for beginning rehabilitation as early as possible is as follows: If the patient can be helped to focus on his return to a satisfying and productive role in life, he will dwell less on his misfortunes, his spirits will improve, and his physical recovery will be hastened.

A related rehabilitation technique involves the use of various *transitional settings:* day hospitals, night hospitals, and halfway houses. Each of these facilities, and its rehabilitation program, is helpful to the patient who is unable to live at home or who, for other reasons, needs some transitional setting before leaving the care and security of a hospital. In the *halfway-house program,* patients who are beginning to recover leave the hospital to live in a community group setting such as a rooming house or small hotel run specifically for such patients. During the day, they work at regular jobs in competitive or sheltered situations. At night, they return to the halfway house, as they later will return to their home. Such halfway-house programs provide a variety of services and often minor treatment facilities in addition to room and board and the security of a ready-made group with which to identify. The ex-patient usually feels and actually is less cut off from the hospital and its helping personnel in such a setting.

Night hospitals are similar to halfway houses, in that patients in night hospitals work in the community by day and return at night to the hospital. The patients may need, on a part-time basis, the care and treatment that can be provided only in a hospital. Special facilities or medications may be needed that cannot be administered outside of a hospital. Thus, the patients who are able leave the hospital and go to some kind of work or other activity during the day. At night, these patients return to the security of the night-hospital setting and receive whatever treatment has been prescribed. In both of these instances, greater care and supervision of the rehabilitant are provided than would be possible if he were to leave the sheltered setting entirely.

Day-hospital programs involve the patient's living at home but spending each day in the hospital, where he may receive continuing treatment, if appropriate, and where other constructive activities may be provided (Epps and Hanes, 1964; Lesser, 1965). Supervision is also an important aspect of this kind of rehabilitation setting. Many of the aged and other chronically disabled persons can be helped by such a setting and rehabilitation program.

Therapeutic-Community Concept. A relatively recent innovation in the psychiatric hospitals in the United States is the notion of the therapeutic community developed by Maxwell Jones (1953), in England, after World War II. This concept assumes that all aspects of hospital life can and should be used to benefit the patient. The therapeutic-community notion implies that a patient's recovery and rehabilitation are related to what happens to him in a social sense, that is, in relation to his family and friends and to hospital personnel. All aspects of the hospital world affect the patient and his family. It follows, then, that strains in this social system will lead to tensions, which, in turn, will affect the patient both physically and psychologically (King, 1962).

Thus, the therapeutic-community concept implies complete flexibility and arrangement of physical facilities that is optimal for the patient primarily and for the staff secondarily. In at least one of the psychiatric hospitals described by Jones (1953), an extension of this concept has resulted in the development of patient government and the complete responsibility of that government, even for deciding on patient discipline and discharge. It must be noted that this degree of patient responsibility is rare in any psychiatric hospital today, and many feel that the dangers in such a plan outweigh the advantages.

Quite often, in psychiatric hospitals, regular (almost daily) "open" group-therapy sessions are a major vehicle of treatment. These sessions are open in the sense that all ambulatory patients are expected to attend and participate as soon as they come on the ward and as long as they stay in the hospital. Since this is a special form of group therapy and is discussed above, in chapter 20, further discussion here is not necessary.

Ex-patient Clubs. This is another widely used way of providing security, help, and guidance to many types of patients who are seeking to become self-sufficient after they leave the hospital or rehabilitation setting. The Alcoholics Anonymous groups represent one of the most widespread and best-known national movements of this type. Former narcotic addicts reportedly have been helped by participation in groups similar to Alcoholics Anonymous. Ex-psychiatric-patient groups, sometimes associated with a hospital and sometimes independent of any formal institution, have been formed and appear to have been helpful in bridging the hospital-community gap (Becker, Murphy, and Greenblatt, 1965).

Workshops. *Sheltered workshops* are increasingly available for all kinds of rehabilitation problems. Such workshops usually involve the manufacture of some kind of product for sale. This manufacturing may be on a subcontract basis in relation to a larger firm (e.g., electrical subcontracting), or it may involve manufacturing or assembling a product (e.g., brooms) from raw materials. Handicapped workers are employed in such settings in accordance with the demands for their skills and the regulations governing the workshop itself. While such workshops are more or less production-oriented, they are usually also supported in part by public or private funds and are meant to provide a sheltered (less competitive and more protected) kind of work situation for the disabled (Feintuch, 1958).

In many instances, patients are able to "graduate" from such sheltered settings to regular jobs in competitive industry. In other instances, it is not expected that the workers will ever leave the sheltered-workshop setting. These latter shops may be called "terminal workshops" and may do a great deal to help the sheltered employee to maintain his self-respect and to feel that he has a reason for living.

There are many kinds of workshops available for a client. Some are oriented primarily toward a specific disabled group such as the blind or the retarded. Other workshops, for example, Abilities, Inc., accept clients with any of many kinds of disabilities (Yanouck, 1962). Since productive work performance usually does not involve the use of all of one's skills and capacities, clients with different disabilities can often work side by side and help each other. For example, a blind worker and a deaf worker can complement each other's capacities and can work as a team—the blind hearing for the deaf and the deaf seeing for the blind (Mase, 1962).

Other Approaches. Another major approach in rehabilitation is exemplified by the *comprehensive rehabilitation center*. These centers provide almost all types of diagnostic and evaluative services that may lead to a better understanding of the patient's problems and a coordinated effort to rehabilitate him to the maximum extent possible. A comprehensive rehabilitation center may include under one roof many or most of the specialists listed in Table 22–1, and more. The more services offered in such a setting, the more comprehensive the center is considered. Housing many specialists together is intended to facilitate their efforts to work together in evaluating and rehabilitating the patient. Case conferences may be facilitated by such a physical arrangement. Also, this arrangement is meant to make it easier to rehabilitate the whole person under one roof and to accomplish this more quickly and efficiently for all concerned. Such comprehensive rehabilitation centers usually have medical specialists, occupational and physical therapists, prevocational specialists, vocational counselors, and a variety of other specialists.

In some instances, a workshop may be associated closely with the rehabilitation center, as an integral part of it. In such a workshop, the patient may be provided with prevocational tasks. From his performance in these tasks, an idea of his skills, needs, and work potential may be obtained. In other parts of the workshop, he may be provided with actual work experiences in a sheltered setting, and he may receive training in job adjustment skills. This training might involve such things as understanding the use of money to meet one's own needs, learning to get to work on time and to work for a full eight-hour day, learning to get along with one's co-workers and supervisors, and, when needed, specific training in personal grooming.

The *state-federal vocational rehabilitation programs* are a major influence in rehabilitation today. Each state, with federal aid on a matching-funds basis through the Vocational Rehabilitation Administration, of the Department of Health, Education, and Welfare, has developed an extensive *vocational* evaluation and rehabilitation program. This may involve, when needed, restorative medical treatment, education and/or job training, job counseling, job placement, and other vocation-related services. Any significantly disabled adult is eligible for this service, providing that there is some likelihood that he can eventually work or return to work. It was estimated that, by the end of the 1965 fiscal year, clients would have been benefiting from the state-federal vocational rehabilitation programs at the rate of 133,000 rehabilitants per year (Hunt, 1964). And this rate is increasing each year! Approximately 10 per cent of those served are mentally retarded or emotionally disturbed. In addition, a significant number of clients are evaluated and served in other ways each year by the state-federal programs but drop out before they are rehabilitated or, in some instances, when it is found that they cannot be vocationally rehabilitated.

These programs have expanded over the years and at present play a major role in the over-all rehabilitation of the citizens of the United States (Switzer, 1956). After a modest beginning, over 40 years ago, there are today state-agency tax-supported vocational rehabilitation departments or divisions in every state. These rehabilitation agencies may be autonomous state commissions, or, more typically, such agencies may be parts of state departments of education, or state welfare departments. They vary in size from relatively small agencies in some of our less heavily populated states to very large ones in Georgia, Pennsylvania, and some of our larger states. The larger state-federal vocational rehabilitation programs usually employ physicians, placement specialists, rehabilitation counselors, and many of the other specialists listed in Table 22–1 (see page 695).

Within the general framework of these state-federal programs, several unusual approaches are being tried. One of the most successful of these is a project at the South Carolina State Hospital, wherein planning for the patient's return to work is begun as soon as he enters the hospital (Chandler, 1963). Vocational evaluation and counseling are followed by specific skill training and work trial evaluations. The vocational specialist becomes a part of the patient's treatment team. Information about each patient is freely exchanged between the traditional treatment team and the vocational rehabilitation staff. Patients are found to stay in the hospital a significantly shorter time and need rehospitalization less often under this coordinated rehabilitation program.

The *Veterans Administration* (VA) focuses its rehabilitation activities both in its medical departments and in a special vocational and educational division that is less illness-oriented and more community-work-oriented than most medical rehabilitation departments. The pioneering efforts of the VA in the use of activities in all aspects of rehabilitation have been carefully documented (Pennington, 1954). The VA also has developed several newer rehabilitation programs, which involve the assessment of a patient's skills and potentials and the development of work and leisure-time activities that help him to meet his needs and to improve his skills. These programs include a member-employee program (Veterans Administration, 1953; Margolin, 1955), wherein the patient, before he is ready to leave the hospital, is assigned to a hospital work group, which may provide services for some aspect of the hospital. The patient may work for pay on a part- or full-time basis in accordance with his needs.

Schillinger and Fridovich (1958) listed the following benefits of member-employee programs: (1) Patients receive evidence of adequacy and develop work skills. (2) Patient responsibility and self-confidence are increased. (3) Patient dependence needs are satisfied. (4) Patients develop good employment habits and a useful recent work history. (5) A vocational assessment situation is provided. (6) Transitional experiences occur that provide a healthy bridge between the hospital and the community. Especially for those patients who have been chronically disabled, the member-employee programs provide for a gradual progression toward self-sufficiency and independence and are a real step forward in rehabilitation practice.

Other rehabilitation approaches utilized by the VA include the placement of chronic but ambulatory patients in private homes, as a means of reintroducing the patient to life outside the hospital. The caretakers into whose homes such patients are placed are paid and supervised in their efforts to work with these patients. Consistent with this program is the growing impression that hospitalization per se does not contribute much directly to a patient's subsequent adjustment in the community once the medical crisis has been dealt with (Berger, Rice, Sewall, and Lemkau, 1965).

Davis and Davis (1964) summarized recent innovations in the VA re-habilitation programs as follows: (1) The hospital is becoming more like a community. (2) Democratic philosophy increasingly pervades all aspects of hospital life. (3) The hospital is being taken into the community. An over-all picture of VA psychological services and activities was provided by Peck and Ash (1964). It is apparent that rehabilitation activities play an increasing role in the VA.

Other rehabilitation approaches include rehabilitation camps, which may provide all kinds of health and restorative facilities in an outdoor, summer-camp-type setting. There is great diversity within the various types of rehabilitation settings and approaches described above, and this is probably healthy. While there are general kinds of programs such as workshops and halfway houses, the differences among these settings are great. There are also great differences in programs within each general category, for example, from one workshop to another. However, in each setting, every effort is made to individualize the evaluation and treatment of the specific patient in order to help him realize his maximum potential for both leisure-time living and employment.

REHABILITATION SPECIALISTS

Rehabilitation cannot be claimed by any one profession, for it belongs to many; nor can it be claimed by the professions alone, for it belongs to the entire community (Mayo, 1959). Nevertheless, some professional specialists are more concerned than others with different phases or aspects of rehabilitation. Specialists most likely to be involved in rehabilitation are listed in Table 22–1. Naturally all of those listed would not neces-sarily be involved with every patient or in every setting. Some of the most frequently involved specialists are described below.

Table 22–1. Specialists Likely To Participate in a Patient's Rehabilitation

Physician, especially	Psychologist
Physiatrist	Social worker
Orthopedist	Chaplain
Psychiatrist	Librarian
Occupational therapist	Nurse
Physical therapist	Aide
Corrective therapist	Audiologist
Music therapist	Workshop supervisor
Recreation therapist	Shop foreman
Speech therapist	Vocational counselor
Industrial therapist	Job-placement specialist

Physicians. Probably, medical specialists are the most centrally con-cerned with rehabilitation (Shields, 1965). They should be particularly involved with the beginning phases of rehabilitation, while the patient is ill or is beginning to recover from his illness or accident. The physician must consider the rehabilitation of his patient as early as possible in the treatment-recovery cycle. The earlier the physician begins to plan for the patient's rehabilitation needs, the more effective the rehabilitation is likely to be.

Authorities feel that there is an optimal time after the disability becomes evident for the initiation of rehabilitation procedures (Dembo, 1956). While plans for rehabilitation should not be initiated too soon after the patient's disability becomes known, there are many instances in which too long a delay in beginning rehabilitation appears to have reinforced unhealthy behavior patterns such as extreme dependence or depression. Thus, after an appropriate "mourning" period, the physician should make sure that rehabilitation is started. While all physicians should be interested in, and informed about, rehabilitation practices, three of the medical specialists are likely to be the best informed and the most active in rehabilitation: the orthopedist, the physiatrist, and the psychiatrist.

ORTHOPEDISTS. Historically, the term *rehabilitation* has referred to the aftercare of physically disabled patients, particularly of those patients with impaired extremities. The orthopedist is the specialist most responsible for the care of this kind of patient. He is and has been especially concerned with disabilities involving paralyses or other kinds of loss of function, especially of the extremities. For example, orthopedists have worked extensively with amputees and polio victims.

PHYSIATRISTS. The physiatrist is a physical-medicine and -rehabilitation specialist. While there are relatively few of these specialists in the country today, this is *the* group of physicians that is the most specifically responsible for the planning and coordination of rehabilitation services for patients with *all* kinds of disabilities. Of all the groups of specialists, this group is probably the most knowledgeable regarding the activities of the other rehabilitation specialists described in this section. The physiatrist usually is the best informed of all the medical specialists about prescriptions for occupational or physical therapy, and about the prescription of appropriate prostheses and orthotics. He is the most likely of the medical specialists to be a knowledgeable captain of the rehabilitation team (Krusen, 1951).

PSYCHIATRISTS. The psychiatrist is the medical specialist responsible for the care and rehabilitation of patients with psychiatric or emotional difficulties. Most psychiatrists are very interested in the newer methods of treating and rehabilitating patients and in returning them to the community as soon as possible. Whereas, in the past, psychiatrists focused almost solely on the treatment of the acute phases of emotional disorders, more recently, many psychiatrists have become interested in helping the patient readjust to his community and home after leaving the hospital. An important part of this readjustment, of course, is the patient's re-employment. Many psychiatrists have become very active in this total treatment cycle from the inception of illness to the patient's return to work (Braceland, 1957).

Nurses. The care of the total person in the hospital has been the traditional role of the modern nurse. Today, the graduate nurse may be the supervisor of less highly trained nurses and sometimes of hospital aides and orderlies. This nursing team is responsible for the physical and psychological well-being of the patient from the time he enters the hospital throughout his inpatient and outpatient contact with the hospital and the rehabilitation service. The nurse occupies a key position in providing for continuity of care over time and across different professional groups (King, 1962).

The *public health nurse* may help to extend this informed concern and care of the patient beyond the hospital into the community and home to which the patient goes after he leaves the hospital. The public health nurse may visit the patient periodically to check on the medications, bandages, and or other aspects of patient care with the family or other persons who are caring for the patient at home. For the chronically ill, the periodic visits of this nurse provide an important service in supervising the patient's continuing care and return to health and well-being to as great an extent as is possible (Anderson, 1965). It was proposed recently (Dinitz *et al.*, 1965) that hospitalization of more than three-fourths of seriously ill schizophrenics could be prevented by regular visits of public health nurses and the use of psychotropic drugs.

Social Workers. This specialist traditionally has dealt with the patient's family, obtaining information from its members about the patient and his life situation. Such information is helpful in understanding and treating the patient's illness and in planning for his rehabilitation (Mayo, 1958). Often, the social worker may not only interpret the patient's background and family to the rehabilitation team but may also interpret to the family what is happening to the patient. Also, the social worker often will interpret the hospital and the medical-care situation to the patient.

The social worker's primary technique is that of the interview. Through the interview, the social worker establishes a relationship with the patient and/or his family. The social worker focuses on the natural history of the disease process, the consequences of the illness in the social functioning of the patient or his family, and the process of health planning (King, 1962).

Vocational Counselors. This specialist is oriented primarily toward helping the disabled client return to a functionally useful role in life. The vocational rehabilitation counselor works with all types of disabled people, helping them to appraise their own assets and liabilities and to understand their own personal needs. In addition to having this counseling function, in many settings, the vocational rehabilitation counselor may act as a co-ordinator of the services needed to help the client achieve the best occupational, personal, and social adjustments of which he is capable. In such a role, the counselor may arrange or otherwise coordinate the services of several of the specialists listed in Table 22–1 or several of the approaches described in an earlier section of this chapter. Thomason and Barrett described in some detail the key role of casework (1959) and placement (1960) in this rehabilitation-counseling process.

Occupational Therapists. Occupational therapy is an integral part of the comprehensive medical care and rehabilitation of all types of patients —the young and the old, the physically and the mentally handicapped. Occupational therapy involves the use of purposeful activities to restore and resocialize the disabled to the maximum of their individual potential for restoration (Dunton and Licht, 1957).

The occupational therapist uses creative arts, manual skills, recreation, education, and prevocational activities as tools for the evaluation and treatment of patients. Occupational therapy for the physically handicapped patient often is used to improve functional hand and arm use by means of the motions required to perform all types of interesting tasks such as crafts. Specific activities may be prescribed in order to provide specific exercises to restore motion and strengthen joints and muscles. Similar activities may be used to improve coordination and build endurance.

Creative, manual, and educational activities may be utilized in the evaluation and treatment of the mentally handicapped. Treatment may be focused on assisting the patient to satisfy his emotional needs, on alleviation of anxiety, on support and maintenance of control while the patient is in other kinds of therapy, and on stimulation of emotional growth. By adapting equipment and the environment to the needs and abilities of the patient, the occupational therapist also is able to help the severely disabled person to become more independent and to perform many of the everyday activities of living. Information related to a patient's potential for employment can be obtained through the evaluation of factors required for the successful performance of various tasks (Ireland, 1957).

Occupational therapy for the child may assist in the development of basic motor skills and in the acquisition of the mental skills needed at school and play. The maturity and development of children can often be determined in part from their performance of various occupational therapy tasks. Various psychological insights regarding the dynamics and thought processes of all types of patients may be gleaned from an examination of the patients' productions with relatively free kinds of materials such as finger paints and building materials.

Physical Therapists. The physical therapist uses special exercise and massage techniques for patients whose disabilities result from fractures, nerve injuries, arthritis, poliomyelitis, cerebral palsy, "stroke," or some other disability or injury of bone, joint, nerve, muscle, or the circulatory system (Rusk, 1964). The physical therapist assists in the analysis of the patient's physical abilities and limitations. For example, he may employ manual or electrical muscle testing.

Prescribed treatment is given by use of exercises, massages, and the remedial properties of heat, light, water, and electricity, applied with specially modified equipment. This therapy is designed to assist in relieving pain and in developing strength, coordination, and purposeful movement. The therapist teaches patients how to help themselves and, where indicated, instructs them and their families in the use and care of braces, crutches, wheelchairs, and other necessary equipment and in therapeutic procedures.

Corrective Therapists. This specialist systematically employs prescribed recreation, play, exercise, and corrective sports to help the physically and mentally handicapped patient. By means of physical activity, the corrective therapist tries to inculcate self-care, personal hygiene, and mobility, to promote muscular tone, to strengthen and develop those muscles needed to attain functional ability, to promote relaxation by the alleviation of physical and mental stress, and to alleviate the psychological effects accompanying disability (Davis, 1964). Like some of the other therapists mentioned in this section, the corrective therapist uses whatever objects and environmental influences he feels are most appropriate in such a way as to help the patient regain his psychological and physical functioning to the maximum possible extent.

Speech Pathologists and Audiologists. The speech pathologist is concerned with understanding and helping those who have failed to develop or have lost the ability to communicate through speech. The audiologist is concerned with the diagnosis and rehabilitation of the person with hearing difficulties. Since the activities of both these specialists are described in detail in Chapter 11 of this volume, they will not be mentioned further here.

THE ROLE OF THE CLINICAL PSYCHOLOGIST

As may be inferred from the description of rehabilitation approaches and settings earlier in the chapter, the clinical psychologist can participate in many ways in almost all aspects of rehabilitation (see Pennington, 1953). An excellent discussion of psychological evaluation and counseling in rehabilitation was presented by DiMichael (1959). One way of considering the role of the clinical psychologist in rehabilitation is in terms of the traditional tripartite categorization of the clinical psychologist's activities: evaluation and diagnosis, therapy and behavior change, and research. Wright (1959), in summarizing a conference discussion of psychology in rehabilitation, added the functions of administration, education, and training.

Evaluation and Psychodiagnosis. Although the psychodiagnostic activities of clinical psychologists were discussed in some detail in Part II of this volume, it is appropriate here to consider specifically how this evaluative function contributes to the rehabilitation process. It should be noted parenthetically that many of the specialists listed in Table 22–1 (the physician, the occupational therapist, the vocational counselor, and others) also provide evaluative information regarding the patient at different points in the treatment-rehabilitation cycle.

The clinical psychologist participates with other specialists in evaluating the strengths and weaknesses, the needs and limitations, and the life situation of the disabled patient. Using his distinctive approaches and tools, psychological tests and techniques, the clinical psychologist provides information that is considered by teams of specialists in deciding on the degree of disability and on how best to help the patient to become a useful and productive member of society. Such information may be of use in the legal determination of disability. All types of interest, ability, and aptitude tests, personality inventories and projective techniques, and other, less formal, approaches can be used by the clinical psychologist to collect his evaluative or psychodiagnostic data.

For example, the psychologist can be very helpful in evaluating the extent of sensory, perceptual, or cognitive impairment. Various tests of communication skills and disorders are often useful in assessing present psychological and rehabilitation potential. The evaluation of personality functioning is usually an important contribution of the clinical psychologist. Certain psychological tests have been developed and normed specifically for certain disability groups. A lucid description of several procedures for assessing emotional and intellectual impairments for the Social Security Administration was provided by Lerner (1963). Since the process of evaluation was discussed in earlier chapters of this book, there is no need to outline it further here.

There are, of course, specific evaluation procedures that were designed to meet particular problems in rehabilitation. One of these procedures, the TOWER System, was developed at the Institute for the Crippled and Disabled. The name "TOWER" stands for Testing, Orientation, and Work Evaluation in Rehabilitation. This work-evaluation system provides for controlled observations and ratings of clients in 13 occupational areas over a period of about three weeks. The specific tasks are related to job requirements, skills, and capacities determined by job analysis to be necessary in different occupations and industries. Rosenberg and Usdane (1963) reported a high reliability for ratings concerning the job placement of 534 clients and based on the TOWER system.

The psychologist then makes his judgments regarding the patient and the specific questions being considered, in a manner similar to that described in earlier chapters of this book. The questions may be quite specific and will usually involve predictions about potential for recovery and return to work. Like the other specialists mentioned above, the clinical psychologist can be helpful to the extent that he is familiar with the situations to which the patient will be returning. Thus, the psychologist should know about the various kinds of rehabilitation facilities and approaches that might be appropriate for a particular patient and that are available to him. The psychologist must be familiar with the culture and the specific life situation from which the patient comes and to which it is hoped to return the patient when he becomes rehabilitated, since these parameters usually impose limitations on what is possible for the patient.

Rehabilitation Therapies. The psychologist can learn to participate in the psychological readjustment of the patient in many of the rehabilitation settings described above. Many of the treatment approaches described in Part IV of this volume can be carried on in rehabilitation settings. One may conduct client-centered therapy, behavior therapy, etc., in a rehabilitation setting just as in a university, hospital, or other setting.

In general, it should be noted that long-term intensive individual psychotherapy is probably not typically employed for rehabilitation patients, since it is very expensive and does not result in a high success rate with patients from the middle- and lower-class subcultures (from which the bulk of the rehabilitation clients come). Other approaches (behavior therapy in a few instances, and more often group approaches of various types) have been found to be more useful in various rehabilitation settings and are certainly more frequently used. Role playing and sensitivity training have been successfully employed by several investigators (Rothaus *et al.*, 1963; Hanson *et al.*, 1964; Rothaus *et al.*, 1964). The focus usually is on specific life adjustment problems such as feelings about one's handicap, family attitudes, and specific problems related to returning to work. As Diller (1958) noted, the therapeutic interests of psychologists in rehabilitation fan out from psychotherapy to the problems posed by environmental and vocational displacement, and even to the problems associated with the perceptual deficits of the brain-damaged.

Research. In this area of activity, the clinical psychologist is uniquely qualified to make a contribution. Most of the specialists listed above in Table 22–1 probably do not have specific research training. The psychologist, if he wishes, may be looked upon as the research specialist in the rehabilitation setting. He is more accustomed to considering research questions, and to questioning as a conceptual activity, than are the other specialists. He is capable and usually experienced in the development of research designs in the behavioral sciences. He has the skills to carry out a research project and has been trained to be interested in evaluating the outcomes and effects of different procedures. For example, one might wish to know what procedures were most effective with different types of patients. This would involve describing both the patients, the procedures, and the settings operationally and in some detail. A survey of psychologists interested in rehabilitation resulted in a list of 316 similar topics about which research was needed (Wright, 1959). It is clear that a major need today in rehabilitation is for more research of every kind.

A 1960 conference on psychological research relevant to rehabilitation (Lofquist, 1963) brought together selected research-visible psychologists, as well as psychologists interested in rehabilitation. At this conference, discussions developed about psychological knowledge and theory as they were related to various rehabilitation problems. The five areas of psychological research discussed were (1) cognitive processes—sensory and perceptual organization; (2) career development and differential psychology; (3) learning; (4) personality, motivation, and clinical phenomena; and (5) social psychology. The implications for rehabilitation of psychological knowledge in each of these five areas were synthesized and presented in some detail in Lofquist (1963).

Kandel and Williams (1964) reviewed and discussed methodological problems involved in the conduct of several studies of ongoing psychiatric rehabilitation research projects. They described problems associated with conflicting commitments of various specialists and gave examples of different approaches and resolutions taken from actual ongoing projects. Their review is strongly recommended to the behavioral scientist and the research-oriented psychologist planning to work in rehabilitation settings.

There is considerable financial support from both public and private sources for research in rehabilitation. Criswell (1964) recently reviewed psychosocial research activities underwritten in part by the Vocational Rehabilitation Administration, as one example of a federal research-support program. Research skill and interest are the specific and unique contributions the psychologist brings to the rehabilitation setting. It is likely that the psychologist will be better able to plan and carry out research on rehabilitation problems after he has immersed himself and participated in some of the rehabilitation activities described above. However, his unique contribution, which others on the rehabilitation team usually are unable to make, is in the research area.

SOME MAJOR PSYCHOLOGICAL CONCEPTS IN REHABILITATION

An extremely important area of interest in rehabilitation is that relating to *motivation* (Wright, 1960; Cowen, 1960; Patterson, 1964). The motivation of patients for rehabilitation remains one of the big unknowns (Barry, 1965a; Barry and Malinovsky, 1965). Some authors (Yuker, Campbell, and Block, 1960) cite motivation as a major reason for the continued re-employment of the handicapped. The best recent general treatment of motivation is that by Cofer and Appley (1964). In their book, and in others focusing on motivation (e.g., Rethlingshafer, 1963; Vroom, 1964), the diversity of approaches and concepts relating to motivation is legion.

Patient motivation is a central problem in rehabilitation (Benny, 1964). Assuming that two patients are grossly similar in their disabilities and other characteristics, when one patient takes advantage of rehabilitation opportunities and returns to a productive life, while the other does not, these different outcomes are very often attributed to motivational differences. A major need in the analysis of all behavior change today is better understanding of such differential phenomena. Research activities in this area have been described briefly by Barry (1965b), by Meyerson (1957), and by many others (see literature review, Barry and Malinovsky, 1965).

Shontz (1957) viewed motivation as a complex of interacting patterns, factors, or dimensions in terms of which all patients can be described. He posited three quantitative and two qualitative factors, which he named: reality orientation, cooperativeness, energy level, breadth of motivation, and ultimate social placement. Shontz (1962) also noted certain motivating pressures imposed upon the client by society: to become less burdensome to the community and to become less helpless. The measurement and manipulation of these factors and pressures should make possible better understanding and control of patient motivation for rehabilitation.

Related and more specific psychological concepts that may prove particularly fruitful in contributing to understanding of rehabilitation are *dependence* and *level of aspiration*. Operational measures of a patient's level of aspiration have been shown to be related to his disability and potential for improvement (Sheehan and Zelen, 1951; Raifman, 1957; Rutledge, 1954). Aspiration level appears both to depend on one's attitudes toward oneself and to subsequently affect such attitudes.

Margolin (1963a, 1963b) and his associates are among the many investigators who are studying patient dependence as a key variable in rehabilitation. Coburn (1964) and others have discussed at length this concept and its importance in understanding of the rehabilitative efforts of patients. Overdependence and extreme reactions to dependence feelings can both interfere with optimum rehabilitation.

Ego strength is another concept related to those already discussed. This notion, growing in part out of psychoanalytic theory, refers to the capacity of the individual to maintain his general adjustment. Ego strength which may refer to a person's resoluteness and strength of character, is usually judged in terms of the degree of reality orientation shown by the client and is conditioned by his general intelligence and drive. Within Maslow's frame of reference (1962), measures of ego strength reflect tendencies toward self-actualization.

A related concept is that of *attitude toward self*. Self attitudes play an important role in a patient's will to recover and return to independent living. Assessments of self attitudes of the disabled can be made with the help of the standard clinical psychological techniques and also by means of specific techniques designed for use with this group (Yuker, Block, and Campbell, 1960). A person's attitudes toward himself are reflected in his feelings of worth and in the degree to which he feels it important to help himself. Of course self attitudes are intimately related to motivation and feelings of dependence.

Still another related notion is the *attitude of others toward the disabled person*. Wright (1964) discussed how the positive or negative attitudes of significant others, as perceived by the patient, influence the patient's attitudes toward himself. The well-known "halo effect" may operate in this instance, distorting the perception of the patient by others and, in turn, the patient's perception of himself. Gellman (1959) described the influence of such feelings on every facet of the patient's life. Those attitudes also may be measured by the specific instrument for measuring attitudes toward the disabled mentioned above (Yuker, Block, and Campbell, 1960).

Patient *expectancy* is a related concept that has been dealt with at the research level by Rotter (1954). He defines *expectancy* as "the probability held by the individual that a particular reinforcement will occur as a function of a specific behavior on his part in a specific situation" (p. 107). Goldstein (1962) reviewed research on counseling and psychotherapy in which patient expectancy was related to various process and outcome variables. Unquestionably, patient expectancy can be an important determinant of any rehabilitation approach.

The use of specific *incentives* to motivate the disabled is only beginning to be widely considered. Meyerson and his associates (1963) described several interesting studies in this area. Storrow (1962) reported the systematic manipulation of financial benefits to motivate clients to return to the world of work. This notion is also a part of such Veterans Administration programs, described above, as for example the member-employee program. Johnson and Lee (1965) described a specific application of graded incentives, designed to motivate patients to participate in a VA rehabilitation program. Hess (1964) reported recent modifications in Social Security regulations, providing for a trial work period during which the disabled person need not risk losing his financial security. All of these developments represent the judicious use of specific incentives to motivate disabled people.

CASE REPORTS

Two case reports illustrate rehabilitation approaches with hospitalized psychiatric patients. The first report concerns a young man suffering from a conversion reaction (monoplegia of the left arm, with numerous anesthesias in other body areas).

The patient, aged twenty-four, first noted his symptoms a few weeks after his return home from military service. Upon entering his mother's house, having just completed his first day at work as a gas-station attendant, he overheard her saying to a visiting cousin, "No, I never expected him back. He sure surprised me. That poor Jones boy up the street got it." Enraged, the patient rushed into the kitchen, and grabbed a chair which he raised high in the air. At this point, his arm became limp, and the chair crashed to the floor a short distance from his mother.

The police were called, and they brought the patient to the hospital. A social service study in the community (with the mother and other relatives) verified the hypothesis suggested above—a running battle between a widowed mother set on selfish control of all in her areas of influence and a rebellious masculinity-proving son. Subsequently, it was established that the mother had repeatedly insisted that her son designate her as his beneficiary in his government life insurance policy while overseas. Instead, he had designated an uncle, his father's brother. In response to this, the mother had threatened, "I'll see you dead before I'll ever let you go through with that."

Psychiatric examination and psychodiagnostic evaluation, both psycho-dynamically oriented and with special reference to the content of the TAT protocols, revealed a robust, emotionally labile young man whose repertoire of adjustment techniques cardinally included what practically amounted to a subliminally triggered aggressiveness toward older women, coupled with strong dependence needs. The latter were overtly camou-flaged by a reaction formation of evident superiority in all athletic con-tests, fist fights, and the like. He had long been unable to control his aggressiveness; a history of abortive physical assaults on women teachers and on one or two athletic coaches during his childhood and adolescence was found, as one would suspect. He appeared to be of high average intelligence, talkative, completely lacking in insight, and showing clearly Janet's famous attribute, *la belle indifférence*, toward his symptoms. In the ward, he acted like a well-adjusted and happy-go-lucky person who "belonged out of here and on the job," as an unperceptive attendant re-marked ill-advisedly and to his own discomfiture.

The diagnostic and therapy-planning conference, after collation and discussion of all the data, prescribed the following approaches. (The reader may wish to formulate the reasons for each.)

First, it was recommended that the patient participate in intensive psychotherapy with a male therapist comparable in age to that of a father figure. Sessions were planned for five days each week. The team also agreed that all requests by the patient to "go home for the weekend on pass" would be denied for the time being. It was decided that the at-tendants, nurses, and other specialists with whom he came in daily con-tact should maintain an objective, somewhat detached, and not unduly sympathetic attitude.

Second, an occupational therapy assignment was arranged in which he was instructed, with a few other patients his age, in the preparation of magazines for binding. The first step in this process required each man to rip and selectively discard covers and other parts of the magazines. The young female therapist was permissive and interfered little. Two weeks later, an older woman was deliberately substituted, owing to the planned transfer of the younger worker to "other duties."

Third, a corrective therapy assignment was outlined in which the rec-reation worker was instructed to teach the patient alone the game of golf. He was instructed at first never to criticize and never to compliment the patient's progress. After a few weeks, constructive criticism was intro-duced in a matter-of-fact way. Later still, an occasional negative com-ment was made. Finally, the patient was introduced to a foursome, one member of which was known not only for his "good golfing" but also as a highly candid and profane critic.

It is noteworthy that, with the therapeutic plan as set forth, no direct attempt was made to treat the monoplegia, which early disappeared in the hospital setting, only to be replaced by the complaint of low back pains. Psychotherapy sessions, analytically oriented, were eventually stormy owing to the patient's release of generalized hostility. The following selected comments come from recordings made at different stages in therapy:

"That golf pro never says anything. Can't he talk? He just lets me blunder along. When I throw the clubs down, he just waits till I pick 'em up."

"Today that guy said I was coming along O.K. First time he's said much. But he only said that after I had made the longest drive yet. Why doesn't he say something else? I'm used to having people holler."

"Today that joker on the golf course told me to sharpen up. I've been playing fairly good, not as good as I did at first. Sharpen up, hell! I can't figure him out. But I'll beat him at his own game; just give me time. You know I landed in a sand trap today. He just stood there. I threw everything every which way and yelled. He asked me if I was practicing my golf or my swearing. I had to laugh. He sorta smiled. I didn't know he could."

"That there witch in O.T. had better shut her trap. I know how to rip covers off stuff. I've had lots of practice. I tore up a whole batch of my mother's stuff when I was a kid. I got whipped, but I had to laugh about it all. She keeps nosin' around, seein' if we're doin' it right. Inspecting, she calls it. I'll inspect her. I'll wop her one sometime."

"That game of golf is fun. I never knew that pro could be halfway decent. I used to think golf was for sissies. Now here I am enjoying it [laughs]. And that joker that swears all the time, he . . . keeps telling us all how to play. I see what goes. He swears like I used to throw things. And while we're on this, why on earth did I ever see Mrs. Johnson in O.T. as being just like my mother? She's not, and that's that. I wonder what she thought of me at first?"

Prior to his discharge, the social worker and the vocational counselor were instrumental in helping the patient implement his strong urge to "get a job and live away from home" with his uncle.

The second case report concerns a forty-five-year-old schizophrenic patient who had failed to show any improvement after various shock therapies and had been hospitalized custodially for the past 12 years. Disoriented as to time, place, and personal identity, he was alternately mute and mildly excited. His neologisms were of such a nature that no member of the ward staff understood him. This was in contrast to the understanding assumed by several fellow schizophrenics who, in better contact, insisted that he was talking about, among other things, how he and his younger brother used to play childhood games with cardboard disks and wooden chips, and how his brother "cheated on him." When any effort to assist him physically toward any activity was made, the patient became mute and immobile.

At a ward conference, it was suggested that supportive psychotherapy be initiated. A youthful staff member was briefed and then asked to make a careful study of the patient's voluminous clinical folder. It was decided that each day the future therapist would casually visit the ward, becoming known to all. At first, the therapist appeared to pay no attention to the patient in question. Gradually, the staff member approached the patient, until one day he was seated next to him. This procedure was intermittently repeated until the latter began furtively to notice the visitor. One day, the therapist sat down and leisurely drew from his pockets brightly colored disks of cardboard and a few wooden blocks. He toyed with these. Several other patients gathered around to ask, "What's them things for?" The therapist merely replied, "You play games with them."

It is impossible here to give a minutely detailed description of the situation that slowly evolved. Suffice it to mention that, one day, a checkerboard was "by chance" found nearby. The therapist placed the brightly colored bits on the board in an indiscriminate manner. The patient, still wary, leaned over and shifted three into positions appropriate for a checker game. This was the beginning. In a few weeks, the patient and threapist were, without verbal exchange as yet, playing checkers with the paper disks and the blocks—a strange sort of game—but playing with objects. Later the patient greeted the therapist by silently handing him a box of red and black checkers the nurse had "found." When thanked for this act, he smiled and blushed. In a year, this man was playing card games, was talking coherently much of the time, and referred less and less to the neologisms that the therapist had in the past ignored or merely nodded to in apparent agreement.

Now, with the patient seemingly unafraid of the therapist, the two proceeded each day to the occupational therapy shop, where they together made another set of checkers for the ward's social room. It was not long until the patient was able to go alone to the rehabilitative assignment, there to meet the therapist. Eventually, by plan, a new therapist was substituted. For a time, this difficult hurdle taxed the ingenuities of all concerned. Shortly, however, the new therapist and the patient could be seen on the golf course—first walking, then putting, and, much later, playing a game.

These case reports illustrate that the chronic, custodial patient often can be made ready for rehabilitative assignment. Many in the "back wards" of hospitals are totally incapacitated and cannot be expected to participate in these programs until prepared for them. Supportive psychotherapy can accompany other rehabilitative techniques, just as the activity therapies can accompany the intensive therapeutic approach.

These and other similar reports suggest the following summary comments: (1) Careful observation of the individual patient may reveal strengths (perhaps relatively primitive ones), which can adroitly be tried as focal points for initiating rehabilitation activities. (2) Professional interest consistently shown and maintained in the service of immediate rewards may slowly redirect the patient's seemingly disorganized response patterns into more constructive channels. (3) Rehabilitative activities, at the outset, must be so clearly and simply arranged, or structured, that early success is experienced, with reward immediately forthcoming. (4) The activity chosen can make a direct or indirect attack on the symptoms by an unobstrusive appeal to the patient's strengths. (5) With some psychiatric patients, the events transpiring in rehabilitation sessions provide material for discussions in individual and group therapy sessions. (6) All members of the rehabilitation staff are from time to time participants in the program developed for an individual patient, with each staff member contributing his own skills to the therapeutic plan and its implementation. (7) Research opportunities for the research psychologist are numerous in this expanding area of treatment, whereby clinically documented observations can be subjected to verification and refinement by rigorous experimental tests.

SUMMARY

In this chapter, rehabilitation approaches, settings, and specialists were described in detail. The rehabilitation philosophy was explained, and its implementation with all types of disabled persons was mentioned. The clinical psychologist should be able to contribute to the rehabilitation of disabled people in many ways. While his diagnostic and therapeutic skills are extremely useful, his unique contribution to this and other kinds of social endeavor appears to be in the research area.

REFERENCES

ANDERSON, ELEANOR M. 1965. Uninterrupted care for long-term patients. *Publ. Hlth Rep.*, **80**, 271–75.

BARRY, J. R. 1965a. Client motivation for rehabilitation. *Rehabilit. Rec.*, **6**, 13–16.

BARRY, J. R. 1965b. Patient motivation for rehabilitation. *Cleft Palate J.*, **2**, 62–68.

BARRY, J. R., and MALINOVSKY, M. R. 1965. *Client motivation for rehabilitation: A review.* Gainesville: Univer. of Florida Press (University of Florida Rehabilitation Research Monograph No. 1).

BECKER, A., MURPHY, N. M., and GREENBLATT, M. 1965. Recent advances in community psychiatry. *New England J. Med.*, **272**, 621–26.

BENNY, CELIA. 1964. Factors affecting motivation for rehabilitation. *Psychiatric Quart. Suppl.*, **38**, 205–20.

BERGER, D. G., RICE, C. E., SEWALL, L. G., and LEMKAU, P. V. 1965. The impact of psychiatric hospital experience on the community adjustment of patients. *Ment. Hygiene*, **49**, 83–93.

BRACELAND, F. J. 1957. Role of the psychiatrist in rehabilitation. *J. Amer. Med. Assn*, **165**, 211–15.

CHANDLER, C. S. 1963. South Carolina rehabilitates psychiatric patients. *Rehabilit. Rec.*, **4**, 26–27.

COBURN, H. H. 1964. The psychological concept of dependency. *Rehabilit. Rec.*, **5**, 37–40.

COFER, C. N., and APPLEY, M. H. 1964. *Motivation: Theory and research.* New York: Wiley.

COWEN, E. L. 1963. Personality, motivation, and clinical phenomena. In L. H. LOFQUIST, (ed.), *Psychological research and rehabilitation.* Washington, D.C.: American Psychological Association.

CRISWELL, JOAN H. 1964. Research needs in the psycho-social aspects of vocational rehabilitation. Paper presented to American Psychological Association, Los Angeles, September, 1964.

DAVIS, J. E., SR. 1964. Corrective therapy, its changing roles. *J. Assn physical Ment. Rehabilit.* **18**, 98–100.

DAVIS, J. E., JR., and DAVIS, J. E. SR. 1964. Psychiatric role of physical medicine and rehabilitation in the third revolution. *Ment. Hygiene*, **48**, 638–43.

DEMBO, TAMARA, LEVITON, G. L., and WRIGHT, BEATRICE. 1956. Adjustment to misfortune: A problem of social-psychological rehabilitation. *Artificial Limbs*, **3**, 4–62.

DILLER, L. 1958. Rehabilitation therapies. In D. BROWER and L. E. ABT (eds.), *Progress in clinical psychology.* Vol. 3. New York: Grune & Stratton. Pp. 197–210.

DiMICHAEL, S. G. 1959. *Psychological services in vocational rehabilitation.* Washington, D.C.: Office of Vocational Rehabilitation, U.S. Department of Health, Education & Welfare.

DINITZ, S., PASAMANICK, B., SCARPITTI, R. R., ALBINI, J. L., and LEFTON, M. 1965. An experimental study in the prevention of hospitalization of schizophrenics. *Amer. J. Orthopsychiat.*, **35**, 1–9.

DUNTON, W. R., JR., and LICHT, S. 1957. *Occupational therapy principles and practice.* (2d ed.) Springfield, Ill.: Charles C Thomas.

EPPS, R. L., and HANES, L. D. 1964. *Day care of psychiatric patients.* Springfield, Ill.: Charles C Thomas.

FEINTUCH, A. 1958. Sheltered workshops: A conceptual framework. *J. Rehabilit.*, **24**, 9–10.

GARRETT, J. F. 1952. Rehabilitation. In D. BROWER and L. E. ABT (eds.), *Progress in clinical psychology.* Vol. 1. New York: Grune & Stratton. Pp. 443–49.

GARRETT, J. F., and LEVINE, EDNA S. 1962. *Psychological practices with the physically disabled.* New York: Columbia Univer. Press.

GELLMAN, W. 1959. Roots of prejudice against the handicapped. *J. Rehabilit.*, **25**, 4–6, 25.

GOLDSTEIN, A. P. 1962. *Therapist-patient expectancies in psychotherapy.* Oxford, England: Pergamon.

HANSON, P. G., ROTHAUS, P., CLEVELAND, S. E., JOHNSON, D. L., and McCALL, D. 1964. Employment after psychiatric hospitalization: An orientation for Texas employment personnel. *Ment. Hygiene,* **48,** 142–51.

HEILMAN, HENRIETTA. 1964. In-hospital vocational training. *Psychiatric Quart. Suppl.,* **38,** 280–89.

HESS, A. E. 1964. Work incentives for the disabled: The Social Security approach. *J. Rehabilit.,* **30,** 15–16.

HUNT, J. V. 1964. The government view. *Proc. Rehabilit. Sympos.* Dallas: Texas Employers Insurance Association. Pp. 92–93.

IRELAND, K. L. 1957. Evaluating work behavior in occupational therapy. *J. Rehabilit.,* **23,** 8–9, 25–28.

JOHNSON, R. F., and LEE, H. 1965. Rehabilitation of chronic schizophrenics. *Arch. gen. Psychiat.,* **12,** 237–40.

JONES, M. 1953. *The therapeutic community.* New York: Basic Books.

KANDEL, DENISE B., and WILLIAMS, R. H. 1964. *Psychiatric rehabilitation: Some problems of research.* New York: Atherton.

KESSLER, H. H. 1964. Medical keynote address. *Proc. Rehabilit. Sympos.* Dallas: Texas Employers Insurance Association. Pp. 9–14.

KING, S. H. 1962. *Perceptions of illness and medical practice.* New York: Russell Sage.

KRUSEN, F. H. (ed.). 1951. *Physical medicine and rehabilitation for the clinician.* Philadelphia: Saunders.

LERNER, J. 1963. The role of the psychologist in the disability evaluation of emotional and intellectual impairments under the Social Security Act. *Amer. Psychologist,* **18,** 252–56.

LESSER, W. 1965. Clinical social work in a therapeutic community: The day treatment centre. *Int. J. soc. Psychiat.,* **11,** 38–45.

LOFQUIST, L. H. (ed.). 1963. *Psychological research and rehabilitation.* Washington, D.C.: American Psychological Association.

MARGOLIN, R. J. 1955. Member-employee program: New hope for the mentally ill. *Amer. Arch. rehabilit. Ther.* **3,** 69–81.

MARGOLIN, R. J. 1963a. The mental patient who wants to fail. *Rehabilit. Rec.,* **4,** 34–39.

MARGOLIN, R. J. 1963b. The failure syndrome and its prevention. *J. Assn physical ment. Rehabilit.,* **17,** 77–78, 82.

MASE, D. J. 1962. Improving the program and image of the sheltered workshop. *J. Rehabilit.,* **28,** 21–22.

MASLOW, A. H. 1962. *Toward a psychology of being.* New York: Van Nostrand.

MAYO, L. W. 1958. Rehabilitation and social work. *J. Rehabilit.,* **24,** 4–5, 15.

MAYO, L. W. 1959. The importance of community planning in the development of rehabilitation. In *Selected papers, Conference of Rehabilitation Centers and Facilities, Inc.* (Eighth Annual Workshop, New York City). Pp. 13–14.

MEYERSON, L. 1957. Special disabilities. In P. R. FARNSWORTH and Q. McNEMAR (eds.), *Annual review of psychology.* Vol. 8. Palo Alto, Calif.: Annual Reviews. Pp. 437–57.

MEYERSON, L., MICHAEL, J. L., MOWRER, O. H., OSGOOD, C. E., and STAATS, A. W. 1963. Learning, behavior and rehabilitation. In L. H. LOFQUIST (ed.), *Psychological research and rehabilitation.* Washington, D.C.: American Psychological Association.

NAGI, S. Z. 1964. A study in the evaluation of disability and rehabilitation potential. *Amer. J. publ. Hlth,* **54,** 1568–79.

NATIONAL REHABILITATION ASSOCIATION. 1965. Statement of professional aims. *J. Rehabilit.,* **31,** 18–20.

PATTERSON, C. H. 1964. A unitary theory of motivation and its counseling implications. *J. indiv. Psychol.,* **20,** 17–31.

PECK, C. P., and ASH, E. 1964. Training in the Veterans Administration. In L. BLANK and H. P. DAVID (eds.), *Sourcebook for training in clinical psychology.* New York: Springer. 61–81.

PENNINGTON, L. A. 1953. Specific psychological contributions to varieties of rehabilitation processes. *J. Assn physical ment. Rehabilit.,* **7,** 12–14.

PENNINGTON, L. A. 1954. Rehabilitation approaches. In L. A. PENNINGTON and I. A. BERG, (eds.), *An introduction to clinical psychology.* (2d ed.) New York: Ronald. 632–60.

RAIFMAN, I. 1957. Level of aspiration in a group of peptic ulcer patients. *J. consult. Psychol.,* **21,** 229–31.

RETHLINGSHAFER, DOROTHY. 1963. *Motivation as related to personality.* New York: McGraw-Hill.

ROSENBERG, B., and USDANE, W. M. 1963. The TOWER system: Vocational evaluation of the severely handicapped for training and placement. *Personnel Guidance J.,* **42,** 149–52.

ROTHAUS, P., JOHNSON, D. L., and LYLE, F. A. 1964. Group participation training for psychiatric patients. *J. counseling Psychol.,* **11,** 230–39.

ROTHAUS, P., MORTON, R. B., JOHNSON, D. L., CLEVELAND, S. E., and LYLE, F. A. 1963. Human relations training for psychiatric patients. *Amer. med. Assn Arch. gen. Psychiat.,* **8,** 572–81.

ROTTER, J. B. 1954. *Social learning and clinical psychology.* Englewood Cliffs, N.J.: Prentice-Hall.

RUSK, H. A. 1964. *Rehabilitation medicine.* (2d ed.) St. Louis: Mosby.

RUTLEDGE, L. 1954. Aspiration level of deaf children as compared with those of hearing children. *J. Speech Hearing Disorders,* **19,** 375–80.

SCHILLINGER, A. A., and FRIDOVICH, D. 1958. The member-employee. *Psychiatric Quart. Suppl.,* **32,** 82–98.

SEIDENFELD, M. A. 1956. Progress in rehabilitation of the physically handicapped. In D. BROWER and L. E. ABT (eds.), *Progress in clinical psychology.* Vol. 2. New York: Grune & Stratton. Pp. 266–94.

SHEEHAN, J. G., and ZELEN, S. L. 1955. Level of aspiration in stutterers and nonstutterers. *J. abnorm. soc. Psychol.,* **51,** 83–85.

SHIELDS, C. D. 1965. Complete medical care includes rehabilitation. *Arch. physical Med. Rehabilit.,* **46,** 161–66.

SHONTZ, F. C. 1957. Concept of motivation in physical medicine. *Arch. physical Med. Rehabilit.,* **38,** 635–39.

SHONTZ, F. C. 1962. Severe chronic illness. In J. F. GARRETT and EDNA

LEVINE (eds.), *Psychological practices with the physically disabled.* New York: Columbia Univer. Press. Pp. 410–45.

STORROW, H. A. 1962. Money as a motivator. *Publ. Welf.: J. Amer. publ. Welf. Assn,* **20,** 199–204.

SWITZER, MARY E. 1956. Role of the federal government in vocational rehabilitation. *Arch. physical Med. Rehabilit.,* **37,** 542–46.

THOMASON, O. B., and BARRETT, A. M. (eds.). 1959. *Casework performance in vocational rehabilitation.* Guidance, Training, and Placement Bulletin No. 1, Rehabilitation Service Series No. 505.

THOMASON, O. B., and BARRETT, A. M. (eds.). 1960. *The placement process in vocational rehabilitation counseling.* Guidance, Training, and Placement Bulletin No. 2, Rehabilitation Service Series No. 545.

VETERANS ADMINISTRATION. 1953. *Member-employee programs in psychiatric hospitals.* VA Technical Bulletin 10–355, Washington, D. C.

VROOM, V. H. 1964. *Work and motivation.* New York: Wiley.

WRIGHT, BEATRICE A. (ed.). 1959. *Psychology and rehabilitation.* Washington, D.C.: American Psychological Association.

WRIGHT, BEATRICE A. 1960. *Physical disability: A psychological approach.* New York: Harper & Row.

WRIGHT, BEATRICE A. 1964. Spread in adjustment to disability. *Bull. Menninger Clinic,* **28,** 198–208.

YANOUCK, R. R. 1962. Efficient utilization of the worker. *Environmental Hlth,* **4,** 432–38.

YUKER, H. E., BLOCK, J. R., and CAMPBELL, W. J. 1960. *A scale to measure attitudes toward disabled persons.* Human Resources Foundation Study No. 5, Albertson, N.Y.

YUKER, H. E., CAMPBELL, W. J., and BLOCK, J. R. 1960. The will to work. *Personnel J.,* **37,** 49–55.

IV

THE CLINICIAN AND RESEARCH

VI

23

Research in Clinical Psychology

Leonard S. Kogan [*]

Debate often arises as to whether the practice of clinical psychology is an art or a science. The fact that clinical psychologists function in a wide range of activities makes it quite difficult to define or even describe the exact role of the clinical psychologist. For the most part, however, the resolution of the debate seems clear enough: Clinical psychology as practiced today is a mixture of both art and science. The sensitivity and integrative capacity demanded of the psychological clinician in carrying out effectively his two major functions, *diagnosis* and *treatment,* make it appear almost axiomatic that his activities can never be reduced to a completely systematic and scientific discipline. Clinical activities transcend formulas and computer-based prescriptions. Artistic components will probably always be desirably present in the pattern of intervention provided by the particular practitioner when dealing professionally with the unique configuration presented by the particular patient or client in his particular environment.

Yet there is every hope that the professional practice of clinical psychology will become more and more of a science-based art through the planned application of creative research effort. Perhaps, the chief function of scientific research in the clinical area is to provide the practitioner with a constantly growing stockpile of tested principles, concepts, and techniques, which will implement and supplement whatever logic, skill,

[*] Leonard S. Kogan, Ph.D. (University of Rochester), Professor of Psychology, and Executive Officer, Doctoral Program in Psychology, The City University of New York.

and empathic talent he possesses in his own right. The analogy between the practicing clinical psychologist and the practicing physician who draws on many kinds of basic and applied research in performing his function needs no elaboration. Possibly, the best defense that the clinical psychologist can present against the bombardment of "theories" and "hints to the practitioner" to which he is continually subjected is to protest, "That sounds plausible, but show me the evidence!"

BASIC APPROACHES

Both the research orientation and the variety of investigatory methods of today's clinical psychologists are the product of many conceptual trends in the history of psychology, psychiatry, and allied professions. One of the most interesting of these trends is what Allport (1937) has called "approaches to the individual within the science of psychology." I shall endeavor to trace briefly how the individual has become a legitimate object of scientific inquiry. It should be emphasized, however, that no implication should be drawn that the approaches described are mutually exclusive.

The Nomothetic Approach. The earliest approach to the individual in the history of psychology as a science was the search for general principles that would be applicable to all human beings. This point of view, promulgated in the experimental studies of Wundt and his students, has come to be known as the *nomothetic approach* and is still characteristic of the investigator's objectives in many phases of clinical psychology. Although the individual as an individual is largely neglected in this approach, there can be little question that, in many fundamental ways, all individuals are alike. Moreover, the underlying assumptions in this approach that psychological phenomena are lawful and susceptible to empirical investigation are the keystones of all psychological research.

The Normative Approach. A second major approach to the individual in psychology stems largely from the pioneering work of Galton, Cattell, and Binet in developing tests of individual differences. In this tradition, discrepancies between the individual and man in general (universal norms) or, more commonly, between the individual and specified groups (group norms) are explicitly recognized. It is presumed that the diagnostic task can best be fulfilled by describing the individuals in terms of the relative degree to which they possess or exhibit common traits, attributes, or functions. This approach has come to be known as the *psychometric, differential, normative,* or *actuarial* point of view because of its emphasis on quantitative measurement, interindividual differences, and group norms as the bases for interpreting individual characteristics or performance.

Research in the psychometric tradition has been most productive in the development of methods for the appraisal of abilities, aptitudes, achievement, attitudes and interests. The typical psychometric instrument consists of a series of structured items designed to elicit responses that can be scored in an objective, that is, mechanical, manner. Paper-and-pencil personality inventories, constructed along psychometric lines, beginning with Woodworth's Personal Data Sheet of World War I, have been the subject of literally hundreds of research endeavors but have generally proved to be of only limited practical or clinical utility (Rotter, 1963).

Part and parcel of the psychometric tradition have been the development and elaboration of the logic and theoretical models underlying the construction and interpretation of mental tests. Most of the criteria we ordinarily use in assessing the utility of diagnostic instruments, such as reliability and validity, are the heritage of this tradition. Similarly, the important role that statistical inference has assumed in psychological research is largely attributable to the influence of the differential approach.

The Idiographic Approach. In the third and most recent approach to the individual, "the individual as such occupies the center of psychological attention and the effort is made to understand him as a unique world of events" (Rosenzweig, 1950). The point of view that the individual as such is a legitimate object of scientific inquiry is known as the *idiographic approach*. A number of different influences have more or less converged to bring the individual to the forefront as a major object of study. Among these are psychoanalysis, with its emphasis on the dynamics and development of the individual personality; field theory and phenomenology, with their concentration on the individual's "internal frame of reference"; and personalism (Allport, 1961), which stresses the unique pattern of organization of the individual.

Diagnostic methods in clinical psychology have been greatly influenced by the idiographic approach, especially in their attention to dynamic-genetic considerations. One of the chief clinical products of this tradition has been the development of projective methods of investigating personality. In contrast to the structured stimulus conditions and predetermined response alternatives generally presented to subjects by psychometric instruments, the essence of projective techniques is to present ambiguous stimuli to the subject under the assumption that his responses will reveal his underlying pattern of motives, conflicts, and mechanisms. Although projective methods of personality evaluation are favored by many clinicians on the basis of personal experience, one of the continuing challenges to clinical research is to objectify and verify systematically the many concepts that are liberally employed in the interpretation of projective test protocols.

The development of appropriate statistical methods for handling data from the individual has become an area of increasing concern for clinicians and clinical research workers. Thus far "statistics for the individual" have been based on the supposition that traditional group-centered statistical methods employing interindividual norms such as group averages and standard deviations can be converted to individual-centered methods by utilizing such concepts as intraindividual norms and the assumption that data for the single case can be treated as an independent universe (Chassan, 1961; Payne and Jones, 1957).

CONCEPTS AND VARIABLES

The stock in trade of the research worker in any field of empirical scientific inquiry comprises the variables he selects for study and the concepts that guide his selection. I am using the term *variables* in the broadest sense to refer to categories, conditions, attributes, or measures. Depending on the frame of reference and purpose of the investigator, such variables may be derived from apparatus-mediated measurement of psychophysiological phenomena, as in electroencephalography (EEG), or, at the other extreme, they may be based on direct clinical judgment (Hunt and Jones, 1962) of very complex psychosocial phenomena such as level of adjustment or quality of transactions between the individual and his environment. One of the most challenging problems that confront the investigator who attempts to carry out research of significance in clinical psychology is that of how to develop and work with concepts and variables that not only meet scientific criteria such as clarity of definition, communicability, objectivity, and mensurability but also are of reasonable relevance to the needs, goals, and interests of clinical practice.

Specifying what variables are important to study in clinical research and how to study them is a particularly difficult and complex task. Since previous chapters in this book have described many clinical concepts and data-collecting techniques such as direct observation, interviewing, and testing, for obtaining empirical information related to these concepts, I shall not duplicate such material in this chapter. It cannot be emphasized too strongly, however, that the methods and models of modern research design and statistical science have stressed rather than minimized the need for adequate conceptualization and theorization within the subject matter of any field of objective research inquiry. From the standpoint of scientific utility, theorization should be judged adequate, not on the basis of the self-evident plausibility of any concept or set of concepts, but only to the degree that empirically verifiable consequences can be deduced from such concepts. By the same token, any particular piece of empirical research takes on significance primarily to the extent that it relates to, reinforces, or extends some more broadly applicable conceptual scheme.

Research of value or potential value for the practice of clinical psychology takes many forms. In some studies, particular problem groups may be the subject of inquiry, for example, juvenile delinquents or alcoholics. Other studies may concern themselves with the relationship between genetic, biochemical, or physiological factors and psychopathology. Even animal studies may be relevant to the formulation of hypotheses about human behavior.

By and large, however, the subjects of most immediate concern to clinical psychology are the personality and adjustment of the human individual. These basic subjects are often masked in research that appears primarily to be concerned with the development and evaluation of either diagnostic devices or therapeutic techniques. On the surface, such research may appear to be test-centered or therapy-centered, but the ultimate objects of concern are the personality and adjustment of the client. This is clearly the case in the epidemiological, etiological, diagnostic, and prognostic aspects of clinical research, but it is also true for the important field of research interest concerned with developing methods for assessing the outcomes and effectiveness of psychotherapy (Zax and Klein, 1960) and behavior therapy (Grossberg, 1964). Fundamentally, all methods for measuring the results of therapy must logically concern themselves with the difference in the personality and adjustment of the patient before and after therapy.

In a recent conference on research in psychotherapy (Strupp and Luborsky, 1962), many variables were discussed as being relevant to assessment of the outcomes of psychotherapy. Luborsky (1962), for example, described 12 variables including anxiety level, severity of symptoms, self-directed aggression, and ego strength, which were being utilized to depict the course and outcome of treatment in the Psychotherapy Research Project, of the Menninger Foundation. In this case, the assessment of the variables was carried out by psychiatrist judges.

Other investigators have used content analysis of electrically recorded interviews as a basis for evaluating the "success" of therapy. Examples of early content-analysis measures were the Discomfort-Relief Quotient (Dollard and Mowrer, 1947) and the Self-Concept Quotient (Raimy, 1948). More recent systems of content analysis were summarized by James Dittes in a book by Dollard and Auld (1959) and by Marsden (1965).

Still other investigators have used psychological tests, both projective and nonprojective, as the bases for evaluating results of psychotherapy or counseling. Muench (1947), for example, attempted to evaluate nondirective psychotherapy by giving the Rorschach, the Kent-Rosanoff Free

Association Test, and the Bell Adjustment Inventory to clients before and after therapy.

As reported in a survey by Reznikoff and Toomey (1959), the tests most commonly used for assessing changes in patients undergoing psychotherapy were the Rorschach, the Thematic Apperception Test (TAT), Draw-a-Person, and the Minnesota Multiphasic Personality Inventory (MMPI).

Additional methods have also been used in studies of the effectiveness of therapy. Berg and Adams (1962) summarized methods of personality assessment relevant to the evaluation of therapy under six main classes: (1) ratings by professionals, self-ratings, and ratings by others; (2) psychological tests; (3) verbal behavior; (4) physiological and organic measures; (5) environmental and achievement measures; and (6) experimentally induced personality change. It is interesting that many of the variables generated by these methods are indirect "indicators," rather than ultimate criterion variables intrinsically relevant to the success of psychotherapy. It would seem that, until there is convincing evidence that measures derived from a particular psychological test or from interview protocols really reflect such things as the client's personal and social adjustment in his home and on the job, use of an indirect method for assessing the outcome of therapy is more an act of faith than an act of objective evaluation.

The problem of ascertaining ultimate criteria related to the validity of diagnostic appraisal and the success of psychotherapy was discussed by Hunt (1949). He suggested, in effect, that such criteria must be based on some as yet unknown method of combining the valuations of therapeutic outcome by (1) the client, (2) other persons whose lives are directly affected by the client, and (3) society in general. It is noteworthy that this conception relegates the judgment of the therapist to the status of an "indicator" needing validation, rather than an ultimate criterion, unless it can be assumed that the therapist's opinion represents the voice of society. By the same reasoning, even the pooled judgments of a jury of therapists would, in turn, have to be validated against a more ultimate set of criteria. If it is essential to find criteria independent of the viewpoints of adherents to various "schools" of therapy, the task of determining such criteria seems almost impossible.

In a rigorously scientific sense, however, there is no logical necessity for finding criteria that satisfy all viewpoints. The only demand one can scientifically make is that the empirical variables specified within any given conceptual scheme as being of significance for assessing the outcomes of therapy be logically related to, that is, deductible from, the given conceptual scheme. Despite this, it can probably be taken for granted that the goals of various "schools" of therapy are closely enough related so that a fair degree of consensus about criterion variables can be reached.

So far, we have discussed only the problem of the establishment of valid indicators of adjustment and psychosocial functioning. These may be regarded as the "dependent" variables in the total task of evaluating the results of therapeutic intervention. The objectives of many forms of treatment are, of course, more concrete than the generalized aim of an over-all improvement in the mental health and functioning of the client. With less ambitious and more circumscribed goals, the task of determining significant indicators is more easily achieved. But, at the same time, it should be clear that the attainment of valid diagnostic methods represents only half of the story if productive effort is to be carried on in the area of evaluative research. Research limited to measurement of results at the termination of therapy—and, of course, we must add at follow-up if we are interested in the degree to which any change is maintained or latent—would have only minimal value for the theory and practice of counseling and psychotherapy.

One might refer here to the problem of solving what could be called the "evaluative equation." One side of this equation consists of dependent variables representing outcomes of the treatment service, while the other side of the equation consists of "independent" variables representing what went into the treatment. In addition to describing variables intrinsic to the client, Watson (1952) described the pertinent classes of variables as situational variables, therapeutic variables, and therapist variables. These variables, in turn, generate "higher-order" variables such as variables relating to patient-therapist interaction (Strupp, 1962). Here again—as in the case of determining variables that depict the outcomes of service—only adequate theory combined with empirical testing can decide which of the host of potential determinants are the significant ones and thus add to our understanding of the therapeutic process.

RESEARCH DESIGN IN CLINICAL PSYCHOLOGY

In the task of developing and assessing concepts relevant to the practice of clinical psychology, it seems clear that considerations regarding experimental design and statistical methods must play a significant role. While the *invention* of hypotheses to be tested is not primarily a statistical operation, it seems almost self-evident that research intended to check the validity of hypotheses and to suggest new hypotheses can be carried out in a more efficient and convincing manner if attention is given to statistical considerations in the design and analysis of studies.

Before describing some of the contributions statistical research methodology can make to investigations in clinical psychology, it is pertinent to indicate the present status of statistics as an organ of scientific method. The last 30 years have witnessed what has amounted to a revolution in the basic principles and concepts of scientific research experimentation. For several centuries, the sole model of scientific method in research was based on the so-called *rule of the single variable*. This rule dictated the simple prescription that, in carrying out a scientific study, all variables but one should be kept constant. This one factor is varied in a controlled manner by the experimenter, and the variation of some designated "dependent" variable is carefully measured. The pattern of covariation between the experimentally controlled "independent" variable and the "dependent" effect variable is then analyzed in order to arrive at a statement of the functional relationship between the two variables. It would be anticipated that, by systematically proceeding from one experimental factor to the next, one could ultimately determine all the essential laws within a selected domain of interest.

This "one variable at a time" model of experimentation, which was developed in the physical sciences, obviously limited the application of rigorous scientific method to the laboratory, since the world outside does not readily lend itself to the arbitrary control of all variables but one. Fortunately, the rule of the single variable, once the only acceptable principle of scientific research, has been amended. The newer logic of scientific experimentation has been due in large part to the influence of the English statistician R. A. Fisher (1935). The scientist qua scientist is no longer confined to the restrictive conditions of the laboratory. Through Fisher's development of the principles of modern experimental design and the associated statistical techniques of analysis of variance and covariance, researchers are now able to do respectable experimental work outside the laboratory, dealing productively with the problem of making valid inferences from studies that involve the simultaneous variation of more than one independent variable.

The newer logic of experimentation deals primarily with the type of research in which it is possible for the investigator to manipulate treatment variables in a controlled manner and to assign subjects at random to treatment groups. I shall refer to this type of investigation as *experimental research*. The other major class of systematic research investigation may be referred to as *survey research*. Although the investigator does not actually manipulate variables in the latter type of research, the same kinds of underlying assumptions are generally made in the analysis of data and the interpretation of results in both experiments and surveys. Investigations that do not meet the formal requirements of experimental or survey research may be described as *exploratory research*.

Sampling Problems. Most investigators, in carrying out investigations in the clinical area, are not content with providing descriptions and drawing conclusions limited to the particular individuals they have directly studied. This is true whether the investigator is engaged in experiments or surveys and whether he is doing cross-sectional or longitudinal research. Since scientific inquiry usually implies a search for general principles rather than for statements that hold only for directly observed data, one of the most important problems in research is how best to draw reasonable inferences about populations on the basis of what is found in samples. The problem of drawing inferences from samples to populations holds not only for the *subjects* who are studied but also for *objects*, for example, stimulus situations, tests, and interviewers (Hammond, 1954). In other words, we must not only think of the particular groups of individuals studied as samples from either real or hypothetical populations, but we must often consider the particular variables studied as samples from populations.

The rules for drawing valid conclusions about populations from observations taken on samples are generally referred to as the *principles of statistical inference*. Detailed consideration of problems of statistical inference is beyond the scope of this chapter, but it is clear that the basic postulate in drawing conclusions about populations from samples is that some element of *randomness* must enter into the sampling process at some point in the investigation. The entire logical structure of statistical inference is built on the notion that each element in a population or subdivision of the population has a known chance of appearing in the sample. This basic postulate obviously imposes two primary demands upon the investigator: (1) a clear definition of the population to which he intends to generalize and (2) a reasonable degree of assurance that the sample studied may be considered a random selection from the specified population.

Unfortunately, the problem of satisfying these two primary requirements for statistical inference is almost insuperable in many areas of clinical research. The populations typically implied in clinical research are persons who have been or would be diagnosed as falling into one or another psychiatric category, personality type, or problem group. Results for samples are usually treated as if they were representative of such categories in general. Even if it were possible to define clinical populations in a satisfactory manner so that diagnostic criteria were fairly consistent from clinic to clinic or from clinician to clinician, the practical difficulties of drawing random samples from such populations would be great. Actually, in most studies, the samples used by investigators are selected on the basis of availability rather than by acceptable sampling procedures from specified populations. Deming (1950) coined the term *chunk* to refer to such samples, which are merely convenient slices of some population, and he emphasized that the usual procedures for statistical inference involving critical ratios, t-tests, chi square, and so on, hold neither for such "chunks" nor for "judgment samples," which are based on the deliberate attempt by the investigator to select a "representative" sample.

The implications for clinical research are clear. In most clinical studies, populations have been poorly defined, if at all, and nonrandom sampling has been the rule rather than the exception. If greater scientific advance is to be made, more attention must be given to sampling considerations. It seems only reasonable to expect that many of the perplexing differences in conclusions reached by investigators independently pursuing research on similar topics would be resolved if problems of population definition and sampling were taken more seriously.

Experimental Research: Classical Evaluative Design. Possibilities for carrying out research in areas of interest to the clinical psychologist in which the investigator is able to manipulate conditions are limitless. Many conclusions based on experiments have already been cited in this book. Although other examples would be simpler, I shall illustrate some of the basic concepts of experimental research by further reference to the problem of evaluating the effectiveness of psychotherapy. What I shall call the *classical evaluative design* is based on the principle, mentioned previously, of keeping all variables but the experimental one constant. In its simplest form, this principle has developed as the *control group design.* One group of clients, labeled the experimental or treatment group, is provided with a designated program of psychotherapy, while a second group, supposedly equivalent to the treatment group in every relevant way, is not treated. Thus all variables are intended to be kept constant except the critical one of therapy, which is varied through two degrees— therapy versus no therapy. Appropriate measures would then be analyzed, yielding a basis for comparison of the treatment and the control group.

Granting the difficult moral and ethical considerations that must be resolved in withholding treatment from the control group and the practical problems of securing comparable data from both groups, one finds there are in addition many methodological problems that must be faced in attempting to apply the control group principle. Assuming that relevant and reliable measures can be obtained, one faces the question of how to set up equivalent groups. The ideal control group design of equating the two groups on *all* characteristics significantly related to the dependent measures under study is unrealistic. Various matching techniques are possible, including (1) *matched pairs,* that is, matching pairs of cases on one or more variables such as sex, age, IQ, or socioeconomic status and (2) the more flexible method of *matched distributions,* that is, allocating cases to the groups so that the frequency distributions of selection variables are comparable. Even when matching takes place on what are presumed to be relevant factors, it is still necessary to randomize within the framework of matching, for example, tossing a coin to decide which of a matched pair of cases goes into each group. In many studies, it seems probable that some complete randomization method, without matching, such as the random allocation of half the cases to each group is not only the most easily accomplished selection procedure but provides the broadest basis for generalizations.

In the execution of the control group study, many administrative and methodological problems present themselves. Among these, for example, are the possibilities of *contamination* (communication between experimental and control subjects) or *differential attrition* (unequal loss of subjects). Other questions have to do with the so-called *placebo effect:* Is the therapy per se doing the job, or are gains primarily a function of the patient's expectations? The extent to which well-known methodological niceties characteristic of drug research, such as the *single-blind* (the patient does not know which drug he is getting, if any) and *double-blind* (neither patient nor doctor knows) techniques, can be adapted to research on psychotherapy remains to be clarified.

Mention has not yet been made of how measures representing effects would be handled to yield a basis for comparing the two groups. Although terminal scores obtained either immediately after the completion of treatment or at some specified follow-up period are sometimes used, the better logic of measurement would dictate that a "before-after" design be employed. In this design, each of the groups would be measured on the same variables before and after treatment. Difference scores or "shifts" in the control group based on the time interval specified for treatment in the experimental group would be a baseline indicating the change to be expected under the usual circumstances of life, including potentiality for spontaneous recovery. Tests of significance of the net difference between the "shifts" within each group would be used to decide whether treatment was effective (Harris, 1963).

The classical evaluative design may be extended to include other treatment groups, each representing further variation in the experimental factor. In this way, several treatment methods may be compared, not only with the control group but also with each other. Other kinds of control or contrast groups may be added to the study. Despite such elaborations, however, a major objection to the classical design is the relative paucity of information supplied to the investigator. In general, results are limited to over-all comparisons among groups. At the conclusion of such an evaluative program, the investigator might be willing to conclude that therapy A is somewhat more effective than therapy B and that each therapy is better than no therapy at all. Even though such a conclusion might be satisfying to proponents of therapy A, there would be little feedback to either theory or practice. Within the classical design, it is difficult to relate variations in outcomes of service to variations in clients and their problems. Similarly, limiting classification of treatment methods to gross categories, for example, client-centered psychotherapy, would preclude finding out whether certain aspects of treatment do better with certain kinds of clients. The "school" of therapy, even when designated by some over-all label, is never a unitary factor. Obviously, the amount and depth of information generated by classical evaluative design are very limited in comparison with the problems and costs of execution.

Experimental Research: Modern Evaluative Design. Our conception of modern evaluative design is based on principles of the factorial experiment. In contrast to the classical rule of varying only one factor, the factorial experiment involves the simultaneous controlled variation of more than one "independent" factor. The advantages of the multifactor study over the single-factor study are considerable. Effects of several factors may be evaluated from no greater a number of observations. The effects of factors in combination may be assessed as well as the effects of single factors. Most important of all, each factor is evaluated, not with other factors kept arbitrarily constant, but over the range of variation of the other factors.

Edwards and Cronbach (1952) furnished a simple illustration of the factorial design in the context of evaluating results of psychotherapy. Let us suppose that we wish to compare two types of therapy provided to two groups of clients, one group with a high degree of initial disturbance and the second with a low degree. If we design this problem as a factorial experiment, discrepancies in response between type of patient and type of therapy show up in what is called "interaction." In the 2×2 table below, the classification at the top, A and B, represents the two methods of therapy while the classification on the side corresponds to the two types of clients. The entries in the four cells of the table are mean scores on the dependent variable selected to designate outcome of therapy.

	Therapy	
	A	B
High disturbance	6	6
Low disturbance	12	8

These data suggest that therapy A is more effective than therapy B. This much would have been obtained from the classical design. The surplus information obtained from the factorial design is the suggestion of an "interaction." The more disturbed clients appear to give the same response regardless of the type of therapy, while the less disturbed clients respond better to therapy A than to therapy B. As a matter of fact, it seems that the apparent over-all superiority of therapy A is due to its superiority for the less disturbed clients. Of course, in an actual study, such inferences would be based on appropriate tests of significance. This example is actually the simplest possible multifactorial design. The student might find it an interesting exercise to attempt to set up a table allowing for evaluation of effects in a design involving three types of therapy, three types of clients, and therapists of two degrees of experience.

Appropriate methods for analyzing results from factorial studies are provided by techniques of analysis of variance. In general, these techniques are simply an elaboration of tests of significance of difference between means. A further extension of such methods is provided in analysis of covariance by means of which it is possible for the investigator to adjust experimental comparisons for the influences of extraneous uncontrolled variables.

Correlational and Factor-analytic Research Designs. One of the most ubiquitous symbols in clinical research is the correlation coefficient. We are using the term *correlation coefficient* in a broad sense to include not only the Pearson product-moment correlation but its many variants such as rank correlation and contingency coefficient. As is well known, the correlation is a summary index of the degree of association or interdependence between sets of paired scores. In general, studies involving correlations may be regarded as forms of survey research rather than experimental research, if by the latter we mean research in which at least one independent variable is manipulated in a controlled manner by the investigator. Correlation coefficients serve many purposes in clinical research, of which the following may serve as examples: test validity based on correlation between test scores and criterion scores; test reliability based on correlation between split halves, repeat tests, equivalent test forms, and so on; judge or observer reliability based on correlation between judges or observers scoring or rating the same cases; correlations used to indicate the relationship between different tests, attributes, or functions; correlations to measure agreement between predicted and actual performance. Correlational approaches have probably most frequently been used in connection with test-construction methodology and in exploratory studies to suggest hypotheses to the investigator. Logically, however, correlational methods may also be used to test hypotheses. Correlation between variables, as the student well knows, does not necessarily imply any direct causal relationship between the variables. In general, imputation of causal relationship is stronger in the case of experimental research than it is in survey research.

Closely related to the correlational approach is the more basic concept of the regression equation. In its simplest form, the regression equation represents a quantitative relationship between a dependent variable and an independent variable that is under the control of the investigator. As generally used by psychologists, however, the designation of which variable is dependent and which is independent depends on the purpose of the investigator. The multiple regression equation is simply an extension of the two-variable regression equation and involves the combination of two or more independent variables in "predicting" a dependent variable. Multiple regression methods have proved especially useful in applied situations where the task is how best to predict performance on a criterion from a knowledge of several prediction variables.

Another extension of correlational techniques, also dependent on principles of multiple regression, is afforded by partial correlation methods. In its usual application, the partial correlation substitutes statistical control of variables for experimental control and is a device for estimating what the correlation between two variables would be if one or more other variables had been kept constant.

Many investigators consider the extension of the correlational approach known as *factor analysis* to be of primary importance in personality research. Factor analysis has been used for many years in a search for underlying "dimensions of mind and personality" and has been a controversial topic ever since its development by Spearman. There are a number of systems for carrying out factor analysis (Harman, 1960; Harris, 1964), but the general aim of all systems is to intercorrelate a number of variables and then determine a smaller number of factors, preferably psychologically meaningful factors, that account for the interrelationships. A summary of factor-analytic contributions to clinical psychology has been reported by Dahlstrom (1957). Cattell (1952a) attempted to integrate the realm of applicability of correlational and factor-analytic studies with his conception of the *covariation chart,* actually a cube with three dimensions: persons, variables, and occasions. The type of correlation that is most familiar and that has been used in most factor-analytic studies is the correlation between two variables derived from paired scores for a sample of persons. This type of correlation, however, is only one of six basic designs for formulating correlations. Although the classification below refers to factor-analytic studies, it should be evident that in many situations the investigator may decide not to carry a particular analysis beyond the stage of drawing conclusions from the observed correlations. Nomenclature is adopted from Cattell (1952a).

1. *R-technique* is based on the traditional correlation between variables on a series of persons. Paired variable scores are obtained for each person; the occasion is presumed to be a constant or irrelevant.
2. *P-technique* is based on the correlation between variables on a series of occasions for one person. Paired variable scores are obtained for each occasion; all scores are derived from one person.

3. *Q-technique* is based on the correlation between persons on a series of variables. Paired person scores are obtained for each variable; the occasion is presumed to be a constant or irrelevant.
4. *O-technique* is based on the correlation between occasions on a series of variables for one person. Paired occasion scores are obtained for each variable; all scores are derived from one person.
5. *T-technique* is based on the correlation between occasions on a series of persons. Paired occasion scores are obtained for each person; all scores are based on the same variable.
6. *S-technique* is based on the correlation between persons on a series of occasions. Paired person scores are obtained for each occasion; all scores are based on the same variable.

While each of these designs and recent extensions (Coan, 1961) is useful, depending on the purpose of the particular study, I shall limit further discussion of these techniques to some of the implications of Q-technique and P-technique for clinical research. Applications of R-technique are readily found in the literature.

Q-technique, also called inverted, transposed, or obverse factor analysis has been strongly advocated by Stephenson (1952) as a modern approach to typology and hypothesis-testing research, and he describes many applications of pertinence to research design in clinical psychology. One of the most interesting adaptations of this approach is the so-called *Q-sort*. In brief, the Q-sort involves having an individual sort a fairly large number of descriptive statements into an ordered series of categories according to specified instructions. For example, the SIO *Q-Sort Test* was developed at the Counseling Center of the University of Chicago for use in studies of client-centered psychotherapy (Rogers and Dymond, 1954). In this application the client sorts a number of self-reference statements, each printed on a separate card, into nine piles running from those which he considers "least like" to those which he regards as "most like." In one sort he is asked to describe himself as he thinks he really is (self-sort). In a second sort he describes himself as he would like to be (ideal-sort) and, in a third sort, he describes what the ordinary person is like (ordinary sort).

Instructions are generally set up so that a normal distribution of items is "forced" by asking the sorter to place a specified number of cards in each pile. Such distributions of sorted items may then be intercorrelated to test hypotheses about changes in the client's perception during the course of therapy; for example, the correlation between the self-sort and self-ideal sort should tend to increase from pretherapy to posttherapy if counseling is successful.[1] In a similar way hypotheses about "identification," "rapport," and so on may be tested by also having the therapist perform Q-sorts and correlating his sorts with those of the client. A critical survey

[1] It might be noted that correlating Q-sorts made by the same individual on different occasions would be an example of O-technique in the Cattell system of nomenclature.

of the contributions of Q methodology has been made by Wittenborn (1961).

The major proponent of *P-technique* in clinical research has been Cattell (1952b), who contends that, when properly coordinated with *R technique*, it represents the most promising research tool available for the description and understanding of the single individual. By repeatedly measuring an individual with respect to a number of attributes and environmental conditions over a fairly long period of time, the claim is made that one can secure a series of correlations among the variables that can be factor analyzed to yield a scientific picture of the unique pattern of dynamics and personality structure for the given individual. Some of the problems involved in P-technique have been discussed by Holtzman (1962).

With regard to study of the unique individual, it has often been pointed out that experimental research employing analysis of variance techniques may be used with the single case. Both Stephenson (1952) and Cattell (1952c) also describe various possibilities for combining experimental research, in which variables are manipulated, with correlational analysis by means of factor analysis.

Profile Analysis. One persistent problem area that has concerned many research workers in clinical psychology is how best to deal with profiles, for example, pattern or "scatter" of Wechsler subtests or scores on the Edwards Personal Preference Schedule (EPPS). Reference has already been made to one technique dealing with profiles by means of multiple regression equations when the problem is that of predicting a single criterion variable from a combination of other variables. In clinical psychology the "profile problem" often takes other forms such as

1. Comparison of the profile of one subject with another, e.g., in a study where it is desirable to match subjects
2. Comparison of the profile of the same subject on different occasions, e.g., pretherapy with posttherapy
3. Comparison of the profile of a subject with one or more standard or normative profiles, e.g., for differential diagnosis
4. Comparison of "average" profiles for different groups, e.g., in determining over-all differences between psychiatric or other diagnostic groups
5. "Clustering" profiles into homogeneous groups, e.g., in establishing syndromes

Various statistical "solutions" to these kinds of profile problems have been summarized by Cronbach and Gleser (1953), Greenhouse and Geisser (1959), Nunnally (1962), and Overall (1964). Many of the methods suggested maintain the traditional conception of a profile as a pattern of points on a two-dimensional surface with three major characteristics: level, shape, and dispersion. For example, the relative similarity between two profiles may be expressed, although not entirely satisfactorily, by means of the correlation between paired variable scores, which is in essence the coefficient previously described in *Q-technique.*

Going beyond the traditional two-dimensional conception of a profile, a more complete *multivariate model* represents a profile of k scores for an individual by a single point in k-dimensional space. Similarly, the average profile for a group may also be conceived as a single point in k-dimensional space. The basis for measuring similarity of profiles then becomes the "distance" between points in k-dimensional space. The multivariate model also provides a method known as *multiple discriminant analysis* for discriminating the typical profiles of different groups and assigning new cases to one of the groups (Beech and Maxwell, 1958). As might be expected, the theory, mathematics, and practical applications of the multivariate conception of profiles is somewhat complex. It is clear, however, that clinical research will find increasing uses for such approaches to profile analysis.

Comparative Surveys. Probably the most common type of study that has been characteristic of clinical research through the years has involved the comparison of various "diagnostic" groups on selected variables. The literature in clinical psychology and related fields is replete with studies in which schizophrenics are compared with neurotics, neurotics with normals, normals with psychopaths, and so on. Such *comparative surveys,* as we shall call them, are sometimes looked upon as pseudo-experiments in which variation in the independent variable, that is, diagnostic classification, is attained by sampling from "criterion" groups rather than by controlled manipulation of conditions. Dependent variables in such studies may be scores derived from well-known instruments such as the WAIS, Rorschach, or MMPI or they may be based on special techniques devised by the investigator.

Discrimination between "criterion" groups is often used as one means of developing and establishing test validity. One of the most common faults that occurs when this is done is failure of the investigator to "cross-validate" his instruments on further independent samples from the same populations to insure that his results are sufficiently stable.

The need for adequate definition of relevant populations and attention to proper sampling procedures is nowhere more clear than in comparative surveys where the investigator aims to test hypotheses or draw general conclusions about differences between diagnostic or psychiatric groups. One of the major difficulties that limits the significance of many such comparative studies is the fact that psychiatric diagnosis has generally been found to be an unreliable criterion (Zigler and Phillips, 1961). Unless there is fairly high agreement from investigator to investigator about the kinds of individuals who will be considered as falling within specified classifications, there is little chance for building up a body of relevant scientific knowledge.

On the other hand, it is important to stress that problems of population definition and sampling are of no greater concern in comparative studies than they are in more experimentally oriented research. As was said before, some element of "randomness" must enter at some point into the sampling process if generalizations are to be drawn about populations from investigation of samples. In an experiment the experimenter himself can introduce the "randomness" necessary for legitimate statistical inference by assigning subjects to, say, either an experimental or control group by some mechanical procedure, for example, tossing a coin. Obviously, "randomness" in a comparative study depends upon the way the investigator has gone about drawing his samples. Nevertheless for both experiments and surveys, if the investigator wishes to draw conclusions beyond the specific individuals who have been the subjects of his study, it is clear that he must have some degree of assurance that the samples he is studying are "representative" of larger populations. The "randomness" introduced by the experimenter in setting up experimental groups in no way absolves him from the necessity for paying attention to the broader questions of population definition and sampling.

Role of Computers. As noted in Chapter 5, by R. M. Dreger, recent years have witnessed the increasing use and influence of high-speed computers in many areas of technology and research, including the social and behavioral sciences. What were once almost prohibitive data-processing problems such as factor analysis or other forms of multivariate analysis with large numbers of subjects and variables (Cooley and Lohnes, 1962) can now be done in seconds and minutes rather than days and months. But, in addition, computers may be programed to prepare stimuli, conduct experiments, and simulate cognitive, decision-making processes or interpersonal relations (Borko, 1962; Green, 1963; Jones, 1963). The utilization of computers in clinical research such as diagnostic classification in schizophrenia (Gerard, 1963; Overall, 1963) and content analysis of psychotherapeutic interviews (Harway and Iker, 1964) is already in evidence. The use of computers as flexible teaching machines programed to respond differentially depending upon the responses of the student has strong implications not only for instructional methods in education but also for the theory and practice of psychotherapy and other techniques of behavior modification.

THE NEED FOR COOPERATIVE ENTERPRISE

The greater part of this chapter has emphasized the importance of coordination between conceptualization and planful research design if scientific inquiry is to be carried out in the clinical area. This emphasis results from the conviction that research in clinical psychology should adhere to the same basic principles of scientific method as other fields of psychological research.

Hints, hunches, and hypotheses of relevance to the operations of the clinical psychologist may arise in many ways. The most important source of such hypotheses has always been the cognitive and problem-solving responses of the clinician to the data that emerge during his contact with clients. Scarcely anyone will deny that the richest conceptualizations about human personality have come from psychoanalysts and other clinical workers. But propositions derived from clinical contact alone do not generally have the status of scientific generalizations. In some instances, for example, variables considered critical in the psychotherapeutic situation may be brought into the laboratory and examined under controlled conditions in what is sometimes called an "experimental analogue of psychotherapy." Or dimensions studied in the laboratory may suggest explanations and better-formulated investigation of the complex transactions occurring in the clinical setting (Bachrach, 1962; Williams, 1964). Research in both the clinic and the laboratory is indispensable for the advancement of clinical psychology. The general task of research in either locale is to formulate propositions in testable form and then carry out the tests under as rigorous and controlled conditions as possible. Such research should, in turn, lead to new and better hypotheses in the endless cycle of successive approximation to the "truth" that is science.

While the service aspects of clinical psychology may be carried out by the individual clinician and it will always be possible for individual investigators to make important contributions to knowledge in the clinical realm, it seems apparent that many of the major objectives of clinical research can be approached only through large-scale cooperative research programs involving both practitioners and researchers of varying disciplines. Research projects that introduce changes in complex social organizations such as social agencies, hospitals, or entire communities generate many kinds of administrative and operational problems (Kandel and Williams, 1964). The traditional interdisciplinary team of psychiatrist, psychologist, and social worker is frequently augmented by sociologist, anthropologist, statistician, and other specialists. But the most important "manpower" ingredient in productive clinical research is the individuals and families who are willing to lend themselves to research and study. Their collaboration is vital to the advancement of our knowledge about man and his environment—knowledge that is the proper basis of the practice of clinical psychology in all of its ramifications.

SUMMARY

The function of research in clinical psychology is to broaden the scientific base upon which the practice of clinical psychology in part depends. By tradition clinical psychology is both research oriented and service oriented. This twofold allegiance to both service and science makes it imperative that the well-rounded clinical psychologist be competent not only in the techniques of clinical practice but also in the methodology of scientific research.

The present chapter has stressed the point of view that productive clinical research is a joint function of logical conceptualization and controlled empirical inquiry. Broadly conceived, the major objective of research in clinical psychology is increased understanding of the personality and adjustment of the client. This major objective takes many specific forms, including the development and validation of diagnostic techniques and evaluation of the process and outcomes of treatment services.

Research design in clinical psychology presents many theoretical and practical difficulties because of the complexity of the subject matter and the ethical issues involved. In general, most investigations may be classified as experimental research, survey research, or exploratory research. Familiarity with modern statistical methods and access to high-speed computers is almost indispensable for the research worker in clinical psychology, but it is clear that many unresolved issues will be resolved only through the development of large-scale multidisciplinary service and research enterprises.

REFERENCES

ALLPORT, G. W. 1937. *Personality*. New York: Holt, Rinehart & Winston.

ALLPORT, G. W. 1961. *Pattern and growth in personality*. New York: Holt, Rinehart & Winston.

BACHRACH, A. J. (ed.). 1962. *Experimental foundations of clinical psychology*. New York: Basic Books.

BEECH, H. R., and MAXWELL, A. E. 1958. Differentiation of clinical groups using canonical variates. *J. consult. Psychol.*, 22, 113–21.

BERG, I. A., and ADAMS, H. E. 1962. The experimental bases of personality assessment. In A. J. BACHRACH (ed.), *Experimental foundations of clinical psychology*. New York: Basic Books. Pp. 52–93.

BORKO, H. 1962. *Computer applications in the behavioral sciences*. Englewood Cliffs, N.J.: Prentice-Hall.

CATTELL, R. B. 1952a. The three basic factor-analytic research designs—their interrelations and derivatives. *Psychol. Bull.*, 49, 499–520.

CATTELL, R. B. 1952b. P-technique factorization and the determination of individual dynamic structure. *J. clin. Psychol.*, 8, 5–10.

CATTELL, R. B. 1952c. *Factor analysis: An introduction and manual for the psychologist and social scientist.* New York: Harper & Row.

CHASSAN, J. B. 1961. Stochastic models of the single case as the basis of clinical research design. *Behaviorial Sci.*, 6, 42–50.

COAN, R. W. 1961. Basic forms of covariation and concomitance designs. *Psychological Bull.*, 58, 317–24.

COOLEY, W. W., and LOHNES, P. R. 1962. *Multivariate procedures for the behavioral sciences.* New York: Wiley.

CRONBACH, L. J., and GLESER, G. C. 1953. Assessing similarity between profiles. *Psychological Bull.*, 50, 456–73.

DAHLSTROM, W. G. 1957. Research in clinical psychology: Factor analytic contributions. *J. clin. Psychol.*, 13, 211–20.

DEMING, W. E. 1950. *Some theory of sampling.* New York: Wiley.

DOLLARD, J., and AULD, F., JR. 1959. *Scoring human motives: A manual.* New Haven: Yale Univer. Press.

DOLLARD, J., and MOWRER, O. H. 1947. A method of measuring tension in written documents. *J. abnorm. soc. Psychol.*, 42, 3–32.

EDWARDS, A. L., and CRONBACH, L. J. 1952. Experimental design for research in psychotherapy. *J. clin. Psychol.*, 8, 51–59.

FISHER, R. A. 1935. *The design of experiments.* London: Oliver & Boyd.

GERARD, R. W. 1964. The nosology of schizophrenia: A cooperative study. *Behaviorial Sci.*, 9, 311–33.

GREEN, B. F. 1963. *Digital computers in research.* New York: McGraw-Hill.

GREENHOUSE, S. W., and GEISSER, S. 1959. On methods in the analysis of profile data. *Psychometrika*, 24, 95–112.

GROSSBERG, J. M. 1964. Behavior therapy: A review. *Psychological Bull.*, 62, 73–88.

HAMMOND, K. R. 1954. Representative vs. systematic design in clinical psychology. *Psychological Bull.*, 51, 150–59.

HARMAN, H. H. 1960. *Modern factor analysis.* Chicago: Univer. of Chicago Press.

HARRIS, C. W. (ed.). 1963. *Problems in measuring change.* Madison: Univer. of Wisconsin Press.

HARRIS, C. W. 1964. Some recent developments in factor analysis. *Educ. psychol. Measmt*, 24, 193–206.

HARWAY, N. I., and IKER, H. P. 1964. Computer analysis in psychotherapy. *Psychological Rep.*, 14, 720–22.

HOCH, P. H., and ZUBIN, J. 1964. *The evaluation of psychiatric treatment.* New York: Grune & Stratton.

HOLTZMAN, W. H. 1962. Methodological issues in P technique. *Psychological Bull.*, 59, 248–56.

HUNT, J. McV. 1949. The problem of measuring the results of psychotherapy. *Psychological serv. Center J.*, **1**, 122–35.

HUNT, W. A., and JONES, N. F. 1962. The experimental investigation of clinical judgment. In A. BACHRACH (ed.), *Experimental foundations of clinical psychology.* New York: Basic Books.

IKER, H. P. 1959. Some theoretical and practical aspects of sampling procedures in research. *J. nerv. ment. Dis.*, **128**, 191–203.

JONES, L. V. 1963. Beyond Babbage. *Psychometrika*, **28**, 315–31.

KANDEL, D. B., and WILLIAMS, R. H. 1964. *Psychiatric rehabilitation.* New York: Atherton Press.

LEDLEY, R. S. 1962. Advances in biomedical science and diagnosis. In H. BORKO (ed.), *Computer applications in the behavioral sciences.* Englewood Cliffs, N.J.: Prentice-Hall.

LUBORSKY, L. 1962. The patient's personality and psychotherapeutic change. In H. H. STRUPP and L. LUBORSKY (eds.), *Research in psychotherapy.* Vol. 2. Washington, D.C.: American Psychological Association.

MARSDEN, G. 1965. Content-analysis studies of therapeutic interviews: 1954 to 1964. *Psychological Bull.*, **63**, 298–321.

MUENCH, G. A. 1947. An evaluation of nondirective psychotherapy. *Appl. Psychol. Monogr.*, No. 13.

NUNNALLY, J. C., JR. 1962. The analysis of profile data. *Psychological Bull.*, **59**, 311–19.

OVERALL, J. E. 1963. A configural analysis of psychiatric diagnostic stereotypes. *Behavorial Sci.*, **8**, 211–19.

OVERALL, J. E. 1964. Note on multivariate methods for profile analysis. *Psychological Bull.*, **61**, 195–98.

PAYNE, R. W., and JONES, H. G. 1957. Statistics for the investigation of individual cases. *J. clin. Psychol.*, **13**, 115–21.

RAIMY, V. C. 1948. Self-reference in counseling interviews. *J. consult. Psychol.*, **12**, 153–63.

REZNIKOFF, M., and TOOMEY, L. C. 1959. *Evaluation of changes associated with psychiatric treatment.* Springfield, Ill.: Charles C Thomas.

ROGERS, C. R., and DYMOND, R. F. (eds.). 1954. *Psychotherapy and personality change.* Chicago: Univer. of Chicago Press.

ROSENZWEIG, S. 1950. Norms and the individual in the psychologist's perspective. In M. L. REYMERT (ed.), *Feelings and emotions.* New York: McGraw-Hill.

ROTTER, J. B. 1963. A historical and theoretical analysis of some broad trends in clinical psychology. In S. KOCH (ed.), *Psychology: A study of a science.* Vol. 5. New York: McGraw-Hill.

RUBINSTEIN, E. A., and PARLOFF, M. B. (eds.). 1959. *Research in psychotherapy.* Washington, D.C.: American Psychological Association.

STEPHENSON, W. 1952. Some observations on Q-technique. *Psychological Bull.*, **49**, 483–98.

STRUPP, H. H. 1962. Patient-doctor relationships: The psychotherapist in the therapeutic process. In A. J. BACHRACH (ed.), *Experimental foundations of clinical psychology.* New York: Basic Books.

STRUPP, H. H., and LUBORSKY, L. (eds.). 1962. *Research in psychotherapy.* Vol. 2. Washington, D.C.: American Psychological Association.

WATSON, R. I. 1952. Measuring the effectiveness of psychotherapy: Problems for investigation. *J. clin. Psychol.,* 8, 60–64.

WILLIAMS, J. H. 1964. Conditioning of verbalization: A review. *Psychological Bull.,* 62, 383–93.

WITTENBORN, J. R. 1961. Contributions and current status of Q methodology. *Psychological Bull.,* 58, 132–42.

ZAX, M., and KLEIN, A. 1960. Measurement of personality and behavior changes following psychotherapy. *Psychological Bull.,* 57, 435–48.

ZIGLER, E., and PHILLIPS, L. 1961. Psychiatric diagnosis: A critique. *J. abnorm. soc. Psychol.,* 63, 607–18.

Name Index

Subject Index